Japan's
Modern Myths

STUDIES OF THE EAST ASIAN INSTITUTE,

COLUMBIA UNIVERSITY

The East Asian Institute is Columbia University's center for research, education, and publication on modern East Asia. The Studies of the East Asian Institute were inaugurated in 1961 to bring to a wider public the results of significant new research on China, Japan, and Korea.

Japan's Modern Myths

Ideology in the Late Meiji Period

CAROL GLUCK

PRINCETON UNIVERSITY PRESS : PRINCETON, NEW JERSEY

Copyright © 1985 by Princeton University Press

Published by Princeton University Press, 41 William Street,
Princeton, New Jersey 08540
In the United Kingdom: Princeton University Press, Oxford

All Rights Reserved

Library of Congress Cataloging in Publication Data will be found
on the last printed page of this book

ISBN 0-691-05449-5
ISBN 0-691-00812-4 (pbk.)

Publication of this book has been aided by the Paul
Mellon Fund of Princeton University Press

This book has been composed in Linotron Bembo

Clothbound editions of Princeton University Press books are printed
on acid-free paper, and binding materials are chosen for strength
and durability. Paperbacks, although satisfactory for personal collections,
are not usually suitable for library rebinding

Printed in the United States of America
by Princeton University Press, Princeton, New Jersey

9 8 7 6 5 4

For Peter

Acknowledgments

WITH APPRECIATION to Professors Mitani Taichirō, Kano Masanao, Irokawa Daikichi, Takagi Kiyoko, Ariizumi Sadao, Yamamoto Tsuneo, Saitō Hiroshi and to Tanabe Sadayoshi, Ichikawa Toshiko, and Kawai Satoru and Teiko for counsel and encouragement. With thanks to Kitane Yutaka of the Meiji shinbun zasshi bunko at Tokyo University, Frank Yorichika of Columbia University's East Asian library, Togasaki Tamiyo of Columbia and International House libraries, and to Gunji Yukiko and Sakuma Mayumi for help and endless patience. With gratitude to Professors Herbert Passin, Paul Varley, Donald Keene, W. T. de Bary, Gari Ledyard, Bernard Barber, Harry Harootunian, Tetsuo Najita, Andrew Fraser, George Akita, J. Victor Koschmann, and especially Herschel Webb for generous reading and conversation. With fond thanks to Deborah Bell, Winifred Olsen, Dorothy Borg, Joan Ericson, and Eric Hyer for fidelity in every sense. With acknowledgment to the Foreign Area Research program of the Social Science Research Council and the East Asian Institute of Columbia University for research support; to Nittsū sōgō kenkyūjo, Kanagawa kenritsu hakubutsukan, Asahi shinbunsha, Mainichi shinbunsha, and Karasawa Tomitarō for the illustrations; to R. Miriam Brokaw for the enthusiasm. And with special recognition to William and Thomas Gluck for walking the dog. To all these both the credit and the indebtedness, to myself alone the faults.

Contents

CONTENTS

Illustrations

(NOTE: Black and white photographs are reproduced
to favor historical accuracy over visual quality)

Japan's
Modern Myths

I

Ideology
and Imperial Japan

THE SUBJECT OF
IDEOLOGY

I

ALTHOUGH no society is innocent of collective notions about itself, some countries have made more of ideology than others. From the time Japan began its deliberate pursuit of "civilization" in the mid-nineteenth century, ideology appeared as a conscious enterprise, a perpetual civic concern, an affair, indeed, of state. Even as the exigencies of institutional transformation were met in the years following the Restoration of 1868, Japanese leaders expressed their sense that institutions alone were insufficient to secure the nation. It was not enough that the polity be centralized, the economy developed, social classes rearranged, international recognition striven for—the people must also be "influenced," their minds and hearts made one.[1]

In 1869, one year after the abolition of feudal rule, traveling missionaries were sent to the countryside to proselytize for the new imperial state. In 1881, a bureaucrat whose own illustrious career was devoted to drafting government legislation, including the Constitution, declared the most urgent national business to be "not government ordinances, but inspiration." While the interest of those in power clearly lay in persuading the population "to yield as the grasses before the wind," the opposition and others outside the political sphere were no less concerned with their own efforts to arouse the universal sentiment of the people.[2] From the 1880s through the first fifteen years of the twentieth century, Japanese sought first to conceive and then to inculcate an ideology suitable for modern Japan.

This proved no easy task. Although many believed in the desirability—and indeed the efficacy—of national exhortation, few agreed on its substance. The state missionaries in 1869 had briefly propagated Shintō as the Great Way of the new era; the legal bureaucrat

3

in 1881 preferred Chinese and German learning as the vessels of inspiration. In the eighties and nineties some suggested imperial loyalty and filial piety, others, the Japanese aesthetic tradition, still others, sociology.[3] In the early 1900s empire abroad and agrarian values at home were offered as the proper content for civic edification. In Japan, as elsewhere, the process of establishing a national ethos in a changed and changing social setting was a trial-and-error affair. Ideologies of the sort imperial Japan produced were neither created ex nihilo nor adopted ready-made. Without a text or a revelation to serve as a canonical source, views of state and society evolved fitfully, often inconsistently, into changing amalgams of past and present, near and foreign. This fitful and inconsistent process—the making of late Meiji ideology—is the subject of this book.

II

IN BOTH Japanese and Western writing it is often a disagreeable subject, since it quickly brings to mind Japan of the late 1930s and early 1940s. During those years of militarism and war, the Japanese were said to be imbued with the notion that Japan was the land of the gods, inhabited by a people uniquely superior in the world, who lived together, the whole nation as a single family, under the benevolent guidance of a divine emperor.[4] This picture of a society mobilized by its mythology in service to the national cause was the backdrop against which the subject of *tennōsei ideorogii*, the ideology of the emperor system, was articulated in the early postwar period. In 1945 and 1946 the Japanese sought to understand the constellation of forces that had brought Japan to war, because they felt, as did their American occupiers, that the past was the obstacle to the future. In order for postwar Japan to begin anew, the first reckoning would be with history. In this turbulent intellectual context attention soon centered on the nature and origins of the prewar emperor system. From Douglas MacArthur to the Japan Communist Party, commentators attempted to identify the elements that had been responsible for the events of Japan's dark years.[5]

Ideology figured prominently in almost every rendering. MacArthur described the Japanese as having been made "abject slaves" to "mythological fiction," and the Occupation attempted to liberate them from "an ideology which contributed to their war guilt, defeat, suffering, privation, and present deplorable condition."[6] Maruyama Masao began his famous essay of 1946 with a similar reference to enslavement, war, and an ideology which "succeeded in spreading a many-layered, though invisible, net over the Japanese people," who

4

had yet to be freed of its hold.[7] Other Japanese felt the s
some to a visceral extent. One writer recalled his chest cc
at the mention of the word "emperor"; the sight of the
spine-chilling tremors through him. The recommended trea
his "*tennōsei* neurosis" consisted of an aggressive pursuit of
of the emperor system until they plagued him, and the cou
longer.[8] Along with the generals, the bureaucrats, the industrialists,
and the landlords, ideology assumed a place on the newly compiled
list of prewar forces whose power had to be both examined and
purged.

In the years since *tennōsei* ideology first appeared on Japan's postwar intellectual agenda, differences of interpretation have generated
lively dispute among Japanese historians. But as with so many other
issues that were defined in the gripping atmosphere just after the war,
the essential nature of the problem has not changed. The outlines of
the argument are these: *tennōsei* ideology was the product of the modern emperor system, of the period from 1890, when the Meiji Constitution established the new political structures of modern Japan,
until 1945, when these structures collapsed with the surrender. The
Meiji government is described as having developed this ideology to
legitimate itself and support its modernizing programs. That is, the
oligarchs, the bureaucrats, and their ideologues, realizing that some
explanation was necessary to secure the cooperation of the people
through the rigors of economic development and international expansion, created a state orthodoxy around the figure of the emperor
and then imposed it upon the people. The orthodoxy was rigid and
flexible at the same time. While its rigidity worked to prevent effective opposition by equating dissent with disloyalty, its vagueness enabled it to adapt its injunctions to different needs, so that sacrifice in
war and savings accounts in peace could both be justified in terms of
the same national myths. By moralizing and mystifying the nature
of the state, politics was depoliticized. All that was required of the
citizen was loyal and willing submission, and this he is said to have
given as a result of an indoctrination that began in his elementary
school years and extended eventually into almost every quarter of his
social life. In one of the most common phrases, the people were
"shackled" (*sokubaku*), and any efforts to escape were met first with
intensified propaganda in the years after World War I, and then with
increasingly repressive measures that culminated in police control of
thought in the 1930s.[9]

For most Japanese writers *tennōsei* ideology represents both internal
psychological constriction and external political submissiveness in

prewar Japanese society. Not only did ideological orthodoxy help ultranationalism and militarism to prevail, but, like the war itself, it represents a blight on Japan's modern experience from which the nation has not fully recovered, even today. The metaphors have changed: what Maruyama called an invisible net became in Irokawa Daikichi's work "an enormous black box into which the Japanese people unknowingly walked."[10] But many of the scholars who study *tennōsei* ideology still do so for therapeutic reasons: they intend to explore whatever national conditions and predispositions enabled the ideology to take hold in the prewar years, and thus prevent its consequences from occurring again. It is for this same reason that Japanese intellectuals keep vigilant watch over what are called "*tennōsei* issues" in Japanese politics today. Whether it is the proposal to revive *kigensetsu*, the anniversary of the legendary founding of the empire and a prewar national holiday, or the move to reinstate government funds for Yasukuni, the shrine of the war dead and an important religious link in the prewar state orthodoxy—any suggestion of ideological recidivism arouses protest and concern.[11]

Tennōsei ideology, defined and established as a scholarly subject in the months after the war, is thus as much a part of postwar intellectual history as it is a reference to the late Meiji period (1890-1912) during which the ideology gradually emerged. But the view from 1945 backward across the decades conferred on the prewar myths a substantiality that they did not possess in the earlier period. The suppression of the late thirties and wartime years had so solidified the civic dogma that it was naturally assumed to have been cohesive, purposive, and effective from the start. Meiji ideology, or for that matter any ideology that stops short of totalitarianism, would not likely have manifested such characteristics in its formative stages, if indeed it ever did. For ideology, like history, is less thing than process.

III

BEFORE the process can be described, some definition of ideology is required, even if a brief and eclectic one. From the theoretical possibilities available to the late twentieth century student of ideology, I draw the outlines of my subject from an approach common to recent anthropological, sociological, and post-Marxist analyses of the relation between ideas and society. For the anthropologist Clifford Geertz, ideology renders social life significant for those who must live it; by both describing and prescribing, ideology provides "maps of problematic social reality" without which the societal arrangement

6

would seem meaningless and the individual's place in it unclear.[12] Any impression that such maps correspond in some geodetic way to the social topography of a given period, however, is misleading. Ideologies not only reflect and interpret the social realities that sustain them; they also, in Berger and Luckmann's term, construct those realities and remain in constant dialectical relationship with them.[13] The study of ideology as process concentrates on that relationship, on what Althusser calls "the *lived* relation between men and their world."[14] Since different people construe their world differently, there is always a multiplicity of ideological formations within a society. The question then arises, which—or whose—set of values and meanings becomes dominant and by what means. Gramsci's conception of hegemony recognizes that when a social group is successful in persuading others of the validity of its own world view, force does not greatly exceed consent. The consent, moreover, so permeates the society that to many it seems commonsensical, natural, and at times invisible. On the other hand, the means by which this permeation occurs are visible indeed. They include the disseminating institutions, both public and private, which though unconnected in their activities—schools and newspapers, for example—help to construct a shared ideological universe.[15] Finally, though one speaks of ideological discourse as if it were singular and static, it is in fact a plural and dynamic field of ideas and practices "within which there are not only continuities and persistent determinations but also tensions, conflicts, resolutions and irresolutions, innovations and actual changes."[16]

Although the sources in this selective recitation differ from one another on many points, they have in common certain emphases that are shared here as well. Each considers ideology an essential social element, "not an aberration or a contingent excrescence of History."[17] All societies, in short, produce ideologies which in turn help to reproduce the social order. These definitions thus avoid the common, but restrictive, equation of ideology with a systematic and manipulative political program. They further refrain from substituting terms like "belief system" or "national myth" in the hope that ideology by any other name would be a different matter. In general, they also relinquish the emphasis on fraudulence that was central to Marx and Engels' definition of ideology as an inversion of reality and a product of false consciousness.[18] This last characterization, however, is the original source of the Japanese term *tennōsei ideorogii*, and the pejorative meaning of ideology predominates in Japanese scholarship, even among those who, like Maruyama or Irokawa, do not consider themselves Marxists. Authors who wish to pursue a "non-

7

evaluative conception of ideology," which was Mannheim's grail, occasionally prefer the word *shisō* (thought), while others may omit *tennōsei* and use *ideorogii* alone in a more neutral sense.[19] Still, the content and immediacy of the particular ideology in question have made Japanese writers understandably reluctant to embrace the contention of recent theory that for those who live it, ideology is both real and "true." The issue of fraudulence aside, both Japanese and Western writers retain the post-Marxist concern with the social determination of ideas, insisting that ideological formations be tied to the social groups that produce and are produced by them. Despite the abstraction of the terms, ideology does not march disembodied through time, but exists in a concrete and particular social history that has not only dates but also names and faces.

Defined in this way, the subject under consideration here is the interpretation of the political and social world as the articulate elite lived it—or imagined they lived it—in late nineteenth and early twentieth century Japan. Since it is the eventually dominant versions that concern us, the focus is on the establishment and the ascendant social orders that constituted the ideological mainstream of the late Meiji period. Shared ascendancy notwithstanding, they were a diverse lot, whose efforts display no sign of a calculated or consistent ideological vision, but splinter instead into a jumble of contending positions. Often self-appointed to the task, they attempted to formulate views of state and society that they themselves could believe in, and then to persuade others to believe in them as well. Not cynical propagandists, they believed utterly in their depictions. The maps they redrew, partly along old, partly along new contours, were also, perhaps primarily, for themselves. Not theorists either, they addressed themselves to the people, interested less in argument than in suasion and its power to create *kokumin* (citizens, or countrymen) of them. Moralists, certainly, they were at home in the hortatory mode, which seemed at once comfortingly Confucian and, in the light of the latest Western treatises on moral education, also reassuringly European. They tackled large issues, defining the meaning of law, the place of politics, the role of the new middle class. They attended to details, the proprieties of imperial ceremony, the reading habits of youth, the extravagance of gold-rimmed spectacles. Impelled almost always by an acute sense of crisis, they prefaced their formulations with dramatic expressions of concern with the present state of social or national affairs. In the gap between what they said—the prefectural governors in 1890 deploring the lack of a unifying moral standard—and what they meant—fearing that the advent of party politics in the first election would unseat them—lay a welter of purposes and cross-purposes in the midst of which different groups and their different views contended.[20]

THE IDEOLOGICAL
PROCESS

I

As THIS general characterization suggests, "ideologues" could be found in many quarters. There was no single group with official, or even unofficial, status as mythmakers to the Meiji state. The so-called "government scholars" (*goyō gakusha*) were not court ideologists but academic consultants who prided themselves on their intellectual independence. No one, in short, did ideology for a living. Instead there was an array of people who did something else for a living but took, one might say, an "ideological" interest—they would have called it public-spiritedness—most often in matters closely related to their work or position. Many were in government, although the leading statesmen who might have been expected to offer guidance in such things seemed, with the important exception of the oligarch Yamagata Aritomo, generally uninterested. A number of upper and upper-middle level bureaucrats in the central ministries, especially Home, Education, and to a lesser extent, Army, and Agriculture and Commerce, attended diligently to ideological enterprise. Their concerns, however, were various. In the years after the Russo-Japanese War, the army wanted its recruits willing and of good physique, while the Home and Agriculture Ministries wished to keep these same rural youth down on the farm working the ancestral lands instead of running off to the cities, "the graveyards of the people."[21] Not only were the doctrines designed to achieve such ends often at odds with one another, but institutional rivalries and bureaucratic regionalism were often so pronounced that instead of contributing to a single orthodoxy, each part of the government vied to produce its own. Also active were provincial bureaucrats at the prefectural and county (*gun*) levels, and a whole range of petty officials, village mayors, and other local notables who, even if they passed in and out of local office, neither thought of themselves nor were thought of by others as links to the central government, but as figures of repute in the locality.

Then, with ideology as with foreign policy in the Meiji period, the strongest views—the hard line—often came from outside the government, from the *minkan*, as it was called, from "among the people." Here "the people" meant journalists, intellectuals, and public figures who produced a disproportionate amount of the "public opinion" (*yoron*) of the period. Influential and possessed of a highly developed national consciousness, their interest in ideological issues seldom flagged. They, too, pronounced on the moral and material welfare of the nation, frequently berating a government which was up to its knees in moral education for insufficient attention to the spiritual well-being of the people. They decried materialism, commended patriotism, questioned socialism, and urged Japan on to greater prestige as a world power, filling the ever-expanding volume of commercial publications with quantities of articulate opinion.

There were interest groups, many of them products of the early Meiji institutional changes, such as the organizations of Shintō priests, of educators, of landlords. In confronting their particular crises—for example, the steady decline in the fortunes of Shintō after the first years of the Meiji period—they publicly urged the universal importance of their contribution to national unity, or to social stability, or—as the Shintoists of 1918 reiterated their perpetual claim—to the cause of "unifying the spirit of the people."[22] Voluntary associations organized for social, economic, or cultural purposes undertook activities in civic education before the central government attempted to coopt them, and afterward as well. The countless societies, study groups, and village organizations pursued their own goals even as the government was instructing them to its purposes.

Government officials, diverse among themselves, thus shared the ideological field with many others in what was a more complex social geography than the term *tennōsei* ideology might indicate. If there were "ideologues"—and this study suggests that the term itself is misleading—they were all around, plying different interpretative trades in different social places. In late Meiji Japan, as in other modern societies, pursuing ideology in process means catching individuals and groups in their ideological aspect, of which they were sometimes intently conscious and sometimes intently not.

II

THE SAME is true of the institutions through which versions of ideology were disseminated to their respective audiences. They, too, were diverse and authentically engaged in one activity—educating children, training soldiers, collecting taxes—at the same time that they possessed an ideological aspect that was more or less overt. Among the most overt in this respect were such state institutions as the schools, army, and local government system, as well as the ple-

10

thora of half-public, half-private organizations which conveyed the impression that imperial Japan was organized from top to bottom, and bottom back to top. Through this hierarchy of interlocking institutions, the wishes of the central government were dispersed to the smallest country hamlet, in what on paper appeared to be the most organized network of social communication imaginable.[23] This of course was precisely the impression that the organizing ministry in question wished to convey, as each claimed full credit for single-handedly mobilizing the nation. Schools, shrines, youth groups, and reservists were each described as the sole effective ideological channel by the part of the government that sponsored them.

To view these channels all together is at least to avoid the pitfall of taking any particular ideological source at its totalizing word. Since the nation that in army documents appears militarized to the last sandal-maker becomes in the annals of the Hōtoku association a country of Sontoku worshippers, it seems wise to remain initially skeptical of grand organizational schemes. This is all the more true when the different institutional hierarchies were claiming the time and commitment of the same people. One suspects that if a farmer had attended the meetings of the score of associations in which his membership was postulated by the Home Ministry in the years after the Russo–Japanese War, he would have had little time left to perform the social tasks assigned him by these various local and national organizations, much less to tend his fields. In fact we know from the laments of provincial officials that local associations competed unsuccessfully for attendance at their meetings by providing saké or food—or the latest magic lantern show—to enliven the prospect of lectures on economic self-help through the raising of leghorns.[24] Audiences tended to be limited and self-selected, and more often than not the lecturers were preaching to the converted. Although this did not necessarily dilute the impact of the message, it suggests a more focused, less total communication than the central bureaucratic sources habitually claimed.

Existing social relations continually interfered with the smooth transmission of ideological messages from the government through its putatively subordinate hierarchy. Moreover, new institutions, once in existence, created their own demands and ideological strategies for self-preservation. The much extolled organs of local self-government (jichi) possessed ideological concerns of their own, some reinforcing, others conflicting with those of the central government. Schoolteachers in charge of creating the "next Japanese" (daini no kokumin) soon acquired as strong an allegiance to their profession as

11

to the government whose citizen-making interests they were hired to serve.[25] The institutional agents of late Meiji ideology were then, and often still are, imagined as conduits through which civic information passed unimpeded to its intended audience. But, neither empty nor direct, the conduits had all manner of kinks in them. Reflecting local economic interests and social relations or alternative views of the shape civilization ought to take, those whom the government appointed as the social custodians of ideology on the local level were not, in a word, reliable. Most strikingly, the local elite (*meibōka, yūshisha*), who were claimed by nearly every government ministry as the "pillars" of its ideological activity in the localities, were often the same entrepreneurial landowners from whose ranks the expanding political parties were gathering their support.[26] Yet to the Meiji bureaucrat in his ideological aspect, party politics was anathema.

Nor were government-sponsored institutions the only purveyors of ideology to the late Meiji population. This was a period of rapidly growing transportation and communication, of an ever more widely diffused press and an expanding printing industry, which published an annual average of nearly 27,000 book titles between 1905 and 1913 (in 1913 only Germany published more titles than Japan; the United States approximately half as many) and produced between 1,500 and 2,000 different magazines in the same period.[27] Increased literacy, a result of the national compulsory education system established in the 1870s, meant that growing numbers of younger Japanese were exposed to a wide diversity of opinion. Travel broadened, entertainment beckoned, and the sources of "education" proliferated. New private institutions such as the political parties and old ones such as the family responded to the times, seeking self-perpetuation with versions of their own importance directed to their members or to society at large. These institutional channels for the dissemination of ideology were thus multiple in number and conflicting in intent. Partial proof of this was the perennial preoccupation with ideological unity. Like sumptuary laws in the Tokugawa period, which were promulgated so often that their reiteration alone casts doubt on their effectiveness, the continued concern with ideology suggests that had the efforts at influence (*kyōka*) gone smoothly, no one need have dealt so copiously with the matter.

III

WITH this thought, the outline of ideological process proceeds to those for whom the impressive range of interpretative effort was ostensibly conducted—the *kokumin*, the countrymen, themselves. For any full history of ideology would necessarily include both the ideologists and the ideologized. Yet the weight of evidence is on the side of the producers, who were by nature expressive and voluble. It is they who tell us of whom and to whom they were speaking. From them one glimpses a hierarchy of ideological value, general and specific versions of civic practice, high, middle, and mass versions, hints or guides (*kokoroe*) for the farmer, the soldier, the rural youth, the taxpayer, the wife and mother. There was something for nearly everyone, though not quite. Unlike the farmers for whom acres of exhortation were cultivated, the growing urban population and the new industrial working class, though they aroused great fear and concern, received little direct ideological attention. That they were slighted is significant, since it helps to explain the nature and the consequences of the ideology that slighted them.

But did the people spoken of by bureaucrats and moralists exist? Or more precisely, did the "rural youth" imagined by the proponents of "social education" in the early 1900s hear what was spoken in their behalf? The view from Tokyo—across the endless vistas of bureaucratic or journalistic paper—suggests a society saturated with ideology, as if no one could have failed to be aware of the civic mission being urged on him by one or another proselytizer from the center. One way to test this perspective is to trace the movement of ideological language from its sources through the institutions of its dissemination to its targets, recognizing always that such sources were as apt to reside in the provinces as in the capital. Some subjects faded from view by the time they reached the village, where silkworms were likely to take precedence over *kokutai* as a topic of lively interest. Sometimes the words and symbols remained the same, but were understood differently in a different social context. In Tokyo, intellectuals and legal scholars theorized about the "deterioration of the family system," quoting from the Confucian "Great Learning" and John Ruskin, for they feared that a deteriorated family would mean rampant individualism.[28] In Tōhoku villages the same phrase meant something more specific: eldest sons were leaving home for the city, and farms and families were going under. If in this instance the ideological messages were reinforcing, in other cases the same groups would receive contradictory counsel. While concord in the community was a constant preachment, so also were Social Darwinist doctrines of competition and personal striving. The rural youth who heard the litany of *wa* (harmony) were equally roused by the call to *seizon kyōsō* (the struggle for survival). Often, of course, their minds were on something altogether less edifying, variously de-

13

scribed—and decried—as the "natural desires" for economic success, larger vistas, and more fun, all of which led them to take the "un-natural" step of departing the countryside for the city.[29] Although the rural youth may have heard the sermons of social education, they clearly heard a great many other things as well.

Without some notion of what these other things were, ideology is deprived of its social environment, over-isolated and over-dram-atized. It is not enough to trace ideology outward from its human sources, whether those sources are national, local, or within the fam-ily. As long as one attends to those who produce it, ideology will appear in every corner, filling the villages, classrooms, and house-holds with billowing vapors of influence. And indeed in the postwar world, *tennōsei ideorogii* was retrospectively likened to a kind of all-enveloping gas.[30] From the view of the people who occupied those corners, however, the late Meiji air swirled with social currents, of which ideology was but one, and a far less important one than its propounders were likely to admit. Here the ideologists can, inad-vertently, be helpful, since they were constantly taking the public pulse, usually to find that it was weak in national spirit. This threat-ening faintness they expressed in a revealing vocabulary of ideologi-cal failure, lamenting the indifference to their words, which—in the most literal of several locutions—like "the east wind in a horse's ear" (*baji tōfū*), hardly grazed the people's consciousness. Because these commentators then went on to identify in colorfully censorious detail the baleful influences to which the people were not indifferent, they offer indirect evidence of other currents of late Meiji social, eco-nomic, and political life that competed with the ideologists for pop-ular attention.

To develop some sense of the fuller canvas and the place of ideol-ogy on it, one looks to sources that are not, properly speaking, "ide-ological" in content. That is, they do not consciously propound a civic view, though they may indeed express one. Village plans (*ze*), teachers' reports, statistical surveys, political speeches, diaries, mem-oirs, popular songs—all offer an opportunity to view the late Meiji experience in a frame larger than the ideologists were wont to sup-ply. They provide a perspective similar to that derived from reading newspapers of the period, which themselves constitute an important source for this study. By embedding ideology more evenly in its context, such sources reduce the disproportionate importance it has for its creators, and, inevitably, for its analysts as well. As an analyst drawn like filings to his subject's magnet, I have not escaped this distortion. Ideology, as it is consciously practiced, still looms larger

14

in studies of ideology than it did in the lives of those for whom it was conceived. Nonetheless, it is occasionally possible to recreate some notion of the ideological view from society at large. This means casting about for as many bits and pieces of social information as possible, conducting an almost phenomenological inquiry into discourse as the late Meiji Japanese experienced it. One wants to know not only how the imperial house was conceived and portrayed in its modern role, but also how the emperor *appeared* to the people; and, further, not only how the people were exposed to the imperial symbol and person, but also to what else they were exposed at the same time. Ostensibly "non-ideological" sources help to situate the civic roles being urged on the people in the context of the rest of their social life, surrounding data of ideological consciousness with the ideas and values that continually competed, reinforced, and conflicted with them. This is particularly important, since a conspicuous characteristic of the ideological process described here is the degree to which influences outside the control of the conscientious ideological producers affected the universe of shared meaning that gradually emerged in the course of the period.

IV

How SUCH shared meanings arose remains a question. Thus far the argument has emphasized diversity, not consensus. A range of "ideologues," genuinely concerned with civic edification, produced multiple, contending views of the late Meiji world. The institutions through which these views were disseminated were equally diverse, their audiences varied. The process itself was uncontrollable. Bureaucrats and publicists responded to reality as they perceived it, with prescriptions designed to serve social or national purposes as they understood them. Their ideas once articulated became public property, social facts in themselves, to be manipulated and communicated in many partial and mutually conflicting ways. *Kokutai*, the concept of a mystical national polity, was turned to many uses; the call for effective local self-government at times rebounded against the interest of the central ministries that originated it. Moreover, much else was happening in the social, economic, and political spheres that caused mutations and divagations unimagined by those who toiled tirelessly in ideological activity.

How then was hegemony wrested from a process which upon close scrutiny appears anything but unified in purpose or cohesive in presentation? The answer depends on a looser construction of ideological discourse than the term *tennōsei ideorogii* suggests. If the discourse is understood to have been diverse within itself, the hegemony plural, then orthodoxy was one element in a dispersed ideological field. Just as it was produced by fits and starts, trials and errors, in the latter part of the Meiji period, so were a number of other versions of reality as it was and ought to be. Some of these, like socialism, were excluded from the dominant view as unacceptable, and were suppressed. But most coexisted, overlapped, or interacted with one another, so that rather than a single ideology, there were several ideologies, each in a constant process of mutual adjustment and change.

Despite the insinuation into the prose of general nouns like "ideologues" and "ideology," the premise here is that neither possessed quite the existential presence that these words imply. Not modern ideology, then, but a congeries of ideologies was the field in which hegemony arose. Indeed the areas of shared agreement, as well as those of shared tension, often appeared in the spaces between the ideological versions, where they seemed so commonsensical as not to merit any comment at all. Who disputed the value of progress, for example, or doubted the moral ambiguity of politics in its modern form? Such views, generalized and naturalized slowly in the course of Japan's modernization, certainly possessed as great a historical significance as the more obtrusive, but often less widely or deeply held, doctrines of the emperor system orthodoxy.

Both are important, however, and most important is the process by which such views were socially created and absorbed. Perhaps because imperial Japan's ideology, like the country itself, developed in comparative isolation, it has frequently appeared unique. One assumption here is that the general process just described is common to complex modern societies, however different the contents of their ideological formulations. On the other hand, no abstract account of ideological process explains the content of a particular ideological form. For that, historicity is responsible. Because Japan's modern myths were made in and from the Meiji period, only the Meiji period can finally account for the nature of the ideologies it generated.

II

The Late
Meiji Period

A TIME OF
SETTLEMENT

ALTHOUGH it makes ready historical sense that ideologies take time
to develop, it is less clear why the particular time in the case of
modern Japan should have been the late Meiji period. In 1868 the
Meiji Restoration had inaugurated the modern imperial state with the
symbolic return of rule to the emperor. Yet what is now called "emperor system" ideology did not begin to emerge in earnest until
around 1890. The delay is sometimes explained in terms of the country's being too caught up in the demanding work of modernization
to bother excessively with political rationalizations or civic blandish-
ments. The concern was there, but not as pressingly as the other
items on the agenda for civilization that Japan had drawn up from
largely Western sources.

Narrative accounts often characterize the first two Meiji decades
(1868-1887) as the pragmatic—and dramatic—years. Epoch-making
political developments included centralization, conscription, tax reform, the movement for parliamentary government, and the drafting
of a constitution. Social change, too, had been considerable, with the
legal leveling of the classes, compulsory elementary education, westernization, leaps in material culture, and increased stature for the rural agricultural elite. Industrialization on a strong agrarian base, an
aggressively entrepreneurial private sector, the chastening experience
of the government deflation in the early 1880s—Japan's capitalist
economy began to take shape during the same period. There would
be accelerations and setbacks, but by 1890 the direction of the economy was clearly set. Equally under way was the development of the
national infrastructure: railroads, communications, financial institutions. Even in the sphere of international relations, where the momentous events lay ahead, the object of the exercise had been clear

17

since the unequal treaties were signed in the late 1850s. It was almost as if the early Meiji scenario for gaining parity with the West were being played out in a late Meiji world, so that treaty revision, the victories over China and Russia, and the alliance with Britain seemed both the successful conclusion to a past quest as well as a departure in imperial power for the future. In all of these areas, then, the development of the structures and directions of Japan's modernity belonged to the first half of the Meiji period.

While it is true that the early Meiji elite were occupied with the pursuit of what they knew as "civilization," they were by no means indifferent to ideology. For "even if we now cause the people to run day and night, we shall not overtake the West in less than a few decades. If such is the case, how much longer will it take if they waste a day each week?" The day in question was Sunday, which if spent in "excess and dissipation" would account for 1,500 lost days in a mere thirty years, "a total of four years and one month of days and nights."[1] Impelled by this and other more consequential concerns, "enlightenment" intellectuals in the 1870s sought to edify the people to prepare them for all aspects of civilization, save perhaps its Sundays. Government leaders who insistently reiterated that the "customs and feelings of the people" (*fūzoku ninjō*) were insufficiently developed to allow for popular sovereignty were, of course, making an equally ideological point.[2] So were the Shintō missionaries in their short-lived heyday in the early seventies. Longer-lived and more important were the slogans that rang through that decade and beyond: *fukoku kyōhei*, a wealthy nation and a strong army, *shokusan kōgyō*, encouraging industry, and *bunmei kaika*, civilization and enlightenment. These phrases were repeatedly wielded as emblems and instruments of national policy during the years of turbulent institutional change. And institutions like the school system and the army were in part conceived, as Yamagata put it, with the thought that "in due course, the nation will become one great civil and military university."[3] From the time the Meiji period began—and in fact well before that—pragmatics had never wholly overwhelmed the urge to influence the population.

Nonetheless, the late 1880s marked an upsurge in ideological activity. The scale changed; more people spoke to the issue, in government, in the opposition, in the press, in the schools, in the provinces. They also spoke to more people, and with greater urgency. To take the speakers at their word, they were prompted in part by a surfeit of change. The nation's eager reach for Western models seemed sometimes to exceed its grasp, as change followed change in the gov-

18

ernment's attempt both to establish new institutions and also to maintain control of them. "Government directives have so often changed or dismantled village administration since the Restoration that it makes a strange historical tale." Moreover, continued Inoue Kowashi in 1886, this institutional fickleness made it difficult to cultivate "the spirit of self-government."[4] By 1890 the local government system had undergone three major reorganizations, in 1871-1872, 1878, and again in 1888-1889, with minor changes in between. In 1891 landlords in the northern provinces, though they "could discern no clear advantage of the new system over the old," urged that "it not be changed again, but left in place long enough for people to become accustomed to it."[5] The same was said of education ordinances, which, it seemed, "had necessarily to receive some revision or alteration with every change of education minister." How then could the "principles of national education" be fixed?[6] This plaint was common outside the government in the late 1880s, in the press, and also in the localities, which, together with the pupils' parents, bore much of the cost of the new compulsory education. Since the original education act of 1872, administrative and curricular change had been dizzying. An administrative structure was first established in 1872 on the highly centralized French model. It then moved in the space of one year (1879) to American-style local control, returned to national intervention in 1880 (though without national subsidies), changed slightly in 1885, and substantially in 1886, to a hybrid European statist system which featured German influence. The elementary curriculum had meanwhile shifted from Anglo-American egalitarian emphasis on the individual intellect, with textbooks literally translated from Willson's *Readers* or Wayland's "wisdom," to a mixture of Confucian and European elitism and moral emphasis that used texts ranging from the most ancient *Analects* to the latest Herbartian example.[7]

The civil code went through draft after Napoleonic draft from 1871 until 1888, only to be rejected after its long-delayed promulgation in 1890. Legal debate, which pitted French against British concepts of civil law and both against indigenous custom, spilled over into public controversy. At issue were the "boundless changes that have attended the reforms in every quarter since our country emerged from feudalism." European models threatened to overwhelm "our distinctive ways and customs," which, such commentators always lamented, had yet to be determined. Moreover, few suggested that they *had* been determined when, in 1898, a civil code, now based on thoroughly German models, was finally put into ef-

19

fect.[8] Since the 1870s, the army had also moved from a French to a Prussian system with major institutional changes occurring again in 1886-1889; the draft law alone underwent a handful of revisions between 1873 and 1889. In 1891 it was suggested that Chinese naval superiority was due to the Ch'ing having "single-mindedly" modeled its navy on England, while Japan had "no stick-to-itiveness (*mikka bōzu*). Last year it learned from France, this year from England, its military drill in constant flux."[9] All these institutional changes—and more—aroused a crescendo of comment in the late 1880s, which called for some fixing and securing of the national sentiment.

In this sense the ideological seizure at the end of the eighties was partly a response to what one contemporary commentator described as the "thunderboltism" of the first two post-Restoration decades.[10] The late Meiji period was less a time of upheaval than one of settlement, less of structural drama than functional adjustment, a time when change was absorbed and some sort of stability was wrested from the aftermath of crisis.[11] The ideological effort to pin things down was one part of this process. But it was by no means a simple reaction, either to the turbulent recent past or—as it is so often suggested—to the westernization that had characterized it. It is a trivialization of their task to regard the ideologists as anti-Western, which the majority emphatically were not, or as apostles of a return to the past, which had little hold on most of them. In fact, the anti-Western reaction of the eighties and early nineties was more complex than the general accounts indicate, both in its socioeconomic origins and its ideological impact. The local movements to boycott Western goods, for example, which were instigated by Sada Kaiseki and his essay on "Lamps and the Ruination of the State" (*Ranpu bōkokuron*) in the early 1880s had involved a Buddhist defense of the faith against Christianity and Copernican theory, as well as an anti-establishment call for self-help in villages suffering the economic consequences of "civilization."[12] This was worlds apart from the interests of such local groups as the Turning the Tide Society (*Kairansha*), which was founded in 1889 to preserve the Japanese spirit against indiscriminate Europeanization. These provincial men of substance, most of them in Western dress, styled themselves "progressive conservatives" and, cherishing the establishment, gathered together to debate the abolition of prostitution, the spirit of independence, Mt. Fuji, Lake Biwa, and patriotism.[13] A newly rising, self-consciously forward-looking middle-class elite, the ideologists were themselves the frequent targets of satirical anti-westernism, their coats and trousers mocked, their "beer, brandy, vermouth" caricatured in song.[14] In any case, by 1890, too much had changed; there was no possibility of going home again. It was partly because so many recognized this—some with fear, others with anticipation—that the ideological momentum gathered as it did in the late 1880s.

A SENSE OF
NATION

I

THERE WERE, however, more direct reasons for the late Meiji outbreak of concern with civic definition. Begun years before in the feudal domains, the long efforts to reconceive the state were finally reaching their institutional culmination. And for those who lived through it, the decade of the eighties had a headlong forward thrust. For every backward glance toward the changes that had transpired in the recent past, there were scores of eyes fixed upon the future, in particular on the year 1890, when the first elected national assembly would inaugurate a new political system. In later years historians concluded that the important moments of structural transition from early modern to modern Japan had occurred in the first two decades of the Meiji period. But in the late 1880s, the social and political elite anticipated that the momentous national events lay just ahead. The promulgation of the Constitution in 1889 would establish the state (*rikkoku*), and whatever else it might bring, the opening of the Diet in 1890 would confirm Japan as a nation among civilized nations (*bunmeikoku no ikkoku*). It was this perception of a beginning that lit the fires of action and opinion—and with them the flare of ideology—in the latter part of the eighties. The subject of change, too, was often presented in this light. If the state were to be established, institutionally and ideologically, then it was time, people said, for imperial Japan to make up its collective mind.

The propulsion toward 1890 gathered variably through the decade—earliest and most doggedly within the central government. In 1881 the oligarchs had promised a constitution and a national assembly. They then spent much of the next nine years making the legal and political provisions necessary to insure that the beginning of parliamentary government would not mean the end of their bureaucratic dominance. A good number of the institutional thunderbolts that came to seem excessive were hurled by the government as part of its race against the day when it would have to share power with the parties. Heightened signs of ideological concern within the government began to appear in the early eighties as well. Yamagata, who was already given to fretting over the effects of politics on the "hearts and minds of youth," spoke increasingly often of "the preparations for constitutional government." It was, he later said, like busily making ready for a journey, one that seemed to him to be fraught with peril. The nearer the constitutional apocalypse, the more he expressed the need "to strengthen the basis of the nation," both institutionally and spiritually.[15]

As the decade progressed, momentum also gathered outside the government. By the late eighties the imminence of the year 1890 seemed, as it were, to hang in the air. For those who expected in some way to be affected by—or to affect—the beginning of constitutional government, the years from 1886 through 1890 were characterized by a sense of both promise and urgency. Opposition parties, though they continued to suffer government suppression, regrouped. Employing the familiar vehicle of protest against the government's "soft" foreign policy, movements against the latest proposals for treaty revision spread across the country in 1887 and 1889, engaging in particular the provincial elite. Landowners who survived the deflation of the early eighties, often with larger holdings and increasingly commercialized enterprises, looked forward to a Diet in which their class would predominate. In anticipation, they—and their sons—took with enthusiasm to "the sea of politics, vast, deep, and mysterious."[16] Other youth, less financially well-off, but privileged by virtue of an up-to-date Western-oriented education, were equally infected by what was called rampant "political fever." They formed small associations in their towns and villages to consider the nation's prospects; they published pamphlet-like journals, some liberal, some conservative, in which they and, typically, their former schoolteachers wrote passionately about national needs.[17] Journalists in Tokyo, who often became honorary sponsors of these local groups, also spoke voluminously to the issue. Some suggested that less political fervor and more national spirit were wanted in a constitutional system. For if "high and low, rich and poor, city and country" were united, they could better "discharge their inherent duties as the people of Japan (*Nihon kokumin*)."[18] Political and moral conservatives founded societies to promote their own versions of the "national doctrine" necessary to a state about to be rent by Western-style parliamentary conflict. Shintō, Confucianism, and Buddhism, advocated one such group in 1888, comprised the "great way," along which, "like a broad street in Tokyo, princes and ministers, samurai, farmers, artisans, and merchants, beggars and outcasts, horses, cattle, dogs, and cats would all together willingly go."[19] And soon—for these arbiters of opinion were conscious always of the pressure of time. In less than two years the nation would have to be ready for the advent of its new political system.

As widespread as the perception of a new beginning was the judgment that in some profound and threatening way Japan was not yet prepared for the task that was upon it. Although the definitions both of the task and of the threat were vastly different depending on the group elaborating them, the collective call was to the people, who lacked, it was said, an adequately developed "sense of nation." Thus the words *kokka* and *kokumin* were suddenly everywhere in the late eighties, coloring the spectrum of opinion from liberal left to moral right with the hues of a nationalism that has been well chronicled.[20] National spirit, national thought, national doctrine, national essence, nationality—this outburst of nation-mindedness included explorations of national character, reassertions of indigenous ways, and projections of Japan into the world order as the nineteenth-century West defined it. Indeed the word "empire" (*teikoku*) became so fashionable in the names of schools, magazines, and insurance companies that one caricature condescendingly warned that "imperial rickshaw pullers" and "imperial nightsoilmen" would be next.[21] This was precisely the point, as the invocations of nation included, more and more pressingly, the effort to draw all the people into the state, to have them thinking national thoughts, to make *kokumin* of them, new Japanese for what was called "the new Japan." And above all, such exhortation attempted to create unity among them, not only against a foreign foe or a loss of national value, but also against the rapidly approaching day when they would constitute the citizenry of a newly constitutional state.

II

THE ideological materials immediately available from the past seemed inadequate to the job, the old rallying cries of little use. By 1889, when the Constitution was promulgated, it was of largely antiquarian interest that the Restoration had been brought about in the name of "loyalty to the emperor and repelling the barbarians." Indeed, as Albert Craig has remarked, "the cupboard of emperor-particularism was almost bare" by the time the interpreters of the Meiji state went to replenish the national supply.[22] The Restoration itself, which, like the Revolution in France, was the epochal dividing mark between the past and the present, had so diminished in meaning that it had

23

practically to be reinvented in order to give modern Japan a historical first principle. New and widely read accounts of the Restoration embodied the concerns of the late eighties and early nineties in their emphasis on unity and sense of nation, the importance of public and popular opinion, and the nature of Japan's great revolution (*daikaku-mei*). Interpreters sought in that revolution the origins of the polity that was only now at hand, and some, such as Tokutomi Sohō, were already calling for a "second restoration" to finish the incomplete work of the first.[23]

The Tokugawa period had grown distant enough for younger generations to rework its legacy and older ones to invoke it with nostalgia. In 1889 the Edo association was established in Tokyo to preserve Edo names and record Edo culture before it disappeared completely. Partly preservationist, partly anti-oligarchy, the defenders of Edo were able to exalt the Tokugawa era as "the period in which Japanese civilization achieved its greatest progress and development" (*shinpo hattatsu*).[24] Thus they filched the most hallowed Meiji claim and applied it to the period that for twenty years had evoked such vile epithets as "feudal" and "antiquated." Also in 1889 Saigō Takamori, the hero of the Restoration—but traitor to the Meiji government—was imperially pardoned and granted court rank on the occasion of the promulgation of the Constitution. If with this act the government had hoped to capture some of Saigō's legendary aura for itself, its proprietary efforts were in vain. For just two years later, in 1891, there was a revival of the sensational rumors that Saigō was alive and would soon reappear in Japan with the Russian Crown Prince or, in another version, return to public life from the mountains. And now opponents from the left and right brandished Saigō's name in criticism of the government that had so recently honored him.[25] By late Meiji, then, the Tokugawa period and the Restoration had receded sufficiently to qualify for the time-honored tradition of using the past to serve, esteem, or blaspheme the present.

The early Meiji period, on the other hand, remained too close and, as is so often the case with the immediate past, too disputed, to provide attractive civic material. The concern with "a wealthy nation and a strong army" had become so entrenched a part of national life that it did not seem capable of rousing people, unless it was to oppose the government which had acted in its name for twenty years. The call to "civilization and enlightenment" had itself been the object of popular protest in the seventies and early eighties as the establishment of conscription, schools, the household registry system, and other paraphernalia of modernity upset the social and economic balance of the countryside.[26] Moreover, the ideological formulations of the first Meiji years had come to seem abstract and limited. The Charter Oath of 1868 had declared that the affairs of state would be administered, "uniting the sentiments of high and low," which in the face of the concrete demands of a constitutional state appeared loftily archaic. In fact, the audience to whom the early Meiji political pronouncements were effectively directed had seldom been the populace at large but rather the feudal aristocracy and a small number of uncommonly risen commoners. By the late Meiji years, however, rhetoric insisted that nothing less than the forty million countrymen (*yonsenman dōhō*) would suffice to make the nation. It became common parlance— probably for the first time in Japanese history—that "just being born and raised in this country is not enough for the masses to be considered citizens (*kokumin*). The prerequisite for citizenship is a sound sense of nation (*kokkateki kannen*)," without which the people remain "*un*patriots" (*hikokumin*), and the nation endangered.[27]

To hear out the ideologists' view of their time requires an additional point, which, like the others, was iterated with awesome redundancy in the late 1880s. The felt need for unity based on suitably modern civic values to meet the challenge of new political institutions was complicated by the fact that it was not yet clear what the stuff of patriotism should consist of. Before it could be communicated to the *kokumin*, national policy in the broadest sense—the *kokuze*— would first have to be established. Was the state to be military or commercial, follow after Bismarck or Disraeli, be Westernized or Japanized?[28] Many "choices" were offered on the oddly innocent assumption that such things as "religion, morality, education, arts, politics, and the system of production" could be chosen, more or less at will.[29] The government had, of course, already made a significant number of the institutional choices that could be made, and was hurrying to make more, passing laws and ordinances at a wholesale rate—336 in the first ten months of 1890, just under the wire before the Diet opened in November.[30] Of this, the nation-minded men in the eighties and nineties were well aware, as they worked to produce "some great books on politics and ethics to supply foundations for the magnificent structures now in the course of construction."[31] The fact that the structures, however magnificent, preceded their foundations only made the task that much more difficult.

From the vantage point of later years it has often seemed that the ideological eruption of the late Meiji period was the culmination of more than two decades of bureaucratic nation-making. Thus, accounts of *tennōsei* ideology commonly suggest that the tenets of orthodoxy were handed down in 1889 and 1890 on the twin tablets of the Constitution and the Imperial Rescript on Education.[32] But the view from 1890, as the ideologues untiringly insisted, was one of chaos and contention. Few yet claimed to understand the two texts of the canon, and those who did disagreed widely about their meaning. In fact, the texts were only the beginning, and, like the United States Constitution and the Pledge of Allegiance to the flag, they depended for civic efficacy on interpretive layers that, in the case of late Meiji Japan, were still to come. Although the analysis here will necessarily deflate much of the ballooning rhetoric of the eighties and nineties to reveal the often unbuoyant meanings contained within it, on this one point at least the perceptions of the ideologists remain sound. Whatever was completed in the years before 1890, ideology in national earnest had more truly just begun.

A COMPLICATED
SOCIETY

I

SINCE ideology is continuously in process, the late Meiji formulations contained threads from earlier years. Indeed, it is a question why strands insistently present over the decades—Shintō as rites of the state, for example—should be long ignored and then suddenly taken up into the ideological fabric, often by the same people who had earlier scorned them. Yet the opposite sort of question is perhaps more compelling. What generates the crisis consciousness that sets men to weaving? In the 1880s, when "the nation" was the ready reply, some were responding to lessons learned from Western nationalism, what Matthew Arnold called "this strange disease of modern life." But others were moved by a profound distrust and fear of politics, to them a stranger and more menacing affliction. It was not an uncommon hope in the eighties and nineties that ideology—in the form of a sense of nation or civic morality—if spread widely and woven tightly enough, might extinguish the steadily flickering impulses toward politics before the parliamentary system reignited them.

Politics and the nation, however, did not remain the only spurs to ideology. Others soon loomed large, provoking the atmosphere of crisis in which ideological activity seems to thrive. For in addition to transmitting the nineteenth-century imperatives of the nation-state, the late Meiji period bequeathed to modern Japanese ideology the less tractable, more disturbing demands of social change. From the late 1890s, when the discovery of social problems (*shakai mondai*) received public attention, through the decade following the Russo-Japanese War (1905-1915), when ideological efforts directed at the social order reached a magnitude as great as the nation-mongering of the eighties and nineties, Meiji ideologues confronted the social results of Japan's plunging rush toward modernity.

Why social change, which had been accumulating noticeably since the early seventies, became the ideological focus in the late nineties and early 1900s is a question to which various answers have been given. At the time it was common for advocates involved with social questions to ascribe their concern to progress. They claimed that Japan had advanced further along a universal modern continuum in which, "once political issues are settled, social issues necessarily arise." The nation's main political business having been concluded with the Constitution and the opening of the Diet, "*shakai mondai* had now become the staple diet of politicians."[33] This 1896 comment by a conservative bureaucrat supporting industrial legislation to forestall social conflict was echoed to a word by opposition activists promoting such conflict in the name of world socialism. Both positions invoked European experience as well as European theory to demonstrate the inevitability of the preeminence of social issues in the years to come.[34] The same press that had offered a litany of nation in the late eighties now brimmed with social preachments and calls for a sense of society (*shakaiteki kannen*). Scholars and journalists agreed that just as Japan had met the nineteenth-century dictates of material progress, national strength, and political rights, it must now attend to the twentieth-century imperatives of social policy and social reform.[35] Others—such as a statistics teacher lecturing to local officials in the provinces—self-importantly pointed out that the latest learning required attention not to "national events" but to "social phenomena."[36] He scorned the obsolete approach of the 1880s, which did not distinguish between upper and lower class by professions (but presumably by feudal class), as manifesting an absence of "*rojikku*." For "logic" in turn-of-the-century Japan had joined forces with progress (*shinpo hattatsu*) to decree a concern with society.

This concern, like the word *shakai* itself, was new to the Meiji period, or so its proponents were proud to claim.[37] They now considered themselves ages distant from the 1870s, when Fukuzawa Yukichi had declared that "in Japan there was a government but no nation (*kokumin*)."[38] By 1900 Japan appeared to them to possess both government and nation but already to be falling behind in the next task of civilization, which was a social one. In an odd symmetry of intellectual comment, Kume Kunitake, a long-lived member of Fukuzawa's generation, asserted in 1921 that "in Japanese history, there was no concept of society (*shakai kannen*)," thus goading Japan onward, as the enlightenment thinkers had always done, by authoritative and unfavorable comparisons with the West.[39] In precisely this sense did many of those who, for varied and conflicting purposes, tackled social issues in the early 1900s feel themselves to be in the very vanguard of intelligent civil concern.

However genuine this feeling of an inevitable shift of concern from state to society, it was scarcely the main reason given by contemporaries for their outpouring of social comment. Less intellectual, more widely heard voices enunciated different stimuli for the sudden importance of social problems. Society, they said, was in disarray, afflicted with ills, beset by economic difficulties, roiled by the struggle for survival, upset by labor problems, exposed to dangerous thought, threatened by socialist destruction, rent by gulfs between rich and poor, city and country, worker and capitalist.[40] Localities, like youth, were delinquent; self-government lay in confusion. Cities were sinks of iniquity leading young people astray and fomenting social strife, even revolution. Customs were degenerating, morals in decline. And the middle classes, the "root and branch" from whom so much civic stability had been expected, had developed "social problems" of their own.[41] In the late 1890s and early 1900s bureaucrats, politicians, local officials, journalists, novelists, and storytellers spewed forth a vocabulary of social cataclysm that to Western ears sounds almost biblical.[42] Compared to the earlier language of national unity, which had looked, if sometimes apprehensively, to the future, the rhetoric of social problems confronted the present and found it everywhere plagued by confusion.

The sources of confusion were judged differently by different people. The government was profoundly anti-socialist; the socialists were devoutly anti-government. Some intellectuals agonized for the rural middle classes, others for the impoverished, usually urban, lower strata.[43] While one group of bureaucrats lamented the decline of self-sufficient agriculture, another berated farmers for their commercial laggardness. Yet together they constituted an ideological chorus which, like the chorus in Greek drama, both participated in and commented upon the scene around it. Its voices, though not in unison, joined in a refrain that echoed with the word *shakai*. Social problems, social reform, social policy, social education, social revolution, social novels, socialism, sociology—the choric theme was clear.

In 1901 the socialist Kōtoku Shūsui, who attacked imperialism, and the genrō Yamagata Aritomo, who advocated it, were both arguing the preeminence of social issues.[44] Instructing Katsura Tarō, the new prime minister and his disciple, in August 1901, Yamagata expressed his feeling that "in the future the source of the government's difficulties will not be foreign, but domestic affairs." Since at that time Yamagata had both Russian expansion in Manchuria and an alliance with Britain on his mind, he had clearly not abandoned his intense concern with foreign issues. Yet his letter stated that his greater worry, which therefore ought to be Katsura's as well, was the consequences of social disorder. Just three months earlier, Japan's first Social Democratic Party had been formed and banned on the same day. Yamagata warned the new prime minister that "society at present is complicated in its every aspect. Slowly and imperceptibly principles and policies are becoming confused, which in the end cannot but alter the course of the ship of state (*Nihonmaru*)."[45] What the socialists were preaching, Yamagata would have Katsura, by staying steady at the helm, prevent.

For ideas of society in the 1900s, like those of the nation in the 1880s, were common ideological property, which did not wholly belong to the government, the opposition, or any single social group. Like the swelling tones of the Greek chorus, ideology gains authority by virtue of its being collectively produced. And for uncoerced hegemony to occur, it is just this widespread harmony of concern, however discordant the individual voices, that is the first essential. The Meiji government's sudden interest in social issues is often portrayed as a reaction to socialism, which in many instances it was. Indeed, in 1911 it was possible to taunt the government for suppressing socialism as an evil while adopting some of the same positions in the unobjectionable name of "social policy."[46] But here, as in the 1880s, simple reaction is too mechanical and Newtonian an equation to explain the processes of ideological formation. The outbreak of concern with social issues, just as with national questions, must be traced to diverse groups who had diverse reasons for their sense of social crisis.

II

THE fundamental reasons were often economic, despite the fact that ideological language tended to substitute "society" for "economy," much as it did "nation" for "politics." Or perhaps it might be said—following Barthes, who described myth as language-robbery—that *because* the problems were economic, their ideological representations avoided the word, as if to obliterate the meaning of economic con-

29

tradictions with talk of social concord.[47] This does not mean that economic questions were ignored, only that in the ideological response to them they were frequently not *named*. They were, however, perceived—and acutely so. It was common to remark, somewhat ruefully, that as a result of "progress in civilization, changes in livelihood, and the rise of new enterprise, social conditions have grown increasingly complicated."[48] Commentators in the late nineties, sounding much like economic historians of later years, pointed out that this complicated society (*fukuzatsu naru shakai*) was a product of economic change that had begun in the 1870s but accelerated sharply in the years since the Sino-Japanese War of 1894-1895. Their counterparts a decade later were certain that in the years after the Russo-Japanese War of 1904-1905 even more dramatic—and unsettling—economic developments were taking place.

Most indicators proved them right. Although a 2.5 percent average annual rate of growth in GNP per capita between 1870 and 1913 placed Japan high, perhaps first, in the world in the rate of economic growth, even those economists who point to relatively smooth growth and long swings with trend acceleration find a "trough" in the late nineties and "faltering" around 1909. Others discuss the advent of Japan's first "modern" recessions, which occurred in 1890, 1900-1901 (with prior signs in 1897-1898), and again in 1907-1908.[49] Those who tried to live and work through them knew these late Meiji cycles as hard times, as each postwar boom led to each postwar bust, prices rose, and taxes increased. Government expenditures, wildly swollen by military costs and also burdened by sharply increased debt and steadily growing administrative expenses, tripled between 1890 and 1900, rising from 66 to 183 million yen, a figure that by 1910 had reached 338 million. In the same period, from 1890 to 1910, the expenditures of local government increased sevenfold, exacerbating the fiscal tug-of-war between central and local administrations.[50]

Taxes not only increased in amount but multiplied in type. Despite the political battle waged by landlords and their parties in the Diet, land taxes were raised in December 1898. But because of increases in existing taxes on saké and income and the institution of new excise and business taxes, the land tax accounted for an ever-dwindling portion of the national income. The land tax comprised 60.6 percent of government revenues in 1890, but in 1899 this had dropped to 32.5 percent and by 1911 to only 17.8 percent. Conversely, indirect taxes, which provided 23.7 percent in 1890, increased to 35.5 percent in 1899, and reached 43.5 percent in 1911.[51] At that point, of course, it was not only landlords but consumers in lower- and middle-income levels as well who claimed the need for relief. Local taxes also increased twelvefold between 1890 and 1912, with the household tax (kosūwari) at the lead. As a result, the combined national and local tax burden of each taxpaying household more than tripled between 1897 and 1912 alone.[52] Inflationary price rises further worsened the situation. Lower-income strata, whether worker or tenant, were particularly hard hit. Despite controversy among economists over whether or not real earnings rose in Meiji Japan, contemporary sources make it clear that a fair number of Japanese *felt* that they were worse off in 1911 than they had been earlier.[53] Too pressed to afford the luxury of the longer view, they felt that "the world belongs to the producers (seisansha)." For despite the growing excess of production, laborers were out of work, "and even in the good years people starved," which was "like suffering from lack of water in the middle of Lake Biwa."[54]

The producers, moreover, were increasingly industrial, since these same interwar decades between 1895 and 1915 comprised what is known as the takeoff period in the development of Japan's modern industrial capitalism.[55] The decennial punctuation of Japanese history by successful wars—the Sino-Japanese War in 1894-1895, the Russo-Japanese War in 1904-1905, and less costly and more profitably, World War I in 1914-1918—worked the leaps in economic scale that such wars often produce. Heavy industry expanded, much of it because of government investment, and the concentration of capital in zaibatsu hands proceeded apace.[56] The rate of industrialization, measured by the ratio of non-primary employment to the total, climbed steadily from 31.2 percent in 1890 to 43.6 percent in 1915, while the industrial share of total production gradually increased. More important perhaps was the sharp rise in the relative percentage of factory production to household or cottage industry, and the gradual increase in employment in the modern sector of the emerging dual economy.[57] Working in factories in town rather than in village paddy fields changed not only the nature of people's livelihood but that of their lives as well.

Yet, the same economists who emphasize the spurt in industrialization in the late Meiji period are also quick to point out that imperial Japan did not reach its "mature" industrial phase until the twenties and thirties. Much of late Meiji industry remained light industry, with textiles averaging one-third the total manufacturing output and more than half the exports throughout the period.[58] In the first factory census in 1909, 52 percent of factory labor were female textile

workers, many of whom were transient employees, who worked—
or were indentured—for a short period, then returned home to
marry.[59] Moreover, as every description of imperial Japan must rit-
ualistically repeat, the economy remained at base agrarian, with 43.6
percent of the GNP derived from agriculture in 1912. If the household industry of 20.4 percent is added to this, even with the sharp
rise in industry, only 36 percent originated in the industrial sector.[60]
The agricultural labor force, too, remained constant in absolute numbers, with the increase in non-primary employment deriving from
what economists call surplus labor from the countryside. In sum, the
retrospective view of the late Meiji economy contemplates the
marked initiation of trends that in some cases had decades to go before they reached the "turning point."[61]

This evolutionary understanding of industrialization was not,
however, available to commentators in the late Meiji period. Had it
been, they might perhaps have been less seized by a sense of social
crisis. In fact, unlike historians who pay at least part of their attention
to continuities, contemporaries (and ideologists in particular) were
wont to fasten theirs almost wholly upon change. Change for the
better, change for the worse—these, though especially the latter,
were the most common prods to ideological production. Often, after
change was more or less absorbed into the social mainstream, ideologists—having writ—moved on. This means that when a new phenomenon like the industrial working class made its initial appearance,
it often provoked greater ideological concern than its numerical presence might seem to warrant. Laborers (rōdōsha), loosely defined, had
reached only 2.5 million by 1909, while by 1935 they were 8 million
strong. Yet to those concerned with labor problems in the late Meiji
period, the relevant figure was that in 1888 there had been only
136,000.[62] The laborers, moreover, were going on strike. Unions had
begun to form in the late nineties as part of the wider social movement of the time. The number of strikes for higher wages mounted
in the post Sino-Japanese War recession that began in 1897-1898,
dropped somewhat, then reached a peak in 1907 during the recession
after the Russo-Japanese War.[63] To the government and others who
shrank from social disorder, the labor disputes, like socialism, were
an unmistakable sign that modern economic life engendered conflict
on a large and unacceptably divisive scale.

Similar thoughts were expressed about other results of economic
change. Urbanization, for example, appeared as a threatening development, not because cities—any more than labor disputes—were
modern inventions, but again because of changes in scale. In the late

1890s and especially during the post-Russo-Japanese War years, more and more people moved to cities, attracted by the opportunities for work and education, for social success and economic survival. The percentage of the population living in cities with more than 50,000 inhabitants doubled from seven to fourteen percent between 1888 and 1913.[64] Although this left Japan still overwhelmingly rural, at the time there were many who considered the rate of urban growth more significant, precisely because of what it would mean for the countryside. Osaka doubled its 1897 population by 1916, reaching 1.5 million people, and in 1911 only forty percent of Tokyo's inhabitants had been born there. Despite the fact that many of these urban migrants were more or less temporary—in Yokohama, for example, approximately sixty percent of the population between 1907 and 1912 retained their household registry in their home location—their numbers swelled the cities.[65] Late Meiji ideologues found this social phenomenon all the more vexing because it was not confined to the capital. The provincial cities were also growing at remarkable rates. And to village officials in rural areas such as Shikoku, the malign effect of Matsuyama city on the "simple and pure customs of the village" seemed every bit as corrupting (*kairan*) as the allegedly iniquitous streets of Tokyo.[66]

For, although the newly urban and industrial Japanese were often the stimulus for ideological activity, the ideology itself was directed not to these groups but predominantly to the countryside. And rural Japan, the persistent focus of concern, was being disrupted not only by the attraction of the cities but by a whole range of social consequences of the economic changes mentioned here. During the eighties and nineties, large landholdings grew larger, and by the turn of the century absentee ownership had sharply increased. During the same period self-cultivating landlords, who were so often looked to for stability as the village middle class, declined in number, and by 1908 tenancy had reached 45.5 percent of cultivated land, the level it maintained until the end of the Second World War.[67] Hardships imposed by the two Meiji wars and by the sacrifices demanded in the name of postwar management (*sengo keiei*) intensified the difficulty at the same time that education and public works were consuming ever larger amounts of local funds. Out-migration and poverty, especially in less economically developed areas like Tōhoku, destroyed some villages and battered many more. Village Japan, which was expected by the authorities to be agriculturally productive, fiscally responsible, and still able to pay the taxes that fell so heavily there, seemed on the verge of failing to meet these age-old tasks, now

33

changed so greatly in nature and scale. Hence the spate of farm legislation in the 1890s and early 1900s.[68] And with the legislation came
the ideological barrage. Bureaucrats intoned the Confucian precept
about agriculture being the foundation of the state, and agrarianists—
presumably intending a compliment—proclaimed the villages "the
fertilizer of the nation."[69] A considerable part of the ideological effort
to shore up the countryside against further inroads of progress proceeded on the assumption that moral suasion could keep men farming
as they once had done, even though this was against all the socioeconomic odds inherent in a rapidly industrializing economy, which by
1910 also had an expanding empire to support.

III

THE LATE Meiji commentators had been correct: progress, as they
called it, had brought them a complicated society. Having recognized
this, they took great pains to record and measure it. Social calculations abounded in the period. Central and local government surveys
were conducted on most of the subjects mentioned here and on many
others as well.[70] Journalists recorded the mounting number of pawnshops, the military totted up the methods of draft evasion, and someone (it is unclear who) counted the rats in Tokyo, which had multiplied by 8.2 million in a mere five years.[71] Such calculations were
often adduced to support the view that social disarray was rampant.
Indeed, the ideological hyperbole that swirled around social questions
is itself significant. For nowhere, verminous Tokyo included, were
the vistas of dire disaster as apparent as they were in the ideologues'
hortatory prose. Also, the social phenomena they so often criticized—the lure of money, of the cities, of advanced education—were
at that time establishing themselves ever more deeply among the people. The word "society," though linked with problems (*mondai*) in
ideological comment, often expressed a positive meaning in popular
usage. An almost universally enrolled population of school-age children, for example, eagerly looked forward to entering society (*shakai
ni deru*) when they finished their studies.[72] Progress, it seemed, had
widened a gulf not only between rich and poor but also between
ideological formulations and social experience.

The nation-mindedness and civic education that began in the
eighties soon naturalized themselves as elements in the ideological
landscape, but the problems posed by socioeconomic change seemed
harder to domesticate. The efforts to produce ideological foundations
for national structures and international ventures appear measured
indeed when compared to the ensuing scramble to retrieve society

34

from the effects of cumulative economic and social change. As with their interpretations of the nation, the ideologues had to evolve their prescriptions for society as they went. But there was less coherence and less agreement among the diverse ideological sources than there had been in national matters. Perhaps it is because social change is less controllable and economic relations more divisive than the call to the nation or the ructions of politics. Or perhaps Japan had been better prepared for the one than the other. To leave these speculations for the moment, it can be said at the outset that the establishment which is generally presumed to have completed the institutional arrangements for the dissemination of *tennōsei* ideology in the decade between 1905 and 1915 was sometimes unsure within itself about the social purposes these institutions were to serve. A vision of the nation in the nineteenth-century mode had come a good deal easier, it seems, than a conception of society that suited twentieth-century needs.

IDEOLOGY
AND ITS TIME

I

THE IDEOLOGICAL chorus that hailed the nation swelled its voices from the late 1880s and, once heard, its chant continued through the decades, if with different echoes. The call for a sense of nation gradually moved out from its nationalist, pre-parliamentary context into the public domain, where it was available for an expanded range of uses. In 1900 the perennial opposition politician Ōkuma Shigenobu argued that the Japanese people needed to acquire a "sense of nation" so that they could lead and protect their less fortunate Chinese brethren from further Western incursions. In 1906 Ōkuma preferred to assert that the government's rhetoric about the need for a "united nation" was meaningless, since "the Japanese now are all a loyal and patriotic (*chūkun aikoku*) people." Their greatest difficulty was not undeveloped ideology but overdeveloped bureaucratic politics (*kanryō seiji*), in which "the number of bureaucrats increases daily and affairs stagnate daily," even as "it rains down laws and ordinances."[73] On each occasion Ōkuma could invoke national consciousness for his own purpose—which was criticism of government policy—because the vocabulary was now widely enough shared to be both immediately understood and unobjectionable. This is one characteristic of established ideology. Another is that those elements that succeed in establishing themselves in one context are transmuted and invoked for different uses in another. An early advocate of youth groups made a "sense of nation" a cardinal point in his boy-scoutish call to rural youth in 1896, while in 1906 a leading bureaucratic apostle of local self-government suggested that the "sense of nation" and public duty aroused in the people by the Russo-Japanese War be turned now to the advantage of village administration.[74] This expansion of ideological usage is accompanied by another characteristic, which is expressed in the incessant claims that the sense of nation was perpetually in danger, never complete, or sharply on the decline. That is, the task of ideology is never finished; the process will continue. But it is important to recognize that the period in which the chorus is first heard in strength sets its own indelible stamp on the content of the subsequent ideological uses of any particular term. Whether invoked to serve the later causes of imperialism, or social order, or local government, the environment of the late eighties and early nineties had set the Japanese representation of national consciousness firmly on its course.

The same is true for the ideological production that centered on social questions. Its chorus of concern began later and bore in its ideological messages the mark of the years in the late nineties and early 1900s, when Japan was beginning its transition to industrial capitalism and a modern middle class and mass society. These social strands, like those of the nation, continued beyond the period when they were initially woven into the ideological fabric, and eventually they exhibited similar characteristics of naturalization of meaning, expansion of usage, and an always elusive completion. And yet, just as there had been a waxing of activity that began the ideological process in the 1880s, it can also be said that a waning occurred in the years after the death of the Meiji emperor in 1912. Ideology, of course, did not disappear and indeed acquired a centrality in the 1930s that would have been unimaginable in the earlier years. But new concerns were generally met with reformulations of ideological material that had come into currency in the late Meiji period, and wholly new elements were rare.

In the late 1880s, in the midst of the sense of beginning engendered by the imminence of new political structures, there had been heightened concern with ideological questions, but few answers. The language of modern ideology had not yet been settled, much less its meanings. The emperor, for example, was a constitutional monarch, and every nation possessed a *kokutai*. By 1912, with the death of the Emperor Meiji, which was widely perceived with what Harry Harootunian identified as "a sense of an ending," the language was pres-

36

ent.[75] The emperor was both a constitutional monarch and a deified patriarch, and the only *kokutai* in evidence belonged to Japan. By 1915 nearly all the institutions that were to disseminate the civic credos and social injunctions were also hierarchically in place. By this time Japan had produced its modern myths, the elements all present, if not yet wholly accounted for.

II

ALTHOUGH much had changed between 1890 and 1915, there is little question that far more had altered in the preceding quarter century. Japan in 1865 bore small resemblance to the Japan of 1890, whereas Japan in 1890 was part, if only the beginning part, of a continuous period that in some ways ended in 1945 and in others proceeds into the present. Geoffrey Barraclough, the British historian, has suggested that the world entered the contemporary era in 1890, the structural aspects that characterize the present being largely on hand by 1900, but scarcely there at all a few decades earlier. By the world—all his intentions to the contrary—Barraclough means the West, but his statement is equally applicable to Japan. And though he wishes to make room for the "branches of extra-European history [that] cut into the past at a different angle," in the case of Japan it might be said that its angle was much the same as that of a number of Western nations of the same period.[76] This is true not only of such phenomena as industrialization, social change, and political process, but also of ideology.

In France from 1870 to 1914—the years corresponding almost exactly to the Meiji period—Eugen Weber has described the process of converting peasants into Frenchmen, of including the people in the national project. Likening the process to colonization, he depicts Paris civilizing the recalcitrant provinces and instilling "a national view of things in regional minds."[77] Although Japan had virtually no independent regional cultures within its borders, the homogeneity of which we hear so much worked no miracles on the nationalization of sentiment. Even on an institutional level, it is possible to argue that Japan had given a greater appearance of centralization since the 1870s than it in fact possessed. That is, the center had charged the localities with a range of national responsibilities, from electing assemblies and collecting taxes to providing police and teachers and building schools. Since the government decreed, but seldom paid for, many of these requisites of state, seventy to eighty percent of local budgets was devoted to executing national tasks on the local level.[78] That the localities did so may have been one of the most important

elements in Japan's nineteenth-century transformation, more important perhaps than the government's measures, which without local
compliance would have meant very little indeed. But the localities
did not comply at once, without cost, or without conflict. What Weber describes in France as "the process by which the language, ges-
tures, and perceptions of national politics penetrated the countryside"
occurred in Meiji Japan as the local elite learned the political lessons,
demanded the fiscal trade-offs, and otherwise began to act on behalf
of local interests within the national political scene.[79] The government, moreover, competed within itself, ministry against ministry,
for control and influence in the provinces, both institutionally and
ideologically.[80] Though the rhetoric of national unity was constantly
wielded as a talisman against the conflict of local interests, in fact,
institutional integration proceeded a good deal more unevenly than
the government was wont to admit.

What was true of political relations between the center and the
provinces was also true of other indices of national integration. Ideologists in Japan, as in Germany of the same time, sought not only
national unity but also an "inner spiritual revival" to help protect the
nation against the potentially threatening social results of modernity.[81] Committed as they were to progress, the old and new Meiji
elite also cherished their position of dominance and craved the social
stability which they thought necessary to preserve it. Thus they
urged patriotism and social harmony as a means of subduing potentially wayward elements. By means of the newly developed catechism of citizenship, all Japanese were to become *kokumin*, assimi-
lated into the dominant society. Not unlike American nativism of the
same period, late Meiji ideology insisted on social conformity as the
binding principle of national loyalty.[82] It may seem odd to compare
such a homogeneous society as Japan to a nation of immigrants. But
in fact Japanese nativism was often invoked for very nearly the same
purpose, except that its targets were those within Japan who appeared to be the bearers of alien ways and thoughts. This included
those who consciously advocated such unacceptable foreign notions
as individualism or socialism as well as those who unwittingly pursued what were characterized as unhealthy Western preoccupations
with materialism and personal success. The United States confronted
a host of foreigners, the Japanese, very few, though their presence
always aroused concern far greater in measure than their number.
But if Americans had real foreigners, the Japanese had metaphorical
ones, and in both cases ideology was considered a prime means of
nationalizing them. To repeat an earlier assertion, this metaphorical

anti-foreignism was not the same as anti-Westernism, but rather a device to gain the day for domestic purposes, social stability in particular. And in this, as in national integration, Japan was far less orderly and coherent than the tenets of *tennōsei* ideology might lead us to believe.

To make these comparisons is not to suggest that Meiji history marched in lockstep with that of Western nations of the same period, though, in terms of modern ideology, this seems a more useful proposition than the frequent comparisons with the third world. There are rather two points here: the first is once again to insist that Japan was in its process of ideological formation a good deal less than unique, and should be seen in the larger context of late nineteenth- and early twentieth-century developments in the newly contemporary world of Barraclough's description. The second is to stress that the process of converting the Japanese into *kokumin* was as complicated and drawn out as turning peasants into Frenchmen, Germans into a Germanic *Volk*, or immigrants into one-hundred-percent Americans. The Japanese, in short, were no instant patriots either, nor was the process as irrevocably thorough as it may sometimes seem. If ideology proposes, or imagines, a relation between men and their world, it is fair to say that the dominant ideology in imperial Japan imagined a nation that was more unified and a society that was more stable than those who lived within them knew to be the case. But since the dominant ideology was not the only one in the field, there arose and persisted an array of ideological formulations which at some points reinforced, and at others contradicted, the official ideological imagination.

Men make their own ideology, but, as Marx may remind us, they do not make it just as they please. The ideologists, official and unofficial, were propelled by the possibilities and confined by the limits of their time. Japan's modern ideology was a product of the Meiji period, which therefore determined the shape and direction that ideology would take. Even the elements drawn from the recent or the ageless past were cast into molds that were newly formed in the Meiji years to suit the needs of the time. And Japan's ideology, like its counterparts in other modern nation-states, reflected the period that produced it. From this point of view at least, "the sense of an ending" that people experienced in the years after the Emperor Meiji's death was not inaccurate. For the late Meiji rendition of modernity was, until 1945, the authoritative one. This, too, is characteristic of ideological hegemony: that by outliving the context that generated it, it becomes an anachronism outpaced—but too entrenched to be easily undone—by change. Another period might perhaps have bequeathed a different ideology to its posterity, but Japan would have to live with its late Meiji heritage, even after it ceased to make the sense it had once commanded.

IN THE ARGUMENT thus far, late Meiji ideology has been approached from four points of view. The first is that of *tennōsei* ideology as it has been formulated in postwar Japan. The second is a theoretical presentation, which assumes that modern ideological process proceeds in roughly similar ways in different national contexts. The third is the ideologues' view of their subject—what the nation-minded men of the eighties and nineties and the social commentators of the nineties and 1900s thought and said they were doing in their efforts to rouse their countrymen. We have given them, so to speak, the first word, in order to see the task of late Meiji ideology as they saw it. The fourth is the brief comparative reference that places Japanese ideology in its temporal frame, the wider international context of which the ideologues themselves were so acutely aware and well informed. Now these representations must be combined in an analysis that seeks to portray not only what the ideological producers were saying but also what they were meaning. They have been permitted, all of them, to speak at once—socialist and bourgeois, bureaucrat and landlord, progressive and conservative—in order to establish their cacophony of common concern. But now their voices must be separated, and further, an attempt made to describe how their reinforcing and conflicting messages worked out in the larger social space beyond the borders of their copious words.

The organization of the study reflects both the evolution and the anatomy of the ideology produced in the late Meiji period. The chronological account begins and ends in ceremony: in February 1889, the "unprecedented event" of the promulgation of the Constitution, and in September 1912 the majestic funeral of the Meiji emperor (and no less majestic suicide of General Nogi on the same day). For Japanese of the period, these two great national ceremonies betokened a promising beginning and a splendid ending to a part of Japan's modern age. Within the general bounds of this chronology, main aspects of the ideological universe are taken up in turn, first those that related to a "sense of nation," and then those concerned with a "complicated society." Although modern views of the nation had been an issue from before the time of the Restoration, they did not take their mature form until after 1889. Conceptions of politics, the imperial symbol of nation and empire, the civil morality of loyalty and patriotism—these national elements constituted the nine-teenth-century basis of *tennōsei* ideology. The ideological results of the social concerns that began in the nineties assumed their full shape in the years following the Russo-Japanese War. In response to the sense of social crisis that seized the ideologues after the war, Japan's agrarian myth was refurbished for modern use, and village and family were reconceived as the social foundations of the state.

The concluding section seeks to reassemble the several aspects, though not into one stupendous whole, since this study denies such a monolithic character even to the full form of *tennōsei* ideology in the Meiji period. The attempt rather is to examine the language of ideology to see how its elements interacted with one another and to suggest the grammar of ideology by which hegemony was ex-pressed. How did state and society appear by the end of the Meiji period, and how did these views relate to the ideological orthodoxy whose doctrines and institutional channels were by then largely in place? And how were these versions of the 1910s to fare in the years to come, when they had in good part survived the context for and in which they were made? Although these are questions that cannot satisfactorily be answered, the attempt helps to provide a sense of the process by which *tennōsei* ideology came into being.

BUT IN LATE Meiji times there was, strictly speaking, no such thing as *tennōsei*. The Japanese of the period knew nothing of an "emperor system," since the new political structures were referred to, over and over again, as *rikkensei*, a "constitutional system."[83] Hence to con-cede to the Japanese of the Meiji period the weight of the world they lived in, it is with the Constitution that the chronicle of the emerging ideology must start.

III

The Body Politic

AN UNPRECEDENTED
CEREMONY

I

AT TEN in the morning of the eleventh of February 1889, the dignitaries assembled in the newly redecorated audience chamber of the imperial palace. Resplendent in formal Western dress, either military uniform or tails, they assumed their places facing the throne. Designed in the European style, it was situated as Eastern tradition dictated at the northern end of the room. To either side of the raised and red-carpeted dais stood high civil and military officials, members of the peerage, prefectural governors, and other specially designated guests. In the gallery on the left were the foreign diplomatic corps and members of the foreign community; in the right gallery stood selected representatives of the press and chairmen of prefectural assemblies, who had been chosen to represent the people on an occasion of such obvious importance to them. At half past ten, the Emperor Meiji, in the uniform of what the foreign press of the day called a generalissimo, entered to the strains of the national anthem. He was accompanied by palace officials, ministers of state, the imperial guard, and followed by the empress in a Western gown with a long train. The assemblage bowed. Then Sanjō Sanetomi, lord keeper of the privy seal, presented a scroll to the emperor, who read aloud from it the Rescript promulgating in the name of "our imperial ancestors" and "for the sake of our present subjects and descendants," "the present immutable fundamental law." From President of the Privy Council Itō Hirobumi—appropriately enough, since he was the oligarch most responsible for its contents—the emperor received another scroll with the text of the document. This he handed to Kuroda Kiyotaka, the prime minister, who had advanced as far as the first step of the dais, though no further, since no one was permitted to look down upon the emperor. The prime minister received the "fundamental law of the state" with a deep bow. The audience was

42

reported to have been moved by its significance, though in truth no one except those who had been involved in its drafting knew yet what the document contained. To the peal of bells and a cannon salute outside and a reprise of the national anthem within, the emperor and his party departed the hall. The guests bowed once again. In less than ten minutes, "the Constitution of the Great Empire of Japan" had been proclaimed. It was, as everyone described it, "an unprecedented ceremony."[1]

Earlier that morning the emperor had performed another ritual in the palace, this time at the inner sanctuaries and clothed in ancient court dress. For the promulgation of the new law of state had been scheduled to coincide with the 2549th anniversary of the legendary founding of the empire, the holiday known as *kigensetsu*. Along with the traditional Shintō offerings to his imperial ancestors, the emperor brought news of the Constitution. In his oath he reported the desirability of such a law "in consideration of the progressive tendency of the course of human affairs and in parallel with the advance of civilization." At the same time he assured the ancestors that this was to the end of preserving the ancient form of government bequeathed by them to the country. After the emperor had placated the ancestral spirits, a Shintō priest delivered the same message to the "myriad gods" at the palace shrine. All that remained was for the imperial messengers, who had previously been dispatched, to report to Ise shrine and to the graves of two special ancestors, the founding Emperor Jimmu and Meiji's father, Emperor Kōmei, who had reigned before him. Thus were the nation's notables and also the gods duly notified of Japan's new Constitution.[2]

The forms of ceremony were revealing. In the throne room the emperor handed down the Constitution, his gesture symbolizing the *kintei kenpō*, a Constitution bestowed upon the nation as a gracious imperial gift. Sovereignty resided in the emperor, whose imperial prerogatives were made explicit in the new Constitution. Yet in ritual fact, the emperor had merely transferred the document from the hands of one oligarch to another; and in political fact, the government would operate in similar fashion. Ministerial decisions would pass through imperial hands for the sanction of legitimacy, remaining, like the scroll, unchanged. The scarcity of party politicians and the preponderance of bureaucrats in the hall fitted the oligarchs' view of the role of the Diet, a view which they would pronounce publicly within the week. The following afternoon Kuroda articulated the principle of transcendental cabinets, and three days later Itō reiterated that the government must stand apart from all parties.[3] From this point of view, the guest list for the occasion reasonably represented the body politic as the government conceived of it in 1889.

The inclusion of the foreigners was of the utmost importance, as were the European-style furnishings and the Western dress. The Constitution was meant in part to demonstrate Japan's credentials as a civilized nation, and most particularly, a nation worthy of the autonomy denied it by the unequal treaties, which had yet to be revised. When copies of the Constitution were distributed among the guests at the end of the ceremony, prepared English translations were on hand for the foreigners. Their reactions, however, proved more mixed than many had hoped. In an admiring article on the "Asiatic Yankees" in the New York *World*, the Japanese were credited with being "an exceedingly progressive race. They have successively adopted our style of dress, our newspapers, our music, our alphabet, our methods of education, as well as our freedom of education and thought." Such gratifying progress notwithstanding, Japan had achieved only a "German constitution," raising the question "as to how far all this can be regarded with any degree of confidence in its stability." The European press, although clearly less disturbed than the Americans by the choice of the Prussian model, expressed similar skepticism.[4] These responses dismayed Japanese intellectuals of the time, and nearly twenty-five years later, when the international mood had shifted, one writer proudly hailed the successful operation of his country's constitutional system "which the foreigners had first regarded as mere apery of the West."[5]

Lest the constitutional occasion be misconstrued as the metamorphosis of the Meiji emperor into a European-style monarch, however, the earlier presentation to the gods and ancestors had served to reaffirm the link between the ruler the Germans called "Kaiser Mutsuhito" and the most venerable of Japanese traditions, the descent of the ruling house from the sun goddess. The religious and moral supremacy which, in the words of the Constitution, made the emperor "sacred and inviolable" was symbolized by the oath he swore to his ancestors to uphold their ancient legacy. This mixture of modern European modishness in protocol and statecraft with mythic appeals to the deepest Japanese past was not confined to the precincts of the palace. Itō, occasionally known in the critical press as "Count Constitution," explained the different provisions of the law by moving in his famous *Commentaries* from examples of legendary gods with names like *Hatsu-kuni-shirasu-sumera-mikoto* ("emperor governing the country for the first time") to disquisitions on the *Reichsgericht* in seventeenth-century Germany and the diplomatic affairs of England's William III.[6] And in the morning, as he was preparing to leave for the promulgation of the Constitution which bore his countersignature, Mori Arinori was assassinated.

Mori, the minister of education known for his westernizing policies, was murdered because of a gesture of disrespect to the imperial house he had allegedly made at Ise shrine over a year before. Members of the government, men of opinion, and the foreign community were appalled at what they viewed as the assassin's act of imperial fanaticism. But as the press printed each sensational detail, a portion of popular sentiment soon went over to the youthful killer. For a time in February and March, Mori, the apostle of "civilization," was eclipsed in the public eye by his murderer, Nishino, the emperor-revering Chōshū samurai, who so lived on in print that the Home Ministry suspended newspapers and banned publications for appearing to encourage his sort of disruptive behavior. The double ceremony of modern monarchy and ancient reverence that had taken place in the palace on the same day seemed to some to reverberate in the contrasting notions of imperial service held by Mori and his loyalist assassin.[7]

II

FOR MOST Japanese, however, the palace ceremonies remained loftily beyond their ken, and even in Tokyo, the popular celebrations moved in a different world. Inside the palace with the gods and the officials, all was stately and solemn. Outside it was chaos, with lanterns, flags, floats, and people filling the streets of the capital, "like the Kanda and Sannō festivals, *bon* and New Year's all rolled into one."[8] Schoolchildren lined the mall in front of the palace, joined by people from the provinces and from other wards of the city. National flags had early sold out, enterprising peddlers hawked oranges at six times the usual cost, and saké wholesalers quickly doubled their prices as the demand jumped dramatically. "Constitution candies" were confected for this, the "celebration of the century."[9] And when the emperor emerged from the palace at Nijūbashi to review the troops at the Aoyama parade ground that afternoon, shouts of *Tennō heika banzai* were heard in his presence for the first time, patterned, as had been advocated, after the European "hooray."[10] That evening while hundreds of guests were entertained at a banquet in the palace, most of Tokyo marked the event in a different style. Instead of the pomp of European ceremony, pinched leather shoes, and glittering chandeliers, the people celebrated with an old-fashioned festival, wearing the traditional high clogs in the light of the lanterns in the

45

street. The excitement, however, was as palpable outside the palace as in. The revelry prompted one dour foreigner to remark that "the great joke is that no one has the least idea of what the Constitution will contain."[11] Nakae Chōmin commented ruefully that "the people are drunk with the name" of a constitution, though they do not yet know whether it is "gold or dross."[12] The Constitution was like the sacred contents of the portable shrine in a Shintō festival which remain concealed even as they are celebrated. The general lack of information confirmed the extent to which the oligarchs had succeeded in keeping the contents of the Constitution a secret until it was safely out of their hands.

An editorial entitled "What sort of thing is a constitution?" pointed out that "though his honor the ward headman states how gracious and auspicious it is, in the back streets it is unclear what is auspicious and gracious and why." The Constitution, the writer went on to explain, was the "rules of the country" (kuni no okite), in much the same way that firms had rules and families had regulations. At this juncture, therefore, he was prepared to identify two auspicious aspects: that after the Constitution officials could no longer do as they pleased and that the Japanese had not had to spill blood to wrest such a law from an unwilling ruler, as was so often the case in the West. With the concluding note that it was not possible to explain the Constitution fully in but one or two editorials, the writer pointed out that he had tried only to supply the rough outlines for the Japanese equivalent of the man in the street (kumakō hachikō), and for further details the readers should consult the Tokyo asahi newspaper in the days after the eleventh of February.[13] Popular entertainers soon developed routines on the subject, a common one centering on the pun that the emperor had bestowed not a constitution (kenpō no happu) but a silken work coat (kenpū no happi). "Sister, when do you suppose they will hand out the silk coats?" "Hmm, probably as souvenirs when the Diet shop opens next year."[14]

In the provinces, where the local notables were fairly knowledgeable about the "Diet shop," ceremonies were held at schools, temples, and shrines at the same hour as the state promulgation in Tokyo. Mock scrolls were employed to suggest the real document which was not yet available for copying. Athletic competitions and fireworks, music, gun salutes, and convivial drinking contributed to the atmosphere of celebration, though there was less general reveling in the countryside and more elite banqueting. Local officials hosted gatherings of their fellow men of influence (yūshi) because, as one announcement urged, it was "better to celebrate the Constitution in a group and so to enjoy lively and pleasant discussion with others."[15] In this way the patriotic spirit would be nourished, which, the speakers often argued, was more important now that "the Constitution has made clear the citizen's right to cooperate and the sharing between the ruler and the people."[16] The word for cooperation (*kyōsan*) used in this speech means approval or sanction, suggesting a more bureaucratic view of parliamentary politics than was held by those members of the audience who had been active in the popular rights movement and who now hoped to gain the right of political participation that they had advocated for so long. Thus in their own way these provincial assemblages were as politically representative as the Tokyo gathering had been.

The meetings were typically described as convocations of "officials (*kan*) and the people (*min*) together." The officials were occupants of prefectural, county, and local offices, and the "people" were the *yūshi*, the landowners, businessmen, journalists, and other leaders of the localities. They would be both the supporters and the adversaries of the government in the new constitutional system (*rikkensei*). Thus their oratory stressed the political role of the citizen, while the oligarchs argued the government's case for impartial preeminence. Educated youth who followed Tokutomi Sohō in considering themselves the young men of Meiji dreamed parliamentary dreams unavailable to the old men of the Tenpō era.[17] One faithful diarist of elite local life, Aizawa Kikutarō, the second son of a landlord in Kanagawa prefecture, was moved by the events of February the eleventh to record the promulgation of the Constitution at unaccustomed length. He even included detailed accounts which he copied verbatim from the newspaper his family had begun to subscribe to just the year before.[18] Tanaka Shōzō, who battled the government both in and outside the Diet for most of his life, first protested that the chairmen of prefectural assemblies had been invited only to "respectfully observe," not—like the bureaucrats and the foreigners—to "attend" the constitutional ceremony in Tokyo. Having noted this insult to the people, the social iconoclast and political activist procured himself a frock coat and wrote three heartfelt poems to celebrate the Constitution, "This gift / From our Lord to his people / Of a priceless jewel!"[19] Other local figures were less excited or informed about the subject: the "certain man of repute" in Iwate prefecture, for example, who declined the invitation to the constitutional ceremony at the local railway station with the polite assurance that he would be delighted to attend "the banquet celebrating the promulgation of next year's Constitution."[20] In general, however, the local elite throughout the country eagerly anticipated the new polity. For whether they were stalwart conservatives or the liberal opposition, they fully expected to have a part in it.

BUT EVEN as the constitutional ceremonies continued, some suggested that the unprecedented event had occasioned more celebration than cogitation. Enough of the uproar (*bakasawagi*), argued one editorial; it was time to begin to prepare for constitutional government (*rikken seitai*).[21] The press reminded its readers that the Charter Oath had promised an assembly and public discussion, and the Rescript of 1881, a constitution and parliament. Now when Japan was about to acquire them, "the typhoon has passed and enthusiasm cooled off completely."[22] Newspapers sought to remedy this with front-page series entitled "Reading the Constitution" and with supplements and extras that included the full text and explanations of each article.[23] Even though the language was technical and the subject difficult enough to daunt the most assiduous reader, commentators continued to be critical of the *kokumin* for ignoring a "law which is necessary to achieve progress and to bring happiness and prosperity to the people." In response to the imperial generosity in bestowing the Constitution, the people were repeatedly urged to exert themselves. The same series of editorials suggested, however, that it would take time to regulate the relationship between the ruler and his subjects. England had had a millenium of experience in political participation, but such practices were quite new to Japan.[24] In this sort of comment, the *minkan* press often unwittingly echoed the government's position that the people were not yet ready to share in the weighty affairs of state. Still the press persevered in its calls to civic duty, exhorting Japanese to take an interest in their Constitution, in order that "the honor of the nation not be stained."[25]

Even so, the audience for such constitutional exhortation remained socially, economically, and politically narrow. The general public, who at this time were not yet newspaper readers, knew of the Constitution by hearsay and celebration, and to some extent from the popular woodblock prints depicting the promulgation ceremony.[26] But the Constitution itself was remote, its connections with familiar political and emotional realities too tenuous to sustain wider popular feeling in its name. When local notables gathered for Constitution reading meetings (*kenpō haidokukai*) in late February and March, of the more than one thousand people who attended one such occasion it was remarked that they were "country gentlemen in Western clothes and high hats, no grooms or rickshawmen or work clothes among them."[27] In late Meiji Japan "grooms and rickshawmen" was the standard social epithet for the lower working classes, usually those who lived in the cities. Though these groups had joined the revelry on the eleventh of February, their interest in having become "the first constitutional people in Asia" was naturally slight. For however much the word *kokumin* was invoked in 1889, its effective meaning was closer to that of the oft repeated *yūshi*—it was the men of influence, and those who could and would join them, who had comprehended the news of their Constitution.

IN FEBRUARY 1889, articulate opinion judged that the possession of a constitution proved that Japan was now fully embarked upon "civilization." For "where there is a nation there is necessarily a constitution, and without a constitution there is no nation worthy of the name."[28] Both the government, fixed on nation-building, and the opposition, hopeful of political power, believed in this constitutional premise. With the promulgation ceremony, the Meiji elite momentarily shared a sense of beginning, of experiencing what was called "a national spring." The wider public, too, celebrating less the law than the season, joined in a mood that compared to that of a coronation, or better perhaps, to Queen Victoria's opening of the Crystal Palace in 1851, in which some had seen "the second and more glorious inauguration of their Sovereign."[29] In 1889 Japanese men of opinion felt that the emperor's bestowal of a constitution enhanced both the nation and its monarch by inaugurating a modern polity known to all as *rikkensei*. Unable yet to foresee how this constitutional system would function, they greeted its establishment alone as cause for celebration.

THE DENATURING OF
POLITICS

I

THE CONSTITUTION, however celebrated, established only the legal shape of the polity. It was the first general election and the opening of the Diet in 1890 that marked a political change, a change in the praxis of politics. What, then, was the conception of politics that accompanied Japan's embarkation as a newly parliamentary state? Ideologically, it was not the constitutional "rules of the country" that were at issue but the political content that would characterize their practical application in the time to come. The ideological agents who

49

projected a view of politics (*seiji*) to the late Meiji population included, first, the government; second, the collective intellectual apparatus known as the "public opinion of the people" (*minkan no yoron*), which in Meiji parlance was not a populist phrase but a reference
to the elite who were not in government, whether they were members of opposition parties, intellectuals, journalists, or local notables;
and, third, the potentially professional politician (*seijika*), an embry-
onic figure who took on new substance with the advent of elections
and a national parliament. Amid the high anticipation that surrounded the promulgation of the Constitution, these three groups
monopolized the open forum on the subject of politics.

> Public opinion, public opinion (*yoron yoron*), they shout and the echo is
> political; the government, the government (*seifu seifu*), they call, and
> their wails too, are political. Are the people of Japan to live by politics
> alone?[30]

Not, certainly, if the government's views prevailed, since in the
1880s before the Constitution and in the 1890s after it, the oligarchs
devoted considerable effort to the denial of politics as a practice acceptable among those who would count themselves as patriotic countrymen.

The background for the denial of politics, in the first instance, was
not ideological but political. That is, the government's suppression
of the popular rights movement and the political opposition it represented had resulted in a series of legal and institutional measures
designed to remove "matters relating to politics" (*seiji ni kansuru jikō*)
from the popular province. A series of suppressive laws in the 1880s
expanded a pattern begun in the 1870s. The government attempted
to control both the formation of political associations and the free
discussion of politics in meetings, publications, and the press. In
short, its legislative targets were the groups who constituted the
"public opinion of the people" (*minkan no yoron*). Certain sectors
were specifically restricted: the Regulations for Public Meetings of
1880 forbade military men, active or reserve, police officers, teachers
and students of public and private schools, and agricultural and technical apprentices to join any political association or to "attend any
meeting where politics forms the subject of address or discussion."[31]
In July 1890, after the first election but before the opening of the
Diet, a new redaction entitled the Public Meetings and Political Associations Law added minors and women to the list of those for
whom public politics was forbidden fruit.[32]

The political result of this legislation of the eighties was simultaneously to cripple and to inspire opposition activity, as parties and publications banded, disbanded, and banded once again. The ideological impact was more subtle but, for a nation approaching a parliamentary era, no less significant. The name of politics, first of all, was displaced. Since political expression was so easily declared illegal, it became common to disavow politics and gather together in ostensible pursuit of the liberal arts (*gakugei*), scholarship (*gakumon*), congeniality (*dōshi*), or education. In the late eighties, with the issue of treaty revision, the establishment of the new local government system, and the anticipation of the Diet, political activity flourished again in the countryside. In Yamanashi prefecture, for example, only fifteen of the once popular speech meetings had been held in 1887, discoursing on 157 topics, eleven of which met with police prohibition. But in 1889, the year of the constitutional excitement, 115 meetings took place, 734 topics were discussed, and eighty-nine of these were banned. By 1890 there was "a piling up of corpses of the associations, which, like the may-fly, had been born in the morning and died in the evening." These corpses, though they had fluttered in politics throughout their short-lived day, bore the euphemistically apolitical names of the eighties. The *Yamanashi dōshikai*, or Fellows Association, was dedicated to the legally unassailable "purposes of basing itself on the principles upon which the state is founded, working for the honor and glory of the imperial house, and advancing the welfare of the people." After the first election the Fellows disbanded, some of them to join the newly formed Yamanashi Political Association (*Yamanashi seisha*). Basking in the new parliamentary light, the association boldly proposed, "according to the doctrines of progress, to base itself on the principles of constitutional parliamentary government, to work for political reform, and to expand the liberty and rights of the people." More often than not, however, local political groups retained their earlier denominations, prompting the comparison between such "lively political organizations" as the *Yamanashi seisha* and the "pitiful social organizations" whose names and stated goals stressed likemindedness (*dōkōkai*) rather than proclamations of principle.[33]

If such purposefully political groups avoided the word "politics," other organizations were even more careful. The journals published by the countless voluntary associations that sprang up all over the country in the mid and late Meiji period confronted the same dilemma that had led to the demise in 1875 of the premier journal of the enlightenment, the *Meiroku zasshi*. At that time Mori Arinori had urged the society to preserve itself in the face of the government's new press and libel laws by acknowledging that "discussions relating to politics were not the original intention" of the Meiroku group. The membership rejected his proposal, and the magazine of the enlightenment ceased publication.[34] By the late eighties and nineties, the laws were stricter and the experience of their application more widespread. So it was that in 1894 a local youth group called the *Agatsuma kyōaikai* changed its name from the Cooperation and Respect Society, which was reminiscent of the political euphemisms of the eighties, to the even more innocuous Agatsuma Alumni Association (*Gakuyūkai*). Its journal then repeated the standard editorial phrase that "the magazine of this association compiles essays and miscellaneous pieces relating to scholarship and education. It is under no circumstances to concern itself with politics."[35]

This kind of evasion was particularly expedient in view of the fact that schoolteachers, who had been forbidden by statute "to meddle in politics," were often among the most active members of such organizations. Moreover, even those professional associations formed for the express purpose of actively promoting educational interests in the public sphere eventually adopted the same course. On the same day that the League for the Establishment of National Education (*Kokuritsu kyōiku kisei dōmeikai*) successfully petitioned the Diet for financial assistance to education in 1893, Minister of Education Inoue Kowashi reacted with the so-called "muzzle order" (*kankō kunrei*). This once again placed "education outside political debate (*seiron*)" and political debate outside permissible bounds for educational associations. The Japan Education Association (*DaiNihon kyōikukai*), the central organization of the hundreds of associations formed on local initiative, promptly cleaned house, sweeping politics out of its purview to concentrate thenceforth on "purely educational affairs."[36] The League, whose more than 10,000 petitions had sparked the issue, responded to the muzzle order by abandoning its frontal political efforts in favor of campaigning for Diet candidates who would be supportive of educational interests. The Ministry of Education then issued another order, this time forbidding teachers to "support or encourage political contests" (*seijijō no kyōsō*) or "to have anything directly or indirectly to do with any parties" in the general elections.[37] Since the directive also stipulated that electoral politics would cost an elementary schoolteacher his job, it was not surprising that education associations and magazines, like so many others, took refuge in the cautious nomenclature of arts and letters.

Displacing the name of politics did not cure the "political fever" of elite youth and the opposition in the 1880s.[38] But the constant association of politics with illicit behavior tended to efface the political from the center of discourse. The members of the Meiji generation born in the 1860s had inhaled politics in their youth like oxygen. When their high political consciousness passed into history, it did so not only because the Constitution established the political structures that had been the issue of their day but also because their younger successors grew up in a different atmosphere. Just as oxygen in certain combinations with hydrogen remains oxygen but is understood—and consumed—as water, politics remained politics but was represented in an ideological molecule whose common name was "nation." Love of nation (*aikoku*), or patriotism, which in the decade of the popular rights movement had signified and been signified by the presence of politics, was increasingly associated with its absence. To a member of the earlier Meiji generation it looked in 1913 as if "the heart had gone out of politics" in the years since the Constitution. "People hardly seem to care whether the Diet is in session or not, and feel no need to join the fray of national debate."[39] One of the reasons for this disinterest was that the fray had been repeatedly declared out of bounds.

II

THE SYSTEMATIC exclusion of certain groups from political activity had the further result of implying that politics was in and of itself undesirable, even noxious. Since the early 1880s, legal restrictions had been accompanied by ideological injunctions. Good soldiers, good bureaucrats, good local officials, and good pupils were to remain unsullied by any connection with politics. In the Rescript to Soldiers and Sailors of 1882 (*Gunjin chokuyu*), the emperor enjoined his military to "neither be led astray by current opinions nor meddle in politics (*seiron ni madowazu seiji ni kakawarazu*) but with single heart fulfill your essential duties of loyalty (*chūsetsu*)."[40] Yamagata conceived the Rescript, later described as a "kind of muzzle order for soldiers," in order to provide a guide to military ethics in "a time of national emergency," which was how the popular rights agitation of 1880-1881 appeared to Yamagata.[41] But like so many state documents of the Meiji period, the Rescript that emerged after several drafts and several drafters betrayed an admixture of viewpoints and interests, even on the single point of the relationship between the military and politics.

In the original draft by the enlightenment thinker Nishi Amane the first of the five soldierly precepts was order (*chitsujo*), with no specific prohibition of politics. It is clear from other contexts, however, that

53

Nishi followed Western military thought in arguing that, for the sake of order and discipline, soldiers on active duty should be separated from political activity, which belonged to the realm of civil, not military, society. Inoue Kowashi, whose hand touched nearly every major document that the Meiji state produced, agreed with Nishi. But his concerns in this instance lay less with the disruptive influence of politics upon soldiers than with the institutional importance of keeping the whole of the army, like the emperor, outside politics. Yamagata felt the same way, though his reasons, too, were slightly different. He was less interested in the constitutional niceties of Nishi and Inoue, both of whom wrote draft constitutions that barred only active military from parliament. Instead, Yamagata instructed that the Rescript be cast as a direct charge from the emperor to his—not the state's—soldiers. For Yamagata, the only means to prevent the sort of dangerous insubordination that had led to the 1878 mutiny in the imperial guard as well as to forestall the political subversion he associated with the popular rights movement was to inculcate the new conscript army with pure and unconditional loyalty to the emperor. Thus, with the journalist Fukuchi Gen'ichirō as stylist, the final version of the Rescript dictated loyalty (chūsetsu), not order, as the first duty of the soldier and added the admonition against politics as part of the definition of this loyalty.[42]

Until the end of the Second World War the Rescript remained the single most important source in the ideological indoctrination of conscripts and the lifelong perpetuation of the "military spirit" among reservists.[43] Three decades after the establishment of parliamentary government, when parties were in power and democracy a political watchword of the 1920s, His Majesty's soldiers and sailors recited by rote their promise to refrain from politics as proof of their deepest allegiance. In the thirties the same code was invoked by the young officers who rebelled not in the tainted name of politics but in the higher cause of imperial loyalty. In 1882 Fukuchi had written that "the thing most to be feared politically is the military in politics."[44] By this he meant that the civilian government should be separated from the military. But because the military was then placed outside government altogether, in direct command of the emperor, the thing most to be feared eventually came true. If the Constitution made this possible structurally, the ideological legacy enabled the military to justify its actions in the prewar years as something other than—and far nobler than—mere politics.

Through universal conscription and the growth of the reservist associations the exclusion and denigration of politics by the military were messages that over the years reached large numbers of Japanese. Other groups for whom politics was interdicted in the 1880s and 1890s added their weight to this cumulative impression. The bureaucracy, like the military an official state apparatus, had been prohibited from participation in political discussions and speechmaking in the 1870s. The ban was lifted only two weeks before the promulgation of the Constitution in 1889, lest government officials be forced to remain mute while the opposition raised its voices in the parliamentary hue and cry.[45] But in the meantime, the 1887 civil service regulations had made it clear that government officials, again like the military, were "His Majesty the emperor's" officials, and not the creatures of partisan politics. Moreover, recruitment practices had established the law faculty at the Imperial University as the privileged entry through the "Dragon Gate" of the civil service examinations.[46] Additional regulations issued in the summer of 1889 provoked the comment in the press that aspiring young bureaucrats were already being directed into the study of law rather than politics. Now with the precise translation of Imperial University grades into entering salary, some complained that "the university was no longer worthy of the name and should call itself a *Kammerschule* or a Bureaucrat Training Institute."[47] Although the Imperial University declined to follow this suggestion, the number of its law graduates entering the civil service steadily increased in the next two decades until they dominated the upper bureaucracy by the end of the Meiji period.[48]

To assure the bureaucratic ranks further immunity from politics, in 1899 Yamagata managed by the fiat of imperial ordinance to restrict appointments to the highest civil service rank effectively to career bureaucrats. This stroke was justified by references to the need for "specialized knowledge" to cope with "the now extremely detailed laws" of the constitutional system. The key passage, however, contended that changing policy officials with each cabinet would result in

> administration losing its character of *impartiality* and *independence* and becoming a tool of *favoritism* and *self-interest*. Thus, if administrative officials are not made to stand—*impartial* and *nonpartisan [fuhen futō]*— apart from politics, one cannot hope to have *fair* and *impartial* administration.[49]

In the unflinching redundancy of the underlined words—which to Yamagata's mind needed no underlining, so obvious was the political ethic they described—lay his enduring conception of political parties. No soldier, no upper-level bureaucrat, or, for that matter, no official in the local government system envisioned by Yamagata in the late 1880s, was to be given the ideological opportunity to associate mere politics (*seiryaku*) with the moral vocabulary of impartiality or fairness (*kōsei*).[50]

During his years as military planner and his long tenure as home minister from 1883 to 1890, Yamagata had presided over the pre-constitutional strengthening of the injunctions against politics. Now as prime minister in 1899 he moved once again, with his usual relentless consistency, to forestall the politicization of the national bureaucracy. Because Yamagata's control was finite, over the years the separation of bureaucrats from politics became increasingly less complete than he had wished. By and large, however, the division in imperial Japan between the career bureaucrats, both military and civilian, and the politicians who moved along electoral paths to the Diet remained sharp enough to preserve the legacy of the 1880s distinction between the officials and the political parties.[51] Politics, the ideological language of the eighties and nineties suggested, took place not within the impartial sanctuary of His Majesty's government but outside in the teeming streets of popular self-interest.

Because some of the newly elected popular representatives saw it differently, the defense of politics as a seemly subject for the citizenry began in the first session of the Diet. Representative Suehiro argued in the Lower House that young people should be exposed to political discussion. For it might have the influence on them that it did on Robert Peel, "who accompanied his father to political meetings in his youth and later became a famous politician." The Representative also challenged the notion that women should be denied political knowledge on the premise that they were "not suited to politics" (*seijijō ni futekitō*). If they were granted the opportunity, he argued, they could be of "help to their husbands," as they had been in the past in Japan and were now in the West. He quarreled with those who said that permitting women to observe the Diet would distract the men and distort their positions. They were judging, he said, by the woman worship of the West, whereas "in Japan the presence of a few women at political discussions would seldom lead men to change their arguments."[52] Kiyoura Keigo, a Yamagata man who was then head of the Home Ministry's Police Bureau, replied for the government. "In view of Japan's history, customs, and mores," he argued, "women have always governed the household and been responsible for the education of the family." Politics would interfere with this; moreover, their involvement was undesirable from the point of view of morality. Like pupils and teachers, "their thought is still immature," and the experience of other countries was, in any case, irrelevant.[53] On this point, the government and the House of Peers stood firm. And indeed it was not until 1922 that women were legally permitted out of the house on political business.

These discussions were repeated in each Diet session in the early 1890s, the House of Representatives favoring relaxation of the restrictions, the Peers voting down the revision every time. In the fourth Diet in 1893, the revised Public Meetings and Political Associations Law that finally passed both houses excluded the same groups as before. In 1897 an amendment striking teachers and pupils from the interdiction passed the Lower House, again to be rejected in the Peers. Vice Minister of Education Makino Nobuaki argued the government's position, insisting that "schools were to have no relation whatsoever with religion and politics."[54] In the context of 1897 this insertion of religion into the argument against politics was neither innocent nor neutral. Religion in the schools had become a controversial issue with the "Conflict between Religion and Education" in 1892-1893. Anti-Christian in origin, this debate resulted in the strengthening of patriotic education and the eventual prohibition under the Yamagata cabinet in 1899 of religious instruction in the schools.[55] Support for this posture was commonly sought in Article 28 of the Constitution, which guaranteed that Japanese subjects should enjoy freedom of religion, "within limits not prejudicial to peace and order, and not antagonistic to their duties as subjects." Yet in the course of the decade Christianity was deemed incompatible with loyalty, and on that basis religion in the schools declared unconstitutional. In 1897, when Makino appealed to the state's "duty to parents" to safeguard their children equally from religion and politics, he thus implied that politics belonged to the same category. It lay, in short, outside the boundaries of patriotism.

The legal language was also similar, in that the Constitution had permitted political activity "within the limits of the law." The laws in question, however, including the Public Meetings and Political Associations Law under debate in 1897, specified the same restriction that had applied to religion—politics was free, within limits not "prejudicial to peace and order." Against this background of suspicion it was easy enough to perpetuate the view that such baleful influences did not belong in the schoolyard. When it was proposed in 1898 that lessons on parliamentary elections be included in elementary school textbooks, the government and its conservative supporters could easily argue that since all talk of politics was forbidden in the schools, elections clearly had no place in the texts.[56] Even on the floor of parliament, politics had repeatedly to be defended as a positive value against the government's implication that legal and ideological strictures were necessary to protect the people from something that in its very nature was harmful to the nation.

II

To COUNTER the opposition in the 1880s the oligarchs had prepared for constitutional government by erecting law as a bulwark against politics. Not only the suppressive legislation but also the constitutional provisions that placed the emperor and the military above politics can be regarded in this light. But the political history of the 1890s made it clear that by the time the Diet opened, the oligarchs had also prepared themselves to operate within the new constitutional system. Even before the Constitution, Inoue Kaoru had formed a political party, and in 1889 the oligarchs attempted to coopt opposition leaders by inviting them into the cabinet. In the course of the nineties, the beginnings of a working arrangement with the Diet emerged, and while Yamagata was bolting the doors of the civil service against the parties in 1899-1900, Itō was forming his own party, the Seiyūkai.[57] Yamagata never would make peace with the notion of parties, although even he anticipated wider political participation and envisaged the new local government system as a training ground for responsible officials.[58] Inoue Kowashi, whose own mind was always divided between constitutional and imperial constructions of the polity, made a manful attempt in 1890 to distinguish between political associations (seisha), which should be controlled as they were in the West, and political parties (seitō), which no parliamentary system could meaningfully exclude.[59] In terms of political theory the principle of transcendental cabinets articulated by Itō and Kuroda in February 1889 was a final byproduct of the politics of the 1880s. But in political practice the principle would be eroded over the next several decades by an evolving accommodation, however uneven, between bureaucratic and party politics.

For ideology, the legacy was different. The negative definition of politics remained current in ideological language. The vocabulary of transcendentalism, for example, had established the government as "His Majesty the emperor's government" and repeated the phrases that associated political parties with private interest. "The government must not work to the interest [ri] of one party faction or the detriment [gai] of another but must be impartial and nonpartisan [fuhen futō]," pronounced Itō in his speech that echoed Kuroda's of three days before.[60] The moral valence of such terms was unmistakable. In the years to come, *ri* and *gai*, combined together as *rigai*, became a standard government pejorative for "interests" in the private, factional, and hence less worthy, sense. Local politicians were accused of acting out of *rigai kankei*, "relations of interest," while the higher value of national impartiality was claimed for the emperor's men. The term *fuhen futō* connoted a nonpartisan neutrality, one which the press had just begun to appropriate for itself, as newspapers undertook the transition from party organs to commercial enterprises seeking the widest possible readership.[61] Repeated assertions of impartiality kept neither the government nor the newspapers free from political alignments, but they did reinforce the contention that any overt pursuit of partisan interests was of questionable moral value.

Added to this devaluation of politics as the pursuit of partial interests was the association of political activity with divisiveness and conflict. This language was particularly strong in the case of Yamagata. In 1888-1890 he presented his views of local government in terms of assuring "harmony" (*chōwa*) and eliminating those "who, calling themselves political debaters (*seironka*), advocate impractical theories and, giving vent to personal dissatisfactions, attempt to throw the social order into confusion." Those who propagated such "arrant foolishness" were responsible for competition, conflict, and disorder that threatened not only society but the state.[62] For Yamagata the denial of politics thus originated in a dual perception of its partiality and its divisiveness, two characteristics that would remain in the ideological presentation of politics in the succeeding years.

The first impulse on the part of the government to give politics a bad name in the 1880s had been defensive: the politically motivated attempt to derogate the actions of the opposition. Legal suppression had therefore been a principal means to this end. The ideological results of displacing the name and excluding the act of politics were secondary. But in Yamagata and others like him, the distaste for politics of the opposition was not their only motivation. For they were equally impelled by their continuing concern with the need for national unity in the international context. Vis-à-vis what Yamagata often called the "external" world, modern Japan required the strength conferred by unity, to which the divisiveness of politics was antithetical. Hence, there was a need not only for legal suppression but also for training and influence. For the purposes of citizen-making, ideology would therefore be primary. And in the ideological construction of the political universe as it came to exist in the gov-

ernment's presentation after 1890, politics retained its negative connotation of private interest and conflict while any positive civic value
it may have had was usurped and absorbed by the word "nation."

In the 1880s the government established the double approach of
legal suppression and ideological suasion that it would use throughout the imperial period in its efforts to control civic values. With
regard to politics, the combined ideological result in 1890 cannot be
characterized simply as apolitical, or as anti-political either. Rather
what the government had achieved was essentially to poison the pot.
By adding something to the political to make it patriotically unpal-
atable, politics was denatured even as the constitutional system was
first beginning to function.

THE *KAN* AND
THE *MIN*

I

ALTHOUGH the oligarchs dominated both the political and
ideological process in the late eighties and early nineties, they were
by no means the sole agents of the denaturing of politics. Outside
the government, amid the "public opinion of the people" (*minkan no
yoron*) appeared another view of political affairs. Different in origin
and contrasting in nature, its effect on the emerging parliamentary
image was also often—and unexpectedly—negative. The opposition,
the intellectuals, and the press were self-appointed spokesmen for the
people (*min*). Yet they too contributed, however unintentionally, to
the defamation of politics that was being carried out by their foes,
the officials (*kan*).

As the arbiters of public opinion expressed it, this dichotomy between the *kan* and the *min* constituted the fundamental structure of
Japanese politics. If the oligarchs' fixed point of departure was party
strife and factional interest, commentators outside the government
generally began with the ongoing struggle between a powerful and
arbitrary bureaucratic clique and an inadequately empowered people.
The *kan-min* distinction, an old one in East Asian political thought,
evoked the division that Fukuzawa had alluded to in 1882 when he
wrote, "A great chasm divides the ruler and the ruled."[63] In traditional governance the separation had been both long established and
unambiguous. For this reason the majority of Meiji Japanese, who
could not have been expected to possess a clear notion of political
parties in the Western parliamentary style, needed little tutelage in

the subject of officials. However much their titles had changed and their numbers increased in the years since the Restoration, the authorities were still the authorities. They included the familiar "honorable officials" (*yakuninsama*) in the local town and village offices (*yakuba*); the famous "great men of state" (*erai kan'insama*) in the capital; and the neither familiar nor famous central, prefectural, and county officials (*kanri*) who passed in and out of local life inspecting, collecting, directing, and otherwise interjecting their bureaucratic presence into the lives of the people.[64] Perhaps because they were neither locally familiar nor nationally famous, this last group was often regarded as the quintessence of Meiji officialdom, the ubiquitous functionaries of the state.

From all these officials, regardless of stature, emanated the aura of government, and experience suggested that government was something the people could little affect. The constitutional system therefore posed an ideological challenge. The traditional bifurcation of the polity into the government and the people had to be adjusted in a new conception of politics that could accommodate the role of an elected assembly. For if the officials were the *kan* and the people were the *min*, what was a parliamentary politician? And how were the people to conceive their role in the new body politic?

Anti-government activists in the late eighties and early nineties stressed the political confrontation between the "parties of the people" (*mintō*) and the oligarchs and their supporting "parties of the officials" (*ritō*).[65] The popular parties sought to rectify ingrained habits of "revering officials and despising the people" (*kanson minpi*). But their chosen means was not harmony between the two (*kanmin chōwa*), as Fukuzawa advocated and government rhetoric frequently echoed.[66] Instead they anticipated a properly parliamentary contest on the floor of the Diet. In the meantime, the old pastime of ridiculing officials, which the 1882 Criminal Code had briefly made a punishable crime, was once again the stock in trade of opposition writers and speechmakers.[67]

> Gentlemen! Most of the men you see exultantly swaggering along or driving carriages around Tokyo, they are officials (*kanri*). And most of those who go strutting about in the countryside, they are also officials. It is enough to make one wonder whether this nation does not altogether belong to the officials.

They strutted and swaggered and, the speaker continued, there were also too many of them. "There are more than 100,000 bureaucrats and a mere 60,000 soldiers. No country has more bureaucrats than soldiers. Only in Japan does one find such a phenomenon."[68] Bureaucrats were so many "little nobles" (shōkazoku) whose tastes for "novels and gambling, Western luxury goods, hot springs and restaurants, Western cuisine and billiards, theater and carriages, and every kind of drink" made them inappropriate "influences" on the people.[69] Such caricatures were commonly used by the popular parties to argue for the reduction of the number of bureaucrats. This would both diminish their unwholesome influence and also alleviate the burdens on the people (minryoku kyūyō), a goal that remained one of the main slogans of the opposition throughout the budgetary battles of the 1890s.[70]

Vernacular references to catfish and river loach (namazu, dojō) reappeared in the popular songs and political theater of the day. Originally the whiskery fish had evoked the moustaches affected by officials in the early Meiji period. "Those idling about with the loach's whiskers, why, they're the catfish's associates," commented an 1877 song about the police and the bureaucrats, while the lyrics of the "Officials Song" (Kan'in uta) suggested that "if growing a beard makes an official, the cats and mice are all officials."[71] Since cats, which popularly meant geisha, were fond of catfish, the allusions were elided until in the political songs of the late eighties a bureaucratic catfish seldom appeared without his feline concubine.[72] Both were further accompanied by accusations of bribery and hints of moral impropriety that titillated both political audiences and newspaper readers of the period. Caricatures of the officials were also central to sōshi shibai (theater of political militants), a rousing combination of acting and speechmaking in behalf of popular rights. The genre reached a peak in 1890-1891 when its most famous actor, Kawakami Otojirō, made the anti-government "Oppekepē Song" famous and presented "an alarm clock to wake the ministers and nobles and a dose of the waters of liberty (jiyūtō) for the catfish and the loach."[73]

The popular parties thus placed politics within the framework of the kan-min dichotomy that had long been familiar to Japanese. Yet, even as they did so, these traditional categories were undergoing change. Schoolboys in the seventies and eighties, for example, dreamed of becoming statesmen, a childhood ambition that had been unavailable to most of their parents in the hereditary feudal hierarchy. Even in the late 1880s, when such dreams were growing fainter, the popular New Year's games (sugoroku) still featured roads to bureaucratic fame. An 1887 "Meiji Officials Competition" began with the horse-drawn carriage of the government elite. It then proceeded, depending on the throw of the die, through frames picturing such figures as Itō, Kuroda, and Yamagata, to the pinnacle that won the game, the imperial noble and military official, Prince Arisugawa.[74] Among those families forced by poverty to far bleaker dreams, the possibility of a daughter's becoming a cat and catching a catfish made the caricatured Meiji officials seem, if passingly, attractive.[75] Moreover, the *kan* and the *min* were less clearly distinguished in general discourse than in political rhetoric. Even the educated youth of the eighties confused them, mixing Napoleon with Abraham Lincoln, or generals and bureaucrats with fiery parliamentarians.[76] Nor could the government, however much it wished to dissociate itself from the factional fray, avoid being identified with politics. In a popularity poll conducted by the press in 1885, Itō Hirobumi won in the "politician" category. Fourteen years later in an 1899 poll, Itō won again, while Yamagata placed in the allegedly apolitical "soldier" category. In neither instance, however, did a politician or soldier even approach the number of votes received by the "journalist" Fukuchi Gen'ichirō and the "businessman" Shibusawa Eiichi in 1885, or the "educator" Fukuzawa Yukichi in 1899.[77] The voting readership, like the Ministry of Education, appeared to prefer cultural or entrepreneurial heroes to the political kind, whether in government or outside it.

The popular image of the *min* was equally inchoate around 1890, especially since the relation between the parties and the wider public had yet to be decided. The question in fact was little discussed, although Nakae Chōmin, perpetually rigorous in his liberal thinking, cautioned that unless a responsive and responsible relationship between the parties and the people developed, the latter were likely to end up obediently enslaved to the Diet. "And whether slaves to the officials or slaves to the Diet, it is slavery all the same."[78] For most members of the opposition, however, the preeminent issue of the day was the conflict with the government, and the masses of *min* were left for the moment politically undefined. The government, for its part, was inconsistent in its definition of the *min*. Ideological language clearly made the people the subjects of the emperor and the countrymen of the nation. The debates over the establishment of the local government system in 1888–1889, however, suggested that the institutional distinction between the *kan* and the *min* fell with a bureaucratic thud at the prefectural and *gun* levels.[79] As the lowest administrative divisions of the central government, headed by appointed prefectural governors and county heads responsible to the bureaucracy, they were the outposts of the *kan* in the countryside.

Below them were the local organs of self-government on the town and village level, whose mayors were the elected representatives of the *min*. Local officials were therefore *kan* to the people (albeit local *kan*) and *min* to the central government, which in 1890 was a politically indeterminate status indeed. Since over the course of the next two decades many of these local officials would become party politicians, the national question of where the politicians were to stand in the *kan-min* split would be repeated at the local level. In the meantime, the relationship of the rest of the population to politics remained, as before, undefined.

II

AGAINST this background as the forces of public opinion (*minkan no yoron*) prepared for the first election, they projected a view of politics that was idealized and jaundiced at the same time. Discussions of the appropriate qualifications for candidates for the Lower House filled the press, and a host of "guides to the election of Diet members" appeared in the months before the election on July 1, 1890. First and foremost, it was argued that the representatives must be of the people (*min*), free from the stigma of "having drunk the waters of the bureaucratic sea."[80] Retired officials, aspirants to office, recipients of government patronage—any association with officialdom was suspect, for "the government and the people have different interests (*rigai*)" and "any ally of the *kan* is an enemy of the *min*."[81] Second, "like railroad engineers," they must have acquired specialized knowledge appropriate to their professional functions as "engineers of the political locomotive of a civilized nation."[82] Fame and good family were insufficient; what was required was an understanding of law, politics, and Japan's contemporary situation. For just as "England has Ireland and the poor as its special problems, Japan has treaty revision and lowering the land tax." The knowledge necessary to cope with these issues should be gleaned from newspapers and translated books. Scholars, however, made unsuitable candidates because they were not used to dealing with "interests" and were also too occupied keeping up with the new theories from abroad to venture into society on errands of politics. Third, on the all-important question of wealth, the ideal Diet member would be a man of independent means who need not follow the government (*kanri*) merely for fear of losing his salary. Money alone, however, was no guarantee of "political thought," nor would it do for the Diet to become a "rich men's club." Hence, most renditions invoked a man of moderate means (*chūtō no seikatsu*), echoing the call of writers like Tokutomi Sohō for an entrepreneurial middle class to come forward as the carriers of the new national politics. Fourth, the candidate must have firm principles (*shugi*) of his own and not merely mouth the general complaint that taxes were heavy and liberty insufficient. Finally, the would-be representative must not seek votes by bribery, whether with money, beer, or sugar, by violence, or by collusion with local officials. Otherwise—and this was the universal reference of the day—the Diet would become but a national version of the prefectural assemblies.[83]

Despite the frequent evocation of European models, it was clear that the ideal Dietman had been fashioned in good part from the negative example of elected politicians of the 1880s. "Look at the provincial assemblies today, they are filled with ordinary men," who have "nought but the knowledge of Tenpō politicians," and "do not know Bentham from Blackstone."[84] Assemblymen were commonly described as self-seeking, toadying, and corrupt colleagues of the *kan*, while the prospective Diet members were imagined to possess every virtue that these provincial representatives lacked. Opposition opinion, no less than the government, had learned its political lessons in the 1880s and conceived the future parliamentary system in the light of that experience. Instead of denying politics as the oligarchs did, the opposition ideologues idealized it. Yet, in the process the picture they drew of politicians could not have been less flattering. By the time the real candidates appeared and began their campaigns in the late spring of 1890, it was as if the politically informed public had been prepared for disillusion. Parliamentary paragons, predictably, were scarce, while the familiar local notables, though they were running for new national office, seemed to be carrying on political business as usual.

For this reason, perhaps, the press responded with acerbic criticism of the candidates, and election abuse (*hiretsu shudan*) became one of the most publicized issues of the campaign. Although the candidates were accused of failing on every count listed in the profiles of the ideal representative, the most common complaints fastened on lack of principles (*shugi*) and unsavory campaign tactics. "What is your *shugi*?" asked a member of the audience at a candidate's speech meeting. "None in particular," replied the candidate. "Any investigations of political affairs?" "Not yet." "What of your future social and political policies?" "No definite prospects as of now." As of now, the commentators argued, too many candidates were interested only in the prospects of fame and profit, to which end "they fawn on the officials (*kan*) and truckle to the people (*min*)."[85] Their motivations and their qualifications both impugned, candidates were ridiculed as "officials who suddenly took it into their heads to become candidates" and "men whose names and faces were unknown in the political world but, had they been known, would have been thought by everyone to be unsuitable in the extreme."[86] Although such characterizations generally referred to the "self-nominated" candidates who sometimes polled fewer than ten votes, these colorful figures received more than their share of press coverage, thus lending to the "election uproar" (senkyo sawagi) an almost carnival air of unprincipled opportunism.[87]

Even more common, however, were the tales of bribery, violence, and collusion that preoccupied the journalists and irritated electoral opponents. Of the three, violence at the hands of sōshi, the hired political ruffians, proved to be somewhat less widespread than either the government or the press had feared.[88] Bribery, on the other hand, was said to have reached new heights of refinement, as candidates vied with one another to give away just enough—but no more than was necessary—to secure the votes of their fellow men of influence. Songs and limericks caricatured the high costs of electoral politics, "Eight hundred yen down the drain in social expenses, not a sen left—flat broke."[89] Examples from the "hotbed of electoral scandals" included "providing refreshments worth thirty sen at banquets with admission fees of only five sen," "candidates who promise free gifts of government forest lands," "anyone who gives away more than fifty sen," and other offenses that straddled the thin line between acceptable hospitality and bribery punishable under the Supplementary Penal Regulations of the Law of Election.[90] Collusion also straddled the line between social custom and electoral impropriety, since the practice of holding pre-election meetings (yosenkai) seemed to some a reasonable means for the local notables to avoid unnecessary conflict. To others, however, these private agreements proved that "the recent electoral commotion was not an open contest among men and opinions but a competition that took place primarily behind the scenes."[91]

In sum, the organs of public opinion in 1890 presented politicians in a light that was only slightly less unfavorable than the harsh beam directed by the government on the allegedly self-interested factionalism of the parties. True, the target of the journalists was not party politics but rather the opportunism and corruption that seemed to them to be "staining the constitutional honor of the nation."[92] But they often used the same critical vocabulary as the oligarchs when they railed against the unseemly conflict of electoral competition (senkyo kyōsō sawagi). When the candidates who had been libeled by their opponents demanded public apologies in the form of "recovery of honor" advertisements in the newspapers, commentators complained of the lamentable extremes of disharmony aroused by parliamentary politics. Post-election meetings of friendly reconciliation (*danshōkai*) were recommended to prevent the conflict among candidates from "tainting and poisoning the establishment of constitutional government." Otherwise, "these public battles were likely to leave the people with a peculiar impression of constitutional politics."[93] It is probable, however, that the press was as much responsible for conveying this impression as the candidates, large numbers of whom were innocent of the charges leveled at their less upstanding fellows.

In fact, the 1890 election is considered by scholars to have gone off rather smoothly, the government impartial in its administration, the candidates responsible in their campaigning, and the electorate enthusiastic in its response.[94] A good part of contemporary opinion, however, judged by a different standard. The discrepancy between the high political ideals nurtured over a decade of parliamentary anticipation and the disappointingly commonplace realities of human political behavior was a source of continuing disillusionment. Even the political novels of the day traded in the romantic idealism of the eighties for muckraking accounts of bribery and violence that held both the *kan* and the *min* responsible for the sad state of parliamentary affairs.[95] When the government brazenly and brutally interfered in the scandalous election of 1892, the object of public clamor was the bureaucracy, not the candidates.[96] Yet, to those not directly involved but exposed nonetheless to public opinion, the abiding impression was the association of politics with corruption. *Kan* or *min*, it appeared that in the first stages of Japan's parliamentary experience, politics in general had what may reasonably be described as "a bad press."

THE GENTLEMEN OF
THE DIET

I

WHETHER frontally proscribed by the government or obliquely diminished in public opinion, politics in 1890 was a subject reserved for the very few. The electorate of 450,000 comprised only 1.1 percent of the population. Because of the enfranchising requirement of 15 yen per annum in direct taxes, rural land-tax-paying property owners were heavily overrepresented and urban dwellers of every economic stratum dramatically underrepresented. The several hundred voters in a given rural district consisted of the local notables (*yūshisha, meibōka*), who were also the village officials, the professionals, the entrepreneurs, or the native sons who had achieved some success in Tokyo and returned, sometimes just to stand for election. When candidates debated or slandered one another and voters gathered to pre-select a candidate, they often knew the men of whom they spoke, if not in person, at least by name or reputation—so tight and narrow a social stratum did they represent. The newspapermen who reported the electoral activities were by virtue of family or achievement linked to this same group, and in fact sixteen journalists stood successfully in the election.

The circle of newspaper readers who kept abreast of political activities was wider, though not by much. At 50,000 copies a day, the *Ōsaka asahi shinbun* had the highest circulation of the time; the three largest Tokyo papers (*Yamato, Yūbin hōchi,* and *Tōkyō asahi*) printed approximately 20,000 each; and the provincial papers far fewer.[97] Although many copies passed through the hands of several readers, the social distribution during this period remained limited to the high elite and the more recently added lower officials, elementary school-teachers, merchants, and others of "middle class society. (*chūryū shakai*)."[98] For these reasons, the election, like the Constitution, was a matter of some interest to a growing bourgeoisie but of direct concern primarily to men of substantial socioeconomic or intellectual influence, who turned out 95 percent of their enfranchised number to vote for their fellows at the polls.[99]

The men they supported became Japan's first nationally elected politicians. Now that politicians existed with full legal status, their character and behavior would also mold the emerging conception of politics in its modern form. Neither the government nor elite opinion, both of which had projected views of constitutional politics in advance of the fact during the 1880s, would be in sole, or even joint, control of the matter once the members of the Diet commenced their parliamentary practice. The first impression created by the new politicians derived from who they were. The popular parties held a majority, 170 of the 300 seats in the House of Representatives, the independents 45 seats, and the much-debated but little-elected parties of the officials only 80 seats.[100] In the narrowly political vernacular of the 1880s the Diet election was therefore a victory for the *min*. Two-thirds of the members were commoners, and one-third were former samurai. Although this meant that there was a higher ratio of the former privileged class in the Diet than in the general population, this disproportion represented the composition of the new Meiji elite rather well. Indeed most of the members were of those generations, nearly two-thirds of them under forty-three years of age at the time of the election.

Like the voters, the new Dietmen were predominantly middle class and largely rural. Tokutomi's "country gentlemen of moderate means" appeared to have come forth as summoned. They were not the richest men in the prefecture, for the fifteen highest taxpayers were represented in the Peers, nor of course were they poor, proletarian, or unpropertied.[101] Many were, simply and quintessentially, *chihō meibōka*, the provincial notables of the period whose individual biographies, proudly enshrined in family and village lore, read like so many local pages torn from a collective provincial book.[102] Whether they were an evolved species of the earlier *gōnō*, or wealthy peasant, class or more recent entrants into the rural entrepreneurial elite, they were locally secure and securely local figures. Many worked a part of the land they owned or undertook commercial enterprises in their hometowns and villages, from the traditional soy sauce and saké manufacture to the newer and quasi-industrial textiles which contributed so substantially to their own wealth and to Japan's growing national product. Not yet absentee, they were the same socioeconomic stratum that had long occupied the top of local society. Only instead of being village headmen, they were national Dietmen now.

Perhaps that is why Mutsu Munemitsu, the highest-ranking state minister elected to the Lower House in 1890, spoke of his colleagues as the "three hundred farmers" (*sanbyaku no hyakushōdomo*).[103] In fact, 68 of the 300 were "little nobles" like himself, as the parties had once satirized the officials. The bureaucrats elected to the first Diet represented the second largest occupational group after agriculture and ranged from Mutsu at the ministerial level to an assortment of ambitious *gunchō*, the county heads identified earlier as the lowest local officials of the national bureaucracy.[104] More telling, however, was the fact that as many as two-thirds of the elected Lower House were former members of prefectural assemblies.[105] Falling far from the political grace evoked by portraits of ideal Diet members, the winners turned out to be "prefectural assembly types," who "went to Tokyo a lot" and otherwise revealed that, whatever profit or position they gained from local soil, their reputation extended at least to the *gun* office and frequently as far as the prefecture.[106] From the viewpoint of the common folk, farmers who wore frock coats, even if they wore them over the traditional *hakama*, were uncommon farmers indeed.

The first impression made by a large number of Diet members thus emphasized that they were the familiar elite, newly dressed and off not to the prefectural capital but to Tokyo. The second impression was of a provincial squirearchy, "country Dietmen who suddenly put on Western clothes like little foreign diplomats," or in the barbed disgust of the "Oppekepē Song," the men "riding in rickshaws, wearing coats and trousers" but "lacking in political thought."[107] When two Dietmen were elected who still wore the samurai topknot, a minor debate ensued over whether they should not adopt a more suitable Western hairstyle in time for the opening of the Diet in November.[108] And on that occasion, the Representatives were reported to have arrived at the opening ceremony in rickshaws, and the Peers in carriages, though many a Representative was also described as traveling about in a carriage even on the country paths at home. Woodblock prints and New Year's games (sugoroku) reinforced the impression of wealth by depicting the Diet members in clothes and conveyances of the greatest expense and modishness.[109] To a people who in 1890 were experiencing their first "modern" depression and a rice price that in June was twice that of a year before, these associations of the "gentlemen of the Diet" (gikai no shinshi) with the extravagances of the rich and noble did little to enhance their reputation as representatives of the people.[110] Nor did the connection with Western fashions, which brought the politicians into range of the reaction against superficial westernization that was both part of the cultural nationalism of the time and, more viscerally, of glaring differences in lifestyle between the social elite and the rest of the population. Even as the government, which had earlier been ridiculed for the fancy dress balls and tea dances held at the Rokumeikan, sold the controversial building in 1890, the new country Dietmen were discovering the pleasures of the Imperial Hotel and Kirin beer, both new in 1890 and both as remote from the lives of most Japanese as a swallowtail coat. As these images suggest, the representatives of the people often appeared to have a good deal in common with the officials whose habits they themselves had roundly criticized for so long.

The third impression that radiated from the new politicians is probably captured by this kan-like aura. Even Tokutomi Sohō—at times an intellectual populist but hardly a man of the people—wrote of the "decadence of the middle class" from whose "country gentlemen" he had expected so much:

Some become village officials, have commerce with county and prefectural officials, and, man being the creature of his environment, are suddenly officialized (*kanka seraru*). Some become members of the prefectural assembly, or of a standing committee, live part or half the year in a small provincial city, and become immediately citified, which means they have gone soft. Some become Diet members, join a petition committee, or become delegates. Recommended by others or on their own initiative, they leave for Tokyo and are instantly urbanized. Or rather it is the opposite, because they are urbanized, they move to Tokyo. . . .

From there extravagance and license took over, leading to the ruin of the pillars of rural society, who then became clerks at the *gun* office, tax collectors, police, usurers, political hangers-on, pettifoggers, journalists, and *sōshi*.[111] In short, the worst of the bureaucratic *kan* and the dregs of the political *min* (plus, interestingly, the journalists) were lumped together as the local products of the new political system. To Sohō the rural elite was "officialized"; to the people the distinction between the clerk at the *gun* office and the new Diet member, who in any given district could conceivably have been the same person, was never that clear. Most Japanese in 1890 knew as little of the Diet as they knew of the Constitution. Yet, though the man in the street may not have been aware that the Constitution provided the "rules of the country," he surely knew a well-off and privileged man when he saw one. As of the time of the first election and the opening of the Diet, a fair number of the new national politicians most resembled the old local elite and, not incidentally, those honorable officials down at the village hall.

II

THE IDEOLOGICAL synergism that occurred among the several views of politics at the beginning of Japan's modern constitutional system was unplanned. The government made a serious effort to deny politics, or at least to restrict it. The *minkan* press attempted to eradicate its baser parts and thus to ennoble it. The Diet members tried their political best to represent and practice it. Oligarchs such as Yamagata and Inoue Kowashi were motivated partly by traditional Confucian notions of governance which denied divisive representations of private interest in favor of public impartiality. They were also affected by the profound fear of disunity common to those members of the Restoration generation for whom the Western threat still influenced their considerations of national policy. In addition, of course, there was the immediate challenge to their own power by the imminent legalization of the opposition. The organs of public opinion drew their sustenance from the long campaign to institutionalize a properly parliamentary opposition. This often led *minkan* commentators in

71

their youth and their frustration both to idealize the practice of politics and to define its essence in terms of the conflict between the *kan*
and the *min*. The new Diet members learned their political lessons
on local ground and came to the Diet prepared to represent their class
and the interests of their district, much as they had in village and
prefectural assemblies, where neither Bentham nor Blackstone had
been of much use. Yet, the combined and reinforcing message of
each of these ideological agents was that politics was divisive and
unpatriotic, corrupt and allied with officialdom, and the property of
a privileged class. In this way were the *kokumin* introduced to their
rights of participation in the new body politic—not perhaps the most
auspicious note on which to embark upon a parliamentary system.

Although the ideological effect of the denaturing of politics would
be considerable, politics per se was seldom the direct object of ideological activity. The government, having excluded politics from its
versions of a civic credo, preferred *not* to speak of it, which further
increased the efficacy of the exclusion. Commentators lamented the
silence, explaining that only one year after the election people had
forgotten about politics. All signs of the "election fever" had subsided, leaving no trace, as in Bashō's poem, "of warriors' dreams,
the aftermath."[112] Politicians, now the new warriors, had just begun
their parliamentary battles and were concerned with mastering—not
defining—the art of politics. Their image, in any case, was in the
custody of public opinion, which never abandoned its skepticism of
politicians as a general breed. The ideological denial of politics thus
remained a negative one, while the positive efforts at citizen-making
concentrated on the sense of nation. And in Japan's newly established
constitutional monarchy, it was the monarch, not the Constitution—
the king, not the compact—that became the center of the emerging
national myths.

The Modern Monarch

CUSTODIANS OF THE
IMPERIAL IMAGE

I

OF ONE LINE for ages eternal, sacred and inviolable, a modern monarch, a living god—with these characteristics the emperor would become the ideological center of the imperial state. In 1889, however, he was not yet clothed for his new role. For the traditional vestments of the imperial office had been vaporous ones, designed for the emperor's long residence "above the clouds," and they would not suffice for his public presence as the ruler of a constitutional state.[1] In terms of ideological process, it required the entire Meiji period to weave the emperor's new clothes and display them effectively before the people. Although the process began in the Restoration years, much of it was completed after the promulgation of the Constitution, and by the time the emperor died in 1912 he was enveloped in an aura of symbolic meaning that held its power through to the end of the Second World War. During the same period the image of both the person and the office became increasingly more visible until most Japanese were familiar with the cut and shape of his new imperial garments.[2]

The ideological transformation proceeded in stages that were linked to the times, to the various custodians of imperial interpretation, and to an intricate layering of legal and moral, regal and religious constructions of the emperor's office. In the first years after the Restoration, from 1868 to 1881, the new government invoked the imperial institution as the symbolic center of the unified nation and displayed the young Meiji emperor as the personal manifestation of the recently wrought political unity. Although the institutional mechanics of direct imperial rule (*shinsei*) remained in flux, the ideological presentation in the 1870s emphasized the direct relation between the emperor and the people.[3] The people included in the first instance the feudal lords and their samurai, without whose "exertions on behalf of the nation" the restoration of imperial rule would mean very little.[4] But they also included commoners whose own visions of the "honorable innovation" (*goisshin*) had been less national than communal and millenial, in that they anticipated not imperial restoration but social betterment, world-renewal (*yonaoshi*), and, sometimes quite concretely, a halving of the tax.[5] To these groups and to any others who might dispute the legitimacy of the new government, the emperor was offered in edicts and in person as proof that—in the language of the Charter Oath—"our country (*wagakuni*) is undergoing an unprecedented change."[6]

The custodians of the throne in its earliest public manifestations were members of the new government, which in the 1870s continued the Restorationist mix of court and state. Samurai such as Ōkubo Toshimichi and Kido Kōin and palace aristocrats such as Iwakura Tomomi and Sanjō Sanetomi were sensitive from the first to the perception that "in Tokugawa times only the shogunate was known to the realm and people were unaware that the imperial house existed. . . . Even now that the realm is at last secured, the imperial will is as yet unknown in the remote and distant parts."[7] And so to the remote and distant parts the emperor was sent. At the age of sixteen in 1868, the new emperor traveled only as far as Osaka. There Ōkubo hoped his imperial appearance might bring the sovereign down from "above the clouds" and remove the impression that "the imperial countenance is hard to look upon and that the imperial person does not set his foot upon the ground."[8] First conceived as a means of separating the emperor from the ancient Kyoto court by moving the capital to Osaka, this early outing was eventually undertaken as a "direct imperial campaign against the rebels."[9] It was the first of the 102 imperial excursions (*gyōkō*) that the Meiji emperor made outside the capital in the forty-five years of his reign. His predecessors had made but three of these imperial progresses in the more than 260 years of the Tokugawa period.[10]

The emphasis on the imperial presence did not belie the ideological purpose of these early travels. As part of the removal of the capital (*tento*) from Kyoto to Tokyo in the autumn of 1868, a mighty imperial procession of 3,300 attendants made the triumphal advance eastward, dramatizing (even before the final military victories that completed it) the goal of "conducting all state affairs by imperial decision."[11] Led by Prince Arisugawa, the Imperial Commander against the Eastern Rebels, the martial procession that chanted "Miyasama, miyasama" not only provided Gilbert and Sullivan with the chorus for their "Mikado,"[12] but also the domains and villages along

74

the way with palpable and impressive evidence of the new imperial presence. This journey became the model for the six Great Circuits (*kunkō*) on which the emperor embarked in 1872, 1876, 1878, 1880, 1881, and 1885. Covering thousands of miles by ship, horse, and palanquin, across steep mountain paths to "remote and distant parts," from Hokkaidō to Kyūshū, the Meiji emperor traveled to see his subjects and be seen by them, spending a total of 273 days on these six journeys.[13] Although members of the court also conceived of these travels as a means to cultivate the young emperor's virtue with knowledge of his realm, the government was equally interested in asserting its own place on the ruling side of the centralized polity in which there was now but one ruler and all the people (*ikkun banmin*).[14]

Supporting the imperial circuit of 1878, Inoue Kaoru argued that "the emperor's visiting all parts of Japan not only informs the people of the emperor's great virtue but also offers the opportunity of displaying direct imperial rule in the flesh, thus dispelling misgivings" about monarchical government (*kunkoku seiji*).[15] But also displayed in the flesh on such travels were prominent members of the government and the court: Saigō, Kido, Ōkubo, Ōkuma, Inoue, Kuroda, Matsukata, Tokudaiji, Iwakura, and Sanjō—all spent some time on the road with the emperor. The quarrels that erupted between the court and the government over who should properly accompany the emperor in his travels in the 1870s reflected the friction in that decade between the two loci of power and also among different views of the imperial institution. Sasaki Takayuki and Motoda Eifu, two palace advisors (*jiho*) who favored the emperor's direct participation in politics with the "advice" of those who held the office that they themselves held, objected to the inclusion of Inoue Kaoru in the imperial entourage in 1878. The palace advisors accused Inoue of "scandalous behavior," which may have referred to his financial views, his Westernism, his recent visit to Paris, or his Chōshū origins. Nonetheless, Inoue, who had just become minister of industry, was permitted to accompany the emperor lest he feel, as Iwakura suggested, "that he was not trusted in his weighty office" which could greatly affect "the future of the government."[16]

This future was precisely what concerned the conservative advisors at court who objected not only to Inoue but to oligarchic power in general. And even as the oligarchs were wrestling with the question of constitutionalism, Motoda and others sought to clothe the emperor in the moral rectitude of a Confucian ruler, graced both with the virtue of authority and the authority of virtue. In political power the court Confucianists proved no match for such oligarchs as Itō Hirobumi, who abolished the office of *jiho* in 1879. But their persistent efforts to assert the moral conception of the imperial office, though muffled by the government in the early period, were finally requited in a different form in the Rescript on Education in 1890.[17] The Shintoists, whose views of the unity of rites and governance (*saisei itchi*) had appeared to prevail in the three years after the Restoration, were more fully eclipsed than the Confucians. For even the gradualists in the government, who opposed the demands of the popular rights movement for the early establishment of an elected assembly, were sufficiently persuaded of Western forms of constitutionalism to reject the theocratic implications of adopting Shintō as a national doctrine.[18] Although in his travels the emperor visited his ancestral shrine at Ise, the repeated assertions of Shintō's importance as an office of state were ignored in the political struggles to define the nature of Japan's constitutional monarchy.

In the 1870s both the formulation of direct imperial rule and the presentation of the emperor in his "manifest ubiquity" promoted national unity against the obtrusions of a feudal past.[19] In the 1880s the ideological reworking of the emperor's appearance concentrated instead on the legal definition of the imperial institution in preparation for the constitutional future. From the Rescript of 1881 which promised the Constitution until the ceremony in 1889 which promulgated it, questions of sovereignty predominated. For the Constitution would make imperial powers legally explicit for the first time in Japanese history. Within the government the two most influential figures in this process were Itō Hirobumi and Inoue Kowashi. Although they differed on some points—Itō, for example, was less taken with Inoue's heritage of late Tokugawa nativism (*kokugaku*) than with his extraordinary grasp of Western legalism—they shared a concern to reconceive the imperial institution in such a way that both the emperor *and* his government would emerge legally and politically sound.[20] This meant asserting the authority of the sovereign against the parties, to whom Itō alluded in his famous speech in 1888 pronouncing the imperial house the "axis of the nation." Without such an axis, "the state will eventually collapse when politics are entrusted to the reckless discussions of the people."[21] Not only the reckless discussions of the *min*, but the vociferous objections of the *kan* had also to be met. For there were members of the government who criticized the Prussian model that Itō favored for the Constitution, while palace bureaucrats like Motoda, joined by conservatives outside the government such as Tani Kanjō, continued to campaign for a more moral and less westernized imperial axis.[22]

Each of these political centers of power in the 1880s put forth its own version of the emperor, as each claimed itself the appropriate content to fill the politically "empty vessel" of the Japanese imperial house. Many of these versions shared a combination of moral and legal attributes that one scholar has characterized as "medieval constitutionalism," whether it took the form of the Confucian moralism in the palace or of the popular rights' statements on imperial loyalty (*kinnō*) and the way of the king (*ōdō*).[23] In the end, the constitutional garb of the emperor was voluminous enough to envelop both moral and legal interpretations of his sovereignty. The first was represented by Hozumi Yatsuka's presentation of imperial sovereignty in the moral context of a family-state, and the second eventually expressed in Minobe Tatsukichi's theory of the emperor as a legal organ of the state.

A similar theoretical tug-of-war occurred in the introduction of the imperial "line unbroken for ages eternal" (*bansei ikkei*) into the first article of the Constitution. In the context of the 1880s the imperial house stood both as a transcendental axis to keep politics at bay and also as a symbol of national unity—what Ōkubo had called in 1873 "the land, customs, manners, and trends of our country (*wagakuni*)," what Itō in 1888 deemed the Japanese equivalent of Christianity in the West, and what Inoue Kowashi in 1889 wrote into the imperial oath announcing the Constitution to the emperor's ancestors as "an exposition in our own day of the grand precepts of government that have been handed down by the Imperial Founder of Our House and by Our Other Imperial Ancestors to their descendants."[24] This definition of the unbroken imperial line was widely shared in the 1880s, even by those most committed to parliamentary and secular views of the polity.[25] Inoue Kowashi, who embraced nativism and constitutionalism at the same time, accommodated both views by insisting in 1890 that Shintō

> rites as national ritual are an affair of society, not an affair of state. The monarch is not only the head of state affairs, he is the paragon (*shihyō*) of society. He entrusts state affairs to the government, while social affairs—ritual, philanthropy, and the like—are performed by the ruling house (*ōke*) itself. Ritual thus belongs to the internal affairs of the ruling house and should not be mixed with affairs of state.[26]

With this comment Inoue admitted nativist views of the imperial line into the emperor's private wardrobe at the same time that he rejected once again the Shintoists' proposal for the establishment of a public department of religion within the new constitutional government.

As a result of the constitutional conception of the imperial institution that was forged from so many—not always compatible—elements during the 1880s, the emperor emerged from the decade institutionally prepared for his new role as a constitutional monarch. His financial and personal status was secured by the consolidation of the greater part of imperial household property in the late eighties and by the enactment of the Imperial Household Law at the same time as the Constitution. Itō was instrumental in both these undertakings, first as imperial household minister from 1884 to 1887 and then as chairman of the Privy Council from 1888.[27] As for the emperor himself, although he had continued to travel, his last circuit was completed in 1885, the year the cabinet system was established. To Itō and Inoue and other political actors of the decade, the definition of the imperial institution had perhaps seemed of greater importance than the display of the imperial countenance. It was also true that by 1889 the displacement of the shogunate by His Majesty's government no longer required imperial visibility to demonstrate it in the flesh. The phase of the "Restoration emperor," which could be said to have begun in 1846 when Emperor Kōmei was drawn into politics over the foreign issue, ended in 1889 when Emperor Meiji was once again raised above politics by the Constitution, which rendered sovereignty but not government within his powers. Yet, though the imperial person was thus returned "above the clouds" whence as a youth he had come, in ideological terms, the fashioning of his new appearance was in many ways just beginning. For it was in the late Meiji period that the Japanese emperor was publicly remade in the image of a modern monarch.

II

THREE characteristics were apparent in the making of the monarch. First, his image replaced his person before the public. Second, the public itself enlarged, both in the sense that the circle of ideological custodians broadened and also that those to whom they addressed themselves now included all the people, the *kokumin* at large. Third, the late Meiji concerns with nation and society determined the symbolic aspect that Japan's modern monarch would present to the people. In general, the late 1880s and 1890s saw the emperor become the manifestation of the elements associated with national progress as the Meiji elite defined it and the symbol of national unity, not of a political and legal, but of a patriotic and civic kind. Then in the period after the Russo-Japanese War, the emperor was also turned toward social ends. As the patriarch of a family-state he became the symbolic representation of harmony and as the descendant of the sun goddess, the deified evidence of the ancestral ethnicity of the Japanese.

This ideological transformation began with the relative sequestering of the imperial person after his bestowal of the Constitution. It was, of course, his earlier visibility that made his later seclusion seem striking, but it is true that more than seventy of the hundred-odd imperial excursions in the emperor's reign took place before 1889.[28] In the late Meiji period his visits were severely limited both in duration and exposure. At first he had traveled to be seen, now only for such specific public purposes as troop maneuvers, naval reviews, or special ceremonies.[29] In the earlier period the people of the provinces had lined the roads to catch a glimpse of His Imperial Highness (*Tenshisama*). They had come from the fields, offered rice stalks, and kowtowed to him in a mix of reverential modes that suggested he was both tutelary god and feudal lord.[30] Now the roads were often cleared of spectators and swept clean before His Majesty the Emperor (*Tennō heika*). Detailed instructions were dispatched that prohibited kneeling or kowtowing and such homely attire as the towels coiled around workers' heads.[31] Earlier the emperor had rested and lodged in the houses of local notables, who had frequently gone to considerable expense to prepare such special facilities as a new entry gate or an imperial privy. These *gōnō* houses—among them those of the family of Tokutomi Sohō in Kumamoto and of the novelist Shimazaki Tōson in the mountains of Nagano—were later preserved, creating the effect of "Emperor Meiji slept here" through the length and breadth of the land.[32] But in the last two decades of his reign, the imperial nights were spent in prefectural halls, military encampments, and other public places. He seldom visited shipyards, attended the openings of railroad lines or bridges, or appeared at local schools as he once had done. Much less was it contemplated, as the press rumored and the palace flatly denounced, that His Majesty would attend the Columbian Exposition in Chicago in 1893.[33] Even on his domestic excursions his audiences were now carefully screened and consisted mainly of prefectural officials and selected members of the local elite. Of these outings it was complained in the press in 1910 that only nobles and men of status were permitted in the imperial presence, when "in a constitutional system the people are supposed to be the bulwark of the throne."[34]

In truth, few of his subjects drew close to the emperor in person in the late Meiji period, which liberated both his official visage and personality from the constraints of reality. After two attempts (the first having displeased His Majesty), an Italian artist captured the emperor in his prime in 1888. The photograph of this engraving was distributed by the palace not only to consulates, ministries, prefectural offices, and institutions of higher education, as had been the

case with earlier likenesses, but also, in the early 1890s, to local offices and elementary schools throughout the country.[35] Thenceforth
in public the emperor scarcely aged. Replaced by his regal portrait—
uniformed and medalled, the hilt of his sword grasped in his hand,
his white-plumed cap on the table beside him—the imperial visage
thus gained a more effective ubiquity than it had in all the earlier
travels.

The immediate custodian of the imperial person was the Imperial
Household Ministry (Kunaishō), whose tight archival security keeps
the secrets of palace management in the Meiji period from too public
a view even today.[36] The "outer" side of the palace bureaucracy, as
David Titus has described it, had charge of the emperor's official
image and, with it, the dignity of the imperial house.[37] Once the
court loyalist Motoda had helped to move Itō out of the post of
imperial household minister in 1887, high court officialdom was
again separated from civil government as it had generally been in
ages past. Yet the office of imperial household minister was occupied
for most of the late Meiji period by two men, Hijikata Hisamoto
(1887-1898) and Tanaka Mitsuaki (1898-1909), both of whom were
Restoration loyalists from Tosa who had had careers in government
before they entered the palace. Their relationship to the government
was therefore distinctive. When it is said that from 1885 to 1912 the
palace leadership was under oligarchic control, this refers in effect to
a situation of mutual influence among a small group of Restoration
compatriots that included, among others, Itō, who was closer to Hijikata, Yamagata, who had more influence with Tanaka, and even in
a sense the emperor himself.[38] These men did not always cooperate
or agree with one another, and it is doubtful that they made concerted decisions of the sort that would have resulted in peremptorily
pulling the emperor back into the palace after 1889. Rather, in ideological matters, their mandates and their interests, although comple-
mentary, were specific to their respective positions.

The Household Ministry sought to guard the autonomy of the
palace and keep the emperor in high repute. The first it did in the
course of jurisdictional squabbles with the government in which the
Kunaishō repeatedly asserted its right to imperial management
against encroachment from the civil ministries. Arguments took
place with the Ministry of Education over which ministry would
distribute and control the imperial portraits and the Rescript on Education; with the Home Ministry over the extent of its role in the
local preparations connected with imperial excursions; and even with
the prime minister, at whose residence Imperial Household Minister

Tanaka declined to appear as summoned since he was not under any orders other than those of the emperor.[39] The ministry fulfilled its second mandate to preserve the emperor's image by exercising careful control over which elements of the empire would be adorned by the imperial name. The objects of imperial benevolence, be they kindergartens, hospitals, or personal "contributions" to the oligarchs, were determined by the palace bureaucracy.[40] The decision to visit Ise, to permit audiences to those who requested them, or, on military maneuvers in 1903, to admit local industrialists into the emperor's company for the first time, so as to take "imperial initiative in encouraging enterprise and urging that imports be checked and exports increased"—these dispositions of imperial favor remained in the province of the Household Ministry and helped to form the image of the monarch that was purveyed to the public in the late Meiji years.[41]

Of the oligarchs closest to the throne in those years, Itō and Yamagata remained preeminent. The emperor personally felt closer to Itō, whom he often consulted on such matters as the details of parliamentary politics: What would the government do if the newly established Diet did not approve (*kyōsan*) its administrative proposals? asked the emperor in February 1890. "Make every effort," Itō replied, "to persuade the Diet to cooperate."[42] For Itō the emperor generally reserved the highest praise and special expressions of solicitude, whether on the occasion of his rickshaw's overturning or of his funeral.[43] But Yamagata, to whom the emperor had shown less personal warmth, was far more influential than Itō in the ideological deployment of the imperial image. This was partly because of the connections Yamagata cultivated within the palace, not only through the late Meiji period but also from 1909 through 1920 when he saw to it that the post of imperial household minister was held by his allies.

A more important reason for Yamagata's influence, however, was his long-standing interest in ideological matters. While Itō saw to the legal and political status of the imperial house in the 1880s, Yamagata was embarked on his preparations for constitutional government, in which the emperor and the loyalty he could command among the people figured strongly. Yamagata played a major part in the two rescripts most closely associated with the imperial charge to his people: the Rescript to Soldiers and Sailors of 1882 and the Rescript on Education of 1890. Yamagata is also said by biographers to have genuinely revered the imperial office—a remark seldom made of Itō—and to have exhibited his devotion even as an old man when he made daily obeisance, rain or snow, to the shrine he had built in his garden in memory of the emperor.[44] Yamagata's awareness of the public importance of the imperial role was revealed in his concern with such details as the proposed cancellation by Tanaka of the emperor's scheduled appearance at a provincial banquet because of an epidemic of dysentery in the area. Yamagata protested that it would not be appropriate to disappoint the local people in this way.[45] In general, however, he preferred rescripts and distant imperial majesty to personal appearances. After attending the coronation of Czar Nicholas II in 1896, Yamagata is said to have voiced his wish for similar mystery and majesty in Japanese court ceremonials.[46] Indeed, for Yamagata, as well as for Itō and others of the Restoration generation, this association of the emperor with one or another of the Western monarchs they had read about or visited in their European tours was perhaps their clearest guide to the appropriate appearance of the emperor in public.

This was also true of many of the *minkan* ideologues, who in the late 1880s had raised their voices in the effort to arouse a sense of nation on the basis of Japan's incomparable imperial line. Although writers such as Kuga Katsunan stressed the incomparability of the imperial house, most were eager to indulge in comparisons of every sort.[47] In his youth Tokutomi Sohō said little of the emperor, and when he began to invoke him in the early nineties it was to do as the Western nations did in looking to their monarchs to provide a source of unity and harmony for society.[48] In 1901 he referred to "the marriage of the Crown Prince in May, 1900, under the new monogamous system and the felicitous birth of a royal heir in 1901" and urged the people to eschew the immoral ways of upper-class society and emulate instead "the imperial model of familial morality and human relations." As the persuasive climax of his brief to his newspaper readers, Tokutomi invoked "the English proverb that 'the royal house is the source of honor' " to suggest the parallel that "the Japanese royal house is the source of social morals."[49]

The most common references to Western monarchs were more concrete. The press supplemented its coverage of daily life at court and the activities of the Japanese royal family with frequent references to their counterparts in Europe. The *Tōkyō asahi shinbun*, which prided itself on its reports from "above the clouds," carefully recorded the progress of imperial mourning for the younger brother of the king of Italy in 1890, and in 1911 the exchange of New Year's telegrams "between our emperor and the monarchs of our imperial allies and other royal houses of England, Germany, Russia, and Austria."[50] Newspapers and magazines included royal gossip from the courts of Europe, a link that English primers of the day expressed by including the words "emperor" and "empress" on the same page as the words for king and queen. Inoue Tetsujirō, a scholar known for his willing service to the government as analyst and ideologue, compared Meiji to his foreign counterparts and found him to be more virtuous than Napoleon or Alexander the Great, both of whom lacked not only feeling (ninjō), but taste, for they did not lend their talents to poetry as the Meiji emperor did. The most apt comparison, Inoue concluded, was Wilhelm I of Germany, although in terms of Japan's progress (wagakuni no shinpo hattatsu) since the Restoration, it appeared that the Kaiser, too, was no match for Meiji.[51] When the emperor died there was scarcely a monarch of past or present to whom he was not compared and found not only similar but superior.[52]

The regal image of the emperor that was so widely projected in the late Meiji period owed a good deal of its persuasive detail to the curiosity of the public. Accounts of the emperor's equestrian and gastronomic interests—the ability of his palate to distinguish between a fish (ayu) from the Katsura River in Kyoto and one from the Tama River in Tokyo—and other imperial anecdotes found wide circulation in the popular culture of the day. The press, the woodblock printers, the manufacturers of fans, scrolls, and mementos with imperial likenesses upon them, and the generally lucrative industry of royal purveyance were always ready to foster and assuage this curiosity with the full-blown exposure and half-baked paraphernalia that royalty is heir to. Although the Kunaishō tried in vain to control unofficial imperial renderings, in fact the Meiji emperor, though above the clouds once again, had become more fully public property than he had ever been before.[53]

THE EMPEROR'S
REGAL ROLES

I

THE IMPERIAL Household Ministry, the oligarchs, the military, the civil ministries, the press, the fanmakers, and the postcard printers all had a share in dressing the Meiji emperor in his monarchical uniform. In the process they cooperated, often unwittingly, in identifying him with the attributes of what the Meiji elite defined as civilization and national progress. This meant not only that the imperial house demanded loyalty and symbolized unity, but also that the emperor became conspicuously associated with some attributes of national endeavor and just as conspicuously disassociated from others.

After his gracious bestowal of the Constitution, which marked his debut in his new role, the emperor's relation to politics was maintained in public on a strictly ceremonial level. He opened the Diet, met with his ministers to hear of political matters, and spoke, as it were, in infrequent rescripts that expressed his government's will in lofty imperial terms.[54] He was reported to peruse cabinet papers assiduously from nine to four o'clock and demonstrate his deep concern (ōmikokoro) for the affairs of state by reading the official gazette and the newspapers every morning. He read, it was noted in the provinces, the provincial press as well.[55] He was described as believing "in the principle of progress (shinposhugi), for only this principle can make the Japanese one of the great peoples of the world." Nonetheless, "he does not decide anything by himself, and though he comprehends the whole of things, he waits instead for the assistance of his ministers."[56] Thus, the ministers were associated with such mundane operations of government as taxation, parliamentary battles, failures in treaty negotiations, and the like. The emperor was credited with "having realized that the Constitution was necessary for the progress of our nation" (wagakuni no shin'un) and other achievements that transcended politics and enhanced the nation, as if the two had little connection with one another.[57] Politics was too ambiguous an endeavor to identify with the symbolic "jewel" that was the emperor, and in the ideological presentation to the people his imperial heart was made to lie elsewhere.

The emperor's presence, for example, was intensified in education, which had been an important aspect of the Meiji design of civilization since the earliest part of the period.

> During his reign the emperor valued learning and attended every graduation ceremony at the Imperial University since 1899. Summoning the minister of education at the time of the Russo-Japanese War, he issued a rescript urging that "education should not be neglected even in times of military crisis and educators should be encouraged in their diligence."[58]

In singling out education as the only imperial accomplishment worth mentioning in this eulogy of 1912, the novelist Natsume Sōseki betrayed his own predilections for humane rather than martial expressions of national pride. But he also portrayed the emperor in a role that had become increasingly familiar since 1889. The emperor's avidity for learning was repeatedly remarked upon, whether in regard to the perspicacity of his questions on such technical matters as radium and airplanes, or his assiduous attention to the lectures on Chinese, Japanese, and Western texts given for his benefit at court. His annual appearances in July at Tokyo Imperial University were well publicized, in particular the moment when the honor graduates received "from his own two hands" an inscribed silver watch as a mark of their achievements.[59] Not only personal but financial patronage was dispensed in the form of grants from the Imperial Household Ministry to educational institutions, both public and private, and scholarly and educational associations. These ranged in magnitude from 50,000 yen to Fukuzawa Yukichi for Keiō University in 1900; 30,000 yen to Ōkuma's Waseda University in 1908; 20,000 to Kokugakuin in 1909 when Sasaki Takayuki was its head; 2,000 annually for ten years to the Japanese version of a national academy, Teikoku Gakushiin, in 1910; 500 to the Japan Education Association in 1891; to a myriad of such smaller tokens of esteem as silver saké cups with the imperial crest bestowed upon educators in various fields.[60]

These evidences of imperial presence and beneficence among the educational elite in the late Meiji period continued a pattern set in earlier years by the Imperial Household Ministry. The emperor's public prominence in the schools, however, was new and owed its effectiveness to the universal distribution of his photographic likeness and the Imperial Rescript on Education, which were linked together in the service of loyalty and patriotism, not by the Kunaishō but by the Ministry of Education. In the late 1880s Mori Arinori had declared that "the emperor is peerless capital, the greatest possible treasure" in the enterprise of fostering loyalty and patriotism (*chūkun aikoku*) in the people toward something as "intangible" as the state.[61] To this end Mori had urged that the two main imperial occasions be properly celebrated in the schools: *kigensetsu*, the anniversary of the legendary founding of the empire by Emperor Jimmu on February 11, and *tenchōsetsu*, the birthday of the Meiji emperor on November 3. Although Mori did not live to see it—having been cut down on *kigensetsu* in 1889 for irreverence to the throne he had himself promoted—the Ministry of Education followed his suggestion in its "Regulations for Elementary School Ceremonies on Festivals and Holidays" in 1891.[62] Obeisance before photographs of the emperor and empress, singing of the national anthem, and reading of the Rescript on Education were followed by patriotic speeches by the principals and other local notables, and frequently also by athletic meets, exhibitions of pupils' compositions, and the distribution of buns and sweets.[63]

85

This mixture of songs, sweets, and patriotism became the model for the eventual intrusion of the imperial presence into every school occasion, from the opening of a new building to the graduation ceremony. Yet the sequence did not originate with the Ministry of Education's ceremonial directive. Instead it had evolved in the schools in the late 1880s, as prefectural offices issued their own regulations and schools vied in their requests to be the first recipient of the imperial photographs in their area. The schoolchildren anticipated these occasions as "bun days" (*manjūmorai no hi*), while some of their parents considered them excuses for keeping the children home and at work in the fields. But in these national festivals, the principals, local educators, and village officials eagerly performed their authoritative roles in much the same way as they did in village shrine festivals. Now, however, their status was enhanced by the association with the emperor and the nation.[64]

Although these local celebrations of imperial holidays were held in many provinces in the late 1880s and early 1890s, they were by no means universal, a fact that the Ministry of Education instructions did not immediately change. School records (*gakkō nisshi*) reveal that schools did not always hold the ceremonies as they were instructed to, and when they did, there was sometimes confusion about their nature. One school in 1897 recorded its closing on February 11 in commemoration of Emperor Kōmei, thus exchanging the founding legend of 660 B.C. for the birthday of the father of Meiji.[65] Also in 1897 the landlord's son Aizawa, who had not yet mentioned *kigensetsu* in the diary he had begun as a youth in his twenties in 1886, became deputy mayor of his village at the age of thirty-one. Perhaps for that reason he recorded the closing of the village office on February 11, though he mistook the founding holiday for *tenchōsetsu*, the Meiji emperor's birthday. From that time forward, Aizawa's diary entries exemplified the pattern of penetration of the imperial ceremonies that was found elsewhere in the countryside.[66] He first mentioned *kigensetsu* parenthetically in 1900 in connection with the announcement of the crown prince's marriage, the main imperial occasion of that year which was widely felicitated in the schools.[67] In 1903 he attended the *kigensetsu* ceremony at the village school for the first time, and from 1905 the ceremony became an annual event for him, as did the banquet that followed and other related activities. In the period after the Russo-Japanese War such local events as reservists' meetings and gatherings to raise funds for new school construction increasingly began to be held in conjunction with the national holiday. When Aizawa became village mayor in 1908, he not only attended but also spoke at the school ceremony, thus enacting the role of the local elite in the manner encouraged by the Home Ministry.

The pattern at work here in the social establishment of national ceremony was a common one. Forward-looking local educators and officials had welcomed the imperial symbol in the 1880s, for it lent their villages, their schools, and themselves additional stature. Outside the schools, however, few villagers were yet aware of the emperor's ceremonial presence. The Ministry of Education then codified and dictated the procedures centrally in the 1890s, but the full penetration of the practices it advocated did not occur until the first decade of the century, most strikingly from the time of the Russo-Japanese War. At that time the number of ceremonies featuring the imperial paraphernalia increased, as schools and local organizations joined to hold victory celebrations, commemorations of the bestowal of the Rescript on Education and the similarly hortatory Boshin Imperial Rescript of 1908, anniversaries of the founding of the school, and other village events with national tasks embedded in them.[68] Other agents of ideology, such as the Home Ministry and the Army, contributed to the ceremonial proliferation, until by about 1910 the imperial rituals had become practiced village habits. Gradually the number of villages in which work was stopped on the three main national holidays (sandaisetsu), which included New Year's and the two imperial occasions, changed from a minority in the late 1880s to a majority in the period after the Russo-Japanese War.[69]

Despite the evident change, local ceremony never quite fulfilled government expectations. Ministry directives and opinions submitted to the Diet continued to complain in the 1910s that the procedures needed further standardization, since the celebrations were not effective in their goal of "unifying the sentiments of the people" (minshin o hitotsu ni shi).[70] In 1911 localities were chastised for continuing to conduct agricultural ceremonies and local festivals according to the traditional calendar of observances (nenjū gyōji). For this meant not only that holidays increased in number, but also that the villages were still following the lunar calendar, which had been abolished in 1873. In a village plan of 1911 it was argued that "the inconvenience of the lunar calendar lies in its not meshing with school and yakuba (village office) holidays; it thus goes without saying that this is an obstacle to village administration and education."[71] The point here was that too many holidays would endanger productivity—the new calendar contained sixty, the lunar calendar seventy, and the latest agronomic theory held that any more than eighty was of serious agricultural consequence. But the emphasis had shifted since the central government directives of the earlier period. The school and administrative holidays that had been decreed by the government in the 1880s had often taken second place, both to traditional observances and to work in the fields. Now the national festivities took precedence in the established routine, and the local issue was focused on holding down the overall number of non-working days. As part of this process by which national ceremony entered the rural calendar of observances, the Meiji emperor—his portrait in its closed cupboard cared for according to strict guidelines from the Ministry of Education—had become inextricably enmeshed in the popular experience of elementary education and the role of the school in village life.

IF EDUCATION was important to the late Meiji conception of progress, so, too, was empire, and the most dramatic increase in imperial exposure occurred not in the schools, but in the context of the two Meiji wars. First, the Sino-Japanese conflict in 1894–1895 brought the image of His Majesty the Commander-in-Chief (*Daigensui heika*) out from the confines of military education and indoctrination into full public light. In September 1894, when the imperial headquarters was moved to the point of embarkation in Hiroshima, the emperor followed "to oversee the important affairs of war," arriving just in time to announce the Japanese victory at Pyongyang.[72] For more than eight months the emperor was described on the front pages of newspapers throughout the country as enduring the privations of a soldier at war. The imperial simplicity (*shisso*) was painstakingly recorded, each phrase beginning with how he "graciously" (*kashikokumo*) occupied a small room, wore his uniform until it was threadbare, declined an arm-chair for a three-legged stool, and on occasion drew his own royal bath. "Uncaring of the inconvenience, the emperor works day and night at military affairs," "rises at six, retires at midnight, and even when he is resting listens to his aides expound on military matters," although one press notice did reveal that there had been time for a little football (*kemari*) in the corridors.[73] In addition to offering military counsel and conducting reviews, the emperor bestowed over 4,000 gallons of saké and 800,000 cigarettes on the troops in 1894, and after the victory distributed cigarettes inscribed as an "imperial gift" to soldiers who were described as "overcome with gratitude."[74] In the press, in the popular magazines—especially the phenomenally successful *Nisshin sensō jikki* [True Record of the Sino-Japanese War] published by Hakubunkan—in woodblock prints, in the numerous magic-lantern shows depicting the victorious battles, the Meiji emperor was suddenly the central public figure.[75]

In the exciting aftermath of victory Japan was declared "a power in the East" (*Tōyō no rekkoku*). Provincial editorials exulted that "after 2,500 years of domestic national accomplishments in culture and institutions . . . now 1895 will be remembered as the year of international recognition."[76] Henceforth the West would "call us as we call ourselves: Nippon, which has a meaning, the rising sun, and there will be no more 'Japan' or 'Japs' in the foreign press."[77] The emperor was closely associated with these momentous achievements, and as children cheered for the emperor (*Tennō heika banzai!*), they also cheered for the empire (*Teikoku banzai!*).[78] After the peace treaty was signed in April 1895, credit was given the emperor for achieving "peace in Asia" and for his trials and guidance at Hiroshima.[79] Within three weeks, however, the emperor disappeared from the front pages as quickly as he had come, retiring into the more formal and reclusive routines of peacetime imperial life.

When he returned as wartime commander-in-chief nearly a decade later, his image appeared quite different. In the Russo-Japanese War of 1904-1905 the imperial headquarters remained in Tokyo. In the Sino-Japanese War the emperor had suffered with the troops; now he worried with the government and presided over imperial conferences rather than maneuvers. From the futile negotiations with Russia through the decisions for war and peace, the emperor was depicted as an active presence whose grave concern for the peril of his people gave him little rest. In part because of the maturity of his reign and in part because of ill health, which was kept from the public during the war, the sympathetic commanding officer was transformed into a statesman. His involvement with the war overflowed the rescripts announcing victories and urging endurance, and spilled over into poetry. Of the more than 90,000 verses the emperor is credited with, he (and perhaps the Imperial Poetry Bureau) composed 7,526 poems during the year and a half of war.[80] This prodigious proof to his subjects of the deep imperial concern for their sacrifice included the famous poem, "Crush the enemy for the sake of the nation, but never forget to have mercy," about which the novelist Tokutomi Roka quarreled with Tolstoy, who criticized it as self-contradictory.[81] But the poetic gist more commonly ran along these lines: "When I think of those in battle, I have no heart for the flowers."[82] This sentiment served the emperor well, and he emerged from the Russo-Japanese War a paragon of statecraft and solicitude. "Since the Russo-Japanese War," it was recorded in a provincial report in 1906, "belief in the imperial house and ancestors is stronger and reverence for the gods deeper as well."[83]

Whether or not "the emperor's will spread through the country like the sound of a bell in this room,"[84] it is probably true that for the Meiji emperor the Russo-Japanese War marked the full meridian of his reign. When he finally did leave Tokyo after two years of attention to national crisis, the emperor traveled to Ise to report the victory at his—and the nation's—ancestral shrine, a journey he had not made after the defeat of China.[85] For victory over Russia lent the emperor an expanded aura, which fused the imperial image with the achievement of international prestige vis-à-vis the West and simultaneously made him the symbol not only of progress but of empire. Like the figure of Britannia, the emperor now represented more than domestic arrangements; he stood for Japan's "advance into the ranks of the world powers."[86] Japan had become a *taikoku*, a "great nation," of which schoolchildren sang: "From Karafuto and the Kuriles in the north to Taiwan and the Pescadores in the south, Korea and all Japan; the nation our *taikun* rules, and the fifty million countrymen over whom waves the flag of the rising sun."[87] Japan had now realized "the ideal it had pursued since the Restoration, that of matching the progress of the West." As the citizens of a great nation (*taikokumin*), Japanese would receive international respect from "countries that turn toward Japan as the sunflower toward the sun."[88] And at the center of the light of empire stood the emperor, the symbol of victory and world power.

Victory was the emperor's, but not the "humiliating peace" that followed it, against which *minkan* activists clamored in September 1905 in the Hibiya riots in Tokyo and elsewhere in the country. Indeed public opinion claimed the imperial will for its own in protest against a government which it accused of betraying the imperial cause by accepting terms less than "what the emperor together with the people had come to expect."[89] As before, the emperor was separated from the failures and credited with the successes of the nation. And now, at the end of a very difficult war that had been presented in an unprecedented explosion of official propaganda and commercial reportage, not only the emperor but empire as well had become a stirring and publicized fact of national life.

II

LESS WELL publicized and also perhaps less stirring were the domestic dimensions added to the imperial image in the years after the Russo-Japanese War, when perceptions of social disarray provoked increasing ideological concern. Although the emperor had long been associated with benevolence (*jin'ai*) and solicitude (*shinnen*), his well-recorded interest from above the clouds in "things below" (*gekai*) now took on a more specific social character.[90] The grants from the Imperial Household purse for relief from floods, earthquakes, and other natural disasters continued, as did the charitable donations, often in the name of the empress, to such socially acceptable institutions as hospitals, orphanages, the Red Cross, and the Patriotic Women's Association (*Aikoku fujinkai*).[91] In 1906, the year of the worst famine in sixty years in Tōhoku, a large imperial gift of 40,000 yen was made, nearly matched in amount by those the English-language press of the day called "the tycoons," Iwasaki, Mitsui, and Yasuda.[92] Although the amount was unusually large, so was the need, and the Imperial Household Ministry was only conforming to the government's preference for private rather than public relief, even in time of unusual hardship. But what inspired unprecedented imperial beneficence in 1911 was neither natural calamity nor economic hardship but the rise of socialism. Two weeks after twelve of the twenty-four leftists sentenced to death in the Great Treason Incident (*taigyaku jiken*) had been executed, the Kunaishō made a grant of 1.5 million yen for drugs and medical treatment for the extreme indigent. The rescript announcing the donation was promulgated on February 11, that most imperial of imperial holidays, *kigensetsu*. It began with the succinct declaration that "as economic conditions change, the hearts of the people are apt to err in their direction."[93] Thus the imperial house, it was suggested in the press, sought to use philanthropy as an antidote to socialism.[94] The Saiseikai, or Relief Association, which was established with the imperial grant and private funds raised in a magnitude of fifteen times the Kunaishō amount, became public evidence of the emperor's new social conscience. Since it was Yamagata, in particular, who regarded the emperor as the appropriate ideological instrument to wield in the suppression of socialism, it was not surprising that the government officials associated with the Saiseikai included such Yamagata men as Prime Minister Katsura, Home Minister Hirata Tōsuke, and his Vice Minister, Ichiki Kitokurō.[95]

The Home Ministry, for its part, was also using the emperor to confront social issues. Rather than meeting an ideological threat with token social relief, however, the Ministry attempted to meet a social threat with an increased dose of imperial ideology. Faced with severe economic hardship in the villages after the war, Home Minister Hirata helped to prepare an imperial rescript expressed in the style of a

Confucian moral ruler. Immediately labeled the "diligence and frugality rescript" by the press, the *Boshin shōsho* of 1908 prescribed hard work, good manners, simple living, and "strenuous effort" (*jikyō*). The emperor enjoined his "loyal subjects" to follow these "teachings of Our revered Ancestors" in order "to keep pace with the rapid progress of the world and share in the blessings of civilization." As Hirata explained to the Prefectural Governors Conference, this increasingly familiar combination of imperial past and future was intended to foster "the harmony of morality and economics" and strengthen "the local organizations which are the basis of the nation" and, not incidentally, of the Home Ministry's programs in the countryside.[96]

In addition to invoking the emperor's moral influence, the Home Ministry frequently reminded its rural audiences of the debt of gratitude that they owed the emperor for his benevolence and how it might best be repaid. "In seven years the Meiji era will be fifty," intoned one Ministry bureaucrat in 1911, "and although we have sacrificed ourselves for the sake of the emperor and the nation in the Sino- and Russo-Japanese Wars, we must do something in times of peace as well." He then suggested to the local officials in his audience that the Kanagawa Local Improvement Association "overcome all difficulties, cooperate to bring about great progress and development, and present the emperor with the results on the fiftieth anniversary of his reign."[97] The Meiji era did not reach fifty, for the emperor died in 1912, and Kanagawa did not overcome all difficulties either, but the name of the emperor and the name of progress were linked together in similar lectures in provincial towns around the country. Combined with the increased emphasis on the ancestral relation of the imperial house as the "great head family" (*daisōke*) of a familial state, these invocations of the emperor contributed to the imperial image of patriarchal benevolence which, it was suggested, could best be reciprocated with local social and economic self-help.[98]

During this same period from 1905 to 1910, the Ministry of Education also laid further claim to the emperor's name on behalf of education. In addition to the effort to promote and hence to share the ideological potential of the 1908 Boshin Rescript, the Ministry presided over a new edition of school textbooks. The 1910 redaction of the elementary school ethics texts increased the emperor's exposure to the point that he appeared more often than any other historical figure (the empress, however, was preceded in frequency by Florence Nightingale).[99] Revised instructions to teachers emphasized the importance of using emperor-centered examples in the classroom. And in the 1911 controversy over the dual legitimacy of the Northern and Southern courts educators insisted that a single imperial line be consecrated as official in the history texts. The fact that this academic issue was politicized only partly explains why the government—Yamagata, Katsura, and Education Minister Komatsubara—reacted so strongly, or why the opposition politician Inukai could stand up in the Diet and assert that for the imperial line to remain unclear was a treason worse than that of the socialists.[100] In the ideologically charged atmosphere that surrounded the emperor in the wake of the events of the Great Treason Incident, a historical issue from the fourteenth century appeared so important because the imperial house was seen increasingly as central not only to the nation but to the fabric of society itself.

THUS BY THE final years of the emperor's reign, his symbolic and regal roles had expanded and increased, and he died in 1912, richly clothed in the garb of a modern monarch. He was associated, at a noble distance, with constitutionalism, much more closely with education, inextricably with victory in war and international prestige, generously with benevolence in small cash grants and large outpourings of concern, personally with culture in the form of poetry and patronage, and always with the achievements of civilization. The emperor was presented as the embodiment of the progressive doctrines of Meiji, the symbol not only of Japan, but of Japan's capacity to propel itself energetically into the forefront of the civilized world. The emperor, pulling his eternal, unbroken line of ancestors behind him, was thus transfigured into the vanguard of progress, with the result that the most traditional of Japanese institutions ended up with its symbolic back to the past.

In this national guise, both the person and the office of the emperor had become increasingly concrete, as ideological sources of every description, from magic-lantern slides to oligarchic pronouncements, reinforced the symbolic imperial content. His role as social benefactor and ancestral patriarch, on the other hand, was less widely communicated, in part because fewer ideological agents participated in its creation, and the reinforcement was therefore fainter. Moreover, safeguarding the emperor from the less desirable aspects of civilization meant not only that he was raised above politics but also that he had comparatively little to do with economics either. Though he opened industrial exhibitions and began to receive industrial entrepreneurs into his presence, in fact the industrial enterprise encouraged by the emperor was generally of the more traditional, familiarly benign sort. Silkworm raising, tea production, saké brewing were frequently mentioned, while copper barons and factory girls were more often screened from his public sight.[101] The darker side of industrialization, whether of the capitalist or the worker, was thus a governmental not an imperial affair.

Indeed His Majesty had been little linked to the harsh realities of life and livelihood in any sector. Hence when the emperor was evoked by Home Ministry bureaucrats and others as a rallying cry for socioeconomic improvement in the countryside, the local reservoir of available imperial association was shallow. Although village Japanese had been familiar with the emperor in the context of national progress, the rigors of war, and the glories of empire, his imperial presence seldom impinged on the rigors of daily experience. For this reason it was perhaps less difficult to project the modern monarch as the symbol of the state than as the patriarch of the paddy field. In late Meiji times at least it was national progress rather than social cohesion toward which the imperial image was first turned to the fullest effect.

LOCAL RENDERINGS OF
THE EMPEROR

THE IMPERIAL image projected by the Kunaishō and the oligarchs, the civil ministries and the *minkan* press was clear in its monarchical silhouette. Less clear, perhaps, was the extent to which this silhouette figured in the lives of the people whose sentiments it was supposed to unite. Local documents suggest that when the ceremonies of peace and war ended and the flags and bunting were down, the emperor disappeared from the village in ways that the state no longer could—whether in the person of its officials or in the form of taxes, conscription, rice inspection, silkworm standards, or new railroad lines. In local speeches, records of local associations, and village plans, even those prepared by officials at the behest of the government, the emperor was seldom mentioned. Instead the nation was generally referred to in terms of its constitutional system, postwar economic recovery, international status as a first rank power, and perhaps most widely, the march of national progress (*wagakuni no shinpo hattatsu*).[102] The *kokuze*, national policy, was frequently invoked; the emperor, rarely so. In one unusually grand introduction to a village plan of 1914, the editors began with world history, suggesting that "England's wealth and Germany's military strength and learning," had not been won overnight. This was true of Japan as well:

94

His Majesty the Emperor Meiji, accomplished in civil and martial matters alike, early reflected on trends in the world and promulgated the
Charter Oath. As a result of the people's working together to achieve
its ends, the promise of the Charter Oath is gradually coming to frui-
tion in the current state of the nation.

"It is the same," they continued, "in the village," which must therefore make a plan as effective as the Charter Oath to assure its own
future.[103] This allusion to the emperor, however, occurred after his
death and reflected the encomia of the Meiji achievements of progress
that followed the end of the era. In general, local sources abounded
with references to *wagakuni*, "our country, Japan" and to progress,
with the imperial rhetoric apparently reserved for special occasions.

Although such negative evidence does not lead to positive conclu-
sions about the nature of village views of the emperor, there are
sources that provide concrete glimpses of the imperial image among
the local elite. Since these men of influence were also the officials and
the imputed carriers of the ideological messages dispatched through
such organizations as the reservists, the youth associations, and the
local government system itself, their renderings of the emperor were
often both local and national in reference. In terms of ideological
dispersal of the imperial image, they functioned in the localities in
ways similar to those of the ministers and *minkan* intellectuals at the
center.

The local elite (*yūshisha, yūryokusha*, or *chihō meibōka*) had been in
the vanguard of popular interest in national and imperial matters
since the 1870s and, in some cases, since before the Restoration.
These were the men who requested the imperial portraits for their
village schools and offices before they were universally distributed
by government decision. And these were the bureaucratic, entrepreneurial, and agricultural elite of the countryside who were proud to
be invited into the emperor's presence when he made his brief appearances in the provinces in the late Meiji years. They donned new
swallowtail coats and sometimes, like "the rural gentlemen of substance" (*shitsugyō taru inaka shinshi*) who appeared before the emperor
in Nagoya in 1890, offered not a Western-style bow from the waist
as befitted their costume, but dropped to their knees and kowtowed
in the old style, their new tails sweeping incongruously along the
floor, much to the amusement of the court assemblage.[104]

These same rural men of substance comprised the majority of the
recipients of the blue medals of merit conferred by the emperor since
1881, when this system of imperial awards was established. In all
there were three colors—green for loyalty, filiality, and virtue, the

recipients of which were often impoverished peasants who endured their misery with particular moral grace; red for saving of lives, a fairly straightforward category; and blue, which had originally been defined in terms of contributions to the "public benefit" (*kōshū no rieki*). For the green and red awards the definition remained unchanged, but the criteria for the blue medals were broadened in April 1890 to include diligence in enterprise (*jitsugyō ni seirei*) and serving as models for the people (*shūmin no mohan*). In July of the same year they were further expanded, specifically to include members of local government and local assemblies, mayors, and those in honorary positions of community service (*kōkyō jigyō*). In 1894 in light of "the great flourishing in the recent course of events and the progress of literature, technology, agriculture, commerce, and industry," these limits were again deemed "too narrow." Added therefore to the roads, dams, schools, and charitable institutions of the past were achievements in arts and technology; construction and repair of public works; improvements in fields, forests, and fisheries; development of agriculture, commerce, and industry; and even the achievements of foreigners in these areas.[105] Foreigners, however, captured few awards; and, as two compendia of recipients published around the turn of the century reveal, the blue medalists were overwhelmingly drawn from the landlord, entrepreneurial, and official class of the countryside, whose achievements in local community service were rewarded with the highest imperial cachet.[106]

Acutely conscious of the importance of such recognition, this same class produced the provincial officials who sometimes revised the biographies of village recipients of imperial favor so that they better accorded with what the officials conceived to be the proper objects of the emperor's notice. In the profile of a poor peasant selected to receive an imperial gift to the elderly, for example, he was originally described as subsisting on a diet of seven parts barley and three parts rice. But for Kunaishō consumption a local official took it upon himself to improve the ratio to half and half. Or, when a farmer was listed as employed full-time in agriculture, tea and silkworm raising were gratuitously inserted into his daily chores as proof of local diligence in agricultural side-employment (*fukugyō*).[107] At work in this social sanitizing by editorial brushstroke were both a bureaucratic sense of local face and a reverence for the honor of the imperial connection.

The rural elite, however, also turned the emperor to local benefit. Visits from members of the imperial family were used as occasions to implement local projects whose budgets were too expansive to manage in ordinary times. In both the 1880s and 1890s these were generally construction projects and public works, and after the Russo-Japanese War such improvements as increasing village savings, repairing roads, and reforming customs were encouraged by the local elite to coincide with imperial visits, often without reference to quite similar injunctions from the Home Ministry.[108] Writing in 1911, Ishibashi Tanzan reproached both palace and local officials for insisting on unnecessary and expensive preparations for the Crown Prince's visit to Hokkaidō—ordering schoolgirls' shoes from Tokyo and arranging for rickshaws in places that had no other need for them. What Ishibashi criticized as the "lack of common sense among provincial officials" had become by 1911 a kind of bureaucratic common sense that took the imperial presence, either in person or by proxy, as a serious charge to the officials' own status as well as that of their locality.[109]

In other cases imperial ceremony was clearly an excuse for a genuinely local enterprise. In 1890, the leading newspaper in Nagano prefecture reported that

> today, as we promised, on the celebration of the anniversary of Emperor Jimmu, we include a drawing of the Ueda bridge completed over the Chikuma river. The opening ceremony will be held today, finally connecting, as we have long hoped, the north and the south [of the prefecture].[110]

In Nagano, of which it was later said that public works were the most serious political business of the prefecture, the bridge was clearly the focus of festivities, and it was announced in the press that "businesses are closed today because of the bridge opening ceremony."[111] The only reference to the imperial occasion was the perfunctory mention of Jimmu. Elsewhere in the prefecture a village banquet was held on Emperor Jimmu's day to honor local contributors to the establishment of evening school. The assemblage concluded with cheers for the emperor and empress, followed by one for night school (*Tennō heika banzai, Kōgō heika banzai, yagakubu banzai!*).[112] Although the center of attention was the night school, for the local elite the conjunction between imperial celebration and local achievements was increasingly a natural one.

In some instances it is possible to discern a difference between the attitude of the local elite toward the emperor and that of more ordinary villagers. For twenty-five years, from 1881 to 1905, farmers of the Kiso valley in Nagano protested the confiscation of their lands and the common land of their villages for conversion into imperial forestlands (*goryōrin*) as part of the consolidation of the imperial estate. They resisted from the start, refusing to witness the boundary surveys in the early eighties, and then petitioned continuously for over two decades. They pulled out survey markers and poached trees from the land whose owners or villages did capitulate, often under pressure, to the "imperialization" of their woods. And while a compromise settlement in the form of a lump sum from the Kunaishō was finally reached in 1905, one farmer, named Ueda, managed to preserve his property until July 1928. Throughout this period the villagers steadfastly argued the case against the confiscation of their lands on economic and legal grounds.

Members of the local elite, however, presented a different point of view.[113] When Shimazaki Hirosuke, a *gōnō* son and the novelist Tōson's older brother, returned from adventuring in China in 1898, he undertook to alleviate "the friction between the officials and the people" (*kanmin no atsureki*) and restore "harmony" between them (*kanmin no chōwa, jōge no enkotsu*) on the question of the Kiso forestlands.[114] Exasperated by the tenacity of the villagers' resistance and despairing of what he called the villagers' "ignorant stubbornness" (*muchi no ganmin*), he warned of disrespect (*fukei*) toward the imperial house. And he expressed concern about the impropriety of litigation involving the emperor and about whether the prefectural governor would lose face with the Kunaishō because of it.[115] The villagers were clear on this point:

> We are not instituting a suit against imperial property (*teishitsu no go-zaisan*). The officials who are supposed to look after imperial property have made an error in the boundaries and confused land owned by the people (*min'yū taru tochi*) with imperial forest. We therefore request that the officials correct the boundary error and turn over the private lands that have been confused with imperial forest. Since this is not a suit against imperial property, but a suit that requests the return of private land to its owners, there is no particular disrespect (*fukei*) involved. Under the transfer of ownership rights guaranteed by Article 27 of the Constitution, we present this suit based on Article 24 of the same law [guaranteeing every Japanese the right to be tried by judges determined by law].[116]

Thus the petitioners refuted the charge of lèse majesté by using the Constitution for their text. Despite Shimazaki's arguments on behalf of loyalty to the throne (*teishitsu ni chūai*), the protestors maintained their position that it was the officials (*kan*) who threatened their land, just as it was the officials who planned the railroad line without compensation for the fields that would be destroyed by the locomotive's black smoke.[117] The villagers had not resisted the imperial forestlands because of disloyalty, nor would they capitulate because of its opposite.

It is probable that Shimazaki's emphasis on imperial loyalty owed its origins in part to the local elite class into which he was born in 1861. His father was a village headman and a follower of Hirata *kokugaku* (nativism), who had believed in the restoration of imperial rule and lost position, wealth, and hope in the course of the transition to the Meiji state.[118] Like others of his class, Shimazaki was educated, and, in his youth, active in the popular rights movement. Unlike his brother or Tokutomi Sohō, who left for Tokyo to make newer, urban careers for themselves, after his time abroad Shimazaki remained active in the local community. He did not disavow his youthful belief in people's rights; indeed he fought for appropriate compensation for the contested property. But he also believed in the importance of respect for the imperial house.

Whether it was the early influence of *kokugaku* or the self-consciousness of the *gōnō* as local leaders with national concerns, Shimazaki displayed a reverence for the emperor that was not uncommon among the rural elite, whose views were well represented in the provincial press. Thus Shimazaki quoted approvingly a local newspaper article in 1905, which argued that especially in time of war "the true duty of the supremely loyal subjects of the Japanese empire" lay in reaching "an accord between the people and the officials (*kanmin itchi kyōboku*) . . . for the sake of the prosperity of the empire and the respect of the imperial house."[119] Here, as in other elements of the emerging ideological discourse, the local elite often revealed themselves to be more closely tied to its tenets than those above them in the prefectural offices or those below them in the village community.

That the villagers were able to separate loyalty to the imperial house from questions of local interest was demonstrated in other prefectures as well. Indeed variations of the Kiso movement to return confiscated lands occurred throughout the country during the Meiji years. The nature of the opposition was nearly everywhere the same. In 1911, for example, the Kunaishō returned a part of imperial land that had been confiscated earlier from village common lands (*iriaichi*) in Yamanashi. In 1912 the prefectural office issued an order that this imperial beneficence be celebrated in the schools so that proper gratitude might be shown. In 1917 another order established March 11 as the "Day Commemorating the Imperial Gift" (*Onshi kinenbi*) for the sake of expressing gratitude and "reforming self-government."

Schools were closed, flags were hung, a song recounting the gracious event was sung, and the ceremonial buns were distributed to the children. Yet the protests against the confiscation of commonage that preceded the imperial benevolence did not cease, for the land had been returned to the prefecture, not to the localities. As before, the issue remained the confiscation of private land by public authorities (*kan*), be they imperial or prefectural.[120]

Such incidents suggest not that village Japanese were disloyal or ungrateful to the emperor but that their respect for him operated on certain planes and not on others. The more overtly ideological expressions of the imperial image arose among the officials and the local elite, while the emperor remained a lofty presence, removed from the immediate concerns of most of the villagers. Yet, from the outpouring of popular expression on the occasion of the emperor's illness and death in 1912, it is possible to discern the general outlines of the people's view of the emperor.[121] First, it appears that by the end of the Meiji period virtually all Japanese were conscious of the emperor's existence for the first time in Japanese history. They were aware at least both of his visage and of his passing: they knew what he looked like and they knew when he was gone. Perhaps because he had been portrayed in such concrete and visible postures—bestowing the Constitution, writing poems, reviewing the troops, even drawing his bath—the popular image of the Meiji emperor was often quite human and personal. In addition, the combination of his constitutional presence, his ceremonial invocation in the army, the schools, and the village, and his statesmanlike image in war conspired to make of him a regal and symbolic figure associated with the Meiji achievement of civilization. However, the moral and religious constructions of the imperial office, which were increasingly emphasized as part of the evolving civic morality, appeared somewhat less prominently in the popular channels of social communication during the late Meiji period. This may be because images of the Confucian sage-king and the Shintō living god paled in comparison with the portrait of the man with the moustache. But whatever the reason, in the popular view the imperial institution seemed less the repository of Japanese traditions than the embodiment of Japanese modernity, less the ancestral manifest deity than the regal symbol of the nation. And the emotional attachment to the emperor that the people expressed upon his death communicated their feeling for a popular monarch very much in the modern mold. This image survived the Emperor Meiji's death, and he remained through the prewar reigns of his son and grandson the quintessential imperial symbol. In the late 1960s a farmer who participated in a latter-day conflict between the state and private lands—the Sanrizuka protests against the Narita airport—explained that he had a photograph of the Meiji emperor hanging next to one of Mao Tse-tung because they were both "great men" (*erai hito*).[122] It was this sort of sentiment that appeared to have established itself by the end of the Meiji era.

IN THE POPULAR iconography of the Meiji period two ubiquitous images gradually emerged as symbols of "civilization": the monarch and the locomotive.[123] Both were associated with progress, even when that progress had its costs, and both contributed to the national and social integration that characterized the modern state. At the beginning of the Meiji period the emperor was a youth carried around the countryside in a palanquin, and the locomotive was an exotic "fire wheeled car" depicted in woodblock prints. By the end of the era the train had chugged its way to the remote and distant parts and become a fact of daily life, while the emperor had been removed from circulation and his image embellished until it was larger than life. For modernity there were to be no two more powerful symbols for a long time to come.

V

Civil Morality

MORALITY AND NATION

I

THE CONSTITUTION and the monarch formed the legal and symbolic bases of the state, but neither alone nor together did they appear to the Meiji elite to be sufficient to weld a people into a nation. To gain the "universal sentiments of the people," a sense of nation and a civic ethos seemed increasingly essential. In the 1880s the impending change in the domestic political system and the intensified focus on treaty revision raised the concern with national unity to a new pitch. Progressives and conservatives alike agreed that a constitutional monarchy depended on a people conscious of their role as citizens (*kokumin*) and subjects (*shinmin*), while survival in an international struggle in which "the strong devoured the weak" required national confidence and pride. Citizenship thus became an issue of the day. Loyalty and patriotism (*chūkun aikoku*), its emerging watchwords, were joined to a social ethic, for shared moral values were considered the surest means of national unity. Drawing on values from the past and the present, the ideologues linked morality and patriotism to define a national ethos that would undergird the legal structures of the constitutional system. Its ideological epitome was the Imperial Rescript on Education of 1890, and the system of national education was the main instrument of its diffusion. In the process of definition and diffusion, *kokutai*, the unbroken imperial tradition, was increasingly invoked as the symbolic embodiment of the nation, and the emperor acquired ever more elaborated roles as the Confucian fount of moral virtue and the Shintō manifestation of a divine ancestral line. Ethical, national, and historical values were gradually intertwined in various renderings, the ideological amalgam of which was a catechism of citizenship that joined code and country in a newly generalized civil morality.

LIKE THE Constitution, the Rescript on Education, which became the focus of this civil morality, represented both an end and a beginning.

102

A product of the 1880s, it was a culmination of the period of complex institutional and ideological sorting out that followed the reforms of the 1870s and preceded the establishment of the new political system in 1890. Although it is frequently described as the conclusion of a successful campaign on the part of traditional moralists to reassert the values of the past against what they regarded as insurgent progressivism, in fact the Rescript emerged from a meandering, often inchoate, process of collective reinterpretation that included many different elements. Court moralists, Western-oriented educators, old conservatives, young progressives, *minkan* nationalists, cabinet ministers, prefectural governors, and, again, Yamagata, were among the ideologues who participated in the sometimes separate, sometimes intersecting debates over national unity and moral education that ultimately resulted in the promulgation of an Imperial Rescript on Education (*Kyōiku chokugo*) in 1890. The Rescript thus reflected a confluence of otherwise divergent ideological currents that flowed around issues of school and nation in the 1880s. Partly because of this, the document itself emerged as a synoptic compendium of attitudes sufficiently common at the time that they appeared unobjectionable in substance and unspecific in meaning. The lack of specificity, however, meant that the imperial pronouncement that ended one period of ideological debate also marked the beginning of another. As ideologues laid layer upon interpretive layer on the text of the Rescript during the 1890s, its meaning was both embellished and sanctified. And the document that had initially expressed commonplace tenets of a civic ethos was increasingly used to define the permissible limits of loyalty and patriotism. In the course of the late Meiji period the Imperial Rescript was gradually enshrined at the core of national education, where it remained until it was finally withdrawn from the curriculum by government order in October 1946.[1]

The origin of the Rescript, or, more properly, of the civil morality it epitomized, was the premise that national education should serve the state. This principle was articulated in the earliest years of the Meiji period and maintained unwaveringly through the dizzying institutional and curricular changes in the education system over the next two decades. Meiji educational policy is often characterized as having been "progressive" in the 1870s, "conservative" in the early 1880s, and "statist" during Mori Arinori's tenure as education minister in the late 1880s. Yet, the various redactions of the education law during these years differed on the means rather than on the ends of national education.[2] The goal of educating and influencing (*kyōka*) the common people, or the general population (*shomin, ippan no jinmin*), had been enunciated in the first months of the new regime.

Nativist scholars at court spoke of the imperial way (*kōdō*) and reformist civil bureaucrats spoke of civilization (*bunmei*). But whatever their differences on the specific content of learning, all agreed from the start that the purpose of the new general education was to serve the nation.

In February 1869, the Meiji government issued a provincial directive in which mention was first made of the establishment of elementary schools. In it the contents of primary education were stated in straightforward terms that revealed the influence of the nativists at court: in addition to the traditional subjects of writing, reading, and reckoning, stories were to be used "to explain the times and the *kokutai*, teach the way of loyalty and filiality, and enrich moral custom."[3] But the nativist influence was short-lived, and within a year *kokutai* disappeared from education edicts, not to reemerge until the Rescript on Education of 1890. Regulations issued in February 1870 described a national system of elementary schools in terms that shifted the ideological emphasis from transmitting native Shintō or Confucian tenets to "seeking knowledge throughout the world" in order to produce learning that was "useful to the nation."[4] What Ōkubo called the "teachings of civilization and enlightenment," Itō defined as the "learning of the world's nations," and Kido regarded as essential "to meet the challenge of the rich and powerful nations in the world." The outward-looking views of these bureaucratic reformers helped to generate an educational policy devoted to "civilization and enlightenment" for the sake of strengthening the nation.[5]

Several months after the Ministry of Education (Monbushō) was created in 1871, it pronounced the establishment of elementary education for the benefit of all, "from noble to commoner," and defined its goals wholly in terms of useful knowledge:

> For enlightenment to flourish and civilization to advance, for people to be secure in their livelihood and preserve their families, each person's talents and skills (*sainō gigei*) must be developed. For this purpose schools are to be established in order that the people will learn.[6]

This viewpoint prevailed in the Education Act (*Gakusei*) of 1872, which established universal compulsory education, mincing no words as to its objective. Its famous preamble openly urged the universal development of character, mind, and talent for the sake of rising and prospering in the world. From the "language, writing, and arithmetic used daily in government, agriculture, trade, and the arts, to law, politics, astronomy, and medicine"—the preamble enumerated the contents of national education without reference to moral influence, either Confucian or nativist.[7] Although the civil bureau-

104

crats were no less emphatic than the court scholars on the relation between education and the nation, their reformist stress on practical knowledge and Western models resulted in the effective eclipse of indigenous national values in the educational policy of the 1870s.

The 1880s marked a period of ideological contention over the substance and methods of national education. Like the constitutional shape of the polity and the institutional role of the monarch, the socio-moral basis for a national ethos was welded together out of bits of reform and reaction, of Western theories and Japanese practices, of enthusiastic anticipation and wary fear of the constitutional future. Throughout the several revisions of education law in the 1880s, the question of moral education (*tokuiku*) was the frequent medium of a debate that in some cases revealed and in others concealed the purposes of the ideologues so vocally engaged in trying to redirect the trends of "influence" in elementary education.

In 1879 Motoda Eifu, the palace official and Confucian tutor to the emperor, issued the formal call to re-establish "our ancestral precepts and national teachings" of "benevolence, justice, loyalty, and filial piety" (*jingi chūkō*) as "the essence of education."[8] Motoda had privately argued this point from the time Western educational models were adopted in 1872, a policy which appeared to him as an "effort to make Japanese into painted replicas of Europeans and Americans."[9] His opportunity for official statement arose when the emperor returned from his circuit of central Honshū in 1878 and voiced concern over the nature of education in the schools he had visited. In the name of the emperor, Motoda drafted a document entitled "The Great Principles of Education" (*Kyōgaku taishi*), in which he lamented the results of the new educational system:

> In recent days, people have been going to extremes. In the name of civilization and enlightenment, they pursue only knowledge and skills (*chishiki saigei*), thus violating the rules of good conduct and bringing harm to our customary ways. . . . While making a tour of schools and closely observing the pupils studying last autumn, it was noted that farmers' and merchants' sons were advocating high-sounding ideas and empty theories, and many of the Western words they used could not be translated in our own language. Even if such people were to return home after their studies, they would find it difficult to pursue their occupations, and with their high-sounding ideas, they would be equally useless as officials. Moreover, many of them brag about their knowledge, scorn their elders and interfere with prefectural officials.[10]

Motoda stated unequivocally that "for morality Confucius is the best guide" and prescribed "morality and skills" (*dōtoku saigei*) as the dual objects of education. The document concluded with two concrete proposals: first, that the illustrations recently introduced into the classroom should portray loyal subjects, filial children, and virtuous women; and, second, that farmers and merchants should study agricultural and commercial subjects "so that when they finish school they will return to their occupations and prosper increasingly in their proper work." Motoda thus expressed dissatisfaction both with Western models and methods and with the social results of educating farmers and merchants beyond the needs of their proper calling.

Although Motoda's views of appropriate social morality were more rigid than most, he was not the only observer vexed by the thought of Japanese schoolchildren in the seventies being guided by such ethics texts as Samuel Smiles' *Self-help* and Aesop's *Fables*, whose author was advertised as "more ancient than Confucius and a hundred years earlier than the Buddha."[11] Among those in government who agreed with Motoda were Nishimura Shigeki, at that time both a Ministry of Education official and an imperial tutor, and Egi Kazuyuki, a Confucian bureaucrat who was then embarking on a long and influential career in the Monbushō, which culminated in his appointment as education minister in 1924.[12] After touring schools in five provinces in 1877, Nishimura reported that "elementary school instruction is circuitous and irrelevant to practical life." He criticized the formalistic application of "question and answer" formats and "object lessons" drawn from American versions of Pestalozzi's pedagogy and based on vocabulary and color charts modeled on Willson's School and Family Charts—the same illustrations mentioned by Motoda in his critique.[13] The translated readers of the seventies were later described by Egi as texts in which "*Goddo*" (God) figured prominently and which "were guaranteed a good reception as long as the word 'Western' (*yōsai*) appeared in their titles."[14] Elementary schoolchildren recited passages about an unfamiliar "God in Heaven," even though in translation this singular God required a plural gloss that listed several deities from Japanese mythology to explain to the pupils who precisely the god in heaven was.[15] This was the period, as one educator later characterized it, when Western notions dominated and "the voices of loyalty and filiality, imperial reverence and patriotism were put away somewhere like bunting after a festival, and, like a roast potato vendor at a fire or an ice stand in the dead of winter, no one would have anything to do with them."[16]

For Motoda, however, it was not only the impropriety of such obvious Western extremes in education but the conception of the emperor as the source of moral authority that was at stake. A Confucian scholar and court official, Motoda advocated a national doc-

106

trine (*kokkyō*) comprised of Confucian morality and ancestral imperial tradition as part of his assertion of the importance of the emperor's role in the new political system.[17] His "Great Principles of Education" was written in 1879, the year in which the oligarchs prevailed in separating the palace from the government and abolished the office of *jiho* (imperial advisor). Indeed, it was Itō Hirobumi, Motoda's main adversary in the battle between court and cabinet, who responded to the *Kyōgaku taishi* with a stiff rebuttal that revealed educational and political concerns of his own.

Drafted by Inoue Kowashi, the legal bureaucrat and frequent amanuensis of the oligarchs, Itō's opinion "On Education" (*Kyōiku-gi*) combined Western notions of a secular state with his animosity toward the court Confucian. Itō's statement declared:

> If we are to blend the new and the old, take the classics into consideration, and establish a national doctrine (*kokkyō*), we are in an area that is not proper for government to control. For this we must wait for a sage.[18]

To this Motoda countered in a written rejoinder that "the emperor is both ruler and teacher. That is his calling, which the cabinet should also serve. What, then, is there to wait for?"[19] Such bickering between court and cabinet aside, Itō's main point lay elsewhere. In fact, he agreed with Motoda that the good customs and mores of the past (*junpū bizoku*) were in decline, although he ascribed the cause to the "changes in the times" rather than to education. The "abuses of custom" that most concerned Itō, however, derived not from a lack of filiality or respect for elders, but from "the excessive number of people involved in political discussion." After casting an aspersion on the Chinese learning favored by Motoda, Itō continued to the heart of the matter:

> In these times, men of even slight talent try to outdo each other in political partisanship. Moreover, today's students are usually trained in Chinese learning, and whenever they open their mouths, it is to argue political theory and discuss public affairs. Thus, when they read Western books, they are unable to set about their tasks with calm and cultivated minds but plunge themselves instead into the radical schools of European political thought. In a whirlwind of empty theory, they fill city and countryside with political talk. . . .[20]

Itō, or more probably his deputy, Inoue, concluded as Motoda had done with the recommendation for more practical learning. But while Motoda would educate farmers and merchants to hold to their proper calling, Itō and Inoue would use education to halt the spread

107

of the political opposition that the popular rights movement represented.

Partly in reaction to the excessive Western emphasis that the conservative moralists decried and also to the popular political agitation that threatened oligarchic power, the guidelines for elementary education were altered in 1880-1881. The Education Ordinance (*Kyōiku-rei*), which had been promulgated in 1879 to replace the original *Gakusei*, was revised in 1880. Under an imperial order engineered by Motoda, Sasaki Takayuki, and others at court, ethics instruction (*shūshin*), which in 1879 had been last in the list of elementary school subjects (after reading, writing, arithmetic, geography, and history), was moved to first in the 1880 revision.[21] At the same time the Ministry compiled a list of unacceptable texts that included translated ethics texts such as Wayland's *Wisdom*, enlightenment tracts by Fukuzawa Yukichi, and political treatises on *kokutai* and constitutionalism by Katō Hiroyuki.[22] The same emphasis on promoting imperial loyalty and indigenous morality while excluding politics also appeared in the "Guidelines for Elementary Schoolteachers," which were drafted by Egi Kazuyuki and issued in 1881. And in 1881 new licensing guidelines for teachers included a provision for the appointment of "erudite scholars and venerable Confucians" (*sekigaku rōju*) for the express purpose of ethics instruction.[23]

Despite the evident conservative turn of such measures, the lack of central control over the schools in the early eighties meant that moral instruction was not uniformly conducted as the Ministry stipulated. Beleaguered by the financial hardships caused by the government's deflationary policy, localities did not always respond to the constantly changing national directives. In addition, the liberal political theories of the popular rights activists, the interest in European philosophy among young schoolteachers, and the influence of the thought of Western pedagogues like Pestalozzi helped to perpetuate the "knowledge-centered" education of the earlier years.[24] On a visit to a provincial middle school in 1884, for example, Egi witnessed an ethics class where skeptical pupils questioned the Confucian parable of filiality in which a son melts the ice with his body to catch fish for his parents. But a person would die before the ice melted, the pupils countered, and when the teacher took refuge from science by ascribing the phenomenon to the will of heaven, they further discomfited him by professing not to understand what that might be.[25] In the same year rural educators read a biography of Pestalozzi in the journal of their local educational association and gathered to hear lectures on Johonnot's theory of moral training. "*Shūshin*," one lecturer explained, "is the basis of happiness in life," an interpretation somewhat different from the Confucianists' invocation of moral instruction as the basis of loyalty and filial piety.[26]

The appointment of Mori Arinori as minister of education in 1885 brought yet another conception of national and moral education to the nation's still fledgling public school system. Once again, the ideological emphasis was changed. The Education Ordinance, which had been revised for the second time in 1885, was replaced in 1886 by a series of School Ordinances (*Gakkōrei*). Mori intended his reforms to train elementary school pupils "to understand their duties as Japanese subjects" (*wagakuni shinmin*), although his reference was to patriotic service to the state on the Western model rather than to the moral obligation between a Confucian ruler and his subjects. Similarly, in moral education Mori emphasized discipline (*kunren*) and character building, disavowing all attempts to establish a particular doctrine or faith in what he called, in English, a "national education."[27] He rejected any association of religion with the state and averred that there were many possible objects of belief—"trees and stones, the sun and the stars, men, gods, the Way, or moral virtue."[28]

This kind of Western discourse was anathema to Motoda, who both favored a moral code sponsored by the state and despised what he called Mori's "American-style" thinking.[29] Thus, in 1890 Motoda still found reason to repeat his plaint, "Ah, but can we Japanese have resigned ourselves to wishing to become foreigners!"[30] And Nishimura, who had also begun to urge the adoption of a national doctrine (*kokkyō*) in the mid-1880s, proposed that moral education be removed from Monbushō jurisdiction altogether and placed in the more safely Confucian haven of the Imperial Household Ministry. He further suggested an imperial rescript as the appropriate means for "establishing the foundation of the nation's moral education."[31]

SINCE MOTODA and Nishimura had been advocating virtually the same position for over a decade, their voices alone did not account for the widespread reawakening of interest in moral education (*toku-iku*) in the 1880s. Indeed, had others not taken up the theme, it is unlikely that the Confucianists' voices would have carried in the ideological din that preceded the promulgation of the Rescript in 1890. But for most of the eighties, educators—both academic pedagogues and practicing schoolteachers—had been engaged in active debate on moral education, generally taking their lead from the latest theories on the subject in the West. They drew on the pedagogy of Johonnot and Spencer in the early part of the decade and then increasingly on

Herbart's theories of character training. They argued the German distinction between *Unterricht* (instruction) and *Erziehung*, which was translated as "the education of character" (*kun'iku*); and they discussed the relevance of Herbart's five *sittliche Ideen* (moral concepts) for the purposes of ethical instruction.[32] Armed with translations of foreign pedagogical theory, contributors to educational journals in Tokyo and the provinces debated the relative importance in moral education of the teacher and the text, and the comparative utility of lessons based on abstract virtues or exemplary individuals.[33] These discussions, which continued throughout the nineties, were peppered with those foreign words that the emperor and Motoda had complained "could not be translated in our language." "*Egoizumu, orijinaru eremento, kosumoporitanizumu, purofuesshonaru man,*" and other such terminology from across the water attested to the genuine cosmopolitanism of these local educators.[34] Thus, many of the teachers for whom the question of moral education was central in the 1880s were as Western-oriented and untraditional as any of the advocates of civilization and enlightenment whose lack of Japaneseness had so enraged Motoda. Yet, despite their starkly different views, the educators and the Confucianists were each advocating the importance of moral education. While the Confucian moralists urged ethical instruction (*shūshin*) in the name of a return to the national past, the educational vanguard advocated "*sittliche Bildung*" (moral education) as essential to the future of progress and civilization.

Not only in educational circles but also in the wider realm of elite opinion, the need for socio-moral bonds to draw the country together under its new constitution had become a commonplace perception by the late 1880s. Reacting against the "materialistic civilization" he witnessed in his travels to the West in 1888-1889, Ozaki Yukio, the young opposition politician, argued the importance of indigenous manners and customs (*fūzoku shūkan*) and morality (*tokugi*) to fulfill the promise of a "more noble, more elegant civilization."[35] While Ozaki considered morality from abroad, others of his youthful contemporaries advocated similar views closer to home. In 1889 the landlord's son Aizawa and his elder brother drafted regulations for a village association "primarily to promote agriculture and sericulture but also to discuss together a good plan for the development of moral education (*tokuiku*)."[36] At the same time in another context, social morality became an issue of heated debate in legal circles. From 1888 to 1892 conservative legal scholars and bureaucrats opposed the proposed civil code for threatening the customary morality of the family with too Western an interpretation of individual rights. They accused the government of being so concerned with establishing a constitutional system and meeting the legal conditions of the Western powers for treaty revision that it was willing to sacrifice the "customs and feelings of the people," to allow "wives to bring suit against husbands, and children to bring suit against parents," and to sanction, in Hozumi Yatsuka's ringing phrase, "the final destruction of loyalty and filial piety."[37]

Indeed, in the late eighties and early nineties talk of morality pervaded public discourse at many levels. Quite apart from the views of such Confucian moralists as Motoda, there was a Victorian sort of moralism abroad among the middle-class elite in the capital and provinces alike. Manners and mores aroused concerned comment, and when the Tokugawa writer Saikaku came into literary fashion again in 1890, the publisher Maruzen reissued his works with censorious circles replacing the phrases that rendered love and sex in too straightforward a manner for "civilized" times.[38] Others reacted to the change in manners that most closely affected their own position. In 1890 the head of one village assembly complained that his fellow assembly members addressed him as "chairman" (gichō) without attaching an honorific, a usage which has since become customary but which he regarded as the extreme of moral decline:

> Whether in moral repute (tokubō) or property, in this village there is no one who can compare with me. And I am older, too. To call me "Gichō, gichō," without the -san, is the height of outrage. Such are the extremes of insolence in these times.[39]

The perception that "civilization" and a constitution without moral foundations would result in the destruction of common social decency and the disappearance of a higher ethical sense was widespread among members of the establishment. Forming associations of like-minded men, they, too, called for the assertion of some familiar moral standard—invoking kokutai, filiality, good manners, and beautiful customs—to see them through the political and social changes that seemed to threaten the order of things and their secure place in it.[40]

II

AT THE SAME time that court moralists and cabinet ministers, Tokyo pedagogues and country schoolmasters, elite youth and established elders debated issues of moral education, other segments of minkan opinion created a corresponding center of ideological argument over definitions of the nation. From 1887 to 1890 intellectuals, journalists, and civic-minded members of the local elite called for the establishment of "a sense of nation" among the people, and as they did, they also emphasized indigenous customs, national culture, and *kokutai*. Their main interest lay with the nation rather than with the schools, with nationalism rather than with moral influence, with foreign policy rather than with education ordinances. Yet, their insistence on national definition and citizenship reinforced the arguments of those concerned with moral education and contributed to the atmosphere of heightened ideological activity from which the Rescript on Education emerged. Moreover, since these *minkan* nationalists often advocated the same native values as the moralists, the two ended up— for different reasons and with considerable mutual disdain—as ideological bedfellows in the process of civic redefinition in the late 1880s. This was true of such publicists as Shiga Shigetaka, Miyake Setsurei, Yamaji Aizan, and Kuga Katsunan, who sought to define what they called Japan's "national essence" (*kokusui*). They argued that this definition of the nation might then become the center of a nationalism (*kokuminshugi*) that would admit Western influence and at the same time preserve Japan's distinctive national character (*kokuminsei*).[41] And it was equally true of the provincial men of influence who formed local associations and published journals with such titles as "Japanism" (*Nihonshugi*), dedicated to cultivating "a sense of nation" (*kokkateki kannen*) for the sake of "conserving what should be conserved and reforming what should be reformed," in the year 1890, "the two thousand five hundred and fiftieth anniversary of the nation and its continuous imperial line."[42]

These proponents of nationalism, who were often labeled conservative by their contemporaries, did not consider themselves as such and criticized the views of moralists like Motoda as "feudal" and "hidebound."[43] Kuga Katsunan, who was perhaps the most articulate of the *minkan* nationalists, condemned the notion of a national doctrine, whether Shintō or Confucian, as unsuitable in a constitutional system.[44] While Kuga himself stressed the importance of customary morality as a stronger national bond than law alone could provide, he also expressed contempt for the moral education associations (*tokuikukai*) and custom reform clubs (*kyōfūkai*) that were in vogue among the elite in the late eighties and early nineties. "Morality and mores belong to the realm of human feeling," he argued, "and it is a mistake to try to cultivate them by forming associations and establishing bylaws."[45] Again, although Kuga considered the imperial household the sole appropriate source of Japanese morality, he decried those who, in opposing European influence, "constantly prate of the way of Confucius and Buddha."[46] Unlike such traditionalists, the *minkan* nationalists argued that they wished neither to expunge the results of civilization gained in the early Meiji westernization nor to revive moral values from the Tokugawa past. Instead they advocated the melding of foreign and indigenous ways and were proud to take their models of national strength and unity from the contemporary West. For that reason a sympathetic writer a decade later described them as having been the true vanguard of the late 1880s. For "the self-styled progressives were those who took the dregs of Western thought of one hundred years before, while those who were called conservatives were in fact in line with the most recent international thinking."[47] Having abandoned such antiquarian "dregs" as British utilitarianism and the ideas of the French enlightenment, the advocates of national essence were thus praised not only for protesting indiscriminate westernization but also for meeting the challenge of the latest Western trend of aggressively assertive nationalism.

Kuga's many editorials on the subject exemplified this particular ideological blend, as in 1889 when he argued the necessity of developing "a sense of nation" (*kokuminteki no kannen*),

> without which it is impossible to make manifest the vitality of the nation as a nation. In terms of national unity, a sense of nation reinforces the vigor of monarchical government. In terms of civilization and progress, it harmonizes with this historical spirit. And in terms of commerce with the powers, it is closely linked to the spirit of independence. Thus if we wish to abandon the abuses of aristocracy, we must manifest a sense of nation. If we wish to guard against the vagaries of individualism, we must manifest a sense of nation. And if we wish to restrain the tendency to dependence, we must manifest a sense of nation.
>
> Outside stimulus always strengthens the sense of self. In every country the development of a sense of nation is now being aroused by the stimulus of international relations. . . . [In Japan] not only is our national autonomy impaired but foreign influence threatens to rush in and buffet our island country about until our manners and customs, our institutions and civilization, our historical spirit, even our national spirit, are swept away. What is to save Japan (*wagakuni*) from these billows? Ah, but a sense of nation![48]

With this hyperbole, which was not unrepresentative, Kuga touched on each of the main concerns of the *minkan* nationalists in the late eighties: the new constitutional system demanded national unity; national unity required the universal sentiment of the people; the universal sentiment of the people must be grounded in indigenous values, which generally meant not only culture and customs but the

113

imperial household and *kokutai*. Indigenous values were the source of national pride; national pride was the source of national strength; from national strength arose independence in the commerce among nations; and in this regard the most pressing need remained the redress of Japan's impaired autonomy through the revision of the unequal treaties.

Since the unequal treaties were imposed upon Japan by the Western powers between 1854 and 1868, the government had sought both by domestic reform and foreign diplomacy to persuade the West of Japan's stature as an equal in international law. And as long as the treaties remained unrevised, they acted as a natural magnet for the political opposition, *minkan* intellectuals and party activists alike. In 1887 the furor over treaty revision in "the public opinion of the people" (*minkan no yoron*) reached a high point of activism in the protests against Inoue Kaoru's draft treaty. Then in 1889 an even higher point of indignation was reached in the hostility aroused by Ōkuma Shigenobu's attempt at revision. Because both Foreign Ministry drafts retained remnants of the extraterritoriality from the original treaties, *minkan* critics were quick to deem them unacceptable to the national honor.[49] In political terms this uproar in the late eighties was the epitome of the "hard-line" in foreign policy that the opposition wielded as an instrument of protest against the government. Just as the imperial loyalists had condemned the shogunate for failing to "repel the barbarians," members of the *minkan* opposition in the Meiji period opposed the government on the issue of treaty revision in the eighties, and mixed residence of foreigners and strict enforcement of treaties in the nineties. *Minkan* politicians, activists, and intellectuals called for war against China in 1894, war against Russia in the early 1900s, and activity and expansion in Asia throughout the late Meiji years. In each case the public criticism of the government's weakness in foreign policy also served the ends of domestic political opposition. Thus, apart from the diplomatic issues involved, the treaty revision controversies in 1887 and 1889 played an important political role in the revived party activity that preceded the establishment of the Diet.[50]

In ideological terms, the treaty revision controversy helped to spread the gospel of national pride beyond the confines of political activity into the wider world of elite public opinion. Provincial newspapers in 1889 bristled with bravado of the sort that demanded that all dealings with foreigners in Japan be conducted in Japanese "to avoid misunderstandings."[51] In the same year Kuga devoted thirty-two editorials to treaty revision in his newspaper, *Nihon*, which received financial support from such anti-government conservatives as Tani Kanjō, and acted as a central organ of *minkan* opposition to the Ōkuma draft.[52] The foreign issue was brought more dramatically to the public's attention when Foreign Minister Ōkuma lost his leg to a bomb thrown by a nationalist zealot in October. And the hapless tale of treaty revision also appeared in fiction and in song. The lyrics of the "Treaty Revision Song" began with the three hundred years of Tokugawa seclusion, lamented the loss of tariff rights, and evoked the more than thirty years of national humiliation that brought "tears of indignation to pelt the cheeks of all red-blooded Japanese men who love their country."[53] With more than a hint of anti-foreignism (and, in the song, such uncomely epithets for Westerners as "red-bearded louts"), this kind of patriotic talk contributed to an environment in which native values were reasserted, sometimes belligerently, as the benchmark of a proper sense of nation.

MORALITY on the one hand and a sense of nation on the other—such were the issues of gathering ideological emphasis in the 1880s. Yet, it was voices from still another quarter that were immediately responsible for the government's decision to promulgate a rescript on education in 1890. At the Prefectural Governors' Conference in Tokyo in February 1890, education became a topic of fervent debate. Komatsubara Eitarō, who was then the governor of Saitama prefecture and would later become one of Yamagata's most active protégés in the field of moral education, presented a proposal on elementary education (*futsū kyōiku*) for consideration by the governors. In it he suggested the implementation of a simplified educational course to relieve the financial burden on local self-government and to lessen the scholastic difficulty of the elementary grades. The discussion, however, veered immediately to the topic of moral education, the governors' enthusiastic interest in which culminated in the drafting of a "Memorial on the Cultivation of Moral Education."[54]

Several positions were aired in the course of the sessions devoted to the question. The importance of moral education based on appropriately native models was argued by several governors. They complained, as Motoda had, that knowledge (*chiiku*) had been stressed at the expense of moral education (*tokuiku*). "The purpose of moral education," stated Matsudaira of Miyagi prefecture, "is to establish the foundations of the *kokutai* and teach the way of patriotism and ethics, thus producing a people who are not ashamed to be Japanese." To achieve this purpose, illustrations from recent events should be utilized, and "if any were lacking, it would be appropriate to use

115

foreign examples as well." Takasaki, the Tokyo governor, agreed, recounting how he had visited a school in his district and asked a pupil of the upper grades about ethics instruction (*shūshin*):

> All he could answer was "proper deportment," and he knew nothing of the way of the five virtues. This is an inevitable result of our single-minded pursuit of "progress, progress" (*kaimei kaimei*) and must be reformed. I myself have repeatedly advocated the importance of moral education to the authorities, but even in the government schools they have been wholly indifferent [the east wind in a horse's ear] to my pleas. . . . I have warned the minister of education that if the current situation continues, the government will end up fostering a generation of nihilists (*kyomutō*).

In expressing his frustration, the Tokyo governor had touched a bureaucratic nerve, and others chimed in to express the need to find a device by which to assert their own authority. "I have said these things to the education minister," stated Shibahara, the governor from Kagawa,

> but nothing happens. We should present our views directly to the prime minister and the education minister, describe the situation in the provinces, and urge that this be done. With things as they are in education today, the world of law (*hōritsu sekai*) will be powerless; only through education can this state of affairs be remedied.

He concluded by lamenting the retreat of moral education since the fall of the Tokugawa, which, he ruefully added, a mere memorial would not likely be able to halt. The suggestion was then made that since "ordinary means cannot be expected to suffice here, we must look to a direct decision by the emperor." Governor Yasuba of Fukuoka, who was a compatriot and relative by marriage of Motoda, agreed: "Just as the army and navy put everything forward by imperial decision, we should do the same in education." The governor from Kagawa voiced his assent, invoking once again the lost Tokugawa past. "In the days of the domains a samurai learned as a child the will to die for his lord, but we cannot hope for that today. Still, we should communicate this point to the prime minister and request an imperial decision." In this context another argument was made by Koteda, the governor of Shimane:

> Since 1872 the principle of education has focused primarily on skills and techniques, so that without realizing it we have neglected morality. If this situation continues, nationalism (*kokkashugi*) will deteriorate. It is said that someone even presented a memorial to the Genrōin that proposed transforming our nation's *kokutai* into a republic. Is this not the

116

behavior of a madman? This kind of person is the result of our intoxication with civilization and the evil of ignoring the state.

The headlong momentum of the discussion had taken it far from the original issues of a simplified elementary course and reduced educational costs. And when one governor asked to add these matters to the emerging memorial, he was squelched with the comment that "moral education is so crucial, it is sufficient to express this concern and leave the other questions for separate proposals." Indeed, the draft that emerged from these discussions articulated the governors' concerns even more clearly than the rhetoric of their debates. Like many documents of ideological purport, the greater part of the memorial—the first three of four manuscript pages—was devoted to colorful enumeration of the evils of the present that the increased attention to moral education was supposed to remedy. "Elementary education," the document began—those words practically the sole vestige of Komatsubara's original statement—"should cultivate the moral character of the people." As a result of an overemphasis on knowledge and skills since the educational system was established in 1872 and a "complete lack of attention to moral education,"

> . . . pupils are proud of whatever small skills they gain in theory and mathematics. They condescend to their parents and incline toward flippancy and frivolity. Those who graduate from upper elementary school forsake their ancestral occupations and wish to become officials or politicians. If they continue further to middle school, even before they have graduated they begin to discuss political affairs. They themselves break school rules but complain of the suitability of the staff and provoke disputes and disturbances. At the worst, they leave school and take up political activities. Although teacher training is in part to blame, so, too, is the educational system. As this situation continues, youth will not value enterprise and will resort instead to lofty opinion. With immature learning and knowledge, they pursue fortune and scorn their elders, thus bringing the social order into confusion and endangering the nation.[55]

The point, in short, was politics. In their oratory the prefectural governors employed the language of moral concern and national unity—of Eastern ethics and "our national polity" (*waga kokutai*)—that had become common in the late 1880s as *minkan* ideologues debated the necessity and substance of a sense of nation. But in their memorial the governors, who were appointed officials, most of them associates in one way or another of the clans and cliques of the oligarchs, used the same language that Itō, Inoue, Yamagata, and Kuroda had used to ward off politics in advance of the Diet.[56] For the prefectural governors met in February, and the first election was less than five months away. Memories of party activism and the provincial movement against treaty revision of the previous three years were fresh in their minds. Hence, their call for moral education had little to do with Confucius, Herbart, or *kokutai*. Rather, it was an expression of their wish to preserve their authority against the imminent appearance of elected politicians. It was in this context that they invoked two of the most commonly repeated fears of the late Meiji ideologues: politics, they argued, would "bring the social order into confusion" and "endanger the nation."

Yamagata was both prime minister and home minister in 1890, and when the prefectural governors submitted their proposal he was immediately receptive. Their memorial accorded with his long-standing interest in civic education as well as with his own grave concern about the divisive consequences of electoral politics. Indeed, Yamagata reiterated these feelings at the same conference in an address to the governors on the nature of the new local government system promulgated in 1888-1889. Yamagata delivered a forceful sermon on the national dangers of party conflict, in which he characterized "the responsibilities of a loyal subject (*chūryō naru shinmin*)" in terms of his striving always for "unity and cooperation (*itchi kyōdō*)." To achieve this end Yamagata enjoined the provincial officials "to give profound attention to educating and guiding the people both for the present and for the future."[57] One month later, in March 1890, Yamagata expanded on his famous foreign policy speech to the Diet in which he had pronounced present national territory to be Japan's "line of sovereignty" and Korea to be Japan's "line of interest." In a written opinion drafted by Inoue Kowashi, Yamagata asserted that the "two elements essential to Japan's policy of preserving its line of interest are military preparation and education." Even in a major foreign policy statement, Yamagata championed the importance of national sentiment:

> The ways of loyalty among the people are the essence of the strength of a country. Unless the people love their country as their parents and are willing to safeguard it with their lives, though there are laws, both public and private, the country cannot exist even for a day. . . .
> Only education can cultivate and preserve the notion of patriotism in the people. In every European country patriotism is inculcated from the earliest stages of the development of knowledge by teaching the national language, history, and other subjects as part of general education. So abundantly is patriotism emphasized that it becomes second nature, and when the youth become soldiers they are brave warriors; when they

become officials they become good civil servants. . . . Despite the existence of factional interests, the people unite in the great principle of making common purpose in the glory of the country's flag and its independence. This is the essence of a nation.[58]

To achieve this patriotic essence, Yamagata had long felt that morality was the most certain means. For just as he feared the divisiveness of politics, he also evinced an uneasiness with what had seemed to him an over-reliance on law in the emerging Meiji state. In his 1879 memorial on the establishment of a national assembly he had written:

> Since the Restoration we have modeled our legal system on foreign laws, and the people now know that we must have laws to preserve society. But we have failed to realize that society must also be maintained with morals and customs (*dōtoku shūkan*).[59]

His list of deteriorating customs had included those enumerated by Motoda in the 1870s, by the prefectural governors in 1890, and indeed perennially by commentators concerned with the rush of social change in the Meiji period. Youth scorned their elders; inferiors had no regard for superiors; affectation and thoughtlessness were common. But Yamagata ascribed these social lapses neither to excessive westernization nor to an overemphasis on knowledge, but to "the tendency to maintain society by relying solely upon law."[60] Even in the military, "laws and regulations are largely external," he argued, and had to be accompanied by exemplary officers who educate and inspire (*kanka*) their men.[61] On the one hand, "square Yamagata," as Tokutomi later characterized him, "impregnable as a fortress," consistently employed law as a bulwark against politics.[62] But on the other, he looked with equal consistency to morality to provide the social and national ethos necessary to "unite the minds of the people."

Prime Minister Yamagata thus responded with favor to the governors' suggestion of an official pronouncement on moral education even though his minister of education, Enomoto Takeaki, appeared indifferent to the proposal. Enomoto replied to the governors by defending the Monbushō, which he pointed out had issued enough directives and instructions on moral education not to be accused of a complete "lack of attention" to ethics instruction. He also reiterated the principle of freedom of religion articulated in Article Twenty-eight of the Constitution. As for an appropriate basis for moral education, he stated only his personal opinion:

119

I think that the teachings we have relied upon since the founding of the nation will have the easiest access to the hearts of the people. What is called the way of the five moral principles, that is, the teachings of Confucius and Mencius—these are suitable for our moral education.[63]

Yamagata in the meantime had taken the matter directly before the cabinet and, according to his later recollections, had conceived of a document similar to the Rescript to Soldiers and Sailors of 1882, a thought he discussed with Inoue Kowashi.[64] Although Yamagata directed Enomoto to produce such a document in March 1890, Enomoto was occupied with yet another revision of the Elementary School Ordinance and was found—probably by Motoda, who meddled where he could—to be "lacking in enthusiasm for a moral doctrine."[65] Yamagata's enthusiasm held, however, and he replaced Enomoto with one of his own men, Yoshikawa Akimasa, who was ordered to preside over the drafting of an imperial rescript on moral teaching (*tokkyō*).

III

THE PROMULGATION of the Rescript on Education was thus an expression of several concerns that had become common ideological coin by 1890: the link between school and state that had been an established premise since the time of the Restoration; the gathering emphasis on moral education in Confucian, pedagogical, and general social comment in the 1880s; the nation-mindedness that pervaded *minkan* opinion in the context of the pre-parliamentary, culturally assertive, and internationally sensitive mood of the late eighties; and, finally, the mistrust of law and fear of politics among some of those for whom the Constitution and parliament appeared as a threat both to themselves and to the nation. The document that emerged from a complex drafting process and many revisions between June and October of 1890 comprehended each of these concerns, but in a form so mixed and homogenized that proponents of all viewpoints could claim it as their own. Indeed, the salient characteristic of the drafting process was the way in which those involved in the editorial tug-of-war proceeded with mutual tenacity and copious corrections in red ink to drive the more extreme expressions out of the text. They worked in this fashion until the participants could more or less agree with the rhetorically overwrought but ideologically moderated phrases that remained in the final version.

The Rescript, given below in the official translation, consisted of a Mito school beginning, which linked *kokutai* with loyalty and filiality; a Confucian center, which enumerated the virtues that inform

120

private and public human relationships, adding a modern injunction to civil obedience and national sacrifice; and an imperial ending, which made the emperor the source of a morality that was said to be both indigenous and universal at the same time.* The two main drafters of this brief but magisterial moral pronouncement were Inoue Kowashi, who had declined the task when first approached, and Motoda Eifu, who had begun to compose without waiting to be asked. After Inoue rejected the assignment, the first versions were prepared for the Ministry of Education by Nakamura Masanao, who produced a discursive essay that melded Confucian morality, Christian ideas of providence, and the British emphasis on character and self-help that Nakamura had absorbed from his translations of the works of Samuel Smiles.[66] When Inoue saw Nakamura's draft, which impressed him as unduly specific and unacceptably religious, he changed his mind and undertook Yamagata's bidding to write his own version.

Inoue then submitted seven guidelines for drafting which reflected his customary predilection simultaneously to promote both moral and legal views of the imperial state. Because "the principles of a constitutional system dictate that the monarch does not interfere with the freedom of conscience of his subjects," Inoue argued first that the Rescript "must be distinguished from a political ordinance and regarded instead as the written pronouncement of the monarch in society (*shakaijō no kunshu*)."[67] Just as he had accommodated nativist views of the imperial line by construing the emperor's ancestral rites as the private affair of the ruling house, Inoue proposed that the

---

The Imperial Rescript on Education (Kyōiku ni kansuru chokugo)

Know ye, Our subjects:

Our Imperial Ancestors (*waga kōso kōsō*) have founded Our Empire on a basis broad and everlasting and have deeply and firmly planted virtue; Our subjects ever united in loyalty (*chū*) and filial piety (*kō*) have from generation to generation illustrated the beauty thereof. This is the glory of the fundamental character of Our Empire (*kokutai no seika*), and herein also lies the source of Our education (*kyōiku no engen*). Ye, Our subjects, be filial to your parents, affectionate to your brothers and sisters; as husbands and wives be harmonious, as friends true; bear yourselves in modesty and moderation; extend your benevolence to all; pursue learning and cultivate arts, and thereby develop intellectual faculties and perfect moral powers; furthermore advance public good and promote common interests; always respect the Constitution and observe the laws; should emergency arise, offer yourselves courageously to the State (*giyūkō ni hōshi*); and thus guard and maintain the prosperity of Our Imperial Throne coeval with heaven and earth. So shall ye not only be Our good and faithful subjects (*chūryō no shinmin*), but render illustrious the best traditions of your forefathers.

The Way here set forth is indeed the teaching bequeathed by Our Imperial Ancestors, to be observed alike by Their Descendants and the subjects, infallible for all ages and true in all places. It is Our wish to lay it to heart in all reverence, in common with you, Our subjects, that we may all thus attain to the same virtue.

The 30th day of the 10th month of the 23rd year of Meiji (1890).

121

Rescript be issued as the personal moral utterance of the emperor and not as a law of state. Indeed, he later suggested that it be delivered as a speech by the emperor to avoid the governmental connection with the Ministry of Education.[68] Inoue's remaining guidelines cautioned, with pressing repetition, against the use of religious, philosophical, and political language, for mention of such subjects would only invite controversy from those who held opposing viewpoints and was in any case inappropriate in the discourse of the monarch. Chinese locutions and Western expressions were similarly to be avoided.[69] Inoue was so concerned over possible constitutional improprieties that he himself deleted the phrase about obeying the laws and respecting the Constitution from one of the drafts, not because he thought it unnecessary, as Motoda did, but because he felt that introducing any even remotely political conception into the moral pronouncement might compromise the separation between conscience and the state.[70] It was along such fine lines that Inoue drew the distinction that enabled him to view the emperor both as a constitutional monarch and a moral repository of native tradition. He was not unaware, however, of the complexities of his position, and concluded his seven cautions with the statement:

> To avoid all these difficulties and fulfill the true substance of the ruler's words will indeed be more arduous than constructing the twelve-story tower of the mountain sages.[71]

Motoda, on the other hand, had immediately begun construction and, even before his counsel was sought, had drafted a document, which he again entitled "The Great Principles of Education" (Kyōiku taishi). In it he combined explicitly Confucian doctrine with formulations of kokutai that echoed those of Aizawa Seishisai of the early nineteenth-century Mito school.[72] As Inoue and Motoda respectfully passed drafts back and forth, each revised a word here, a phrase there. Motoda, for example, changed Inoue's word for "the people" from shūsho (all the people) to shinmin (subjects), explaining to Inoue that the peers and government officials had previously objected to being included in such a plebeian appellation.[73] Inoue, for his part, mercilessly excised Motoda's Chinese allusions and Confucian terminology with marginal notes questioning his style, repetitiveness, and even the authority of his classical references.[74]

That each accepted the other's schoolmasterish corrections may have been partly due to their mutual respect and their common origins in Kumamoto, but more likely it was because the court Confucian and the legal bureaucrat agreed on the essential points, however different their reasons for that agreement. Motoda advocated Confucianism as a "national doctrine" because it was the way of the sages and of the Japanese past. Inoue supported Confucian ethics precisely because he wished to avoid all semblance of a "national doctrine" and the kind of religious strife that the link between Christianity and the state had engendered in the West. He had argued in this fashion since his travels to Europe in the mid-seventies, and in the early 1880s praised Confucianism both as a "teaching that does not rely on the deity" and as the closest counterpart in Japan to "the science that in the West is called 'philosophy.' "[75] Motoda and Inoue also shared adjacent interests in the Mito and nativist traditions, Motoda because Mito learning located "the fundamental character of our Empire" in the imperial institution, Inoue because he felt that "national classics (koten-kokuseki) are essential to the governance of the nation and the education of the people, and do not serve one religion or any one party."[76] Thus Inoue, the constitutional drafter, legislative expert, and proponent of Prussian political theory, argued that "the national classics are the father, Confucianism is the teacher."[77] Combined with Inoue's emphasis on the ancestral tradition of the unbroken imperial line, this meant that even his most critical editorial remarks did not do radical violence to Motoda's text.

In addition to the main drafting work carried out by Inoue and Motoda, Education Minister Yoshikawa made several emendations. He is said to have restored the phrase that Inoue had deleted about respecting the Constitution and obeying the laws. Yamagata and the emperor saw the drafts at various points, and other education and cabinet officials tinkered a bit here and there. When they were finished, Motoda prevailed in the argument over the means of promulgation, and the Rescript was promulgated as a chokugo, a transcript of an oral pronouncement by the emperor, but one which was separated from the status of what Inoue called an ordinary political ordinance (chokurei) only by the lack of a minister's countersignature.[78]

Yet, apart from Inoue's legalistic scruples and the foreign minister's concern about negative foreign reaction, it appeared that an imperial pronouncement on morality was regarded at the time as neither legally untoward nor constitutionally out of place.[79] This had not been the case with the new Elementary School Ordinance (Shōgak-kōrei) that was promulgated three weeks before the Rescript. This latest redaction of education legislation replaced Mori's law of 1886, setting the goals of elementary education firmly on their subsequent half-century course of moral, national, and intellectual education—in that order. At the behest of the Privy Council, the statute was issued in the form of an imperial ordinance (*chokurei*) rather than as a law (*hōritsu*), which meant that it would remain outside the control of the Diet.[80] Members of the government and the press criticized this decision as inappropriate in a system that would be parliamentary within the month.[81] But while they argued that in a constitutional system national education belonged within the purview of law, they offered no objection to the Imperial Rescript on Education. Indeed, the affirmation of the emperor's role as a source of moral virtue seemed both familiar and, judging from the reception in the press, also welcome.

The Rescript was greeted with favor by journalists and educators, although even for the informed elite its announcement was not an event remotely approaching the magnitude of the promulgation of the Constitution, the latest attempt at treaty revision, or the first election. Those who had been involved in the drafting expressed immediate pleasure with the results of their work. At court Motoda told Sasaki that although the Rescript "is not as I conceived it, in spirit it is no different," and Yoshikawa wrote to Inoue of his "great satisfaction" with the favorable reception in the press and among the principals of government schools.[82] Editorials praised the Rescript, nearly always harking back to the confusion that had characterized the decades since the Restoration, when there had been "no principle in society, no policy (*kokuze*) in the nation."[83] Commentators noted with apparent relief that "educational policy, which has been in constant flux, changed in five years, revised in three, altering entirely even in the space of a single year," was now settled and would cease its wild fluctuations from Western morality to Confucianism back to Western ethics and thence to nationalism.[84] It had settled, wrote another, "in a word, on our *kokutai*, which derives from our national history and is now to be the center of our national education."[85]

The Rescript was frequently described in terms of its making "good citizens" (*zenryō naru kokumin*) and serving as the basis for loyalty and patriotism (*chūkun aikoku*), not only in the schools but in society at large. Kuga commended its sentiments for laying the moral foundations for patriotism:

> A constitutional system is a polity of loyal and patriotic people (*chūkun aimin*), in which high and low yield to and respect one another, and ruling the country with civility is the way of good government (*ōdō*).[86]

He also expressed the hope that the Rescript would inspire the teachers who were "no longer educators but technicians," applying the latest theories of Spencer instead of cultivating the distinctive morality of the Japanese.[87] The educators, for their part, made learned references to Bluntschli and Aristotle, immediately incorporating the Rescript into the kind of theoretical discourse that Kuga decried.[88] In regard to the curricular content of education, the Rescript was widely considered to have righted the imbalance which, according to one writer, "had been nine parts moral to one part intellectual education before the Restoration," and then shifted to "eight or nine parts knowledge to only one of morality." But this was also unacceptable because Japan, unlike the West, could not look to religion for ethical guidance and had to rely upon the schools for moral training. The writer warned, however, that knowledge and skills must remain important, lest Japan "fall behind in the competition for wealth and power and be humiliated by the stronger nations."[89]

In regard to the particular morality enshrined in the Rescript, the reception was everywhere rather calm. "There is nothing novel about the Rescript," commented the *Tōkyō asahi* at the end of an enthusiastic editorial. "These are the precepts of the imperial ancestors and the tangible expression of our national customs and mores."[90] Others, such as Tokutomi, explained that "by means of the emperor's reverent pronouncement, existing principles have been clearly imprinted in the minds of the people; no particularly new educational policy has been presented."[91] And although the virtues enumerated in the Rescript were Confucian enough to satisfy Motoda, general commentators demurred at the association with Confucianism. For while the ethic itself was well received, the term "Confucianism" (*jukyōshugi*) still carried the taint that Fukuzawa and others had attached to it in the seventies and eighties as the obsolete doctrine of the feudal past.[92] In 1889 even Nishimura Shigeki, who was urging the adoption of "the Confucian Way" as the basis of moral education, advised the minister of education not to use the word Confucianism. For "the name Confucianism has for some time been disliked by the people, so that there are many who would not believe in the substance because of the name."[93]

Although the name did not indeed appear in the Rescript, Tokutomi, who had earlier opposed Confucianism as fusty and antiquated, was quick to assert that the "Way" mentioned in the Rescript did not refer to Confucianism alone, but to "the ordinary morality of the Japanese that has been transmitted from earliest times, even before there was Confucianism or Buddhism."[94] And another journalist explained that "although the five virtues are also taught in Confucianism, since the Rescript describes the subjects' loyalty and filiality as the principle of our *kokutai*, here they are not Confucianism but

125

kokutai-ism." Moreover, he argued that where Confucians valued morality at the expense of knowledge, the Rescript expressly urged the development of knowledge and skills.[95] Even Inoue Kowashi minimized the Confucian connection. In a pseudonymous article published in the newspaper *Nihon* just after the Rescript was promulgated, he lamented the tendency of "people to think that ethics (*rinri*) is the special possession of Confucianism," when in fact it "is derived from the organization and structure of human physiology." He argued that familial relationships were the same "in the past and the present, among people East and West," and that the relationship between the ruler and his subjects depended on the universal fact that "as the Greek philosophers said, man is a political animal."[96]

This disavowal of the Confucianism of the obviously Confucian virtues in the Rescript was not uncommon among self-consciously forward-looking intellectuals in the 1890s. Reflecting on the history of three Meiji decades from the vantage point of 1897-1898, commentators described the eighties as a period of reaction against Western civilization in which "old-fashioned Confucianists" attempted a revival that failed. In 1897 Yokoi Tokio, a Christian who had to defend his own faith against charges of disloyalty to the sentiments expressed in the Rescript, described "the moral crisis in Japan" in the 1880s in these terms and concluded:

> It was at this juncture in 1890 that the Emperor's rescript on morals appeared. The document was noble in style, catholic in sentiment, candid in tone. On all sides it was hailed as a welcome shower in the sultry moral atmosphere of the time. Some desperate attempts have indeed been made by the reactionists to wrest the rescript from its proper and moral interpretation, but the document remains to this day the earnest of the Emperor's fatherly counsel to his loyal subjects in the essentials of sound morality. Characteristically the rescript contains at its close a sentence which must be a perpetual stumbling block to all reactionary interpreters: "These principles, infallible for all ages, and true in all places."[97]

In the same year an article in a provincial education journal similarly divided the Meiji years into three periods of moral education. The first, in the 1870s, the writer labeled the period of "chaos," when civilization was conceived in material terms, learning was linked to rising in the world, and moral education was scarcely mentioned. The second period in the 1880s he described as a decade of indecision which revolved around the question, "What was to be the standard of moral education: Christianity, Buddhism, Shintō, or Confucianism?" This question, he continued, was answered in 1890 by the Rescript on Education, which ushered in the third period of moral education when the influence of Herbart prevailed.[98] Indeed, as the influence of Herbartian methods reached a peak in the 1890s, the German pedagogue's five *sittliche Ideen* were said by his supporters to correspond to the five Confucian virtues enumerated in the Rescript.[99] Thus the Rescript that Motoda saw as a vindication of Confucius, the pedagogues preferred to construe as the basis for the triumph of Herbart.

While scholars and intellectuals engaged in erudite argument on behalf of the scientific universality or historical comparability of the Confucian virtues that they preferred to call by other names, the generally matter-of-fact reception of the Rescript supported Tokutomi's contention that in the context of 1890 the morality enunciated by imperial proclamation was considered "ordinary." Injunctions to filiality, affection, harmony, modesty, and benevolence—whether labeled Confucian or not—were indeed part of the familiar code of customary social morality. And the exhortation to loyalty and the link to the imperial ancestors and *kokutai*, though not part of the ethos of "all the people," were common enough in elite opinion not to excite great comment. The Rescript, in short, met Inoue's standards of unexceptionable generality, leaving the imperial injunctions doctrinally vague, or in Inoue's words, "as vast as the waters of the ocean."[100] The brief, ornate text offered little to suggest that the Rescript would not flow into the sea of Monbushō documents without raising a swell.

Yet, instead the Rescript acquired an interpretive apparatus that by 1940 included 595 book-length commentaries, hundreds of Ministry of Education directives and teachers' guides, and countless evocations in print and oratory.[101] Not only were the interpretations increasingly elaborate and doctrinaire, relentlessly specifying the meanings of a document whose ambiguity had been carefully crafted, but the Rescript itself was raised to the status of a civic creed. What began as an assertion of native values and social ethics became a civil morality: an index of loyalty and patriotism (*chūkun aikoku*) not only for the schools, but for wherever allegiance to the state was at ideological issue.

PATRIOTISM AND THE USES
OF FOREIGNERS

I

WHAT the Rescript on Education had provided, in fact, was a national text. Available to ideologues of any persuasion, it soon served as a basis for a variety of civic sermons. While the Ministry of Education laid immediate institutional claim to the Rescript as a means to assert its bureaucratic and curricular authority over the schools, commentators outside the government continued to seize the ideological initiative in the 1890s. In the context of growing concern and continuing fear over Japan's prospects in the international arena, a mixed group of scholars, publicists, and *minkan* conservatives shifted the advancing edge of civic definition away from moral education and a sense of nation to issues of loyalty and patriotism. The earlier terms of the eighties did not of course disappear. Moral education was established both by statute and usage as part of the curricular triad in elementary education of moral, intellectual, and physical training (*tokuiku, chiiku, taiiku*). And by virtue of similarly repetitive reinforcement, the phrase "a sense of nation" had become a cliché of public language. But the focus now was sharper, less the general assertion of the need for citizenship than the specific boundaries of patriotism. In the process of demarcation, *minkan* ideologues formed a phalanx of defensive nationalism and attacked what was foreign as a means of staking out the home ground of what was Japanese. As they did, those whose attention was riveted on Japan's uncertain niche in the late-nineteenth-century world order were joined by others more apprehensive about their own travails at home. After two decades of being pushed into the wings while alien ideas held center stage, Buddhists and Shintoists were quick to grasp the opportunity to reassert their presence by defending native creeds and denouncing foreign ways. They thus contributed to the seizure of patriotic evangelism that resulted in the first interpretive steps toward the sanctification of the Rescript and the civil morality it represented.

Among those who engaged in this ideological controversy in the 1890s were the academics sometimes known by the epithet *goyō gakusha*, or scholars in service to the state. Their premier representative was perhaps Inoue Tetsujirō, who became one of the most prolific ideologues of civil morality in the late Meiji period, acting in the academy much as Yamagata did in the upper reaches of the government or Tokutomi in the press.[102] Like Yamagata and Tokutomi, Inoue engaged in ideological activity because he believed both in its necessity and its substance. Even when he worked on government assignment, as he did in 1891 when the Ministry of Education commissioned him to write the first official commentary on the Rescript on Education, Inoue regarded himself as an independent scholar who toiled in the service of philosophy and the nation, rather than of the state. Indeed, uninhibited by bureaucratic caution, academics such as

Inoue, Katō Hiroyuki, and Hozumi Yatsuka often led the ideological charge, while the Ministry of Education followed after with a backup barrage of directives and manuals that imprinted, but seldom initiated, the patriotic message in official form.

The Monbushō selected Inoue Tetsujirō to write a commentary on the Rescript for use "as a textbook in the regular curriculum of ethics and morals" because, as Egi later recalled, Inoue "was neither infatuated with the West nor of course was he of the old conservative school."[103] In 1890 Inoue had just returned to a post at the Imperial University after six years of study in Germany, imbued with his mission as a philosophical scholar in the latest European mode. "East of Suez," he is said to have boasted at the time, "there is no philosopher who surpasses me."[104] Although he is probably better known in academic history for his later compilation of the works of Tokugawa Confucianism than for his treatises on "*Identitäts-realismus*," or "phenomenon-qua-reality," his abiding ambition was "to study and compare the philosophy of East and West, and then construct a philosophical system superior to both."[105]

Thus equipped with what he regarded as the armaments of philosophical and scientific reason, Inoue approached the Rescript, asserting with confidence that "in the past, Chinese and Japanese scholars unquestioningly recounted the virtues which men must practice, but now I have explained *why* these virtues constitute the center of human morality."[106] Whether or not his often utilitarian explanations fulfilled this claim, Inoue's commentary on the Rescript (*Chokugo engi*), of which some four million copies were eventually printed, laid an interpretive basis for the years to come.[107] In it Inoue fabricated the rudiments of the family-state ideology from Confucian analogies of ruler to father and Western organic theories of the state.[108] And in keeping with his intention to "weld the ethics of East and West into one," he stressed the universal applicability of the virtues enumerated in the Rescript.[109] But he also emphasized the importance of the citizen's obligation to the state and, in the preamble to the commentary, revealed in resonant phrases that what underlay his philosophical argument was not only a rationale for moral universality but the sense of crisis regarding the nation that he shared with so many others in the late eighties and early nineties:

> In the world today Europe and America are of course great powers, while the countries settled by the Europeans have all prospered as well. Now only the countries of the East are capable of competing with the progress of these nations. Yet, India, Egypt, Burma, and Annam have already lost their independence; Siam, Tibet, and Korea are extremely

129

weak and will find it difficult to establish their autonomy. Thus in the Orient today Japan and China alone have an independence stable enough to vie for rights with the powers. But China clings to the classics and lacks the spirit of progress. Only in Japan does the idea of progress flourish, and Japan has it within its means to anticipate a glorious civilization in the future.

Japan, however, is a small country. Since there are now those that swallow countries with impunity, we must consider the whole world our enemy. Although we should always endeavor to conduct friendly relations with the powers, foreign enemies are watching for any lapse on our part, and then we can rely only upon our forty million fellow countrymen. Thus any true Japanese must have a sense of public duty, by which he values his life lightly as dust, advances spiritedly, and is ready to sacrifice himself for the sake of the nation.

But we must encourage this spirit before an emergency occurs. "Making a rope to catch a thief only after he shows up" is obviously foolish. The purpose of the Rescript is to strengthen the basis of the nation by cultivating the virtues of filiality and fraternal love, loyalty and sincerity (*kōtei chūshin*) and to prepare for any emergency by nurturing the spirit of collective patriotism (*kyōdō aikoku*). If all Japanese establish themselves by these principles, we can be assured of uniting the hearts of the people.[110]

This was the language both of national citizen-making and fear of international danger. Inoue continued, "If we do not unite the people, fortifications and warships will not suffice. If we do unite them, then even a million formidable foes will be unable to harm us." Over and over again in his commentary Inoue linked Confucian virtues with "collective patriotism," thus making patriotism, a word that did not appear in the Rescript, the sum meaning of the moral text.

Talk of fortifications and warships, formidable foes and patriotic sentiment was very much in the air of public opinion at the time. In the spring of 1891, the press condemned the spreading rumors that the forthcoming trip of the Russian Crown Prince was not an ordinary visit of state but a pretext "to look over our military preparations, locate strategically defensible sites, and prepare for future encroachment into East Asia."[111] The military implications of the trans-Siberian railroad, the ground-breaking ceremony for which occasioned the Russian heir's journey to the East, aroused comment and apprehension. When the Crown Prince arrived in May, he was stabbed by a Japanese zealot, ostensibly because of the foreigner's "betrayal and insult" to the emperor, whom he failed to greet at the start of his visit. This caused an uproar in both the government and the press over the possible foreign consequences of such an act. And while the newspapers may have exaggerated in their reports that "there is no Japanese in all the length and breadth of the country who is not distressed and disturbed by this calamity," the fear aroused by the incident was nonetheless considerable.[112] As a demonstration of official concern, the emperor journeyed to Kyoto to pay the wounded prince a personal visit. The press lamented the attack as the deed of a "madman," and more than ten thousand letters were reported to have been delivered to the bedside of the recovering prince.[113]

In July 1891 the arrival of China's Peiyang fleet provoked another flurry of concern over the ulterior purpose of such a martial display as well as over the imposing firsthand evidence of the naval superiority of the Ch'ing.[114] In the same month the *Tōhō kyōkai*, or Oriental Society, was founded by a group whose board members included the journalists Kuga and Miyake, the scholars Sugiura Jūgō and Inoue Tetsujirō, the party politician Hoshi Tōru, and the Pan-Asian activist, Oi Kentarō. One of the many *minkan* associations formed in the nineties to promote treaty revision, expansion in Asia, or a hard line in foreign policy in general, the society proposed to consider conditions in "neighboring Asian countries" for the sake of "preserving the balance between Eastern and Western nations in the Orient."[115] While such organizations expressed their concerns in journals or learned debate, similar sentiments also appeared in the popular narrative songs of the day:

> England in the West,
> Russia in the North.
> Don't be caught off guard,
> Countrymen!
> The treaties that bind on the surface
> Do not plumb the depths of the heart.
> International law though there may be,
> When the time comes,
> We must be prepared—
> For with brute force,
> The strong devour the weak.[116]

A song entitled "The Future of Asia" recounted the fate of other Eastern nations:

> Civil unrest unrelenting,
> Afghanistan, Baluchistan,
> Annam, Burma, India,
> And other countless small countries, too.

131

> All these are colonies of England or of France.
> If this continues, the Orient
> Will be trampled under
> By the power of the West.
> And no country will retain
> Its place of equality.

Unlyrical perhaps but persuasive, the song echoed the theme of the preamble to Inoue's commentary on the Rescript and concluded with a rousing patriotic vision:

> England, France, Germany, Russia—
> Should all the enemy be struck down
> And the glorious Flag of the Rising Sun
> Wave o'er the Himalayan peaks,
> What fun! What joy![117]

II

AGAINST this background of perceived foreign peril and assertive national pride in the early nineties, *minkan* ideologues precipitated one patriotic controversy after another. In 1891 journalists and scholars accused the Christian Uchimura Kanzō of lèse majesté when he refused to bow before the Imperial Rescript on Education at its ceremonial presentation to the students and faculty of the First Higher School in Tokyo. Christianity, which after centuries of proscription had enjoyed favor among the elite in the seventies and eighties both as a personal faith and as the religion of "civilization," was again under attack. As a result of his "disrespect incident" (*fukei jiken*), Uchimura resigned his teaching position.[118] "Buddhists, Shintoists, Confucians, and Infidels are uniting against Christians," he wrote, as he watched with bewilderment while his "personal affair . . . passed into the general question of the Relation of Christianity to the Nation and the Imperial Court."[119]

In 1892 nativist scholars and Shintoists hounded the historian Kume Kunitake out of the Imperial University for his scholarly treatise on Shintō as "an ancient custom of heaven worship."[120] In the same year that Kume stood accused of "disrespect to the imperial name and to the *kokutai*," the Presbyterian minister Tamura Naoomi was denounced by the press and fellow Christians for his unpatriotic criticism of the indigenous family system in his book, *The Japanese Bride*.[121] And also in 1892 Inoue Tetsujirō led the frontal attack on the loyalty of Japanese Christians in the controversy that became known as the "Conflict between Religion and Education," in which Inoue took the Rescript on Education as his text for the assault.[122]

132

The Emperor Meiji (1888)

The Promulgation of the Constitution (11 February 1889)

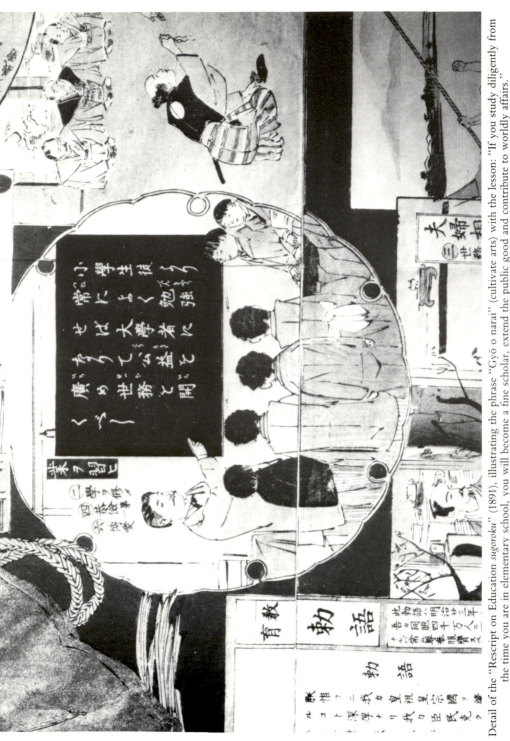

Detail of the "Rescript on Education *sugoroku*" (1891), illustrating the phrase "Gyō o narai" (cultivate arts) with the lesson: "If you study diligently from the time you are in elementary school, you will become a fine scholar, extend the public good and contribute to worldly affairs."

In what a sympathetic Buddhist writer called the first "thunderous fusillade from the citadel of academe at the flagship of Christianity,"[123] Inoue fired the ideological cannon with his customary assurance:

> The meaning of the Rescript, in a word, is nationalism (*kokkashugi*). But Christianity lacks nationalistic spirit. Not only is it poor in nationalistic spirit, it is opposed to nationalistic spirit. The conclusion is therefore inescapable that Christianity is incompatible with the nationalism of the Rescript.[124]

Thus the Rescript, whose meaning, "in a word," in 1890 had been morality, or, at most, moral education, now signified nationalism. And since "Christians value the kingdom of Heaven while the Rescript is concerned with the nation here on earth," they stood accused not of religious heresy but of "non-nationalism" (*mukokkashugi*).[125] Moreover, "Japan's indigenous morality" began with filiality and the family and then extended to the nation in the form of loyalty and patriotism (*chūkun aikoku*). But Inoue averred that Christ spoke seldom of loyalty and filiality and stressed instead undifferentiated universal love.[126] That contemporary Europeans evinced the spirit of patriotism (*aikokushin*) Inoue ascribed to the surviving pre-Christian heritage of Greece and Rome and suggested that Western science owed its recent progress to the decline in the power of the church.[127]

> In sum, Christianity is unnationalistic (*hikokkashugi*) and attaches no importance to loyalty and patriotism. Its followers do not differentiate between their own ruler and the rulers of other countries and hold what are tantamount to cosmic beliefs. For these reasons Christianity is fundamentally at odds with the spirit of the Rescript.[128]

The controversy that ensued was voluminous in quantity and, among the Buddhists, often vituperative in tone. Between Uchimura's refusal to bow in 1891 and the beginning of the Sino-Japanese War in 1894, 76 volumes and 493 articles appeared that argued the case for and against the loyalty of Christians.[129] Such prominent Christians as Ebina Danjō, Honda Yōichi, and Yokoi Tokio defended their love of country, which even in Uchimura's case was not much in doubt. The man who had spoken in 1888 of Christ and patriotism (*Kirisuto aikoku*) as his principles and later wrote of the "two J's," Jesus and Japan, as the twin centers of his faith, was a patriot.[130] Nor, as Uchimura commented, was the attack a "religious controversy which you often see in America," but rather "the heartless attack of a 'philosopher.'"[131] Indeed, with rare exceptions, issues of faith and religious freedom were buried in the avalanche of accu-

133

sations that with Christianity came republicanism, individualism, socialism, and colonialism.[132]

Many of these charges originated with the Buddhists, who, having themselves suffered the attacks of the philosophers, remained in deep institutional decline. The relentlessly secular orientation of the political and intellectual establishment since the mid-seventies had proved as inhospitable to organized Buddhism and Shintō as it had to any suggestion of an official association of religion with the government.[133] While political theorists like Inoue Kowashi stood on the legal ground of separation of religion and the state, Meiji intellectuals tended to maintain what they regarded as a properly modern "scientific" distance from religion.[134] Even as the Buddhists supported Inoue Tetsujirō's attack on Christianity, he carefully disavowed partiality for their religion, or for any other.[135] It was because Japan was "free of any religious affiliation," he later argued, that it could "conduct a pure form of moral education," and in this respect had the civilizational advantage over Asian and Western nations alike.[136] Thus, though he judged Buddhist polytheism and doctrines of male superiority to be more congenial to Japan's tradition than the Christian God or assertion of equality between the sexes, he also criticized Buddhism for "pessimistic tendencies" unsuitable to the march of progress and "civilization."[137]

This attitude drove some late Meiji defenders of the faith to sincere eclecticism of the sort practiced by the Buddhist philosopher Inoue Enryō in his ceremony to the four sages, Buddha, Confucius, Socrates, and Kant.[138] Many, however, attempted to revive the flagging fortunes of Buddhism not by doctrinal debate but by nationalistic propaganda. In attacking Christianity they therefore stressed that Buddhist countries did not colonize and that Christianity was injurious to the *kokutai*.[139] Consorting with Christianity, which the Sinologist Naitō Konan had likened to Japan's betraying its proper wife with a painted woman, was compared by the Buddhist activist Ōuchi Seiran to a child trying to "change his mother" for another.[140] It was unnatural, immoral, and, considering the attendant foreign danger, a failure of national nerve.

However different their motivations, these emotional representations of the Buddhists echoed the assertions of the philosophers and the nationalists. In each case what was *not* patriotic was invoked to establish what was, so that Christianity was as much a vehicle as a target. As one academic forthrightly confessed: "I do not say Christianity is opposed to the purpose of national education because it is not nationalistic but rather because it is foreign."[141] In effect, Japanese

Christians in the early nineties served the ideologues as metaphorical foreigners in whose alien reflection the silhouette of patriotism emerged that much more clearly.

This ideological use of foreigners had two aspects. Not only was the foreign used to define the native, but once defined, the native was used to nationalize the foreign. Thus Christianity served as a means to enshrine the civil morality expressed in the Rescript, which then became the test of Christian loyalty. Christians were permitted to continue being Christian, provided they were also willing to take the oath as Japanese. Indeed, by 1912 when the socialists had become the main metaphorical foreigners of the day, Inoue Tetsujirō commended Christianity for "not having contravened the *kokutai* in recent years," which he attributed to its having been "Japanized." He then advocated a "national ethic" comprised of Confucian benevolence, Buddhist compassion, and Christian altruism.[142] In the same year the Home Ministry organized its "Meeting of the Three Religions" (*sankyō kaidō*) to engage Christians, Buddhists, and Shintoists in the cause of "uniting religion and the state" and promoting "national morality."[143] Christianity, now Japanized, seemed benign in comparison to the greater and more menacingly alien threat of socialism, and the government was ready to enlist religion, which it had earlier eschewed, into ideological service. On this occasion it was the religionists and the press who objected to the government's injecting matters of faith into affairs of state, and the "three religions" movement quickly subsided.[144] The Rescript, however, continued to function in much the same way, held up against individualists, socialists, and other metaphorical foreigners to declare them beyond the pale of patriotism and outside the bounds of civil morality.

III

WHILE metaphorical foreigners presented one kind of ideological mirror, real foreigners served as another. When the Sino-Japanese War of 1894–1895 offered the Chinese against whom to test Japan's patriotic mettle, the attack against the Christians was soon forgotten. The press, popular magazines, schoolteachers, and local orators expressed contempt for the cowardly "Chinamen" (*chan-chan bōzu*) from "pigtail land" (*tonbikoku*) who "ran from battle disguised in women's clothes."[145] And the Ch'ing fleet that had seemed so impressive just four years earlier was depicted as sinking and in flames. Woodblock prints, war songs, magic-lantern shows, and New Year's games raised the stock of the Japanese by denigrating their enemy.[146] Casting the war as a conflict between civilization and barbarism, *min-*

kan ideologues praised the level of Japan's civilization, while even in popular song China became the "enemy of civilization," against which Japan fought a "righteous war."[147]

Abetted by the rousing and often rabid stance of the press, the war inspired a spirit of national unity (*kyokoku itchi*) that the ideologues had sought but could not alone have produced. As the tone of swaggering national assurance that suffused *minkan* comment was echoed in the schoolyards and local celebrations around the country, Japan's victory was ascribed to bushidō, to the Japanese spirit (*Yamato damashii*), and to the patriotic willingness for self-sacrifice enjoined by the Rescript on Education. In 1897 the writer Takayama Chogyū, who with Inoue Tetsujirō was a leading proponent of Japanism (*Nihonshugi*) at that time, wrote that the war had transformed the people's understanding of the Rescript on Education and changed the spirit of loyalty and patriotism from empty theory and half belief into concrete "national consciousness."[148] It had also enhanced national confidence and pride of empire at the expense of an age-old cultural respect for China.

At the same time that China served as a whetstone on which to sharpen Japan's image of itself in the world, another group of real foreigners became the focus for patriotic definition within Japan. On the eve of the Sino-Japanese War in 1894 the unequal treaties with the Western powers were finally revised, lending the old issue of "mixed residence" (*naichi zakkyo*) new urgency. For when the revised treaties went into effect in July 1899, the legal restrictions on foreigners would be lifted and commerce and residence permitted anywhere in the country. The ideological challenge was to prepare for the day when foreigners—nearly always conceived of as Westerners—would be loosed upon the countryside and thus threaten the morals and customs of the Japanese.[149]

Politicians and intellectuals had debated this question since the 1880s, joining political and diplomatic considerations with concern for the ideological preparation of the Japanese to meet the foreigners. In 1889 Inoue Tetsujirō had warned against mixed residence, arguing Japanese inferiority on the basis of the latest scientific references to a cranial capacity smaller than that of the Europeans.[150] In 1893 Ozaki Yukio took a prouder tack, explaining first that the Japanese were a big-headed race, who though shorter in stature than the Caucasians, found European hats much too small for them. He then argued that the best preparation for mixed residence was not the study of Western table manners—indeed, a good deal was written about the importance of not slurping the soup or using a toothpick at table when in the company of foreigners—but rather the strengthening of the morals of the Japanese to resist the incursion of foreign ways.[151] The Buddhists were prominent in this campaign as well, expounding the importance of loyalty, patriotism, and Buddhism as native antidotes to the "foreign insects poisoning the nation."[152] In the spirit of "know yourself, know your enemy," as these ideologues repeatedly pronounced, the best defense was a detailed, "objective" analysis of the foreigner and, in his reflection, of the Japanese. To this end commentators compared "Western and Eastern morals," identifying such undesirable foreign customs as materialism, equality between the sexes, shaking hands, and kissing. Practical advice was offered on how to distinguish foreign gentlemen from foreign scoundrels by the presence of a pipe or a topaz ring and how to protect one's land and women from foreign greed and lust.[153] To protect the women Ōkuma Shigenobu suggested cultivating the conscience of the people; to protect the land one popular guide proposed doubling its price to foreigners.[154] To protect the kokutai, most orators recommended the Rescript, education, and national spirit as the most effective native resources.[155] Whether in inflammatory pamphlets or earnest speeches, the appeal, "Ah! the first of July!" signified yet another ideological opportunity to measure Japanese—cranial capacity and "beautiful customs"—against the foil of the foreign.[156]

Foreigners, metaphorical and real, were the ideological means to a patriotic end. And once the end was temporarily gained, the ideologues lost interest in them for a time as the intensely defensive nationalism of the nineties ebbed and an increasingly aggressive imperialism took its place. Westerners, for example, who were in fact already present in Japan before 1899, proceeded about their business without incident, and mixed residence—like kissing—ceased to be an ideological issue.[157] The Westerners themselves had never been the point; what had mattered was the idea of the West that the Japanese had created for purposes of self-definition. The real West was irrelevant; in the imagined West people were incapable of loyalty and filiality, and this was sufficient to define these traits as essentially Japanese.

Similarly, the religious controversy of the nineties served an ideological purpose that was quite different from its consequences for the religionists involved. The Ministry of Education's Order Number 12, which prohibited religious instruction in the schools in 1899, disadvantaged Christian and Buddhist schools alike. Some of the private Christian schools were moved to adopt the Rescript on Education rather than the Bible as the basis of moral education.[158] For the

Buddhists, their role in the anti-foreign commotion had not produced the renascence they had envisioned. When Buddhism and Christianity both began their slow recovery of stature, strength, and doctrinal dynamism in the early 1900s, they did so with less ideological controversy and more attention to theology and organization. The Buddhists emulated the practice of their Christian rivals, expanding charitable institutions in Japan and undertaking colonial missionary work in Taiwan and Korea.[159] And just as the Buddhists abandoned their single-minded stress on Buddhism as a native faith, the Christians further muted the foreign origins of Christianity. For both had made their accommodations with the civil morality as the Rescript defined it. Because the morality was secular, Buddhism, like other institutional religions, was denied an official place, and because the morality was native, Christianity had had to become more insistently Japanese. For ideology, however, the significant result was not the effect on religion but the strengthening of the civil morality to which all loyal and patriotic Japanese of any faith had now necessarily to subscribe.

"THE GLORY OF OUR *KOKUTAI*"

I

Shintō could be expected to have thrived in an ideological environment where indigenous values and patriotic loyalty were in the ascendant. For Shintō, as the Shintoists tirelessly pointed out, was more native than Buddhism and more intimately imperial than any doctrine available to the Japanese. But the ideological process by which Shintō was eventually woven into the fabric of civil morality was a complicated and, for the Shintoists, an arduous one. It was complicated because in order for Shintō to be admitted as imperial ritual in a secular morality, it had been declared not to be a religion. It was arduous because the Shintoists were simultaneously advantaged by their privileged position and threatened by the obvious difficulty of maintaining shrines and a priesthood without acknowledgment of their traditional religious function.

The institutional vicissitudes of Shintō had begun with the Restoration. After a brief period as the established religion of state, Shintō and the "unity of rites and governance" (*saisei itchi*) fell victim to the secularizing policies of the early Meiji leadership. As part of the government's response to Western demands for religious freedom—a prerequisite for treaty revision—Shintō was disestablished as a national teaching in the early seventies. Then, in 1882, Shintō priests of national shrines were forbidden to conduct funeral services or to hold the office of religious guide (*kyōdōshoku*). By this "separation of rites (*saishi*) and religion (*shūkyō*)" the government proposed to preserve Shintō in its function as imperial ritual without violating the constitutional dictates of the separation of church and state.[160] While the Shintoists did not reject this logic, it left their status uncomfortably ambiguous. Thus, for decades—indeed from the 1880s through the 1930s—Shintō priests and scholars labored to retrieve the position that Shintō had once held and lost. They began to organize in the late eighties, gradually establishing local priests associations, national confederations, a public relations office in Tokyo, and in 1898 the National Shintō Priests Association (*Zenkoku shinshokukai*). On behalf of a priesthood now nationally organized for the first time in its history, these groups lobbied long and hard for the revival of the *Jingikan*, the Department of Shintō that had been abolished in 1871; for the restoration of government funds for local shrines and priests' salaries; and for some acceptance of the supplicative and religious functions performed by the shrines. In their efforts to repair the institutional damage to their position, the Shintoists conducted an ideological crusade whose goal was public recognition of Shintō as the official rites of the state (*kokka no sōshi*).[161]

For this purpose the Rescript on Education of 1890 offered the Shintoists an opportunity more promising than any since the Restoration. In its initial phrase, *waga kōso kōsō*, which meant "our imperial ancestors from Amaterasu and Jimmu through the unbroken line of historical emperors," Shintō and nativist scholars found an official confirmation of their national importance. The Rescript promulgating the Constitution and the Imperial Household Law of 1889 had both made the same reference, and the Rescript on Education brought the imperial ancestors into full public light. Inoue Kowashi, whose hand had touched each of these three documents, praised Shintō rites as "the foundation of the nation" and "the source of custom," but insisted that Shintoists themselves not be favored by the state.[162] Shintō ideologues, however, regarded the imperial texts of 1889-1890 as a basis for re-establishing Shintō's importance in present-day court ritual and emphasizing its association with Japanese history from the beginning of national time. If the ancestral founding of the nation was "the glory of our *kokutai*" (*kokutai no seika*), as the Rescript on Education pronounced that it was, the Shintoists reasoned that the prospects for government funding and support of Shintō would inevitably be brighter.[163]

These expectations were partly fulfilled and partly foiled. In the nineties the Shintoists continued to press their claims for the institutionalization of Shintō as a separate office of state, and the government continued to be unreceptive. The Shintoists presented over 600 petitions and memorials to the Genrōin in 1890 alone; from 1890 to 1895 they petitioned each session of the Diet and lobbied Diet members both in Tokyo and in their home districts. Yet when a resolution for the revival of a *Jingikan* passed both houses in 1896, the government declined to act on it, declaring the matter "under investigation." In the early nineties the cabinet offered treaty revision as the reason for denying the Shintoists' request; in the late nineties the official argument was the necessity of establishing the legal and administrative basis of the shrines before responding to the Diet's resolutions. In vexation the Shintoists despaired of ever "making the authorities understand the importance of imperial Shintō (*teikoku jingi*)," and in 1899 resorted to the press to publicize their grievance.[164] At that point pressure from the Shintoists coincided with the government's concern to separate religion from the schools and to regulate religious organizations in preparation for the mixed residence of foreigners. Thus in 1900 the government established a Shrine Bureau (*jinjakyoku*) in the Home Ministry, and in the next years promulgated ordinances that separated the shrines and public offices from religious affairs, which were removed to a separate bureau. The Shintoists, however, regarded the victory as partial, since the shrines had been granted preferential administrative treatment but neither ideological preeminence nor substantial financial support.[165] They thus resumed their efforts to revive the *Jingikan* and institutionalize the shrines as a system of national worship.

Since the professional Shintoists steadfastly advanced the same causes, their effectiveness depended as much, or probably more, on changes in the surrounding environment as on their own persistence. "The Sino- and Russo-Japanese Wars helped," reported the organ of the Shrine Association (*Jinja kyōkai*) in a retrospective article in 1906, "for they brought the shrines to public attention."[166] The government's promotion of the shrines, especially Yasukuni, the national shrine of the war dead, had served the cause of wartime mobilization and enhanced Shintō's national functions at the same time. But when the priests complained during the Russo-Japanese War that "the Buddhists have a monopoly on funerals," and debated whether funerals should be considered "religious" or not, the authorities remained, as before, unresponsive.[167] The government was more forthcoming after the war, as the Shrine Bureau of the Home Ministry undertook to implement its administrative control over the localities through reorganization of local shrines. Priests, however, commented on the callousness to local gods who had been summarily evicted from their homes, and lamented the Shrine Bureau's tendency to treat the shrines as "monuments," as if they were so much rural furniture to be moved about without regard for their religious and emotional meaning.[168]

The Home Ministry bureaucrats who headed the Shrine Bureau between 1904 and 1921—Mizuno Rentarō, Inoue Tomoichi, and Tsukamoto Seiji—promoted the ideological function of the shrines in unifying the sentiments of the people in the spirit of "reverence for the gods and respect for the ancestors" (keishin sūso). At the same time they insisted that Shintō was not a religion, its priests were public officials, and its administration determined by law.[169] Yet in 1912 when the Vice Home Minister Tokonami Takejirō sought to combat socialism with national morality, he did not hesitate to include Shintō in the "Meeting of the Three Religions." Four years later, a Ministry representative offhandedly remarked that Buddhist criticisms of the role of the shrines in the Taishō coronation ceremonies were unwarranted, since people were free to regard shrines as they wished; but as for the government, it chose to view them as "non-religious."[170] Christians and Buddhists railed at the inconsistency of the government's urging the people to pray at the shrines for victory during World War I and simultaneously declaring that no supplication occurred at Shintō shrines, only expressions of gratitude and "repayment of ancestral debt" (hōhon hanshi). And the Shintoists found this attitude of the government inexcusably "passive" and redoubled their efforts for preferential treatment in the years following the First World War.[171]

By that time the Shrine Bureau had evolved into a center of ideological activity on behalf of Shintō that sometimes paralleled, sometimes intersected, and sometimes conflicted with the objectives of the Shintoists. From the Shintoists' point of view, the bureaucrats remained capricious allies, rallying round in times of national and social crisis, and dismissing Shintō claims when they were inconvenient or could not be turned to the government's own purposes. Nonetheless, the combined result was the increased prominence of Shintō in the civic catechism. The Ministry of Education instructed schools to include shrine visits in the children's schedules, so that the imperial ancestors and the local ancestors were linked not only in textbooks but in practice.[172]

A similar reinforcement of Shintō's national importance was provided by some of the same minkan ideologues who represented what

141

Shintoists lamented as "the logical tendency of the intellectual world" that led to the disparagement of religion in general and of Shintō in particular.[173] In his attack on Christianity in 1893, for example, Inoue Tetsujirō had inserted the cautious phrase, "*We call* Amaterasu the greatest of the Gods, the ancestor of the Imperial House," thus evoking the possibility that this was not true in fact.[174] In 1907 Inoue, intending a compliment, wrote that "Shintō as vulgar Shintō is mere superstition, but as the ancestor worship (*sosenkyō*) of the Japanese, it possesses great power."[175] By 1912 in his compendious work on national morality, Inoue was arguing that "as a religion Shintō is primitive, but it is not merely a religion; in its relation to Japan's *kokutai* it is related to Japan's fate as a nation." Shintō, he asserted, was Japan's "national religion" (*kokkateki shūkyō*).[176] Equating Shintō with imperial and ancestral tradition, secular intellectuals such as Inoue and Hozumi Yatsuka incorporated the way of the gods into the way of loyalty and patriotism, fostering Shintō even as they redefined its character.

The interaction of Shintoist, bureaucratic, and *minkan* ideologues resulted in the gradual establishment of shrine Shintō as a national rite. This does not mean, of course, that the constructions of the ideologues were immediately apparent to those who worshipped at local shrines. In the late Meiji period the public impact of the rites performed by the emperor privately at court was limited, and Shintō ideologues complained, for example, that "people do not know about the New Year's or Harvest Festivals or of their importance as rites of state."[177] At the local level the problem faced by Shintō was not the lack of knowledge or popular participation in shrine activity, which was part of customary practice, but the difficulty of infusing local and familial tradition with national ideological content. It remains unclear, for instance, whether the prefectural governor or village mayor who served as "imperial envoy" presenting ceremonial offerings at local shrines was perceived by villagers as an emissary of the center or simply as a prefectural governor or village mayor—a representative of the *kan* therefore rather than of the court.[178]

The Meiji emperor, whom Shintō scholars described as a manifest deity (*arahitogami*), the living representative of a divine imperial line, did not appear to his subjects in so distinct a theological definition. The emperor was known both to be "sacred and inviolable" (*shinsei ni shite okasu bekarazu*), in the formidable words of the Constitution, and also to be an awesome personage before whose photograph one bowed one's head in reverence. But the emperor was not formally worshipped in Shintō shrines, since legally he could be enshrined

142

only after his death. He was first enshrined in fact at Meiji shrine in 1920. During his lifetime there were instances, however, in which the emperor was worshipped as a living god (*ikigami*)—that is, a god-like man, or a man worshipped as a god—in the folk tradition. In most cases this took place at private shrines constructed by imperially minded members of the local elite to commemorate sites the emperor had visited in his early travels.[179] In one shrine in a remote Nagano village, the Meiji emperor was actively worshipped as a living god during his lifetime, though in the guise of the then permissible "hall for worshipping from afar."[180] In addition, some of the popular "new religions" included the emperor or the ancestral deities in their teaching, but in ways distinctive from and often conflicting with the views of Shintō.[181]

The emperor's appearance as an object of reverence in folk tradition and popular religion thus strengthened sentiment toward the ruler, but it did so at first outside the ranks of shrine Shintō and with different religious meaning than that put forward by the official Shintō establishment. Recognizing this, the Shintoists persisted in the quest to promote their version of emperor worship and institutionalize Shintō. As the ideological environment changed in their favor in the 1930s, they were more successful. But as before, the Shintoists owed this success to the efforts of others, in particular, the military, academic, and *minkan* ideologues who amplified the significance of the imperial line in the increasingly doctrinaire context of a national morality (*kokumin dōtoku*). And finally, after almost seventy years, a separate office of Shintō (*Jingi-in*) was re-established in the government in November 1940, giving State Shintō an institutional center that lasted until the Occupation authorities abolished it five years later.[182]

II

WHETHER villagers perceived their local shrines as performing "rites of state" in the late Meiji period remains a question. There is little doubt, however, that Shintō itself was effectively enshrined in civil morality because of its link with the myth of *kokutai*, the continuous ancestral tradition of the imperial house. Not only in connection with Shintō but with moral education, patriotism, nationalism, and imperialism—in ideological speech of every civic description—the term *kokutai* was invoked with increasing frequency in the late Meiji decades. And by the end of the period it had become a symbolic rebus that, whatever its context, stood unmistakably, if indefinably, for the nation.

As before in Japanese history, the precise definition of *kokutai* mattered less than the ideological uses to which it was put.[183] In late Tokugawa times, *kokutai* had served as a rationale for imperial restoration. Then, after a brief ascendancy at court, the Mito and nativist conception of *kokutai*, like Shintō, was submerged by the tides of civilization and enlightenment, whence *kokutai* emerged, unchanged in mythic essence, to function as a benchmark against which to measure institutional change.

In 1875, Fukuzawa argued for the adoption of Western civilization to strengthen *kokutai*, which he conceived in terms of the social, historical, and geographical attributes that constituted the essence of a nation—what "in Western language they call 'nationality.' " He wrote that every nation possessed a *kokutai* which each sought to preserve, and "ultimately the existence of a *kokutai* depends on whether a nation loses its political sovereignty or not."[184] In this usage *kokutai* was jeopardized from without and would be secured by the adoption of Western civilization. In the constitutional debates of the 1880s conservatives like Motoda spoke of *kokutai* as jeopardized from within and argued that it must be secured by establishing direct imperial rule. The political system (*seitai*) might change, but not so the *kokutai*. Others expressed the same point to different ends, using *kokutai* to reassure conservatives that the political change that resulted from the Constitution would be "compatible with the *kokutai*."[185] Similar arguments were made in the debates over the local government system and the civil code, and *kokutai*, whether expressed in terms of indigenous customs or imperial continuity, was the standard against which to define the acceptable limits of domestic change.

The way in which *kokutai* was used in the eighties is illustrated by an episode in 1884 when Sasaki Takayuki, the court official, wrote to Kaneko Kentarō, who was then Itō's private secretary, asking him to clarify the meaning of the word *kokutai* that suddenly seemed to be on everyone's lips. Sasaki wrote that he had always thought it referred to "the unbroken imperial line, but people are now speaking of land, people, language, and Western nations," which gave him grave misgivings. In a discussion that Sasaki had with Itō about the nature of *kokutai*, Itō had described *kokutai* as "changing with the times" and therefore with the new constitution. This had shocked Sasaki, who as an imperial advisor might have expected to be authoritative on a subject such as *kokutai*.[186]

Kaneko's response was erudite and somewhat flippant, with citations from the Mito school and Edmund Burke, designed to reassure

Sasaki that though the *seitai* might change, the *kokutai* would endure. Although Sasaki had requested that Kaneko destroy the letter, as it was a matter of "some personal embarrassment," Kaneko showed it instead to Itō and found to his surprise that Itō was not amused. Itō lectured him for over an hour on Kaneko's erroneous assertion that *kokutai* was immutable. *Kokutai*, pronounced Itō, using the English words, was the "national organization," a "general name for the land, people, language, clothing, shelter, and institutions of a state, and as such it was only natural that it change with the times." In response to Kaneko's attempt at rebuttal, Itō silenced him with the command to reflect on it until he better understood the matter.[187]

In the late eighties, however, as *minkan* ideologues began to invoke *kokutai* in their discussions of the nation, they, like Kaneko, emphasized its immutability and distinctiveness, omitting references to historical change in language and custom and to the comparable *kokutai* of America or Holland. As if an unchanging *kokutai* were something both to cling to and be proud of through the domestic turmoil of a constitutional system and the international struggle for survival, members of local patriotic societies spoke of "the need for unity to make manifest our *kokutai*" and to "spread knowledge of our sacred *kokutai* within Japan and to the world."[188] *Minkan* writers produced numbers of tracts and books essaying to define *kokutai*, and by 1892 one such author complained that *kokutai* was getting lost among all the new interpretations.[189] By the end of the 1890s when *kokutai* was described with newly imperialistic confidence as "the unique principle of each nation," Japan's *kokutai* was then compared to England's or China's and found by virtue of its immutability to be, as it were, "more" unique.[190]

In these and later *minkan* representations, *kokutai* was characterized in terms of its age, with frequent reference to Japan's more than 2,500 years of history. "To talk of the present," recounted one lecturer, "one must begin with the past, just as a traveling haiku master writing a poem on the full moon will begin with the crescent. So it is with my talk." He then began with ancient emperor Kammu, eventually to reach his contemporary topic, "the glory of our *kokutai*."[191] That "there was no nation as old as Japan" was alleged and supported with examples of age without national continuity, as in India or China, and national identity without age, as in Germany or Italy.[192] By generalizing the living emperor into a timeless series of emperors-in-sequence, *kokutai* seemed to offer the abstract grandeur possessed by such notions as *patrie* or *Vaterland* in the West. *Kokutai* provided a past that was ageless, continuous, and secure in its ancestral tradi-

145

tion. Amuletic and ambiguous, eventually *kokutai* served to identify the nation and separate "them" from "us."[193]

Thus in 1908 when Itō made a speech on the occasion of the twentieth anniversary of the promulgation of the Constitution, he recollected that no matter how the scholars had argued about the Constitution and *kokutai* in the eighties, his own position had remained categorically firm: "I maintained that constitutional government could never change the *kokutai*, only the political structure (*seitai*)." Itō then mentioned the unbroken line since the legendary emperor Jimmu and other by then familiar references to the grandeur of Japan's ageless past.[194] Kaneko, who was in the audience, was so pleased with his belated victory on the question of *kokutai* that he recorded the exchange that had occurred two decades earlier. In terms of the ideological use of *kokutai*, Itō's apparent reversal was revealing. "Round Itō," as Tokutomi characterized him, cared little for the niceties of ideological definition and instead easily rolled along with the trend of the times.[195] Seldom the ideologue and always the politician, Itō had found a changeable *kokutai* opportune in the early eighties' debates over a constitution. As the constitution took shape, it was Itō who invoked the imperial household as an axis to unite the people and maintain the bureaucratic prerogative amid the politics of a parliamentary system. And in 1908 Itō was content to pronounce *kokutai* immutable since this had by then become the accepted interpretation. Kaneko in the meantime had taken to arguing that "with the substitution of the stars and stripes for the emperor, the methods of moral education in Japan might well be translated to American soil."[196] Both politicians had kept abreast of the times, for the *kokutai* mentioned in the Rescript was now immutable and its glory was taught as part of the civil morality with much the same symbolic meaning as the stars and stripes.

THE SCHOOLS
AND CIVIL TUTELAGE

I

WHILE *minkan* ideologues assumed the lead in interpreting and proliferating the meanings of civil morality, the Ministry of Education worked to institutionalize them in the schools. The operation was by no means automatic, since the articulation of new educational policy at the center did not guarantee immediate implementation in the localities in 1890 any more than it had in earlier decades. Indeed, in the

1890s and 1900s the Monbushō was still occupied with the task of establishing its authoritative control over the nation's public education. Thus at the same time that the Ministry sought to standardize moral education based on the Rescript, it also used the Rescript's imperial authority to bolster its own bureaucratic weight.

In the interests of both standardization and control, the Monbushō acted first to institutionalize the Rescript by distributing copies to the schools and laying down guidelines for their storage, handling, and ceremonial reading.[197] Then, as a result of pressure in the Diet to standardize the textbooks in the late nineties and of the impact of the textbook scandal of 1902, the Ministry was authorized to take over the compilation of elementary school textbooks from the private publishers. In this regard the conservative resolutions in the Diet had specifically called for the national regulation of moral education "to develop the spirit of loyalty, filiality, and patriotism and advance the nation's civilization."[198] From the time the first government texts appeared in 1903 through four subsequent redactions until the end of the Second World War, the schools used uniform and official national texts, not only in ethics but also in history, language, and geography.[199] In order to regulate the teaching as well as the texts, rules and guidelines for teachers and for normal school education were produced in abundance.[200] With the Rescript as a moral basis, a corpus of national textbooks and a body of publicly trained and employed teachers, the Monbushō pursued its mission of civic education.

The schools, along with the army, clearly constituted the most pervasive tutelary apparatus of the state. The ideological message purveyed to elementary schoolchildren was probably the most codified in content and single-minded in goal of any to which late Meiji Japanese were exposed. Yet, even in this most purposeful of all ideological endeavors, official control was neither easily effected nor complete. The ideologues who thrashed out the substance of civil morality in the elite controversies of the eighties and nineties did so in a rarefied and relatively confined social atmosphere. But the dissemination of the civic values that they endorsed occurred on many levels of the provincial bureaucracy, relied on the interpretation of many teachers, and reached an audience of enormous diversity. National uniformity thus proved easier to decree than to realize, and the Monbushō worked for decades to impose ideological consistency in the schools.

The Ministry's efforts to establish the Rescript as the basis of moral education were conducted without statutory support. Despite the repeated requests of the Privy Council that a provision mentioning the Rescript be inserted into education ordinances in the late nineties, the government resisted this as constitutionally inappropriate. In the end, the Rescript appeared by name only in the colonial education ordinances established for Korea in 1911 and Taiwan in 1919 and, in response to the rise of Korean nationalism, was deleted even from these in 1922.[201] To institutionalize the Rescript, the Ministry relied therefore not on legal but on imperial authority. It was partly for this reason that school ceremony became almost as important an ideological instrument as formal ethics instruction in the classroom.

The standardization of school ceremonial occurred in a process of bureaucratic and ideological interchange that was typical of education policy in the late Meiji period. The regulations for school ceremonies originated as a central directive from the Monbushō in 1891. Next in the general progress of bureaucratic paper were the instructions issued by the prefectural governments in 1892 and 1893, which echoed the Monbushō directive with little or no change in language. Then the prefectural regulations were further specified and often embellished at the level of the county office, by the county association of school principals, or by other local education officials. In the course of the decade individual schools developed their own, often very elaborate, ceremonial guides for reading the Rescript and revering the imperial portraits that hung behind the Rescript in its lacquer or wood box. In addition to "reverence in their hearts," for example, the pupils in one school were instructed—at a level of physical detail that resembled the explanation of a golf stroke—to "stand straight, hands at the side, fingers together, palms slightly forward, little fingers touching the thigh."[202] That this elaboration of national education directives occurred at the local level was also typical, as was the fact that the specificity introduced by local educators often appeared in later instructions from the Monbushō. School principals who had vied to receive the imperial portraits now competed to receive the first copy of the Rescript in their district. Indeed, it was often the enthusiasm and self-importance of local principals that first imbued the ritual reading of the Rescript with its sanctified formality.[203]

As the ceremonial forms were gradually established around the country in the nineties, schoolchildren heard the principal intone the Rescript on each national holiday, each school ceremony, and at special monthly convocations held expressly for the purpose. In the lower three grades the children repeated the words after the teacher in *shūshin* class; in fourth grade and above they were expected to recite it from memory. The ceremonial recitation of the Rescript, like the Pledge of Allegiance to the flag in the United States, became an emblematic moment in school ritual. It was associated with the principal and the emperor—that is, with both local and national authority—and with obedient demeanor and solemn sanctity.[204]

The Rescript proved easier to establish in school ceremony, however, than in the curriculum. The process began in 1891 when the "Fundamental Principles and Rules for Elementary School Teaching" made the Rescript the basis of moral instruction (shūshin), and texts and simple commentaries on it appeared almost immediately.[205] The uninspiring habit of rote recitation from these sources prompted Inoue Kowashi, who had become minister of education in 1893, to issue a directive inveighing against the tyranny of the text and urging "the guidance of the teacher" instead.[206] In fact, under the teacher's guidance the three compulsory hours devoted to shūshin instruction each week were a decidedly mixed offering in the 1890s. Lesson plans and pupils' notes reveal that manners and morals occupied a fair portion of class time. In connection with the Rescript's injunction to filiality, first graders were instructed to be sure to tell their parents whenever they left or returned home. In the fourth grade, topics for discussion on the same subject included "how caring for parents is different from caring for a dog or a horse." Third graders learned how to read a book sitting and standing and how to clean the classroom just as they would their own home. Older children were told to omit needless words in conversation, lest they be disliked and therefore not achieve their goals. Shūshin lessons on "the spirit of public morality" undertook to prepare pupils for the advent of the mixed residence of foreigners, and individual teachers drew on textual examples as disparate as Smiles' Self-help and traditional fairy tales.[207]

The Rescript, taught phrase by phrase, was often illustrated in class by tales of historical heroes and folk legends. This was true outside school as well, where the Rescript was a popular subject in illustrated books, magic-lantern shows, and New Year's games (sugoroku): "if you make a mistake in reading the Rescript, you miss a turn."[208] The pious phrases of the Rescript were even matched to the adventures of the fairytale hero Momotarō, the "peach boy" who was loyal and filial as he quelled the denizens of Demon Island.[209] This presentation of the Rescript in terms of heroes and homilies both in and outside school was haphazard enough to explain the results of a local poll of conscripts in 1913, who were then twenty years old and would have attended elementary school around the turn of the century. Of the 1,343 conscripts who had completed six years of upper elementary school, two more years than were compulsory at the time, only 30 percent understood the meaning of the Rescript and could recite substantial parts of it. Middle school graduates, of whose elite number there were but 167 in the district, fared better, in that 70 percent were reported capable of reciting most of the Rescript.[210]

In middle schools the problem was perhaps less lack of instruction than lack of interest. The youth who wrote a composition on "The Utility of Learning" in 1894 was typical of his peers at the time. Beginning with the inspirational thought that learning had made it possible for James Watt to invent the steam engine, he continued exuberantly, "and now there are locomotives on land and steamships at sea, making transportation and transport convenient." He made the obligatory mention of the virtues of the Rescript, noting the importance of "being loyal to the nation, filial to parents, friendly to brothers and sisters, and true to friends," and asserted that the "emperor pays special attention to such things." At that point his teacher inserted in red ink the missing reference: "And thus His Majesty has graciously bestowed the Rescript to guide us, his subjects."[211] But for the pupil in the 1890s, James Watt, whose achievements figured as one of the success stories in Samuel Smiles' *Self-help*, was both better known and more inspiring than the gracious imperial origins of the Rescript. And the student's confident conclusion that "perfecting virtue and extending knowledge will make us useful to the nation when we grow up" reflected the combination of patriotism and ambition that had been communicated in the 1870s and had not lost its appeal.

II

PATRIOTISM of the sort preferred by ideologues in the 1890s swept the schools during and after the Sino-Japanese War, although less as a result of the ideologues' efforts than as a consequence of the fervor of war among the teachers and the students. In September 1894 the Monbushō issued a directive in which it encouraged the singing of war songs to raise the proper spirit of vigor among the pupils. But the martial atmosphere soon grew so thick with mock military drill and enemy hostility that educators lamented what they called the schools' craze for "*shōbu, shōbu*" (martial spirit, or militarism). And in December the Monbushō issued another directive, this time warning against the excessive singing of war songs in the schools.[212] Not only was this instruction to no avail, but the spirit of martial patriotism remained high for two or three years after the war, while the content of ethics instruction continued as before on its uneven course.

150

When the first national *shūshin* texts were published in 1903, one source of the confusion was removed, but not the most important one. For it was not the texts but the teachers who introduced the element of greatest unpredictability into the well-laid plans of education officials, both national and local. Indeed, no sooner had the new textbooks appeared than progressive educators criticized them for an insufficiently Herbartian approach to character training, while conservatives and moralists judged them heavy enough on character development and unacceptably scant on loyalty and patriotism.[213] In the meantime the teaching profession was in the throes of a transition that brought new kinds of teachers into the classroom and made ideological uniformity that much more difficult to achieve.

By 1900 the salary, supply, and status of full-time professional schoolteachers had sunk to a point unthinkable in earlier Meiji decades. During the depression years of the late nineties teachers' salaries compared unfavorably with those of artisans and laborers. In 1899, when Yokoyama Gennosuke published his famous survey of the Tokyo lower classes, those he classed as middle-rank laborers were not quite able to make ends meet with an average monthly wage of 16.25 yen for a family of three. Yet an elementary schoolteacher with a wife and child earned an average of only 13 yen.[214] Economic hardship and poor prospects thus made the profession less attractive just at the time when elementary school enrollments were rising at a rapid rate. The resulting shortage of teachers in turn necessitated the hiring of increased numbers of temporary and part-time personnel, many of whom had not been trained for the classroom. These included the so-called *koshikake kyōshi*, or "stopgap" teachers, who taught for a short time and then moved on to something else and the *demo kyōin* and *taran sensei* (would-be teachers) who taught because they had nothing better to do.[215] Indeed, employment guides at the end of Meiji urged middle school graduates temporarily to escape the "struggle for survival" by finding a relative or a friend who would recommend them for a teaching job.[216] Teachers of dubious caliber and qualifications joined the pedagogical ranks when they could, and at a licensing exam in Yamagata city in 1907 one youth was appalled at his motley fellow examinees, who appeared to him to be "a veritable exhibition hall of the unfit."[217]

A further corollary of the shortage of teachers was the rapid turnover in staff of any given school, as the teachers who "teach at A school in the morning, by evening have moved to B; or yesterday employed at a school in one province, today are at work in another."[218] Even among the 43,593 full-time professional teachers in

151

1897, more than 14,000 had been employed for less than five years in their school, and almost 6,000 had worked in one place for less than a year.[219] In 1908 when the supply of properly trained teachers had begun to increase, only 26 percent of licensed teachers were graduates of the strict training and socialization of the nation's normal schools. And two of the common motives for entering normal school were poverty, since tuition was paid, and draft evasion, since graduates employed as teachers exchanged two years in the army for a mere six weeks. Thus in times of recession the number of applicants to normal school increased, and as soon as the economy recovered even professional teachers left their jobs for more lucrative employment.[220]

As a result of the low pay, uneven quality, and high turnover, the status of schoolteachers fell far below the ideal of either the educational profession itself or the localities which were paying their salaries. During the 1890s and 1900s pedagogues accordingly called for higher salaries, government subsidies to pay them, and the raising of professional standards. To replace the seemingly lost notion of teaching as a calling (*tenshoku*), some educators in 1907 called for "professionalism" (*shokugyōshugi*), while others sought to reinvigorate the profession with new ideals of teaching as a mission (*seishoku*).[221] Unfortunately for the government, this professional crisis occurred at just the same time that the bureaucracy was looking to elementary schoolteachers to serve as local pillars of ideological dissemination. In the years after the Russo-Japanese War, when not only the Ministry of Education but the Home Ministry and the army as well were building the schools into their respective ideological networks, the available teaching personnel were often pedagogically untutored and ideologically unreliable. The elementary school principals, whom the teachers sometimes regarded as "bureaucratic" (*kanryōteki*), were the more trustworthy ideological stalwarts. Indeed, in position and outlook they had rather more in common with the local officials than with their own underpaid and temporary teaching staff, who were little inclined to see themselves as the bannermen of civil morality.[222]

While variety in the preparation and quality of schoolteachers was one source of ideological inconsistency, another was the susceptibility of teachers, particularly the younger ones, to the latest intellectual trends of the time. In the 1900s youthful teachers in their late teens and twenties were less apt to draw their inspiration from Herbart or Confucius than from Tolstoy, Ibsen, and "Hamuretto" (Hamlet). Often these teachers were middle school graduates who confronted what were known as "employment difficulties" after the Russo-Japanese War. No longer able to proceed directly into the higher civil service or other such prestigious careers as their predecessors had done, they turned, some of them temporarily, others permanently, to teaching. While the villagers around them "talked of raising silk-worms and making money," as the barely fictional country school-teacher in Tayama Katai's novel commented, these educated youth brought their own tastes for Russian novels, naturalist literature, and social idealism into the classroom.[223] And when they attended the compulsory local lectures on ethics instruction sponsored by the Monbushō, they responded according to their own lights.

After listening to a lecture on *kokutai* and national morality in 1912, one teacher wrote that he had found three points unacceptable: first, the theory that *kokutai* and national thought (*kokumin shisō*) were un-changeable; second, the assertion that Ibsen's Nora had lost all chance for happiness by abandoning her husband and children; and, third, that learning and action could be separated in moral education. The *kokutai*, he argued, had been changing for two thousand years and would clearly continue to do so. The importance of the unity of knowledge and moral action had been posited by Wang Yang-ming and proved in Japan by the events of the Meiji Restoration. And as for Nora, he explained—with more eloquence and passion than he expended on either *kokutai* or Wang Yang-ming—individualism was acceptable in the West, Nora should not be judged by Japanese stand-ards, and happiness, in any case, was a personal matter.[224]

This cheerful and open eclecticism was common at the time, and twenty-five years later this same teacher reflected that schools at the end of the Meiji period were places of instruction, not indoctrination, "where no one harped on Japanism or such doctrines."[225] A similar recollection in 1934 of a 1907 graduate of a provincial normal school suggested that this was true even in those bastions of pedagogical discipline:

> [the authorities] now have become very strict on ideological issues (*shisō mondai*), which they go to great trouble to control. But in those days control was difficult, and since it was hopeless anyway, they called it something acceptable like "self-government" and in reality just left us to our own devices.[226]

Control continued to be difficult through the 1910s and 1920s, as teachers espoused liberal politics and pedagogy, formed unions, or gravitated toward socialism.[227] Over time the teaching profession sta-bilized. Normal school graduates who were products of standardized training came to predominate in the elementary schools, and educational job mobility decreased so that teachers no longer moved freely from position to position. The prevalence of teachers of the so-called "normal school type," who were regularly attacked by critics for their unimaginative intellect and mechanical moralism, gradually helped to foster greater ideological conformity in the schools.[228] But it was only with the severe and rigid ideological controls of the 1930s that the government was able to suppress the diverse intellectual and political enthusiasms of its teachers.

III

THE ELUSIVE uniformity of civic education was thus a perpetual topic of discussion among education officials, conservative politicians, and *minkan* social critics. By the end of the Meiji period the Rescript on Education had moved out of the schools into public ceremonies and associations where, as a Diet resolution had suggested in 1900, it was intended to check the "deterioration of moral teaching" among the population at large.[229] When the official English translation of the Rescript appeared in 1907, foreign educators praised its "highest kind of principles, ethical and moral."[230] Yet in the same year the vocal opposition critic Ōkuma Shigenobu called the constant invocation of loyalty and filiality "an empty piety," and in 1912 the journalist Ukita Kazutami commented that "though the Rescript on Education is known and memorized throughout the country, it is only mouthed. Even the educators recite it like a sutra without understanding its meaning."[231] The ever-patriotic Christian Ebina Danjō similarly criticized the educational world as "formalistic," citing the warning of a Tokyo University professor that the constant stress on the Rescript might have an effect opposite of the one intended. As people became accustomed to it, they would no longer feel gratitude toward the emperor, but merely "mouth the words 'loyalty and filial piety.' "[232] In 1909 the *Asahi* judged the Rescript "inadequate for teaching Japanese the principles of right and wrong," since loyalty and filial piety alone were insufficient moral armament against the political and financial corruption of the day. Another rather more ironic comment in the press in 1911 questioned the necessity for "all the talk about the need for cultivation (*shūyō*) and the disparagement of current manners and morality." Youth, after all, had been instructed in the Rescript on Education for twenty years, and "unless education is a totally ineffective affair, cultivation should need no further strengthening."[233]

In fact, educators were continually questioning the efficacy of *shūshin* instruction. "Everyone agrees," wrote a leading pedagogue in 1914, "that ethics instruction is ineffective in the early grades," and a middle school graduate of 1911 observed that "you cannot make a living in Osaka with the ethics learned in middle school, trivial as it is and lacking in common sense."[234] In the wake of the Great Treason Incident of 1910-1911 there was a widespread demand for reevaluation of the entire enterprise of "moral education." In a reprise of the arguments of the 1880s, Yamagata, the Monbushō, members of the Diet, and other men of opinion called for national morality (kokumin dōtoku) to unify the thought of the people and protect the kokutai, this time against the socialists, who were the new enemy within.[235] To meet the challenge it was suggested that the content of moral education be updated, and commentators examined the different possibilities anew. One writer concluded that both Confucianism and bushidō were obsolete in the present age, "for we have to compete with the powers, and all the samurai had to do was be frugal."[236]

No new moral basis, however, was agreed upon by the ideological establishment, and the Rescript was invoked once again. This same ideological cycle was repeated several times in the course of the following decades, and in 1935 a quasi-official source on education commented that "the educational world of the Meiji and Taishō periods, like the general intellectual world of the time, lacked the driving force to establish the honored meaning of the Rescript," which therefore remained in the mid-thirties the "most pressing educational issue" just as it had been forty years before.[237]

If the schools did not always fulfill the ideological expectations of their parent ministry, they nonetheless succeeded in conveying the general outlines of civil morality to successive generations of children. In a 1934 poll in which children were asked the origin of the Rescript on Education, three-fifths located it in the general imperial domain, including one-third who correctly answered the Meiji emperor, the others offering the present emperor, the imperial household, and the Imperial Household Ministry. Of those who guessed wrong, 11 percent understandably attributed the Rescript to the Ministry of Education, and one child revealed a precocious grasp of the lines of local bureaucratic power by answering, "the people at city hall."[238] The link of loyalty and patriotism with the emperor and national authority was more or less complete, even if the almost incomprehensibly elaborate charts and interpretations of the content of the Rescript largely remained an arcanum of the ideologues.[239]

THE CIVIL morality that had been wrought in good part by minkan ideologues and disseminated by the Ministry of Education and official organs of many kinds was thus gradually established among the wider population as the indispensable minimum of civic allegiance. The Confucian social ethic, which in the 1930s was labeled by its proper name, set the bounds of secular moral conformity within which "loyal and patriotic" Japanese were to locate themselves, or at least were expected not publicly to contravene. Reverence for ancestors, a deeply familiar social custom, reverberated with allusions to the unbroken imperial line, and through overlapping and reinforcing repetition, the imperial line and *kokutai* were linked to nation and empire. This joining of customary socio-moral tradition with the grandly imperious values of the state made of the new civil morality a bond both unremarkably familiar and relentlessly demanding at one and the same time.

Social Foundations

SOCIAL FEVERS

I

IN THE DECADE from 1905 to 1915 efforts to "influence" the people intensified as ideologues responded to what they viewed as a crisis in the social order. The earlier outburst of ideological activity in the late eighties and nineties had been motivated both by a fear of parliamentary politics and a perceived need for national unity. In anticipation of a new constitutional system, ideologues had undertaken to foster "a sense of nation" among the Japanese as citizens and countrymen. Now both the perception of social disarray and the fear of social disorder impelled commentators to attempt to retrieve some semblance of past concord and orderliness in what appeared to be an increasingly "complicated society." Like most ideological tasks, the older work of citizen-making was never thought to be done, and such elements as *chūkun aikoku*, national morality, and Shintō were reinterpreted in the context of these new social concerns. But after the Russo-Japanese War the main focus of ideological expression shifted from national issues to social problems. For the social questions that had attracted attention since the late 1890s seemed to have changed so greatly in magnitude that they appeared to many to constitute a new threat to the state.

Indeed, the war was described as a watershed, after which Japan was said to be faced with social difficulties equal to the national challenges it had met in the nineteenth century. This perception, which pervaded political rhetoric and intellectual opinion in Tokyo, was not by any means confined to the capital. Provincial officials sounded the same themes, often in otherwise workaday bureaucratic documents:

> The trail of cannon smoke over Uraga Bay at the end of the Tokugawa era broke the long dream of the people and heralded the end of the policy of seclusion. In its place the national policy (*kokuze*) of progress was established. Now with the results of the war against Russia the great tasks of the Meiji Restoration have been completed and a new

157

national policy has emerged. . . . The Russo-Japanese War blossomed and bore fruit for the nation, but to flower and bear fruit in peacetime requires the encouragement of industry. In foreign affairs the nation has progressed, and the future of the empire lies clear before it. Now we must turn inward, cultivate the empire's power at home . . . and nurture the social foundations of the state.

Comparing Japan to England after the Napoleonic wars, this provincial official then warned that as domestic matters began to take precedence over foreign affairs, special attention must be paid to the towns and villages. He argued that when, after its remarkable industrial development, England realized that agriculture must not be neglected, it was already too late. Japan had therefore to strive "to unite the sentiments of high and low" in order to progress in both industry and agriculture with the same spirit as in wartime.[1]

The war served as a benchmark against which the present was to be measured. Victory was credited with having demonstrated Japan's status as a first-rank power (*ittōkoku*) as well as expanding the empire (*DaiNihon teikoku*) to include Sakhalin, Korea, and Manchuria within its sphere of influence. Yamagata proposed that these achievements be celebrated with the construction of an arch of triumph, and New Year's retrospectives in 1907 commented proudly on international recognition of the empire. One writer compared Meiji Japan in its fortieth year to Confucius in his, for just as at forty the sage had no more doubts, Japan now believed in itself. And as at fifty Confucius knew the will of heaven, Japan, too, would soon know its mission as a great power.[2] Yet, one year later in the midst of the severe postwar depression, it appeared as if "the pleasant dreams of victory" had faded in the face of increased tax burdens, economic hardship, fiscal incompetence at home, and "anti-Japanese immigrant fever" abroad.[3] The Russo-Japanese conflict, which had been a large and difficult foreign war, seemed to have bequeathed equally large and difficult problems in domestic postwar management (*sengo keiei*).[4] In the calls for a "second restoration," now the reference was neither to national nor international issues but to social and economic ones—problems of livelihood (*seikatsu mondai*) in general and of the agricultural sector in particular.[5]

Before the problems could be treated, Inoue Tomoichi argued, they had to be identified, "just as when a doctor would administer medicine he first examines the patient." In arguing this point, Inoue, one of the leading Home Ministry ideologues of the countryside, was advocating the careful investigation of village conditions that he associated with Ninomiya Sontoku's movement for agricultural im-

provement in the early nineteenth century.[6] Others, however, conducted examinations of a more general sort, which frequently
resulted in diagnoses of various social "fevers."

"City fever" (*tokainetsu*) was diagnosed in the rural youth who
abandoned their ancestral occupations (*sosen denrai no hongyō*) for
schooling and jobs in urban areas, both in the provinces and in Tokyo. "Now is the age of the cities. From those who have learning
and seek honor to those who want to make money or to sell their
labor—everyone and his brother is setting out for the cities, as if
gripped by a kind of fever."[7] In the decade between 1898 and 1907,
from 40,000 to 60,000 people moved to Tokyo each year, and 20,000
to 40,000 to Osaka.[8] By 1908 the population of metropolitan Tokyo
had risen to 2 million, of a total national population of 50 million.
Of the 1.6 million who now lived within the city proper, nearly 60
percent were described as *inakamono*, having come to Tokyo from
the country, the largest number from the prefectures of Chiba, Saitama, Niigata, Ibaraki, and Kanagawa.[9] And 1908 is considered to
have marked only the beginning of a decade of intensified urban migration that continued through the end of the First World War.[10]

As more rural Japanese succumbed to this fever, the ideological
concern for the countryside mounted. "Ah, the money and the people are going to the capital!" lamented one apostle of *jichi* in a poem
rhapsodically entitled "Local Self-Government."[11] Despite the fact
that Japan's farming population remained constant in absolute numbers from the late 1880s to the 1920s, a steady increase in the birthrate
meant that there was a continuous outflow of rural youth whom the
ideologues saw as "recklessly pressing into the cities to pursue 'some
scheme' and 'make some money.' "[12] The eldest sons of landlords
who left home for higher education in Tokyo; the daughters who
went to marry in the provincial city and live "beneath the castle"
rather than in a neighboring village; the second and third sons of poor
farm families who constituted the majority of migrant urban labor
and who statistically were more likely to remain and not return to
the village; their sisters who worked away from home in textile factories for several of their teenage years—these and other youth were
considered particularly vulnerable to city fever.[13] And those who returned to the village, having been exposed to the "epidemic (*ryūkōbyō*) of urban temptations," were condemned for inflicting a blight
on the "beautiful customs" (*bifū*) of the countryside.[14]

While the ideologues made frequent reference to youth, they were
also describing the general economic and demographic trends that
accelerated in the decade between 1905 and 1915, as rural out-migra-

159

tion and a rise in the number of non-farming families combined to change the nature of the village. Whole families, as well as individuals, moved in or out of villages, resulting in a continuing increase in household mobility. In a village of 365 households in Aichi prefecture, for example, 20 families moved into the community from other parts of the prefecture in the 1890s and 1900s, and in the course of the Meiji period a total of 36 households left the village, half to the cities of Nagoya, Toyohashi, and Tokyo. This migrating 10 percent of the population was comprised of poorer farmers who were not able to make agricultural ends meet, first in the deflationary years of the early eighties and then again during the periods of recession and inflation in the 1900s.[15] In 1910 a local mayor in Shiga prefecture reported a similar phenomenon in his locality. He identified three periods of economic change in his town, which in the Tokugawa period had been a commercial entrepôt on the route to Kyoto and Osaka. The first period resulted from "the changes in the world after the Restoration and the development of the railroad. These had a great influence on the people's occupations, and they could no longer manage their expenses as they once had." The second period of change occurred in the eighties and nineties as lands were sold into tenancy, and disputes between landlords and tenants occurred, "leaving us behind in such things as agricultural improvement." The third period was both the most recent and the most dire:

> There is presently little economic value in agricultural income. As industry in the city grows, it requires a large number of workers, and the people who move to other prefectures increase each year. Their number has now reached 1,400, and not a few of them have surrendered to landlords the lands tilled by their ancestors. As a result the town's agricultural production has decreased, and commerce and industry, of course, do not flourish.[16]

In other cases, not only the poor, but prosperous farmers of the sort Yanagita Kunio praised as "the most industrious, the most vital, and the most knowledgeable of the villagers" also "abandoned" the country for the city, contributing to the "social illness" (*shakai no yamai*) that Yanagita identified with this kind of migration. "As civilization progresses" and "farmers become townsmen," he argued, "their descendants turn into vagabonds (*hyōhaku*) and both agriculture and the nation suffer."[17]

Equally significant, however, were the changes in livelihood among farm families who remained in the same location but whose members began to work as wage laborers—as carpenters or tradesmen close to home, or as temporary workers (*dekasegi*) in firms and factories either in neighboring towns or distant cities.[18]

> Together with the progress of the times . . . great changes have occurred in the budgets of farm households. In the 1880s rice was the general standard for prices, and farm families could afford to buy commodities in a relatively stable environment. But in the years since the late 1890s, with the exception of ordinary grains and foodstuffs, everyday items like fertilizer, oil, salt, tobacco, soy sauce, and saké must all be purchased, and in each case the prices have risen to the point that the value of rice will no longer cover them. Moreover, children's education and other social expenditures require enormous outlays, quite apart from the so-called political expenses in these areas. Even for those who remain in the villages and faithfully work in agriculture, it is difficult today to meet household expenses with the time-honored Japanese methods of rice cultivation alone. And if this is true, what can be said of the future? It will become increasingly necessary to concentrate the family's efforts in generating as much cash income as possible.[19]

Thus the change in the village that the ideologues associated with youth and their fatal attraction to the city was in fact a phenomenon of considerably wider socioeconomic provenance.

The same was true of "enterprise fever" (*jitsugyōnetsu*), another malady that appeared to the social diagnosticians to be spreading in the years following the war. Its various strains affected different social strata in different ways, none of which was considered beneficial to the national health. While industrial magnates were criticized for letting their business fever (*kigyōnetsu*) lead them to invest in such profitable but less than urgent enterprises as the construction of railroad and streetcar lines to scenic or religious sites, the more general complaint was directed at those who "laid down their plows" and succumbed to "get-rich-quick market fever" (*ikkaku senkin no sōba netsu*).[20]

> In the flush of victory after the war, business fever became rampant. The world of speculation gave rise to numbers of nouveaux riches, fueling rumor and giving people the impression that there was nothing like speculation for getting rich. Those who dreamed of easy fortune (*ikkaku senkin o yume miru*) laid down their plows and with a glass in one hand and a cigarette in the other gave no thought to where they might end up. And as they pursued extravagance (*shashi*) and ostentation (*fuka*), the evil ways of the city (*tokai no akufū*) swept over the length and the breadth of the land.[21]

The charges of enterprise fever and mammon-worship that the *minkan* moralists had made in the wake of the economic development after the Sino-Japanese War in the late 1890s now became common among educators, civilian and military bureaucrats, and social commentators in general.[22] Some addressed themselves to farm youth whose success fever (*seikōnetsu*) led them to abandon their ancestral occupation; others to middle-class youth of both town and country in whom "small-success fever" (*shōseikōnetsu*) resulted in easy satisfaction with superficial materialistic achievement. That money was also worshiped in the United States was of small comfort to one writer, since he felt that America at least had the spirit of a Theodore Roosevelt, while Japan's "Yamato spirit" seemed to him to have passed with the two Meiji wars.[23] The spirit of enterprise in the countryside, however, had grown steadily in the late Meiji years, and now even the agricultural side-employments (*fukugyō*), which the government had encouraged since the 1870s, were sometimes considered a threat to the ancestral property (*sosen denrai no zaisan*). Farmers trapped by "the delusion that sericulture is a get–rich–quick enterprise" overextended their resources and fell into debt. Others embarked on silkworm raising without the necessary knowledge of the worms and cocoons.[24] Even usury was not what it used to be "before the Restoration when pawnshop owners understood the needs of the people and conducted their affairs with virtue," instead of profiting mercilessly as they now did from the farmers' enthusiasm for enterprise.[25]

Not only the ancestral property of individual households but the wholesome customs and simple mores of entire villages were judged to be the casualties of the materialism and money worship (*haikinshugi*) that accompanied civilization and "the struggle for survival." One village plan lamented that "as a result of the trends of the time (and perhaps because we are near a city), extravagance and luxury are steadily increasing." Another plan explained that "in recent years as the currents of civilization have swelled, farmers have lost the virtues of diligence, and there are many who indulge in luxurious consumption." Yet another plan stated that "the villagers used to be simple and unsophisticated (*shitsuboku*), but now, affected by recent social trends, they dislike labor and incline toward extravagance." Even the youthful graduates of a provincial agricultural school lamented the predilection of their peers to "abandon the ancestral pursuit of agriculture to become merchants, factory workers, or bureaucrats." Currently enrolled students in the same school discussed ways in which "the extreme development of material civilization corrupts the social atmosphere, as farmers pursue luxury, developing a dislike for work and a taste for pleasure."[26] And the closer the village to a

162

city, the more exposed it was thought to be to the extravagance and ostentation associated with civilization and urban life.

Thus the railroad that in the 1880s had been protested by the farmers for depredating the land and welcomed by the local elite for its easy transport of freight to and from the provinces was now described by rural-minded ideologues as the conveyor of provincial youth, newly infected with urban idleness and a distaste for agricultural toil, who sported such affectations as white *tabi* and gold-rimmed spectacles.[27] But as military officers and agrarian moralists were warning against the effect of the railroad on rural life, the general population was becoming increasingly more enchanted with "the sound of the whistle." The "Railroad Song," whose first installment—the Tōkaidō line in sixty-six verses—appeared in 1900, had become one of the most popular songs in the country. Magazines catered to the growing interest in rail travel with issues that combined maps and statistics on lines and stations with handy travel guides to the points of interest along the way.[28] As the railway expanded, new installments were added to the song, handier guides were published, and more people traveled.[29] And as they did, the temptations of enterprise and the seductions of the city penetrated more deeply, until their symptoms were discovered "not only in the upper and middle strata of village society, but in the lower classes (*teikyū*) as well." By the end of the Meiji period it was remarked that only "where transportation is inconvenient are customs simple" and only in the remote mountain areas (*sankan hekichi*) were the materialistic effects of "so-called civilization" (*iwayuru bunmei*) still contained, although it was common to add that this was unlikely to remain the case for very much longer.[30]

II

LIKE MANY social issues of national import in the Meiji period, city and enterprise fever were linked to education. The diagnostic accounts of postwar maladies included two symptoms in particular that suggested the existence of education fever as well: first, the increased demand for and debate over elementary education among the people and, second, the appearance of "educated idlers" (*kōtō yūmin*) among middle school graduates of the middle class. After decades of promoting school enrollments, the Ministry of Education proudly reported an increase in the initial enrollment of school-age children from 64 percent in 1889 to 98 percent in 1906.[31] Partly on the basis of this nearly universal enrollment and in light of "the recent expansion of our national fortunes," in the same year the Ministry prepared for the extension of compulsory elementary education from four years to six. In its proposal to the cabinet, the Monbushō argued that an instructional span of only four years made it "extremely difficult to create the necessary basis of moral and civic education and to provide the knowledge and skills of elementary education that are essential to the people's livelihood." Moreover, compulsory education ended too early (at age ten or eleven), leaving the children "in the middle of life's most impressionable age when mind and body are most effectively molded." Thus, for the sake of the people's "discipline" and "common sense," the time had come to implement the extension which educators had actively discussed since the late 1890s.[32]

Anticipating resistance to the extension, the Ministry postponed the enforcement of the two additional years until 1908 and even then was prepared to be lenient with localities that could not muster the necessary facilities. In an effort to mute parental opposition, one principal in Hirosaki invited the parents of fourth-graders to school in 1907 to persuade them that establishing a fifth grade was beneficial to the pupils, to the nation, and to his own reputation as an educator. Since the four years of compulsory education had finally become free in 1900, the principal expected that few would welcome an additional year with school fees of thirty sen and was surprised to find that fifty-four out of sixty parents signed up their children immediately.[33] All over the countryside, occasionally in the same localities where farm families had vehemently, sometimes violently, opposed the imposition of compulsory education in the 1870s, parents registered little apparent complaint about the two new grades.[34] Sawayanagi Masatarō, the vice-minister of education, later recalled that "the extension was implemented more easily than the authorities had thought, with no obstacle at all and with remarkable completeness throughout the country."[35]

One of the reasons for the unexpectedly prompt compliance was that in 1906 three-quarters of the schoolchildren were already continuing to fifth grade, even though the government did not require them to do so.[36] Society, it seemed, had kept abreast of the government in comprehending the importance of education. As one father commented in 1904,

> it used to be that all a parent had to do was bring children up without their going hungry. . . . Now that they have to be educated, the so-called burdens of parental duty are burdensome indeed. Especially today when every occupation, whether farming, industry, commerce, or office work, requires education to get anywhere at all . . . it is not merely

duty to the nation, but the personal feeling of a parent for his child. If you let a child grow up ignorant and illiterate, you consign to the depths of misfortune the life of a child, that which is "more precious than silver or gold." If a parent has the heart to do this, I don't think there is anything in the world that he would stop at doing.[37]

The preamble of the original Education Act of 1872 had declared learning the key to success in life, which none could afford to neglect. Now, after thirty years of promoting education as the means both of self-help and national progress, schooling had become so entrenched a part of social life that it seemed to many to be a law of human nature.

The people, however, did not always agree with the educational establishment on the contents of compulsory schooling. While the government and educators called for more emphasis on moral and spiritual education,[38]

> the present demand among teachers and pupils seems to be that "primary education must fill present-day needs." In response to what precisely these present-day needs are, fishermen and small farmers reply, "What the children learn in school is of no use in our work." The merchants say, "School education should be more utilitarian." Among those who are educated themselves, some say that upper elementary schools [seventh and eighth grades] are unnecessary, and technical schools would be of more direct benefit. Everyone, whatever his position (shugi), discusses education. But the emphasis on the "present-day" has as its basis immediate and selfish benefit. The people do not think of elementary education in terms of moral, intellectual, and physical education (tokuiku, chiiku, taiiku) but give first priority to knowledge.[39]

Not only in Tokyo, where this report originated in 1913, but also in the villages, people were making demands for "present-day" knowledge in elementary education. Village plans, reflecting the administrative and fiscal importance of education in local concerns, called for more work in "practical subjects" and an increased emphasis on technical, or vocational, education (jitsugyō kyōiku), not only in the technical schools but at the lower levels. Literary skills were valuable, but even more important was the agricultural knowledge "necessary to the development of each family's affairs." Village plans also reflected the fact that enrollment rates cited by the Monbushō were not matched either by rates of daily attendance or by successful graduation of the allegedly enrolled pupils. This was especially true in the poorer farming areas, where it was stated that increasing the practical value of schooling would help to raise attendance and encourage completion of elementary school.[40]

Similarly, the technical continuation schools (*jitsugyō hoshū gakkō*) for elementary school graduates that proliferated in the post-Russo-Japanese War period were often initiated at the village level. Established in response to the "present-day" needs of small owner-farmers and tenants, these supplementary programs enabled their sons to have more vocational education without leaving the farm while they acquired it.[41] Thus the attitude among the villagers was often different from that of such social diagnosticians as the visiting military officer who complained that "education weighted toward knowledge" had resulted only in the "remarkable progress of graffiti by elementary school pupils." He pointed out that once they had scrawled simple phrases in chalk here and there on doors and walls, but now they wrote elegant prose in pencil on every shop shutter in town.[42] Yet, the knowledge that he and others decried, whether it was expressed on shop shutters or in family account books, was precisely what village officials and the local elite were endeavoring to promote in their localities.

This local enthusiasm provoked criticism in the press and also from the Home Ministry, whose own plans for postwar management included stringent fiscal constraints on local expenditures.[43] Education consumed by far the largest portion of town and village budgets, averaging 43 percent nationally in the years between 1906 and 1911, while administrative expenses, the next largest expenditure, amounted to less than 20 percent. And the local cost of education had quadrupled between 1890 and 1911.[44] In some towns and villages both the percentages and the actual expenditures were considerably higher than the national average, occasionally reaching 70 percent of village expenses. Construction costs of new buildings to accommodate the advanced grades became an issue. Provincial observers, for example, criticized Toyama prefecture, where "because of local pride among the prefectural assemblymen, schools have been recklessly constructed in every *gun*." In Nagano, competition among hamlets for new construction or for additions to existing schools was deemed financially irresponsible, although the local newspaper commented that fine buildings were doubtless a good thing, as "all the visiting Chinese remark upon them."[45] For fiscal reasons, then, the provinces were criticized for building too many schools.

To relieve the budgetary strain of construction and other educational costs, the Home Ministry urged that more private contributions be solicited from local men of influence and even from the villagers themselves. That this time-honored method employed by the central government to extract private funds for public purposes

166

continued to be at all effective was due in part to the local commitment to education. It was even possible to utilize this sentiment in the service of tax collection, the teacher confronting villagers at school meetings and pleading for payment so that "the expenses of one child's education" might be defrayed.[46] The Home Ministry was less pleased, however, when this commitment spilled over into political battles and village uprisings, as it did, according to one count, at least ninety-seven times between 1906 and 1911.[47] A dispute, for example, over whether two or three schools should be established to accommodate the two new grades erupted into violence in Okazaki—rubble was thrown at the opposition, and four policemen were injured in the melee.[48] Even when there was no violence, the polarization of a village assembly in Niigata into a "construction faction" and a "postponement faction," which called meetings at 2 a.m. to catch its opponents off-guard, did not coincide with the government's conception of harmonious self-government.[49] Nonetheless, because the Home Ministry, no less than the Monbushō and the army, regarded the village schools as central to the provincial social order, the voices that criticized the localities for excessive enthusiasm for elementary education had perforce to remain somewhat muted.

When this enthusiasm reached beyond elementary education, however, the voices of the social diagnosticians grew shrill. In his address to the prefectural governors on the extension of compulsory education in 1907, Minister of Education Makino Nobuaki emphasized that elementary school was to be considered "complete and independent education that has virtually no relation to higher levels of schooling." The problem, he argued, was that

> teachers think that elementary school is the first stage of education and forget that for the majority it is the final one. Then pupils and parents are also drawn into this vogue, and young people indiscriminately proceed to middle school. Thus we are faced with the evil of too many people harboring hopes of higher education.[50]

Harboring hopes of higher education was undesirable on several counts. First, it drove rural youth to the city, often to Tokyo, where they fell victim to the depravity of city life. Educators and agrarian ideologues alike discouraged village youth from "going up to the capital" (jōkyō), for when and if they returned, it was considered that the higher their level of education, the worse their manners and morals, the more clever their draft dodging, and the less likely they were to wield a hoe. The second objection to middle school hopefuls was their inclination toward such agriculturally unuseful careers as teach-

167

ing, journalism, and the civil service. Doctors, too, "were increasing like bamboo after the rain."[51] Young women who insisted on too much education and attended women's higher schools were described as less marriageable, less prepared for their role as "good wife, wise mother," and in general as "females not suited to the countryside."[52] But if they would end up "tutors and old maids as in the West," a worse fate awaited their male counterparts who would often find no work at all. Because of their "irrelevant learning" and the scarcity of positions in the careers for which they thought themselves suitable, these youth became clerks at the village office, insurance salesmen, or spent their time uselessly, thus earning themselves the less than charitable epithet, "human fertilizer machines."[53] The employment difficulties (shūshokunan) of these "educated idlers" were said to derive from too much higher education and to result in a serious social problem.[54] Indeed one agrarian ideologue listed middle school graduates, along with traveling actors, degenerate monks, and others among the ten "bacilli" infecting village life.[55]

If the number of this particular "bacillus"—male graduates of the five-year middle school course of elite education—increased threefold between 1900 and 1909, it was partly due to the Middle School Act of 1899, which established the three basic routes to higher education. The other two forms, the four-year women's higher schools and the three-year vocational schools, grew even more rapidly in the first decade of the twentieth century, both in the number of schools and the number of pupils. This numerical growth was impressive, yet in 1909 when 6.4 million children attended elementary school, there were only 118,000 males in middle school, 51,700 females in women's high schools, and 60,000 vocational students. And in the same year the middle school graduate "bacilli" increased their number by a nationwide total of only 11,652.[56] Numbers alone therefore did not account for the degree of ideological concern with education fever.

That the preponderance of middle school pupils belonged to the middle class was of particular importance. These included elite rural youth of the landlord class, many of them second and third sons who would not inherit the family property, but also eldest sons who would. Since this class was expected to provide the pillars of local society, the defection of its progeny threatened the structure of village leadership. As middle school education "turns the middle classes of our country (wagakuni no chūtō minzoku) into idlers of most inferior character, what is throwing society into confusion is not the poor people of the lower classes but the middle classes of considerable property and status."[57] Also of concern was the increase in the number of ordinary peasant children who wanted further education, even if they could not afford the expensive middle school course.[58] One such child, the only son of a poor tenant farmer in Fukuoka prefecture, graduated from elementary school in 1914 and later recalled that

> it was natural for the rich children to go on to middle school, which meant about one in ten. Of my class of seventy-two, six continued to middle school or girls' school. Some went to agricultural school and others to teacher training, but most remained at home. . . . For a long time study had been regarded as a nuisance, but now people began to wake up and realize that learning was the root of success. Even farming parents warned that "if you don't learn your letters, you'll be in trouble when you grow up." And every year the number of middle school hopefuls grew, and some even began to go to normal school and university.[59]

Since education was viewed as the path to rising in the world (*risshin shusse*), it followed that the more education, the higher the rise. Popular New Year's games of the late 1890s and 1900s illustrated an ideal course where the player began in kindergarten—another flourishing development of the 1900s—and won the game with successful entrance into university, where the student was pictured playing pingpong and tennis, the late Meiji epitome of fashionable sport. Hopes of middle school led to hopes of higher school, which was the preparatory course for university. As the words of a popular song in 1912 expressed it,

> I will be a doctor of laws.
> You a doctor of letters.
> So let's go to the pleasure quarter.
> Our parents in the country are digging yams.[60]

Although few indeed realized this ideal, that young Japanese of yam-digging parents aspired to it was enough to cause the ideologues concern. Elementary school was one thing, they seemed to be saying, while the feverish craving for higher education was quite another.

In this connection the social commentators after the Russo-Japanese War discovered yet another affliction, for it appeared to them that "indiscriminate reading" was generating "unhealthy thoughts" which poisoned the minds and the morals of the people. Again, youth were considered most susceptible, attracting the concern of the Ministry of Education, the Home Ministry, and the army. The so-called "morals directive" (*fūki kunrei*) issued by Minister of Education Makino in June 1906 set the tone for the promotion of wholesome thought (*kenzen naru shisō*). It sought to combat spiritual "despondence," moral "decadence," and licentious "self-indulgence" on the one hand, and socialism and the "poison" of radical ideas on the other. Both were linked to "the recent publications that have increasingly tempted young men and women with dangerous opinions, world-weary attitudes, and depictions of the baser sides of life." To prevent the erosion of school and familial authority and the disruption of the "foundations of the state" and of "the social order," Makino instructed educators to "scrutinize the contents of books read by students and pupils. Those that are deemed beneficial should be encouraged, while those likely to arouse unwholesome results (*furyō no kekka*) should be strictly prohibited both in and out of school."[61]

The press, in the main, was sympathetic to the minister's concern with student morality, in part because the disaffection among educated youth was recognized as a social problem in itself. Those whom the "morals directive" characterized as despondent, "anguishing over daydreams," and "neglecting their duties in life" belonged to the barest pinnacle of youth who received an advanced education. In 1906 less than 5,000 were enrolled in the public higher schools, which then numbered seven, and roughly the same number attended the two imperial universities.[62] *Minkan* commentators admitted that the exquisite agony (*hanmon*) that made students of the elite higher schools retreat into literature, pessimism, or suicide, was a phenomenon confined to the "upper strata of society."[63] Yet, because extravagance (*shashi*) and world-weariness (*ensei*), like the "dangerous thought" of socialism, were considered "contagious," their spread would result in "a grave and serious illness in the nation."[64] Indeed, the contagion was already apparent: rural youth were reading novels and popular magazines, which exposed them to the "fleshly aroma of naturalist writing." They read newspapers that thrived on accounts so scurrilous that no "parent who understood education could read the paper aloud in front of the children without leaving parts out." Adultery, pornography, "nauseatingly vulgar fiction"—newspapers were socially dangerous, like the "hanging pine" that gave people who passed it the unaccountable urge to destroy themselves on it as others had done.[65] On behalf of the young women whose "vanity was being fanned" by the frivolities of popular magazines, one letter to the editor asked plaintively if there was not some way to control such wanton "reading outside the curriculum."[66]

Intellectuals criticized the notion of government control of reading matter, suggesting that "not all Monbushō bureaucrats are men of noble virtue" whose ability to distinguish wholesome from unwhole-

170

some prose could go unchallenged.[67] Yet, the government persevered in its efforts. Makino's successor was Komatsubara Eitarō, a Yamagata man who headed the Ministry of Education in the Katsura cabinet from 1908 to 1911. Concerned with the state of national morality (*kokumin dōtoku*), Komatsubara became known as the "directive minister" for his many pronouncements in the area of popular, or social, education (*tsūzoku kyōiku*). To counteract the deleterious effect of what he called the "love and lust" in popular fiction, "the popularity of naturalism and the penetration of socialism," he directed that "wholesome reading beneficial to public morals" be encouraged through the establishment of libraries and the promotion of lecture, storytelling, and film programs in social education. Even after the Great Treason Incident of 1910-1911, when fear of radical activism heightened the ideologues' sense of social crisis, Komatsubara continued to speak of naturalist literature and socialist doctrine in the same breath and to associate both of them with misguided and unbridled reading.[68] In the decade between 1905 and 1915, the Home Ministry and the army joined the effort to stop the spread of Tolstoy, unwholesome thrillers, and works that corrupted morals and incited the "spirit of speculation." In their stead youth associations were urged to purchase heroic war stories (*bidan*), sericultural manuals, and tales of loyalty and patriotism to circulate to their members.[69] Through these printed instruments of social education the central government attempted to channel the reading fever of youth who were old enough to be beyond the influence of public-school textbooks but within the reach of potentially disruptive social information.

This proved a Sisyphean task, especially since it was clear that the reading habits in question were not confined to youth. The Russo-Japanese War, like the war with China a decade earlier, had resulted in a remarkable expansion of the publishing industry. The number of newspapers tripled between 1897 and 1911, when 236 papers were published in Tokyo and the provinces and the circulation of the seven largest dailies each surpassed 100,000.[70] Commercial competition was fierce, and journalists were quick to respond to government criticism of the scandalous content of their papers with the rejoinder that "few people buy newspapers out of charity." If a socially beneficial press were wanted, they suggested that the government had better start with the public, whose tastes ran rather to multiple murders and adultery than to moral uplift.[71]

New book titles were published in astonishing numbers, among them the highly successful pocketbooks. These included a popular

"Pocket Analects" and the long-selling Tachikawa Bunko series, in which fictional Edo heroes lived by sincerity and the sword.[72] Magazines also flourished in the 1900s. The publisher Hakubunkan blanketed the nation with the products of its empire, diversifying to serve different age and interest groups, some of whom may not have been aware of their collective identity until Hakubunkan defined it for them by publishing such magazines as *Youth World, Coed World, Middle School World, Agricultural World,* and the like. Its flagship journal, *The Sun (Taiyō)*, had begun, like the railroad, to penetrate even the remotest villages.[73] Local reports on "reading tastes" mentioned these and other popular magazines such as *Jitsugyō no Nihon (Business Japan)* as well as newspapers, swashbuckling fiction, and the best-selling novel of the Russo-Japanese War, *The Human Bullet (Nikudan)*.[74] The first home encyclopedias sold widely. In the successful Fuzanbō version, which sold 70,000 copies from newspaper advertising before it was even published in 1906, the longest section was devoted to a clinical exegesis of exotic Western foods, the present-day *tonkatsu* (pork cutlet) and *omuretsu* (omelet) thus reaching provincial housewives through its pages.[75]

The quantitative expansion in publishing coincided with an extension of readership that was made possible by a steady increase in the ability to read. For by the end of the first decade of the twentieth century the results of compulsory education were becoming more and more apparent. Simple tests of scholastic skills conducted at draft physicals revealed a rise in literacy that very nearly matched the increase in the rate of enrollment in elementary school. In part this represented a minimal achievement of the sort that gratified army officers charged with the training of new conscripts.

> In 1893 one third of the recruits [in Osaka] were illiterate and the majority could not distinguish left from right, which meant that before they could enter training, they had to be taught basic skills. . . . Last year [1906] there was hardly anyone who could not write his name, so military education could begin immediately.[76]

It was true that of an annual average of 12,500 recruits in Ōsaka-fu between 1902 and 1912, the percentage of raw illiteracy dropped from 24.9 percent to 5.5 percent in that decade; and other parts of the country showed roughly similar decreases.[77] More significant for the expansion of the reading public, however, was the ability and desire to digest simple prose on subjects of interest. The establishment of the written colloquial language (*genbun itchi*) and the widespread use of *furigana* glosses increased the accessibility of newspapers and popular works. Then the Russo-Japanese War provided the excitement that sold papers in unprecedented numbers as the press conducted its own "war of extras," and the avid public followed the siege of Port Arthur and the progress of Russia's Baltic fleet toward its doom in the Tsushima Straits.[78] The results of compulsory schooling were thus more than matched by the willingness of the publishing industry to cater—indeed some said, to pander—to the interests of the expanding literate sector of the population.

Although expanding literacy did not guarantee that a graduate of six years of elementary school could, or would, read the daily press, it is clear that newspapers were reaching a wider social audience than ever before. The fad for "postcards to the editor" that swept the commercial press in the late nineties produced voluminous response, not only from middle-class men of letters but from laborers, farmers, soldiers, and apprentices. Like the shopboy who complained that his boss considered "newspapers the archenemy of business," some sneaked time from the store to read them and write such thoughts to the editor. Others used the *furigana* glosses in the newspapers to learn to read, thus pulling themselves up by their scholastic bootstraps in order to rise in the world.[79] Commercial guides to "prose for Japanese soldiers," as well as for industry, agriculture, and commerce, soon appeared to provide models for the kinds of colloquial writing necessary for what was described as "occupational success."[80]

In the villages the "itinerant readers" of the early Meiji period no longer appeared to unravel the intricacies of a written text for the unlettered, their place taken by educated residents, often of the younger generation. The local elite, landlords and officials, and usually also the schoolteachers subscribed to the provincial paper and often to a metropolitan daily as well.[81] Because of the subscribers' position in the community the news—and sometimes the paper itself—was quickly carried to the rest of the village. Young men read magazines and newspapers in the small library collections of their village youth associations, and women and children of the subscribing elite snatched the paper from the head of the house who in earlier years had considered it his private property.

In the cities people saw the papers in such public locations as barbershops, milk bars, or their places of employment. Newspapers, like beer, were now a widely available commodity. And just as the new beer halls were described as "a separate world in which the classes are truly equal, rickshawmen mix with gentlemen, laborers with clerks, frock coats with uniforms," so too by 1900 had the news-paper-reading public "moved downward to the lower social strata . . . from small tradesmen, younger students, grooms and rickshaw-men in attendance to the whores in the brothels."[82] Although this magazine writer's mention of grooms, rickshawmen, and prostitutes was standard social hyperbole in the Meiji period, there is evidence nonetheless that urban laborers had begun to read the papers, some-times in factory reading rooms and even, according to one account of Tokyo tenement life in 1904, by subscription.[83] This increase in readers of the "lower social strata" was the reason, the magazine writer continued, that papers printed so many sensational scandals on their feature pages (sanmen kiji). His condescension was perhaps un-warranted in the light of a local report in 1908 that complained of similar interests among schoolteachers who, "though they intend to glance at the foreign cables and other news, are apt in fact to read only the fiction (kōdan) and the sanmen kiji."[84]

In this way as information flowed further and deeper into society, the recipes for omelets and pork cutlets, to which the government did not greatly object, and the pornography and the socialism, to which it did, found increasingly wider audiences than the bureaucrats themselves could be certain of reaching in their efforts at wholesome social "influence."

III

IN THEIR ministrations after the Russo-Japanese War the ideologues confronted not only a series of feverish afflictions but also what ap-peared to them to be a plague (yakubyō). Its symptoms were the increasing signs of social conflict, whether in the form of strikes, mass demonstrations, the "widening gap between rich and poor," or the doctrines of socialism. Since the late 1880s a number of commen-tators both in and outside the government had warned of the inevi-tability of social discord, for the experience of Western nations showed that labor unions and socialism appeared together with "the progress of civilization."[85] Western models also suggested in the 1890s that such preventive social policy as production cooperatives (sangyō kumiai) and factory legislation could help to forestall the "calamity" of class divisions before it occurred.[86] Similarly, in regard to socialism, it was argued that "since the German Kaiser is using every possible means to proscribe it, it seems appropriate for Japan to adopt the same policy." In 1901, Yamagata's Home Minister Sue-matsu Kenchō thus advocated the use of suppressive legislation as a

174

means to control the danger to the state, in this case invoking the Peace Police Law of 1900 to ban the Social Democratic Party on the day it was formed.[87] Yet, despite this historical acquaintance with social problems, the reaction of the ideologues to the social eruptions after the war suggested that the calamity was proving even worse than they had feared.

Before the Hibiya riots against the Portsmouth Treaty erupted in mob violence in September 1905, Prime Minister Katsura wrote Yamagata of his concern that the lower classes (*kasō no jinmin*) "are mixing politics with social questions, and now, from grooms and rickshawmen to small tradesmen, the people are raising a hue and cry about an indemnity, though they know nothing of the issue."[88] The 1906 demonstrations against the rise in streetcar fares repeated scenes of violence similar to those at Hibiya, as did the Tokyo riots at the time of the change of government in 1913. Because the city was considered to be the vanguard of social disruption—"if they set streetcars on fire in Tokyo," it was said, "they will then do the same in the provinces"—these assertions of "the power of the general populace (*ippan minshū*)" in the capital made the ideologues fear for the country as a whole.[89]

The same was true of strikes, especially in the tumultuous year of 1907:

> Beginning with the Ashio copper mine riot, the disturbances at the Koike coal mines and the Uraga docks have followed one upon the other, and now there is the violence at the Horonai mines. Even though the Ashio incident was not an event of grave proportions, there is no doubt that this year is the year of the strike.[90]

The spread of the contagion was the more likely as industrialization intensified and the number of factory workers began to increase, which they did rapidly, nearly tripling in number to one million nationally between 1900 and 1917, and doubling to 80,000 between 1903 and 1912 in privately owned factories in Tokyo alone. Wages were low, the average hovering around a monthly income of twenty yen, which was officially defined as the poverty level in Tokyo in 1911; the average length of employment per regular factory worker in Tokyo was still only twenty-two months in 1914; and there were nearly four times as many day laborers, many of them from the provinces, whose livelihood was even more uncertain.[91] At the same time that the Ministry of Agriculture and Commerce and the Home Ministry conducted extensive surveys of labor conditions, the gov-

175

ernment continued its dual policy, culminating its Meiji phase in 1911 with both the passage of the factory law and the police suppression of the Tokyo streetcar strike.[92]

In the same years, from 1907 to 1911, the ideological concern with socialism mounted, as socialists participated in union-organizing and anti-government activity. The press explained the rise of socialism in terms of conflict between capital and labor, the government's dilatory handling of labor problems, and once again, an oversupply of middle school graduates.[93] At the same time the Katsura government, urged on by Yamagata, seized on the Red Flag Incident of 1908 and the Great Treason Incident of 1910-1911 to suppress what Yamagata called "social destructionism" (shakaihakaishugi). In a document of that title drafted with the aid of the scholar Hozumi Yatsuka in 1910, Yamagata presented the views on socialism that informed government policy on that subject, in part because such Yamagata-line bureaucrats as Katsura Tarō, Hirata Tōsuke, Komatsubara Eitarō, Ichiki Kitokurō, Kiyoura Keigo, and Ōura Kanetake were responsible for implementing it. The document began:

> In considering the changes in popular sentiment that occur in modern society, the people (minshū) begin by claiming political rights, and, once they are allotted these, they demand food and clothing and wish for the wealth of society to be equally apportioned. Realizing that such demands are incompatible with current national and social institutions, they first turn their efforts to the destruction of the foundations of the state and society. Herein lies the genesis of what is called socialism. Its immediate causes are the extreme division between rich and poor and the marked changes in ethics that accompany modern culture. It is now urgently necessary both to construct a policy that will remedy this affliction at its roots (byōkan) and also, for the sake of national and social self-preservation, to exercise the strictest control over those who espouse its doctrines. The spread of this infection (byōdoku) must be prevented; it must be suppressed and eradicated.[94]

The message was clear: "to preserve order and stability" the "contagious epidemic" (ryūkō densen) of socialism must be forcibly crushed. Yet, as was usually the case with Yamagata, the endeavor involved more than suppression.

> The first essential in the eradication of socialism is the diffusion of full and complete national education and the cultivation of moderate thought (onken naru shisō). After that the next task is material relief in the form of what is known as social policy (shakai seisaku).[95]

176

First came the ideological measures—which here included such increasingly familiar dicta as "developing national thought and excluding individualism," cultivating "healthy thought" in teachers, pupils, and texts; "expanding vocational education to eliminate the educated unemployed idlers"; and "promoting wholesome and beneficial reading"—and then the promotion of social provisions for the poor, the sick, and the disadvantaged. Thus, the Boshin Rescript urged frugality in the name of strenuous effort in the same year that the government called for the establishment of social reform and relief measures (*shakai kyūsai jigyō*). Both together constituted the efforts of the ideologues to meet the spread of disruptive social symptoms, lest "socialism become anarchism as the common flu turns to pneumonia."[96] Confronted by such afflictions as "individualism, internationalism, socialism . . . husbands addressing their wives with the honorific '*san*,' and the light Japanese cuisine being overwhelmed by heavy Western food,"[97] the social physicians responded with calls for harmony and cooperation, reverence for ancestral customs, familial virtues, and public spiritedness. Thus they prepared ideological nostrums to return society to what they regarded as its former state of health.

As SOCIAL DOCTORS they were not unaware of the etiology of the several fevers and maladies that they diagnosed in late Meiji society. These were the results of the "progress and development of our country": the ills that civilization brought (*bunmeibyō*). Urbanization, commercial and industrial capitalism, the diffusion of education, the expansion of transportation and communication, the mass expressions of social protest—the fevers represented a veritable catalogue of the attributes of a modernizing society. In the case of Japan they were but the economic, social, and technological results of the early Meiji reforms. It was as if the nation's eager pursuit of civilization had involved it in a process whose consequences lay far enough beyond the limit of contemporary vision that they now appeared to be a series of plagues unleashed upon Japan by some force that had not been reckoned with. Although the late Meiji ideologues did not regard cities, enterprise, education, and reading as social ills in themselves, they were nonetheless unprepared for the consequences of their diffusion, especially when these were associated with the breakdown of the agrarian order in the countryside and the emergence of new forms of social conflict in the cities and factories. Confronted with a modernity that threatened to shake the social foundations of

177

the nation, the ideologues turned to the verities of the past—the village and the family, social harmony and communal custom—to cure civilization of its fevers so that society as they envisioned it might yet survive.

THE AGRARIAN MYTH
AND *JICHI*

I

SINCE society as they envisioned it had so much to do with the village, the ideologues turned to the countryside with a fervor that swept many concerns before it. One of its ingredients was a reawakened agrarian vision that set the country against the city in a way that was age-old and, at the same time, up-to-date. As Raymond Williams has described in a study of a similar phenomenon in England, the contrast of city and country is often used to express an unresolved conflict between the experienced present and the remembered or imagined past.[98] Whether the indigenous communal spirit, the alleged simplicity of a natural economy, or just the good old days, the order symbolized by the countryside seemed suddenly to be disappearing. In a country like Japan where agrarian symbols were strong, each generation was wont to feel that the final loss of the rural past was occurring in their lifetime. As village life seemed about to change utterly, it was recalled and exalted as part of a critique of the less congenial present, which was associated with the cities.

In the early eighteenth century Ogyū Sorai, gazing with distaste at Edo, had decried the city as the center of unwelcome "changes in the manners and customs of the times," which then "spread to the peasants in the country."[99] In the late nineteenth century and increasingly after the Russo-Japanese War, late Meiji commentators declared the city to be a "destructive force in society," the origin of evil ways and dangerous thoughts, and the "Rome" dragging the empire into decadence and downfall.[100] Some of the proffered antidotes for urban maleficence even echoed Sorai's wishful proposal that the samurai be relocated in the countryside. Tokutomi Sohō suggested in 1900 that "men of rank and wealth spend a part of the year in the country" to "increase the circulation of social classes" and "cultivate pastoral tastes as in England."[101] Thus, the agrarian myth that had been a pious hope in the eighteenth century was resurrected once again as the ideal image of the social order in the twentieth.

The ideologues contributing to this resurrection were a varied lot,

178

who sometimes had little in common apart from their evocation of the countryside as the source of positive social value. Some *minkan* agrarianists—Maeda Masana in the 1890s, Yokoi Tokiyoshi and Yamazaki Enkichi in the 1900s—were also dedicated agriculturalists, whose careers were spent largely in the service of agronomic education and technical improvements in farming. When they argued, as they did indefatigably, that "agriculture is the foundation of the nation" (*nō wa kuni no moto nari*), they echoed the classical Confucian formulation of agriculture as the root, trade and industry as the branches of the natural economy. But their advocacy further reflected the long years of effort to assure farming a place in an evolving national policy (*kokuze*) that appeared to be leaning increasingly toward industry.

Maeda had championed the agricultural cause from his posts in the Ministry of Agriculture and Commerce (*Nōshōmushō*) in the early eighties and again in the late eighties and early nineties. In the early eighties he had been opposed by Matsukata of the Finance Ministry, who favored support of industry. In the late eighties Maeda's agrarian views fell victim to the political infighting among the oligarchs in advance of the opening of the first Diet. In 1890 Maeda was ousted as vice-minister of agriculture, and Yamagata assigned the position of agriculture minister to Mutsu Munemitsu, the bureaucrat who later condescended to "the three hundred farmers" sitting in the Diet. Two years after Maeda's departure from the Ministry, he embarked on an ideological and organizational crusade as what he professed to be a "private Nōshōmushō." He participated in the establishment of twelve different farming organizations, including the National Agricultural Association (*Zenkoku nōjikai*), and from 1893 to 1897 published the journal *Sangyō*, the "industry" of its title referring to what he called "indigenous manufacturing" (*koyū kōgyō*) of such local and semi-agricultural products as tea and silk. In the late 1890s he led the campaign to encourage villages to produce their own plans (*ze*) based on local facts, not foreign theory, arguing that on the basis of town and village policy (*chōsonze*) a more appropriately agricultural national policy (*kokuze*) might be constructed.[102] His was a struggle, in short, between farm and industry, between the hoe and the machine.

Like Maeda, who was a farming landlord himself, Yamazaki and Yokoi were professionally concerned with agriculture. Both taught in agricultural schools, Yamazaki in Aichi prefecture, Yokoi at the government agricultural college in Tokyo. They were thus agrarianists by trade. Yamazaki described the farmers as "the mother of *fukoku kyōhei* (a rich nation and a strong army)," and "the bulwark of *kokutai.*" He lectured that country people were more virtuous than city people and invoked farming as a sacred calling, adducing as partial proof the fact that after his great success George Washington devoted the rest of his life to the soil.[103] Yokoi argued that farming was the profession best suited to preserve the nation and that *nōgyōdō*, the Way of agriculture, was the heir to bushidō, the Way of the warrior.[104] He suggested that

> Cities are extremely weak in the ability to produce their own population and thus have no recourse but to absorb the population they need from the countryside. This means that cities depend on the country for their existence. Without the country where could the cities obtain the population they require? If the country were somehow to go on strike and resolve no longer to supply any population at all, the population of the cities would become purely urban (i.e., urban children of two urban parents). The birthrate would steadily decline, and at its extreme would dwindle to zero. With one more step, it would be negative, and in the end the cities would be bound to collapse.[105]

The idea of the country's staging a demographic walkout until the cities collapsed was peculiar perhaps to Yokoi. Among the advocates of agrarianism (*nōhonshugi*), a word he is said to have coined in 1897, Yokoi was conservative in the extreme.[106] Yet the extremity of his remarks and those of other *minkan* agrarianists derived in part from the increasingly difficult situation of agriculture. For if farming had been threatened by commerce and industry in the 1880s, in the 1900s it seemed besieged. In its defense the agrarianists propounded an ideology that attempted to persuade both the government and the farmers that the countryside must remain the economic foundation of the state.

At the same time, other commentators were rediscovering in the villages the communal foundations of Japanese national experience that were being undermined by the advance of civilization. Yanagita Kunio, himself a Nōshōmushō bureaucrat from 1900 until 1902, disagreed both with *minkan* agrarianists like Yokoi and also with the central government's bureaucratic policies toward the countryside. Yanagita regarded Yokoi as extreme and anachronistic, and the Home Ministry as administratively manipulative of village life. Yet, as he traveled around the countryside in the 1900s, wearing the traditional straw sandals that Maeda had also worn when he embarked as an agricultural "pilgrim" in 1892, Yanagita was making his own pilgrimage to the cultural "native place" (*kyōdo*) of the Japanese. He and other intellectuals such as Nitobe Inazō combined erudite treatises on agricultural administration and economics with romantic evocations of the countryside as the repository of ancestral custom.[107] Their writings and lectures thus contributed, if unintentionally, to the same agrarian myth that the government was finding useful.

While Yanagita embarked on his folkloric forays into the rural origins of Japanese ethnicity, others invoked village custom for different purposes. The army, though not institutionally inclined to pastoral sentimentalism, praised the "manners and mores of the people" (*ninjō fūzoku*) in the villages remote enough from cities and civilization to have preserved the rustic, simple ways (*junboku na kifū*) of the past.[108] Village conscripts were said to be physically stronger, while the physiques of youth in general, weakened by the sedentary pursuits of education and non-agricultural occupations, were reported to be in continuous decline.[109] Rural youth, especially in the poorer areas, were described as less inclined toward draft evasion of the "unabashed" sort found in the capital. In Tokyo one educated youth "calmly" announced that the poor vision he had claimed probably did not show up at his physical because it varied with his frequency of masturbation, and another just as "coolly" reported "twenty or thirty siblings" from his father's "I don't really know how many mistresses."[110] As "draft evasive behavior" appeared in the countryside, and local people evinced what was described in the post Russo-Japanese War years as new coolness, mistrust, and even dread (*kyō-fushin*) of military service, leading military advocates of social education like Tanaka Giichi of the army called more frequently for the preservation of the disappearing customs of the rural community.[111] Both the Imperial Reservists Association (*Teikoku zaigō gunjinkai*) created in 1910 and the National Youth Association (*DaiNihon seinendan*) established in 1915 depended on a nationwide network of local branches, which Tanaka expected would foster "harmony between the military and the people."[112] For despite the army's constant criticism of the farmers' lack of public spirit (*kōkyōshin*), in contrast to the cities or to those youth corrupted by "citified" ways, the main hope for the military spirit (*gunjin seishin*) appeared to lie in the perpetuation of cooperative custom in the village.

The use of custom, in particular the "manners and mores of the people," as an ideological index of change was itself an established custom. In the early Meiji period, whether in drafting the civil code or debating the Constitution, the preliminary stage of institutional reform was often an inquiry into Japanese custom. It was argued that customary usage must be determined so that the new institutions of civilization could be made consonant with it. The 1879 compendium of social practices that preceded the initial attempts to draft a civil code, for example, contained images of the countryside that derived naturally from Tokugawa times and endured, somewhat unnaturally, into the late Meiji period. "Peasants in general live in their ancestral homes (*sosen denrai no ie*) and rarely change their place of residence," pronounced the report.[113] Although this was not altogether true even in Tokugawa, by the end of Meiji when newspaper columns offering popular advice on legal questions explained "how to register land when A sells to B and B to C," the notion that farmers did not move was more hallowed myth than fact.[114] Nonetheless, the ancestral customs invoked by the late Meiji ideologues often revived such myths to serve as a benchmark against the deterioration of the village order.

Yet, there were differences, too, that were indicative of the changes that had taken place in the attitude toward the villages. In the debates in 1895 over yet another draft of the civil code, the question arose as to *which* customs should become the basis of the marriage and inheritance sections of the law. The conservatives Hozumi Yatsuka and Yokota Kuniomi argued that "the customs of farmers should not be considered customs"; the true and relevant customs were those of the samurai or the nobility.[115] Once the samurai model of the patriarchal family had been adopted, however, Yanagita made a different conservative point, complaining that the more flexible traditional marriage customs of the peasants had been ignored in modern law. "Although we speak of the equality of classes (*shimin byōdō*), we have imitated the samurai in every way possible, and would instead do better to reflect on the virtues of the peasant life of old."[116] And throughout the period customary usage, like social morality, was considered as important as law—and in the case of someone like Yamagata, more important—for holding society together.[117] Hence, when rural society appeared to be threatened, the customs of the farmers rather than those of the samurai were now enshrined by the ideologues as the usages that must be preserved against the encroachment of social change.

If Yanagita's folkish views of village customs unwittingly reinforced those of the agrarianists and the imperial army, other, still stranger bedfellows contributed to the overlapping evocations of the countryside. Disaffected intellectual youth sometimes romanticized the countryside as a pastoral refuge from the emptiness of modern life or looked to it to provide popular energies for reform. In the late 1890s writers such as Tokutomi Roka and Kunikida Doppo had written romantic exaltations of nature, which were widely read by educated youth in the following years. Doppo's famous poem of 1897, "Freedom is found in the mountains and forests," became an emblem of their often Wordsworthian longing.[118] The enthusiasm for Tolstoy in the 1900s brought the virtues of simple peasant life to the minds of young intellectuals, and sometimes even the most urban and urbane writers contributed to the redisovery of the countryside. Tayama Katai, for example, who regarded Yanagita's work as "an extravagance of affected rusticity," produced his own evocations of rural society in such novels as *Furusato (Hometown), No no hana (Flowers of the Field)*, and the account of a late Meiji *Country Schoolteacher (Inaka kyōshi)*.[119] The poet Ishikawa Takuboku wrote of the need for the revival of the countryside, although he, like other social idealists, sometimes despaired of the popular potential for improvement that he sought in provincial society. In 1909 Takuboku, who wrote that he regarded "the awakening of one small village as far more valuable than all the great plans in the heads of the officials," admired the flourishing agricultural activities in Shizuoka and commented disparagingly of his native Iwate prefecture: "In Iwate all they have adopted is the slogans. Even if a young man were to organize a radish fair, there would be no one in Tōhoku capable of continuing the effort."[120]

Such comments among resident intellectuals or temporary émigrés from the cities were generally well-intentioned in comparison to the condescension among government bureaucrats for the farmers whose lives and livelihoods were central to their ideological efforts. Like Sorai's distaste for the cities, this attitude had a long Tokugawa history. What in 1649 had been rendered as "peasants are people without sense or forethought," in 1912 became "farmers are deficient in logical memory, do not like to think, and are unable to grasp concepts."[121] Peasants were said to lack a sense of nation, motivation for progress, adequate powers of observation, and an ability to socialize that was sufficient to civilized times.[122] These attributes were adduced as arguments for the importance of social education for farmers, often when the ideologues were addressing the local elite but sometimes even when speaking to the farmers themselves. The criticisms were coupled with exhortations to more strenuous self-improvement in village mores and family farming, as if such social flagellation would arouse the peasants to abandon their obdurate boorishness and join the march of progress.

This attitude also accounted for the other side of the ideological coin of custom. For at the same time that ideologues insisted that the "simple and beautiful customs of the village be preserved in the face of industrialization," they berated the people for persisting in the backward social practices of the rural past.[123] Since the beginning of the Meiji period, custom reform (*fūzoku kairyō*) had periodically been encouraged in the name of progress. In the early 1870s such traditions as nakedness, wild dances at the mid-summer *o-bon* festival, fox worship, topknots, and horse races were forbidden as part of the "civilization and enlightenment" of the provinces. In the 1880s custom reform was advocated by private organizations like the "haircut clubs" formed in Tokyo to bring feminine coiffures into the Western mode, and meat-eating associations that worked to strengthen Japanese physiques in advance of the residence of foreigners.[124] By the 1900s these and other Western fashions were also appearing in the countryside, where they were opposed by the ideologues as destructive of the beautiful customs of the village. Such high-collar (*haikara*) accoutrements as hats, overcoats, and silk scarves were criticized by Home Ministry and army officials as materialistic and extravagant. And in the post Russo-Japanese War period this evidence of rural civilization and enlightenment became the object of a renewed campaign of custom reform (*fūzoku kyōsei*).[125]

While in these instances the customs in question had been introduced in the course of the Meiji period, in other cases the alleged defects in provincial mores had hardly changed since the Tokugawa. Where once the shogunate has chastised farmers for spending too lavishly at weddings, drinking too convivially at New Year's, and gambling with a heavy hand, now the Home Ministry bureaucrats and local officials urged the organization of "moral reform clubs" (*kyōfūkai*) to rectify the profligacy that such practices encouraged.[126] In addition to criticizing the villagers' penchant for social ostentation, officials compiled lists of time-honored "moral abuses"—"graffiti on the walls and pillars of shrines and temples, nightsoil buckets left on the grounds"—as well as newer transgressions such as "failing to display the flag on holidays" and "village and school holidays not coinciding."[127] Another routine concern was punctuality, in which farmers were said to be particularly deficient. When local "punctuality associations" (*jishukai*) were formed, the Home Ministry praised them. Clocks, which had been quintessential symbols of civilization in the early Meiji period, were regarded as obvious aids to punctuality. Provincial officials thus encouraged them, landlords sometimes mounted them on the gable ends of their houses to make tenants aware of the time as they worked in the fields, and some village plans counted the number possessed by families in the community. Yet, in the 1900s when rural recruits began to appear at the draft physical with gold pocket watches and farmers purchased clocks as "ornaments," the custom reformers betrayed a new ambivalence toward timepieces, inveighing against them on behalf of the spirit of savings (*chochikushin*) and frugality.[128] When a Tōhoku village established "Regulations for custom reform in Ihō village" in 1911, for example, regulation number four was "giving up watches altogether," while number eleven was "punctuality at all gatherings."[129] And whether for want of watches or not, what was regarded as the peasants' customary and unprogressive disregard for time remained a perturbation and sometimes a rationalization for the ideologues. Thus, an army officer in Chiba in 1913 complained that villagers arriving late at youth and Hōtoku association meetings was one reason why the organizations were languishing. He further recorded disdainfully that the elite were even tardy at town and *gun* assemblies, which did not conduce to the working of effective self-government.[130]

A different disdain for the countryside appeared in the urban context, since not everyone in late Meiji Japan was a true believer in the superiority of village life. In addition to Nagai Kafū, whose literary elegies evoked old Edo, there were other intellectuals who hailed the city. Indeed, in an essay on urban planning for Tokyo in 1899, the writer Kōda Rohan roundly criticized his fellow "poets and novelists who tend to treat the city as a sink of iniquity and exalt the hamlet as paradise incarnate."[131] And the tradition of urbane culture and provincial vulgarity (*tohi gazoku*) was an even more venerable cultural value than the agrarian myth.[132]

In terms of ideology, a certain condescension toward the countryside appeared in the social education programs in Tokyo that were briefly supported by the government at the end of the Meiji period.[133] Katō Totsudō, one of the most active lecturers on this circuit in Tokyo and elsewhere, appealed to his urban audience's pride in their native place. In his city lectures, however, the native place was not the village community but plebeian Tokyo, the hometown of Edo. He argued that the customs of old Edo had been destroyed by country bumpkins (*inakamono*). First the samurai rustics from the outlying domains had moved to Tokyo in the 1870s, and more recently country people had come pouring in to work in the factories. Because of them, Tokyo had been "vulgarized" and countrified, losing the "beautiful customs" that properly characterized the capital of Japan. Thus Tokyoites were urged to develop love of city (*aishishin*) and—the concluding exhortation echoing that to their provincial counterparts—reform their customs and make the capital a worthy model for the nation.[134] And while agrarianists appropriated bushidō for the farmer, Katō claimed it for the printer, the draper, and the rickshawman. He argued that Japan had now become a nation of samurai—

the very phenomenon that Yanagita decried—and that the citizens of plebeian Tokyo were now all soldiers, equal in their rights and duties and service to the "glories of the *kokutai*."[135] Native place, beautiful customs, soldiering, and *kokutai*—this urban appropriation of ideological values generally associated with the countryside in itself revealed the pervasiveness of the rural formulations. Indeed, despite these oratorical efforts in Tokyo, the ideological attention to urban Japanese remained half-hearted, overwhelmed by the dominant view of cities as the source of social affliction, whose spread to the villages evoked the greater concern. And the more the cities grew, the more insistent became the ideological fixation on the countryside.

IT WAS AGAINST the background of these intersecting expressions of agrarian value that the ideological offensive against social change took shape in the period after the Russo-Japanese War. The emphasis on the village that seemed to arise from every quarter meant that Shintoists, for example, found a more receptive audience for Shintō's role as an ideological vessel of the state. The Home Ministry initiated the shrine merger movement in 1906 for the sake of unifying village administration and cutting administrative expenses as part of its policies of postwar management. Thus the Shintoists, who had urged their cause for more than thirty years, now became the beneficiaries of a policy that commended the shrines for having "helped to promote public morals and civil administration."[136]

Ancestor worship, like Shintō, also received increasing emphasis in the context of the concern with the village between 1905 and 1915. The legal scholar Hozumi Yatsuka had already contended in 1892 that "ancestor worship (*sosenkyō*) is the source of public law" and repeated in a work for general audiences in 1897 that "ancestor worship is the foundation of Japan's distinctive *kokutai* and of its national morality."[137] At that time, however, Hozumi's contentions were of little relevant interest to other ideologues engaged in fostering a sense of nation. And his assertion thus remained ideologically isolated in much the same way as the earlier claims for attention on the part of the Shintō priests association. But in the 1900s as part of the response to the departure of village youth and the bankruptcy of individual farm families, Nōshōmushō bureaucrats, *minkan* agrarianists, local officials, the Home Ministry, the army, and intellectuals like Yanagita Kunio repeatedly invoked the phrases, "ancestral land," "ancestral property," and "ancestral occupation." Indeed, "ancestral" (*sosen denrai*) was used almost as a pillow word, the Japanese version of the Homeric epithet. Because it seemed invariably to preface the men-

186

tions of land, family property, and farming, it immediately evoked the countryside. Once the economic continuation of the family and the social survival of the village order were at stake, the notion of ancestor worship resonated with these "ancestral" concerns and became more widely established in the ideological landscape.[138]

The concept of the family-state (*kazoku kokka*) reverberated in similar ways. From the 1870s through the 1890s the traditional family (*ie*) had both retained its social centrality and also undergone considerable change. The household received new legal articulation in the Household Register Law of 1871 and the Civil Code of 1898, which strengthened the legal position of the household head in terms of property ownership and social authority. At the same time the family figured in ideology in the form of Confucian renderings of family and society, the emphasis on the imperial line, moral precepts of loyalty and filiality, and the familial relationship expressed in the Rescript on Education.[139] Metaphorical invocation of the family was also standard in ideological usage. The founder of the modern Japanese police, Kawaji Toshiyoshi, had declared in 1876 that "the nation is a family, the government the parents, the people the children, and the police their nursemaids." In his promotion of the local plans (*ze*) in the 1890s Maeda Masana commonly referred to "the autonomy of one town or village as a family." And scholars such as Hozumi Yatsuka and Inoue Tetsujirō developed abstract formulations that compared the *ie* to the Japanese state.[140] There was thus no shortage of attention to the family in the decades before the Russo–Japanese War.

Throughout this earlier period, however, the concepts and customs of the ancestral *ie* had remained the dominant form of familial relations in the countryside. Now the traditional *ie* appeared to be threatened in two ways. First, rural migrants to the cities, especially those of the poorer groups, were increasingly living in conjugal units, sundered both from the kin and the property associated with the existence and continuity of the rural family. One scholar in 1911 labeled these households "small families" to distinguish them from the "large families" of landowning farmers.[141] Without the property, the social stability, and the economic role in the division of agricultural labor, neither the household nor its head possessed the moral or economic authority of the traditional *ie*. In the meantime, among the urban middle classes, what Komatsubara called the "individual-centered" morality of the West was undermining paternal power, as youth set off on their own course, irrespective of family needs or position.[142] Second, and more important to the ideologues, was the appearance of similar changes in the countryside. Family members, generally between the ages of sixteen and thirty-five, were disappearing from home (*iede*), in what one newspaper series on the phenomenon in 1911 entitled "the effect of social disaffection—a revolutionary time in the view of the family."[143] More commonly, the transfer of land from independent owner-farmers to larger landlords meant that the "mainstay owner-farmers" (*chūken jisakunō*), as Hirata Tōsuke had called them in the nineties, either tilled smaller and smaller plots or ended up as tenants, driving from home family members whom they could no longer employ or support.[144] Confronted with this phenomenon, the ideologues declared not only the village, but the nation to be in danger:

> The spiritual blow caused by the destruction of the owner-farmers who constitute the middle class is so profound it is frightening even to contemplate it. In sum, it means, first, the loss of the patriotic spirit, which forms the axis of our national character; second, the penetration of extreme individualism, which is the enemy of nationalism; third, the outbreak of socialism, which execrates those in power. And these three are alike in being inimical to the nation (*hikokkateki*), and together they will destroy our national character.[145]

These were strong words, both for the *Tōkyō asahi* newspaper and for the owner-farmers on whom this burden of patriotism allegedly rested. Yanagita's allusion to "domicide," the killing of the house by migration to the cities, was of similar valence, for he considered this destruction of the family a simultaneous blow to the state.[146] So, too, was the movement among legal scholars in 1910-1912 to enact a Japanese version of a Homestead Act. For if the inalienability of landownership were established, the *ie* would not lose the property that secured it economically and socially to the village and patriotically to the nation.[147] As the traditional rural *ie* seemed to be disappearing, the connection between family and nation was increasingly stressed and the concept of the family-state evolved as much in the name of the family as of the state.

It was also in this context that educators began in the 1900s to emphasize the role of the home (*katei*) in education, in order to enhance the family and the schools at the same time. Presenting the case that "one wise mother is worth ten teachers," a local elementary school notice argued simply but persuasively to parents that since "when children grow up they care for their parents and raise the fortunes of the family (*ie*) as well as exert themselves loyally for the ruler and the country," there is nothing as important as their education. Without education at school and discipline at home, children end up "bringing sorrow to their parents, ruin to the family, and harm to the nation." To prevent these dire consequences, mothers were to "speak to their children of their father's kindness higher than the mountains, and fathers to speak of their mother's bounty deeper than the sea." And both were to help cultivate in their children the virtue of public-spiritedness, an area in which "the Japanese are inferior to Westerners and hence often at a disadvantage in commerce with other nations."[148] The army, too, began to look to the family for discipline and public-spiritedness of a different kind. Military educators argued that young people were being brought up deficient in martial spirit (*shōbu no seishin*). "Conscripts come from families whose rules are not only lax and habits dissolute but who foster misunderstandings about the military that have a baneful effect on military education." To remedy this, the officers argued that the home should be turned from a "destroyer of military education to its supporter." And "since the women secretly possess the real power in the house" and are "the real teachers," the army sought to engage mothers in this effort.[149]

In these and other ways the family became increasingly prominent in discussion. "The home, the home (*katei katei*), everywhere in the country people are paying attention to it now," commented a magazine article in 1906. "Whether one talks of state or society, the foundation is the home, where all social reform must originate." The argument continued that the "spirit of love and duty" was the essence of the authentic meaning of family.[150] Indeed, as the absolute patriarchal authority of the household head ebbed, this appeal to sentiment as the wellspring of obedience was heard more frequently.[151] Lest the family, and with it the village, end up in the world that they had lost, the government and the *minkan* ideologues enshrined these values together at the heart of the nation-state.

II

IN ADDITION to this collective creation of a social ideology to combat social change, the ideologues of the countryside worked toward two further and related ends in the period after the Russo-Japanese War. The first was improvement of agricultural technology and production; the second, the strengthening of the localities so that they could continue to play the administrative and fiscal roles demanded of them by the state. In the first instance, the government implemented farm programs of the sort encouraged by the *minkan* agrarianists in the 1890s. The Home and Agricultural Ministries continued their support of measures designed to bolster the position of agriculturalists.

189

Production cooperatives (*sangyō kumiai*) were initiated under the Nōshōmushō in 1900, the law establishing them supported by two Yamagata men, Hirata Tōsuke and Shinagawa Yajirō, both of whom believed in the social and economic importance of the "mainstay owner-farmer." In 1905 these local organizations were united under Hirata's direction into a central organization and, by 1914, there were 11,160 cooperatives representing ninety percent of the localities nationwide. Similarly, the local agricultural associations (*nōkai*), which tended to be dominated by larger landlords, were codified by law in 1899. In 1910 they were brought under the central umbrella organization of the Imperial Agricultural Association (*Teikoku nōkai*).[152] Dedicated to providing credit and encouraging farm improvements, these agricultural programs were generally implemented with less ideological fanfare than other rural programs undertaken by the Home Ministry in the 1900s.

Government encouragement of the rural Hōtoku societies, for example, employed ideology in equal measure with organizational and technical programs to promote what its leading *minkan* advocate, Tomeoka Kōsuke, ritually called "the harmony of morality and economics."[153] Local Hōtoku societies had been founded by progressive landlords in the early Meiji period. Invoking the example of the Tokugawa agricultural moralist, Ninomiya Sontoku, they encouraged technical improvements and the repayment of virtue (*hōtoku*) through honesty, diligence, and communal cooperation.[154] The Home Ministry began to support these societies in 1903, when Inoue Tomoichi asked Tomeoka to report on the "Influence of Hōtoku in the Localities." Not surprisingly, Tomeoka found that in towns and villages where "the spirit of *hōtoku* is active, the results of self-government are accordingly positive," an assertion that was later supported by the home front actions of Hōtoku societies during the Russo-Japanese War. In the name both of productive agriculture and of harmonious self-government, the Home Ministry encouraged the formation of additional local societies and, true to the government pattern, gathered them together under a central organization, the *Hōtokukai*, in 1906.[155]

The activities of the local Hōtoku societies included lecture meetings, in which peripatetic Home Ministry officials such as Tomeoka, Ichiki, and Hirata spoke about Sontoku, public-spiritedness, agricultural self-help, and the problems of the poor in Britain. Attendance usually numbered in the several hundreds, although the magazine of the central association, *Shimin*, recorded a series of lectures in Hiroshima in 1908 at which the lowest attendance was 6,700 and the highest 12,130.[156] *Shimin* also carried inspirational articles on "Theodore Roosevelt as agricultural reformer" and news of successful rural enterprises like the "egg savings association" in Chiba, which raised chickens to pay school tuition for the two new compulsory years and deposited any surplus in postal savings.[157] Hōtoku society members were often praised by the entrepreneurial elite because they "worked hard, saved money, made sandals at night to earn more money to save, put one quarter of their income into savings, and met monthly to discuss the teachings of Sontoku and methods of cultivation."[158] This sort of circular relation between economics and ethics helped to bring Ninomiya Sontoku into the Monbushō's canon of educational heroes as well. From the 1910 redaction of elementary school textbooks until the end of the Pacific War, Sontoku and the Meiji emperor are said to have been the most frequently mentioned figures.[159] And statues of Sontoku still adorn the grounds of elementary schools in different parts of the country. As for the Hōtoku associations themselves, they appeared to flourish in prefectures like Shizuoka, where they had been strong before the government promoted them, and to remain somewhat less vital in areas where their establishment was artificially induced by the diligent encouragement of prefectural and *gun* officials.[160]

The second postwar objective revolved around the government's attempt to cast its ideological net over the provinces (*chihō*) for the purpose of rousing the localities to more effective administration and fiscal "self-government" (*jichi*). The Home Ministry (Naimushō) assumed the central ideological role, while the army, the Monbushō, and the *minkan* agrarianists sometimes cooperated and sometimes competed in the efforts to "influence" the *chihō*. The word *chihō* was variously defined in agricultural, geographical, or political terms. To Yamazaki Enkichi it meant "the opposite of the cities, a place where farmlands and farmers are numerous and agriculture is conducted."[161] More frequently, it was used to mean any place outside Tokyo—the provinces, as the French use the word. This was sometimes modified to signify the non-urban provincial areas, as when Tomeoka Kōsuke, lecturing in Okayama, corrected his Tokyo-centered definition by adding that of course "when one is in Okayama, *chihō* refers to anything outside Okayama city." "Local improvement (*chihō kairyō*)," he added, "means the reform of the towns and villages. . . . The total number of cities, towns, and villages is 12,566, so that this is the same as saying 'Japan.' "[162] Despite this flattering oratory, it was clear that in Home Ministry usage, while the *chihō* were indeed predominantly rural, the more immediate connotation was the admin-

191

istrative distinction between the center and the localities. The *chihō* lay outside Tokyo, not because the provinces were rural and rustic and Tokyo urban and urbane, but because they were local entities which the national government sought to control and upon which it depended.

Thus the main Naimushō watchword was neither farm nor village but local self-government (*chihō jichi*). The term itself had gained prominence in the late 1880s when it became the basis of the new local government system (*chihō jichi seido*) established between 1888 and 1890. The word *jichi* first entered public language as the Japanese translation of the German *Selbstverwaltung*, or local "self-administration." Its institutional formulation was derived from the theories of the Prussian Rudolf Gneist, which were transmitted to Japan by Albert Mosse after his arrival in 1886 as an employee of the Japanese government.[163] His views received the enthusiastic support of Yamagata, who regarded local self-government, like the conscription system, as a safely apolitical means of national integration—what he called "strengthening the foundations of the state." In his often-quoted speech to the Prefectural Governors Conference in February 1890, Yamagata reiterated his conception of the local government system as

> the foundation of the state, because it gives the localities control over their affairs, within the limits of the law. The establishment of self-governing units and the cultivation of the spirit of *jichi* will train people in the administration of public affairs and enable them to be entrusted with national affairs.

Moreover, and for Yamagata more important as the time of the opening of the Diet drew near,

> whatever political turmoil may arise at the center, the localities will remain undisturbed. They will stand outside the currents of political party strife and thus escape the evils of partiality in their administrative affairs.[164]

In Yamagata's thinking, the local government system was another area of national life from which politics and parties were to be excluded, at the same time that the localities were to be groomed to serve the needs of public administration. Other discussions of *jichi* prior to the promulgation of the Constitution pointed to the dangers inherent in the concept of local self-government. In 1888 Inoue Kowashi wrote that the *chihō* were "the places where the orders of the center do not reach." He warned that unless this situation was remedied institutionally, "local self-government might evolve into demands for national self-government," which "American and British scholars consider another name for a republic." Should this development occur, "it might result one hundred years hence in the destruction of our ancestral *kokutai*."[165] In this sense *jichi* had had a double meaning from the first, for it emphasized the localities' administrative self-governance at the same time that it denied any semblance of political autonomy and tied the *chihō* as closely as possible to the center.

Thus the provincial cities, towns, and villages had long been enjoined to conduct a selfless kind of self-governance, to manage their own fiscal and administrative affairs but to do so always and only in accordance with the needs of the state. Although local political and economic realities had belied this administrative vision from the start, the situation after the Russo-Japanese War appeared to the ideologues to present a crisis of new dimensions. The most pressing issue was economic. In a time of national financial difficulty caused in great part by the costs of war, the localities were called upon not to spend but to retrench, and at the same time not to look to the government for funds but to engage in more effective community self-help. Again—and also at the same time—the localities were expected to continue to perform their allotted national tasks, which included tax collection, draft administration, education, and relief.[166]

In an effort to rouse the localities to meet this considerable challenge, the ideological appeals to "the spirit of *jichi*" took on new fervor. The term itself expanded in meaning. Without losing its earlier institutional meaning of local administration or its ideological implication of apolitical national integration, *jichi* was now extended to include moral exhortations in the name of economic and social programs of local self-improvement. Naimushō bureaucrats—Inoue Tomoichi, Hirata Tōsuke, Ichiki Kitokurō, Tokonami Takejirō, among others—were instrumental in effecting this expansion of usage. Inoue, whose *Jichi yōgi* of 1909 was called the "Bible of Self-Government" when it appeared, spoke of *jichi* as a gift which, like the Constitution, had been bestowed by the emperor. "Through the operation of *jichi*, local administration is perfected, the foundation of the state strengthened, neighborly friendship deepened, and thereby the mores of the country are restored."[167] Specific functions of self-government enumerated in the "bible" were police and fire protection; the administration of "influence" (*kyōka*), which included schools and social education, and of "morals" (*fūki*), which ranged from children's curfews and the encouragement of savings to promoting "amusements appropriate to the progress of civilization"; the administration of relief for the poor and the sick; the administration of public health, both through preventive and ameliorative measures; construction and maintenance of transportation facilities; encouragement of agriculture in the form of side-employments, farmers clubs, and credit unions; and, finally, financial administration.[168] In their discussions of *jichi*, Inoue and other Naimushō bureaucrats made constant reference to examples of self-government in the West and often traveled abroad, searching for relevant foreign models of local administration in such places as the garden cities of Britain, the peasant areas of Lombardy, and the "agricultural city of Chicago," for which the Ministry predicted "a bright future." In Home Ministry guides to provincial reform, agrarian references to the Tokugawa villages of Ninomiya Sontoku appeared side by side with comparisons between Paris and the provinces, the reconstruction of the city of Cleveland, and the like.[169]

In their compendia of the tasks of *jichi*, Home Ministry ideologues nearly always invoked the Russo-Japanese War as a time in which, in Inoue's words, "a sense of nation, a spirit of public service (*hōkō-shin*) and cooperation (*kōkyōshin*) had prevailed."[170] And, according to Tokonami,

> the period of greatest progress of *jichi* was during the war against Russia. . . . Whether in meeting military expenses or in home front support, everyone in the country worked in complete unity (*kyokoku itchi*). Not only military matters but local affairs such as tree planting and savings that are not satisfactorily carried out in ordinary times were undertaken even in the midst of that busy period. Postal savings had amounted to 5,600,000 yen before the war, but since the war they have sharply increased and have now risen above a hundred million. I think that the people then were imbued with the sense that if they did not consolidate hamlet finances or plant trees, we could not win against Russia . . . it is wholly a result of *jichi* that the Japanese resolved to take charge of national affairs.[171]

Taking charge of national affairs was indeed the issue, for as Tokonami argued,

> the country and the localities are like parent and child. When the children are young and can do nothing for themselves, the parents must care for them until they are about ten. But gradually, as the years pass, the children become able to take care of themselves. . . . The relation between national government and the *chihō* is exactly the same . . . as the country acquires civilization, society grows complicated, and the government's tasks have increased. Thus it divides these tasks among the provinces and makes the localities perform what they can.[172]

These local tasks were clearly stated in Tokonami's lectures: "*jichi* is the foundation of the state," and "tax collection is the local citizen's highest duty."[173] According to this definition towns and villages were declared "delinquent" and *jichi* said to be "in disarray," when they were afflicted with "local officials of poor quality, inferior tax collection, improperly tended land, and party strife." To remedy such delinquency, which was "harmful to the development of the nation," the ideologues urged that *jichi* be perfected and the national duties thus fulfilled.[174]

At the same time that Naimushō ideologues emphasized the national duties of local administration, the term *jichi* was increasingly used both by bureaucrats and others to represent not only effective fiscal management but also the social harmony and cooperation associated with the idealized village community. This was particularly true in the exhortations of the *minkan* agrarianists, whose main interest lay as much with the village as with the state. Yamazaki Enkichi compared "local figures" (*chihōteki jinbutsu*) to their "national" counterparts. Local citizens "remain in their native place, thus securing the foundation of the nation; they continue in their ancestral occupations and do not fail to perform the ancestral rites." They were thus as much responsible for "progress and development" as those who left the village in pursuit of fame or fortune.[175] Like Yanagita and Yokoi, Yamazaki did not share the Naimushō's enthusiasm for administrative tidiness, the late Meiji result of which was the merger of shrines, villages, and common forestlands, often without regard for hamlet identity or the usages of custom. Yanagita objected to the shrine mergers, and Yokoi warned localities of the disadvantages of being designated a "model village" by the Home Ministry, since the expenses of entertaining visitors strained village resources to no good cause.[176] The concern of these men for the village led them to less bureaucratic solutions for its problems than those advocated by the Naimushō.

As the accompanying illustration reveals, Yamazaki's rendering of what resembles an agrarian mandala placed agriculture at the center of the nation. "The contentment of cooperation, cultural flourishing, collective advancement, the perfection of *jichi*"—these elements would contribute to the "establishment of the village." Although all the local institutions, from schools to markets to public works, were pictured as part of the larger framework of "national progress" and "social welfare," the central government was nowhere included.[177]

Jichi means, just as it reads, to govern oneself by oneself. . . . Village *jichi* therefore means that the village works to promote its own interest

195

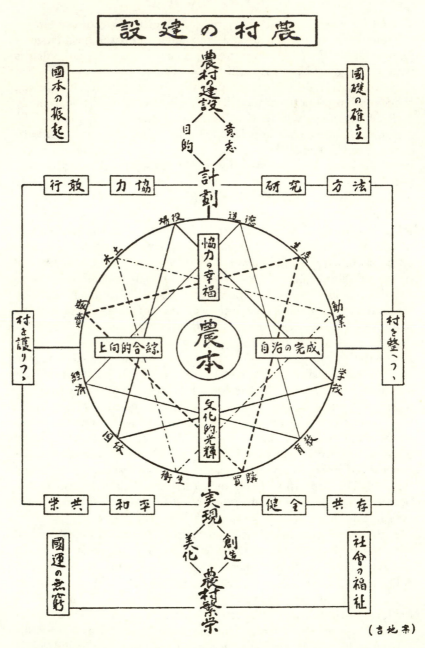

"Construction of a Village": portraying the social, economic, administrative, and moral aspects of agriculture, "the foundation of the nation." (Yamazaki Enkichi, "Nōson kensetsu," 1927)

196

(*rieki*). By itself the village operates to advance its happiness; it undertakes its own progress and advances its own development. It goes without saying that the village must itself enhance its domain.[178]

In such invocations of self-reliant local communities *jichi* sometimes appeared as part of a mystical panacea for the problems of rural Japan, which hinted at a kind of communal autonomy independent of the hierarchical bureaucratic state. Thus, between the bureaucrats and the agrarianists—with reinforcement from military educators and the increasing number of officials who worked in the institutions of "self-government"—*jichi* gradually became the *kokutai* of local government, a notion that could be invoked to many purposes because it accommodated many meanings. And just as *kokutai* signified the ideological essence of the nation, *jichi* stood as a public sign of the countryside.

THE PERFECTION of *jichi*, and with it the securing of the village, required local institutions and local leaders. Each of the bureaucratic agents of rural ideology—the Army, the Home, Education, and Agriculture Ministries—turned to one type of institutional mechanism and one stratum of local leaders. The institutional solution was nearly always a local organization (*chihō dantai*). The Local Improvement Movement (*chihō kairyō undō*), formally initiated by the Home Ministry in 1909, had among its goals "improvement of the affairs of *jichi*, financial reorganization, the development of the economy and production, establishment of institutions of moral education and custom reform, and encouragement of savings."[179] And in nearly every case the means to these social, economic, and ideological ends was an association. Thus, in 1911, Ujimura, in Okayama, one of the hundred designated "model villages," listed the village's voluntary organizations as examples of its achievements in creative collectivity:

Thrift and Savings Union (*Kinken chochiku kumiai*)
Agricultural Association (*Nōkai*)
Custom Reform and Youth Association (*Kyōfū seinenkai*), with its subsidiary, the Custom Reform Youth Association Evening School Club
Household Head Association (*Koshukai*)
Women's Association (*Fujinkai*)
Shiminkai
Hōtokukai
Reservists Association (*Zaigō gunjinkai*)
Martial Association (*Shōbukai*)
local membership in national organizations, including the Patriotic Women's Association (*Aikoku fujinkai*) and the Red Cross.[180]

Also in 1911, a Toyama village plan laid detailed claim to a

Self-government Association (*Jichikai*)
Agricultural Association (*Nōkai*)
Landlord Association (*Jinushikai*)
Buddhist Youth Circle (*Shūtokukō*)
Youth Association (*Seinendan*)
Middle School Alumni Association (*Kōyūkai*)
Martial Virtue Veterans Association (*Shōtoku dōsōkai*)
Boshin Women's Club (*Boshin fujinkai*)
Martial Association (*Shōbudan*)
School Cooperative (*Gakkō kumiai*)
Production Cooperative (*Sangyō kumiai*)
Industrial Cooperative (*Kōgyō kumiai*)
Education Association (*Kyōikukai*)
Respect for the Aged Association (*Keirōkai*).[181]

In addition to these organizations, most of which were standard, other localities supported *Boshinkai*, dedicated to the promotion of morality and economics as dictated in the Boshin Rescript; innumerable custom or moral reform associations (*Kyōfūkai*); special interest groups like the "club for purchasing new fishing boats" in Hyōgo prefecture; and miscellaneous associations like the "Prince Shōtoku circle" near Hakodate, which had begun in 1902 with only 50 members but in 1911 reported an "increase to 230 after the promulgation of the Boshin Rescript and the encouragement of 'local improvement.' "[182]

Although the bureaucratic ideologues referred most frequently to the organizational effectiveness of the home front during the Russo-Japanese War, the associations of which they spoke were largely of earlier origin. Some, such as youth associations and the religious circles, had Tokugawa antecedents. Others—for example, the custom reform clubs and farm associations, including the Hōtoku societies—often dated from the 1870s. The education associations began to appear around the country in the 1880s and school alumni groups in the late 1880s and 1890s. At this time, too, it was common for youth groups to change their names from the earlier *wakamono-gumi* to the more modern *seinenkai*, or *seinendan*. Credit and production cooperatives were products of the 1890s and 1900s, and the various martial groups emerged in number after the Sino-Japanese War. It was because of this existing basis of flourishing voluntary associations that the government was able to create national organizational hierarchies with such apparent ease. The prior existence of these groups, however, also meant that the establishment of prefectural and central um-

198

brella organizations alone did not guarantee homogeneous institutional performance throughout the country. Such quasi-governmental organizations—or half-*kan*, half-*min*, as Ishida Takeshi has labeled them—required considerable time and orchestrated bureaucratic effort before they functioned in anything close to the local form indicated on the organizational chart at the center.[183]

The *seinendan*, or youth associations, typified the pattern, both in their late Meiji phase and their later evolution. Like so many other programs promoted after the Russo-Japanese War, the modern form of the youth association owed its origins to *minkan* ideologues, in this case the particular efforts of Yamamoto Takinosuke. Having written a treatise on "Rural Youth" (*Inaka seinen*) in 1896 and another entitled "Local Youth" (*Chihō seinen*) in 1904, Yamamoto was known for his active support of youth groups. When Home Minister Yoshikawa Akimasa returned from a provincial tour in 1905 impressed by the wartime work of local youth organizations, he had Inoue Tomoichi seek Yamamoto's counsel on the matter.[184] The combination of Yamamoto's activism and the government's postwar concerns with the countryside led eventually to the establishment of the National Youth Association (*DaiNihon seinendan*) in 1915, with the support, for different and not always mutual reasons, of the Home and Education Ministries and the army.

In 1906 the Education Ministry took up the issue of local youth associations, while the Home Ministry revealed its own concerns in a directive that was later released under the title, "*Chihō jichi* and youth associations." In 1907 Education Minister Makino spoke to the prefectural governors on the reform of *seinendan*; in 1908 Home Minister Hirata addressed them on the same subject. In 1910 the government was questioned on *seinendan* policy in the House of Peers, and Minister of Education Komatsubara announced the first Monbushō awards to *seinendan* for "excellence in supplementary education." Hirata, who was still Home Minister, issued a directive at the Prefectural Governors Conference warning against *seinendan* abuses, and both Education Minister Komatsubara and Vice-Home Minister Ichiki addressed the All-Japan Youth Association meeting in the same year. In 1911, in the wake of the Great Treason Incident, the Education Ministry included the *seinendan* as an important mechanism of social education, and the Home Ministry made its own awards to *seinendan* selected for "excellence in the practice of *jichi*."[185] In 1914–1915 Tanaka Giichi and Terauchi Masatake argued the army's case for a national youth association, partly by referring to the fact that "all the European powers are now engaged in an effort to cultivate youth, and we are falling behind in this." More to the point was Tanaka's contention that just as the Reservists Associations were charged with continuing military education for men from the ages of twenty to forty, so must the army have some way of reaching young men from the time they left school at twelve or thirteen until the age of conscription at twenty.[186]

Each source of support for the *seinendan* had its own institutional interests, and cooperation among them was sometimes strained. While Yamamoto Takinosuke frequently referred to the British Boy Scouts—"each day a good deed" and the like—Tanaka Giichi argued for the necessity of physical training, military drill, and "guiding the thought of the *kokumin*."[187] The prominence of Yamagata's protégés among the supporters of the *seinendan* meant that the youth associations possessed an avowed ideological purpose in addition to their educational, local, or military activities. But the influence of such a powerful oligarchic mentor, whose own concern with the "minds and hearts of youth" had been well established in the early 1880s, did not guarantee smooth cooperation among bureaucratic branches in the 1910s. The Home and Education Ministries issued frequent joint directives and did occasionally suggest a division of labor, in which the regulations and educational activities of the *seinendan* came under Monbushō jurisdiction, and the relation between the youth associations, local government, and the local elite belonged under Naimushō purview.[188] Since there was likely to be only one youth group in a given village, however, this division was more form than fact. Moreover, the combined opposition of the two civil ministries, the press, and the Diet to the army's militarizing activities resulted in the establishment by the army of an independent military training system for youth in 1926. In the meantime the local *seinendan* increased their membership until, by 1935, forty percent of the nation's eligible youth were enrolled, although as with other national networks of local organizations—including the reservists—participation was always markedly higher in the countryside than in the city.[189]

The ideological aspects of the *seinendan*, as well as of other organizations such as the reservists and the agricultural associations—which served more specific and less divided institutional purposes—were frequently subsumed under the category of social education (*shakai kyōiku*). In the post-Russo-Japanese War period the Ministry of Education briefly used the term popular education (*tsūzoku kyōiku*), and the army sometimes preferred the phrase military education (*guntai kyōiku*), but the common meaning was the effort to "influence" sections of the population who were otherwise out of range of such state institutions as the schools and the army.[190] Nearly every one of the local organizations had "enterprises of social education" as part of its charge. In the villages this usually involved supplementary education, in the form of lecture meetings (*kōshūkai*) on everything from the spirit of reverence for the gods (*keishin no seishin*) to the organized disposal of trash (*kuzumono seiri*), as well as extended programs of evening school.[191] One particularly enterprising *minkan* advocate of social education even suggested that "morning schools" be established for ladies of the night, although the more common educational target was rural youth in their teens and twenties.[192]

For a short time after the Russo-Japanese War, the Home and Education Ministries extended a portion of this ideological attention to the city and supported social education for the general populace (*ippan na minshū*), or the common people (*shomin*), of Tokyo. Impelled first by the urban unrest in 1905-1906 and then, with greater force, by the Great Treason Incident of 1910-1911, the government began to apply similar techniques of social education to the capital as it did to the *chihō*. In 1910 Home Minister Hirata Tōsuke, one of Yamagata's closest protégés at the time, called for "national character education" (*kokumin kun'iku*) and offered subsidies for popular storytelling and lecture meetings sponsored by the Tokyo Education Association.[193] The *Miyako shinbun*, then the widely read newspaper of plebeian Tokyo, commented in 1911:

> The Ministry of Education is working hard these days to hold popular lecture meetings and such. The point is this: in commoner society (*heimin shakai*), we are not yet up with civilized times. Trapped by harmful customs and mores, as the years pass we are increasingly unable to meet present-day tasks and make progress as our children do. The Ministry is concerned that just as the children are being taught, we should receive some guidance as well.
>
> Since the Great Treason Incident the Home Ministry is emphasizing the education of the common people (*shomin kyōiku*). Apart from its efforts to spread the concept of reverence for gods (*keishin shisō*), it is considering and implementing surveys of the poor (*hinmin*) and reform of the "special hamlets" [of the former outcaste class].[194]

Between 1910 and 1914 popular lecture meetings flourished in Tokyo, and in the peak year of 1912 it was recorded that 32,000 people attended sixty functions, which amounted to four people per one hundred households in the fifteen wards of the city.[195] These included general gatherings as well as special lectures for merchants and businessmen, and a program for the poor (*saimin*) and the lower classes

201

of downtown Tokyo. "Popular education" was described by its supporters as more interesting than "education that had the smell of education" and hence capable of exerting "a good influence on people without their realizing it."[196] Yet, this painless education turned out to be more attractive when the patriotic and hortatory sermons were accompanied by magic-lantern shows and, increasingly, motion pictures. When lectures alone were held, between three and four hundred people attended, but when the dose of "influence" was sweetened with entertainment, more than twice that number showed up.[197] Whether or not this kind of suasion was effective in the plebeian sections and slums of Tokyo, the government withdrew its subsidies for urban lecture meetings in the early Taishō period, a result in part of the fickleness of its ideological concern for the cities. Also important, however, in the lack of concerted interest in the cities was the absence of a readily available stratum of local urban leaders who could serve as community custodians of ideology.

For the fact remained that ideological efforts, both *minkan* and government, still depended in the post-Russo-Japanese War years, as they had since early Meiji times, on the presence of a local elite. The "provincial men of influence"—*yūshisha, yūryokusha, chihō meibōka, tokushika*—were referred to by the ideologues in various ways but nearly always with the same implication of impartial, generous, and selfless service to the locality. Yamagata's definition of the provincial elite had emphasized apolitical service to the community. In Yamagata's plans for local government in the 1880s, the *chihō meibōka* figured as the village mainstays who would occupy unsalaried local office and administer *jichi* while remaining aloof from party politics. But some *meibōka* had now become Diet members and joined political parties, and others were trafficking with party leaders like Hara Kei, who expanded the influence of the Seiyūkai by trading promises of government funds for local projects in exchange for the *meibōka*'s support of the party.[198]

Although political abstinence soon proved an unrealistic demand on the local elite, the more common and more accurate description alluded to their high social and economic status in the community. In 1889 definitions of local notables included such statements as "the *yūshisha* are people with capital." They "have influence in the provinces as a result of land, family status, or wealth. Or, if they are without wealth or family, they possess some learning. And because they have no land, they then make a success elsewhere and return. These, too, are *meibōka*."[199] The notables were further described as generous both with their money and their community spirit. In 1890

202

yūshisha were praised for such public service as donations for school construction, for school fees for poor children, for social succor on the occasion of a rice riot, and for building "a splendid public meeting hall that mixed Japanese and Western styles and was the best in the prefecture."[200] Local men of influence were also described as concerned with the education of their fellow villagers, participating, as the diarist and landlord son Aizawa did, in Associations for Development and Cooperation (*Hattatsu kyōwakai*) to further the fortunes of their fellow villagers and the village as a whole.[201] In socioeconomic terms the local notables were landlords, often wealthy peasants (*gōnō*) of the early Meiji period, who survived the deflation in the 1880s and accumulated land in the process. They had been the local supporters of "encouragement of industry" (*shokusan kōgyō*) in the seventies and had expanded their own financial horizons, first into provincial commercial activities, and then, in the 1890s and 1900s, into urban capital investment and securities. As they did, their ties to the village loosened, so that by the post-Russo-Japanese War period, the ideological definition of the local elite had also changed, lest the elite in question be insufficiently "local."[202]

It is true that in the 1900s the Home Ministry continued its appeal to the wealthier landlords. They were urged to solicit contributions from their peers instead of using public funds for victory celebrations during the war or for excessive construction of schools and public works during the period of stringent postwar management.[203] Ideologues encouraged—and sometimes flattered—these provincial plutocrats, implying that their public good works, because they were performed by the people (*min*), had a value beyond those undertaken by the government. When a prominent public-spirited landowner in Shizuoka prefecture, Kinbara Meizen, donated trees for a barren section of imperial forest, the trees he planted were reported to be thriving, while the Imperial Forest Bureau's saplings died. In addition to praising Kinbara's spirit of repaying virtue (*hōtoku*), the magazine *Shimin* reported that "tasks performed by the government (*kan*) always cost more than private undertakings (*mingyō*) and the results are not as good."[204]

Social munificence as great as Kinbara's, which was said to run to tens of thousands of yen, was not available in every locality, and as local needs expanded in cost and complexity, ideologues began to broaden their definition of local leadership. Inoue Tomoichi invoked the Confucian notion of exemplary moral action: "with one man's virtue, the improvement of the whole village." He contributed speeches and articles on the "beautiful enterprises of 'local benefactors' (*chihō tokushika*)."[205] But praise of the benefactors was increasingly joined by mentions of village figures who contributed in other ways: the mayor—wealthy or not—the elementary school principal, local officials, small landlords, police, teachers, reservists, Shintō priests, and Buddhist monks.[206] Along with the landed notables of old, now such petty functionaries as schoolteachers became the recipients of Home Ministry awards for achievements "in the fields of *jichi*, custom reform, influence, and economics."[207] This was different both from the earlier period and from the models suggested by "the American *yūshisha* (man of influence), Andrew Carnegie."[208]

Yet, the expansion of the definition of the local elite notwithstanding, late Meiji ideologues often suggested that in the ideal scheme of things, the village mayor would possess sufficient wealth and influence to serve as mayor, honorary chairman of the *seinendan*, the reservists association, the agricultural association, and still generate sufficient income to make financial donations to the appropriate causes. But since the same wealthy landed and increasingly non-resident rural class was called upon by each of the central sources of ideological activity, as well as by the political parties and the notables' own personal and local connections, the "local elite" of the old style often could not fulfill the range of tasks allotted to them. For the early Meiji model of self-generated local beneficence was no longer capable of meeting the demands of an increasingly complex state, in which society, the localities, and the *meibōka* as well were fast outgrowing the village community of the past.

IDEOLOGIES OF STRIVING
AND SUCCESS

LATE MEIJI ideologues attempted to secure the countryside by reinvoking the values and customs of the past to serve the ever more complicated present. In the post-Russo-Japanese War years these efforts intensified and diversified, generating both the ideological substance and the institutional forms of an official social ideology for years to come. The official ideology of rural folk and family, however, was not established smoothly, nor was it the only one available to the late Meiji villager. From his perspective, both the substance and the process appeared somewhat different.

Local officials and landlords sometimes regarded the Home Ministry as meddlesome, with its "gratuitous advice" (*yokei na sewa*) on merging village shrines and common lands. In some parts of the country its programs were protested by the villagers in demonstrations against government interference in local customs and livelihood.[209] Provincial editors commented that "the farmer is the victim of the city" and criticized the government for too little "attention of the sort that would bring telephones and water systems to the localities."[210] Suggestions on "how to save the *chihō*" commonly ran to tax relief for the burdened villagers and "heavier assessments on the cities where capital concentrates."[211] Ideological programs of the government were sometimes rebuffed, as when the prefecture cut its appropriation for the Naimushō's Local Improvement program in half from 1,200 to 600 yen in Yamanashi in 1915. The assemblyman who protested the appropriation stated that "most of us are from the area (*chihō*) and work day and night toward the advancement of *chihō jichi* . . . broadly speaking, most of the prefectural budget is for Local Improvement (*chihō kairyō*)," and, he concluded, there was thus no reason to set such a sum aside especially for this purpose.[212]

On the village level the Home Ministry programs sometimes engendered conflict at the same time that they called for harmony and cooperation. This was particularly true when retrenchment in capital expenditures was urged. Since retrenchment occurred in the budget of the administrative village, the debates over cutbacks were deflected to the hamlet level, as hamlets wrangled over the location and funding of the schools, roads, and public works.[213] When these disputes occurred, Home Ministry officials and military officers blamed them on the contentiousness of "*chihō meibōka* of the second and third rank," whose fixation on "their own narrow community interest betrayed a distressing lack of cooperative spirit."[214] The local press was more apt to blame the low quality of the officials of *jichi* on an excessively centralized bureaucracy: "The government appoints university graduates as county heads (*gunchō*) and academically inclined people as village mayors. And the people are not involved in selecting their own leaders."[215] The villagers, for their part, protested fraud and corruption on the part of local officials both by petition and demonstration.[216] And the ideologues, who had invoked local pride to urge the local elite to build schools and roads in the eighties and nineties, now rigorously chastised them for competing with one another in local accomplishment.[217] Thus the supposed harmonies of *jichi* were constantly challenged by the press of local politics and interests.

Just as the government was not wholly in control of the local self-government system, it also had less than omnipotent influence in the local associations. The *seinendan* and local reservist branches, many of which were newly established in the early 1910s, were criticized by the press and district military officers for "existing in form in Hiroshima prefecture but not in substance, except to compete for which association will hold the largest number of meetings." Or again, in Okayama, "*seinendan* exist but they are self-centered (*jiko hon'i*); few come to the meetings and those who do, arrive late." And, it was commonly remarked, "without food and liquor," attendance was next to nil.[218] The efficacy of ideological communication was also questioned. In the same local poll in 1913 where the Rescript on Education was little known, the Boshin Rescript, which the ideologues had fervently promoted in social education and local organizations since 1908, fared even worse. Of 1,343 graduates of upper primary school of conscript age, "those who could give a rough explanation of the Boshin Rescript and recite from it" amounted—as the writer departed from his customary mathematical percentages and resorted to words to express his chagrin—to "only a single person" (*tada hitori arishi nomi*).[219] Such evidence of less than full ideological compliance does not suggest that the ideologues worked in vain, but that their effectiveness was not necessarily always what it appeared to be in their speeches and directives.

More important than this negative evidence, however, was the manifestation among late Meiji Japanese of what might be called an alternative social ideology to the official one of collective cooperation within the family and the community. This congeries of attitudes toward education, employment, and rising in the world (*risshin shusse*) amounted to a social ideology of success that enjoined not cooperative community spirit but personal striving and brandished the language not of social harmony but of the Darwinian struggle for survival (*seizon kyōsō*).

The goal of rising in the world was scarcely a new one. Its modern form was as old as the Meiji program of civilization and enlightenment, its Tokugawa antecedents as venerable as the neo-Confucian principle of the samurai and the bourgeois profit of the commoner. But the course of "lofty aspiration" (*seiun no kokorozashi*) in the Meiji period had not run smooth, and the decades since the Restoration had seen several transformations in the nature of the dreams dreamt by Meiji youth.[220] This was particularly true of elite youth, who had early responded to the promise of "civilization" with visions of themselves as statesmen and other figures of great fame and fortune. Easily persuaded of the link between education and success, their numbers swelled the ranks of students who "went up to Tokyo" in the 1880s.[221] By the nineties their goals had begun to include a greater emphasis on material success, often of a less grandiose sort. One sixteen-year-old scion of a *gōnō* family confided to his diary in 1890: "My goal is already decided. I will become rich, and the means to this end is agriculture." Although he contemplated "making a million" in Hokkaido, the avenue to agronomic riches still led through higher education in Tokyo. His father periodically scolded him for bookishness and in one fit of anti-scholastic pique "threw my beloved *Hakkenden* into the privy." The young man survived the loss of Bakin's *Biography of Eight Dogs* and went on, not to make a million in Hokkaido but to become a pillar of the local community. After the Russo-Japanese War, while he was still in his thirties, he became leader of the credit cooperative and mayor of the town.[222]

It was just at this time, however, that his counterparts in the next generation were facing a greater diminution of opportunity, as the employment difficulties (*shūshokunan*) of the postwar years shrank their hopes and lowered their sights. Employment guides counseled middle school graduates not to scorn low-status jobs in banks, post offices, and even the police. Anticipating a negative reaction to this last recommendation, one guide soothed the social pretensions of educated youth:

> But do not worry; middle school graduates do not end up as patrolmen. They become such things as inspectors, the "imperial princes" of the police force. Being a patrolman, however, is the first step, like going to school. . . . Think of it as going to school while earning a salary.[223]

This consoling metaphor of further education to ease the pain of lowly employment was of little use to graduates of higher schools and universities who were experiencing similar setbacks in mobility. In a series of articles devoted to the issue of the "educated idle," Abe Isoo offered three suggestions, each more exotic than the last: establish a small independent business, like one Waseda graduate who was prospering in wood and charcoal; go to the countryside, which lacks "knowledge and brains," and flourish like the law graduate of Kyoto Imperial University who took up farming in Izu; go to America, a surpassing place to make money, and become an automobile driver. This job only seems beneath a university graduate by Japanese standards; in America they are democratic (*heiminteki*) and do not make such distinctions.[224] So saying, Abe and many others attempted to spur youth whose heads were full of themselves and Tolstoy to succeed in late Meiji times, of which the much-repeated refrain of the popular song complained, "Ah! It's a money world!"[225]

Few, however, decried this materialism in the manner of a Home or Education Ministry bureaucrat. Instead the literature of success proposed ways to get along in "the money world," while advancing a rung or two on the social and economic ladder. And if this applied to the small number of overeducated, underemployed middle class elite, it was even more true of ordinary youth. Since they had not aspired to be "officials and scholars" in the first place, they had little aversion to the business enterprise (*jitsugyō*) that by the 1900s was widely promoted as the "safest and easiest" route to rising in the world. More and more of the seemingly countless employment guides—or sometimes, "gospel for job seekers"—were directed toward youth of poor family with an elementary school education, or even with no formal schooling at all. Their low estate, they were told in simple, but inspirational language, was an advantage:

> You are fortunate indeed. Look. Many rich men's sons squander the legacy of their ancestors in idleness . . . lose the family property . . . and end up like beggars. And if you look at those who have succeeded in past or present, most are youth from poor families. . . . You at least are free of extravagance and loose living and are well able to endure hardship. You probably don't realize that Heaven gave you these virtues instead of lending you the fees for education—you are in the happiest position in the world.[226]

It is doubtful that either writer or reader quite believed this, since the rest of these guides inevitably consisted of copious advice on how to escape from this happy heavenly allotment.

Elementary school graduates who wanted the highest salary were urged—without apology—to become policemen, wardens, streetcar conductors, postmen, and in nearly every case, factory workers, preferably at the government arsenal in Tokyo, where "since people are always quitting, there are usually openings." Job-seekers in the cities were advised not to look down on day labor as a way to an eventual full-time factory position, and provincial youths who had come to the capital to find their fortune were warned in almost Dickensian tones against employment agencies that specialized in fleecing countryfolk. On the other hand, youths of a commercial bent were counseled to go to the countryside and practice a little fleecing of their own, peddling secondhand shoes to people who had not thought of buying them or, "since the people of Meiji are many," selling food, "which is always a safe business." Teaching, nursing, and working as telephone operators were mentioned for young women, but factory girl (*jokō*) was the nearly universal recommendation. In guides designed as "factory bibles" or "women's sutras," the girls were told to send their money home, which would raise the fortunes of their families, and to obey the factory rules, since "in four or five years you will be married, and the experience of following rules will help you as a bride." And for those seeking the "four roads to success" without paying education fees, the choices were the military, small business, working their way through school, or taking a job at a low salary and persevering. In all these recipes for *risshin shusse*, tilling the ancestral lands was an ingredient conspicuous in its absence.[227]

Also absent was talk of community and concord. Giving proof to the comment by a lecturer to an erudite audience that "everyone today is talking and writing about the struggle for survival (*seizon kyōsō*), even the proverbial four-year-olds all know about it," the popular literature of success was replete with references to the "battlefield of *seizon kyōsō*."[228]

> In this age of the struggle for survival, as civilization expands, so does the struggle. Those who live in this society must progress with progress. One day spent in idleness is a day behind. Once behind the progress of society, a person cannot catch up, but remains a weakling in the struggle for survival. In other words, he is not a man like other men.[229]

"Civilization," like society, was said to be "truly complicated, and in the end only the fittest survive (*yūshō reppai*)." Napoleon was cited for his keen understanding that "competition is the basis of progress," which only the individual's strong will and healthy body could withstand.[230]

In the 1890s, when the struggle for survival had been among nations, Momotarō of the fairy tale was transformed into a boy who slew the demons "for the sake of our country." Now in the 1900s the struggle for survival was "among classes and among individuals," and Momotarō once again struck out on his own to bring back the treasure.[231] Small wonder then that commentators accused those who, like the Peach Boy, seemed to forget the greater good of village and empire of an unbecoming "ordinariness" (*heibonshugi*). For "rather than loving their nation, they think it more important to love money and their families" and "are content to make a good home and lead a peaceful life, extremely ordinary and as pleasurable as possible."[232]

Thus the late Meiji Japanese were heir to a wider range of social meanings than the ideologues dispensed or could control. Moreover, in this respect the ideologues had themselves been guilty of dispatching contradictory messages. Advocating the harmony of morality and economics, they had legitimized economic goals even as they emphasized moral conduct. For they argued that morality—or bushi-dō—was the best means to material success, and they praised *Self-help* as an ethics text to "elevate the minds of the students."[233] Although scholars like Inoue Tetsujirō belatedly attempted to separate virtue (*toku*) from wealth (*tomi*), the two had been linked too long and too insistently to be rent apart. In his criticism of the aggressive "go! go!-ism" (*yareyareshugi*) that characterized society in recent years, Inoue invoked the samurai discipline and restraint of the Tokugawa era.[234] But he neglected the folk morality of the same period that had joined moral worth and economic benefit and indeed produced the very Ninomiya Sontoku of whom Home Ministry officials and others were so fond.

Similar contradictions were evident in the materials used in the crusade for social education in the period after the Russo-Japanese War. The "educational storytelling" (*kyōiku kōdan*) sponsored by the Home and Education Ministries in downtown Tokyo and elsewhere laced traditional narrative tales of Edo commoner horse sense with didactic digressions about the latest conveniences of civilization. When the protagonist's shop burns down and leaves him penniless, the narrator explained that "in the old days there were no banks or fire insurance companies" to protect him against the loss. Unable to raise the capital for a new shop, Kichibei, as he was called, works as a palanquin bearer, thus providing the opportunity to recount the history of transportation from palanquins to airplanes. And when, as is inevitable in a townsman's tale, the talk turns to the importance of money, the dialogue sounds like the lyrics of "Ah! It's a money world." In another popular *kōdan* of the same genre, a more forceful protagonist named Jinbei stalks financial success like one of Saikaku's merchant millionaires. Entitled "The Horse's Sandals: The Rise of a Young Man," the tale follows the poor country boy from Mikawa who, unable to afford straw sandals, picks up a horse's discards. He then makes his way to Edo, where with "frugality and saving, he amasses capital," a "self-made youth" (*seinen no risshi*) of the old school. But what was the late Meiji audience to make of a hero so parsimonious that he picks up orange peels on the street and sells them to the apothecary, or refuses to light a lamp in his entryway, thus forcing his guests to stumble around in the dark looking for their clogs? No doubt they made of him just what Edo audiences had before them: here was a man who made a profit and more power to him; his was a morality of his own.[235]

The ideological messages to the countryside, which were far more numerous than the *kōdan*, also conveyed mixed signals. One "Map of Society" proposed by a provincial educator as conducive to "local improvement" ingeniously charted the possible pitfalls awaiting Japanese youth on the twisting, winding road to success. Graduates of compulsory education might cross the "Bridge of Pleasure" and end up back in their birthplace, living in a section called "Ordinary Street" (*Heibonchō*). Others might sojourn in Extravagance City, which would lead them to Poverty Village. Those who passed the Metropolis of Upper Elementary Education might then embark on the Bay of Society, or, if sidetracked by dreams of fast fortune into Moneylending Quarter, they, too, would find themselves back in Extravagance City. Those few who made it up the Hill of Effort to middle school, which was characterized as the most perilous ascent of all, might continue across the Pass of Ambition to the Metropolis of Higher Education. Heading toward the Lamp of Success as their landmark into Diligence Row, they would pass hill and vale and, meeting all difficulties, end up triumphantly in the City of Wealth. Failing that, they might find themselves in Extravagance City, with the others whose education was inadequate, or worst of all, back in Poverty Village.[236]

Although the educator did mention that Hōtoku thought—not Christianity—was an appropriate guide to the social map, his allegory of educational success was a far cry from the ideologues' urging youth to remain in what amounted to "Poverty Village," tilling the ancestral lands. Even as the Home Ministry published this map, hapless youth were setting out on the road to the Cities of Wealth and Extravagance. And while they may have traveled by train, they probably did not see their journey as another leading pedagogue did: "the tracks are morality, the engine knowledge," and any derailment means ending up a "loser in society."[237] For no matter how creative the metaphorical effusions that appeared with the imprimatur of the Home Ministry, they constituted but a part of the array of social influences to which late Meiji youth were prone.

THUS THE OFFICIAL social ideology co-existed with and was belied not only by political conflict and economic hardship, but also by a widely diffused ideology of individual success. In the effort to sustain the familial, communal, and customary verities of the past, the ideologues were attempting to scale their own Hill of Effort, struggling against the winds of social change. As they did, however, they emphasized an ethos that reinforced deep values associated with the village and familial collectivities, and, by making individual striving

211

officially suspect, managed to contain a good part of that striving within the bounds of the social group. This ideological reinforcement of community was a lasting and important effect of late Meiji ideology, even if the ideology itself was never able to cure the social fevers of modernity.

VII

End of an Era

AN UNPRECEDENTED
CEREMONY

I

AT EIGHT in the evening of the thirteenth of September 1912, the funeral cortege emerged from the imperial palace at Nijūbashi. Amid cannon and gun salutes, the 108 times tolling of the temple bells, and the plaintive notes of the processional dirge, the cortege began its solemn progress to the specially constructed hall on the parade ground at Aoyama. In the faint flickering light of torches and newly installed electric lamps, the procession of more than 20,000 stretched along the Tokyo streets, now freshly strewn with gravel, for a distance of two and a half miles. Throngs of people lined the streets, having gathered in the course of the day from nearby Tokyo neighborhoods and remote country towns. Yet the autumnal night air was hushed and silent as the cortege passed. After more than two hours the imperial hearse reached Aoyama, although it took another hour before the full procession had entered the ground. Honor guards and military bands, including a naval band from "our ally England," escorted the cortege, as did court musicians wearing the robes and bearing the instruments of antiquity. Attendants in court dress with bows and halberds, fans and staffs, preceded imperial princes, palace officials, the genrō, government ministers, high-ranking civil servants and the nobility, many of them in glittering full-dress uniform. Members of the two houses of the Diet followed in black tailcoats, "like river loach after goldfish, or penguins after golden pheasants," remarked one of the thousands of "special worshipers" awaiting the cortege in the funeral grounds. Although the same commentator considered his fellow guests a mixed group displaying "strange contrasts" of class and dress, most of the men were themselves in tails, by then the accepted formal uniform of the Meiji middle class elite.

The dignitaries seated in the stands included foreign diplomats and, more important, special envoys from the courts and governments of

213

the West. Among those who had graciously "crossed the distant seas" for the occasion were princes of England and Germany and Secretary of State Knox of the United States. Representatives of the Japanese in Korea, Taiwan, and Sakhalin were on hand to manifest the new length and breadth of the empire. Members of the Tokyo city government, its chamber of commerce, prefectural officials, mayors, school principals, religious leaders—the customary roster of late Meiji notables was present, though in numbers greater than ever before. More than ten thousand people paid their respects as the ceremony began with trumpets' sound near midnight. The new emperor, son of the emperor Meiji, dressed in the uniform of a generalissimo, spoke a brief eulogy, followed then by Prime Minister Saionji and Imperial Household Minister Watanabe. After the service ended, the imperial casket was transferred to the funeral train, which departed at 2 a.m. for Kyoto. The emperor and the train, twin symbols of the era, traversed the 340 miles of the Tōkaidō line, the tracks lined the whole way with revering subjects. Upon the train's arrival late in the afternoon, further services were held, and on the morning of the fifteenth, interment took place in the imperial tomb at Momoyama. So ended the funeral of the emperor who "for forty-five years had bestowed his generous rule upon his people" and "had constructed a great and majestic Japan such that no one had imagined in the early years of Meiji." It had been, as everyone described it, "an unprecedented ceremony."[1]

On the thirteenth, "ceremonies from afar" (yōhaishiki) were held all over the country, in town and village offices, schools, temples, and other public places. There the selection of notables duplicated in local miniature the assemblage in Tokyo. Representatives from the schools, the village assembly, the police, the local associations from the Reservists to the Red Cross gathered in front of schoolchildren and other villagers. They then paid their respects and heard their mayor pronounce a eulogy. The diarist Aizawa Kikutarō, who had become mayor of his village in 1908, gave a speech extolling the benefits of civilization (bunmei no ontaku) conferred on the people by the benevolence of the last emperor.[2] In Tochigi, at the hour the funeral began in Tokyo, Tanaka Shōzō, the embattled anti-government activist, faced south toward the capital and for more than an hour "sat erect, silent and motionless as a stone."[3]

The ceremonies, public and private, were but the latest in a series of local memorial services that had begun just after the emperor's death on July 30. Guided by numerous and detailed instructions from the central ministries and prefectural offices, the practices of national mourning had made the emperor's death a palpable presence even in the smallest villages. There were to be no drums, no *bon* dancing, no athletic competitions, no drunkenness. Black crepe was quickly bought up and sold high, and "beggars became rich" selling each newspaper extra banded in black, although when enterprising merchants peddled celluloid mourning bands on trains, the authorities decreed such materials inappropriate to the dignity of Meiji.[4] By September, there were occasional comments that further closings during the funeral would be bad for business. Nevertheless, even rickshawmen did not work, as towns and villages were stilled on the thirteenth for the funeral ceremonies that were solemnly reproduced across the nation.[5]

OF THE TOKYO ceremony it was often remarked that the forms of ritual had combined pure Japanese ceremonial with the latest flourishes of European pomp. By Japanese ceremonial the chroniclers meant court tradition, for their impressions were overwhelmingly secular. The Shintō installation of the spirit, which had taken place in the palace precincts in the early morning of the day of the funeral, was little mentioned, though the press did report that after the ritual the imperial family and high ministers, Yamagata among them, had partaken of the departed emperor's favored foods, *ayu* and European wine. Compared to the earlier unprecedented ceremony promulgating the Constitution in 1889, the imperial funeral did appear to manifest an easier blend of old and new ritual forms, as if the state had grown more comfortable in its ceremonial skin. It is also true that palace practices protecting the emperor's private life had become that much more public with his illness and death. "Until then," recalled one journalist, "court life had been utterly above the clouds, the people given no opportunity to know of it. But this time they broke with age-old custom and published daily bulletins on His Majesty's condition."[6] Newspapers felt free to suggest that the prohibition on viewing the imperial cortege from elevated heights be removed, since the gallery public was already permitted to look down on the emperor each time he attended the opening session of the Diet.[7] By and large, the events surrounding the imperial death suggested less the deification of the emperor than the apotheosis of his reign.

For Meiji—the emperor and his reign—was now credited with the full achievement of modernity. At the funeral ceremony the Taishō emperor spoke in vague imperial phrases of the emperor's beneficence and the people's loyal solicitude, while Prime Minister Saionji presented the government's concrete views of his—or more properly its own—accomplishments. The Meiji Restoration, the Charter Oath, and the abolition of the feudal domains led the list. In domestic affairs, the Constitution; abroad, treaty revision and the expansion of Japan's interests—these the emperor achieved even as law codes were established, industry encouraged, the military developed, education and letters supported. In this way the prime minister fashioned his eulogy into an official history of the Meiji period that retains authority even today. The imperial household minister, for his part, spoke of the rather more modest activities of the emperor that remained under his institutional control. In the palace view, Meiji had strengthened imperial rule, distributed titles and orders, encouraged meritorious deeds, reviewed his troops, traveled around the country, and helped those in distress with gifts from the imperial coffers. Indeed, on the day of the funeral, a total of one million yen from the privy purse was doled out to the prefectures and the colonies to commemorate the benevolence of their late sovereign.[8]

The foreign reaction, always so important to Meiji Japan's view of itself, proved forthcoming, even effusive, on the occasion of the emperor's passing. The Western press that had two decades earlier expressed skepticism about Japan's constitutional mimicry of the West now outdid itself in full-blown praise of the "world monarch" and his modern nation.

> Thus ends the era of the Meiji, the reign of "Enlightened Peace." Japan was an unknown, hidden land, trampled under the heels of a feudal militarism, and the sport of a succession of Shoguns, when his Majesty, in his 15th year, ascended the throne occupied in unbroken line by his ancestors since the days when Tyre and Sidon were in their glory, Carthage was flinging her yoke over the inhabitants of Northern Africa, and the wise men of the East were still straining their eyes for the Star of Bethlehem. The Emperor has passed away, in his modern Palace in Tokyo, in the full knowledge that under his inspiration, and with the devoted aid of his statesmen, the red disc of the national flag which, in the words of a great Japanese, was the wafer over a sealed island, has become the emblem of the confident hope of a united nation which has won its place among the Great Powers of the World. In the history of civilisation there is nothing more wonderful than the evolution of this island kingdom.[9]

So in its wisdom did the London *Daily Telegraph* place Japan in historical context. More laconic, but no less overstated was the Viennese comment, "Stolz könnte Kaiser Mutsuhito sagen, er habe in einem Menschenalter eine Grossmacht aus nichts geschaffen."[10] Few Japanese shared the notion that the Meiji Emperor had created "a great

216

power out of nothing," any more than they would have believed a contemporary American judgment that the Japanese capacity for progress was proof of "possession of distinctive Aryan qualities."[11] But like the appearance of distinguished foreign envoys at the funeral, these statements were taken much to heart by the chroniclers of the era just ended. As further proof of international respect, the press noted that the September 14th performance of Gilbert and Sullivan's *Mikado* in London had been canceled as a sign of deference to the emperor on his funeral day.[12] Less cognizance was taken of the dissenting opinions expressed in certain Chinese organs, one of which rejoiced in the fact that "fortunately Heaven has visited Japan with a scourge and killed her emperor."[13] With foreign opinion as with foreign policy, the majority of Japanese commentators preferred to glimpse their national reflection in the mirror of the West.

Yet, the funeral ceremonies also showed that foreign opinion was less the anxious center of concern in 1912 than it had been in 1889. Definitions of modernity, like tailcoats, had come to seem indigenous, and the eulogists of Meiji produced reams of self-confident prose on the pride of the era (*Meiji no hokori*). The press of August and September was given over to lengthy reminiscences and front-page histories of the achievements since the Restoration.[14] A representative example by Yamaji Aizan listed five accomplishments: uniting the people, advancing democracy (*heiminshugi*), awakening to Japan's mission in the world, the rise of capitalists, and changes in the people's beliefs. As a result of this last achievement, Ibsen and Tolstoy were "no longer foreigners," the Japanese partook of global sentiment, and Japan had become a "province of the world."[15] Some compared the emperor to Shōmu and other Japanese emperors of the past, while others ranked him with Napoleon and Queen Victoria.[16] The modernity identified with his reign nearly always emphasized the same essentials: the Charter Oath, the Constitution, and empire. They were thus not far removed from the prime minister's characterization at the funeral. There was also a strain of instant nostalgia, as writers referred to the last reign as if it were lost in the golden ages of antiquity. "Now everyone is extravagant, but in the last reign they were parsimonious and wore their clothes with soiled neckbands until they were threadbare, and only then did they make new ones."[17] Barely three weeks had passed, and not only the reign but the habits forced by poverty had been transmogrified.

Commentators who had heralded the constitutional beginnings of modernity in 1889 now trumpeted its completion. Their attitude toward the people, however, remained similarly didactic. On the eve of the Constitution they had urged the *kokumin* to fulfill the demands of national awareness and patriotic spirit; now they cautioned them against excessive displays of sentiment for their late monarch. The hundreds of thousands of country people who would press into Tokyo for the funeral were admonished to correct their misguided notions of loyalty and patriotism, forsake such "fanaticism," stay home instead and worship from afar.[18] The people's lack of experience of national ceremony might lead them to misbehave, thus "staining the honor of the state" instead of producing "a model funeral" not only for Japanese history but for the world.[19]

If the tone was similar, the audience had, however, changed considerably. The effective public for constitutional and parliamentary concerns—those whom the press had exhorted to civic responsibility in 1889—had represented a socially small and economically privileged sliver of the population. But the Japanese who responded to the death of the emperor belonged in the widest sense to the *kokumin* at large. Moreover, when officials and journalists referred to public misbehavior during the funeral in Tokyo, they envisioned not the scattered outbursts of the political rowdies (*sōshi*) of the eighties and nineties, but the mass and often violent eruptions of such demonstrations as the Hibiya riots of 1905. Awareness of the passing of Meiji was a national phenomenon that made "the people" into a larger, more inclusive group than had been spontaneously affected by any previous national event, with the exception perhaps of war. Indeed, many commentators spoke of the sense of national unity (*kyokoku itchi*) engendered by the emperor's death as reminiscent of the two Meiji wars.[20] Others at the time, and a great many more in later recollections, claimed the national mood to be unprecedented. "Never before had the entire people, their deep concern knowing no distinction of high and low, city and country, been so captured by the same sentiment as on this occasion."[21]

This sentiment, though everywhere expressed, was of a more general nature than the retrospective that swamped the world of oratory and print. It is true that the popular appetite for accounts of the demise of Meiji was enormous, suggesting to one provincial commentator that "from the time of the emperor's funeral people's reading ability seems to have increased by leaps and bounds."[22] Special commemorative issues of magazines sold tens of thousands, sets of picture postcards of the funeral became immediate collector's items, and the press, which had been admitted to the ceremonies in numbers, found a ready audience for every recorded detail. The ceremony promulgating the Constitution had been depicted in woodblock prints, a form no longer in common use as a medium of visual communication. The emperor's funeral, on the other hand, was preserved in endlessly reprinted photographs that even captured, with a new camera's blinding flash, the ceremonial by night.[23] That commercial publishing was able to exploit the opportunity was due partly to its flourishing expansion since the Russo-Japanese War and partly to an interest among the people that also appeared unprecedented.

That interest centered first on the emperor—hence the curiosity about the minutiae of his last living and first posthumous days. People all over the country had prayed for him in his final illness, which had been sudden, while in Tokyo mournful crowds had gathered by the tens of thousands in front of the palace.[24] Upon his death they had attended services, sent condolences, and otherwise expressed shock and regret. Some gave up drink, others fasted, and many talked with one another in subdued tones of disbelief. The emperor's death, it was remarked, only confirmed the saying that "the gods, the Buddhas, the college professors were none of them a match for mortality."[25] The press commented that mourning bands were universal, worn "by townspeople of course, but also by farmers . . . and even in the fields." In a similarly fawning tone, the Home Ministry police reported that socialists who never flew the flag of the rising sun had hung the flag of mourning, responding to the emperor's death "in the same way as the general population."[26] This was true, not because farmers or socialists had been transformed into imperial patriots by the event, but because they, like so many others, were mourning the death of "our familiar, dear, revered, and much-relied upon" monarch.[27] These words of the self-described "free thinker" Tayama Katai help to explain why so many intellectuals who otherwise eschewed risings of national sentiment also confided their own emotional condolences in private and in print.

They were, first of all, mourning a man, not a government. For this reason Tokutomi Roka, who had recently protested the harsh treatment of the socialists in the Great Treason Incident, could also write movingly of his personal sense of loss at the emperor's death. Uchimura Kanzō, the Christian who had disavowed the establishment but not the nation, wrote that he felt as if he had lost a father, while Ebina Danjō offered a Christian prayer for him whom "God had protected as a father."[28] Natsume Sōseki made plain his disgust both with the government in its zealous rush to close down the amusements of the common people as an imposed sign of reverence for the dying emperor, and also with the press which reported the imperial demise in such sycophantic detail. But, like the others, Sōseki separated the emperor, whom he eulogized in poetry and prose, from "the authorities" who manipulated him, and thus also from the state.[29] In this sentiment, the intellectuals were representative of most Japanese at the time, whose responses indicated the extent to which the emperor and the government were separately viewed by the people. Due partly to political structure, partly to ideology, and partly to the power of a popular monarch to remain unsullied by the unpopular actions of his officials, the Meiji emperor died well and widely mourned, while the oligarchs went far more quietly—and in the sense of national iconography, almost silently—to their graves.

As widely shared as this sentiment for the departed monarch was the equally apolitical sense that, as Sōseki expressed it in a famous passage in *Kokoro*, "the spirit of the Meiji era had begun with the emperor, and had ended with him," leaving those who had been brought up in that era "to live as anachronisms."[30] That is, the people seemed to be responding not only to the emperor's death, but as much or more to the unexpected transition from one era to another. The change in era name had been announced the afternoon the emperor died, and as suddenly as the forty-fifth year of Meiji ended, the first year of Taishō had begun. Dates were expressed differently, though "with a slip of the pen," people still wrote Meiji through force of long habit.[31] Businesses changed their name to Taishō to avail themselves of the advertising value of the new era, and with the precise usage that Japanese apply to all demarcations of time, references to the past, however immediate, became "the last reign" or "the age of the previous emperor."[32] Confronted daily with the denomination of a new age, many older people felt that their own time had passed with Meiji. Tokutomi Roka wrote:

> When the emperor dies the era name also changes. . . . I knew this perfectly well, but still I felt as if the name of Meiji would continue forever. I was born in October of the first year of Meiji, the year when the Meiji Emperor ascended the throne and the month when he first went from Kyoto to Tokyo. . . . I am accustomed to thinking of Meiji's age as my own, and being the same age as Meiji has been both my pride and my shame.
>
> The emperor's death has closed the book of Meiji history. When Meiji became Taishō, I felt as if my own life had been broken off.[33]

There were younger Japanese as well who, having known no other period, felt temporarily displaced. One student described himself as one of those "whose sole pride was as the new men and new women of Meiji." Now he realized that "we are not a new breed after all and will meet the same fate as those born in the Tenpō era."[34] The phrase that became common in later years—Meiji has faded into the past (*Meiji wa tōku narinikeri*)—was already keenly felt in the summer of its passing.

II

THE UNITY of sentiment engendered by this sense of closure as well as the three-day funeral ceremony that marked it were both shattered by news of General Nogi's suicide. At 7:40 p.m. on September 13, just as the funeral cortege was preparing to leave the palace, the military hero Nogi Maresuke and his wife Shizuko seated themselves in front of the imperial portrait in their home and committed ritual suicide, he disemboweling himself with a military sword, she stabbing herself in the heart with a dagger. In notes left before their death there were poems that spoke of "following the lord" and references to Nogi's having lost the regimental colors in the Satsuma Rebellion of 1877.[35] When rumors of the suicides began to circulate during the funeral ceremony, they were greeted with derisive disbelief. Then, as the first extras appeared in the streets at 2 a.m., the derision turned to shock, but the disbelief remained.[36] On first hearing it did not seem possible that one of the best-known figures in Meiji national life had committed *junshi*, the custom of following one's lord into death. In a nation in the midst of a solemn celebration of its modernity, its foremost soldier and hero of the Russo-Japanese War had followed a custom that had been outlawed by the Tokugawa shogunate as antiquated in 1663.

Soon it was noted that "nothing has so stirred up the sentiments of the nation since the vendetta of the forty-seven *rōnin* in 1703."[37] The comparison was apt, partly because Nogi in his loyalty and purity of heart was so often likened to the avenging samurai in popular expressions, and partly because Nogi's act, like that of the forty-seven *rōnin*, aroused heated debate over its ethics and appropriateness among the intellectuals of the day. The emperor's death had briefly united national sentiment; Nogi's suicide rent it apart. The press exploded with praise for this "splendor that adorns the end of the glorious reign of Meiji" and censure for this "retrograde custom" that contravenes the entire "national policy of progress and development (*shinpo hattatsu no kokuze*)."[38] "Ah! General Nogi!" enthused some; woe to a nation that condones an act hostile to all the "ways of civilization," lamented others. For each of these expressions, there were immediate letters and articles taking the opposite position, which were also printed.[39] When one journalist sought the opinion of scholars of ethics, he was told that "while suicide is surely a bad thing in ethical terms, in Nogi's case it cannot be lightly judged. . . . If you plan to publish this in your newspaper, I really don't know what to say." It was, the journalist commented, an even larger problem for the newspapers.[40]

The question of coverage was simply handled, as voluminous biographies and reminiscences of Nogi reduced mention of the recently buried emperor to a miscellaneous paragraph or two. The difficulty lay rather in the editorial comment. Since the Russo-Japanese War, suicide among youth had been a controversial issue, criticized far and wide as a disease of civilization (*bunmeibyō*). Also, when a score of lesser personages had committed suicide in the wake of the emperor's death in July, "this foolish custom" had been roundly denounced as inappropriate in one of the "world's first-ranking countries" in the twentieth century.[41] Yet, in Nogi's case, it could not be lightly judged, as the same newspaper equivocated barely one month later:

> General Nogi's death marked the completion of Japan's bushidō of old. And while emotionally we express the greatest respect, rationally we regret we cannot approve. One can only hope that this act will not long blight the future of our national morality. We can appreciate the General's intention; we must not learn from his behavior.[42]

This masterful ambivalence was typical of the immediate response. Commentators tried to separate Nogi's *junshi*, which they found unacceptable in a modern state, from his samurai loyalty and bushidō, which might serve as an "unintentional moral lesson."[43] The foreign press further compromised such distinctions with florid praise of bushidō that instantly found its way into the Japanese press. The London *Times*, which had prophesied "a spiritual crisis" at the time of the emperor's death, now pronounced Nogi's suicide to have demonstrated that "the spirit of Japan is not extinct."[44] This, of course, was precisely what Nogi's critics were afraid of.

Even those Japanese who expressed emphatic condemnation were discomfited by recent occasions when after the emperor's death they, too, had made affirmative, albeit metaphorical, use of the term *junshi* to exhort their countrymen or criticize the government. One paper, for example, which was sharply critical of Nogi in September, had argued in August that "the genrō and court officials, who thought nothing of spending millions of yen from the privy purse to build their own houses," should by all rights slit their wrinkled bellies (*shiwabara o kakikirite*) in order properly to praise the late emperor's

222

virtue. "But since present morality does not permit *junshi* . . . they should at least resolve to perform its spiritual counterpart and obliterate their personal desires."[45] The writer doubtless invoked *junshi* for dramatic effect, never for a moment contemplating its reality in the present age. Yet, metaphors are also real, and the forward–looking journalist so confident of Japan's modernity was in fact contributing to the currency of the concept of *junshi*. Perhaps he would have argued that in the summer of 1912 he felt perfectly safe in doing so. Nonetheless, he and the readers who several weeks later so vociferously defended Nogi's loyal and traditional act inhabited the same universe of discourse. Indeed, Nogi seemed to many of them that much more commendable for having actually accomplished a deed that for almost everyone else was but a rhetorical relic of the past.

If this was true of *junshi*, whose limited relevance meant that its mention was infrequent, it was far more true of bushidō, which had gathered increasing momentum as a term of common parlance since the Russo-Japanese War. When Nogi was called "the flower of bushidō," the reference evoked not only his martial exploits and his spartan educational philosophy at the Peers School, but a whole range of expanded meanings that enhanced the moral value of his suicide. And some of those appalled by Nogi's death had themselves contributed to that expansion of meaning. Ukita Kazutami, for example, the leading writer at *Taiyō*, the most widely read and influential magazine of opinion of the period, was by his own definition a Christian and a constitutionalist (*rikkenshugisha*). In 1908 he had identified inferior business ethics as a major problem for Japan and proposed as its solution "the infusion of bushidō into the business world."[46] He, too, was wielding a traditional metaphor in an unexceptionably modern context. But when Nogi died, it appeared that, like the ethics professors, Ukita did not quite know what to say. He judged the act admirable but inapplicable to today's "complicated society" (*fukuzatsu naru shakai*) and suggested that though it might influence the military, it could hardly be expected to arouse repentance "in the politicians who buy votes in their electoral districts or in the voters who sell them." Nor could one hope for it to make high-minded men of "the officials consumed with their own vainglory, or the entrepreneurs wallowing in worldly pleasures." For that purpose it might have been better had the general lived to educate a "genius" capable of continuing such formidable tasks.[47] Moving back and forth in this way between respect and disapproval, like a shuttle on a loom, Ukita wove his argument of ambivalence. Having advocated

223

entrepreneurial bushidō with confidence that his readers would at least understand, and perhaps even applaud, his reference, Ukita might have expected people to be awestruck when Nogi displayed what everyone described as the real thing. Other Christians, who mourned the emperor and admired Nogi, criticized his suicide as "theatrical bushidō" and "bushidō of an earlier age."[48] But bushidō it was, nonetheless. The intellectuals who trafficked in such language, whether nonchalantly or with critical intent, unwittingly helped to perpetuate the popular phenomenon they so decried.

Nogi's suicide aroused contradictory responses in other quarters as well. The army, whose public image was at a low ebb at the very moment that it wanted budgetary approval for two new divisions, could be expected to have rejoiced in Nogi's heroics. The government, for both political and ideological reasons, was no more likely to refrain from a wholehearted response. Nogi, however, had complicated his heroism by including in his testament a provision that with his death the Nogi house was to end for all time, a prerogative the authorities did not wish to encourage among the peers. They therefore suppressed that part of Nogi's note, but were scooped by the press. Tokutomi Sohō's *Kokumin shinbun* began to hawk its extra in the streets even as the government spokesman was announcing the censored version. The opposition then accused the government of betraying Nogi's wishes, creating a political issue that flared again in 1914 when, despite the General's testament, the Nogi house was officially restored. The imperial government looked with favor on the emergence of an apotheosized image of Nogi and, apparently unconcerned that others might emulate his disruptive behavior, did not ban the twenty-eight volumes on him that appeared before the year was out, nor the additional ninety-seven published between 1913 and 1942. It did, however, feel constrained to suppress the full police medical report of the suicides, perhaps because it, like the testament, contained clinical facts that might spoil the emerging heroic fiction.[49]

In popular expressions Nogi also emerged as a hero, but one whose final act lost much of the ambivalence and didacticism of the more ponderous versions.[50] It was Nogi—not the emperor—who became the embodiment of the Meiji period in popular culture. Along with the forty-seven *rōnin*, he appeared as the ubiquitous protagonist of *kōdan* and *naniwabushi*, the narrated and chanted tales that were the most popular entertainment of the time. Indeed *naniwabushi*, which were originally a street amusement associated by the elite with the "lower orders," rode to the peak of their popularity in 1912 and 1913 on the crest of an interest in the tale of General Nogi that knew no convenient social distinctions.[51] And while the emperor Meiji headed the list of the most frequently mentioned figures in elementary school texts of the imperial period, according to one tabulation he did not appear at all in *Shōnen kurabu*, the widely read young people's magazine published by Kōdansha. Instead, leading the roster of youth's heroes were Kusunoki Masashige, the forty-seven *rōnin*, the fictional Yaji and Kita of *Hizakurige*, and General Nogi. Nogi also figured in the textbooks, outranking Kusunoki in the language texts, for example. This curricular appearance and the much more popular renditions of the "private ministry of education," as the immensely successful Kōdansha was sometimes called, combined to assure Nogi a premier place in the pantheon.[52] His wife, whose dying was equally accomplished, received much less attention. Perhaps she might have expected this, having proved her loyalty to a man whom one eulogist described as disliking three things: priests, merchants, and women.[53]

Nogi's death also stimulated literary responses from such writers as Mori Ōgai and Akutagawa Ryūnosuke.[54] But whether the works defended the suicide as Ōgai's did, or satirized it in the manner of Akutagawa, they betrayed the ambivalence of the intellectual's reaction. For them Nogi was a "Japanese Don Quixote" who both impressed and disturbed them at the same time.[55] Yet, despite the outburst of opinion, Nogi's importance for most Japanese should not be exaggerated. For all who expressed their views of the suicide, there were many more who remained silent. For them *junshi* was cause for neither censure nor celebration, but an exotic act irrelevant to their lives. Indeed, youth were taken to task for not understanding the general's death, since they seemed to take little "inspiration" from it.[56] And there was a great difference between the national and deeply felt response to the death of the emperor and the more controversial but less universally expressed reaction to Nogi's suicide.

OF THE TWO ceremonies that took place on the night of September 13, 1912, one was a national ritual that signified the end of an era. The Meiji period had been long in years and even longer in the perception of those who experienced it. It could be said of the emperor that, like Queen Victoria, he shared his name with an age, imposing "an illusory show of continuity and uniformity on a tract of time where men and manners, science and philosophy, the fabric of social life and its directing ideas, changed more swiftly perhaps, and more profoundly, than they have ever changed in an age not sundered by a political or religious upheaval."[57] In Japan the illusory continuity and the underlying changes were now identified with both the reign and the monarch and given the further name, "modernity." Neither Meiji nor modernity met with universal approval. The devoutest wish of some progressive youth was to be quickly quit of Meiji so that modernity could move ahead, while the direst fear of many of their elders was that Meiji's end would enable modernity to swamp the remains of their familiar world. But both shared the sense of the passing of an age and the certainty that they were living in indisputably modern times.

Nogi's ceremony upset this certainty for some, leaving intellectuals with a queasy ambivalence about the nature of Japan's modernity. For others, including the army, the schools, and private proponents of Nogiism (*Nogishugi*), it provided a symbol for loyalty and self-sacrificing service to the state. To popular culture it offered a modern example of the heroic samurai suicide.[58] Although Nogi's act divided national sentiment in this way, the division was also a legacy of Meiji. Like the assassination of Mori Arinori by an imperial loyalist on the morning of the promulgation of the Constitution, Nogi's suicide was as much a product of the times as the splendid pomp of the "world monarch's" funeral. In 1889 the emperor had bestowed the Constitution on the nation in the name of his ancestors, whose most sacred shrine was Ise. An assassin had rectified a slight to the imperial ancestors by murdering the education minister. Logically—or ideologically—one act invoked the other. In 1912 the established equation of imperial loyalty with patriotism and the outpouring of sentiment upon the emperor's death created an atmosphere in which Nogi's *junshi* made a bizarre but irrefutable sort of sense. The modern constitutional monarch and the traditional expression of loyalty were not only equally available, they were also linked by the person of the emperor. Those who preferred constitutionalism to bushidō were appalled at Nogi's suicide, yet they, too, participated in the same universe of discourse. Innocent use of metaphor often proved reckless, and a genuine feeling for Meiji, the man and the era, brought even the voices of dissent into harmony—a dissonant harmony, but harmony nonetheless—with the larger chorus. In the decades to come this dual ideological legacy would affect not only the militarists and the radical right but the democrats and socialists as well. Vocabularies of constitutionalism and emperorism intersected and overlapped, producing resonances between right and left, between parliamentary politics and terrorist assassination, between those who manipulated the symbols and those who were manipulated by them. The end of

226

the era did not so much close the book of Meiji history as set the stage for the decades to come.

THE NEW POLITICS
OF TAISHŌ

I

THE EMPEROR's death did not alter what Yamagata called "the course of the ship of state," though he appeared to fear that it might, and took pains to assure himself access to the ear of the new and inexperienced Taishō emperor.[59] At the same time, in August 1912, Yamagata removed Katsura from the arena of politics by arranging his appointment to a dual position in the imperial household. There his prominent disciple might serve Yamagata's bidding in the palace and, more important, be prevented from pursuing what Yamagata regarded as Katsura's disloyal flirtation with political parties.[60] In December, when the genrō were recalled to action to select a new prime minister, "Japan's master at destroying cabinets"—as the press reviled Yamagata for his role in toppling the Saionji government—rose to the political occasion.[61] Sounding his familiar themes of the "disorder and disorderliness" associated with the parties, Yamagata warned of "entanglements following upon disturbances as the genrō are attacked in speeches and newspapers and the sentiments of the people agitated and led astray."[62] Although his by now formulaic protest that he was "a mere soldier, not a politician" must have fallen on deaf ears, he did resort to full martial metaphor as public clamor rose against the government in January.

> [The opposition] has raised the banner in the name of eliminating cliques and protecting the Constitution. Their strategy, which is to mislead and inflame the people and draw the government down into the maelstrom of attack and siege, is providing them with increasing gains. To save the nation the sole avenue of escape is to charge them at the center (*chūō tokkan*).[63]

But Katsura, who was being called upon to lead the charge, chose instead to surrender and form his own flank of what to Yamagata would always be the enemy, the parliamentary parties. For if Yamagata still persevered in the rocklike stance he had held for four decades, the currents of the political world now flowed past him with increasing force. The events of the Taishō political change (*Taishō seihen*), which saw two changes of cabinet in two months in the winter of 1912-1913, reveal the extent to which the practice of politics

227

had altered since 1890.[64] The political turnover at the beginning of Taishō thus affords the opportunity to assess—in the standard phrase of the time, "now that more than twenty years have passed since the establishment of constitutional government"—how the visage of politics appeared as one era ended and a new one began.[65]

ALTHOUGH the emperor's death had signified closure of a national, monarchial, and even personal sort, in political discourse the future beckoned more than the past, and hopes of a new beginning outweighed retrospection in the first months of the Taishō period. Indeed the mood among political commentators and party politicians resembled the anticipation with which those same sectors of the elite had awaited the opening of the Diet in 1890. Once again the public opinion of the people (*minkan no yoron*) called for a "second restoration," this time a Taishō restoration to fulfill the constitutional promise that Meiji had satisfied "in form but not in spirit or substance."[66] Since the categories of ideology, once entrenched, carry forward from their formative period, the essential political division still fell between the *kan* and the *min*: "*Kan ka min ka?*" Which side of the dichotomy of the 1880s would prevail in the new politics of Taishō, the bureaucratic heirs of the oligarchs or the political parties of the people?[67]

Within these categories, however, the evolved rhetoric of the opposition parties reflected a confidence born of the experience of the first two constitutional decades. The first of the twin slogans of the heralded Taishō restoration—"destroy clique government" (*batsuzoku daha*)—was as old as the "old men like Yamagata, Inoue, Ōyama, and Matsukata, the elder statesmen of the Meiji Restoration who are still at their manipulations even now that it is Taishō."[68] The new era thus lent its force to "thirty years of accumulated public anger" at the oligarchic cliques and the genrō, "those great blights upon the nation," whose end—the orators asserted with climactic enthusiasm—had belatedly but finally come.[69] The second slogan of the anti-bureaucratic forces—"protect constitutional government" (*kensei yōgo*)—belonged more to the Taishō present than the Meiji past. By appropriating for the new popular politics (*minsei*) the force and authority of the Constitution, they used the word "constitutional" (*rikkenteki*) synonymously to mean the position and demands of the parties. In 1889, when constitutional government was still an abstraction, the government claimed transcendental impartiality, and the parties, free and popular representation. Widely referred to as the

右ヨリ
信前村長
井村
隣貝調査委
賞組貝
台顧貝
常開長
務
堀堀
拝事
調
査
委
貝農作
廣向万九郎ッコ
（羽織ット）

左ヨリ
最景
信縣
用隣賀組台
賀技長
組手
調
査中
委員川
堀滋
三治
平（セビロ）
（半ヨロ服）

日委員調是村ニ於ケ掘ニ内邸氏作ニ堀ニ是村前

Members of the Village Plan Investigation Committee Gathered at the House of Former Village Mayor Hori Nisaku (Yokota village, Toyama prefecture, 1911). See chapter 6, footnote 201

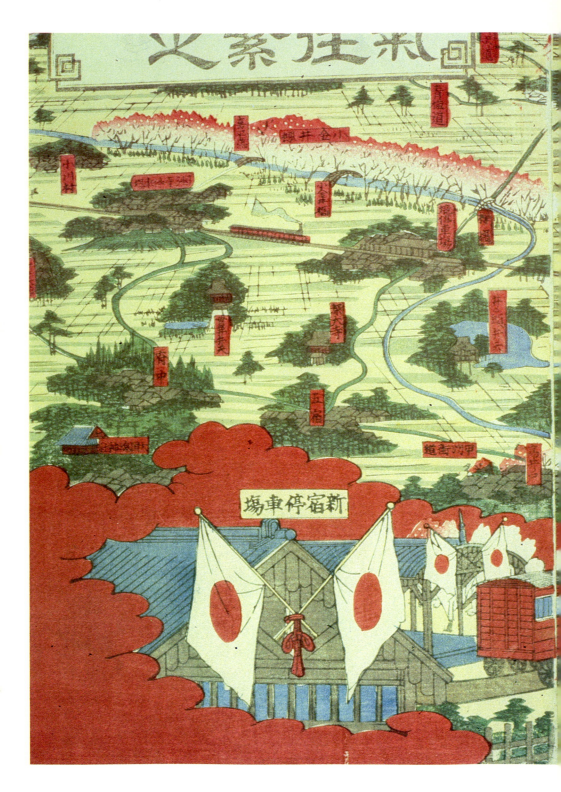

"Picture of Prosperity with Locomotives Running Back and Forth" (1889):
the opening of the railway line from Shinjuku to Tachikawa

Midnight funeral cortege of the Meiji Emperor (13-14 September 1912)

kintei kenpō, the "imperially bestowed Constitution" belonged, if to anyone, to the oligarchs who had controlled its drafting and hoped to control its operation. Now in 1912-1913, the political parties, each of which included the word *rikken* in its official name, rhetorically claimed possession of the Constitution, while the government's every action was met with the quickly established epithet "unconstitutional" (*hirikkenteki*).[70] Just as the Minobe-Uesugi debates of this same time wrenched the preponderant authority of constitutional interpretation from Itō's *Commentaries*, so did the parties take the name of the Constitution upon themselves, infusing the ideological division between the *kan* and the *min* with the now mature formulations of constitutional politics.

Although the facts did not match the formulations of those who expected the "constitutional crisis" to result in the "Sekigahara of the war for constitutional government," the Taishō change did make it clear that the battles between the bureaucratic *kan* and the political party *min* would now be joined by more participants on more fronts than had been the case in the Meiji period.[71] Neither the genrō nor the cliques obliged by departing the field, for, as the press rightly noted, getting rid of Katsura did not mean the end of oligarchic influence in the bureaucracy, the peers, and the military.[72] These sectors continued to provide particular sources of support for Yamagata, who also remained personally influential through much of the decade until his death in 1922. Nonetheless, the power of the genrō was waning, and Katsura was not the last of Yamagata's men who sought to assure their political future through association with the parties. As Tanaka Giichi and others made their accommodations, the distinction between the *kan* and the *min* continued to blur at the highest levels of government. The distinction between the emperor and parliamentary politics, on the other hand, was sharpened when the parties, in Ozaki Yukio's famous words, made it impossible for the bureaucrats to continue "using the throne as a parapet and imperial rescripts as bullets."[73] The military, which had largely worked through the genrō during the Meiji decades, emerged as an independent force that could and would bring cabinets down to gain its ends. Those ends also became increasingly apparent at this time. For the Chinese Revolution of 1911, described by both Tanaka and Yamagata as "a golden opportunity," spurred the army's plans for continental expansion and affected domestic politics in the form of the two divisions issue.[74] The voice of business, too, was heard more insistently in the political arena, as entrepreneurial leaders and the

League of Chambers of Commerce took part in the movement to protect constitutional government and, not incidentally, to lower the business tax.[75]

The expanded constellation of political actors in 1912-1913 represented what Tokutomi Sohō called the forces of military, financial, and popular rights (*heiken, zaiken, minken*).[76] The last, the *min*, still referred to the political parties, whose growth in size and influence the events of the Taishō change made publicly apparent. In 1890 the combined popular parties had won a parliamentary majority, but from 1908 to 1915 one party—indeed the same party, the Seiyūkai—controlled the Lower House. Moreover, the earlier stark and stalwart opposition between the popular parties and the bureaucracy had given way to the conciliating results of Hara Kei's "politics of compromise" and "mutual understanding."[77] The Seiyūkai, though it remained a party of the people (*mintō*), was now also a government party, a party in power (*yotō*), which traded favors with the bureaucrats in exchange for parliamentary support. From December 1912 to February 1913, when the Seiyūkai opposed Katsura's short-lived cabinet, it became the opposition party (*yatō*). In February it resumed its position as the government party during Yamamoto Gonnohyōe's bureaucratic cabinet, and the anti-Seiyūkai party (the Kenseikai), so recently and loudly criticized as bureaucratic, now carried the banner of the opposition. The Taishō change thus prepared the way for an exchange of power from party to party, instead of from bureaucracy to party as had been the case in the Meiji period.[78]

But this development, which was natural enough in a parliamentary system, did not altogether redound to the credit of the parties—or of politics in general. The persistence of bureaucratic cabinets in what was not in fact a wholly parliamentary system was one reason for this. Another was that the entrenched categories of Meiji political discourse compromised the politics of compromise, since it appeared that the long-avowed representatives of the *min* had made common cause with the long-reviled bureaucratic *kan*.[79] As a result of their metamorphosis from "protestors" to "respectables," as Peter Duus has described them, the parties crossed the line into the political establishment.[80] Indeed, from Taishō on they were known less as the *mintō*, the popular parties, than as the *kisei seitō*, the established parties. And in expressions of public opinion they were often lumped together with the bureaucracy in the category of those whose business was politics, not representation. Already in 1912-1913 the negative vocabulary conventionally applied to the government was being transferred to the parties. Critics warned that, rhetoric to the contrary, the parties were neither constitutional nor popular and that "bureaucratic clique politics" would only be followed by "party clique politics."[81] Trapped in the bifurcation of an earlier age, party politicians appeared to confirm the general impression that, however much they talked like *min*, they acted more like *kan*. As before, this conception excluded from the operational realm of constitutional politics the emperor, who by being further removed from direct political manipulation became more available to those who would invoke him for allegedly pure and "apolitical" purposes. It also excluded the wider population, who, though they semantically remained *min*, still lacked an effective political definition of themselves in that capacity.

Outside the bright but narrow spotlight focused on parliamentary politics, however, the Taishō change gave evidence that other forms of public action had also established themselves on the wider reaches of the political stage. The mass meetings and riots that occurred in conjunction with the Movement to Protect Constitutional Government in early 1913 were of dual ancestry. They were heirs both of the speech meetings of the elite "men of influence" of the eighties and nineties and also of the urban, often violent, mass protest that characterized the strikes and demonstrations of the last Meiji decade.[82] Indeed the demonstration of February 10, which "suddenly turned the area around the Diet into a battlefield scene," was repeatedly compared to the Hibiya riots against the Portsmouth Treaty in 1905, although the violence was judged to be greater this time. Mobs again burned police boxes and stormed government-line newspapers in Tokyo and in the provinces.[83] Government figures, especially such Yamagata men as Tanaka Giichi, were quick to see socialism's gain and the specter of anarchy in the mass demonstrations.[84] The two threats they so much feared separately—popular political action and mass social protest—were here combined together. To them, the period from December to February appeared, in the words of another Yamagata disciple, Hirata Tōsuke, as "a time in which national disintegration is taking place before our very eyes."[85] In fact what they were witnessing were the effects of national *integration*, as political action and expression reached and included a larger portion of a rapidly changing and industrializing society.

The expanded political scale was apparent in other sectors as well. The press had long been important in galvanizing public action, whether it was provincial meetings of several hundred local *yūshisha* to protest the government's proposed treaty revision in 1887 or street mobs responding to widely publicized cries of "national humiliation" in regard to the treaty of 1905. During the agitation of December

1912, Tokutomi Sohō complained that "all the press does is stir up popular sentiment," a somewhat disingenuous remark since his own *Kokumin shinbun* attempted the same on behalf of the government and was once again rewarded with bricks and shouts of "*Goyō shinbun!*"[86] By 1912 the political organs were long defunct, and more papers were claiming to be "impartial and nonpartisan" (*fuhen futō*)—although for a time the *Ōsaka asahi* eschewed the phrase, possibly on the ground that its long association with oligarchic transcendentalism gave it too much of a government taint.[87] Political figures competed for the favors of the press, and even Yamagata could be unwontedly obsequious in expressing his interest in Tokutomi's newspaper, whose support of the government earned it not only Yamagata's "rejoicing" at increased circulation but also unofficial monthly subsidies.[88]

Despite the assertions of editorial impartiality, during the Taishō change most of the press was actively anti-government, both in printed denunciations of the genrō and in participation of reporters in the constitutional movement. Journalists not only joined others, but took the lead in organizing their own rallies in January and February 1913.[89] This activism prompted Tokutomi's *Kokumin shinbun*, the five other "bureaucratic" dailies, and a score of provincial newspapers to form an association of "Press to Promote Constitutional Government" (*Kensei sokushin kishadan*). Its aim was to support Katsura's cause against the opposing parties—and against the other newspapers as well. The anti-government press, however, was far more influential. Indeed, the combined effect of the journalists' activism and adversarial reporting led one scholar later to conclude that for the first time the anti-government press propelled the parties rather than being propelled by them.[90] This pattern of successful "agitation" was repeated during the Rice Riots of 1918, when the *Ōsaka asahi* fanned the discontent over government financial policies across the country and suffered government suppression in the White Rainbow Incident of the same time.[91]

Two characteristics of the twentieth-century Japanese press were therefore becoming apparent as Meiji turned to Taishō. One was the steady expansion of scale reflected not only in increased overall circulation but in the trend toward large national dailies which, because they combined serious reporting with popular features, were able to attract a widely diverse readership. The *Asahi*, the prototype of this genre, and the *Mainichi*, its larger competitor, both grew enormously during Taishō. The *Ōsaka asahi* increased its circulation from approximately 250,000 in 1913 to 800,000 in 1923; the *Ōsaka mainichi* grew from 300,000 to 920,000 in the same period.[92] The circle of newspaper readers, still so small in 1890, had broadened beyond the confines of middle-class elite opinion into an increasingly mass audience which was also national in scope. At the same time the distinctive editorial stance that still characterizes Japanese journalism also emerged more decisively. It combined frequently crusading anti-establishment positions—often as critical of the parties as of the government—with an ever-stronger insistence on "impartial and non-partisan" editorial policy. Even the aggressively progressive *Ōsaka asahi* adopted the motto that it had earlier avoided and became *fuhen futō* in the aftermath of government suppression in 1918.[93] But this combination of conscientious opposition with the sometimes herculean effort to remain editorially unaligned was not a product of censorship alone. Rather, like the censorship itself, it was a legacy of Meiji politics and ideology: the stance of opposition was inherited from the long popular crusade against the government, and that of non-alignment from the cumulative effects of the identification of party politics with civically unworthy partisanship.

II

THE EVENTS of 1912-1913 also demonstrated that the expansion of the field of politics at the national level had been matched in the provinces. Although the constitutional movement is said to have been "switched on" by activists at the center, only the changes in local society and politics can explain why the switch ignited with so bright and instant a flash.[94] The numbers of "constitutional youth" associations, for example—some of which were anti-government in the name of the parties, others anti-government in the name of the emperor—proved that the ideological sequestering of youth from politics had not been wholly successful. The phenomenon was soon diagnosed in the press as a symptom of the "political fever" that now afflicted female as well as male students.[95] Like the political youth (*seiji seinen*) of the 1880s, the constitutional youth (*rikken seinen*) of 1913 were the product of the political consciousness of a new generation. One regional military officer described them as lapsed farmers and idlers who succumbed to "half-understood constitutional theories and the agitation of ambitious politicians."[96] In fact, these local youth were often knowledgeable activists who, despite their early ideological schooling in apolitical patriotism, took part in organized political activism of one sort or another throughout the Taishō period.[97]

While a number of Taishō youth were being newly politicized,

233

their elders among the local elite were by 1913 well versed in the ways and means of party politics. Local government, intended by Yamagata to remain "outside the turmoil of central politics," had been engulfed by the "party strife" against which he had repeatedly warned.[98] In language that echoed Yamagata's every speech on the subject in the eighties and nineties, the same army officer who criticized the constitutional youth of his district lamented the riven state into which *jichi* had fallen in 1913:

> Political party fever flourishes surprisingly in the district. Party and factional coloration is found not only among the middle classes and above but even in people of the lower strata. Efforts to incriminate the opposition have become part and parcel of people's daily business. This means that where there is only one party faction in a town or village things are comparatively tranquil. But where two parties compete within the same locality, every issue of self-government is laced with factional conflict, whether it is the usual roads and schools or, beyond these, agricultural facilities and management of shrine finances. It is as if whatever the other party advocates must be opposed at all costs, no matter the merits of the case. *It is just like national politics* and harmful in every instance. Political party fever is poisoning the provinces. I have argued that this intrusion of party conflict into *jichi* should be considered a violation of public morality (*kōtoku ihan*). . . .
>
> During the fourteen months that I have been here, in the two cities and 193 towns and villages in the district, eight cases of offenses committed by public officials have come to court, eleven have been investigated and reported in the newspapers but not brought to court, and who knows how many more have not even seen the light of day. Although this is doubtless due to the corruption of officials, they also say that incrimination by the opposition party is often responsible. I therefore believe that true village cooperation is impossible until this extreme political fever cools and the agitation of ambitious politicians ceases.[99]

Such political cooling was little likely, as the parties established themselves further at the prefectural, county, and local levels. In the midst of his political troubles of January 1913, Katsura received a letter from Yamagata that urged him to solicit firsthand reports on the provinces. "Conditions there are different from what they used to be," noted Yamagata in epistolary understatement, "and governors, administrators, police, and other officials appear to hold divergent views."[100] Indeed it was true that prefectural governors, once the safely bureaucratic arm of the government in the provinces, now included more and more appointees congenial to the Seiyūkai among their ranks. And although Hara Kei's attempt to abolish the county (*gun*) was foiled by Yamagata in 1906-1907, the county heads were also not impervious to party influence in the years before Hara finally succeeded in removing the *gun* from the local government system in 1921.[101] In the course of the late Meiji period the distinction between *kan* and *min* had blurred in local politics just as it had at the center. As Yamagata feared, the provincial *kan* were infiltrated with party *min*, and it was no longer possible to allege with confidence where the *kan* ceased and the *min* began. Nor, from the viewpoint of villagers and townsmen, was it clear where the *min* stopped and the *kan* commenced, since the local leaders occupied official posts and supported parties at the same time. Like their counterparts in the Diet they appeared as politicians, a profession so often associated with the governing *kan*, not the governed *min*.

In addition to the mixture of party and bureaucratic personnel in each other's bailiwick, divisions along party lines gradually appeared in prefectural, county, and village assemblies, as changes in local economic structure made the parties' presence there increasingly indispensable. The *gōnō* of the early and mid-Meiji period had for the most part worked within the village, both in their agricultural livelihoods and in their roles as local leaders. Their late Meiji counterparts increased their commercial activities, enlarged their land holdings, and functioned as a provincial elite—the often invoked *chihō meibōka*—whose political horizons spread to the prefectural level and beyond to the Diet. Many of them were landlords of middle rank who became the local mainstay of the expanding Seiyūkai and the beneficiaries of its pork-barrel "positive policy." By the mid-Taishō period, however, landlord absenteeism was loosening ties to the village, as tenant problems worsened and growing commercial and industrial interests reduced the political strength of the agricultural sector. At that point even the large landlords who could afford to remain aloof from parties in the Meiji period and rely instead on personal influence to gain their ends now often looked to the parties (frequently of the anti-Seiyūkai line) to support their interests, which in any case had become less and less "local."[102]

The localities, meanwhile, had undergone a similar transition which made it clear that they could no longer manage their fiscal affairs independent of outside aid. What in the early 1890s had sometimes been resisted as government "interference" in local matters became by the end of the Meiji period an essential dispensation of prefectural and national funds for road and school construction, flood control, and all manner of public works.[103] Demands that for so long had flowed with magisterial authority from the center to the localities were now flowing contentiously in both directions. With experienced assurance, local leaders pursued those "relations of interest" (*rigai kankei*) that the oligarchs had condemned as partisan subversiveness in 1889. This meant in effect that they concentrated their efforts on the representation of local benefit (*rieki daihyō*) that the Home Ministry had habitually labeled the enemy of *jichi* in the years since the Russo-Japanese War.[104]

At the same time that the central government was attempting to reduce its overextended budget in 1912, the localities were laying their own, often expansive, fiscal plans. In Nagano prefecture, for example, one town was embarked on a three-year 60,000-yen construction of two new elementary schools. The hamlets of another village wrangled among themselves over funds for the repair of river embankments. And yet another village planned capital increases in village assets, school budgets, and road building in commemoration of the fiftieth year of the emperor's reign.[105] Although Meiji's reign did not survive the summer nor the Saionji cabinet the year, the government lasted long enough for the Home, Education, and Agricultural Ministries to issue joint instructions in October in the name of local financial readjustment (*chihō zaisei seiri*). This demand for retrenchment was greeted with resentment and, in one Nagano paper, a cartoon showing the central government sweating with a wooden mallet to squeeze every grain of extravagance and government subsidy from sacks that contained local budgets for education and public works.[106] Not only did local officials and organizations resist the government's administrative bludgeon, but they looked to the political parties to fatten the sacks with increasing shovelfuls of prefectural and national funds. And the frustration occasioned by the discrepancy between the government's simultaneous demands for local retrenchment, its calls for increased military expenditures, and local expectations aroused by the Seiyūkai's "positive policy" was partly responsible for the flash of party support that ignited around the country during January and February of 1913.

Thus had national integration—which had been largely administrative and hortatory in the first half of the Meiji period—become political. The center and the provinces were now linked by channels of mutual demands brokered by a local elite who were increasingly tied to the parties. No longer the village patrons who dispensed paternalistic favors and raised funds among their fellows for disaster relief or school construction, the *meibōka* had outgrown the socioeconomic confines of the locality. The locality, meanwhile, had outgrown them, its own list of priorities requiring a degree of capital and of regional, even national, interconnectedness that no local men of influence could provide. Local politicians and politics alike required the extra-local mediation that the parties were ready to supply. The shift from the "land-tax politics" of the 1890s to the "railroad politics" of the post Russo-Japanese War period epitomized this changed relation between the parties and the rural elite.[107]

In early twentieth-century Japan, as in France of the same period, a politicization of the provinces had taken place. National politics now entered local life in such a way that the local elite could turn the needs and demands of the government to their own interests.[108] Equally important in the case of Japan was the injection of local politics into the national government, a phenomenon that Yamagata and others had diligently worked to prevent. The appearance of centralization projected by the early Meiji state had gradually been transformed into the reality of a nationally integrated institutional structure. And what made the structure work was not the exercise of administrative impartiality but the grease of political interest. The planners in the 1880s who intended the local government system to "strengthen the base of the nation" by keeping it productive and non-partisan had tried to meet the needs of integrated national administration without the intrusion of integrated national politics. Now politics had caught up with their plans and made Japan modern in a way that they had long hoped to avoid.

A PARLIAMENTARY
IDEOLOGY

I

THE EVENTS of the Taishō change confirmed two results of the interaction between politics and ideology in the late Meiji period. First, the ideological denial of politics on the part of the government had not prevented politics from flourishing. New participants had been attracted to its pursuits; its partisan representations had established themselves in the assemblies and penetrated the bureaucratic recesses of central and local government. Ideology, however impartial, however transcendental, could not stay the momentum of politics in its newly constitutional context. Second, what in one sense appeared to be the political denial of ideology on the part of the opposition was in fact the establishment of an alternative ideology. Its construction of the state situated the practice of parliamentary politics at the center and imperial authority at the legitimating circumference, rather than the reverse. By the end of the Meiji period this "parliamentary ide-

237

ology" had taken a permanent place within the dispersed ideological field that also contained, but was not wholly commanded by, the imperial view of the state.

The parliamentary conception of politics was distilled in the first instance from the cumulative political experience of the opposition in the decades since the Restoration. It thus in part encompassed such formulations as freedom and popular rights in the 1880s, constitutionalism in the 1910s, and democracy in the 1920s. But it was by no means a product of the critical opposition alone. If the parliamentary ideology owed its origins to the tradition of popular opposition, it owed its maturity to the "election uproar," "relations of interest," and "politics of compromise" that constituted political practice in the late Meiji period. By 1913 it was the property less of the critics than of the politicians, both local and national, who had learned to operate in party and parliamentary channels. They believed in the efficacy of these channels at the beginning of Taishō, throughout the twenties and thirties, and in the postwar period, too. Furthermore, as leading bureaucrats became involved with party politics, the parliamentary ideology became the increasingly necessary property of successful government figures as well.

For this reason what is here called a parliamentary ideology is not synonymous with the political ideals evoked by the words *Taishō demokurashii*. Indeed in important respects it was not even shared by some of the liberal theorists and activists of the democratic movement, who were often as critical of parliamentary politics as it was practiced as of the bureaucracy it was allegedly practiced against. For the ideology of politics this became and remained a significant difference. For while the ideas of a leading democratic theorist such as Yoshino Sakuzō could be considered "potentially antipolitical,"[109] those who inhabited the parliamentary universe described here were committed—heart, soul, and pocketbook—to the practice of politics.

Theirs was the section of the evolved ideological field in which the events of the Taishō change had their meaning. The parliamentary ideology imbued the participants in the constitutional movement in 1913 with optimism about the future. The further expansion of politics through the movement for universal manhood suffrage and the continuing fight for responsible party cabinets occupied a good part of the parliamentary field of vision and of the political history of the next decade. The achievement of both—suffrage in 1925 and the "normal constitutional government" of Katō Kōmei in the previous year—testified to the strength of the parliamentary view. But it remained a narrowly based strength confined to a social stratum which, though larger in number than in 1890, was still predominantly rural and propertied. Moreover, by 1913 it was already clear that even among the politically active elite the parliamentary conception of politics had limited appeal.

Both the socialist left and the nationalist right abandoned parliamentary action as part of their own "denial of politics"[110] and conducted their considerable activism in the name of society or of the nation. By the 1930s radicals of the left and right condemned the parties along with the government as the source of "abuses" inimical to the welfare of the people, whether they were defined as the propertyless masses or the agrarian Volk. Other members of the educated elite rejected public politics altogether. Often critical of the state, they displaced this criticism in the moral search for personal cultivation, the aesthetic pursuit of culture, or in the case of Yanagita Kunio, the collective representation of custom. Yanagita saw indigenous communal custom as a means of transcending the partial interests (*rigai*) associated with politics and the majority rule of only "half the people plus one."[111] In each of these cases the parliamentary conception of politics was first acknowledged as dominant, then abandoned as unworthy. Among the wider population, for whom the Taishō change was no change at all, parliamentary politics remained, as before, irrelevant. For if one legacy of Meiji ideology was the failure to prevent politics in practice, another was the success in diminishing its civic value.

II

THE GOVERNMENT, since the 1880s the most deliberate agent of the devaluation of politics, had compromised politically. Yet, ideologically, it had stood firm. Unable to depoliticize national or local government, the oligarchs and the ministries had accommodated partisan politics in the transcendental halls of power and accepted the political presence of an expanded bourgeoisie. In effect bureaucratic politicians were forced to recognize the parliamentary ideology as part of the modus operandi of practical politics. Outside this sphere, however, for the *kokumin* at large, the imperial ideology prevailed, as bureaucratic ideologues unswervingly pressed the importance of national unity and the supreme charge of undivided, unpolitical loyalty. Within the government these two positions were frequently combined. Where Itō epitomized the Meiji bureaucrat as politician and Yamagata the Meiji bureaucrat as ideologue, Tanaka Giichi managed, somewhat schizophrenically but not untypically, to be both. A military bureaucrat who manipulated first one political party, then the other, to gain the army's ends in the 1910s, Tanaka reached the highest post of his career in the late twenties as prime minister and president of the Seiyūkai.[112] At the same time that he jockeyed with the parties for political power in a way that would have been familiar to Itō, he also lavished considerable energy on ideological endeavors of the sort that his mentor, Yamagata, had always promoted. Directing his efforts toward youth, conscripts, and reservists, Tanaka warned them tirelessly against politics. "It is fine," he acceded in a concession to constitutionalism absent in the earlier period, "for you as individuals to assert your rights and duties, but if as an organization the reservists become involved politically, you will be poisoning the nation."[113]

The contamination of the body politic appeared the more lethal because of the social expansion of political sentience and activity to include members of a new generation of youth and both urban and rural elements of the masses. The expanding web of youth associations and reservist organizations was therefore added to those sectors of the population for whom political activity was interdicted. National unity and local harmony were the ideological antidote to the dangerous divisiveness of politics, which remained, as before, denatured. Thus, at the same time that the bearers of the new politics of Taishō stressed the Constitution and the parliamentary future, government ideologues invoked the emperor and the communal past. They propounded a view of national unity based on undifferentiated homogeneity, as if an ever more strenuous insistence on spiritual unity might provide an alternative to the increasingly political integration of the nation and make, the emperor willing, politics subside. When it did not, and the political currents of the 1920s drew teachers and tenants, students and workers, and also some *seinendan*, into the vortex of political activism, the government responded with a renewed combination of legal suppression and ideological suasion. In the same year that the universal manhood suffrage bill was passed and during the regime of "normal constitutional government," the Peace Preservation Law of 1925 laid the statutory basis for thought control. In the mass arrest of communists in 1928 the law was applied and strengthened under then Prime Minister Tanaka, who remained ever vigilant against the poisonous effects of evil thought (*aku shisō*).[114] Throughout the imperial period, and with increasingly severe consequences, the government reiterated its ideological point that politics, whether radical or electoral, was an improper arena for patriots.

Outside the government, the arbiters of public opinion continued to make the opposite point, attempting to raise the political consciousness of their countrymen. Toward the end of the Meiji period commentators frequently complained that the Japanese lacked an adequate awareness of themselves as a constitutional people (*rikken kokumin*).[115] As a remedy Ukita Kazutami once suggested that

> one way to make the people understand the origins, significance, spirit, and ideals of the Constitution is to explain to them that the Constitution, like our *kokutai*, is sacred (*shinsei*). Only through the realization and advancement of the Constitution can *kokutai* be assured of perpetuity. Anyone who values our *kokutai* should therefore regard the Constitution as sacred and pray for its fulfillment and harmonious advance.[116]

More common than Ukita's proposal to sanctify the Constitution, however, was the advocacy of wider dissemination of knowledge of its provisions. Diet members had continued to submit periodic memorials to the Lower House demanding more attention to electoral politics and constitutional thought in national education. In the wake of the constitutional movement in 1913, the Diet did finally pass a provision that called for the Rescript Promulgating the Constitution to be read aloud in schools and village offices on the anniversary of the promulgation each February.[117] But the Constitution had been promulgated on *kigensetsu*, the anniversary of the legendary founding of the empire and an important imperial holiday. And since the Rescript itself described the Constitution as a presentation from the emperor and his sacred imperial ancestors, this legislative provision for constitutional edification resembled Ukita's suggestion perhaps more than its sponsors intended.

A similar paradox was brought into public view in the constitutional debates between the legal scholars Minobe Tatsukichi and Uesugi Shinkichi, which occurred at the time of the political changes of 1912-1913 and were also directed toward a "clarification of the fundamental spirit of the Constitution."[118] In his arguments for the organ theory of the emperor, constitutional restraints on imperial prerogatives, and the legal and corporate nature of the state, Minobe laid the theoretical underpinnings for parliamentary government. The people must be educated so that they might participate, preserve their rights, and resist the despotism of bureaucratic government. Uesugi, following in the footsteps of his teacher Hozumi Yatsuka, emphasized the emperor as sovereign, the constitution as his imperial gift, and the historical and moral nature of the state. The people must be educated so that they might develop a strong national spirit, be

241

obedient, and preserve the *kokutai*. Together these polar positions—their proponents seated simultaneously on the law faculty of Tokyo Imperial University in the 1920s—established the universe of interpretative discourse on constitutional matters in imperial Japan. In 1913, the Movement to Protect the Constitution (*kensei yōgo*) drew on Minobe's views to help move the parties closer to power. In 1935, the League for the Protection of *Kokutai* (*kokutai yōgo*) presented Uesugi's arguments to force Minobe's resignation from the House of Peers in the name of "the clarification of the national polity."[119] While both poles of Meiji constitutional theory remained available for future political use, what they had in common was more significant for ideology. Just as Uesugi supported the law, so did Minobe support the emperor. And it was precisely this mixture of *kensei* and *kokutai*, of constitutional body politic and imperial national polity, that characterized the political shape of imperial Japan as most Japanese came to know it.

For despite complaints that the people were constitutionally untutored, by the beginning of Taishō few remained wholly ignorant of the Constitution. Without attending to the intricacies of constitutional debate that appeared in the newspapers and magazines, the wider public in 1913 was aware, in a way that it had not been in 1889, that it inhabited a constitutional state. The interpretative layers that had formed around the Constitution and the Rescript on Education were now conveyed, not only through schools and government-sponsored organizations, but also through print and every manner of social communication. Generally, the Constitution was associated with law, with obligations of civic obedience, and—in the phrase that had become so familiar that even Tanaka included it in warning the reservists against politics—with the "rights and duties" (*kenri gimu*) of the Japanese as subjects and countrymen. One of the common sermons addressed to audiences by lecturers in social education credited the Meiji emperor with "having established the Constitution to make clear the rights of the people." Whereas the farmers and townspeople of old could be cut down by samurai without recourse, one prominent lecturer argued, now that they were the people of a constitutional system they were both protected from such discrimination and granted the right of official recourse and political participation.[120] Viewed from this perspective, few would gainsay the benefits of the emperor's constitutional beneficence or reject the duties exacted in exchange for the rights bestowed. Military officers stationed in the provinces reported that the people's sense of their rights (*kenri shisō*) was increasingly well developed, an unwelcome result, suggested some, of education and freedom of the press.[121] Students accused their teachers of being "unconstitutional" when their commands contravened school rules, and geisha said the same of customers who insulted them.[122] In the vernacular of 1913 these expressions reflected the vague, but widespread sense of reciprocal obligation that attached to *rikkensei* as it was commonly understood. Thus, the difficulty confronting those who wished to instill parliamentary views in the people was less an ignorance of the constitutional polity than a well-learned dissociation of the emperor's law from politics.

The gap between imperial patriotism and practical politics was further widened by the organs of public opinion which, even as they heralded the new politics of Taishō, continued the defamation of politicians that had been steady public fare since the 1880s. The national election of May 1912 produced the familiar laments about corruption and money politics (*kinken seiji*). The press excoriated candidates who offered bribes and voters who accepted them—sometimes from both sides—and then did not even vote.[123] Those who did vote were criticized for treating the election, not as a public but as a personal matter, and for "choosing Dietmen no differently than they would a wife or bride." The bride's family background was at least investigated, but the Diet member was chosen without any consideration whatsoever of principles or character.[124] By the time government interference made the 1915 election the second most corrupt polling in Japanese history, the newspaper-reading public was long familiar with the bribery and transgressions of electoral politics. Although the critics intended their portraits of public iniquity to inspire nobler forms of parliamentary behavior, in effect the anti-government commentators were only reinforcing the government's efforts to compromise politics' good name.

The ridicule heaped on corrupt Dietmen (*fuhai giin*), delinquent representatives (*furyō daigishi*), and the truly grand decadence (*erai daraku*) of politicians now resembled the mockery once reserved for officials.[125] "Blockhead, dunce, milk sop," fools became Dietmen in popular song, and a former young man of Meiji warned Taishō youth not to crave politics as his generation had twenty years before. Considering the spectacle of the elite carrying on in the riots at Hibiya, Dietmen leading attacks on the government like grooms and rickshawmen, the writer condescendingly concluded that business would have made a higher calling.[126] Though the whiskers were gone and the carriages transformed into motor cars, the professional politicians had taken the place of the bureaucratic catfish and loach as the objects of satirical opprobrium. The bureaucracy, meanwhile, again beckoned to educated youth. In a time of diminishing employment opportunities, university graduates gravitated to the status—and security—of the civil service, low ranks as well as high.[127] And popular employment guides invariably recommended that elementary school graduates in the provinces become policemen and clerks at the local village, town, and county offices, where after four or five years one moved up a grade and "could with study even overtake one's seniors."[128] Although bureaucratic cliques were out of fashion, not so the officials, whose popular reputation appeared somewhat repaired, while the Dietmen were the new black sheep (shūrui), leaving "great stains on the history of the empire."[129]

III

THE PRACTICE of politics had changed; the ideology of politics had not. Outside the parliamentary sphere, which was remote from the experience of the majority of Japanese, neither the government nor the "public opinion of the people" had altered their separate but mutually reinforcing stances on the moral ambiguity of politics. The combined effect on popular political culture was, first, the perpetuation of the gulf between the people and politics. When Yamaji Aizan commented in 1910 that "four kinds of men of influence (yūryokusha) constitute Japan's privileged classes: the aristocracy, the society of officials (yakunin no shakai), the political parties, and the wealthy," his purpose was to argue that they be regarded "not as enemies but as allies of all the people."[130] In fact, his statement, not excluding the hostility, was a fair representation of the popular view of both politics and privilege. Government, on the one hand, remained the province of the kan. Bureaucratic politics (kanryō seiji), though "it did not appear in Aristotle's definition of politics," nor "could it be found in any foreign text on political theory," was established in law and in expertise.[131] On the other hand—and in part because the popular parties had had to accommodate themselves to the bureaucracy—the alleged representatives of the min now constituted a class of professional politicians who shared the business of government with the officials.[132] In popular perception the parties had joined the bureaucrats on the governing side of the chasm that still divided the rulers and the ruled. Together, like the kan of old, they were the subjects of politics, while the masses of Japanese considered themselves, as the min always had, to be its objects.

"While I do not understand much of politics," wrote an elderly reader to the newspaper in 1914, "what are the government's honorable high officials (okami no erai yakuninsama) doing at this moment?" Prices are high, he explained, and though the rich can afford a luxurious life, "in the middle and below we can no longer support our families. They say the laws and regulations have made us freer than in the old days, but living more comfortably would be the best freedom. Although regulations are fine, in real life money comes first, and without money laws do us no good either."[133] This attitude toward government as something done by "them" to "us" was repeatedly criticized in the press as unprogressive indifference (reitan) toward politics.[134] Why, asked Ōkuma, with customary rhetorical flourish, were the people indifferent to the representation of their interests (rigai) in the Diet: "Are they inexperienced, are they naive, or are they asleep?"[135] If anything, they were anesthetized, trained, "like the monks of medieval Europe, to take the transcendental view" and live in a parliamentary system without feeling the sensation of politics.[136] In this respect, the pre-Meiji distinction between the kan and the min remained fundamentally unchanged, and what Abe Isoo called the castration of politics by the government resulted in an inculcated sense of unconnectedness (mukankei) between the larger population and the affairs of state.[137]

Parliamentary politics, moreover, had been publicly devalued. Electoral politics was associated with unenlightened self-interest, lack of principles (shugi), and the dominance of personal relations over social good. Parties carried the stigma of partial, partisan, and factional representation; great things, it was said, were as little likely to be expected from politicians and ministers as the proverbial fish from trees.[138] This collective portrait contributed to an abiding ambivalence toward the worth of politics which, like widespread disinterest (mukanshin) in political affairs, is still considered characteristic of the Japanese electorate today.[139] That alternative forms of political action—whether class protest or patriotic terrorism—openly rejected parliamentary politics was perhaps less distinctive than the denigration of the existing political system by the dominant ideology, an ideology produced not only by the government bureaucracy, but also by minkan intellectuals most committed to the constitutional cause.

In terms of ideological process two points are suggested by this joint denaturing of politics. First, however much the imperial ideology did to moralize the nation and depoliticize the state, what it did not do to change the relation between the ruler and the ruled was of equal significance. Unconditional loyalty to the emperor accounted for only a part of the national credo. The other part, which included both the displacement of politics from civic discourse and the distaste for politics in practice, cut as deep and lay as wide as the myth of the

245

kokutai. Although not unconnected, one did not necessarily require the other. Had the emperor become a wholly constitutional monarch neither morally nor divinely cloaked, parliamentary politics might still have acquired its ambiguous reputation. For the reluctance to enshrine public mechanisms for regulating interests and resolving conflict at the center of the ideological construction of the state was not confined to the imperial ideologues. Although it is customary to say that in imperial Japan nearly everyone, left, right, and center, admitted the emperor into his view of the state, it is also true that hardly anyone, left, right, or center, cherished an utterly whole-hearted, undisillusioned allegiance to parliamentary practice. In the dominant part of the ideological field, the clear and many-voiced commission of the imperial myth was accompanied by an equally clear, if mute, omission of a restructuring of political consciousness to embrace the politics of parliamentarism.

Second, the ideological acts of commission and omission were achieved, as it were, in unison. Despite the differences of position and intention among the several ideological agents involved in the construal of modern politics, more often than not they shared an aversion to the partisan representation of partial interests associated with political parties. Arising in part from the Confucian disavowal of self-interest in the public sphere, in part from the alternative forms of resolving conflict and pursuing interests embedded in the Japanese social system, and in part from the institutional structure of the Meiji state, the resistance to partisan politics was widespread enough to be the product of mutual consent, if unintentionally so. While bureaucratic motives for the ideological denial of politics were instrumental and realistic, those of the opposition, the press, and the intellectuals were critical and idealistic. But both contributed. And just as the emperor-centered ideology alone cannot explain the popular acquiescence to the imperial state, neither can the government be held solely responsible for the displacement of politics. It is when hegemonic ideology is also the product of shared consent that it has its greatest impact. In contemporary Japan, though the emperor once divine is now symbolic, the press, the intellectuals, and the public continue to share a simultaneous belief in and disaffection for the practice of parliamentary politics. Whether this is a legacy of the Meiji state or a Meiji codification of deep social structure, the ambiguity of political value was then established and now abides.

VIII

The Language of
Ideology

THE GRAMMAR OF
IDEOLOGY

I

BY 1915 Japan possessed a public language of ideology that retained currency through the end of the Second World War. Produced in the course of the Meiji decades, the ideological vocabulary, meanings, syntax, and usage were now collectively maintained in much the same way as other parts of the evolved vernacular language. On the most general level of the social evolution of language, elements once confined to the few had become the property of the many. The model of a "fire wheeled car" that Putiatin and Perry offered in the 1850s as miniature proof of the might of the West had been domesticated, technologically and linguistically, into the ubiquitous Japanese locomotive which no longer stopped at a *suteishon* (station) but an *eki*. The railroad now represented convenience and movement to the people and the Japanese version of the serpent in Eden to the moralists.[1] The Meiji emperor, who began the period in the ancient and cloistered privacy of the court, had been transformed into a modern monarch whose symbolic presence belonged universally to his subjects. Only fifty years earlier neither railroad nor emperor had yet impinged on the experience of most Japanese. From split-skirted *hakama* to pinch-necked *haikara*; from the privileged learning of *gakumon* to the familiar windowed, wooden village school (*gakkō*); from the homely native, even regional, sense of *kuni* to the grandly imperial *teikoku*—just as Meiji Japanese made these socio-linguistic transitions in common life and speech, they also came to share a universe of ideological discourse. The language describing state and society, while in unevenly active use among different members of the population, in the passive sense at least was widely and mutually understood.

247

Like any language, the whole of Meiji ideology was larger than any one person could speak or possess, nor indeed was anyone exposed to the full range of ideological expression available at a given time. Instead, specific versions were directed to specific audiences by the ideologues who, in a society increasingly specialized in its economic and organizational structure, spoke not to the society or community at large, but to their particular clienteles and for their particular institutional purposes. As preached to conscripts and reservists, the military view of the nation centered on the emperor and the village. The emperor was invoked to inculcate a soldierly spirit of loyalty and bushidō. The village was used to create military-mindedness in rural youth disinclined to soldiering as well as in the local farmers whose vexing coolness to the army meant that, in maneuvers specifically designed to impress them, "the only ones roused by the sound of the guns are the sparrows."[2] The nation presented to the farmers by agrarianists and bureaucrats, on the other hand, was less imperial than familial. The rural prescriptions emphasized ancestral property, the "spirit of savings," and the village as the unit of the state (*kokka no tan'i*).[3] For both household and village were threatened by the same "economic demon of non-productive property that begets no economic offspring but devours them," as consumer expenses and school budgets swallowed ever increasing proportions of the productive "foundation of the nation."[4] While the rural *meibōka* were regaled with the virtues of hierarchy and their responsibilities as the local elite, the rickshawmen and shop clerks of downtown Tokyo were lectured on the benefits of the social equality conferred on them since the Restoration. "Now that all men are samurai (*bushi*)," they were urged both to cultivate "manly obedience" and to emulate the integrity of Rothschild and Mitsui.[5] It was not suggested to the carpenters of Hongō that the farmers were the backbone of the nation, nor to the farmers that factories promised not only urban degradation but a steady, if low, living wage. Such specific versions, whether for rural or elite youth, schoolteachers, local officials, Hōtokukai members, wives and mothers, or shoemakers, were directed by ideologues to the sector that most concerned them. Like dialects of the wider ideological language, they were commonly spoken in certain social places at the same time that they were rarely heard in others.

Although these specific versions often appeared to their proponents to be coherent and sufficient to express the whole, their representations remained partial and specialized. Stated goals and overstated claims notwithstanding, neither the Ministry of Education nor the Shintoists, the *minkan* nationalists nor the moralists were able to control the purity of their respective dialects. The reservist was more than likely to be a farmer as well, familiar with the sometimes competing, sometimes reinforcing vocabulary of both army and agrarian ideologues. Moreover, ideological messages were continually scrambled by the overlapping, crisscrossing lines of social communication that characterized an increasingly integrated modern society. It is therefore not the specific versions alone, but the interactions among them that account for the ideological lingua franca that had emerged by the end of the Meiji period.

II

THREE KINDS of interactions can be identified in the process that produced a universe of shared significance from diverse ideological formulations. The first emerged from the stressed parts of ideological speech, what is here called the "middle of the message"; the second from the unstressed elements that often appeared as the "dependent clauses" of ideological utterance; and the third from the unarticulated elements, identified here as the "deep social meanings" that made ideological discourse comprehensible to those who participated in it. These interactions, like a grammar of ideology, characterized the process by which the common ideological language was continuously produced.

The first and most obvious kind of interaction was the most overt—the repetitive, stressed meanings that appeared in a variety of sources. Constituting the "middle of the message," these were elements so common that their constant repetition lent them a cumulative weight. Just as intersecting circles of different colors produce a common sliver of deeper hue in their overlapping segments, ideological expressions which otherwise were different in content and purpose shared elements whose presence was intensified by layer after layer of reinforcing appearances. In this category fall many of the signs, symbols, and myths that are now associated with *tennōsei* ideology and were then invoked to solve the perceived civic riddles of national unity and social order.

The Meiji emperor, as monarch to whom allegiance was due and symbol of modernity, appeared in virtually every context. In his regal form the imperial presence was thus everywhere apparent. As a manifest deity, however, the emperor remained in the more parochial reaches of public expression, in those parts of the circles that were socially fainter because they less often overlapped. *Kokutai*, in its elemental aspect as a myth of continuity that signified Japan's national distinctiveness, also appeared in the middle of intersecting ideological messages. But the same surpassing vagueness that contributed to its currency as a referent for the nation may also have prevented *kokutai* from accreting the layers of descriptive detail that clung so easily to the emperor. Although by the end of the Meiji period, *kokutai* was generally understood as a synonym for Japan, it was less commonly mentioned than the ruler whose line and state it symbolized. The phrase *chūkun aikoku*, loyalty and patriotism, had also become a civic cliché by virtue of its similarly repetitive presence. Standing for a certain minimum of secular social conformity, the phrase could be summoned to many purposes since, like *kokutai*, it required not precise definition but undifferentiated general assent. While ideologues continued to emphasize *chūkun aikoku* as the goal of moral education, others invoked it in the name of such causes as party loyalty, the entrepreneurial imperative to rise in the world, or the promotion of the sales of domestic—rather than imported—beer.[6] The incessant mention of empire, on the other hand, resembled that of the emperor, in that *teikoku* acquired an increasingly concrete presence in the public language of all social dialects. In this case, it was not the ancient founding myths of empire or the latest justification of constitutionalism at home and imperialism abroad that accumulated in the middle of the message, but the constant evocation of the Great Empire Japan (*DaiNihon teikoku*). Of 1,592 youth surveyed in one locality in 1913, only two in ten elementary school graduates knew why the sun goddess was important, and no more than three in ten could identify the founding holiday of *kigensetsu*.[7] But the crossed flags of the Imperial Army and Navy appeared everywhere, in the town halls, in popular magazines, illustrations, and on crockery. And the "fifty million countrymen" who now spread from "Karafuto to Taiwan" appeared in texts, oratory, and popular song. Like the modern monarch, they were invoked as concrete evidence of Japan's new status as a "first-class nation" (*ittōkoku*) which had "joined the ranks of the powers" and become an empire in the East.[8] These elements— emperor and empire, *kokutai* and *chūkun aikoku*—were the patriotic concentrate that emerged from the vast amounts of ideological effort devoted to developing "a sense of nation."

In the attempts of the ideologues to cope with "a complicated society," the middle of the message contained the village in the place of greatest ideological depth. Whether the administrative village of *jichi* that was invoked as the local locus of citizenship, the national village preached by the army as the cradle of the military spirit, or the folkish village of agrarian romantics, the symbols of meaningful community were concentrated in the countryside.[9] Related elements, such as the evocation of "beautiful customs" (*bifū*) which suggested native Japanese ways or the invocation of harmony as Japan's greatest social virtue, appeared most often in the rural context.

> The customs of our childhood have become mere formalities . . . the old homemade gifts replaced by strange Western-style sweets imported from Nagoya and wrapped in gaudy paper with names like "chrysanthemum mist" written on it. . . . The worship of local gods, once the most important organ of village solidarity (*nōson danketsu*) . . . now deteriorated into meaningless ceremony, the festivals into brawls (*kenka matsuri*) . . . family members into birds searching frantically outside the home for a place to light. . . .

"Relations of interest" (*rigai kankei*), vulgar entertainment, city life, and Ibsen's Nora—all threatened the unity of the family, the solidarity of the village, and thus, "the superiority of the Japanese people."[10] The widely shared association of socialism with destructiveness also suggested that the social order most imperiled by such doctrines was that of the village community. Like the prejudice against partisan politics, which was another product of the middle of the message, the distrust of socialism and individualism as alien notions was generally couched in terms of their anti-social character, and the society in question, more often than not, was the village.

The reiteration that gave the family its social centrality in ideological language also appeared in close conjunction with the concern for village life. Bureaucratic diatribes against rural youth who sought unseemly amounts of education were echoed by the farmers themselves. Forbidden by his father to stand for the teaching examinations, one eldest son studied on the sly, stood secretly for the exams, and passed, to which news the neighbors reacted with such condoling remarks as "That's the end of that family." And with that family, other families, and with other families, the fabric of the village—in this case in Tōhoku in the desperate years after the Russo-Japanese War—was also threatened. The schoolteacher's family, former samurai who became owner-farmers at the time of the Restoration, fell deeply into debt and finally into bankruptcy, two years after the "village heretic" had sneaked off to his examinations. As if to prove the contagion of the heresy, other youth also became teachers, or policemen, station attendants, nurses, and midwives, and "things became very different in the village than they had been several years ago."[11] Thus, in an overlapping and reinforcing way, were family and village added to the densest area of ideological concentrate. That the concentrate contained four parts nation to two parts society reflected a

251

relative difference, not in concern with the two issues, but in the available inventory of values and, most important, in the effective extent of shared communication.

Shared communication of this sort is not, properly speaking, the same thing as consensus.[12] If agreement or convergence of opinions produces consensus, then the arbiters of public opinion who opposed the government in the name of a "hard line" in foreign policy represented a consensus on that subject. Ideologically, however, their position remained a partial version. Those committed to the issue agreed in a broad consensual fashion, while those to whom the issue did not "speak" heard little of it at all. In the middle of the message, the situation was very nearly the reverse. Everywhere except in the reinforcing center, the ideological expressions were more or less in disagreement. And those for whom the surrounding issue was irrelevant were likely to hear *only* the common refrain. Though they may not have been listening for it, it became so familiar that it could not help but be "overheard."

The ideological presence of the emperor, for example, was therefore not the product of consensus. The political parties festooned their campaign meetings in 1890 with contradictory banners proclaiming "Liberty Forever," "Sincerity Moves Heaven," and "Long Live the Emperor"; the constitutional rallies in 1913 denounced every action of the government that claimed his majesty's authority, then closed the proceedings with vigorous shouts of Tennō heika banzai![13] Kita Ikki argued in 1906 that political relationships should be transformed so that the people belonged not to the emperor but both emperor and people belonged equally to the state, while textbooks and popular readers phrased the emperor familially as the mother and father of the Japanese.[14] Although these—and many other—diverse sources of divergent opinion had the emperor in common, they neither agreed with one another as to his nature nor held opinions that converged at the point that the emperor entered their discourse. Instead they could be said to have been committed to separate issues but engaged with the same symbols.[15] And the more these symbols were stressed and repeated, the more other people became engaged with them as well. The result was that these words, as if capitalized, were used like universal proper nouns in the shared ideological language. Large numbers of Japanese came to acknowledge them, at the same time that their symbolic valences remained general enough to be variously interpreted and mutually reinforced. Earlier in the Meiji period commentators had suggested that monarchies, like mountains and rivers, were "naturally formed," and that the emperor, like Mt.

Fuji, would inspire patriotic sentiment as Niagara Falls did in America.[16] Niagara Falls aside, it is true that by the end of Meiji, the emperor and other elements from the middle of the message were established in the landscape. Socially created symbols, they had been transformed by time and circumstantial ubiquity into the ideological equivalent of natural monuments.

III

THE NATURALIZATION of meaning also took other, equally repetitive but less obvious forms. Indeed a second and very effective kind of interaction among the different versions of state and society occurred in the *un*stressed parts of ideological speech. Parse an ideological sentence, and it will frequently be found to have begun with a dependent clause that stated the reason for the main proposition. In it the speaker revealed why he felt impelled to enjoin as he did, and what imperfect condition or crisis roused him to public utterance. Since he was identifying the problem for which the main statement was his solution, this was often the most eloquent—and for the historian, most informative—part of his message. But for the speaker it was also the part that he expected his audience most readily to understand. He assumed they would agree that "since so many youth are led astray by the ways of the city . . . ," some melioration of the problem was necessary, and he happened to have one to hand. He then spent a fair portion of his public time expounding the virtues of, say, night schools in the provinces, hoping to persuade local educators, youth, or their parents of the merits of his proposal.

For the ideologue the main interest of his presentation lay in night schools, not the perils of urban life. For the student, or grammarian, of ideology, it is often the other way around. This is because the dependent clauses of ideological utterance, be they sentences, paragraphs, or volumes, contained the meanings socially held in common. These were elements assumed to be intelligible and meaningful, the common ground from which, once rhetorically surveyed, the speaker could launch his distinctive cannonade. Some ground, however, was more common than other ground, and even a cursory review of dependent clauses reveals that otherwise divergent introductory statements frequently contained meanings so universal that they appeared to be nothing more than common sense. "As civilization progresses" (*bunmei no shinpo to tomo ni*), it brought with it socialism—or the evils of the city, changes in ways of living, a rise in the suicide rate, or lefthandedness—and so the ideologues proposed their several solutions.[17] And the more such notions as "civilization" and "progress" appeared in these dependent clauses, the less remarkable, the more commonsensical they seemed. But common sense, as has been observed, is never as unremarkable as it seems. It, too, is a social product, a collective gloss on experience that seems natural or self-evident only because it is so widely shared.[18]

Indeed, some of the elements that constituted ideological common sense at the end of the Meiji period were either absent or arcane just fifty years before. *Bunmei*, or civilization, which had begun the Meiji era as a word foreign in form and European or Western in meaning, was gradually naturalized. First it acquired the adjectives "new" or "Japanese" before it, and then it shed even those.[19] By the end of the period, "civilization" appeared as an indigenous fact of social life that possessed the same descriptive transparency as any unmodified common noun.

In the process of naturalization, *bunmei* migrated from the main to the dependent clause of ideological speech. In the 1870s civilization and enlightenment were articulated as part of a conscious program to adopt and adapt Western ways. In those years the apostles of civilization often initiated their exhortations with some variety of the phrase, "for the sake of national strength and expanding national power."[20] For this was one of the most common dependent clauses of the mid-nineteenth century, while the injunction to "civilization" constituted the main purport of the sentence. Overtly stressed and repeated as the central proposition of many utterances, over the years the association of Japan with civilization accumulated almost subliminally in the listener. By the 1900s even those displeased with the effects of *bunmei* were not free to dismiss the notion, any more than they could—or would—roll up the railroad tracks that were the material epitome of its achievement.[21] At that point "civilization" appeared most often in the dependent clauses. It was offered as a preamble—which though "it goes without saying," was nonetheless said—in the introductory parts of ideological statements. There, like salutations and other common furnishings of social intercourse, *bunmei* was taken for granted in such a way that it was used, as it were, subliminally by the speaker.

Available for any context, applicable in any situation—as an ideological salutation, "civilization" was now everywhere in use. Social critics suggested that its "evil consequences" led to extravagances that were to be cured with frugality, while in its "underside" lay temptations that could be thwarted with belief in the gods and Buddhas. The "ornaments" of civilization were said to encourage materialistic concern that only the spirit of familial love and duty could remedy, and its "empty trappings" were blamed for misleading the government, which should reform by "using money to encourage local industry."[22] More general mention of the ills of civilization (*bunmeibyō*), or even just "so-called civilization" (*iwayuru bunmei*), was enough to set the ideological train of thought in motion. Other references alleged that the "trappings" of civilization included a factory law, and that its "ways" (*fūzoku*) could accommodate Nogi's suicide. In the exhilarating context of "warring civilizations," writers urged that Japan must become first in the world, and that "in today's civilized times," stones should not be thrown at trains. In the most familiar phrase of all—"as civilization progresses"—commentators explained that economic issues become naturally more complex, which suggested, for example, that "the government should pay off local debts."[23]

Perhaps the largest number of allusions to *bunmei* occurred in more neutral statements that purported to describe the evident consequences of civilization. "As everyone knows," or "it goes without saying"—these were delivered in a bland and factual manner, as if the speaker, his audience, and indeed all intelligent beings would surely know that civilization results in increasing professional specialization, higher government expenditures, an intensified "struggle for survival," or airplanes.[24] In 1902 a local village plan stated simply that although in the past people abided by the proverbial number of three or, at most, four children, "those born since the laws of civilization were promulgated are all being brought up, and it is now not uncommon to raise as many as seven or eight children."[25] The issue here was the means to increase farm production to cover the ever higher costs of rearing and educating children. And the simple declarative statement alluding to what may have been a significant decrease in infanticide slipped by as yet another commonplace result of "civilization." A village plan of 1914 traced the recent increase in bankruptcies to the same cause. "Although the failures arise from reverses in enterprises undertaken by the people who have breathed too deeply of the air of material civilization, the immediate cause is the rise in the standard of living and the fall in savings and diligence which has caused us to forget our allotted measure."[26] In this instance the aim was the encouragement of parsimony to keep farm families from selling their lands and moving to the cities. Rising expectations among the peasants were mentioned, but only in passing, as another self-evident consequence of civilization.

Such indications that *bunmei* was perceived as a social fact of life, however, do not imply that Meiji Japanese "agreed" on its meaning or value. Indeed, just as with the stressed elements of ideology, the unstressed, seemingly commonsensical aspects could sustain diverse interpretations and engender controversy and disagreement. Nonetheless, civilization had become part of the late Meiji world to which Japanese of the time had frequent collective, though not harmonious, reference. Thus, while the new men and women of Meiji criticized the morality of their elders for being unscientific and uncivilized, the socialist Kōtoku Shūsui decried the ways of civilization as mere hypocrisy.[27] But good or bad, hailed or defamed, the existence of "civilization" was itself no longer a question.

The unquestioned elements that reverberated in the dependent clauses therefore constituted an important part of the common ideological language that had emerged by the end of the Meiji era. Although seemingly less assertive than stressed national symbols like the emperor or social referents like the village, it is possible that these understood values were both more widely uttered and more deeply heard than the overtly belabored refrains. The idea of progress, for example, the general theorem of which civilization was but the Meiji application, was ubiquitously invoked. The phrase *wagakuni no shinpo hattatsu*, literally "the progress and advance of our country," appeared so often that specific meaning was largely drained from it. So many things were said to have occurred "together with progress," so much urged "for the sake of progress," that progress itself was taken for granted. Indeed one of the progressive intellectuals who criticized the "spiritual shallowness of Japanese civilization" as the Meiji era ended, deplored the fact that such criticism was overshadowed by the "eulogists of the present" (*jisei ōkasha*) and thus had virtually no influence on most Japanese. "On the contrary the majority of the people anticipate further national progress (*koku'un no shinpo*) and are optimistic about contemporary civilization."[28] And those who, like this writer, were less than optimistic, sought not to halt the march of progress, but only to redirect it.

Constitutionalism was another element that migrated from the main proposition to the dependent clause in the course of the Meiji period. In the 1870s and 1880s the issue of the constitutional system (*rikkensei*) had been the programmatic focus of political debate. Introduced by such dependent clauses as the "necessity of the trend of the times" or "in the name of liberty and popular rights," modern conceptions of constitutionalism gradually emerged. In the late 1880s and 1890s as the constitutional system was implemented and interpreted, the notion of *rikkensei* gained increasingly broader social currency. By the time of the Taishō change in 1913, constitutionalism itself was no longer the issue. From geisha to bureaucrats, Japanese applied it to their world, each perhaps meaning something different but presuming enough semantic common ground to make the usage comprehensible. Like civilization and progress, constitutionalism was an element new to general parlance in the mid-nineteenth century that by the early twentieth century had come to seem part of the very structure of things.

Other elements in the dependent clauses were not new but transmuted. The striving for success in the world (*risshin shusse*), which was the Meiji doctrine of progress expressed on the level of the individual, had earlier origins in Tokugawa social thought. In 1872 it received its first official formulation in the Education Act that linked learning to success and, in the following years, its popular reinforcement in the inspirational tales of Smiles' *Self-Help*. In 1912 this message had so permeated society that "in order to rise in the world" had become the common justification for all manner of individual striving, including that for more education than the government was by then prepared to encourage. Still other elements in the dependent clauses were as old as the nation. In particular, the word *wagakuni*, "our country," or in effect, Japan, formed an ancient incantation familiar in such degree to the ideological elite that it had appeared from the first among the commonplaces of their introductory phrases. By virtue of a half-century of unstressed but constant reiteration, however, these words and others of similar meaning were now as natural to vast numbers of Japanese as they once had been to the learned few. The nineteenth-century myths of progress, the Meiji dogmas of civilization, the political doctrines of constitutionalism, the social morality of success, the national and ethnic sense of being "we, Japanese"—these generalities may have been as beguiling (and in the end as inescapable) as the more obvious elements of what was later called *tennōsei* ideology. For if the emperor was the ideological counterpart of a natural monument, familiar to everyone at a distance, here was the ideological ground on which he and his subjects stood, the ordinary terrain that seemed less remarkable for its always being underfoot.

IV

EVEN LESS remarkable, and in general unremarked, were the social meanings that enabled ideological expressions to "make sense" in the context in which they were articulated. Neither monuments nor ordinary terrain, these elements lay in the deepest strata of Japanese society. They seldom occurred in either the stressed or the unstressed

257

parts of ideological utterances but filled the unspoken spaces between them. These were the fundamental values that did indeed go without saying, yet were indispensable to the meaningfulness of anything being said. Thus they contributed to the third kind of interaction by which a common ideological language was produced. Just as linguists assert that acquaintance with the vocabulary, sentence structure, or dialects of a language is not sufficient to account for effective communication among its users, in ideology, too, it is the shared and assumed, though often unarticulated, meanings embedded in social practice that make the spoken language of ideology intelligible.

Because community was a positive value collectively expressed and practiced in the Japanese social system, appeals to community spiritedness (*kōkyōshin*) and cooperative unity (*kyōdō itchi*) on the local level made sense in that context. Those local citizens who were judged by frustrated army officers to be "poor in cooperative unity" or to possess "absolutely no spirit of community" understood what was meant by such terms even if they did not always choose to exemplify them in their behavior.[29] Similarly, without the established notions of self-improvement that characterized Confucian thought and popular social morality of the Tokugawa period, neither the doctrines of *Self-Help* nor the association of education with personal success would have fallen on so many ready ears. Confirmed attitudes toward authority made the separation of *kan* and *min* comprehensible and amplified the preference for law over politics as a means of regulating the relationship between the ruler and the ruled. And the preference for morality and mores over law as the guarantees of civic order emerged against the background of the communitarian ethos that was the most familiar and practiced socio-moral form of the majority of the Japanese.

From these collective attitudes arose not only the areas of deeply shared agreement but also the areas of deeply shared tension and ambivalence that characterized the ideology of imperial Japan. The competing claims of community and hierarchy expressed in traditional social relations were echoed in the insistence on egalitarian opportunity in education or enterprise and, simultaneously, on maintaining the ranks of social position and bureaucratic expertise. "Self-government" stressed the community both as a social end in itself and as a unit in the national hierarchy of institutional authority. The Boshin Rescript described the people—the sentiments of high and low united—as a moral community of subjects under the emperor. At the same time they were also cast as hierarchically subject to the authority of local, prefectural, and national bureaucracies. Conflicting notions of personal striving and social harmony appeared in the ideological contradictions between the sometimes reluctant endorsement of individual economic competition and the always insistent exhortation to place the common welfare of the family or village before that of any of its members. A venerable Confucian ambivalence toward getting and spending underlay the ideological queasiness toward money, which concealed entrepreneurial aggressiveness in the spiritual armor of bushidō and muted the emphasis on business that might easily have suited a surging capitalist economy. Familial conceptions of the state and folkish views of the nation rested congenially with communitarian values that less readily accommodated either raw individualism or representations of class conflict. On the other hand, neither state nor nation made the same kind of immediate sense as the economic and social imperatives of personal success and family survival. Indeed, the unrelenting efforts of the ideologues to assert the preeminence of public values revealed that it was often the private ones that constituted the stronger personal motivation. The continued tension between the public and the private poles of civic value arose in part because Japan's deepest social meanings did not readily dispose people—whether blindly or with forethought—to make "the leap to the state."[30]

These same social meanings, however, accounted for some of the public behavior for which ideology is occasionally credited. Ideologists were frequently pleased to conclude that the effective functioning of village organizations or the evident patriotism of landlord elites was due in part to the success of their considerable efforts to "influence" the people. Others were forever lamenting—this time in dirge-like refrain at the ends of their sentences—that the popular indifference (reitan) toward their ideological ministrations was regrettable, deplorable, most grievous, and not easily borne.[31] The former claim asserted the power, the latter the powerlessness of overt ideological suasion to produce results in social practice. In fact, social practice produced its own results. Voters gathered to pre-select their candidate; villagers participated en masse in demonstrations lest refusal result in the traditional attack on the non-participant's house; women marched out with their neighbors in wartime to plant the required number of trees; and prefectural assemblymen voted a trifling sum for the Home Ministry's "local improvement" program so as not to appear wholly uncooperative.[32] The responsiveness, or lack of it, owed less to ideology than to what one Meiji theorist of social education called the moral power of social sanction. After all, he added, bushidō had developed "from the samurai's desire not to be laughed at," and even in the twentieth century when money reigned supreme, society possessed its powers of moral sanction, if only it would use them.[33]

Society did use them, if not directly in service of the state or the "true spirit of bushidō," at least in pursuit of its own diverse interests, to which questions of money remained germane. Not only social sanction but a practiced sense of collective benefit moved local organizations and national professional associations to lobby aggressively for funds or favors. Villages that vied with one another in building elementary schools in the 1870s competed for selection as the site of a prefectural middle school in the 1910s. The Ministry of Education applauded their efforts in the first instance and deplored them in the second. The villages, however, remained consistent, intent throughout on the "pursuit of their own advantage (yūri)."[34] When the advantage conflicted with national exhortation, they were charged by the officials with uncivil indifference; when the response coincided with the latest directives, Ministry bureaucrats awarded citations of merit and claimed the credit for themselves. Often, in the relation between ideology and conduct what ideologists considered their own doing was instead the result of a high degree of shared social meanings and motivations that sometimes supported and sometimes conflicted with the specific ideological formulations.

Like all elements of social systems, these collective attitudes placed certain limits on ideology, both because the ideologists shared them and also because any wild deviation from them would have set a given formulation too much at odds with conventional social wisdom. Like syntax in language, the deep social meanings determined what ideologists would and could say, but were neither all-determining nor unchanging. Although a language accepts new vocabulary far more easily, syntactical change also occurs. Discussions of prewar ideology sometimes inadvertently suggest that such was not the case in the social language of rural Japan. Analyses of the social basis of ultranationalism and militarism or accounts of "the moral authority of the collectivist ethic" in connection with "the rural origins of Japanese fascism" occasionally convey the impression of a tenacious substratum of social tradition that ran rock-hard under the newer ideological edifices built upon them in the modern period.[35]

Yet the fundamental conceptions of social relations were also changing, albeit far more slowly than the ideological surface with which they interacted. For ideology, these interactions made a difference. Unspoken, even unthought, but enacted in social behavior— conceptions of the relation between self, family, and community, for example, rose from deep within the social system to connect with learned socio-moral formulations like filiality and more program-matic injunctions like the admonition against forsaking the ancestral lands. Yet, fundamental familial values were also in the process of slow movement and change, the nature of which was affected by new attitudes introduced into the rapidly altering social order. As the permanence and the settled roles of the members of a rural farm family were loosened by the currents of social and economic change, age-old conceptions of the family were perforce transmuted. Simi-larly, the social meaning of community clearly influenced the devel-opment of a modern ideology that became bourgeois communitarian rather than bourgeois individualist. Social relations, however, were also changing, sometimes in ways quite contrary to the increasing aversion to the "bourgeois" values on the part of ideologues in the prewar decades. That postwar Japan eventually became one of the most "middle-class" of industrial capitalist societies was due in part to changes in social value that were proceeding even as the official ideology in the 1930s glorified the farmer and the soldier.

FROM THESE interactions among the stressed, unstressed, and unartic-ulated parts of ideological "speech" the common language of ide-ology emerged. Here speech includes not only the spoken and writ-ten words of the ideologists of every persuasion, but the array of social symbols from which Meiji Japanese gathered their reinforcing meanings. These included railroads, the "engines of civilization" that suggested mobility of goods and persons, the latter, when they were village youth, seemingly less welcome than the former. Tokyo streetcars stood as the new plebeian vehicles of the metropolis as well as embodiments, together with police boxes, of the apparatus of wealth and power that became the object of mass rage during strikes and demonstrations. In the countryside the farmer saw in the silk-worm both the emblem of the economic difficulties that confronted him and a partial if ever elusive remedy for them. From the elemen-tary schools now universally established in the heart of the village beckoned the possibilities of success through education, at the same time that continuing to middle school remained beyond the economic means of most of the pupils' families. In wars the meaning of empire and sacrifice were both writ large, while smaller rites in the village tied emperor and nation to the ceremonial coattails of the local elite. These and many other social symbols communicated partial render-ings of state and society that resonated with those of the ideologues. Together, these were the echoes of the chants of the ideological chorus that hailed the nation in the 1880s and bewailed society in the 1900s, the concerns of the late Meiji period reverberating widely well beyond their time.

THE CONTEXT OF
IDEOLOGY

I

THE TIME remained all-important. For the ideologues were responding to the late Meiji world which then set its stamp on their every utterance. Thus the ideological language they produced depended in good part on that world for its efficacy. At this point the examination of ideology necessarily shifts from the grammatical to the contextual. In an analysis of language the grammarian can perhaps stop with the interactions that form the discourse and enable it to be mutually understood. In a discussion of ideological process, however, a further step is necessary. This is because ideologues intend their speech to be not only understood but also believed and even acted upon. And for ideology to be credible, something more than common currency is required.

Unless ideological formulations possess a certain congruence with the experience of those to whom they are directed, any hegemony that occurs is likely to be fragile. Whether in the emphatic middle of the message, the unstressed dependent clause, or the deep and silent social meanings, the more ideological elements appear to "fit" the political, social, and economic realities as people know them, the more unexceptionable they seem. Something that seems, however deceptively, to be unexceptionable settles into the social landscape smoothly enough not to obstruct the view. An element might be as deeply engrained as the Confucian social ethic which was suddenly raised to an imperial dictum in the Rescript on Education, or as manipulative as the amuletic invocation of national unity to ward off politics before the opening of the Diet. But in the context in which these views were advanced, neither, in essence, was "hard to believe." Indeed, filial piety and national unity scarcely seemed to require active belief; the avoidance of overt disbelief was for the most part sufficient. Congruence, in short, contributed to the "apparent invisibility" of ideological values.

Since the congruence, like the invisibility, was always more apparent than real, Meiji ideology never wholly fit the reality it purported to describe. Yet the ideological language that had emerged in

Japan by 1915 possessed enough congruence with the world that produced it that it appeared generally plausible and in a number of aspects even commonsensical. This meant that Meiji Japanese could share basic premises without undue contention or coercion and argue instead over the specific formulations that most concerned them. Within this framework of general credibility, however, some parts of Meiji ideology seemed to rest more easily than others in the experience of Japanese of the period. And differences in congruence, loosely conceived, may help to explain why the views of the nation appeared more unexceptionable than the views of society in the context of the late Meiji period.

In matters of timing, the ideological efforts to create "a sense of nation" which gathered momentum in the late 1880s appeared to some extent after the political fact. That is, the early Meiji changes had established the national structures for which the late Meiji ideologues were attempting to provide a civic ethos. In another sense, however, in 1890 the constitutional system was just beginning, national integration was in the process of transition from an asserted condition to political actuality, and the international stature that Japan had sought since the 1860s still lay in the future. Thus, as the concerned commentators plied their diverse ideological trades, their work coincided to some degree with the evolution of the systems that they were interpreting. This contemporaneity of historical change and ideological construction lent to late Meiji views of the nation of initial advantage in congruence. The nineteenth-century projects of nation and empire that impelled the ideologues were simultaneously impelled by them, and in the dialectic between experience and ideology, the relationship between description and prescription was relatively close.

Views of the nation were also unexceptionable because they seemed to suit and indeed fulfill nineteenth-century phenomena both within Japan and in the world. The modern monarch, national unity and national distinctiveness, a secular morality of citizenship, and the increasingly assertive boast of empire did not much strain late Meiji credulity. Long sought and oft discussed, these national values rested familiarly and unimposingly, not only in the government's house but in many corners of the plural social field. The considerable history of concern with the nation was matched by a rich inventory of values available both from within Japanese tradition and from the newer stock appropriated from the West. Moreover, in the quarter century between 1890 and 1915, events appeared for the most part to corroborate the widely communicated views of nation and empire. People became accustomed to perceiving themselves as *kokumin*. Successful wars confirmed Japan as an expanding nation in the world. And the encomia after the emperor's death expressed both international recognition of and national satisfaction with "Japan's achievement in forty-five years of what had taken several hundred in the West."[36] In their most general sense the nineteenth-century views of the nation were not ultimately disconfirmed until the defeat in 1945, and some, such as the civic "sense of nation," continue into the present.

In addition to timing, a suitable inventory of values, and historical corroboration, immediacy—or rather, the lack of it—may also have contributed to the relatively effective communication of the Meiji sense of nation. Collective assent to national values was perhaps more easily gained because they impinged less immediately on people's lives. Except in war, few Meiji Japanese consciously confronted the nation when they awoke each morning. The resentment they felt toward such national impositions as tax collection and conscription was generally directed at the bureaucratic intermediaries who administered them. Draft evasion, which in the late Meiji years had its gods to whom families prayed for their sons' failure in the physical examination, was not inconsistent with popular reverence for the emperor.[37] Withholding information on family property, budgets, tax payments, and debts from inquiring officials—keeping "secrets" from "science," as one mayor of a model village expressed it—did not conflict with the family members' performance of their other national duties as army reservists or "patriotic women."[38] Requests and grievances continued to be expressed to the officials, at the same time that displaying the flag and cheering the monarch came relatively easily by the end of the period.

In the case of political values, the situation was somewhat different. The discrepancy between the ideological efforts to contain politics and the establishment of an effectively functioning parliamentary system grew more apparent with time. Politics pervaded the localities in the form of parties and "relations of interest," increasing the tension between ideology and experience. In national politics the government itself propagated one line and practiced another. Evidence of these strains in congruence appeared in the formulation of a parliamentary ideology that postulated a thoroughly political sphere as an alternative to the depoliticized official version. Yet since politics was remote from the experience of the majority of Japanese, this discrepancy was less obtrusive than it might have been had the dichotomy between the *kan* and the *min* not remained so sharp.

Compared to the views of the nation and even to those of politics, late Meiji views of society were less congruent from the first. This was in part a result of timing. For when the ideological elite raised their voices in concern over "a complicated society," it was in response to social change that they felt had somehow got ahead of them. The social and economic consequences of "civilization," which became increasingly manifest in the decade between the two Meiji wars, presented the ideologues with a twentieth-century project that was already under way when—with apparent surprise and no little chagrin—they began to respond to it. In this case the late Meiji figures appeared to be running after reality, constructing their versions of society on the heels of social change. Often the result was a gap between the situation they described—or, typically, the ills they diagnosed—and the prescriptions they offered to remedy them. Appearing after the social phenomena that provoked them, late Meiji views of society sometimes seemed perceptibly behind the times.

In national matters, the ideologists had generally attempted to impel change; in social issues, many hoped to restrain it. For an industrializing economy they reinvigorated an agrarian myth, and in an urbanizing society they apotheosized the village. In the face of gesellschaft, gemeinschaft was invoked; confronted with increasing individuation and even anomie, ideologues enshrined the family—the hyphenated metaphor of the family-state in effect sanctifying the family at least as much as it domesticated the state. As the Darwinian struggle for survival was absorbed into popular morality, even rural Japanese sought to gird themselves for the arena with the help of guides "to increase your memory-power" and home remedies for "the nervous prostration (*shinkei suijaku*) that inevitably accompanies civilization."[39] But for the same affliction, agrarianists—arguing that cities functioned by competition (*kyōsō*), but villages operated on a different social principle—prescribed instead cooperative unity (*kyōdō itchi*), communal striving, and a cessation of higher education.[40] For rural economic difficulties, commonly proffered solutions included frugality, fertilizer, and *fukugyō* (agricultural sidelines such as sandal-making and sericulture), while fiscally strapped localities heard lectures on austerity and more effective community self-help.[41] As the rural men of moderate means so often invoked in the eighties and nineties disappeared into the "citified, officialized" provincial elite and the salaried urban middle class increased in number, ideologists spoke more and more critically of middle-class self-interest and idleness. And of the working class, they generally preferred not to speak at all. Meanwhile, the spirit of bushidō was preached to the petit bourgeois, and reverence for the gods to the farmer.[42]

265

This frequent evocation of the social past was appealing and straining at the same time. For it postulated the retrieval of a world that beckoned even as it was disappearing. An inventory of familiar values that included family, village, and social custom did not in itself lack credibility, especially in the countryside, where these homely values originated and the majority of people still lived. But the traditional verities could no longer be propped up in the corners of social life and, because in daily use, taken familiarly for granted. The more experience gave them the lie, the more they were scrubbed and polished and enshrined. To maintain them in the face of the socioeconomic changes that accompanied Japan's transition to a mature capitalist economy and a mass industrial society would require considerable effort. And since this transition was in fact just then beginning, the discrepancy between the official social myths and an urbanizing, industrializing society with an increasingly vulnerable agricultural sector only widened with the years. More often than not, therefore, experience disconfirmed ideological constructions whose congruence had been problematic from the start.

Late Meiji views of society suffered a disadvantage, not only in terms of timing, a predominantly rural inventory of values, and the consequent lack of historical corroboration, but also in terms of immediacy. Unlike national values, the social exhortations often flew in the face of everyday socioeconomic realities as the Japanese experienced them. The frequent injunctions against materialism, enterprise fever, and get-rich-quick speculation (*ikkaku senkin shugi*) conflicted with the owner-farmer's economic common sense that any promising commercial scheme would be preferable to another year's poor crop in rice or barley. Sermons on the sanctity of the ancestral occupation were less persuasive to the poorer rural population than the economic difficulties (*seikatsunan*) that drove increasing numbers of second and third sons from the farms to migrant labor, jobs in the cities, or overseas to Korea and North America. In some villages as many as one-fifth of the population were resident elsewhere, and others had several "America widows" who, in the temporary but long absence of their husbands, were considered a moral threat to the men who remained.[43] Whether or not this was the case, the government officials and itinerant moralists who delivered these sermons often spoke at odds with the experience of their local audiences. Villagers were understandably skeptical of the repeated charges of extravagance leveled at them. Commentators who praised the days when only the headmen had *tatami* mats on the floor of their houses and criticized the tenants for expecting such luxuries in 1913 were engaged in an uphill battle against economic interest and social change.[44] Since these were issues that people did confront in their daily life, ideological incongruity was immediately apparent, not only to them but also to the ideologues, who continued to cast around for solutions to a "complicated society" long after their "sense of nation" had taken its essential shape.

Because they seemed to tug against the direction of socioeconomic change, the views of society settled less unexceptionably into the late Meiji landscape than the views of the nation. And yet, in 1915, this disparity was still a relative one. Despite the fact that ideologues often invoked the rural past as society itself was moving toward a different future, even the social formulations were not unbelievable in the context of the present. Village Japan, after all, still predominated: close to three-fifths of the gainfully employed population worked in agriculture in 1915; in 1913 nearly three-quarters of the Japanese lived in localities with less than 10,000 in population; and half remained in towns and villages of under 5,000.[45] A 1910 survey of land tenure in twenty-one prefectures had been expected to reveal sharp increases in concentration of ownership. Instead it concluded that transfer of land between 1899 and 1908 showed "no remarkable signs" and was instead "remarkably stable."[46]

However much its imminent disappearance was lamented, the agrarian tradition was sufficiently vital that people could believe—or at least hope—that its best aspects might be preserved and even that its lost virtues might be recovered. The strains between their hopes and their experience were contained within the possibilities of the time. This was true of other elements of the ideological language as well. The reassertion of familial virtues, the confident cultural condescension toward China and Korea, the harsh suppression of socialism—all made suitable sense to large numbers of Japanese. Even those who were unlikely to articulate these and other such positions felt little need to dispute them. It was this momentary congruence between ideology and experience as much as it was the voluminous efforts of the ideologues to influence the people that accounted for the apparent credibility of the late Meiji myths. They lay, as it were, still lightly in the air.

II

As THE MEIJI period passed, so did this momentary congruence. While it is predictable that the ideological expressions that suited one age might not necessarily suit another, the conservative disposition of much of Meiji ideology intensified the later strains in congruence and credibility. To examine the conservative nature of the dominant ideological language is partly to address the question: *whose* ideology was it? In terms of generation, social composition, and collective concerns, the figures who dominated the process of ideological interpretation constituted a distinctive group. Like the views they propounded, they were very much the product of Meiji times.

In general, the ideologists belonged to two generations, both of which possessed an extraordinary longevity of influence. The events of the Restoration thrust the first generation, born in the 1830s and 1840s, into positions of power very early in their careers. And there many of them stayed, long after they had been called "the old men of Tenpō." Yamagata, their premier ideological representative, lived from 1838 until 1922. From his thirties until his eighties he played a preeminent role in government and ideology throughout the long and eventful period between the early Meiji reforms of the 1870s and the years following the First World War. The second generation, the "young men of Meiji," were born in the 1860s and 1870s. Like Tokutomi Sohō, who gave them this label, they also rose to prominence when they were young.[47] Where those of Yamagata's generation had risen to fill a vacuum of leadership, this next generation rushed in to fulfill what they had been brought up believing was the promise of Meiji. The years of their prime coincided with the late Meiji period, from the 1880s through the 1910s.[48] Thus this age group produced many of the most active ideologues, including the younger bureaucratic and military disciples of Yamagata, the career officials who occupied middle-level posts in the central bureaucracy, and the men of influence who constituted and perpetuated the ranks of the local elite. This was true of the so-called "public opinion of the people" as well, since the *minkan* commentators of this generation contributed their views to the emerging ideology in the same years. Tokutomi himself remained active through the 1940s, long enough to be arrested by the Americans as an "imperialist intellectual" after the war. He died at the age of 94 in 1957.[49]

These two generations both produced and were products of the changes of the Meiji era. As they aged, the personnel of the newly constituted institutions aged with them. In 1911 Ōkuma Shigenobu lambasted the House of Peers for being "an old age home for bureaucrats" and the Lower House for having "too many old faces to represent properly the new and fresh concerns of the citizens."[50] Although this charge was typical of Ōkuma's perennial and often opportunistic criticism of those in power, he was correct in his assessment of the age of Diet members. In 1890, 45 percent had been elected in their twenties and thirties, and only 17 percent of the Lower House were fifty or over. By 1924, a full 56 percent were in their fifties or older, and a mere 10 percent of the representatives were under forty.[51] This same aging occurred in the higher ranks of the bureaucracies, both central and provincial, and in the upper reaches of the political, intellectual, and entrepreneurial elite. Positions that had often been held by men in their thirties in the 1870s were frequently occupied by men in their forties in the 1890s. By the 1920s senior positions were largely held by persons in their fifties, a pattern that, once established, has continued to the present.[52] Similarly, the local elite of the Meiji period were often a younger group in the 1880s than they were by the 1910s, and frequently the same occupants grew old in office. The landlord and diarist, Aizawa Kikutarō, who lived from 1866 to 1962, was active in village self-help organizations as a young man in the late 1880s. He became deputy village mayor in 1897 at the age of thirty and held the office of mayor from 1908 until 1920, when he became president of the local bank until he retired in 1935 at the age of nearly seventy.[53]

Although Yamagata, Tokutomi, and Aizawa outlived most members of their generation, they had in common with many of them a longer period of professional prominence than later career patterns generally displayed. Because of the magnitude of institutional change in the decades following the Restoration, the two Meiji generations rose earlier and therefore remained influential longer than would most of their successors in the mature institutional system.[54] For ideology this generational length meant that many of the same people who responded to the perceived need for a sense of nation in the late 1880s also reacted to what they saw as a crisis in social order in the early 1900s. It is therefore not surprising that they were unequally prepared for the two tasks, each of which belonged to a different time.

As a generation the late Meiji ideologues also bore the mark of the unusual degree of social change that accompanied the reforms following the Restoration. In terms of feudal class they were a mixture of former samurai and commoners. Those of samurai origin were often from a lower status within their class than the commoners who came from the ranks of landlords and wealthy peasants (gōnō). Both gained much of their professional success through their own achievements rather than through the status of their ancestors. And the "samurai consciousness" that is identified in the Meiji emphasis on

loyalty and nation was as much a property of the commoner ideologues as of the former samurai.[55] In terms of social class, they were
a mixture of the traditional rural elite and the emerging modern middle class. In their ideological expressions, the distinction between city
and country often appeared to be absolute. But as a class, the bureaucrats and journalists in Tokyo and the local notables who remained, more or less, in the provinces often shared a similar outlook
on national and social issues. This was partly because the urban middle class was composed of new migrants from the rural areas, and
partly because both had experienced and contributed to the institutional and economic developments of the Meiji period. It was *their*
period, so to speak, and they retained a proprietary interest in the
preservation of its national achievements and its social institutions.
Neither aristocracy nor peasantry, nor again a bourgeoisie on the
European model, the Meiji ideologues represented a social hybrid of
an old and a new elite of the middle strata. They were the Meiji
manifestation of what would become the dominant social formation
in modern Japan: a middle class that both prided itself on mobility
through education and achievement and also maintained itself
through meticulous attention to existing social relations and social
status.

Similarly, the collective concerns of the Meiji ideologues grew directly out of the times in which their formative experiences occurred.
That those experiences had been vastly different from the world in
which the Japanese lived in the 1910s was widely remarked at the
time. The new generation of youth, those who had been born since
the 1880s, were often glad of the difference, pleased to live in an age
in which

> the word "modern" has a kind of strange appeal. In contrast to the
> intolerable anguish and displeasure it arouses in people of middle age
> or older and in some intellectuals, youth in general and others in the
> intellectual world appear exultant over the triumph that has been gained
> under the banner of modernism (*kindaishugi*).[56]

In the 1910s the "people of middle age or older" belonged to the first
two Meiji generations, and they were less impressed with the
triumphs of modernity. One writer commented that all the great
changes occurred in the decades around the Restoration, when principles (*shugi*) were clear, and in the name of imperial loyalism or
constitutional government men engaged in national rather than personal affairs.[57] Another lamented that "the more people utter the
phrase loyalty and filial piety, the more moribund its meaning" and

270

concluded that "of the Japanese alive today only those over fifty years old possess sincerity."[58]

Now the early Meiji period, which had previously been neglected as a source of ideological inspiration, became the object of proud praise and some nostalgia. A Home Ministry official enumerated the reforms of the 1870s and 80s, concluding that "there was nothing so glorious as Meiji in all our 2,500 years."[59] The Chinese Revolution of 1911 revived considerable talk of Japan's early Meiji reforms as a useful model for a turbulent China. And in a historical work of 1905 the post-Restoration changes were described by a member of the second Meiji generation, not as the mere reform of political institutions, but as a "revolution of the whole (*sōtai no kakumei*), spiritually and materially, a fundamental revolution."[60] During the same period national history in general became a more conscious and increasingly institutionalized concern. In 1908 Japanese history first appeared as a separate subject in the fifth and sixth grades of the expanded compulsory curriculum, and in 1911 the official collection of historical materials relating to the Restoration was begun under the direction of the Ministry of Education.[61] In the closing years of Meiji the preservation of national monuments also became an issue. In view of the fact that "the United States is doing this, though it is the most recently founded nation," one supporter of the preservation movement argued that Japan must also begin to attend to its far more venerable cultural tradition and historical sites.[62]

In the course of this national reflection at the end of Meiji, the earlier Meiji period was established as a historical subject. The Charter Oath of 1868 appeared more and more frequently as the emblem both of the intent and the success of the imperial government's reforms. Its phrases, which had seemed too abstract for ideological purposes in the 1880s, were revived in the 1900s. Word for word the language of the Charter Oath reappeared in the Boshin Rescript of 1908, asserting once again the importance of "uniting the sentiments of high and low."[63] Although the Constitution and the Rescript on Education would provoke more interpretation and commentary in the ensuing decades, the Charter Oath probably became the best-known statement of modernity as the ideologues conceived it. Already by the 1910s it seemed to belong to the heroic past. Those who had no wish to revive that past nonetheless agreed that "we were born in a different age than the pioneers of Meiji" and that the period of the great legislative achievements of Prince Itō and his generation "have become a dream of the past."[64] Others praised the "incomparable political figures" of the decades between the Restoration and the Constitution. For what they lacked in knowledge and experience was more than compensated for by their "genuine sense of nation."[65]

Indeed, it was the lack of a sense of nation among the later generations of Meiji youth that disturbed men like Yamagata and Tokutomi. For decades they had framed their purposes in terms of national affairs. In the voluminous correspondence Yamagata conducted throughout his lifetime, the phrase *kokka no tame* appeared as a constant refrain. "For the sake of the nation" was the highest justification he knew and, sincerely or not, he invoked it in nearly every context. The death of Inoue Kaoru, the abolition of the *gun*, the rise of dangerous thought were regrettable for the sake of the nation; the quieting of Tokyo after the streetcar strike, bureaucratic unity in confronting the Diet, a record agricultural harvest were gratifying for the sake of the nation; and each of his correspondents was urged by all means to take care of his health "for the sake of the nation."[66] Similar references abounded in Tokutomi's published works, in the popular columns he called "sermons" that were collected as his Sunday chats, and in his historical studies.[67] In 1913 he told a gathering of youth that "while I appear to have been simply relaxing, in fact my mind has been filled with thoughts of concern for the nation."[68] Indeed such thoughts had become reflexive for many members of his generation.

The objective that animated Yamagata's career during the Restoration and early Meiji years had been the preservation of Japan's autonomy against the threat of the West. In the late Meiji period Tokutomi and others strove to advance Japan's status as a power in the world. By the last years of the Meiji era both goals had been attained. Yet to commentators of these generations they seemed perpetually threatened. Annual New Year's retrospectives described the progress of civilization since the mid-nineteenth century when the nation was in danger and imperial rule was restored. These essays often concluded with the sober thought that, without extraordinary efforts in the future, "the miracle of 1906" (or whatever the year in question) could not be expected to continue.[69] A similar sense of the fragility of national success permeated the statements of Yamagata's later years. The end of World War I presaged a racial conflict in the Far East as "the white races unite against us," while the Russian revolution abroad and the rice riots at home caused him "to be very concerned and anxious about the future of Japan."[70] Tokutomi concluded his speech to the gathering of youth in 1913 with ruminations about Japan's future in a world that "is now putting heavy pressure upon us. We thus cannot afford to be careless, even though there may be temporary respites. Japan must be prepared in all things . . . ready for any eventuality."[71] The perception that what had been gained "for the sake of the nation" could also be lost remained deeply engrained among ideologues of the two older Meiji generations.

This fear was reinforced by their concern with the results of increasing social change. By the post Russo-Japanese War years the greatest threat to the nation appeared to them to come from within. In this context the ideologists propounded views of society designed to assure that national strength would be preserved rather than squandered in disorder and decline. They therefore reflected on the past as if to identify the characteristics that had held the key to Japan's success thus far. The village, the family, social morality, frugality, the spirit of bushidō, agriculture, Shintō—an amalgam of such attributes appeared to have served the country well enough in the early Meiji period. Thus might they also serve as bulwarks against the disintegration of society in the future.

This fear that the negative social consequences of progress might undo its positive national results provoked much of the ideological effort to restore the communal unity of decades past. Yamagata's perpetual concern with the "feelings, customs, and thought" of the people led him to commission a report from each of the army's seventy-two domestic regimental commanders in the wake of the Taishō change in 1913. The result was a frequently devastating portrait of the inroads of civilization into the countryside. Of the many notations that Yamagata made in the manuscript, some concerned the divisive presence of party politics in village self-government, but most related to the patriotic deficiencies and extravagance of youth. Occasionally, Yamagata noted the widespread incidence of trachoma among conscripts. More often, however, he underlined entries that recorded the frequency of rural recruits sporting silk scarves and gold-rimmed spectacles—even, in the case of one Tōhoku youth, *without* lenses in them. The low level of civic education disturbed him, as did the sophisticated attempts at draft exemption. Although Tokyo youth were not illiterate and could handle calculations and practical business language, many graduates of upper elementary school knew nothing of Ise shrine, and when asked by an officer, one of their teachers could not explain it either.[72] The landlord Aizawa recorded similar chagrin at the "unruly, even oafish" behavior of the local youth on the solemn occasion of their draft physical.[73] The disorderliness, extravagance, and youthful self-absorption were regarded by Yamagata and others as social evidence of a national peril. "The consequence of this growth of materialism is the vulgarization of society and social unrest," wrote Tokutomi after World War I. "Vulgarity is perhaps tolerable, but social unrest is something that threatens the nation."[74] The suppression of socialism occurred against this same background, for as it was commented, "just the word 'destruction' is enough to make the government fearful."[75]

What made the Meiji ideologues increasingly fearful in the 1910s was the future. They had begun their careers in the nineteenth century committed to progress for the sake of the nation. Along the lines of conservatism as described by Mannheim, they had been gradualists who preferred to pull the present out of the past without too radical a break. Their aggressive pursuit of change was contained within the existing social system, which they assumed would be preserved. "We are neither conservatives nor destructive radical revolutionaries," declared one of the leading *minkan* nationalists in the late 1880s. "We are reformers (*kaikakusha*), who work to strengthen the system from within."[76] Thus they often argued that the time was not yet ripe for a constitution, a parliament, mixed residence, and the like. In the name of national progress, however, they judged that these changes and many others could eventually be contemplated. Then as the social changes that resulted from the earlier reforms became evident in the later Meiji years, the ideologues began to suggest that the time was overripe, society in decline, and the nation accordingly in danger. The point at which their attitudes shifted was when it seemed to them that social change might destroy the national gains Japan had achieved. Their ideological attempts to retrieve the social past and their sometimes obsessive concern with the degradation (*daraku*) of youth derived from a profound fear that "the glories of Meiji" might prove ephemeral.

The ideologues were not alone in this perception. On the one hand, it was felt in the closing years of the era that Meiji would continue forever, as popular magazines prophesied another half century and villages laid plans for the 100th Meiji year.[77] On the other hand, the 1910s were commonly viewed as "an age of transition" to a future whose outlines appeared uncertain.[78] Many of the Japanese of the Meiji period had experienced an unusual rapidity of change in their lifetime, the kind of change that one Western observer wrote "makes a man feel preternaturally old."[79] The author of a compendium on national morality condescendingly suggested in 1916 that "most conservatives are old; their psychology is retrospective . . . they lose understanding and sympathy with the present age."[80] He, of course, like most of the elite, regarded himself as a progressive, even though his book was devoted to expounding the tenets of ideological orthodoxy, from *kokutai* to the family-state. Age was less the issue than the uncertainty of the future. For far from losing sympathy with the present, a large number of Japanese wished mainly to preserve it. They were thus susceptible to ideological views that promised to "immobilize the world," as Barthes once portrayed the role of myth.[81] As before in Japanese history, the resistance to radical transformation combined with the incorporation of change into the status quo to make Meiji ideology conservative in the name of the preservation of progress.

ORTHODOXY AND DIVERSITY

THE COMMON ideological language that emerged in the course of the late Meiji period was the result of a process of interaction among the different versions of state and society. The language gained hegemony because of its relative congruence with the experience of Meiji Japanese, many of whom shared the impulse to conserve the present that was felt so strongly by the older generations of ideologues. These men had both convinced themselves and persuaded others of the general tenets of civic value. And although their considerable efforts to "influence" the people had not wrought the "unity of sentiment" so often invoked since the Restoration, a commonality had been achieved. Part of this commonality was reflected in the tenets of what is now called *tennōsei* ideology, which in the late Meiji period constituted an orthodoxy of the sort described by George Orwell when he wrote:

> At any given moment there is an orthdoxy, a body of ideas which it is assumed that all right-thinking people will accept without question. It is not exactly forbidden to say this, that, or the other but it is "not done" to say it, just as in mid-Victorian times it was "not done" to mention trousers in the presence of a lady.[82]

In this sense many Japanese accepted the emperor and the nation "without question," just as they knew that it was "not done" to mention social protest in the presence of an official. Partly because these attitudes emerged from and resonated with late Meiji experience they often appeared self-evident to Japanese of the period. This seeming naturalness notwithstanding, the orthodoxy was socially learned and transmitted.

As the transmission continued, late Meiji ideological formulations were perpetuated, sometimes carrying nineteenth-century concerns forcefully over to twentieth-century society. This was due in part to the generational lag among the dominant ideologues. But institutional momentum also played its role, since many of Japan's public institutions were newly established during the Meiji period. Once established, these organizations tended to maintain themselves and the values that sustained them. And these values naturally bore the mark of the period in which the organizations first were formed. This was true not only of such state institutions as the army, the educational system, and local government, but also of partly public, partly voluntary associations like the youth organizations and the landlord associations. When the ideological and institutional momentum of the Meiji period became the ideological and institutional inertia of the decades to come, the structures of orthodoxy were thereby strengthened.

Nonetheless, the argument here has suggested that orthodoxy—emperor, loyalty, village, family-state—occupied but a portion of the wider ideological landscape as Meiji turned to Taishō. Precisely because its common values were largely unexceptionable and exceedingly general, they coexisted with a diversity of ideological formulations that were often very different from the dominant one. In the 1880s government ideologues had reacted to their fear of politics with an emphasis on national unity. Yet neither the politicians nor the politically active public feared politics in the least, and their parliamentary ideology gradually took its place alongside the imperial construction of the state. In the 1900s ideologues both in and outside government had responded to their fear of social disorder with visions of communal harmony and collective self-sacrifice. But younger generations believed as much or more in the social ideology of competition and personal success as they did in the agrarian myths. Disaffected intellectuals who shared neither the values of communalism nor those of material success seceded from the ideological mainstream altogether. Preferring culture to civilization, they developed their own ideology of self-cultivation (shūyō) and intellectual pursuit. The socialists, though suppressed in the Great Treason Incident of 1910-1911, had produced an ideology of radical dissent that would continue throughout the prewar period, despite increasingly brutal control by the government. In the 1910s the older generations had confronted their fear of the future with an effort to conserve the achievements of the past. While they now hailed the Meiji Restoration as a revolution, however, younger generations considered it a failure and sought to reincarnate its promise in a restoration of the right or a revolution of the left. In short, the plural postures associated with different moments of prewar Japanese history were simultaneously present in the dispersed ideological field of the late Meiji period.

The same was true of the institutions that were the social carriers of ideology. Even state institutions could be turned to purposes different from those of orthodoxy. The penetration of local government by politics and of the Taishō schools by liberal ideas of education proceeded despite the original intentions and the later efforts of their parent bureaucracies. In the partly public, partly private sector, some Taishō youth organizations promoted socialism, and a number of landlord associations acted as unions to protect landlords rather than as government instruments to promote the resolution of tenant disputes.[83] Moreover, the organizational experience that had accumulated during the Meiji decades prepared local groups for many different kinds of activity. The sericulture associations and journals that sprang up in the late Meiji period had been constituted "to convey the gospel [of sericulture] to ordinary commoner silkworm households." Some of these later became the silk-raising cooperatives and unions of the late teens and twenties and, as the silk market collapsed with the depression, the local supporters of right-wing agrarianism in the thirties.[84] The institutions, like the ideology, did not remain within the control of the ideologues who originated or manipulated them.

Conceiving of orthodoxy as one series of formulations among others in a plural ideological universe helps to explain the subsequent course of such values in the ensuing decades. What sometimes appears as a succession of independent and seemingly unconnected phenomena—from Meiji conservatism to Taishō liberalism to Shōwa fascism—becomes instead a continuously evolving ideological landscape in which one or another of the dispersed versions gained increased authority. In part because of the preponderance of accounts by the ideologues themselves, it often seems as if orthodoxy wholly dominated the public landscape in the late Meiji period. In fact, however, the imperial orthodoxy coexisted with rival formulations, of which only socialism was emphatically excluded from the realm of permissible civic discourse. And ideologically even socialism survived in the following decades. Perhaps because the orthodoxy was relatively credible in the context of the times, it gained common assent without excessive coercion and could tolerate considerable diversity without losing its hold. In later years as the orthodoxy lost

its unforced credibility and others of the available alternative formulations threatened to assume dominance, this kind of diversity was
disallowed. In the late Meiji period, however, the discourse was
loosely wrought. Indeed it is likely that elements outside the orthodoxy, such as the commitment to social progress and individual success, contributed significantly to its apparent effectiveness.

If ideologies of the sort produced by modern nation-states consist
of the common values by which state and society perpetuate themselves, at most these values may rouse the people to active support
for the system and at least prevent them from rising up to subvert
the state. An effective modern ideology is further charged with extending this minimal common assent to the whole of society rather
than to the elite alone. Late Meiji ideology in the broader, plural
sense can be said to have provided and communicated this kind of
common ideological language. Although few ordinary Japanese, as
Sōseki expressed it, sold their bean curd for the sake of the nation,
equally few wished wholly to secede from society as it was then
constituted.[85] On a continuum of civic participation that might range
from active self-sacrifice or resistance at one pole to passive indifference at the other, most Meiji Japanese probably fell somewhere in
between. They could be active social participants even when they
were ideologically passive. This meant, for example, that they may
have gone to the village meetings for the saké and the society, rather
than for the moral and agrarian uplift. On the other hand, many
shared both the promise and the yoke of "civilization" and conceived
of modernity in personal rather than national terms. Given this lati-
tude, it was possible for larger numbers of Japanese to participate in
this comparatively uncoerced civic practice than ever before in Japanese history. Neither the lack of coercion nor the relative credibility
of the orthodoxy, however, would long outlive Meiji, the era during
which the modern language of ideology was established.

IX

Epilogue:
Ideology and Modern
Japan

IN THE THREE decades between the end of Meiji and the end of the
Second World War, ideological effort did not flag. For from the
viewpoint of later generations of ideologues, the task of influencing
(*kyōka*) the people remained ever incomplete. And during the years
of militarism and increasing state control in the 1930s the content and
apparatus of ideology reached an intensity that required police enforcement and culminated in the "spiritual mobilization" for war.
Thus the ideological process that had begun in the Meiji period continued. Yet it is also true that in the course of the prewar years few
wholly new elements appeared. Instead, the late Meiji formulations
were reinvoked and reinterpreted to meet whatever current crisis
most concerned commentators in the government or the arbiters of
the "public opinion of the people."

In the context of economic difficulty in the early 1910s, the *kokuze*,
or national policy, was again debated. Bureaucrats and intellectuals
argued their respective cases for a commercial, an industrial, and of
course an agricultural basis of the state.[1] Taishō educators spoke of a
moral crisis in the face of "progressivism" (*kakushinshugi*) and once
again sought its solution in the strengthening of moral education.[2]
Sounding much like their counterparts in the late 1880s, they argued
that moral education was necessary to instill in youth a properly civic
"sense of nation," a need that was "recognized even in the schools
of Republican France and was more pressing in Japan now that worship of the West was so widespread."[3] Moral education would further serve to protect young people from such encroaching "abnormalities of thought" as materialism, individualism, and socialism.[4]

The turbulent years after the First World War appeared to be the
incarnation of the ideologues' earlier fears of social disorder, as rice
riots, strikes, and the calls for reform made the post Russo-Japanese

279

War fevers seem mild in comparison. In response, the ideological call to unite the sentiments of the people (*jinshin tōitsu*, or *shisō tōitsu*) was sounded again by the Shintoists, the Education and Home Ministries, and members of the provincial elite.[5] This recurrent concern was greeted with skepticism by some:

> Uniting the sentiments and thoughts of the people has been frequently advocated of late, but are people's sentiments or thoughts so easily united? And in what way are they to be united? It is difficult to understand what these people are driving at.[6]

Nonetheless, ideological efforts intensified. Prefectural assemblymen and local educators complained of the influence of democratic thought (*demokurashii no shisō*) on school pupils and of the impact of the increase in women workers on social mores.[7] The Home Ministry confronted the evident rise of labor and of class conflict with its customary combination of ideology, preventive social legislation, and police control of strikes. With the establishment of a Social Section in 1919, the word "society" first appeared in the organization of the Home Ministry, and one year later this section became the Social Bureau (*shakaikyoku*), charged with such issues as unemployment and relief. Also in 1919 the Ministry established a government-sponsored union called the *Kyōchōkai* (Conciliation Society), from whose name Yamagata himself had excised the words "labor and capital" because of their too overt reference to class struggle.[8]

To a countryside increasingly distressed, first by lack of growth in the twenties, then by depression in the thirties, the central government continued to offer its "positive" administrative policy. In 1919 the Home Ministry promoted a movement to "cultivate national resources." This program followed the pattern of the late Meiji local improvement movement in its ideological efforts "to foster a sense of nation"; "to cultivate the concept of *jichi*"; and, "by arousing the beautiful customs of diligence and strenuous effort and increasing production capital, to secure the livelihood of the people."[9] Although the names were sometimes changed from self-government (*jichi*) to self-effort (*jiriki*) or from local improvement (*chihō kairyō*) in the 1900s and cultivation of national resources (*minryoku kan'yō*) in the 1920s to economic regeneration (*keizai saisei*) in the 1930s, the general mix of ideological and organizational encouragement remained the same throughout the period.[10] As one scholar commented on the local impact of the "economic regeneration movement" of the mid-thirties, "the more difficult the economic self-help, the more strongly the ideological aspects were emphasized."[11] Indeed, even in the midst of the terrible deprivation of wartorn society in late August 1945, the central government was promoting a postwar rural program that depended on spiritual and organizational resuscitation through the local agricultural associations.[12]

The ideological meanings and institutions established between the 1880s and the 1910s thus continued to be employed in subsequent decades. The subsequent decades, however, were increasingly different from the late Meiji times in which these meanings and institutions had emerged. The discrepancy between the dominant ideology and the world it purported to describe grew wider with the years. Other formulations in the plural ideological landscape contended with the orthodoxy in an effort to make sense of the changed and changing realities. After World War I, while some were urging moral education and spiritual unification, many more of the elite (liberal, left, and right) were calling for democracy, revolution, restoration, and—in a word common to nearly all these positions—reconstruction (kaizō).[13] In the 1920s the official textbook version of the state confronted considerable competition from these other legacies of the Meiji ideological process.[14]

The 1930s, the decade in which the term "tennōsei" was coined, was also the one in which its ideological orthodoxy rigidified. A description of the process by which this occurred would require the kind of contextual exploration of the ideologists and their time that has been attempted here for the Meiji period. For the moment two observations may be made. The first relates to congruence and is prompted by the increasingly coercive nature of official ideology during the thirties. Late Meiji ideology, while by no means spontaneous, had emerged through a process in which suasion outweighed coercion as a means of establishing ideological hegemony. The suasion was sometimes moral, sometimes social, and sometimes institutional, as it was in the schools and the military. And in each of these cases coercive forces of varying degree were also at work. But the overall effect was that of an orthodoxy as Orwell described it: powerful because widely held and widely held because it made sense to people at the time.

In the course of the twenties and thirties some of the ideological formulations appeared to be increasingly at odds with the experience of those to whom they were directed. This was especially true of the views of society that had strained against change from the first. Already in 1912, as one commentator argued, in an age when families did not always live together and husbands and wives worked in different factories, the five Confucian relationships enumerated in the

Rescript on Education no longer sufficed to encompass social morality.[15] Between 1910 and 1935 the proportion of gainfully employed
workers in the industrial and service sectors of the economy increased
steadily, and the urban population doubled, until 30.8 percent were
living in cities of over 50,000.[16] Yet during these same years the
agrarian myths through their very momentum received as much—or
perhaps even more—attention as before. Rural Japan, moreover, had
also changed. The ideological invocation of the village had originally
depended on the presence of a local elite whose most powerful members by the twenties had become increasingly absentee. These were
also the years of hiatus between a traditional agrarian paternalism that
was disintegrating and a modern industrial paternalism that was still
in its formative stages. The landlords were no longer offering succor
to distressed tenants, and the companies were not yet acting in a
paternalistic role on any significant scale.[17] Thus the government's
periodic calls for local self-help seemed more and more feeble in the
face of the economic troubles in the countryside. In this context programs set forth by the socialists in the twenties or the agrarianists of
the radical right in the thirties seemed to some to offer more hope
for effective "self-effort" than the government's familiar exhortations
to cooperative spirit or imperial loyalty.[18]

   This increasing disparity between ideology and experience meant
first that parts of the ideology were not as unexceptionable as they
once had been. No longer perceived as natural, more artifice and
force were required to maintain their dominant position. As the imperial ideology lost what might be called its "apparent invisibility,"
it became more obtrusively present, more insistent, and more intol-
erant of diversity than it had needed to be in the late Meiji period.
To assure its ideological hegemony, the government eventually had
to "control the good with the bad," censor scientific treatises on
"Insect Society" along with political tracts on proletarian society, and
suppress minor doctrinal deviations from imperial orthodoxy just as
it did such major subversions as armed rebellion by the military
against the civilian center of the state.[19]

   At the same time that this disparity led to increased coercion, it
also helped to provoke the intensification of efforts at suasion and
"influence" that characterized ideology in the 1930s. The ideologues
appeared to be working harder, as earlier general elements became
increasingly elaborate and doctrinaire. This was especially true of
such originally ambiguous concepts as *kokutai*. "Altering the *kokutai*"
was first included as a crime against the state in the Peace Preservation Law of 1925. Directed against the Communists and suggesting

a meaning similar to that of the word "un-American" in the United States, its inclusion transformed *kokutai* into a legal term, albeit one that even the drafters of the law had difficulty in defining.[20] By the late thirties, *kokutai* appeared in lofty, mystical, and sometimes impenetrable description in lower school textbooks as well as in ideological tracts. *Kokutai no hongi*, the 1937 manual of patriotic education which had been distributed in millions of copies by the end of the war, offered the "national polity" in one of its most ornate and all-encompassing manifestations. In a translation that takes its awkwardness from the original, the first paragraph read:

> The unbroken line of Emperors, receiving the Oracle of the Founder of the Nation, reign eternally over the Japanese Empire. This is our eternal and immutable *kokutai*. Thus, founded on this great principle, all the people, united as one great family nation in heart and obeying the Imperial Will, enhance indeed the beautiful views of loyalty and filial piety. This is the glory of our *kokutai*. This *kokutai* is the eternal and unchanging basis of our nation and shines resplendent throughout our history. Moreover, its solidarity is proportionate to the growth of the nation and is, together with heaven and earth, without end. We must, to begin with, know with what active brilliance this fountainhead shines within the reality of the founding of our nation.[21]

Although, as one scholar later recalled, no one in the 1940s was expected to know anything about *kokutai* but everyone was supposed simply "to feel it," the treatises devoted to the subject suggested the dimensions of the ideological effort expended to produce this feeling.[22] What after the war was called "the warped theory of *kokutai* of the past several years"[23] was a product of the period in which government and *minkan* ideologues responded to socioeconomic strains at home and an increasingly unfavorable international situation by rigidifying the imperial orthodoxy. It was as if the unique glory—and the reassuring immutability—of *kokutai* became that much more important as the world fell away around it.

As the world seemed about to collapse altogether in the closing weeks of the war in the summer of 1945, the government clung to the "preservation of the national polity" (*kokutai goji*) as its condition for accepting surrender. And in his radio broadcast informing the people of the end of the war, the emperor announced that the *kokutai* had indeed been preserved. Later in 1946 conservatives in the government and the Diet asserted that the new postwar Constitution would not result in a change in *kokutai*.[24] By this time, however, the meaning of *kokutai* had begun to wither. In 1946 the conservatives identified *kokutai* as the "basic characteristic of the nation," which they defined in terms of the existence of the imperial institution.[25] Their usage thus resembled the definition of national polity of the 1880s more than it did the florid *kokutai* of the immediate prewar years. In time the prewar concept of *kokutai* crumbled away altogether. Younger Japanese in the postwar period, hearing a word that sounds the same as *kokutai* but is in fact an abbreviation for *kokumin taiiku taikai*, are said to have assumed that it could only mean the National Athletic Competition that is widely celebrated every year.[26]

This postwar history of the prewar myths suggests a second observation concerning the role of *tennōsei* ideology in prewar Japan. In the period immediately following the end of the war, the Occupation authorities and the Japanese together abolished both the general tenets and the specific versions of *tennōsei* ideology. In its place state and society were reconceived in the name of democracy (*minshushugi*). The enthusiasm with which many Japanese abandoned *kokutai* for democracy in the short space of several months suggests, among other things, that prewar ideology had overreached itself. Not only had the imperial orthodoxy become strikingly incongruent with social and national realities but it had rigidified to the point that it appeared to defy common sense. Indeed it contradicted not only such obvious facts as urban industrial capitalism and, later, the unmistakable signs of military defeat, but it defied elements of ideological common sense as well. The denial of individualism, for example, had intensified to the point that all economic and educational striving was considered suspect unless wholly sublimated to the needs of the state. Although from the Meiji period Japanese had been exposed to an official ideology that defined personal success and material improvement in terms of national progress, they had seldom been willing to abandon the former for the latter. Yet now their work was to be done with "minds set on guarding and maintaining the prosperity of the Imperial Throne" alone.[27] The nativist insistence on Japanese tradition—in the wartime texts not only was Japan the country of the gods and the emperor a deity but even Mt. Fuji was said to be divine—was coupled with an often stridently anti-Western bias, whether it was expressed in the notion of "overcoming the modern" or of the superiority of the Japanese spirit.[28] This anti-Westernism, which after the war disappeared even more quickly than *kokutai*, ran against the grain of the Japanese experience, from the Meiji adoption of civilization through the cosmopolitan pursuit of the modern in the years between the two world wars. Arguing backward in time, the rapid disappearance of *tennōsei* orthodoxy in 1945 and 1946 suggests that the relation between experience and ideology had become so strained that the official ideology was relatively easy to abandon once the institutional apparatus that sustained it was dismantled.[29]

If this was generally true, it was by no means universally so. Imperial enthusiasts in the thirties and forties were legion, and they were actively responsible for the dissemination and implementation of the ideological injunctions. Throughout these years the orthodoxy appeared amply capable of galvanizing society for the purposes of the state. Even in this period, however, a plural rendering of ideology suggests that an interaction of elements rather than the official construction alone may be needed to explain civic behavior. Despite the ever-increasing power of the state, it seems likely that the pattern of earlier years continued. This would mean that the prevailing ideological formulations were the product not only of official indoctrination but of mutual manipulation among diverse ideologists, some official, others not. And if orthodoxy mobilized society, it is probably also true that society continued to mobilize itself, its deep social meanings operating to hold society together before, during, and after the war. In what ways *tennōsei* ideology moved prewar Japanese to act as the state would have them act and in what ways it prevented them from acting differently are questions that must still be asked of the ideological process in the Shōwa period.

It may be found in answering them that the view from 1945 backward across the imperial decades understandably exaggerated the power of ideological orthodoxy. In part this is because the postwar commitment to an utterly different future required a prompt identification of the forces responsible for the cataclysm of the immediate past. In this context *tennōsei* ideology, so palpably potent and distasteful, was reified, given a substance, a prominence, and even an efficacy that it may not in fact have possessed. This study at least suggests that orthodoxy—the combination of government indoctrination, suppression, and control—may prove no more or less important than other parts of the ideological discourse that interacted with it, not all of which were created by the prewar state nor could be abolished by its postwar successor.

For after the war the elaborated monuments of *tennōsei* ideology were either razed to the ground by legal or institutional reform or reduced, as the emperor and Mt. Fuji were, from divine quintessences to more naturally scaled symbols. In terms of their Meiji origins as I have described them, what disappeared in 1945 were the *tennōsei* elements that had originally emerged in the middle of the message and by the war had expanded to drive other aspects of the earlier plural rendering out of permissible parlance. These other aspects, however, often survived the war. Among the dependent clauses of Meiji ideological utterance, postwar Japanese can scarcely be said to have discarded their belief in progress, whether in terms of Japan as a whole or of individual social and economic betterment. The sense of nation, of being Japanese, was transmitted to the whole of the *kokumin* for the first time in the Meiji period and is not much diminished today. Nor is the postwar pride in the national achievements and international status of "our country, Japan" (*wagakuni*), although the status of joining the ranks of the imperialist powers has been replaced with that of gaining preeminence among the economic and cultural ones. And on the unspoken level of deep social meaning, the defeat did not of course obliterate evolving but solidly rooted Japanese attitudes toward the individual and the collectivity. Nor did a new political system, which enshrined rather than denatured parliamentary politics, wholly remove the social disinclination for public resolution of conflict of partial private interests.

The year 1945 thus saw the end of some of the ideological elements established in the Meiji period and the continuation of others. The ideological process that resumed in a different spirit after the war continues to the present. Indeed the postwar decades have witnessed efforts at reinterpretation of state and society that are not dissimilar to the process that occurred in the late Meiji period. And like late Meiji ideology, ideology in postwar Japan has not been created ex nihilo or adopted ready-made. Instead, as with so many other aspects of Japan's modern experience, contemporary ideology remains heir to the interpretations of the political and social world as the Meiji Japanese imagined they were living it.

Bibliography

To FACILITATE its use for reference, the bibliography is divided into categories presented in increasing order of accessibility for readers outside Japan. To help locate works in the bibliography, identifications are inserted in the notes as follows: letters and manuscripts are marked [ms]; town and village plans contain the word *ze* in their titles; newspapers and magazines are divided into Tokyo and provincial publications, the latter identified by the title or in parentheses; pamphlets, many of which can be found in the Special Collections at the National Diet Library, are marked [P]; miscellaneous materials are primarily visual and include *sugoroku* and magic-lantern presentations; Meiji-Taishō publications are identified by their date of publication (1868-1926); collections, reprints, and reminiscences are largely primary sources written, collected, or reprinted since 1926, many of them in recent editions; secondary sources in Japanese and English-language sources are self-explanatory. The place of publication of Japanese works, unless otherwise cited, is Tokyo.

LETTERS AND MANUSCRIPTS

Aichi kenchō monjo. Monbushō shiryōkan, Tokyo.

Chiba-ken tsūzoku kunkai bunko tosho mokuroku. Chiba, Higashi-gun, September 1908. Chiba prefectural library, Chiba.

Chihōkan kaigi giketsusho narabi hikki, 1890, 1891, 1892, 1894, 1907, 1910, 1911, 1912, 1913. Tōkyō-to komonjokan.

Hirata Tōsuke monjo. Kensei shiryōshitsu, National Diet Library, Tokyo.

Hōten chōsakai minpō giji sokkiroku. Minpō shinzokuhen sōzokuhen hikki. Faculty of Law, Tokyo University.

Inoue Kaoru monjo. Kensei shiryōshitsu, National Diet Library, Tokyo.

Kakurentaiku kannai minjō fūzoku shisōkai no genjō, I-VII, December 1913. Faculty of Law, Tokyo University.

Katsura Tarō monjo. Kensei shiryōshitsu, National Diet Library, Tokyo.

Kōshaku Sasaki Takayuki-kun shokan: kokutai mondō. Shoryōbu, Imperial Household Agency, Tokyo.

Naimushō. Shuppanbutsu torishimari ni kansuru tsūchō (October 1910). Microfilm courtesy of Uchikawa Yoshimi.

BIBLIOGRAPHY

Shimofusa-no-kuni Sōma-gun Fujishiro-mura Iida-ke monjo. Monbushō shiryōkan, Tokyo.

Shinano-no-kuni Saku-gun Shimokaise-mura. Tsuchiya-ke monjo, Monbushō shiryōkan, Tokyo.

Terauchi Masatake kankei monjo. Kensei shiryōshitsu, National Diet Library, Tokyo.

Tokutomi Sohō monjo. Sohō kinenkan, Ninomiya, Kanagawa. Courtesy of Itō Takashi.

Yamagata Aritomo. Taishō seihenki. Kensei shiryōshitsu, National Diet Library, Tokyo.

Yamagata Aritomo monjo. Kensei shiryōshitsu, National Diet Library, Tokyo.

TOWN AND VILLAGE PLANS (*CHŌSONZE*)

Aichi-ken Kaitō-gun Ifuki-mura sonze, 1904 (National Diet Library).

Ehime-ken Unsen-gun Yoto sonze chōsa shiryō, 1903 (Hitotsubashi University).

Fujii Masata. *Gunshichōson hattensaku gunshichōsonze chōsa hyōjun.* Himeji: 1910. (National Diet Library).

Fukuoka-ken Ikeba-gun Himeji sonze, 1897 (National Diet Library).

Fukuoka-ken Yame-gunze, 1900 (Hitotsubashi University).

Fukushima-ken Iwase-gun Nishibukuro-mura sonze chōsa, 1902 (Hitotsubashi University).

Fukushima-ken Kawanuma-gun Oikawa-mura sonze, 1911 (Hitotsubashi University).

Fukushima-ken Minami Aizu-gun Koyana-mura, Yahata-mura, Fusawa-mura sōgō sonze chōsa, 1905 (Hitotsubashi University).

Fukushima-ken Sōma-gun Kamimano sonze, 1907 (Hitotsubashi University).

Fukushima-ken Tamura-gun Koizumi-mura sonze chōsasho, 1902 (Tokyo University).

Gumma-ken nōkai sonze chōsasho. Gumma-ken nōkai, 1911 (National Diet Library).

Hyōgo-ken Iibo-gunze narabi ni chōsonze. Hyōgo Iibo-gunyakusho. Himeji: 1908. (National Diet Library).

Ibaraki-ken Inashiki-gun Numazato sonze, 1913 (Hitotsubashi University).

Ibaraki-ken Kita Sōma-gun Omonma sonze, 1914 (Hitotsubashi University).

Ibaraki-ken Kita Sōma-gun Takai sonze, 1916 (Hitotsubashi University).

Ibaraki-ken Naka-gun Sano-mura sonze chōsasho, 1912. (Katsuta-shishi hensan iinkai, ed., *Katsuta-shi shiryō*, vol. 3. Katsuta-shishi hensan iinkai, 1973.)

Ibaraki-ken Nishi Ibaraki-gun Kita-Kawane sonze, 1912 (Hitotsubashi University).

Ibaraki-ken Sashima-gun Yumata sonze, 1912 (Hitotsubashi University).

Kōchi-ken Agawa-gun Hata sonze chōsasho, 1914 (Hitotsubashi University).

Miyagi-ken Natori-gun Oide-mura sonze chōsasho, 1902, 1908 (Hitotsubashi University).

Nara-ken Ikoma-gun Kita-Yamato sonze, 1905 (Tokyo University).

BIBLIOGRAPHY

Niigata-ken Iwafune-gun Sekidani-mura sonze, 1918 (Hitotsubashi University).
Saitama-ken Iruma-gun Toyooka-chō chōze chōsa yōroku, 1904 (Hitotsubashi University).
Shiga-ken Kōga-gun Ishibe chōze, 1910 (Hitotsubashi University).
Shizuoka-ken Haibara-gun Katsumata-mura sonze chōsa. Katsumata-mura nōkai, 1903 (Hitotsubashi University).
Toyama-ken Imizu-gun Yokota sonze chōsasho, 1911 (National Diet Library).
Zenkoku nōkai. *Chōsonze chōsa hyōjun. Ishikawa-ken, Ishikawa-gun, Yasuhara sonze*, 1900 (Hitotsubashi University).

NEWSPAPERS AND MAGAZINES

Unless otherwise noted, all newspapers and magazines can be found in the *Meiji shinbun zasshi bunko*, Faculty of Law, Tokyo University.

1. Newspapers published in Tokyo
Chōya shinbun (1889-1893)
Chūgai shōgyō shinpō (1889-1912)
Hōchi shinbun (1895-1912)
Jiji shinpō (1889-1913)
Kokkai (1890-1895)
Kokumin shinbun (1889-1912)
Mainichi shinbun (1889-1906)
Miyako shinbun (1894-1919)
Nihon (1889-1913)
Niroku shinpō (1893-1904)
Tōkyō asahi shinbun (1889-1914)
Tōkyō denpō (1888-1889)
Tōkyō mainichi shinbun (1890-1891, 1906-1913)
Tōkyō nichi nichi shinbun (1889-1913)
Yamato shinbun (1905-1912)
Yomiuri shinbun (1889-1913)
Yorozu chōhō (1894-1895, 1897-1913)
Yūbin hōchi shinbun (1889-1894)

2. Provincial newspapers
Akita sakigake shinpō (Akita, 1889-1912)
Chōshū nichi nichi shinbun (Bōfu, 1910-1912)
Fukui nippō (Fukui, 1912)
Fukuoka nichi nichi shinbun (Fukuoka, 1889-1913)
Fukuryō shinpō (Fukuoka, 1890, 1895)
Geibi nichi nichi shinbun (Hiroshima, 1910-1912). National Diet Library
Gifu nichi nichi shinbun (Gifu, 1889-1912)
Hokuriku seiron (Toyama, 1890-1892, 1893-1899)
Ibaraki (Mito, 1892, 1903, 1909)
Kōbe yūshin nippō (Kōbe, 1889-1899, 1912)

289

Kōchi nippō (Kōchi, 1889-1890)
Kyūshū nichi nichi shinbun (Kumamoto, 1889-1912)
Kyūshū nippō (Fukuoka, 1900-1912)
Niigata shinbun (Niigata, 1892-1912)
Ōsaka asahi shinbun (Ōsaka, 1889-1913)
Ōsaka mainichi shinbun (Ōsaka, 1888-1890, 1905-1906, 1910-1913)
Ōu nichi nichi shinbun (Sendai, 1894-1895, 1901, 1904)
San'in shinbun (Matsue, 1889-1912)
San'yō shinpō (Okayama, 1890, 1904-1905, 1908-1913). National Diet Library
Shimotsuke shinbun (Utsunomiya, 1907, 1909). National Diet Library
Shinano mainichi shinbun (Nagano, 1889-1890, 1901-1913)
Tōhoku shinbun (Sendai, 1892-1903)
Wakayama shinpō (Wakayama, 1910-1913)

3. Magazines published in Tokyo
Bōken sekai (1910)
Chūgaku sekai (1898-1912)
Chūō kōron (1899-1914)
Dokuritsu hyōron (1903, 1908)
Fūzoku gahō (1889-1913)
Gakusei kurabu (1901)
Jindō (1905-1906)
Jinja kyōkai zasshi (1900-1913)
Jitsugyō no Nihon (1897-1912)
Jogaku sekai (1904-1908)
Kaikōsha kiji (1909-1913)
Kaitsu zasshi (1888-1891)
Kaji setsuyō (1902-1903)
Kannagara (1890)
Katsusekai (1890-1891)
Kokumin no tomo (1888-1895)
Kokumin zasshi (1910-1913)
Kōyūkai zasshi [Daiichi kōtōgakkō kōyūkai] (1910-1912)
Kyōiku jiron (1888-1897, 1906-1913)
Kyōikukai (1906-1907)
Meijikai sōshi (1888-1897)
Nichiro sensō jikki (1904-1905)
Nihonjin (1888-1906); *Nihon oyobi Nihonjin* (1907-1913)
Nihon kōdōkai sōki [also, *Nihon kōdō sōki, Kōdō*] (1889-1912)
Nihon kokkyō daidō sōshi (1888-1890, 1906-1913)
Nihonshugi (1897-1901)
Nisshin sensō jikki (1894-1896)
Rikugō zasshi (1891-1893)
Rōdō sekai (1897-1901)
Seikō (1912)
Seishin (1892)

Sekai no Nihon (1896-1900)
Sen'yū (1910-1913)
Shimin (1906-1912)
Shinjin (1903-1912)
Shinkōron (1906)
ShinNihon (1911-1915)
Shōnen sekai (1895-1915)
Taiyō (1895-1915)
Teiyū rinrikai rinri kōenshū (1900-1912)
Tensoku (1890)
The Far East (1897)
Tōkyō-fu kyōikukai zasshi (1910-1913)
Yūben (1910-1912)
Zenkoku shinshokukai kaihō (1899-1918)

4. Provincial magazines
Agatsuma kyōiku [also, *Agatsuma kyōikukai zasshi*] (Gumma, 1888-1898)
Aichi zasshi (Gifu, 1891)
Aikoku (Gifu, 1893-1894)
Aikoku (Kōfu, 1890)
Aimin (Nagano, 1889)
Daifukuchō [Ōsaka mainichi shinbunsha] (Ōsaka, 1904-1906)
Fūzoku kairyō zasshi (Ōsaka, 1892-1893)
Giyūkai kaihō (Ibaraki, 1901)
Jikyō (Ibaraki, 1910)
Jōmō seinenkai zasshi (Gumma, 1888-1889)
Kenritsu Nakonojō Nōgyō Gakkō kōyūkaihō (Gumma, 1906-1912)
Kokufukai kōgiroku (Nagoya, 1891)
Kokuhonkai kaihō (Saga, 1897-1899)
Kyōfū (Tochigi, Ashikaga, 1894)
Kyōfū zasshi (Ōita, 1895-1901)
Meijikai kaihō (Chiba, 1900-1901)
Nihonshugi (Gumma, Maebashi, 1890)
Shimo Ina-gun seinenkaihō (Nagano, 1913)
Shinano kyōiku (Nagano, 1890-1897, 1908-1915)

PAMPHLETS

Arita Kansan, ed. *Ebara-gun seinenkai kengakushi*. Tōshūsha, 1912
Awasen jikki. Tokushima: 1895
Danjo hikkei: shūshoku annai. Eirakudō, 1905
Gyōkei kinen jigyō. Fukui: 1909
Hirao-mura kigensetsu kenpō happu shukuenkai kiji. Nagano, Shimo Takai-gun: 1889
Ibaraki-kenchō. *Meiji yonjūnen tokubetsu daienshū: gyorinkō kinenchō*. Mito: 1908

Ishikawa Tōji. *Kokkai giin senkyo kokoroe.* 1889
Ishimura Teiichi. *Rikugun: gunjin tokuhō seimon engi.* 1907
Itō Giichirō. *Shina seibatsu: yamatodamashii.* Chūō seinen kurabu, 1895
Itō Keidō. *Shūshoku tebikigusa.* Tōkyō kōbunkan, 1909
Itō Samon. *Nihon no hikari: kokutai engi.* Mie-ken, Kawasaki-mura: 1893
Jokō tokuhon. Jitsugyō kokumin kyōkai, 1911
Kagoshima shiyakusho. *Gyōkei nikki.* Kagoshima: 1908
Kaku Kinjirō. *Kinen: San'indō gyōkeiroku.* Matsue: 1907
Kakubari Eisaburō. *Nisshin sensōshi no hanashi.* Uedaya honten, 1895
Katō Totsudō. *Bukkyō kokumin: zakkyogo no kokorue.* 1898
Kenpō kyōiku kenkyūkai. *Godai chokuyu ryakkai.* 1909
Komura Torakichi, ed. *Nihon gunjin tokuyū seishinron.* 1910
*Kyōiku chokugo Boshin shōsho haidoku shiki oyobi dainikai chihō jigyō kōrōsha
    hyōshō shiki kiji.* Yokohama: Kanagawa-kenchō, 1911
Maekawa Torahiro. *Naichi zakkyo shōsōron.* Maebashi: 1893
Maruta Misao. *Tsūzoku Nisshinsō mondō.* Chūyūgikai, 1894
Misono Kintarō. *Kokumin kyōiku senji kōwa.* Nihon shoseki, 1905
Miyamoto Muraji. *Chōhei tekireisha kokoroe.* 1905
Mori Tsunetarō. *Sonchi jikkendan yōryō.* Chiba-ken, Izumi-gun: 1911
Morooka Tadashi. *Kokkai giin shina sadame.* Jōsō zasshisha shikyoku, 1889
Naimushō. *Senji kinen jigyō to jichi keiei.* Seitō shobō, 1906
Nōshōmushō nōmukyoku. *Tochi shoyūken idō no jōkyō.* Nōshōmushō, 1910
Okazaki Yasukichi. *Mohanteki chihō seinendan no shishin.* 1910
Ōno Seitarō. *Kokkai giin sentei kagami.* 1890
Ōtsuka Kajima-gunchō sonchō ni taisuru enjutsu. Ishikawa-ken, Kajima-gun-
    yakusho, 1894
Saikin chōsa shūshoku no tebiki. Seibunsha, 1911
Saishō shihon: shinshokugyō annai. Tanizaki hanbaibu, 1909
Sakuma Gōzō. *Kokumin kokoroe.* Kyōikushobō, 1886
Seikōdō henshūbu. *Shōgaku sotsugyō kugaku seikō shūshoku tetsuzuki: risshin
    annai.* Seikōdō, 1910
"Senji ni okeru nōka no kokoroe," *Tōkyōfu nōkai gōgai.* Min'yūsha, 1904
Shichigatsu koi!—Naichi zakkyo kokoroe. 1898
Shokugyō annai zensho. Tōkyō jitsugyōsha, 1911
Shūshoku no hiketsu: kyūshokusha no fukuin. Yokohama, 1910
Sōtei kyōiku: nyūei junbi dokushūsho. Hōbunkan, 1907
Sugi Kenji. *Meiji Tennō gotaisō.* Shiseisha shuppanbu, 1912
Suzuki Jun'ichirō. *Kokumin yōi: naichi zakkyo kokoroe.* 1894
Takayanagi Junnosuke. *Shōgaku sotsugyō risshin annai.* Gakuyūsha, 1907,
    1910
Tamura-ō, sonchidan. Shimane-ken: Ikinoshima nōkai, 1908
Tomeoka Kōsuke. *Chihō kairyō kōen sokki.* Okayama: 1912
Tsūzoku Nisshin sensō mondō. 1894
Yamazaki Enkichi. *Chihō jichi kōshū hikki.* Shimane-ken, Daitō-chō: 1912
Yoshikawa-mura seinen kōkyōkai hōkoku. Yamaguchi-ken: 1894

BIBLIOGRAPHY

MISCELLANEOUS MATERIALS

DaiNihon kokkai gijidō sugoroku. 1890
DaiNihon teikoku gikai no zu. 1890
Danshi gakkō kyōiku sugoroku. 1900
Danshi kyōiku shusse sugoroku. 1890, 1906
Gentō ōyō: shūshin eiga setsumeisho. 1889
Gentō ōyō: zen'aku jidō no kekka setsumeisho. 1890
Jōkisha ōfuku han'ei no zu. 1889
Katei kyōiku gakkō mawari sugoroku. 1906
Kenpō happu no zu; Kenpō happushiki no zu; Kenpō happu shukusaizu. 1889
Kyōiku chokugo Boshin shōsho zukai. 1908
Kyōiku chokugo gentō eiga setsumeisho. 1894
Kyōiku chokugo sugoroku. 1890, 1891, 1893
Kyōiku chokugo zukai gentō. 1891
Kyōiku hitsuyō gentō shinbun sugoroku. 1890
Meiji kan'inkyō sugoroku. Yokoyama Enshō, 1887
Nakamura Shinzaburō. *Kyōiku chokugo zukai.* Kōseidō, 1912
Nichiro sensō sugoroku. 1905, 1906
Nisshinsen kōhitsu gentō eiga setsumeisho. 1895
Nisshin sensō gentō eiga setsumeisho. 1895
Nisshin sensō: gentō eiga setsumeisho daiikkai mokuroku. 1895
Nisshin sensō gentōkai. 1895
Nisshin sensō sugoroku. 1894, 1895

MEIJI–TAISHŌ PUBLICATIONS

Aichi kyōikukai. *Sengo shakai kyōiku ni kansuru chōsa.* Nagoya: 1906
Anesaki Masaharu. *Nanbokuchō mondai to kokutai no daigi.* Hakubunkan, 1911
Bōkyūkai. *Naichi zakkyo ni taisuru shotaika no iken.* Kōeki tosho, 1899
Fukasaku Yasufumi. *Kokumin dōtoku yōgi.* Kōdōkan, 1916
Haga Yaichi. *Kokuminsei jūron.* Fuzanbō, 1908
———— and Shimoda Jirō, eds. *Nihon katei hyakka jii.* Fuzanbō, 1906
Hamanaka Nisaburō, ed. *Chihō jichi seinen dantai mohan jiseki.* DaiNihon go-
    kokukai, 1910
Hayakawa Jōsui. *Kyōiku kōdan.* 3 vols. Ōe shobō, 1919
Hibino Hiroshi. *Kokumin hitsudoku: Nihon shindō.* Kinkōdō, 1910
Hirata Tōsuke. *Jikyō sadan,* ed. Nakamura Chiyomatsu. Shōbundō, 1911
Hōrei zensho. Naikaku kanpōkyoku, 1880, 1889–1890
Hoshijima Jirō, ed. *Uesugi Hakase tai Minobe Hakase saikin kenpōron.* Jitsugyō
    no Nihonsha, 1913
Hozumi Yatsuka. *Kokumin dōtoku: aikokushin.* Yūhikaku, 1897
Ibaraki-ken senji jōkyō ippan. Mito: Ibaraki kenchō, 1906
Ikeda Gengo. *Boshin shōsho to chihō jiseki.* Sapporo: Ikeda shoten, 1911
Ikeda Jōtarō. *Mohan chōson no genkyō.* Yomiuri shinbunsha, 1911

Inage Sofū. *Gendai kyōikusha no shinseikatsu.* Daidōkan shoten, 1913
————. *Wakaki kyōikusha no jigaku to kokuhaku.* Naigai kyōiku hyōronsha, 1912
Inoue Kamegorō. *Nōmin no shakai kyōiku.* Kinkyōdō, 1902
Inoue Tetsujirō. *Chokugo engi.* Keigyōsha, 1891
————. *Jinkaku to shūyō.* Kōbundō, 1915
————. *Kyōiku to shūyō.* Kōdōkan, 1910
————. *Kyōiku to shūkyō no shōtotsu.* Keigyōsha, 1893
Inoue Tomoichi. *Inoue Meifu ikō.* Ed. Ōmi Masao. Sanshūsha, 1920
————. *Jichi yōgi.* Hakubunkan, 1909
Ishida Denkichi. *Jichi sōsho: mohan chōson to yūryō shōgakkō.* Daigakkan, 1910
————. *Risō no mura.* Shōyōdō, 1914
Kanagawa-ken tōkeisho. Kanagawa-ken, 1908, 1911
Kanbe Tsutomu. *Chihō no kairyō.* Teikoku chihō kairyō kyōkai, 1913
Katō Kyūtarō. *Zaishoku yonenkan.* Chiba: Jichi kenkyūkai, 1911
Katō Totsudō. *Shakai kyōiku: tsūzoku kōwa.* Bunseidō, 1918
————. *Shūyō shōhin.* 1915
Keishichō tōkeisho. Keishichō, 1902-1910.
Kishimoto Nobuta. *Nihonjin no go tokushitsu.* Min'yūsha, 1902
Kobayashi Ōri. *Meiji bunmeishi.* 1915
Kōchi-ken naimubu. *Kōchi-ken chōson jiseki ippan.* Kōchi: 1905
Kokumin hyakka jiten. Fuzanbō, 1908
Kokumin to hikokumin. Min'yūsha shuppanbu, 1911
Komatsubara Eitarō. *Komatsubara Bunshō kyōikuron.* Ed. Tateishi Komakichi. Nishōdō shoten, 1911
Komatsubara Eitarō-kun jiryaku. Kinoshita Ken, 1924
Ko Motora Hakase tsuitō gakujutsu kōenkai. *Motora Hakase to gendai no shinrigaku.* Kōdōkan, 1913
Kyōiku sōranbu. *Meiji sanjūshichihachinen sen'yaku: chūyū bidan.* 5 vols. Tōkyō kaikōsha, 1907
Matsuzaki Tenmin. *Kisha zange: ningen hitsugo.* Seikōkan, 1924
Miyagi-kenchō. *Meiji Tennō sekishi.* Sendai: 1925
Miyake Setsurei. *Meiji shisō shōshi.* Heigo shuppansha, 1913
————. *Seinenkun.* Shūdō bunko, 1915
Mochizuki Kotarō. *Sekai ni okeru Meiji Tennō.* Eibun tsūshinsha, 1913. (Published in English as *The Late Emperor of Japan as a World Monarch.* Tokyo: Liberal News Agency, 1913.)
Mohan senshō: Okayama-ken Kawakami-gun Ujimura chiseki. Okayama: 1911
Monbushō. *Shūsei kokutai kyōkasho: hensaku shuisho,* vol. 2. Monbushō, 1910
Monbushō futsū gakumukyoku. *Zenkoku seinendan no jissai.* Monbushō, 1921
Mori Tsunetarō. *Chōsonze chōsa shishin.* Teibi shuppansha, 1909
Motoda Eifu. *Motoda Sensei shinkōroku.* Ed. Yoshimoto Noboru. Min'yūsha, 1910
Naimushō. *Chihō kairyō jigyō kōenshū.* 2 vols. Hakubunkan, 1909
————. *Chihō kairyō jiseki.* Shinshinsha, 1910
Naimushō chihōkyoku. *Chihō jichi yōran.* Naimushō, 1907

————. *Chihō kairyō jitsurei.* Hakubunkan, 1912

————. *Mohanteki chōsonji.* Naimushō, 1903

Naimushō kanbōkyoku. *Meiji kokumin kikan.* Kokkōsha,1902

Nichiro sensō no jikyoku to kokumin: gunkoku no kinken chochiku. Kōbundō, 1904

Nihon kōdōkai shijūnenshi. Nihon kōdōkai, 1918

Nishisonogi-gun kyōikukai. *Shōgakkōchō kōshūkai kōenroku.* Nagasaki: Jūseisha, 1918

Noda Sentarō. *Shichōsonze.* Shichōson zasshisha, 1903

Oka Minoru. *Kōjōhōron.* Yūhikaku, 1913

Ōkuma Shigenobu. *Kokumin tokuhon.* Hōbunkan, 1910

————. *Ōkuma Haku shakaikan.* Ed. Tateishi Komakichi. Bunseisha, 1910

Ozaki Yukio. *Naichi gaikō.* Hakubunkan, 1893

Ozaki Yukio zenshū. Vol. 3. Heibonsha, 1926

Saitō Mankichi. *Nōgyō shikin: jitchi keizai.* Aokisūzandō, 1911

Sakurai Tadayoshi. *Nikudan* (1906). (Translated as *The Human Bullet* by Masujirō Honda. Boston: Houghton Mifflin, 1907.)

Sasagawa Kiyoshi. *Ganzen shōki.* Keibunkan, 1912

Seki Kōsaku, ed. *Inoue Hakase to Kirisutokyōto: "kyōiku to shūkyō no shōtotsu" no tenmatsu oyobi hyōron.* 3 vols. Tetsugaku shoin, 1893

Shinbun sōran. Nihon denpō tsūshinsha, 1911

Sugimoto Shōjirō, ed. *Meiji chūkō setsugi den: Tōyō risshihen.* 5 vols. Kuni no ishizuesha, 1898

Takayama Chogyū (Rintarō). *Chogyū zenshū.* 5 vols. Hakubunkan, 1905

Takekoshi Yosaburō. *Jinmin tokuhon.* Fuzanbō, 1913

Tanaka Giichi. *Shakaiteki kokumin kyōiku.* Hakubunkan, 1915.

————. *Sōtei tokuhon.* Teibi shuppansha, 1915

————. *Tanaka Chūjō kōenshū.* Fuji shoin, 1916

Tanaka Hozumi. *Seikatsu mondai to nōson mondai.* Jitsugyō no Nihonsha, 1913

Tani Kanjō ikō. Ed. Shimanouchi Toshie. Vol. 2. Seikensha, 1912

Tatebe Tongo. *Boshin shōsho engi.* Dōbunkan, 1908

Tokonami Takejirō. *Chihō jichi oyobi shinkōsaku.* Jitsugyō no Nihonsha, 1912

Tokushima-kenfu. *Meiji sanjūshichihachinen: Tokushima-ken senjishi.* Tokushima: 1907

Tokutomi Ichirō (Sohō). *Jimu ikkagen.* Min'yūsha, 1913

————. *Nichiyō kōdan,* 11 vols. Min'yūsha, 1900-1911

————. *Sohō bunsen.* Comp. Kusano Shigematsu and Namiki Sentarō. Min'yūsha, 1915

————. *Taishō no seinen to teikoku no zento.* Min'yūsha, 1916

————. *Taishō seikyoku shiron.* Min'yūsha, 1916

————. *Seikatsu to shosei.* Min'yūsha, 1900

Toyama-ken kyōikukai. *Seinendan shidō chōsa hōkoku.* Toyama: 1918

Toyama Kakusuke. *Nihon no Nihon.* Hakubunkan, 1892

Tsubotani Zenshirō. *Kakkoku toshi jigyō ippan.* Tōkyō shiyakusho, 1909

Tsūzoku kyōiku kenkyūkai. *Tsūzoku kyōiku ni kansuru jigyō to sono shisetsu hōhō.* Tsūzoku kyōiku kenkyūkai, 1911

Wada Shinjirō, ed. *Kōshitsu yōten*. 1913
Yamada Taiichirō. *Senji nōka hikkei*. Nagoya: Aichi-ken nōkai, 1905
Yamaji Aizan. *Aizan bunshū*. Ed. Uchiyama Shōzō. Min'yūsha, 1917
Yamamoto Takinosuke. *Chihō seinen dantai*. Rakuyōdō, 1909
Yasuda Kyūshū. *Zakkyo junbi yūkoku no namida*. Kokkōsha, 1897
Yokoi Tokiyoshi. *Yokoi Hakase zenshū*. Ed. DaiNihon nōkai. Vols. 4-9. Yokoi Hakase zenshū kankōkai, 1925
Yokoyama Masao. *Chōsonze chōsa kōyō*. Morioka: Iwate-ken naimubu shomuka, 1909
Yokoyama Tokujirō. *Shōgaku kagai kyōzai oyobi kyōhō*. Hōbunkan, 1907
Yoshida Kumaji. *Waga kokumin dōtoku to shūkyō*. 1912
Zenkoku minji kanrei ruishū. Shihōshō, 1880

COLLECTIONS, REPRINTS, AND REMINISCENCES

Abe Isoo, ed. *Teikoku gikai kyōiku giji sōran* (1932), vols. 1-3. Rinsen shoten, 1961
Abe Yoshishige. *Waga oitachi: jijoden*. Iwanami shoten, 1966
Aizawa Kikutarō. *Aizawa nikki*. 5 vols. Sagamigahara: Aizawa Yoshihisa, 1965-1977
Andō Yoshio and Yamamoto Hirobumi. *Kōgyō ikenta: Maeda Masana kankei shiryō*. Kōseikan, 1971
Aoki Keiichirō, ed. *Shiryō: Kiso goryōrin jiken kōshōroku*. Shinseisha, 1968
Chiba-ken shihan gakkō. *Sōritsu rokujū shūnen kinen: Chiba-ken shihan gakkō enkakushi*. Chiba: 1934
Egi Kazuyuki-ō keirekidan kankōkai. *Egi Kazuyuki-ō keirekidan*, vol. 1. 1935
Fukuzawa Yukichi zenshū. Ed. Keiō gijuku. Vols. 4-5. Iwanami shoten, 1959-1960
Hara Kei nikki. Ed. Hara Keiichirō. Vols. 1-6. Kangensha, 1950-1951
Hōchi shinbunsha tsūshinbu. *Meishi no shōnen jidai*. 3 vols. Heibonsha, 1930
Hoshino Takeo, ed. *Meiji Tennō gyōkō shiroku*. Ushio shobō, 1931
Hoshino Tōru, ed. *Minpōten ronsō shiryōshū*. Nihon hyōronsha, 1969
Hozumi Yatsuka Hakase ronbunshū. Ed. Hozumi Shigetaka. Yūhikaku, 1943
Inoue Kowashi den, shiryōhen. Ed. Inoue Kowashi denki hensan iinkai. 6 vols. Kokugakuin daigaku toshokan, 1966-1977
Inoue Tetsujirō. "Meiji tetsugakukai no kaiko" (1912). In *Gendai Nihon shisō taikei*. Vol. 24, *Tetsugaku shisō*. Ed. Shimomura Toratarō and Furuta Hikaru. Chikuma shobō, 1965
Inoue Tomoichi. *Inoue Hakase to chihō jichi*. Ed. Inouekai zenkoku chōson chōkai, 1940
Ishibashi Tanzan zenshū. Ed. Ishibashi Tanzan zenshū hensan iinkai. Vol. 1. Tōyō keizai shinpōsha, 1971
Ishikawa Takuboku. *Takuboku zenshū*. Vols. 3-4. Chikuma shobō, 1967
Itō Hirobumi kankei monjo. Ed. Itō Hirobumi kankei monjo kenkyūkai. Vol. 8. Hanawa shobō, 1980
Karasawa Tomitarō. *Hanga sugoroku*. Mainichi edishonaru sentā, 1972

Katsuta-shi shiryō. Vol. 3. Katsuta-shishi hensan iinkai, 1973

Kindai Nihon shiryō kenkyūkai. *Nihon shakai undō shiryō*. 2d ser. Vol. 2-1. *Tokubetsuyō shisatsunin jōsei ippan*. Meiji bunken shiryō kankōkai, 1957

Kiyoura Keigo. *Keigo yawa*. 1939

Kōda Rohan zenshū. Ed. Kagyūkai. Vol. 27. Iwanami shoten, 1954

Kodaira Namihei. *Kōnan nikki*. Kodaira Namihei-ō kinenkai, 1954

Kōtoku Shūsui, ed. *Chōmin Sensei-Chōmin Sensei gyōjōki*. Iwanami bunko, 1960

Kuga Katsunan zenshū. Ed. Nishida Taketoshi and Uete Michiari. 9 vols. Misuzu shobō, 1969

Kumagai Tatsujirō, ed. *Seinen yomimono ni kansuru chōsa*. DaiNihon rengō seinendan chōsabu, 1928

———. *Zenkoku seinendan kihon chōsa*. DaiNihon rengō seinendan chōsabu, 1934

Kusumoto Tōkichi. *Mura no kurashi: aru kosakunin no nikki*. Ochanomizu shobō, 1977

Kyōgakubu. *Kyōiku ni kansuru chokugo kanpatsu gojūnen kinen shiryō tenran zuroku*. Naikaku insatsubu, 1941

Kyōiku chokugo kanpatsu kankei shiryōshū. 3 vols. Kokumin seishin bunka kenkyūjo, 1939

Makino Nobuaki. *Kaikoroku*. Vol. 2. Chūkō bunkō, 1978

Matsumoto Sannosuke, ed. *Kindai Nihon shisō taikei*. Vols. 30-31, *Meiji shi-sōshū I, II*. Chikuma shobō, 1976

Meiji bungaku zenshū. 90 vols. Chikuma shobō, 1966-1972

Meiji bunka zenshū. Ed. Yoshino Sakuzō (1927-1930). Reprinted in 27 vols. and 4 supplements. Ed. Meiji bunka kenkyūkai. Nihon hyōronsha, 1967-1974

Meiji daizasshi. Ryūdō shuppan, 1978

Meiji Tennō goshū. Ed. Meiji jingū. Kadokawa shoten, 1967

Meiji Tennō gyōkō nenpyō (1933). Ed. Nihon shiseki kyōkai. Tōkyō daigaku shuppankai, 1982

Meiji Tennōki. Ed. Kunaichō. 12 vols. and index. Yoshikawa kōbunkan, 1968-1977

Meiji Tennō seiseki. Monbushō, 1935-1936

Meiji Tennō shōchoku kinkai. Ed. Meiji jingū. Kōdansha, 1973

Miyake Setsurei. *Dōjidaishi*. Vols. 2-4. Iwanami shoten, 1950

Miyauchi Yosaburō. *Meiji Taishō Shōwa kaisō 86-nen*. Tōkyō-to kyōikukai, 1968

Mori Arinori zenshū. Ed. Ōkubo Toshiaki. Vols. 1-2. Senbundō shoten, 1972

Muramatsu Shōfū. *Akiyama Teisuke wa monogataru*. Kōdansha, 1938

Naimushō chihōkyoku shakaikyoku. *Saimin chōsa tōkeihyō* (1912, 1914, 1922). Keiō shobō, 1973

Naimushō keihokyoku. *Kinshi tankōbon mokuroku* (1888-1934). Vol. 1. Kohokusha, 1976

Naitō Konan zenshū. Ed. Kanda Kiichirō and Naitō Kenkichi. Vol. 1. Hakkōsha, 1970

Nakae Chōmin shū. Ed. Matsunaga Shōzō. Chikuma shobō, 1974

Natsume Sōseki zenshū. Vol. 10. Chikuma shobō, 1972; *Sōseki zenshū.* Vols. 13–15. Iwanami shoten, 1966–1967

Nihon kyōkasho taikei, kindaihen. Ed. Kaigo Tokiomi. Vols. 2–7. Kōdansha, 1962

Nitobe Inazō zenshū. Ed. Nitobe Inazō zenshū henshū iinkai, 16 vols. Kyōbunkan, 1969–1970

Nōshōmushō. *Shokkō jijō* (1903). Ed. Ōkōchi Kazuo. Kōseikan, 1971

Rōdō undō shiryō iinkai. *Nihon rōdō undō shiryō.* Vol. 2. Tōkyō daigaku shuppankai, 1963

Sasakawa Rinpū. *Meiji sakigaeshi.* Ajiasha, 1946

Sawayanagi Masatarō. *Sawayanagi zenshū.* Vols. 1 and 6. Sawayanagi zenshū kankōkai, 1925; *Sawayanagi Masatarō zenshū.* 11 vols. Sawayanagi Masatarō zenshū kankōkai, 1975–1980

Shinbun shūsei Meiji hennenshi. Ed. Shinbun shūsei Meiji hennenshi hensankai. Vols. 7–15. Zaisei keizai gakkai, 1935–1936

Shinbun shūsei Taishō hennenshi. Vol. 1. Taishō Shōwa shinbun kenkyūkai, 1966.

Suzushino Tsutomu. *Saikushi.* Vol. 3. Tategu kōgeisha, 1965

Tashiro Kōji, ed. *Tashiro Zentarō nikki, Meijihen.* Sōgensha, 1968

Tayama Katai zenshū. Vols. 2, 14, 15. Bunsendō shoten, 1972

Tayama Katai. *Inaka kyōshi* (1904). Iwanami shoten, 1972

Tokutomi Ichirō (Sohō). *Sohō jiden.* Chūō kōron, 1935

———. *Waga kōyūroku.* Chūō kōron, 1938

Tokutomi Kenjirō (Roka). *Roka zenshū.* Vol. 8. Roka zenshū kankōkai, 1929

Toyohara kenkyūkai. *Zenji nisshi: Yamagata-ken Shōnai heiya ni okeru ichi nōmin no nisshi* (1893–1934). Tōkyō daigaku shuppankai, 1977

Ubukata Toshirō. *Meiji Taishō kenbunshi.* Chūō kōronsha, 1978

Uchimura Kanzō zenshū. Vols. 2, 20, 21. Iwanami shoten, 1932–1933

Ueda Shōzaburō. *Seinen kyōshi no sho.* Kenbunkan, 1936

Watanabe Masamori. *Seinen kyōshi jidai.* Tōyō tosho, 1937

Yamagata Aritomo ikensho. Ed. Ōyama Azusa. Hara shobō, 1966

Yamaji Aizan. *Kirisutokyō hyōron, Nihonjinminshi.* Iwanami shoten, 1966

Yamakawa Kikue and Sakisaka Itsurō. *Yamakawa Hitoshi jiden: aru bonjin no kiroku.* Iwanami shoten, 1961

Yamamoto Takinosuke zenshū. Ed. Kumagai Tatsujirō. Nihon seinendan, 1931.

Yamazaki Enkichi zenshū. Vols. 1–6. Yamazaki Enkichi zenshū kankōkai, 1935

Yanagita Kunio shū (Teihon). Vols. 4, 16, 24, supp. 3. Chikuma shobō, 1962

Yanagita Kunio. *Kokyō shichijūnen.* Asahi shinbunsha, 1974

Yokoyama Gennosuke. *Nihon no kasō shakai* (1898). Iwanami shoten, 1978

Yokoyama Gennosuke zenshū. Ed. Sumiya Mikio. Vol. 1. Meiji bunkan, 1972

BIBLIOGRAPHY

SECONDARY SOURCES

Akita kindaishi kenkyūkai. *Kindai Akita no rekishi to minshū*. Akita kindaishi kenkyūkai, 1969

Andō Yoshio. *Kindai Nihon keizaishi yōran*. Tōkyō daigaku shuppankai, 1975

Anzu Motohiko and Umeda Yoshihiko, eds. *Shintō jiten*. Hori shoten, 1968

Aoki Kōji. *Meiji nōmin sōjō no nenjiteki kenkyū*. Shinseisha, 1967

Arichi Tōru. *Kindai Nihon no kazokukan—Meijihen*. Kōbundō, 1977

Ariizumi Sadao. "Meiji kokka to minshū tōgō." *Iwanami kōza Nihon rekishi*. Vol. 17, *Kindai* 4. Iwanami shoten, 1976

―――. "Meiji kokka to shukusaijitsu." *Rekishigaku kenkyū*, no. 341 (October 1968): 61–70

―――. *Meiji seijishi no kiso katei*. Yoshikawa kōbunkan, 1980

Asahi shinbunsha shashi henshūshitsu. *Asahi shinbun no kyūjūnen*. Asahi shinbunsha, 1969

Asakura Haruhiko and Inamura Tetsugen, eds. *Meiji sesō hennen jiten*. Tōkyō shuppan, 1965

Banno Junji. "Keien naikaku to Taishō seihen," *Iwanami kōza Nihon rekishi*. Vol. 17, *Kindai* 4. Iwanami shoten, 1976

―――. *Meiji kenpō taisei no seiritsu: fukoku kyōhei to minryoku kyūyō*. Tōkyō daigaku shuppankai, 1971

―――. *Taishō seihen: 1900nen taisei no hōkai*. Minerubua shobō, 1982

―――. "Taishō shoki ni okeru rikugun no seitōkan: Tanaka Giichi o chūshin to shite." *Gunji shigaku* 11, no. 4 (March 1979): 54–62

Chiba Toshio. *Meiji no shōgakkō*. Hirosaki: Tsugaru shobō, 1969

"Chōsonze to sono shozai ni tsuite." *Chihōshi kenkyū* 9, no. 4 (August 1959): 55–59

Chūō Hōtokukai. *Fukensei gojūnen o kataru*. Chūō Hōtokukai, 1941

Dōkōsha henshūbu. *Meiji no hyōka to Meijijin no kanshoku*. Dōkōsha, 1967

Ebihara Haruyoshi. *Gendai Nihon kyōiku seisakushi*. San'ichi shobō, 1965

Emori Itsuo. "Meijiki no Hōtokusha undō no shiteki hatten." In *Nihon sonraku shakai no kōzō*. Kōbundō, 1976

Endō Shunroku. " 'Mohanson' no seiritsu to kōzō." *Nihonshi kenkyū*, no. 185 (January 1978): 33–60

Fujita Shōzō. *Tennōsei kokka no shihai genri*. Miraisha, 1966

Fukaya Masashi. *Gakurekishugi no keifu*. Reimei shobō, 1969

Fukuchi Shigetaka. *Shizoku to shizoku ishiki: kindai Nihon o okoseru mono horobosu mono*. Shunjūsha, 1967

Fukushima-ken. *Fukushima kenshi*. Vol. 4, *Kindai* 1. Fukushima: Fukushima-ken, 1971

Furushima Toshio et al., eds. *Meiji Taishō kyōdoshi kenkyūhō, Kyōdoshi kenkyū kōza*. Vol. 7. Asakura shoten, 1972

Fuwa Kazuhiko. "Nichiro sengo ni okeru nōson shinkō to nōmin kyōka, I." *Tōhoku daigaku kyōiku gakubu kenkyū nenpō*, no. 25 (1977): 123–44

Fuzanbō. Fuzanbō, 1932

"Gendai ni okeru tennō to tennōsei." *Gendai to shisō (tokushū)*, no. 15 (March 1974)

"Gendai tennōsei." *Hōgaku seminā (zōkan)*, (February 1977)

Gifu-ken. *Gifu-kenshi. Tsūshihen, Kindai.* Vol. 2. Gifu: Gifu-ken, 1972

Gotō Seiichi. *Kyōiku chokugo kankei bunken mokuroku.* Kyōiku chokugo hō-senkai, 1940

Gotō Yasushi. "Kindai tennōsei ron." In *Kōza Nihonshi.* Vol. 9. Ed. Reki-shigaku kenkyūkai and Nihonshi kenkyūkai. Tōkyō daigaku shuppankai, 1971

Haga Noboru. *Meiji kokka to minshū.* Yūzankaku, 1974

———, ed. *Gōnō Furuhashi-ke no kenkyū.* Yūzankaku, 1979

Hakubunkan gojūnenshi. Hakubunkan, 1936

Hamada Toshihiro. "Mohanson ni miru chihō kairyō jigyō no jittai to sono rekishiteki igi." *Saitama minshūshi kenkyū*, no. 4 (March 1978): 46-71

Harada Katsumasa and Aoki Eiichi. *Nihon no tetsudō: 100-nen no ayumi kara.* Sanseidō, 1973

Hashikawa Bunzō. *Yanagita Kunio: sono ningen to shisō.* Kōdansha, 1977

Hayashi Hideo, ed. *Seiun no kokorozashi to zasetsu, Chihō bunka no Nihonshi.* Vol. 8. Bun'ichi sōgō shuppan, 1977

Hidaka Rokurō, ed. *Sengo shisō no shuppatsu.* Chikuma shobō, 1968

Hirayama Kazuhiko. *Seinen shūdanshi kenkyū josetsu.* Vol. 2. Shinsensha, 1978

Hitotsubashi daigaku keizai kenkyūjo, Nihon keizai tōkei bunka sentā. *Gunze, chōsonze chōsasho shozai mokuroku.* Hitotsubashi University Library. Mimeo. 1964

Hōjō Hiroshi. *Mura to iriai no hyakunenshi.* Ochanomizu shobō, 1978

Horimatsu Buichi. *Nihon kindai kyōikushi: Meiji no kokka to kyōiku.* Risōsha, 1972

Ienaga Saburō. "Kyōiku chokugo seiritsu no shisōteki kōsatsu." *Shigaku zas-shi* 56, no. 12 (December 1946): 1-20

Ikeda Ranko. *Onna mon.* Kawade shobō, 1960

Ikeda Susumu and Motoyama Yukihiko, eds. *Taishō no kyōiku.* Daiichi hōki shuppan, 1978

Inada Masatsugu. *Kyōiku chokugo seiritsu katei no kenkyū.* Kōdansha, 1971

———. *Meiji kenpō seiritsushi.* 2 vols. Yūhikaku, 1962

Inō Tentarō. *Jōyaku kaiseiron no rekishiteki tenkai.* Komine shoten, 1976

Inoue Kiyoshi. *Tennōsei.* Tōkyō daigaku shuppankai, 1952

Inumaru Giichi. "Sengo tennōsei kenkyū no seika." *Rekishi hyōron* (April 1967): 27-41

Irokawa Daikichi. *Meiji no bunka.* Iwanami shoten, 1970

Ishida Takeshi. *Meiji seiji shisōshi kenkyū.* Miraisha, 1954

Ishikawa Hisao. "Meiji kōki Taishōki no iwayuru mohanteki nōson jichi." *Hōseishi kenkyū*, no. 22 (March 1973): 127-50

Ishitoya Tetsuo. *Nihon kyōinshi kenkyū.* Kōdansha, 1967

Isoda Kōichi. *Shisō to shite no Tōkyō: kindai bungaku shiron nōto.* Kokubunsha, 1978

Itoya Toshio. *Nihon shakaishugi undō shisōshi*. Hōsei daigaku shuppankyoku, 1979
——. *Zōho kaitei taigyaku jiken*. San'ichi shobō, 1970
Kaigo Tokiomi. *Inoue Kowashi no kyōiku seisaku*. Tōkyō shuppankai, 1968
——. *Kyōiku chokugo seiritsushi no kenkyū*. Kōtokusha, 1965
——. *Motoda Eifu*. Bunkyō shoin. 1942
—— and Yoshida Kumaji. *Kyōiku chokugo kanpatsu igo ni okeru shōgakkō shūshin kyōju no hensen*. Kokumin seishin bunka kenkyūjo, 1935
Kajiyama Masafumi. "Meiji makki no tokuiku rongi—Taigyaku jikengo no teikoku gikai." *Nihon shisōshi*, no. 7 (1978): 112-33
Kamijō Hiroyuki. *Chiiki minshūshi nōto*. Ginga shobō, 1977
Kamishima Jirō. *Kindai Nihon no seishin kōzō*. Iwanami shoten, 1961
Kamiya Chikara. *Ie to mura no hōshi kenkyū: Nihon kindaihō no seiritsu katei*. Ochanomizu shobō, 1976
Kanagawa kenritsu kyōiku sentā. *Kanagawa-ken kyōikushi*. Yokohama: 1972
Kanagawa-ken toshokan kyōkai. *Kanagawa-ken toshokan shi*. Kanagawa kenritsu toshokan, 1966
Kaneko Kentarō. *Itō Hirobumi den*. 3 vols. Shunpo kōtsui shōkai, 1940
Kanno Tadashi. *Kindai Nihon ni okeru nōmin shihai no shiteki kōzō*. Ochanomizu shobō, 1978
Kano Masanao. *Shihonshugi keiseiki no chitsujo ishiki*. Chikuma shobō, 1969
Karasawa Tomitarō. *Kyōkasho no rekishi: kyōkasho to Nihonjin no keisei*. Sōbunsha, 1956
——. *Kyōshi no rekishi*. Sōbunsha, 1968
——. *Meiji hyakunen no jidōshi*. Vol. 1. Kōdansha, 1968
——. "Nihon ni okeru jidō bungaku no kindaiteki hatten to sono kyōikushiteki igi: Meiji-Shōwaki no jidō zasshi o chūshin ni." *Nihonjin no kindai ishiki keisei katei ni okeru dentōteki keiki to seiōteki keiki. "Nihon kindaika" kenkyūhō*, no. 2. Tōkyō kyōiku daigaku, 1968
Katō Fusazō, ed. *Kōshaku Hirata Tōsuke den*. Hirata Tōsuke denki hensan jimusho, 1927
Kawasaki Fusagorō. *Meiji Tōkyō shiwa*. Tōgensha, 1968
Kawashima Takeyoshi. *Ideorogii to shite no kazoku seido*. Iwanami shoten, 1957
Kidota Shirō. "Kenze, gunze oyobi chōsonze no seisaku to nōka jikkō kumiai." *Keizaigaku kenkyū nenpō* 39, no. 4 (March 1978): 93-112, and 40, no. 1 (July 1978): 47-69
Kikegawa Hiroshi. *Jichi gojūnenshi seidohen*. Bunsei shoin, 1977
——. *Meiji chihō jichi seido no seiritsu katei*. Tōkyō shisei chōsakai, 1955
Kikuchi Kunisaku. *Chōhei kihi no kenkyū*. Rippū shobō, 1977
Kimura Ki. *Hiroshima daihon'ei no Meiji Tennō*. Sekkasha, 1966
——. *Meiji Tennō*. Shibundō, 1956
Kimura Shōshū. *Meiji shōnen bungakushi hanashi*. Dōwa shunjūsha, 1949
Kindaichi Haruhiko and Anzai Aiko, eds. *Nihon no shōka: Meijihen*. Kōdansha, 1977

Koike Zenkichi. "Meiji kōki ni okeru chihō seinen no shisō to kōdō I, II: Gumma-ken Agatsuma-gun tōbu chihō no seinen ni tsuite." *Gumma daigaku kyōyōbu kiyō* 10, 11 (1976, 1977): 71-95; 69-91

Kokuritsu kyōiku kenkyūjo. *Nihon kindai kyōiku hyakunenshi.* 10 vols. Kyōiku kenkyū shinkōkai, 1974

Kokutetsu rekishi jiten. Nihon kokuyū tetsudō, 1973

Komota Nobuo et al. *Nihon ryūkōkashi.* Shakai shisōsha, 1970

Kōmoto Mitsugi. "Shisō konnan to jinja." In *Nihon ni okeru kokka to shūkyō.* Ed. Shimode Sekiyo Sensei kanreki kinenkai. Daizō shuppan, 1978

Konishi Shirō, ed. *Nishiki-e Bakumatsu Meiji no rekishi.* Vols. 10-11. Kōdansha, 1977

Kubo Yoshizō. *Tennōsei kokka no kyōiku seisaku.* Keisō shobō, 1979

Kumagai Tatsujirō. *DaiNihon seinendan shi.* Nihon seinenkan, 1942

Kuno Osamu and Kamishima Jirō, eds. *"Tennōsei" ronshū.* 2 vols. San'ichi shobō, 1974-76

Kurauchi Shirō. *Meiji makki shakai kyōikukan no kenkyū: tsūzoku kyōiku chōsa iinkai seiritsuki.* Kōdansha, 1961

Kurasawa Takashi. *Shōgakkō no rekishi.* 3 vols. Japan raiburarii byūrō, 1963-70

Kurata Yoshihiro. *Meiji Taishō no minshū goraku.* Iwanami shinsho, 1980

Kusama Shunrō. "Meiji Tennō no gyōkō to zuikō o meguru uchiwake: shinshiryō ni motozuku uchiwake kaiketsu no rimenshi." *Nihon rekishi,* no. 334 (March 1976): 38-40

Kuwabara Makoto. "Meiji-Taishō no Hokkaidō ijū." *Atarashii dōshi* 7, no. 5 (1969): 1-15

Kyōikushi hensankai. *Meiji ikō Nihon kyōiku seido hattatsushi.* 13 vols. and index. Kyōiku shiryō chōsakai, 1964-1965

Machida Masami. *Kiso goryōrin jiken.* Nagano: Ginga shobō, 1982

Maeda Ai. *Kindai dokusha no seiritsu.* Kōbundō, 1973

Maki Masami. *Nihon kyōin shikaku seidoshi kenkyū.* Kazama shobō, 1971

Mainichi shinbunsha. *Mainichi shinbun hyakunenshi, 1872-1972.* Mainichi shinbunsha, 1972

Maruyama Masao. *Nihon no shisō.* Iwanami shinsho, 1961

Masumi Junnosuke. *Nihon seitō shiron.* Vols. 2-3. Tōkyō daigaku shuppankai, 1966

Matsumoto Sannosuke. *Kindai Nihon no seiji to ningen.* Sōbunsha, 1966

———. *Tennōsei kokka to seiji shisō.* Miraisha, 1969

Matsushita Yoshio. *Meiji gunsei shiron.* 2 vols. Yūhikaku, 1956

Matsuura Rei. *Nihonjin ni totte tennō to wa nan de atta ka .* Henkyōsha, 1974.

Matsuura Shigejirō. *Okada Ryōhei Sensei shōden.* 1935

Meiji shiryō kenkyū renrakukai. *Minkenron kara nashonarizumu e.* Ochanomizu shobō, 1957

Mikuriya Takashi. *Meiji kokka keisei to chihō keiei.* Tōkyō daigaku shuppankai, 1980

Mitani Taichirō. *Nihon seitō seiji no keisei.* Tōkyō daigaku shuppankai, 1967

————. *Taishō demokurashiiron.* Chūō kōronsha, 1974

Miyachi Masato. *Nichiro sengo seijishi no kenkyū: teikokushugi keiseiki no toshi to nōson.* Tōkyō daigaku shuppankai, 1973

Miyagawa Torao. *Seikatsu no naka no kokka.* Vol. 8, *Nihon seikatsu bunkashi.* Kawade shobō, 1974

Miyakawa Tōru et al. *Kindai Nihon shisō ronsō.* Aoki shoten, 1971

Miyata Noboru. *Ikigami shinkō: hito o kami ni matsuru fūzoku.* Hanawa shobō, 1970

Miyatake Gaikotsu. *Meiji enzetsushi.* Bunbudō, 1926

Mizuno Hiroshi and Hirano Kazuko. "Meiji shoki no 'urban-rural' jinkō ni tsuite." *Tōkeikyoku kenkyū ihō,* no. 30 (March 1976): 1-27

Monbushō. *Gakusei hyakunenshi.* 2 vols. Teikoku chihō gyōsei gakkai, 1972

Mori Senzō. *Meiji Tōkyō itsubunshi.* 2 vols. Heibonsha, 1969

Motoyama Yukihiko. *Meiji kyōiku yoron no kenkyū.* Vol. 2, *Kyōiku seiji keizai kairon.* Fukumura shuppan, 1972

Murakami Shigeyoshi. *Kokka Shintō.* Iwanami shinsho, 1970

Nagano-ken jinjachō. *Nagano-ken jinja hyakunenshi.* Nagano-ken jinja sōdai-kai, 1964

Nagano-ken kyōikushi. 16 vols. and 2 supplements. Nagano-ken kyōikushi kankōkai, 1972-82

Nagaoka Shinkichi. *Meiji kyōkōshi josetsu.* Tōkyō daigaku shuppankai, 1971

Nagata Hiroshi. *Meiji no kisha.* Kōtsū Nihonsha, 1978

Naka Arata. *Meiji no kyōiku.* Shibundō, 1967

————. *Meiji shoki no kyōiku seisaku to chihō e no teichaku.* Kōdansha, 1962

Nakamura Kichisaburō. *Meiji hōseishi.* 3 vols. Shimizu kōbundō shobō, 1971

Nakamura Masanori. *Kindai Nihon jinushi seidoshi kenkyū: shihonshugi to ji-nushisei.* Tōkyō daigaku shuppankai, 1979

Nakamura Takafusa. *Senzenki Nihon keizai seichō no bunseki.* Iwanami shoten, 1971

Nakatsuka Akira. *Nisshin sensō no kenkyū.* Aoki shoten, 1968

Namekawa Michio. *Nihon sakubun tsuzurikata kyōikushi I.* Kokudosha, 1977

Nihon joshi daigaku joshi kyōiku kenkyūjo. *Meiji no joshi kyōiku.* Kokudosha, 1967

Nihon kokuyū tetsudō. *Nihon kokuyū tetsudō hyakunen shashinshi.* Kōtsū kyōryokukai, 1972

Nihon kokuyū tetsudō sōsaishitsu shūshika. *Tetsudō ryakunenpyō.* 1961

Nihon shoseki shuppan kyōkai. *Nihon shuppan hyakunenshi nenpyō.* Nihon shoseki shuppankai, 1968

Nishida Taketoshi. *Meiji jidai no shinbun to zasshi.* Shibundō, 1961

Nishimura Sensei denki hensankai. *Hakuō Nishimura Shigeki den.* 1933

Nojiri Shigeo. *Nōson rison no jisshōteki kenkyū* (1942). Nōson gyōson bunka kyōkai, 1978

Ogi Shinzō. *Tōkyō shomin seikatsushi kenkyū.* Nihon hōsō shuppan kyōkai, 1979

Oguri Junko. *Nihon no kindai shakai to Tenrikyō.* Hyōronsha, 1969

Ōhama Tetsuya. *Meiji Kirisutokyōkaishi no kenkyū.* Yoshikawa kōbunkan, 1979

———. *Meiji no bōhyō: Nisshin Nichiro uzumoreta shomin no kiroku.* Shūei shuppan, 1970

———. *Meiji no gunshin: Nogi Maresuke.* Yūzankaku, 1972

Ohkawa Kazushi et al. *Chōki keizai tōkei: suikei to bunreki (LTES).* Vol. 8, *Kokumin shotoku.* Tōyō keizai shinpōsha, 1974

Oka Toshirō. "Kindai Nihon ni okeru shakai seisaku shisō no keisei to hatten: 'kokka seiji' kara 'shakai seiji' e." *Shisō,* no. 558 (December 1970): 69-88

Oka Yoshitake. "Nichiro sensōgo ni okeru atarashii sedai no seichō." *Shisō,* no. 512 (February 1967): 1-13, and no. 513 (March 1967): 89-104

———. *Yamagata Aritomo: Meiji Nihon no shōchō.* Iwanami shinsho, 1958

Ōkuma Kō hachijūgonenshi. 4 vols. Ōkuma Kō hachijūgonenshi kankōkai, 1926

Ono Hideo. *Meiji wadai jiten.* Tōkyōdō shuppan, 1968

———. *Nihon shinbunshi.* Ryōsho fukyūkai, 1948

Ono Noriaki. *Nihon toshokan shi.* Genbunsha, 1970

Ōsaka-shi. *Meiji Taishō Ōsaka-shishi.* Vol. 2. Nihon hyōronsha, 1934-1935

Ōsato Katsura, ed. *Meiji ikō honpō shuyō keizai tōkei.* Nihon gentō tōkeikyoku, 1966

Ōshima Mitsuko. *Meiji no mura.* Kyōikusha, 1977

Ōya Sōichi. *Honoo wa nagareru.* Bungei shunjū, 1972

Ozaki Mugen. "Meiji matsunen ni okeru kyōiku no kōzō henka ni tsuite." *Meiji makki ni okeru shakai shisō, Shakai shisō* 2, no. 4 (Winter 1972): 937-53

Ozawa Saburō. *Uchimura Kanzō fukei jiken.* Shinkyō shuppansha, 1961

Rekishi chiri gakkai. *Meiji kōki no rekishi chiri. Rekishi chirigaku kiyō,* no. 8 (1966)

Sagamigahara-shishi hensan iinkai. *Sagamigahara-shishi.* Vol. 3. Kanagawa: Sagamigahara shiyakusho, 1968-1969

Saitō Hiroshi. "Hōtokusha undō no kuronorojii." *Mita gakkai zasshi* 64, no. 8 (August 1971): 219-34

Saitō Tsuyoshi. *Meiji no kotoba: higashi kara nishi e no kakehashi.* Kōdansha, 1977

Sakai Yūkichi. "Meiji kenpō to dentōteki kokkakan o megutte." In *Nihon kindai hōshi kōgi.* Ed. Ishii Shirō. Seirin shoin shinsa, 1972

Sakata Yoshio. "Meijiki no tennōkan." *Sandai hōgaku* 9, nos. 2 and 4 (September 1975, March 1976): 20-44, 35-54; 10, no. 4 (March 1979): 17-38; 12, no. 1 (June 1978): 60-85

Sakeda Masatoshi. *Kindai Nihon ni okeru taigai kō undō no kenkyū.* Tōkyō daigaku shuppankai, 1978

Sakurai Masashi. *Meiji shūkyōshi kenkyū.* Shunjūsha, 1971

Sasaki Yutaka. "Chihō kairyō undō to sonze chōsa." *Nōson kenkyū* 40 (March 1975): 76-87; 41 (September 1975): 49-59; 43 (September 1976): 61-72; 44 (March 1978): 64-74

Satō Hideo. "Wagakuni shōgakkō ni okeru shukujitsu daisaijitsu gishiki no keisei katei." *Kyōikugaku kenkyū*, no. 30 (March 1963)

Shashi hensan iinkai. *Mainichi shinbun shichijūnen*. Mainichi shinbunsha, 1952

Shima Yasuhiko, ed. *Chōson gappei to nōson no henbō*. Yūhikaku, 1958

Shindō Haruo. *Kyōiku chokugo shinnyū katei ni okeru seiji to kyōiku*. Fukuoka: Fukuoka-ken rekishi kyōikusha kyōgikai, 1970

Shintō bunkakai. *Meiji ishin Shintō hyakunenshi*. 5 vols. Shintō bunkakai, 1966-68

————. *Sengo Shintō ronbun senshū*. Shintō bunkakai, 1973

Shisō no kagaku kenkyūkai. *Yume to omokage*. Chūō kōronsha, 1950

"Shisō to shite no tennōsei." *Kagaku to shisō (tokushū)*, no. 7 (January 1973)

Soda Osamu. *Chihō sangyō no shisō to undō*. Minerubua shobō, 1981

————. *Maeda Masana*. Yoshikawa kōbunkan, 1973

Soeda Tomomichi. *Enka no Meiji Taishōshi*. Iwanami shinsho, 1963

Sorimachi Shōji. *Tetsudō no Nihonshi*. Bunken shuppan, 1982

Sumiya Mikio. *Nihon shihonshugi to rōdō mondai*. Tōkyō daigaku shuppankai, 1967

Suzuki Jūzō. *Meiji tetsudō nishiki-e*. Kōtsū kyōikukai, 1971

Suzuki Masayuki. "Nichiro sengo nōson saihen seisaku no tenkai ni kansuru ichikōsatsu: nōson shōgakkō mondai o chūshin ni." *Ibaraki-kenshi kenkyū*, no. 27 (December 1973): 11-28

————. "Teikoku kenpō happu kinen yōrō shikin kashisha raireki: kakinaosareta sonmin raireki." *Chihōshi kenkyū*, no. 129 (June 1974): 68-75

Suzuki Shūji. *Bunmei no kotoba*. Bunka hyōron shuppansha, 1981

Suzuki Toshio. *Shuppan: kōfukyōka kōbō no isseiki*. Shuppan nyūsusha, 1970

Tabata Shinobu. *Katō Hiroyuki (Jinbutsu sōsho, vol. 29)*. Yoshikawa kōbunkan, 1959

Tachibana Yūichi. *Meiji kasō kiroku bungaku*. Sōjusha, 1981

Taikakai. *Naimushōshi*. 4 vols. Chihō zaimu kyōkai, 1970-1971

Takahashi Yūsai. *Meiji keisatsushi kenkyū*. 3 vols. Reibunsha, 1963

Takaku Reinosuke. "Meijiki chihō meibōkasō no seiji: Kawahara Yoshio shōden." *Shakai kagaku*, no. 22 (December 1977): 168-217

Takane Masaaki. *Nihon no seiji eriito*. Chūō kōronsha, 1976

Takeda Katsuzō. *Saiseikai gojūnenshi*. Saiseikai, 1964

Takeda Kiyoko. *Ningenkan no sōkoku: kindai Nihon no shisō to Kirisutokyō*. Kōbundō, 1959

————. *Tennōsei shisō to kyōiku*. Meiji tosho, 1964

Takeda Tsutomu. "Meiji kōki Setouchi ichi nōson ni okeru nōminsō no bunka." *Nōgyō sōgō kenkyū* 17, no. 4 (October 1963): 39-97

Takizawa Hideki. *Mayu to kiito no kindaishi*. Kyōikusha, 1979

Tanba Tsuneo, ed. *Nishiki-e ni miru Meiji Tennō to Meiji jidai*. Asahi shinbunsha, 1966

"Tennōsei." *Shisō (tokushū)*, no. 336 (June 1952)

"Tennōsei." *Shisō no kagaku (tokushū)*, no. 37 (April 1962)

"Tennōsei to Nihon no kindai." *Rekishi kōron*, no. 8 (August 1977)

Tokutomi Ichirō. *Katsura Tarō den*. 2 vols. Katsura Kōshaku kinen jigyōkai, 1917

———. *Kōshaku Yamagata Aritomo den*. 3 vols. Yamagata Aritomo Kō kinen jigyōkai, 1933

Toshitani Nobuyoshi. "Meiji minpō ni okeru 'ie' to sōzoku." *Shakai kagaku kenkyū* 23, no. 1 (1971): 30-104

Tsuda Shigemaro. *Meiji seijō to shin Takayuki*. Jishōkai, 1928

Tsunemitsu Kōnen. *Meiji no Bukkyōsha*. 2 vols. Shunjūsha, 1968

Uchida Yoshihiko. "Chishiki seinen no shoruikei." In *Nihon shihonshugi no shisōka*. Iwanami shoten, 1967

Uchikawa Yoshimi. "Shinbunshihō no seitei katei to sono tokushitsu—Meiji kōki ni okeru genron jiyū henshitsu no ichi sokumen." *Tōkyō daigaku shinbun kenkyū kiyō*, no. 5 (1956): 59-96

Uchiyama Sōjūrō. *Meiji haikara monogatari*. Jinbutsu ōraisha, 1968

Ueda-shishi hensan iinkai. *Ueda kindaishi*. 1970

Umetani Noboru. *Meiji zenki seijishi no kenkyū*. Miraisha, 1963

Umihara Tōru. *Meiji kyōinshi no kenkyū*. Minerubua shobō, 1973

Ushiyama Keiji. *Nōminsō bunkai no kōzō: senzenki*. Ochanomizu shobō, 1975

Wakamori Tarō. *Ryūkō sesō kindaishi*. Yūzankaku, 1970

———. *Tennōsei no rekishi shinri*. Kōbundō, 1973

Watanabe Ikujirō. *Kōshitsu to shakai mondai*. Bunsensha, 1925

———. *Meiji Tennō*. 2 vols. Meiji Tennō shōtokukai, 1958

———. *Meiji Tennō no hohitsu no hitobito*. Chikura shobō, 1938

———. *Meiji Tennō no seitoku: kyōiku*. Chikura shobō, 1941

———. *Nisshin Nichiro sensō shiwa*. Chikura shobō, 1937

Watanabe Kazuo. *Jitsuroku gōgai sensen*. Shinbunjidaisha, 1963

Watanabe Makoto. *Nihon nōson jinkōron*. 1938

Watari Shōsaburō. *Kyōiku chokugo to gakkō kyōiku*. Meikeikai, 1930

———. *Kyōiku chokugo shakugi zenshō*. Chūbunkan, 1934

Yamada Mamoru. *Keihin toshi mondai*. Kōseisha kōseikaku, 1974

Yamagishi Haruo. "Meiji kōki nōson ni okeru jitsugyō hoshū gakkō: Miyagi-ken no baai." *Kyōiku shakaigaku kenkyū* (Tōhoku daigaku) 32 (September 1977): 139-49

Yamamoto Nobuyoshi and Konno Toshihiko. *Meijiki gakkō gyōji no kōsatsu: kindai kyōiku no tennōsei ideorogii*. Shinsensha, 1973

Yamamoto Shigeru. *Jōyaku kaiseishi*. Takayama shoin, 1943

Yamamoto Shirō. *Taishō seihen no kisoteki kenkyū*. Ochanomizu shobō, 1970

Yamamoto Taketoshi. *Kindai Nihon no shinbun dokushasō*. Hōsei daigaku shuppankyoku, 1981

———. "Meiji kōki no riterashii chōsa." *Hitotsubashi ronsō* 61, no. 3 (March 1965): 345-55

———. "Meiji sanjūnendai zenpan no shinbun dokushasō." *Shinbungaku hyōron*, no. 16 (1967): 98-123

———. *Shinbun to minshū*. Kinokuniya shinsho, 1973

Yamamoto Tsuneo. *Kindai Nihon toshi kyōkashi kenkyū*. Reimei shobō, 1972

Yamanaka Einosuke. *Nihon kindai kokka no keisei to kanryōsei*. Kōbundō, 1974

Yamanashi-ken gikai jimukyoku. *Yamanashi-ken gikaishi*. Vols. 2-3. Yama-nashi-ken gikai, 1973

Yoshida Kyūichi. *Nihon kindai Bukkyō shakaishi kenkyū*. Yoshikawa kōbun-kan, 1964

————. *Nihon kindai Bukkyōshi kenkyū*. Yoshikawa kōbunkan, 1959

————. *Nihon shakai jigyō no rekishi*. Keisō shobō, 1960

Yoshida Noboru. "Meiji jidai no jōkyō yūgaku." in Ishiyama Shuhei, ed., *Kyōiku no shiteki hatten*. 1952

Yoshikawa Masamichi. "Meijiki no chiiki shakai shūdan no ichi kōsatsu sei-nendan shi josetsu." *Shakai mondai kenkyū* 20, nos. 1-3 (October 1970): 72-85

Yoshimoto Takaaki. "Tennōsei o dō miru ka," *Yoshimoto Takaaki zenchosaku shū*, vol. 13. Keisō shobō, 1972

ENGLISH–LANGUAGE SOURCES

Akita, George. *Foundations of Constitutional Government in Modern Japan, 1868-1900*. Cambridge: Harvard University Press, 1967

Baelz, Toku, ed. *Awakening Japan: The Diary of a German Doctor: Erwin Baelz*. Bloomington: Indiana University Press, 1974

Banno Junji. "The Taishō Political Crisis and the Problem of Japanese Gov-ernment Finance, 1906-1914." *Papers on Far Eastern History*, no. 19. Aus-tralian National University, 1979

Beckmann, George M. *The Making of the Meiji Constitution: The Oligarchs and the Constitutional Development of Japan, 1868-1891*. Westport, Ct.: Greenwood Press, 1957

Braisted, William R., trans. *Meiroku Zasshi: Journal of the Japanese Enlighten-ment*. Cambridge: Harvard University Press, 1976

Chamberlain, Basil Hall. *Things Japanese*. London: John Murray, 1905. Re-printed as *Japanese Things: Being Notes on Various Subjects Connected with Japan*. Tokyo: Tuttle, 1971

Craig, Albert M. "Fukuzawa Yukichi: The Philosophical Foundations of Meiji Nationalism." In *Political Development in Modern Japan*, ed. Robert E. Ward. Princeton: Princeton University Press, 1968

Dore, Ronald P. "The Modernizer as a Special Case: Japanese Factory Leg-islation, 1892-1911." *Comparative Studies in Society and History* 11 (1969): 433-50

————, and Tsutomu Ōuchi. "Rural Origins of Japanese Fascism." In *Di-lemmas of Growth in Prewar Japan*, ed. James W. Morley. Princeton: Prince-ton University Press, 1971

Friedell, Wilbur M. "Government Ethics Textbooks in Late Meiji Japan." *Journal of Asian Studies* 29, no. 4 (August 1970): 823-34

————. *Japanese Shrine Mergers, 1906-12*. Tokyo: Sophia University Press, 1973

Fukuzawa Yukichi. *An Outline of a Theory of Civilization* (1875). Trans.

David A. Dilworth and G. Cameron Hurst. Tokyo: Sophia University Press, 1973

Hackett, Roger F. *Yamagata Aritomo in the Rise of Modern Japan, 1838-1922*. Cambridge: Harvard University Press, 1971

Hall, Ivan Parker. *Mori Arinori*. Cambridge: Harvard University Press, 1973

Hall, John Whitney. "A Monarch for Modern Japan." In *Political Development in Modern Japan*, ed. Robert E. Ward. Princeton: Princeton University Press, 1968

Hall, Robert King, ed., and John Owen Gauntlett, trans. *Kokutai no hongi: Cardinal Principles of the National Entity of Japan*. Cambridge: Harvard University Press, 1949

Havens, Thomas R. H. *Farm and Nation in Modern Japan: Agrarian Nationalism, 1870-1940*. Princeton: Princeton University Press, 1974

Holtom, D. C. *Modern Japan and Shinto Nationalism: A Study of Present-Day Trends in Japanese Religions*. Chicago: University of Chicago Press, 1943

————. *The National Faith of Japan: A Study in Modern Japan* (1938). New York: Paragon Book Reprint, 1965

Howes, John Forman. "Japan's Enigma: The Young Uchimura Kanzō." Ph.D. dissertation, Columbia University, 1965

Hozumi Nobushige. *Ancestor Worship and Japanese Law*. Tokyo: Maruzen, 1912

Huffman, James L. *Politics of the Meiji Press: The Life of Fukuchi Gen'ichirō*. Honolulu: University of Hawaii Press, 1980

Ishiguro Tadaatsu, ed. *Ninomiya Sontoku: His Life and "Evening Talks."* Kenkyūsha, 1955

Ishii Ryosuke. *Japanese Legislation in the Meiji Era*. Trans. William J. Chambliss. Tokyo: Pan-Pacific Press, 1958

Itō Hirobumi. *Commentaries on the Constitution of the Empire of Japan*. Trans. Itō Miyoji. Igirisu hōritsu gakkō, 1889

Itō Takashi, and George Akita. "The Yamagata-Tokutomi Correspondence: Press and Politics in Meiji-Taishō Japan." *Monumenta Nipponica* 36, no. 4 (Winter 1981): 391-423

Jansen, Marius B. "Monarchy and Modernization in Japan." *Journal of Asian Studies* 36, no. 4 (August 1977): 611-22

Keene, Donald. "The Sino-Japanese War of 1894-95 and Japanese Culture." In *Landscapes and Portraits: Appreciations of Japanese Culture*. Kōdansha, 1971

Kinmonth, Earl. *The Self-Made Man in Meiji Japanese Thought: From Samurai to Salary Man*. Berkeley: University of California Press, 1981

Kishimoto Hideo. *Japanese Religion in the Meiji Era*. Ōbunsha, 1956

Koschmann, J. Victor, ed. *Authority and the Individual in Japan: Citizen Protest in Historical Perspective*. Tokyo: University of Tokyo Press, 1978

Marshall, Byron K. "Professors and Politics: The Meiji Academic Elite." *The Journal of Japanese Studies* 3, no. 1 (Winter 1977): 71-98

Maruyama Masao. "Theory and Psychology of Ultra-Nationalism" (1946). In *Thought and Behaviour in Modern Japanese Politics*, ed. Ivan Morris. London: Oxford University Press, 1963

Mason, R.H.P. *Japan's First General Election: 1890.* Cambridge: Cambridge University Press, 1969

McLaren, W. W., ed. *Japanese Government Documents, Transactions of the Asiatic Society of Japan* 42, 1st ser., pt. 1 (1917)

Miller, Frank O. *Minobe Tatsukichi: Interpreter of Constitutionalism in Japan.* Berkeley: University of California Press, 1965

Minami, Ryoshin. *The Turning Point in Economic Development: Japan's Experience.* Tokyo: Kinokuniya, 1973

Minear, Richard H. *Japanese Tradition and Western Law: Emperor, State, and Law in the Thought of Hozumi Yatsuka.* Cambridge: Harvard University Press, 1970

Mitchell, Richard H. *Thought Control in Prewar Japan.* Ithaca: Cornell University Press, 1976

Morioka Kiyomi. "The Appearance of 'Ancestor Religion' in Modern Japan: The Years of Transition from the Meiji to the Taishō Periods." *Japanese Journal of Religious Studies* 4, nos. 2-3 (June-September 1977): 183-212

Morse, Ronald A. "The Search for Japan's National Character and Distinctiveness: Yanagita Kunio (1875-1962) and the Folklore Movement." Ph.D. dissertation, Princeton University, 1975

Natsume Sōseki. "My Individualism." Trans. Jay Rubin. *Monumenta Nipponica* 34, no. 1 (Spring 1979): 21-48

Najita, Tetsuo. *Hara Kei and the Politics of Compromise, 1905-1915.* Cambridge: Harvard University Press, 1967

———. *Japan.* Englewood Cliffs, N.J.: Prentice Hall, 1974

Naka Kansuke. *The Silver Spoon (Gin no saji,* 1913). Trans. Etsuko Terasaki. Chicago: Chicago Review Press, 1976

Notehelfer, Frederick G. *Kōtoku Shūsui: Portrait of a Japanese Radical.* Cambridge: Cambridge University Press, 1971

Ohkawa Kazushi, and Shinohara, Miyohei, eds. *Patterns of Japanese Economic Development: A Quantitative Appraisal.* New Haven: Yale University Press, 1979

Okamoto, Shumpei. *The Japanese Oligarchy and the Russo-Japanese War.* New York: Columbia University Press, 1970

Ōkuma Shigenobu, comp. *Fifty Years of New Japan.* Vol. 2. London: Smith, Elder, 1909

Patrick, Hugh, ed. *Japanese Industrialization and its Social Consequences.* Berkeley: University of California Press, 1976

Passin, Herbert. *Society and Education in Japan.* New York: Teachers College Press, 1965

Pierson, John D. *Tokutomi Sohō, 1863-1957: A Journalist for Modern Japan.* Princeton: Princeton University Press, 1980

Pittau, Joseph. "Inoue Kowashi, 1843-1895, and the Formation of Modern Japan." *Monumenta Nipponica* 20, nos. 3-4 (1965): 253-82

———. *Political Thought in Early Meiji Japan, 1868-1889.* Cambridge: Harvard University Press, 1967

Pyle, Kenneth B. "Advantages of Followership: German Economics and Japanese Bureaucrats, 1890-1925." *Journal of Japanese Studies* 1, no. 1 (Autumn 1974): 127-64

————. *The New Generation in Meiji Japan: Problems of Cultural Identity, 1885-1895.* Stanford: Stanford University Press, 1969

————. "The Technology of Japanese Nationalism: The Local Improvement Movement, 1900-1918." *Journal of Asian Studies* 33, no. 1 (November 1973): 51-66

Roden, Donald T. *Schooldays in Imperial Japan: A Study in the Culture of a Student Elite.* Berkeley: University of California Press, 1980

Scheiner, Irwin. *Christian Converts and Social Protest in Meiji Japan.* Berkeley: University of California Press, 1970

Shively, Donald H. "The Japanization of the Middle Meiji." In *Tradition and Modernization in Japanese Culture,* ed. Donald H. Shively. Princeton: Princeton University Press, 1971

————. "Motoda Eifu: Confucian Lecturer to the Meiji Emperor." In *Confucianism in Action,* ed. David S. Nivison and Arthur F. Wright. Stanford: Stanford University Press, 1959

————. "Nishimura Shigeki: A Confucian View of Modernization." In *Changing Japanese Attitudes Toward Modernization,* ed. Marius B. Jansen. Princeton: Princeton University Press, 1965

Silberman, Bernard S., and H. D. Harootunian, eds. *Japan in Crisis: Essays on Taishō Democracy.* Princeton: Princeton University Press, 1974

Smethurst, Richard J. *A Social Basis for Prewar Japanese Militarism: The Army and the Rural Community.* Berkeley: University of California Press, 1974

Smith, Warren W., Jr. *Confucianism in Modern Japan: A Study of Conservatism in Japanese Intellectual History.* Tokyo: Hokuseido Press, 1959

Spaulding, Robert M., Jr. *Imperial Japan's Higher Civil Service Examinations.* Princeton: Princeton University Press, 1967

Staubitz, Richard. "The Establishment of the System of Local Self-Government (1888-1890) in Meiji Japan: Yamagata Aritomo and the Meaning of 'Jichi' (Self-Government)." Ph.D. dissertation, Yale University, 1973

Strong, Kenneth. *Ox against the Storm: A Biography of Tanaka Shōzō, Japan's Conservationist Pioneer.* Vancouver: University of British Columbia Press, 1977

Takane, Masaaki. *The Political Elite in Japan.* Berkeley: Institute of East Asian Studies, University of California Press, 1981

Titus, David Anson. *Palace and Politics in Prewar Japan.* New York: Columbia University Press, 1974

Tokutomi Kenjirō [Roka]. *Footprints in the Snow (Omoide no ki, 1901).* Trans. Kenneth Strong. Tokyo: Charles Tuttle, 1971

Tsunoda, Ryūsaku, Wm. Theodore de Bary, and Donald Keene, comps. *Sources of Japanese Tradition.* New York: Columbia University Press, 1958

Tsurumi, E. Patricia. "Meiji Primary School Language and Ethics Textbooks: Old Values for a New Society?" *Modern Asian Studies* 8, no. 2 (1974): 247-61

Waswo, Ann. "In Search of Equity: Japanese Tenant Unions in the 1920s."

In *Conflict in Modern Japanese History: The Neglected Tradition*, ed. Tetsuo Najita and J. Victor Koschmann. Princeton: Princeton University Press, 1982

————. *Japanese Landlords: The Decline of a Rural Elite.* Berkeley: University of California Press, 1977

Webb, Herschel F. "The Development of an Orthodox Attitude Toward the Imperial Institution in the Nineteenth Century." In *Changing Japanese Attitudes Toward Modernization*, ed. Marius B. Jansen. Princeton: Princeton University Press, 1965

Wray, Harold J. "Changes and Continuity in Japanese Images of the Kokutai and Roles Toward the Outside World: A Content Analysis of Japanese Textbooks, 1903-1945." Ph.D. dissertation, University of Hawaii, 1971

Yamazaki Masakazu, and Miyakawa, Tōru. "Inoue Tetsujirō: The Man and his Works." *Philosophical Studies of Japan* 7 (1966): 111-25

311

NOTES

CHAPTER ONE

1. *Kyōka* was the word commonly used for influence, or civic education. Uniting the sentiments of the people was *shōkakokoro o itsu ni shi* in the Charter Oath of 1868, *jinshin o hitotsu ni su* in many early Meiji sources, and by the 1900s such variants as *kokumin shisō tōitsu*. Examples of imperial language: *Meiji Tennō shōchoku kinkai*, ed. Meiji jingū (Kōdansha, 1973), 114-16, 239-40, 1377-79. Government language of "social education": Naimushō chihōkyoku, *Chihō kairyō jitsurei* (Hakubunkan, 1912), 72-114.

2. Shintō missionaries (*senkyōshi*): Murakami Shigeyoshi, *Kokka Shintō* (Iwanami shinsho, 1970), 91-98. 1881 statement by Inoue Kowashi: "Jinshin kyōdō iken an," *Inoue Kowashi den, shiryōhen*, ed. Inoue Kowashi denki hensan iinkai, vol. 1 (Kokugakuin daigaku toshokan, 1966), 248-49. Inoue glossed his word *fūdō* (literally, the moving wind) with the phrase *jinshin o michibiku* (guiding the sentiments of the people). The liberal opposition: e.g., the phrase *jinmin mina dōshin nareba nari*, "Minsen giin setsuritsu kenpakusho" (1874), in *Jiyūtōshi*, ed. Itagaki Taisuke (1910), 90; also in *Sources of Japanese Tradition*, comp. Tsunoda, de Bary, and Keene (New York: Columbia University Press, 1958), 683-85. Enlightenment thinkers on the same subject: *Meiroku Zasshi: Journal of the Japanese Enlightenment*, trans. William R. Braisted (Cambridge: Harvard University Press, 1976); also, *Meiji bunka zenshū*, ed. Meiji bunka kenkyūkai, vol. 5, *Zasshihen* (Nihon hyōronsha, 1968), 43-268.

3. Loyalty and filial piety: Ch. 5 below. Aesthetic tradition: Ozaki Yukio, "Ōbeimanyūki" (1888-90), *Ozaki Yukio zenshū*, vol. 3 (Heibonsha, 1926), 163-88. Sociology, "the Confucianism of the new age": Tatebe Tongo, "Meiji shisō no hensen," *Nihon*, 23 Mar. 1898.

4. For an expression of these doctrines: *Kokutai no hongi: Cardinal Principles of the National Entity of Japan* (1937), ed. Robert King Hall, and trans. John Owen Gauntlett (Cambridge: Harvard University Press, 1949).

5. 1945-1946 *tennōsei* debates: Hidaka Rokurō, ed., *Sengo shisō no shuppatsu* (Chikuma shobō, 1968), 95-168. Communist Party statement on the overthrow of the emperor system: "Jinmin ni utagau" (*Akahata*, 20 Oct. 1945), ibid., 245-47. Also, Kuno Osamu and Kamishima Jirō, eds., *"Tennōsei" ronshū*, vol. 1 (San'ichi shobō, 1974), 7-40. The general Occupation position: Charles L. Kades, "Representative Government in Japan," in Supreme Commander for the Allied Powers, *Political Reorientation of Japan, September 1945*

to September 1948, Report of Government Section, vol. 1 (Washington: U.S. Government Printing Office, 1949), xxiii–xxxv.

6. MacArthur, "Statement First Anniversary of Surrender" (2 Sept. 1946), SCAP, *Political Reorientation of Japan* 2:756–57, and "Message to American People Concerning the Surrender" (2 Sept. 1945), 2:737. Official statement on ideological liberation: SCAP memorandum, "Abolition of Governmental Sponsorship, Support, Perpetuation, Control and Dissemination of State Shinto" (15 Dec. 1945), 2:467–69.

7. "Theory and Psychology of Ultra-nationalism," in *Thought and Behaviour in Modern Japanese Politics*, ed. Ivan Morris (London: Oxford University Press, 1963), 1. Originally printed in *Sekai* (May, 1946), which the previous month had published Tsuda Sōkichi's controversial article, "Kenkoku no jijō to bansei ikkei no shisō." Although Tsuda criticized *tennōsei* and its ideology for suppression of the people, he defended the imperial house as a cultural institution that the Meiji government had distorted, and this brought him severe censure. See 1946 issues of the journals *Sekai hyōron, Jinmin hyōron, Rekishi hyōron,* and *Nihon rekishi* for other scholarly articles critical of the emperor system.

8. Yoshimoto Takaaki, "Tennōsei o dō miru ka," *Yoshimoto Takaaki zenchosaku shū,* vol. 13 (Keisō shobō, 1972), 460.

9. Characterization based on works of major writers on the subject. "Maruyama school": Maruyama Masao, *Nihon no shisō* (Iwanami shinsho, 1961), 28–52; Fujita Shōzō, *Tennōsei kokka no shihai genri* (Miraisha, 1966); Ishida Takeshi, *Meiji seiji shisōshi kenkyū* (Miraisha, 1954); Kamishima Jirō, *Kindai Nihon no seishin kōzō* (Iwanami shoten, 1961), 17–164; Matsumoto Sannosuke, *Tennōsei kokka to seiji shisō* (Miraisha, 1969), 254–308. Also, Matsumoto, "The Roots of Political Disillusionment: 'Public' and 'Private' in Japan," in *Authority and the Individual in Japan: Citizen Protest in Historical Perspective*, ed. J. Victor Koschmann (Tokyo: University of Tokyo Press, 1978), 31–51. A Marxist résumé: Inoue Kiyoshi, *Tennōsei* (Tōkyō daigaku shuppankai, 1952). However, Marxist historiography has generally concentrated on political and economic structures, with less attention to ideological aspects: see Inumaru Giichi, "Sengo tennōsei kenkyū no seika," *Rekishi hyōron* (Apr. 1967): 27–41. "*Minshūshi*" view: Irokawa Daikichi, "Tennōsei to shite no ideorogii," *Meiji no bunka* (Iwanami shoten, 1970), 263–335; Kano Masanao, *Shihonshugi keiseiki no chitsujo ishiki* (Chikuma shobō, 1969), 259–625; and to some extent, Yasumaru Yoshio, who practices Weberian analysis on earlier origins of *tennōsei* ideology, *Nihon no kindaika to minshū shisō* (Aoki shoten, 1974). Representative postwar writings on the emperor system: Kuno and Kamishima, *"Tennōsei" ronshū,* 2 vols. Changes in *tennōsei* scholarship over time: "Tennōsei," *Shisō,* no. 336 (June 1952); "Tennōsei," *Shisō no kagaku* , no. 37 (Apr. 1962); "Shisō to shite no tennōsei," *Kagaku to shisō,* no. 7 (Jan. 1973); "Gendai ni okeru tennō to tennōsei," *Gendai to shisō,* no. 15 (Mar. 1974); "Tennōsei," *Dentō to gendai hozuban* (1975); "Gendai tennōsei," *Hōgaku seminā (zōkan),* (Feb. 1977); "Tennōsei to Nihon no kindai,"

Rekishi kōron, no. 8 (Aug. 1977). Brief bibliography of postwar *tennōsei* writings: Wakamori Tarō, *Tennōsei no rekishi shinri* (Kōbundō, 1973), 8-12.

Western writers have treated the subject less directly, though most often in general agreement with interpretations of scholars like Maruyama, e.g., Robert Bellah, "Values and Social Change in Modern Japan," *Beyond Belief: Essays on Religion in a Post-traditional World* (New York: Harper and Row, 1970), 114-45.

10. Irokawa, *Meiji no bunka*, 265. The "black box" is Marx's *camera obscura*, the device of optical inversion here enlarged to its original sense of a chamber large enough to enter (hence to be unaware of the ideological distortion within).

11. E.g., among many, "Tennōsei ideorogii—'Meiji hyakunen' hihan," *Rekishigaku kenkyū*, no. 341 (Oct. 1968); Matsuura Rei, et al., *Tennōsei to Yasukuni o tou* (Chikuma shobō, 1978); Wadatsumikai, *Tennōsei o toitsuzukeru* (Chikuma shobō, 1978). Other *tennōsei* issues include the textbook trials, the celebration of the fiftieth anniversary of the emperor's reign, the institutionalization of the reign name system (*gengōsei*), etc.

12. Clifford Geertz, "Ideology as a Cultural System," *The Interpretation of Cultures* (New York: Basic Books, 1973), 216-20.

13. Peter L. Berger and Thomas Luckmann, *The Social Construction of Reality: A Treatise in the Sociology of Knowledge* (New York: Anchor Books, 1966), 123-28. A discussion of similar issues in more philosophical terms: Paul Rabinow and William M. Sullivan, eds., *Interpretive Social Science: A Reader* (Berkeley: University of California Press, 1979), 2-8, and passim.

14. Louis Althusser, *For Marx*, trans. Ben Brewster (London: NLB, 1969), 233-35.

15. Antonio Gramsci, *Selections from the Prison Notebooks*, ed. and trans. Quintin Hoare and Geoffrey Nowell Smith (New York: International Publishers, 1971), 12-13, 80, and passim. Also, Althusser, "Ideology and Ideological State Apparatuses," *Lenin and Philosophy and Other Essays*, trans. Ben Brewster (New York: Monthly Review Press, 1971), 142-47.

16. Raymond Williams, *The Sociology of Culture* (New York: Schocken Books, 1982), 29.

17. Althusser, *For Marx*, 232. In a different tradition, see Geertz's refutation of ideology as a "radical intellectual depravity," "Ideology as a Cultural System," 193-200. The argument for ideology as a "persistent functional component of all social systems" is made in each of the dialects of social science. E.g., Bernard Barber, "Function, Variability and Change in Ideological Systems," in *Stability and Social Change*, ed. Bernard Barber and Alex Inkeles (Boston: Little, Brown and Co., 1971), 251; Joseph LaPalombara, "Decline of Ideology: A Dissent and an Interpretation," *American Political Science Review* 60, no. 1 (Mar. 1966): 7; Rolf Schulze, "Some Socio-Psychological and Political Functions of Ideology," in *Towards the Sociology of Knowledge: Origin and Development of a Sociological Thought Style*, ed. Gunter W. Remmling (New York: Humanities Press, 1973), 115-28.

18. Karl Marx and Friedrich Engels, *The German Ideology* (1920) (New York: International Publishers, 1970), 47, 65-66. Although less emphasized, there are other non-pejorative mentions of ideology in Marx's work, e.g., "A Contribution to the Critique of Political Economy" (1859), *The Marx-Engels Reader*, ed. Robert Tucker (New York: W. W. Norton and Company, 1972), 5.

19. While hardly a rigorous distinction, see, for example, Ariizumi Sadao's preference for the term *ideorogiiteki tōgō* (ideological unity): "Meiji kokka to minshū tōgō," *Iwanami kōza Nihon rekishi*, vol. 17, *Kindai* 4 (Iwanami shoten, 1976), 222ff. For Karl Mannheim: *Ideology and Utopia* (New York: Harcourt, Brace and World, 1936), 84-108.

20. "Meiji nijūsannen nigatsu chihō chōkan kaigi hikki" (1890), *Chihōkan kaigi giketsusho narabi hikki*, transcript, Tōkyō-to komonjokan (ms).

21. *Kokumin no bochi*: "Nōson jichi no kenkyū" (1908), *Yamazaki Enkichi zenshū*, vol. 1 (Yamazaki Enkichi zenshū kankōkai, 1935), 21-22.

22. *Kokumin seishin tōitsu*: Sakurai Tōhoku, "Jingi ni kansuru tokubetsu kanga no setchi wa teikoku kokuze no saikyū saiyō bubun nari," *Zenkoku shinshokukai kaihō*, no. 232 (Feb. 1918): 2.

23. Representative accounts: Kano, *Shihonshugi keiseiki*, 429-80; Ishida, *Meiji seiji shisōshi kenkyū*, 180-202; Sumiya Mikio, "Kokuminteki bijon no tōgō to bunkai," *Kindai Nihon shisōshi taikei*, vol. 5 (Chikuma shobō, 1960), 22-30.

24. E.g., reservist youth groups offering food and liquor: *Kakurentaiku kannai minjō fūzoku shisōkai no genjō*, III, Sakura, Dec. 1913, Faculty of Law, Tokyo University (ms). Encouraging evening school, Shintō youth meeting: *Shinano mainichi shinbun*, 1, 9 Apr. 1890; on the suitability of leghorns: 6 Apr. Such *enzetsu gentōkai* (speech and magic-lantern meetings) were common in the 1890s.

25. Literally, "the number two citizens," a standard phrase, e.g., "Rikken kokumin no kyōiku," *Tōkyō mainichi shinbun*, 17 May 1907; "Kyōikujō no shinfukuin," *Shimin* 6, no. 2 (7 May 1911): 55.

26. See Ariizumi, "Meiji kokka to minshū tōgō," 247-54.

27. Nihon shoseki shuppan kyōkai, *Nihon shuppan hyakunenshi nenpyō* (Nihon shoseki shuppankai, 1968), 1064; Suzuki Toshio, *Shuppan: kōfukyōka kōbō no isseiki* (Shuppan nyūsusha, 1970), 123.

28. "Katei to keishin kannen to no kankei," *Nihonjin*, no. 446 (5 Nov. 1906): 15.

29. "Yokubōjō yori mitaru nōson kaihatsu saku," *Kokumin zasshi* 3, no. 3 (1 Feb. 1912): 12-15, and no. 4 (15 Feb. 1912): 20-22.

30. Takeuchi Yoshimi, "Kenryoku to geijutsu," *Shinpen Nihon ideorogii, Takeuchi Yoshimi hyōronshū* (Chikuma shobō, 1966), 378-84.

CHAPTER TWO

1. Kashiwabara Takaaki, "On Sunday," speech reprinted in *Meiroku zasshi* 33 (Mar. 1875), Braisted, 406-7.

2. E.g., Ōkubo Toshimichi, "Rikken seitai ni kansuru ikensho" (1873), *Kindai Nihon shisō taikei*, vol. 30, *Meiji shisōshū I*, ed. Matsumoto Sannosuke (Chikuma shobō, 1976), 5-7.

3. *Yamagata Aritomo ikensho*, ed. Ōyama Azusa (Hara shobō, 1966), 52; Roger F. Hackett, *Yamagata Aritomo in the Rise of Modern Japan, 1838-1922* (Cambridge: Harvard University Press, 1971), 65. Many of Yamagata's opinions on conscription, most probably including this one, were drafted by Nishi Amane. See Tokutomi Ichirō, *Kōshaku Yamagata Aritomo den*, vol. 2 (Yamagata Aritomo Kō kinen jigyōkai, 1933), 267-69.

4. "Chihō seiji kairyō iken an," *Inoue Kowashi den* 1:480.

5. "Kaku chihō jikkyō hōkoku," (*Yomiuri shinbun*, 14 Feb. 1891), a DaiNihon nōkai investigation conducted among *rōnō* (experienced farmers), the agricultural elite of the provinces. On local government reorganization: Kikegawa Hiroshi, *Meiji chihō jichi seido no seiritsu katei* (Tōkyō shisei chō-sakai, 1955); Ōshima Mitsuko, *Meiji no mura* (Kyōikusha, 1977); Kurt Steiner, *Local Government in Japan* (Stanford: Stanford University Press, 1965), 19-40.

6. "Shōgakurei to shinnin monbudaijin," *San'in shinbun*, 26 May 1890; also, e.g., "Gakkō kyōiku to seikai fūha no soto ni tataseru koto ni tsuite," *Mainichi shinbun*, 15 Apr. 1888.

7. Kokuritsu kyōiku kenkyūjo, *Nihon kindai kyōiku hyakunenshi*, vol. 1 (Kyōiku kenkyū shinkōkai, 1974), 59-150; Karasawa Tomitarō, *Kyōkasho no rekishi: kyōkasho to Nihonjin no keisei* (Sōbunsha, 1956), 49-149; Ivan Parker Hall, *Mori Arinori* (Cambridge: Harvard University Press, 1973), Chs. 9, 10.

8. Hōgakushikai, "Hōten hensan ni kansuru hōgakushikai no iken" (May 1888), *Minpōten ronsō shiryōshū*, ed. Hoshino Tōru (Nihon hyōronsha, 1969), 15; DaiNihon kyōikukai chōsa hōkoku, "Hōten to rinri no kankei," *Nihon*, 24 Sept. 1892. For a partial view of the controversy: Richard Rabinowitz, "Law and the Social Process in Japan," *Transactions of the Asiatic Society of Japan* 10, 3d ser. (1968): 7-39.

9. "Nihon Shina kaigun no hikaku," *Mainichi shinbun*, 16 July 1891. On the military system: Matsushita Yoshio, *Meiji gunsei shiron*, 2 vols. (Yūhi-kaku, 1956); Ernst L. Presseisen, *Before Aggression: Europeans Prepare the Japanese Army* (Tucson: The University of Arizona Press, 1965).

10. *Raidenshugi*: Ozaki Yukio, "Eibei no idō" (1889), *Ozaki Yukio zenshū* (1926) 3:190.

11. For this suggestion in a different historiographical context: Theodore K. Rabb, *The Struggle for Stability in Early Modern Europe* (New York: Oxford University Press, 1975), 147-51.

12. Honjō Eijirō, "Sada Kaiseki no kenkyū," *Nihon keizai shisōshi kenkyū*, vol. 2 (Nihon hyōronsha, 1947); Tsunemitsu Kōnen, *Meiji no Bukkyōsha*, vol. 1 (Shunjūsha, 1968), 71-82. Ōhama Tetsuya, *Meiji Kirisutokyōkaishi no kenkyū* (Yoshikawa kōbunkan, 1979), 85-89.

13. *Nihonshugi* (Gumma-ken, Maebashi), no. 1 (11 Feb. 1890): 1-2, 23-24.

14. "Oppekepē," Soeda Tomomichi, *Enka no Meiji Taishōshi* (Iwanami shinsho, 1963), 22-23. This was one of the best-known dramatic *sōshi* songs

of 1890; such refrains were sung about bureaucrats, rural gentlemen, and opposition politicians.

15. Politics and youth: e.g., letter to Itō Hirobumi (July 1878), Itō Hirobumi kankei monjo kenkyūkai, *Itō Hirobumi kankei monjo*, vol. 8 (Hanawa shobō, 1980), 95. Preparing for constitutional government: e.g., "Shisei chōsonsei gunsei fukensei ni kansuru genrōin kaigi enzetsu" (Nov. 1890), *Yamagata Aritomo ikensho*, 190; "Chōheiseido oyobi jichiseido kakuritsu no enkaku," ibid., 394.

16. "Isasaka shoshi o kishite dokusha ni tsugu," *Aikoku* (Yamanashi-ken, Kōfu), no. 1 (7 May 1890): 2; "Yamanashi ni okeru seiji shisō," 5-6.

17. Political fever, *seijinetsu*, or *seinetsu*. Examples include journals supporting political parties, e.g., *Aimin* (Nagano), Apr. 1889, *Heiminshugi* (Chiba), May 1890; organs of local youth associations, such as *Jōmō seinenkai zasshi* (Gumma-ken), Jan. 1888, with which Taketoshi Yosaburō and Tokutomi Sohō were associated; and those of the local education associations that also proliferated at this time, e.g., *Agatsuma kyōiku* (Gumma-ken, Agatsuma-gun), July 1888; and conservative "Japanist" publications such as *Nihonshugi* (Maebashi), Feb. 1890 (Meiji shinbun zasshi bunko collection, Faculty of Law, Tokyo University).

18. Kuga Katsunan, "Sōkan no ji," *Nihon* (11 Feb. 1889), *Kuga Katsunan zenshū*, ed. Nishida Taketoshi and Uete Michiari, vol. 2 (Misuzu shobō, 1969), 1-2.

19. National doctrine *(kokkyō): Nihon kokkyō daidō sōshi 1*, no. 1 (25 July 1888), 1, journal of the Nihon kokkyō daidōsha, founded in 1889 by Kawai Kiyomaru, Torio Koyata, and Yamaoka Tetsutarō, and published until 1917. Another enduring conservative organization, Nihon kōdōkai, was founded in 1887 by Nishimura Shigeki and others. Its journal, variously named, was published throughout the prewar period and continued after the war. See *Nihon kōdōkai shijūnenshi* (Nihon kōdōkai, 1918).

20. Sense of nation is *kokkateki kannen*, or *kokuminteki kannen*. On nationalism: Kenneth B. Pyle, *The New Generation in Meiji Japan: Problems of Cultural Identity, 1885-1895* (Stanford: Stanford University Press, 1969); Donald H. Shively, "The Japanization of the Middle Meiji," in *Tradition and Modernization in Japanese Culture*, ed. Shively (Princeton: Princeton University Press, 1971), 77-119. Representative Japanese works include Maruyama Masao, "Meiji kokka no shisō," *Nihon shakai no shiteki kyūmei*, ed. Rekishigaku kenkyūkai (Iwanami shoten, 1949), 181-236; "Kuga Katsunan to kokuminshugi," *Minkenron kara nashonarizumu e*, ed. Meiji shiryō kenkyū renrakukai (Ochanomizu shobō, 1957), 192-209; Motoyama Yukihiko, "Meiji nijūnendai no seiron ni arawareta nashonarizumu," *Meiji zenpanki no nashonarizumu*, ed. Sakata Yoshio (Miraisha, 1958), 37-84.

21. *Mainichi shinbun*, May 4, 1888.

22. Albert M. Craig, "Fukuzawa Yukichi: The Philosophical Foundations of Meiji Nationalism," in *Political Development in Modern Japan*, ed. Robert E. Ward (Princeton: Princeton University Press, 1968), 144.

23. Especially well known were Takekoshi Yosaburō, *ShinNihonshi* (1891-

92), *Meiji bungaku zenshū* 77:3-225; and Tokutomi Sohō, *Yoshida Shōin* (1893), ibid., 34:159-243. Takekoshi stressed *Nihon kokumin taru shisō*, e.g., p. 7; Sohō, *kokumin kannen, kokuminteki tōitsu no seishin*, e.g., p. 174. Takekoshi analyzed the revolutionary nature of the Restoration (pp. 134-42); Sohō shared this view, but in a thorough revision of the work in 1908 abandoned it. See John D. Pierson, *Tokutomi Sohō, 1863-1957: A Journalist for Modern Japan* (Princeton: Princeton University Press, 1980), 292-94. Sohō's call for a "second restoration" was widely echoed in the speeches and press of the early nineties, e.g., "Daini ishin no ki o kaisō seyo," *Katsusekai*, no. 10 (27 Mar. 1891): 5-7. See also, Shimada Saburō, *Kaikoku shimatsu* (1887), which related Restoration history to the contemporary treaty revision issue (*Meiji bungaku zenshū* 77:287-311). For remarks on this and two earlier histories, Taguchi Ukichi's *Nihon kaika shōshi* (1877-82), and Fukuzawa Yukichi's *Kyūhanjō* (1877): ibid., 429-36. Also on Meiji historians: Ienaga Saburō and Kano Masanao, *Nihon no rekishika* (Nihon hyōronsha, 1976), 2-59.

24. The Edokai's organ, *Edokai zasshi*, and the *Edo shinbun*, from which this quotation comes, both began publication in 1889. According to Ogi Shinzō, this activity marked the first conscious retrospective use of Edo as a place-name and cultural artifact. *Tōkyō shomin seikatsushi kenkyū* (Nihon hōsō shuppan kyōkai, 1979), 11-23.

25. *Tōkyō nichi nichi shinbun*, 5 Apr. 1891; *Saigō Takamori-kun seizonki* (1891); Ubukata Toshirō, *Meiji Taishō kenbunshi* (Chūō kōronsha, 1978), 25-26; *Chōya shinbun*, 10 Feb. 1889.

26. Hirota Masaki, *Bunmei kaika to minshū ishiki* (Aoki shoten, 1980), 56-81.

27. *Taiyō* 3, no. 20 (20 Oct. 1897): 58-59.

28. Katō Hiroyuki, "Nihon no kokuze ('bukokushugi' o toranka, mata 'shōkokushugi' o toranka)," *Tensoku* 1, nos. 1-2 (Apr.-May 1889); unsigned, "Ikkoku no kokuze o ittei seyo," *Katsusekai*, no. 19 (27 Mar. 1891); Shiga Shigetaka, "Nihon zento no kokuze wa 'kokusui hozon shigi' ni sentei sezaru bekarazu," *Nihonjin*, no. 3 (May 1888).

29. Shiga Shigetaka, "Nihonjin no jōto o sensu," *Nihonjin*, no. 1 (Apr. 1888); Pyle, *New Generation*, 64.

30. *Tōkyō nichi nichi shinbun*, 12 Oct. 1890.

31. Yokoi Tokio, "The Moral Crisis in Japan," *The Far East* 2, no. 4 (20 Apr. 1897): 157.

32. General narratives written in the postwar period simply state this; for a sophisticated analysis: Fujita Shōzō, *Tennōsei kokka no shihai genri*, 7-35.

33. Soeda Juichi, "Dai ikkai nōshōkō kōtō kaigi giji sokkiroku: shokkō no torishimari oyobi hogo ni kansuru ken," *Meiji bunka shiryō sōsho*, vol. 1, *Sangyōhen* (Kazama shobō, 1961), 55. Partially quoted in Oka Toshirō, "Kindai Nihon ni okeru shakai seisaku shisō no keisei to hatten: 'kokka seiji' kara 'shakai seiji' e," *Shisō*, no. 558 (Dec. 1970): 69-88.

34. Bureaucrats: Oka, ibid., and Kenneth B. Pyle, "Advantages of Followership: German Economics and Japanese Bureaucrats, 1890-1925," *Journal of Japanese Studies* 1, no. 1 (Autumn 1974): 127-64. Socialists: Oka, 71, and

Kōtoku Shūsui, "Jūkyūseiki to nijūseiki," *Nihonjin*, no. 129 (Dec. 1900): 13-15.

35. Hisamatsu Yoshinori, "Shakaiteki kanken ippan," *Nihonjin*, no. 109 (Feb. 1900): 12-14.

36. Not *kokka no jiken*, but *shakai no dekigoto*. Yokoyama Masao, *Chōsonze chōsa kōyō* (Morioka: Iwate-ken naimubu shomuka, 1909), 3-9.

37. The Chinese compound *shakai* in its modern sense of "society as a whole" first established itself in Japan in the late 1870s among enlightenment intellectuals, but did not come into common use until the 1890s. Saitō Tsuyoshi, *Meiji no kotoba: higashi kara nishi e no kakehashi* (Kōdansha, 1977), 175-228.

38. Fukuzawa Yukichi, *An Outline of a Theory of Civilization* (1875), trans. David A. Dilworth and G. Cameron Hurst (Tokyo: Sophia University Press, 1973), 144. Similarly, in *An Encouragement of Learning* (1874), trans. David A. Dilworth and Umeyo Hirano (Tokyo: Sophia University Press, 1969), 25.

39. *Kaihō* (Apr. 1921), quoted in Saitō, *Meiji no kotoba*, 177.

40. The vocabulary of social disarray (*shakai no konran, shakai no ranchō*) is found throughout contemporary comment. A wide-ranging sample is provided by the military in Kakurentaiku kannai minjō fūzoku shisōkai no genjō, I-V (ms). For representative specific examples: Social ills (*shakai no yamai*): Yanagita Kunio, "Tsuka to mori no hanashi," *Shimin* 6, no. 10 (Jan. 1912): 48. Diseases of civilization: Tokutomi Sohō, "Bunmeibyō" (1906), in *Sohō bunsen* (Min'yūsha, 1915), 933-36; *ryūkōbyō*, in Sawayanagi Masatarō, "Gakusei no fūki mondai," *Jindō* 1, no. 6 (Sept. 1905): 7. Typical presentation of economic difficulties (*seikatsunan, shūshokunan*): the *zappō* of *Kokumin zasshi*, vols. 1-3 (1910-12). Struggle for survival (*seizon kyōsō*): Hozumi Yatsuka, *Kokumin dōtoku: aikokushin* (Yūhikaku, 1897); speech by Oishi Masami, *Kokumin shinbun*, 15 Feb. 1907; Kaneko Chikusui, "Kindaishugi no engen," *Taiyō* 17, no. 14 (1 Nov. 1911): 18-19. Labor problems (*rōdō mondai*): Yokoyama Gennosuke, "Rōdō undō no shomaku," *Chūō kōron* (Aug. 1899); the journal of the establishment's Social Policy Association, *Shakai*, vols. 1-3 (1899-1901). Dangerous thought (*kiken shisō*): Makino Nobuaki, "Gakusei seito no fūki shinshuku ni kansuru," *Kunrei* no. 1 (June 1906), in *Gakusei hyakunenshi*, ed. Monbushō, vol. 2 (Teikoku chihō gyōsei gakkai, 1972), 35; Hirata Tōsuke on the Boshin shōsho of 1908, in *Kōshaku Hirata Tōsuke den*, ed. Katō Fusazō (Hirata Tōsuke denki hensan jimusho, 1927), 119-28; Komatsubara Eitarō on social education (Apr. 1911): *Komatsubara Bunshō kyōiku-ron*, ed. Tateishi Komakichi (Nishōdō shoten, 1911), 309-23; Muramatsu Tsuneichirō, "Kiken shisō bōshisaku ni kansuru shitsumon" (Lower House, 9 Mar. 1911), in *Teikoku gikai kyōiku giji sōran*, ed. Abe Isoo, vol. 3 (Rinsen shoten, 1971), 48-62. Socialist destruction (*shakaihakaishugi*): Yamagata Aritomo (drafted by Hozumi Yatsuka), "Shakaihakaishugiron" (1911), *Yamagata Aritomo ikensho*, 315-22; in general usage, *Tōkyō nichi nichi shinbun*, 14 June 1908. References to the gulf between rich and poor (*hinpu no henkaku*, etc.) are found in nearly all of the above.

41. Delinquent localities (*furyō naru chōson* and *jichi no bunran*): "Seiseki furyō naru chōson gyōsei seiri suru ken" (Fukushima: 1908), in Fuwa Kazuhiko, "Nichiro sengo ni okeru nōson shinkō to nōmin kyōka, I," *Tōhoku daigaku kyōiku gakubu kenkyū nenpō*, no. 25 (1977): 17. Criticism of the portrayals of Tokyo as a sink of iniquity (*zaiaku no sōkutsu*): Kōda Rohan, *Ikkoku no shuto* (1899), *Kōda Rohan zenshū*, vol. 27 (Iwanami shoten, 1954), 8-9. The dangers of cities: Yokoi Tokiyoshi, "Tokai to inaka," *Yokoi Hakase zenshū*, ed. DaiNihon nōkai, vol. 4 (Yokoi Hakase zenshū kankōkai, 1925), 531-652. Customs and morals (*fūzoku taihai, fūki fuhai*): Higashi Kan'ichi, "Fūzoku taihairon," *Nihonjin*, nos. 52-55, 57 (5 Oct.-20 Nov. 1897); and esp. the controversy surrounding the "*Gakusei fūki kunrei*" (June 1906), e.g., *Kyōiku jiron*, nos. 761-71 (June-Nov. 1906). Middle class: "Chūtō shakai no sekinin," *Tōkyō mainichi shinbun*, 16 Jan. 1907; "Kyōiku aru yūmin no shochi mondai," *Chūō kōron* (July 1912): 75-90.

42. Social reportage and social novels: Tachibana Yūichi, *Meiji kasō kiroku bungaku* (Sōjusha, 1981).

43. The common terms were *chūtō kaikyū* (middle classes), which was in wide use since the 1880s, and *kasō shakai* (lower social strata) which gained currency at the turn of the century, in good part as a result of Yokoyama Gennosuke's pioneering study, *Nihon no kasō shakai* (1898) (Iwanami shoten, 1978).

44. Kōtoku Shūsui, "Kiken wa uchi ni ari" (1901), *Kōtoku Shūsui zenshū*, vol. 3 (Kōtoku Shūsui zenshū henshū iinkai, 1968), 217-20; *Nijūseiki no kaibutsu teikokushugi* (1901), *Kōtoku Shūsui shū, Kindai Nihon shisō taikei*, vol. 13 (Chikuma shobō, 1975), 34-78; also, Frederick G. Notehelfer, *Kōtoku Shūsui: Portrait of a Japanese Radical* (Cambridge: Cambridge University Press, 1971), 55-87.

45. Yamagata to Katsura, 11 Aug. 1901, Katsura Tarō monjo (70-12), Kensei shiryōshitsu, National Diet Library (ms).

46. Kiyama Kumajirō, "Nisan no seinenron," *Teiyū rinrikai rinri kōenshū*, no. 101 (Jan. 1911): 78-79.

47. Roland Barthes, *Mythologies* (New York: Hill and Wang, 1972), 131-42.

48. *Chōshū nichi nichi shinbun*, 7 July 1912.

49. GNP calculations vary and, like all Meiji economic statistics, are the subject of controversy. In Nakamura Takafusa's reckoning, Japan led the United States and Canada in real GNP per capita; others place Japan just below these countries, although still in the highest group. (*Senzenki Nihon keizai seichō no bunseki* [Iwanami shoten, 1971]. 2-9). Long swings and faltering: Kazushi Ohkawa and Henry Rosovsky, *Japanese Economic Growth: Trend Acceleration in the Twentieth Century* (Stanford: Stanford University Press, 1973), 19-43. Recessions: Nagaoka Shinkichi, *Meiji kyōkōshi josetsu* (Tōkyō daigaku shuppankai, 1971), 2-11.

50. Ohkawa Kazushi et al., *Chōki keizai tōkei: suikei to bunseki* (LTES), vol. 8, *Kokumin shotoku* (Tōyō keizai shinpōsha, 1974), 178; Andō Yoshio, *Kindai Nihon keizaishi yōran* (Tōkyō daigaku shuppankai, 1975), 18-19. These

are nominal figures, used here because they, rather than real figures, were what contemporaries were reacting to.

51. Andō, *Keizaishi*, 18; Banno Junji, *Meiji kenpō taisei no seiritsu: fukoku kyōhei to minryoku kyūyō* (Tōkyō daigaku shuppankai, 1971), 146-74, 243. The land tax was raised again in 1904 and 1905.

52. Local (city, town, and village) taxes increased the most dramatically; when prefectural taxes are included, all non-national taxes increased nearly ninefold. National taxes in 1912, on the other hand, were 5.5 times what they were in 1890 (Ōsato Katsura, ed., *Meiji ikō honpō shuyō keizai tōkei* [Nihon gentō tōkeikyoku, 1966], 136-7, 150-1). Burden per household: Nakamura Masanori, *Kindai Nihon jinushi seidoshi kenkyū: shihonshugi to jinushisei* (Tōkyō daigaku shuppankai, 1979), 46-49.

53. Andō, *Keizaishi*, 27; Tsutomu Noda, "Prices," in *Patterns of Japanese Economic Development: A Quantitative Appraisal*, ed. Kazushi Ohkawa and Miyohei Shinohara (New Haven: Yale University Press, 1979), 219-28. For the neoclassical view that the standard of living rose: Allen C. Kelley, Jeffrey G. Williamson, and Russell J. Cheetham, *Dualistic Economic Development: Theory and History* (Chicago: University of Chicago Press, 1972), 130-75. Few Japanese economists accept this view.

54. "Seisansha no tenka, juyōsha no kutsū," *Kokumin zasshi* 2, no. 2 (1 Feb. 1911): 9.

55. Ōishi Kaichirō and Miyamoto Ken'ichi, eds., *Nihon shihonshugi hattatsushi no kiso chishiki* (Yūhikaku, 1975), 114-334; Nakamura Takafusa, *Senzenki Nihon keizai*, 14-201; Kazushi Ohkawa and Henry Rosovsky, "A Century of Japanese Economic Growth," in *The State and Economic Enterprise in Japan: Essays in the Political Economy of Growth*, ed. William W. Lockwood (Princeton: Princeton University Press, 1965), 66-81; and Kozo Yamamura, "The Japanese Economy, 1911-1930: Concentration, Conflicts and Crises," in *Japan in Crisis: Essays on Taishō Democracy*, ed. Bernard S. Silberman and H. D. Harootunian (Princeton: Princeton University Press, 1974), 299-328.

56. Nakamura Masanori estimates the post Sino-Japanese War percentage of government-capitalized industry at 30 percent by 1897. After the Russo-Japanese War, this reached 51 percent by 1907. In Ōishi and Miyamoto, *Nihon shihonshugi hattatsushi*, 115-16.

57. Ryoshin Minami, *The Turning Point in Economic Development: Japan's Experience* (Tokyo: Kinokuniya, 1973), 25; Andō, *Keizaishi*, 8; Nakamura Takafusa, *Senzenki Nihon keizai*, 70-73.

58. Gary R. Saxonhouse, "Country Girls and Communication Among Competitors in the Japanese Cotton-Spinning Industry," in *Japanese Industrialization and its Social Consequences*, ed. Hugh Patrick (Berkeley: University of California Press, 1976), 98; Ippei Yamazawa and Yuzo Yamamoto, "Trade and Balance of Payments," in *Patterns of Japanese Economic Development*, ed. Ohkawa and Shinohara, 135.

59. Robert E. Cole and Ken'ichi Tominaga, "Japan's Changing Occupational Structure and Its Significance," in Patrick, *Japanese Industrialization*, 59. For other figures, Nōshōmushō, *Shokkō jijō* (1903), reprint, ed. Ōkōchi

Kazuo (Kōseikan, 1971), 17; Sumiya Mikio, *Nihon shihonshugi to rōdō mondai* (Tōkyō daigaku shuppankai, 1967), 90-104.

60. Gotō Yasushi, "Kindai tennōseiron," in *Kōza Nihonshi*, ed. Rekishigaku kenkyūkai and Nihonshi kenkyūkai, vol. 9 (Tōkyō daigaku shuppankai, 1971), 192.

61. Between 1872 and 1914 the agricultural force remained stable at approximately 16 million, while the average rate of contribution from agriculture to nonagricultural employment was around 70 percent in the same period. Mataji Umemura, "Population and Labor Force," in *Patterns of Japanese Economic Development*, ed. Ohkawa and Shinohara, 244-46; Cole and Tominaga, in Patrick, 57-63; also Minami, *The Turning Point*, 105-12, 225-26. Minami postulates that the "turning point" in labor supply did not occur until the 1950s (225-53).

62. Gotō, "Kindai tennōseiron," 188. Estimates vary, but total population was approximately 40 million in 1888, 52 million in 1912, and 68 million in 1935. Calculated according to sector, Andō gives the percentages of employed population as follows (*Keizaishi*, 25):

	Primary	Secondary	Tertiary
1887	78%	9%	13%
1912	62	18	20
1936	45	24	31

It is the doubling in the secondary sector between 1887 and 1912 that aroused the kind of concern mentioned here.

63. Rōdō undō shiryō iinkai, *Nihon rōdō undō shiryō*, vol. 2 (Tōkyō daigaku shuppankai, 1963), 3-173; Sumiya, *Nihon shihonshugi*, 115-19, 159-60.

64. Cities, moreover, were growing at a rate 2.5 times the rate of increase in the total population. Hiroshi Ohbuchi, "Demographic Transition in the Process of Japanese Industrialization," in *Japanese Industrialization*, ed. Patrick, 330-37.

65. Ōsaka-shi, *Meiji Taishō Ōsaka-shishi*, vol. 2 (Nihon hyōronsha, 1934-5), 118-20; "Tōkyō-shi no jinkō," *Kokumin zasshi* 3, no. 10 (15 June 1912): 59; Yamada Mamoru, *Keihin toshi mondai* (Kōseisha kōseikaku, 1974), 22-26.

66. Mori Tsunetarō, *Chōsonze chōsa shishin* (Teibi shuppansha, 1909), 180. For a sample of provincial growth rates: Mizuno Hiroshi and Hirano Kazuko, "Meiji shoki no 'urban-rural' jinkō ni tsuite," *Tōkeikyoku kenkyū ihō*, no. 30 (Mar. 1976): 1-27; Unno Fukujū, "Kōgyō hatten to toshi no dōkō," in *Meiji Taishō kyōdoshi kenkyūhō*, *Kyōdoshi kenkyū kōza*, ed. Furushima Toshio et al., vol. 7 (Asakura shoten, 1972), 148.

67. Nakamura Masanori, *Kindai Nihon jinushi*, 123; Ann Waswo, *Japanese Landlords: The Decline of a Rural Elite* (Berkeley: University of California Press, 1977), 66-88.

68. See Thomas R. H. Havens, *Farm and Nation in Modern Japan: Agrarian Nationalism, 1870-1940* (Princeton: Princeton University Press, 1974), 56-110.

69. Speech by Yamazaki Enkichi, *Chihō jichi kōshū hikki* [P] (Shimane, Daitō-chō: 1912), 9.

70. The most famous examples of these surveys include Nōshōmushō, *Shokkō jijō* (1903), reprint, ed. Ōkōchi Kazuo (Kōseikan, 1971); Naimushō chihōkyoku shakaikyoku, *Saimin chōsa tōkeihyō* (1912, 1914, 1922), reprinted, 1973. For a brief outline of the genre of local government plans known as *ze*: Soda Osamu, *Chihō sangyō no shisō to undō* (Minerubua shobō, 1981), 159-73.

71. Draft evasion: Kikuchi Kunisaku, *Chōhei kihi no kenkyū* (Rippū shobō, 1977), pts. 2, 3; pawnshops and rats: *Kokumin zasshi* 2, no. 1 (1 Feb. 1911): 89-91.

72. A representative selection of "social problems": Yokoyama Gennosuke, "Shakai mondai no bokkō" (*Mainichi shinbun*, 14 Jan., 24 Feb. 1889), *Yokoyama Gennosuke zenshū*, ed. Sumiya Mikio, vol. 1 (Meiji bunken, 1972), 518-26. For popular usage, the countless employment guides for graduates: e.g., Seikōdō henshūbu, *Shōgaku sotsugyō kugaku seikō shūshoku tetsuzuki: risshin annai* [P] (Seikōdō, 1910); Takayanagi Junnosuke, *Shōgaku sotsugyō risshin annai* [P] (Gakuyūsha, 1910).

73. Ōkuma Shigenobu, "Kyorai ryōseiki ni okeru sekai rekkoku to Nihon to no ichi," *Taiyō* 6, no. 8 (15 June 1900): 2; speech to Shinpotō taikai, *Mainichi shinbun*, 22 Jan. 1906.

74. Yamamoto Takinosuke, "Inaka seinen" (1896), *Yamamoto Takinosuke zenshū*, ed. Kumagai Tatsujirō (Nihon seinendan, 1931), 4-11. Inoue Tomoichi, "Ōsei jichi no taikan" (1906), *Inoue Hakase to chihō jichi*, ed. Inouekai (Zenkoku chōson chōkai, 1940), 19.

75. Harry D. Harootunian, "Introduction: A Sense of an Ending and the Problem of Taishō," in *Japan in Crisis*, ed. Silberman and Harootunian, 3-10.

76. Geoffrey Barraclough, *An Introduction to Contemporary History* (Baltimore: Penguin Books, 1976), 9-42.

77. Eugen Weber, *Peasants into Frenchmen: The Modernization of Rural France, 1870-1914* (Stanford: Stanford University Press, 1976), 485-96.

78. Ōshima, *Meiji no mura*, 170-79.

79. Eugen Weber, "Comment la Politique Vint aux Paysans: A Second Look at Peasant Politicization," *The American Historical Review* 87, no. 2 (Apr. 1982): 358.

80. For a detailed study of intra-government conflict over institutional control of local government in the 1880s: Mikuriya Takashi, *Meiji kokka keisei to chihō keiei* (Tōkyō daigaku shuppankai, 1980).

81. George L. Mosse, *The Crisis of German Ideology: Intellectual Origins of the Third Reich* (New York: Grosset and Dunlap, 1964), 1-9.

82. John Higham, *Strangers in the Land: Patterns of American Nativism, 1860-1925* (New York: Atheneum, 1973).

83. The Meiji term was *rikkensei*, or *rikken kunshusei* (constitutional monarchy); the term *tennōsei* dates from the thirties, its locus classicus, the Comintern's "1932 theses," which identified the absolutist emperor system as the object of communist overthrow (*tennōsei datō*). Ishidō Seirin and Yamabe Kentarō, *Kominterun Nihon ni kansuru tēze shū* (Aoki shoten, 1961), 76-101.

The term *tennōsei* originated in and has to a great extent retained this sense of opposition to the Japanese imperial system, both in its pre- and postwar forms.

CHAPTER THREE

1. Description of the ceremony drawn from eyewitness accounts in *Jiji shinpō* and *Tōkyō nichi nichi shinbun*, 11-12 Feb. 1889; *Fūzoku gahō*, no. 2 (Mar. 1889); Miyake Setsurei, *Dōjidaishi*, vol. 2 (Iwanami, 1950), 358-65; Toku Baelz, ed., *Awakening Japan: The Diary of a German Doctor, Erwin Baelz* (Bloomington: Indiana University Press, 1974), 81-83; *Meiji Tennō shōchoku kinkai*, 821-40; and woodblock prints of the period, e.g., "Meiji nijūnen nigatsu jūichinichi Nihon kenpō happushiki no zu," in *Nishiki-e ni miru Meiji Tennō to Meiji jidai*, ed. Tanba Tsuneo (Asahi shinbunsha, 1966), 56. The word "unprecedented" was used in most accounts, often in the phrase *mizou no seiten*, an unprecedented ceremony.

2. Account of the *saiten*, or *kigensetsu* ceremony, is drawn from *Meiji Tennō shōchoku kinkai*, 817-20; Miyake, *Dōjidaishi* 2:358-65. *Kigensetsu*, or anniversary of the founding of the empire, was a modern holiday declared in 1873. Translations of the oath (*kōmon*) to the gods and the rescript (*chokugo*) read to the human assemblage at the state ceremony described above: appendices to Itō Hirobumi, *Commentaries on the Constitution of the Empire of Japan*, trans. Itō Miyoji (Igirisu hōritsu gakkō, 1889), 151-54.

3. Both speeches were reprinted widely in the press. For political background of transcendentalism (*chōzenshugi*) within the government: Banno, *Meiji kenpō taisei no seiritsu*, 1-6; Mikuriya, *Meiji kokka keisei to chihō keiei*, 204-20; George Akita, *Foundations of Constitutional Government in Modern Japan, 1868-1900* (Cambridge: Harvard University Press, 1967), 68-75.

4. *The World*, 13 Feb. 1889; similarly, *The Washington Post*, *The Times* (London), *Le Temps*, etc.

5. *Saru no monomane*—literally "monkey-like imitation": Takekoshi Yosaburō, *Jinmin tokuhon* (Fuzanbō, 1913), 10; also, Baelz, *Awakening Japan*, 85-89 and passim.

6. "Kenpō Haku," *Shinano mainichi shinbun*, 3 Apr. 1890; Itō, *Commentaries*, 3, 23, 27.

7. Typical press coverage: *Tōkyō nichi nichi shinbun*, 13 Feb.-10 Mar. 1889; *Jiji shinpō*, 14-27 Feb. 1889. Representative responses: *Mori Arinori zenshū*, ed. Ōkubo Toshiaki, vol. 2 (Senbundō shoten, 1972), 277-367; Hall, *Mori Arinori*, 1-16. Banned titles: Naimushō keihōkyoku, *Kinshi tankōbon mokuroku*, vol. 1 (Kohokusha, 1976), 80.

8. "Kenpō happu tōjitsu no ichi no nigiwai," *Tōkyō nichi nichi shinbun*, 13 Feb. 1889; "Kenpō happu zenjitsu toka no keikyō," *Tōkyō nichi nich shinbun*, 11 Feb. 1889.

9. *Yomiuri shinbun*, 8 Feb. 1913; Kawasaki Fusagorō, *Meiji Tōkyō shiwa* (Tōgensha, 1968), 243-46. Fūgetsudō, the famous confectionery, sold *kenpō*

okoshi from street carts (Asakura Haruhiko and Inamura Tetsugen, eds., *Meiji sesō hennen jiten* [Tōkyō shuppan, 1965], 289).

10. "Seiten ni 'banzai' hassei no hyōgi," *Chūgai shōgyō shinpō*, 8 Feb. 1889; for Imperial University Professor Toyama Masakazu's decision on the correct pronunciation of the cheer: Wada Shinjirō, ed., *Kōshitsu yōten* (1913), 503-5.

11. The oft-quoted remark is Baelz's. *Awakening Japan*, 81. For the banquet: Miyake, *Dōjidaishi*, 360.

12. Gold or dross, literally gems or tiles, from the proverb *tama to natte kudaku tomo kawara to natte mattakuraji*. Kōtoku Shūsui ed., *Chōmin Sensei-Chōmin Sensei gyōjōki* (Iwanami bunko, 1960), 17-18. Also, "Kenpō happu no seiten ni tsuite jinmin no kietsu," (*Jiyū shinbun*, 10 Feb. 1889), *Nakae Chōmin shū*, ed. Matsunaga Shōzō (Chikuma shobō, 1974), 288-89.

13. "Kenpō to wa ikanaru mono ka," *Tōkyō asahi shinbun*, 7 Feb. 1889. Similarly, in the provincial press: e.g., *Gifu nichi nichi shinbun*, 9 Feb. 1889.

14. "Kenpō no okōshaku," *Tōkyō asahi shinbun*, 5 Mar. 1889.

15. *Hirao-mura kigensetsu kenpō happu shukuenkai kiji* [P] (Nagano, Shimo Takai-gun: 1889), 2. Representative accounts of local ceremonies: *San'in shinbun*, 13-17 Feb. 1889; *Akita sakigake shinpō*, 19-22 Feb.; *Gifu nichi nichi shinbun*, 13-20 Feb.; *Shinano mainichi shinbun*, 16 Feb. and 5 Mar.; "Happu tōjitsu no zenkoku kakuji no moyō to sono denpō," *Jiji shinpō*, 12 Feb.

16. *Gifu nichi nichi shinbun*, 24 Feb. 1889.

17. Tokutomi Ichirō (Sohō), *Shin Nihon no seinen* (1887) was the most influential work (*Meiji bungaku zenshū* 34:112-158). A good literary example of such youth is found in Tokutomi Kenjirō (Roka), *Footprints in the Snow* (*Omoide no ki,* 1901), trans. Kenneth Strong (Tokyo: Charles Tuttle, 1971), 106-7, 262-63, 270-73. See also Pyle, *The New Generation*, 23-52; Earl Kinmonth, *The Self-Made Man in Meiji Japanese Thought: From Samurai to Salary Man* (Berkeley: University of California Press, 1981), 81-116.

18. Aizawa Kikutarō, *Aizawa nikki* (Sagamigahara: Aizawa Yoshihisa, 1965), 131-35. Aizawa's diary covered nearly eighty years, from 1885 to 1962. Also, Ubukata, *Meiji Taishō kenbunshi*, 23-24.

19. Kenneth Strong, *Ox against the Storm: A Biography of Tanaka Shōzō, Japan's Conservationist Pioneer* (Vancouver: University of British Columbia Press, 1977), 59-62.

20. *Tōkyō asahi shinbun*, 10 Nov. 1889.

21. *San'in shinbun*, 13 Feb. 1889. Similar remarks were heard among the intellectuals, e.g., Kuga Katsunan, "Kenpō happugo ni okeru Nihon kokumin no kakugo," (*Nihon*, 15 Feb. 1889), *Kuga Katsunan zenshū* 2: 8-9; political dissent was voiced in such journals as *Seiron*, 4-18 Mar. 1889, and in political meetings, e.g., "Kenpō ni kansuru kanjō," *Chōya shinbun*, 6 Mar. 1889. Nakae Chōmin expressed his dissent from the uproar by a near month of unaccustomed silence in the *Shinonome shinbun*, while the rest of the press expatiated at length on the constitution in an enthusiastic mood. Censorship was applied to negative criticism deemed guilty of *lèse majesté*, including the constitutional issue of Miyatake Gaikotsu's satirical magazine, *Tonchi kyōkai*

zasshi, no. 28 (1889), whose editor, artist, and printer were fined and imprisoned.

22. *Gifu nichi nichi shinbun*, 20 Mar. 1889.

23. E.g., "Teikoku kenpō o yomu," *Akita sakigake shinpō*, 20 Feb.-12 Mar. 1889; "DaiNihon teikoku kenpō yōron," *Shinano mainichi shinbun*, 22 Feb.-5 Mar.; "DaiNihon teikoku kenpō hyōron," *Chōya shinbun*, Feb.-Mar. Typical of the extra and supplement combination was *Kōchi nippō*, 12, 15 Feb.

24. *Akita sakigake shinpō*, 19-21 Feb. 1889.

25. The same warning was repeatedly offered in the period from the promulgation of the constitution through the first election. E.g., *Fukuryō shinpō*, 1 July 1890.

26. Newspaper readership: Yamamoto Taketoshi, *Shinbun to minshū* (Kinokuniya shinsho, 1973), 130-34 and passim; Nishida Taketoshi, *Meiji jidai no shinbun to zasshi* (Shibundō, 1961), 149-205. Woodblock prints, which were all a little different because the artists were not themselves present at the ceremony: Konishi Shirō, ed., *Nishiki-e Bakumatsu Meiji no rekishi*, vol. 10, *Kenpō happu* (Kōdansha, 1977), 28-33; Tanba, *Nishiki-e ni miru Meiji*, 55-56. Prints were also used to illustrate the chapter on the constitution in prewar elementary ethics texts: Kaigo Tokiomi, ed., *Nihon kyōkasho taikei*, vol. 3, *Kindaihen* (Kōdansha, 1962), 57 (1903 text), 110-11 (1910), 204-5, (1918). The 1941 texts replaced the prints with a photograph of the Diet building (489-90).

27. Gifu-ken, *Gifu-kenshi, Tsūshihen, Kindai*, vol. 2 (Gifu: Gifu-ken, 1972), 186.

28. *Shinano mainichi shinbun*, 8 Feb. 1889.

29. *The Times*, 2 May 1851, quoted in David Thomson, *England in the Nineteenth Century* (London: Penguin Books, 1950), 99. Yamagata had written from Berlin that the occasion could be considered "a third restoration [the second having been the abolition of the domains]. In slightly over twenty years our political and cultural life has made great progress . . . an advance unparalleled in the world." (Hackett, *Yamagata Aritomo*, 116).

30. Editorial, *Tōkyō shinpō*, 4 Sept. 1889, quoted in Oka, "Kindai Nihon ni okeru shakai seisaku shisō," 69.

31. Regulations for Public Meetings (*Shūkai jōrei*, 1880, revised 1882). *Hōrei zensho* (Naikaku kanpōkyoku, 1880), 57-61; English translation in W. W. McLaren, ed., *Japanese Government Documents, Transactions of the Asiatic Society of Japan* 42, 1st ser., pt. 1 (1917): 495-501. For a brief summary of this legislation, including the Peace Preservation Law (*Hōan jōrei*, 1887), the Public Meeting and Political Association Law (*Shūkai oyobi seishahō*, 1890), and Peace Preservation Police Law (*Chian keisatsuhō*, 1900): Nakamura Kichisaburō, *Meiji hōseishi*, vol. 1 (Shimizu kōbundō shobō, 1971), 209-20, and 2:51-84). Also, brief mention in Ishii Ryosuke, *Japanese Legislation in the Meiji Era*, trans. William J. Chambliss (Tokyo: Pan-Pacific Press, 1958), 262-63, 465-70, 556-57.

32. *Hōrei zensho*, no. 7 (1890), 165-70.

33. Yamanashi-ken gikai jimukyoku, *Yamanashi-ken gikaishi*, vol. 2 (Ya-

manashi-ken gikai, 1973): number of meetings, 36; corpses, 44; *dōshikai*, 46; *seisha*, 65; comparison of organizations, 73. Also Ariizumi Sadao, *Meiji seijishi no kiso katei* (Yoshikawa kōbunkan, 1980), 201-7.

34. Mori Arinori, "Meirokusha daiichinenkai yakuin kaisen ni tsuki enzetsu," *Meiroku zasshi*, no. 30 (Feb. 1875), Braisted, 367-68; see also, xii-xliv. For politics Mori used *seiji*, "political matters," which in the early seventies was still used interchangeably with *seiji* "political governance," the compound that eventually dominated. See Suzuki Shūji, *Bunmei no kotoba* (Bunka hyōron shuppansha, 1981), 107-14.

35. Koike Zenkichi, "Meiji kōki ni okeru chihō seinen no shisō to kōdō I: Gumma-ken Agatsuma-gun tōbu chihō no seinen ni tsuite," *Gumma daigaku kyōyōbu kiyō* 10 (1976): 83-86.

36. Petitions: Abe, ed., *Teikoku gikai* 1:81-96. Text of the muzzle law (*Kunrei* no. 11, Oct. 1893): Kyōikushi hensankai, *Meiji ikō Nihon kyōiku seido hattatsushi*, vol. 3 (Kyōiku shiryō chōsakai, 1964), 978; also Kaigo Tokiomi, *Inoue Kowashi no kyōiku seisaku* (Tōkyō daigaku shuppankai, 1968), 782-88. For the debate: *Kyōiku jiron*, no. 308 (15 Nov. 1893).

37. Kyōikushi hensankai, *Hattatsushi* 3:978. Also, Umihara Tōru, *Meiji kyōinshi no kenkyū* (Minerubua shobō, 1973), 192-99.

38. See Diet debate on amendment of the Public Meeting and Political Association Law (Dec. 1890) in Abe, ed., *Teikoku gikai* 1:33.

39. "Heart gone out of politics," literally, the political world (*seitai*) had lost the bones, or essence, of political discussion (*seiron*). Miyake Setsurei, *Meiji shisō shōshi* (serialized in *Ōsaka asahi shinbun*, 1913, then published by Heigo shuppansha) in Kano Masanao, ed., *Nihon no meichō*, vol. 37 (Chūō kōronsha, 1971), 418.

40. "Rikukaigun gunjin ni tamawaritaru chokuyu," *Meiji Tennō shōchoku kinkai*, 657-61; partial translation in Tsunoda, et al., *Sources of Japanese Tradition*, 705-07.

41. Miura Keigo's comparison of the Rescript to a muzzle order, which he did not mean unfavorably: Umetani Noboru, *Meiji zenki seijishi no kenkyū* (Miraisha, 1963), 214; Yamagata's *kokka kikyū no toki*: letter to Itō Hirobumi, 6 Oct. 1881, *Itō Hirobumi kankei monjo* 8:104.

42. Umetani, *Meiji zenki seijishi*, 178-240; Thomas R. H. Havens, *Nishi Amane and Modern Japanese Thought* (Princeton: Princeton University Press, 1970), 200-16; Hackett, *Yamagata Aritomo*, 83-86; James L. Huffman, *Politics of the Meiji Press: The Life of Fukuchi Gen'ichirō* (Honolulu: University of Hawaii Press, 1980), 139-54. Fukuzawa Yukichi took a similar position on the military and the emperor in "Teishitsuron" (May 1882), *Fukuzawa Yukichi zenshū*, ed. Keiō gijuku, vol. 5 (Iwanami shoten, 1959), 259-92.

43. Richard J. Smethurst, *A Social Basis for Prewar Japanese Militarism: The Army and the Rural Community* (Berkeley: University of California Press, 1974), 154-65.

44. "Rikukai gunjin wa seiji ni kanshō subekarazu," (*Tōkyō nichi nichi shinbun*, 27 Feb. 1882), Umetani, *Meiji zenki seijishi*, 236.

45. 1878 proscription by the Dajōkan: Miyatake Gaikotsu, *Meiji enzetsushi*

(Bunbudō, 1926), 37. 1889 *kunrei*: "Toku ni seigen serarezaru kanshi wa kōshū ni taishi seijijō gakujutsujō iken o enzetsu shi mata wa jojutsu suru koto o e," (24 Jan. 1889), McLaren, *Japanese Government Documents*, 505.

46. Service Regulations for Government Officials: "Kanshi fukumu kiritsu," (Chokurei, 29 July 1887). Also, Yamanaka Einosuke, *Nihon kindai kokka no keisei to kanryōsei* (Kōbundō, 1974), 8-9, 277-85. Imperial University: Robert M. Spaulding, Jr., *Imperial Japan's Higher Civil Service Examinations* (Princeton: Princeton University Press, 1967), 78-99.

47. "Teikoku daigaku no kamerarizumu," *Chōya shinbun*, 6 Aug. 1889.

48. Masumi Junnosuke, *Nihon seitō shiron*, vol. 2 (Tōkyō daigaku shuppankai, 1966), 47-54.

49. Tokutomi, *Yamagata Aritomo den* 3:371-72 (emphasis added). Also, on the 1899 amended ordinance (*Bunkan nin'yōrei*): Spaulding, 111-20.

50. Yamagata's admonition to local government officials: Naimushō kunrei (Dec. 1889), McLaren, *Japanese Government Documents*, 419-22.

51. For a tabulation of the two career paths: Takane Masaaki, *Nihon no seiji eriito* (Chūō kōronsha, 1976), translated as *The Political Elite in Japan* (Berkeley: Institute of East Asian Studies, University of California, 1981), 123-44.

52. Suehiro Shigeyasu (Tetchō), "Kyōin seito mo seidan shūkai ni kaigō shite sashitsukaenai" (Lower house, 20 Dec. 1890), *Teikoku gikai*, ed. Abe, 1:32-34. Both a political and a literary activist, Suehiro wrote several of the most popular political novels of the eighties. See *Meiji bungaku zenshū* 6:111-321.

53. "Kyōshi seito no seisha kan'yū wa fuka de aru" (Lower house, 1 Mar. 1891), ibid., 37.

54. "Gakkō wa seiji shūkyō no soto ni okitai" (Lower house, 2 Mar. 1897), ibid., 309. For full run of debates: ibid., 32-38, 45, 58-59, 62-66, 308-10.

55. For the controversy: see below pp. 259-62. For Order no. 12: "Ippan no kyōiku o shite shūkyōgai ni tokuritsu seshimuru no ken" (Aug. 1899), *Gakusei hyakunenshi* 2:35.

56. "Senkyo kokoroe o shōgakkō kyōkasho ni hennyū suru no kengi" (Lower house, 28 May-1 June 1898), *Teikoku gikai*, ed. Abe, 1:353-58.

57. On the eighties: Mikuriya, *Meiji kokka keisei to chihō keiei*. On the nineties: Banno, *Meiji kenpō taisei no seiritsu*. Also, Akita, *Foundations of Constitutional Government*.

58. Speech to the prefectural governors conference (13 Feb. 1890): *Meiji bunka zenshū*, vol. 10, *Seishihen* 2:149-52.

59. "Seitō iken" (to Itō Hirobumi, 14 Nov. 1890), *Inoue Kowashi den* 2:288.

60. Itō's speech to presidents of prefectural assemblies (15 Feb. 1889) and Kuroda's to prefectural governors (12 Feb.): *Meiji bunka zenshū*, vol. 10, *Seishihen* 2:36-42. Although at this time Itō and others also referred to national interests (*zenkoku no rigai tokushitsu*) in comparison to prefectural interests, in the following years this vocabulary attached itself less to national and more to local or factional interests.

61. Yamamoto, *Shinbun to minshū*, 69-86.

62. Speech to Genrōin (20 Nov. 1888): Kikegawa Hiroshi, *Jichi gojūnenshi seidohen* (Bunsei shoin, 1977), 321.

63. Fukuzawa Yukichi, *An Outline of a Theory of Civilization* (1875), 143. Although their romanized forms are homophones, note that *min* (people) and *kan* (officials) are written with different characters than *minkan*, which literally means "among the people" and refers to those outside the government.

64. For a homely rendition of these feelings: Tokutomi Kenjirō, *Yadorigi*, which is in fact the reminiscences of Shinohara Ryōhei (1881-1908), whose father became mayor of a Tōhoku village in 1889. *Roka zenshū*, vol. 8 (Roka zenshū kankōkai, 1929), 29-55.

65. The *mintō* included the liberal (*Jiyūtō*) and progressive (*Kaishintō*) parties and factions. The *ritō* (also known as *kankentō*) included Inoue Kaoru's moderate conservative *Jichitō*, Torio Koyata's extreme conservative *Hoshu chūseikai*, and after the election, the amalgamation of pro-government factions, the *Taiseikai*.

66. "Jiji shinpō no kanmin chōwaron" (1893), *Fukuzawa Yukichi zenshū* 13:650-76.

67. According to the Criminal Code (*Keihō*) put into effect in Jan. 1882, a verbal insult to an official (*kanri bujoku zai*) was punishable by imprisonment of one month to one year and a fine of five to fifty yen. Asakura and Inamura, *Meiji sesō hennen jiten*, 202.

68. *Shin enzetsu*, no. 15 (1 Dec. 1889): 36.

69. *Katsusekai*, no. 5 (17 Feb. 1891): 2-5.

70. See Banno, *Meiji kenpō taisei*, 47-100.

71. "Oyama kachanrin" (1875) and "Kan'inuta," Komota Nobuo et al., *Nihon ryūkōkashi* (Shakai shisōsha, 1970), 201; also, 18, 198. For other references, *Kōko shinpō* (18 Nov. 1880), Ono Hideo, *Meiji wadai jiten* (Tōkyōdō shuppan, 1968), 129; Kurata Yoshihiro, *Meiji Taishō no minshū goraku* (Iwanami shinsho, 1980), 51-52.

72. For one of the most famous satirical renditions, "Yatsukero bushi" (1890): Soeda Tomomichi, *Enka no Meiji Taishōshi*, 16-19; Komota *Nihon ryūkōkashi*, 211.

73. Kurata, *Meiji Taishō no minshū goraku*, 104-9. Contemporary accounts of *sōshi shibai*: *Tōkyō asahi shinbun*, 9 Sept. 1890; *Shinonome shinbun*, 23 June 1889. "Oppekepēbushi": Soeda, *Enka no Meiji Taishōshi*, 23-24. "The waters of liberty" was a pun on the name of the opposition Liberal party (*Jiyūtō*).

74. *Meiji kan'inkyō sugoroku* (Yokoyama Enshō, 1887). Also, Karasawa Tomitarō, *Hanga sugoroku* (Mainichi edishonaru sentā, 1972).

75. Kurata, *Meiji Taishō no minshū goraku*, 52.

76. Kinmonth, *The Self-Made Man*, 86, 115-16.

77. *Konnichi shinbun*, 5 May 1885. "Meiji jūniketsu," *Taiyō (rinji zōkan)* 5, no. 13 (June 1899): 1-560.

78. Nakae Chōmin, "Senkyonin mezamashi" (Apr. 1890), *Meiji bungaku zenshū* 13:156.

79. The debate over the prefectural and county system, one battle that

Yamagata lost: Kikegawa, *Jichi gojūnenshi*, 295-356; Richard Staubitz, "The Establishment of the System of Local Self-Government (1888-1890) in Meiji Japan: Yamagata Aritomo and the Meaning of 'Jichi' (Self-Government)," (Ph.D. diss., Yale University, 1973), 172-223. Strengthening of the bureaucratic authority of the *gunchō* under Yamagata in 1899: Kikegawa, 434-41.

80. Ishikawa Tōji, *Kokkai giin senkyo kokoroe* [P] (1889), 60.

81. *Shinano mainichi shinbun*, 1 Apr. 1890.

82. Ishikawa, *Kokkai giin senkyo kokoroe*, 6-8.

83. Collective portrait drawn from Ōno Seitarō, *Kokkai giin sentei kagami* [P] (Apr. 1890); Morooka Tadashi, *Kokkai giin shina sadame* [P] (Dec. 1889); Ishikawa, *Kokkai giin senkyo kokoroe* [P] (1889); "Giin senkyo no kokoroe o ronjite senkyonin shokun ni tsugu," *Nihonjin*, no. 48 (3 June 1890); *San'in shinbun, Akita sakigake shinpō, Tōkyō nichi nichi shinbun*, Mar.-June 1890.

84. Ishikawa, *Kokkai giin senkyo kokoroe* [P], 31-43.

85. *San'in shinbun*, 24 Apr. 1890. The *shugi* exchange occurred in Ishikawa prefecture but, as was common practice, was reprinted here and elsewhere in national and provincial papers.

86. *San'yō shinpō*, 1 July 1890; *Fukuryō shinpō*, 21 June 1890.

87. For a comprehensive account: R.H.P. Mason, *Japan's First General Election; 1890* (Cambridge: Cambridge University Press, 1969); also, Suematsu Kenchō, "Nijūsannen no sōsenkyo," *Meiji bunka zenshū*, vol. 10, *Seishihen* 2:200-21.

88. Mason, 174-85.

89. *Tōkyō nichi nichi shinbun*, reprinted in *San'yō shinpō*, 29 June 1890.

90. *San'in shinbun*, 16 May 1890; *Akita sakigake shinpō*, 12-28 June; also, Mason, 167-73. For the Supplementary Penal Regulations, which forbade bribery, intimidation and abduction of voters, innuendo, assembly in groups and using bells, horns, or bonfires to stir up the people, "Shūgiin giin senkyo bassoku hosoku" (30 May 1890), *Hōrei zensho*, no. 7 (1890), 106-7; Mason, 53, 219.

91. "Shūgiin giin senkyo no kekka," *San'in shinbun*, 12 June, 5 July 1890; also, *Shinano mainichi shinbun*, 12 June; *Tōkyō nichi nichi shinbun*, 27 June.

92. *Fukuryō shinpō*, 1 July 1890.

93. *San'in shinbun*, 20 Apr., 22 May, 1 July 1890; *Fukuryō shinpō*, 3 July; *Tōkyō nichi nichi shinbun*, 15-30 June.

94. Mason, 185-205. A typical contemporary report: *Tōkyō nichi nichi shinbun*, 2 July 1890.

95. Yanagida Izumi, "Seiji shōsetsu no ippan (2), "*Meiji bungaku zenshū* 6:454-56. Particularly popular were the fictional exposés written by Fukuchi Gen'ichirō, whose enormous political experience lent both credibility and bitterness to the discrepancy between earlier ideals and later realities. (*Meiji bungaku zenshū*, vol. 11).

96. Press coverage: *Tōkyō nichi nichi shinbun*, 14-28 Feb. 1892; *Nihon*, 12 Feb.; *Tōkyō asahi shinbun*, 16 Feb.-4 Mar.; also, Takahashi Yūsai, *Meiji keisatsushi kenkyū*, vol. 3 (Reibunsha, 1963), 207-340.

97. Meiji circulation figures are notoriously imprecise, though the figures

are agreed upon in general. Basic sources include *Naimushō tōkei hōkoku, Keishichō tōkeisho*, and claims of the individual papers, which with the exception of *Ōsaka asahi*, which has systematic records, are sporadic at best and often inflated. For figures cited here: *Kuga Katsunan zenshū* 2:805; Asakura and Inamura, *Meiji sesō hennen jiten*, 644-45; Yamamoto, *Shinbun to minshū*, 130-33.

98. "Shinbun dokusha no hensen," *Chūō kōron* (May 1900): 85-86.

99. Statistics on the electorate: Mason, 30-31, 185; Suematsu, "Nijūsannen no sōsenkyo," *Meiji bunka zenshū* 10:201-21.

100. The remaining five seats were won by the conservative *Kokumin jiyūtō*, which was dissolved in 1891. These were the alignments as of the opening of the Diet in November. Immediately after the election the results, though incomplete, were as follows: *mintō*, 144; *ritō*, 35; independents, 87 (Mason, 190-95).

101. E.g., Tokutomi Sohō, "Inmitsu naru seijijō no hensen," pt. 2, *Kokumin no tomo*, no. 16 (17 Feb. 1888): 1-6; pt. 3, no. 17 (2 Mar. 1888): 1-7. For tax figures: Mason, 195-98; Suematsu, "Nijūsannen no sōsenkyo," *Meiji bunka zenshū* 10:204-5.

102. E.g., Takaku Reinosuke, "Meijiki chihō meibōkasō no seiji: Kawahara Yoshio shōden," *Shakai kagaku*, no. 22 (Dec. 1977): 168-217.

103. Letter to Inoue Kaoru (20 Dec. 1893), Inoue Kaoru monjo, Kensei shiryōshitsu, National Diet Library (ms).

104. "Shūgiin giin senkyo no hyōron," *Meiji bunka zenshū*, vol. 10, *Seishihen* 2:221; *Kokumin shinbun* (6 July 1890) lists the names and positions of forty bureaucratic winners.

105. Masumi Junnosuke, *Nihon seitō shiron* 2:88. Mason follows *Nihon* (15 July 1890) and gives 158 for this figure, which likely excluded those who had been assembly members in the past, but were not at the time of the 1890 election.

106. *San'in shinbun*, 5 July 1890.

107. *Tōkyō asahi shinbun*, 30 Oct. 1890; Soeda, *Enka no Meiji Taishōshi*, 22. Satirical remarks were common, e.g., description of a newly-elected provincial Diet member who distributed a photograph of himself to the press, prompting the comment that "his stylish frock coat is worthy of an eight-hundred-yen-a-year salary to be sure, but somehow or other he got his celluloid collar on backwards and from the front looks just like a pup in a collar." *Tōkyō nichi nichi shinbun*, 21 Aug. 1890.

108. *Tōkyō nichi nichi shinbun*, 7, 13 July 1890.

109. *Tōkyō nichi nichi shinbun*, 30 Nov. 1890. Prints: Tanba, *Nishiki-e ni miru Meiji Tennō*, 56-59; Konishi, *Nishiki-e Bakumatsu Meiji* 10: 70-77. For *Sugoroku: Danshi kyōiku shusse sugoroku* and *DaiNihon kokkai gijidō sugoroku*, both 1890 and both with the Diet chambers as the object of the game.

110. On the depression: Nagaoka Shinkichi, *Meiji kyōkōshi josetsu*, 26.

111. Tokutomi Sohō, "Chūtō kaikyū no daraku," *Kokumin no tomo*, no. 172 (13 Nov. 1892): 3-4.

112. Election fever and the Bashō quotation: editorial, *Nihon*, 1 July 1891.

CHAPTER FOUR

1. For the Tokugawa imperial institution and restorationist ideology: Herschel F. Webb, *The Japanese Imperial Institution in the Tokugawa Period* (New York: Columbia University Press, 1968); H. D. Harootunian, *Toward Restoration: The Growth of Political Consciousness in Tokugawa Japan* (Berkeley: University of California Press, 1970); Herschel F. Webb, "The Development of an Orthodox Attitude Toward the Imperial Institution in the Nineteenth Century," in *Changing Japanese Attitudes Toward Modernization*, ed. Marius B. Jansen (Princeton: Princeton University Press, 1965), 167-91.

2. Basic sources on the Meiji emperor: *Meiji Tennōki*, ed. Kunaichō, 12 vols. and index (Yoshikawa kōbunkan, 1968-77); and *Meiji Tennō shōchoku kinkai*, ed. Meiji jingū (Kōdansha, 1973). Also, John Whitney Hall, " A Monarch for Modern Japan," in *Political Development in Modern Japan*, ed. Robert E. Ward (Princeton: Princeton University Press, 1968), 11-64; David Anson Titus, *Palace and Politics in Prewar Japan* (New York: Columbia University Press, 1974).

3. Imperial pronouncements of 1867-68, esp. "Ōsei fukko no daigōrei" (9 Dec. 1867) and "Meiji ishin no shinkan" (14 Mar. 1868): *Meiji Tennō shōchoku kinkai*, 63-65ff; 116-18ff. For views of the emperor in this period: Sakata Yoshio, "Meijiki no tennōkan," *Sandai hōgaku* 9, no. 2 (Sept. 1975): 20-44.

4. "Meiji ishin no shinkan" (14 Mar. 1868), *Meiji Tennō shōchoku kinkai*, 118.

5. On *goisshin* and *yonaoshi*: Ichii Saburō, *"Meiji ishin" no tetsugaku* (Kōdansha, 1967), 119-44; Tanaka Akira, *Mikan no Meiji ishin* (Sanseidō, 1968), 3-19; Haga Noboru, "Goisshin to ishin," *Meiji kokka to minshū* (Yūzankaku, 1974), 3-26. For "halving of the tax" (*nengu hanmetsu*) and the "counterfeit army" of Sagara Sōzō: Takagi Shunsuke, *Ishinshi no saihakkutsu: Sagara Sōzō to uzumoreta sōmōtachi* (Nihon hōsō shuppan kyōkai, 1970).

6. "Gokajō no goseimon," *Meiji Tennō shōchoku kinkai*, 115. This phrase occurs after the five articles and is omitted from the translation in Tsunoda et al., *Sources of Japanese Tradition*, 643-44.

7. "Zenkoku yōchi kunkō no kengi" (May 1872), *Meiji Tennōki* 2:674.

8. Ōkubo Toshimichi, "Ōsaka tento ni kansuru kengisho" (23 Jan. 1868), in Sakata, "Meijiki no tennōkan" (Sept. 1975), 26.

9. *Meiji Tennōki* 1:602-03, 611, 655-94.

10. The exact number of *gyōkō* is disputed. The most complete record is *Meiji Tennō gyōkō nenpyō* (1933), ed. Nihon shiseki kyōkai (Tōkyō daigaku shuppankai, 1982). Figures cited here from Haga Noboru, "Meiji kokka to chihō," *Meiji kokka to minshū*, 101. For an abbreviated list: "Meiji gyōkō nenpyō," *Meiji bunka zenshū*, vol. 17, *Kōshitsuhen*, 632-41.

11. Eastward progress (*tōkō*): *Meiji Tennōki* 1:831-66; *Meiji Tennō gyōkō nenpyō*, 4-13 and "Kaidai," 2-3. "Conducting all state affairs by imperial decision" (*banki o shinsai shi*): "Tōkyō kaishō no sho," *Meiji Tennō shōchoku kinkai*, 133.

12. For "Miyasama, miyasama," the first words of the song "Ton'yare

bushi," which Shinagawa Yajirō and Ōmura Masajirō are said to have written: Komota, *Nihon ryūkōkashi*, 16, 197.

13. For the circuits: *Meiji Tennō gyōkō nenpyō*; Haga, *Meiji kokka to minshū*; Tanaka Akira, "Tennō kunkō," in *Seiun no kokorozashi to zasetsu, Chihō bunka no Nihonshi*, ed. Hayashi Hideo, vol. 8 (Bun'ichi sōgō shuppan, 1977), 43-70.

14. Cultivating the emperor's virtue (*kuntoku baiyō*): e.g., Motoda Eifu, "Iwakura Udaijin e jōsho: kuntoku hodō no yō," *Motoda Sensei shinkōroku* (Min'yūsha, 1910), Introduction, 21-26; also, Sakata, "Meijiki no tennōkan" (Mar. 1976), 35-40. *Ikkun banmin*: Ichii Saburō, *"Meiji ishin" no tetsugaku*, 198-215.

15. "Tennō shinsei o manoatari ni miseru" was his phrase: Kusama Shunrō, "Meiji Tennō no gyōkō to zuikō o meguru uchiwake: shinshiryō ni motozuku uchiwake kaiketsu no rimenshi," *Nihon rekishi*, no. 334 (Mar. 1976): 38. The 1878 circuit was of the Hokuriku and Tōkai districts of Honshū.

16. Ibid., 39.

17. For Motoda: Donald Shively, "Motoda Eifu: Confucian Lecturer to the Meiji Emperor," in *Confucianism in Action*, ed. David S. Nivison and Arthur F. Wright (Stanford: Stanford University Press, 1959), 302-33. For Sasaki: Tsuda Shigemaro, *Meiji seijō to shin Takayuki* (Jishōkai, 1928). For the *jiho* and the oligarchs: Titus, *Palace and Politics*, 16-33.

18. For Shintō as a national doctrine (*kokkyō*): Murakami, *Kokka Shintō*, 85-119; and below, pp. 138ff.

19. "Manifest ubiquity" is Harootunian's phrase: *Toward Restoration*, 299.

20. See Inada Masatsugu, *Meiji kenpō seiritsushi*, 2 vols. (Yūhikaku, 1962); also, Joseph Pittau, *Political Thought in Early Meiji Japan* (Cambridge: Harvard University Press, 1967), 159-95.

21. Itō's speech to the Privy Council, which included the phrase *kokka no kijuku*: Kaneko Kentarō, *Itō Hirobumi den*, vol. 2 (Shunpo kōtsui shōkai, 1940), 614-17; excerpted in Titus, *Palace and Politics*, 36, and Pittau, *Political Thought*, 177-78.

22. See Matsumoto Sannosuke, "Meiji zenki no hoshushugi shisō," *Kindai Nihon no seiji to ningen* (Sōbunsha, 1966), 93-127; Akita, *Foundations of Constitutional Government*, 64-66. Itō Hirobumi's retrospective on the subject: "Some Reminiscences of the Grant of the New Constitution," in *Fifty Years of New Japan*, comp. Ōkuma Shigenobu, vol. 1 (London: Smith, Elder, & Co., 1909), 122-32.

23. Sakai Yūkichi, "Meiji kenpō to dentōteki kokkakan o megutte," in *Nihon kindai hōshi kōgi*, ed. Ishii Shirō (Seirin shoin shinsha, 1972), 80-85. Although Sakai does not mention Chiba Takusaburō's *Ōdōron*, it is a good example of similar views: Richard Devine, "The Way of the King: An Early Meiji Essay on Government," *Monumenta Nipponica* 34, no. 1 (Spring 1979): 49-72.

24. Ōkubo Toshimichi on *tochi, fūzoku, ninjō*, and *jisei*: "Rikken seitai ni kansuru ikensho" (1873), *Kindai Nihon shisō taikei*, ed. Matsumoto, 30: 5-7

(differently translated in George M. Beckmann, *The Making of the Meiji Constitution: The Oligarchs and the Constitutional Development of Japan, 1868-1891* [Westport, Ct.: Greenwood Press, 1957], 112). Itō: see above, note 21. Oath (*kōmon*) to the imperial ancestors: *Meiji Tennō shōchoku kinkai*, 817-18; with a slightly different translation in Itō, *Commentaries*, 152.

25. The imperial line in private drafts of the constitution: Irokawa, *Meiji no bunka*, 264-78.

26. "Jingiin setsuritsu no kengi ni tsuki iken," *Inoue Kowashi den* 2: 281-82.

27. See Titus, *Palace and Politics*, 65-69, 41-46.

28. Again these numbers differ slightly according to source: *Meiji Tennō gyōkō nenpyō*; Haga, *Meiji kokka to minshū*, 101; Titus, *Palace and Politics*, 48.

29. An example of this difference as it appeared in Nagano-ken: Kamijō Hiroyuki, *Chiiki minshūshi nōto* (Ginga shobō, 1977), 288-316.

30. Miyata Noboru, "Minkan shinkō to tennō shinkō," *Dentō to gendai*, no. 29 (Sept. 1974): 113-32; also, Wakamori, *Tennōsei no rekishi shinri*. In imperial records: *Meiji Tennōki* 1:847-48, etc.; also, *Meiji Tennō seiseki* (Monbushō, 1935-36), *passim*.

31. In addition to official chronologies, there are many detailed records of Meiji *gyōkō*, the most complete of which were often published by the localities through which the emperor passed: e.g., Miyagi-kenchō, *Meiji Tennō sekishi* (Sendai: 1925); Ibaraki-kenchō, *Meiji yonjūnen tokubetsu daienshū: gyorinkō kinenchō* [P] (Mito: 1908). Also, Hoshino Takeo, *Meiji Tennō gyōkō shiroku* (Ushio shobō, 1931), though here most of the detailed records pertain to the earlier circuits. Similarly for the late Meiji travels of the Crown Prince (*gyōkei*): e.g., Kaku Kinjirō, ed., *Kinen: San'indō gyōkeiroku* [P] (Matsue: 1907); Kagoshima shiyakusho, *Gyōkei nikki* [P] (Kagoshima: 1908).

32. These lodging or resting places (*anzaisho*) began to be commemorated locally in the late Meiji period and were recognized nationally by the Ministry of Education in the early 1930s; see *Meiji Tennō seiseki*. On the 1872 circuit to Kyūshū, the emperor visited the house of the Tokutomi family (who were *gōshi*, or country samurai); the house is now part of the Tokutomi Kinen'en in Kumamoto. The Okuya, the house of the *gōnō* Shimazaki branch family of Tsumago in Nagano, was visited on the 1880 circuit and is preserved as a museum, including the imperial privy elegantly modeled on one in the Katsura detached palace. Other lodging places are detailed in the sources cited in note 31. In 1948, Occupation authorities declassified 379 sites commemorating the Meiji emperor: William Woodward, *The Allied Occupation of Japan and Japanese Religions* (Leiden: E. J. Brill, 1972), 171.

33. *Tōkyō nichi nichi shinbun*, 12 Apr. 1892.

34. *Ōsaka asahi shinbun*, 2 Feb. 1910.

35. *Meiji Tennōki*: 1888 portrait of Chiossone 7:7-8; earlier distributions, 2:789-90, and 3:134, 156; schools, 7:424, 644.

36. Materials in the *Shoryōbu*, the archives of the present Imperial Household Agency (Kunaichō) are plentiful but fragmentary. Secondary sources by those close to the Palace tend to encomia rather than factual description.

The central writer here is Watanabe Ikujirō. See his *Meiji Tennō no hohitsu no hitobito* (Chikura shobō, 1938); *Meiji Tennō no seitoku: kyōiku* (Chikura shobō, 1941); *Nisshin Nichiro sensō shiwa* (Chikura shobō, 1937); and *Meiji Tennō*, 2 vols. (Meiji Tennō shōtokukai, 1958), which is said to be a short version of the definitive chronicle he was preparing when Japan lost the war and with it the need for an account of the victorious empire.

37. Titus, *Palace and Politics*, 63-74.

38. See Titus, 24-26, 118-32. Also, Watanabe, *Meiji Tennō* 2:302-35.

39. Differences with the Monbushō: *Meiji Tennōki* 7:644; Watari Shōsaburō, *Kyōiku chokugo to gakkō kyōiku* (Meikeikai, 1930), 1-61. Naimushō role: Taikakai, *Naimushōshi*, vol. 3 (Chihō zaimu kyōkai, 1971), 757-92. Tanaka's refusal to visit Katsura and other examples of jurisdictional friction: Titus, *Palace and Politics*, 124-25.

40. Ibid., 128.

41. Imperial Household Minister Tanaka and the industrialists: *Meiji Tennōki* 10:397-98.

42. Ibid., 7:471.

43. For these and other late Meiji examples of Itō's relationship with the emperor: *Meiji Tennōki* 7:648, 652; 8:160, 469; 12:299. Also, Watanabe, *Meiji Tennō* 2:302-25.

44. Oka Yoshitake, *Yamagata Aritomo: Meiji Nihon no shōchō* (Iwanami shinsho, 1958), 120-21; Hackett, *Yamagata Aritomo*, 247.

45. 1902 in Kumamoto: Tokutomi, *Yamagata Aritomo den* 3:1215-18.

46. Kimura Ki, *Meiji Tennō* (Shibundō, 1956), 260.

47. On Kuga's version of "medieval constitutionalism": Sakai, "Meiji kenpō to dentōteki kokkakan," 66-69.

48. Tokutomi Sohō, "Risōteki rikken kunshusei," *Kokumin no tomo*, no. 200 (23 Aug. 1893): 8-10.

49. The phrase was *wagakuni no teishitsu wa shakai fūkyō no sengen*: "Teishitsu to shakai no fūkyō," *Nichiyō kōdan*, vol. 2 (Min'yūsha, 1902), 7-11.

50. *Tōkyō asahi shinbun*, e.g., "Unjō no gantan," 1 June 1911. Italy: 23 Jan. 1890; New Year's telegrams: 9 Jan. 1911.

51. Inoue Tetsujirō, "Meiji Tennō heika no gojinkaku," in *Jinkaku to shūyō* (Kōbundō, 1915), 275-328.

52. E.g., Emperor Shōmu: *Shinano mainichi shinbun*, 31 July 1912. Napoleon and Victoria: "Meiji Tennō goichidai goseitokuki," *Taiyō* 18, no. 13 (Sept. 1912): 7-12, etc.

53. E.g., sales of photos to mark imperial birthdays: *Gifu nichi nichi shinbun*, 2 May 1912. Permission to reproduce goods with the imperial crest: *San'in shinbun*, 20 Apr. 1890. Kunaishō efforts at control: *Meiji Tennōki* 3:229; 4: 606; 5:276.

54. Marius Jansen has described an "epistolary slowdown" in the 1880s, when the number of imperial rescripts, like imperial journeys, dropped markedly: "Monarchy and Modernization in Japan," *Journal of Asian Studies* 36, no. 4 (Aug. 1977): 616.

55. On his reading habits: *Kokumin shinbun*, 18 Nov. 1892. Provincial press: *Agatsuma kyōikukai zasshi* (Gumma-ken), no. 117 (Sept. 1898): 12.

56. "Meiji Tennō heika no kōtei," *Sekai no Nihon* (Oct. 1896): 3.

57. *Akita sakigake shinpō*, 19 Feb. 1889.

58. Natsume Sōseki, "Meiji Tennō hotō no ji," *Natsume Sōseki zenshū*, vol. 10 (Chikuma shobō, 1972), 165. The rescript, which Sōseki quoted verbatim, was "Rokoku to kōsenchū monbudaijin ni tamawaritaru chokugo" (11 July 1904): *Meiji Tennō shōchoku kinkai*, 1270.

59. Anecdotes on the imperial interest in learning abound: e.g., Watanabe, *Meiji Tennō*, 492-95. Lectures: *Tōkyō asahi shinbun*, 4, 11 Jan. 1911. Graduations: *San'in shinbun*, 15 July 1899, *Tōkyō asahi shinbun*, 11 July 1912, etc.

60. Keio and Waseda: *Meiji Tennō shōchoku kinkai*, 1273-74. Kokugakuin and Gakushiin: Watanabe, *Meiji Tennō* 2:500. DaiNihon kyōikukai: *Tōkyō nichi nichi shinbun*, 26 Apr. 1891. Saké cup and other mementos: "Kōshitsu to kyōiku," *Kyōiku jiron*, no. 764 (5 July 1906): 44. These and others are also recorded in *Meiji Tennōki*.

61. "Kakugian" (between 1887-89, date unclear): *Mori Arinori zenshū* 1:345. "Intangible" (*mukei*): Kaimon Sanjin, *Mori Arinori* (Min'yūsha, 1897), 81-82.

62. Yamamoto Nobuyoshi and Konno Toshihiko, *Meijiki gakkō gyōji no kōsatsu: kindai kyōiku no tennōsei ideorogii* (Shinsensha, 1973), 67-74, 81-82.

63. For a compendium of these occasions, including sample speeches: Yokoyama Tokujirō, *Shōgaku kagai kyōzai oyobi kyōhō* (Hōbunkan, 1907), 47-65 and passim.

64. Yamamoto and Konno, *Meijiki gakkō gyōji*, 86-109; Satō Hideo, "Wagakuni shōgakkō ni okeru shukujitsu daisaijitsu gishiki no keisei katei," *Kyōikugaku kenkyū*, no. 30 (Mar. 1963): 48-54.

65. Shindō Haruo, *Kyōiku chokugo shinnyū katei ni okeru seiji to kyōiku* (Fukuoka: Fukuoka-ken rekishi kyōikusha kyōgikai, 1970), 10-12.

66. Aizawa Kikutarō, *Aizawa nikki, Zoku Aizawa nikki, Zokuzoku Aizawa nikki, Zōho Aizawa nikki*, 11 Feb. entries. For this argument: Ariizumi Sadao, "Meiji kokka to shukusaijitsu," *Rekishigaku kenkyū*, no. 341 (Oct. 1968): 63-66.

67. For a literary example: Tayama Katai, *Inaka kyōshi* (Iwanami shoten, 1972), 50-51; or, *Tayama Katai zenshū*, vol. 2 (Bunsendō, 1974), 366.

68. E.g., Yamamoto and Konno, *Meijiki gakkō gyōji*, 122-27.

69. For an approximate comparison: Ariizumi, "Meiji kokka to shukusaijitsu," 63, 68.

70. "Sandaisetsu gishiki ni kansuru seigan" (Mar. 1910), *Teikoku gikai*, ed. Abe, 3:30.

71. *Fukushima-ken Kawanuma-gun Oikawa-mura sonze* (1911), in Ariizumi, "Meiji kokka to shukusaijitsu," 68. Other examples: *Miyagi-ken Natori-gun Oide-mura sonze chōsasho* (Sendai: 1902); *Aichi-ken Kaitō-gun Ifuki-mura sonze* (Aichi: 1904).

72. *Tōkyō asahi shinbun*, 13-19 Sept. 1894.

73. Examples drawn from *Tōkyō asahi shinbun*, *Ōu nichi nichi shinbun, San'in shinbun*, and *Kokumin shinbun*, Sept.-Nov. 1894. Quotations from *Tōkyō asahi shinbun*, 5, 24 Oct. 1894, 6 Jan. 1895. See also Watanabe Ikujirō, *Nisshin Nichiro sensō shiwa*, 151-54; Nakatsuka Akira, *Nisshin sensō no kenkyū*

(Aoki shoten, 1968), 252-54; and a fictionalized version, Kimura Ki, *Hiroshima daihon'ei no Meiji Tennō* (Sekkasha, 1966).

74. *Tōkyō asahi shinbun*, 26 Feb. 1895; *Miyako shinbun*, 26 Apr. 1895.

75. *Nisshin sensō jikki* was published from Aug. 1894 to Jan. 1896. The first issue was reprinted 23 times and sold 300,000 copies; by the 13th issue the magazine had reached the unprecedented circulation of 3 million. See Tsuboya Zenshirō, *Hakubunkan gojūnenshi* (Hakubunkan, 1937). Woodblock prints: Tanba, *Nishiki-e ni miru Meiji*, 145-54; Konishi, *Nishiki-e Bakumatsu Meiji* 11:1-104. Narration booklets that accompanied magic-lantern shows: *Nisshin sensō gentō eiga setsumeisho* (Mar. 1895); *Nisshin sensō: gentō eiga setsumeisho daiikkai mokuroku* (1895); *Nisshin sensō gentōkai* (1895), *Nisshinsen kōhitsu gentō eiga setsumeisho* (Apr. 1895). The slides often concluded with a cheer by narrator and audience, *"Daigensui heika banzai!"*

76. For *Tōyō no rekkoku: Miyako shinbun*, 27 Apr. 1895. The year 1895: *Fukuryō shinpō*, 15 May 1897.

77. "Sekai ni okeru Nihon no kokumin," *Sekai no Nihon* (25 Oct. 1896).

78. E.g., "Nisshin sensō sugoroku," *Shōnen sekai* (Feb. 1894); "Kan Nisshin gentōki," *Eisai shinshi*, no. 906 (5 Jan. 1895): 3. Also, magic-lantern shows cited in note 75.

79. *Miyako shinbun*, 23 Apr., 5 May 1895.

80. *Meiji Tennō goshū*, ed. Meiji jingū (Kadokawa shoten, 1967), 237.

81. Roka and Tolstoy: *Meiji Tennō shōchoku kinkai*, 1461.

82. *Meiji Tennō goshū*, 83.

83. Aichi kyōikukai, *Sengo shakai kyōiku ni kansuru chōsa* (Nagoya: 1906), 280.

84. Lecture by the vice home minister, Tokonami Takejirō, printed in his *Chihō jichi oyobi shinkōsaku* (Jitsugyō no Nihonsha, 1912), 13.

85. *Tōkyō asahi shinbun*, 15 Nov. 1905. On the same day ceremonies were held in schools and administrative offices were closed. *Aizawa nikki (Zokuzoku)*, 120.

86. *Rekkoku no narabi ni resshite, rekkyō no nakamairi*, etc., were common expressions. A representative summary: Haga Yaichi and Shimoda Jirō, eds., *Nihon katei hyakka jii* (Fuzanbō, 1906), 1031-33.

87. "Dōhō subete gosenman," in *Nihon no shōka: Meiji hen*, ed. Kindaichi Haruhiko and Anzai Aiko (Kōdansha, 1977), 284. The textbook version: *Nihon kyōkasho taikei* 7:226.

88. Takekoshi Yosaburō, *Jinmin tokuhon* (1913), 212-13.

89. For *Heika to kokumin to tomo ni kitaeshitamaeru: Ōsaka asahi shinbun*, 1 Sept. 1905. Provincial activists also discussed submitting memorials to the emperor: e.g., *San'in shinbun*, 10 Sept. 1905. Other examples of this use of the emperor: Shumpei Okamoto, *The Japanese Oligarchy and the Russo-Japanese War* (New York: Columbia University Press, 1970), 203-12.

90. *Yorozu chōhō*, 18 Aug. 1904.

91. For a résumé: Watanabe Ikujirō, *Kōshitsu to shakai mondai* (Bunsensha, 1925), 205-15. Disaster relief, and the exact sum donated, was always reported in the press: *Tōkyō asahi shinbun*, 2 Nov. 1894, 28 Sept., 16, 30 Oct. 1899, etc.

92. *Japan Chronicle*, 7 Feb. 1906.

93. "Seryō saisei no chokugo" (11 Feb. 1911), *Meiji Tennō shōchoku kinkai*, 1427.

94. "Jiji nisshi," *Taiyō* 17, no. 5 (Apr. 1911).

95. Takeda Katsuzō, *Saiseikai gojūnenshi* (Saiseikai, 1964), 1-9, 15-78, 1147-48. Also, Yoshida Kyūichi, *Nihon shakai jigyō no rekishi* (Keisō shobō, 1960), 228-29.

96. "Boshin shōsho" (13 Oct. 1908), *Meiji Tennō shōchoku kinkai*, 1377ff. Press response to the *kinken no shōsho: Tōkyō nichi nichi shinbun, Tōykō mainichi shinbun, Tōkyō asahi shinbun, Kokumin shinbun* (with English translation of the rescript), 15-17 Oct. 1908. Hirata Tōsuke's speech to the governors: *Nihon shinbun*, 15 Oct. Hirata on the rescript: *Jikyō sadan* (Shōbundō, 1911), 135-90.

97. *Kyōiku chokugo Boshin shōsho haidoku shiki oyobi dainikai chihō jigyō kōrōsha hyōshō shiki kiji* [P] (Yokohama: Kanagawa-kenchō, 1911), 65.

98. E.g., Sawayanagi Masatarō, "Wagakuni no kyōiku" (1910), *Sawayanagi zenshū*, vol. 1 (Sawayanagi zenshū kankōkai, 1925), 425-33.

99. Karasawa, *Kyōkasho no rekishi*, 672-76. The emperor's role in the 1910 texts remained that of the secular modern monarch; the four lessons devoted wholly to him discussed the Charter Oath, the move of the capital to Tokyo, the education system, the military, the two wars, the Constitution, the annexation of Korea, and a quantity of benevolence. *Nihon kyōkasho taikei* 3:110-11.

100. Nanchō seitō kankei shokan, Yamagata Aritomo monjo, no. 20 (1911), Kensei shiryōshitsu, National Diet Library (ms); Tokutomi, *Yamagata Aritomo den* 3:767-76. For a full account, including Inukai's speech (p. 3): Shigaku kyōkai, *Nanbokuchō seijunron* (Shūbunkaku, 1911); also, H. Paul Varley, *Imperial Restoration in Medieval Japan* (New York: Columbia University Press, 1971), 176-85.

101. E.g., emperor's visits to several *Naikoku kangyō hakurankai* in the late Meiji period—the third, Ueno, Tokyo (Apr. 1890); the fourth, Kyoto (May 1895); the fifth, Osaka (Apr. 1903): *Meiji Tennōki* 7:594, 606; 8:821; 10:406-17. For an example of the "industrial enterprise encouraged by the emperor": *Meiji yonjūnen tokubetsu daienshū: gyorinkō kinenchō* [P], 7-8.

102. E.g., *Jikyō* (Ibaraki-ken Tsukuba-gun shiminkai), no. 1 (Jan. 1910); *Hyōgo-ken Iibo-gunze narabi ni chōsonze* (Himeji: Hyōgo Iibo-gun'yakusho, 1908); *Kōchi-ken Agawa-gun Hata sonze chōsasho* (Kōchi: 1914).

103. *Ibaraki-ken Kita Sōma-gun Omonma sonze* (1914).

104. *Mainichi shinbun*, 8 Apr. 1890.

105. The *hōshō jōrei* and its amendments: *Meiji Tennōki* 5:584; 7: 541, 599; 8:366. These changes were also covered in the press.

106. Sugimoto Shōjirō, ed., *Meiji chūkō setsugi den: Tōyō risshihen*, 5 vols. (Kuni no ishizuesha, 1898); Naimushō kanbōkyoku, *Meiji kokumin kikan* (Kokkōsha, 1902). Of the 617 winners between 1882 and 1897, this work includes biographies of 335, 159 of whom were blue medalists, (e.g., pp. 27-28). See also Takeda Kiyoko, *Tennōsei shisō to kyōiku* (Meiji tosho, 1964), 50-57.

107. Suzuki Masayuki, "Teikoku kenpō happu kinen yōrō shikin kashisha raireki: kakinaosareta sonmin raireki," *Chihōshi kenkyū*, no. 129 (June 1974): 68-75.

108. E.g., Miyagi-kenchō, *Meiji Tennō sekishi*, 483-510, 610-23; *Gyōkei kinen jigyō* [P] (Fukui: 1909); Kaku, *Kinen: San'indō gyōkeiroku* [P] (Matsue: 1907).

109. Ishibashi Tanzan, "Kunaikan to chihōkanshi" (*Tōyō jiron*, Sept. 1911), *Ishibashi Tanzan zenshū*, ed. Ishibashi Tanzan zenshū hensan iinkai, vol. 1 (Tōyō keizai shinpōsha, 1971), 182-85.

110. *Shinano mainichi shinbun*, 3 Apr. 1890; also, *San'in shinbun*, 1-3 Apr.

111. Nagano and public works: *Kokumin zasshi* 1, no. 2 (Jan. 1911): 99-100.

112. *Shinano mainichi shinbun*, 8 Apr. 1890.

113. This account is based on the diary, discovered in 1967, that Shimazaki kept from 1901 to 1905. Aoki Keiichirō, ed., *Shiryō: Kiso goryōrin jiken kō-shōroku* (Shinseisha, 1968).

114. Ibid. Phrases on friction and harmony are repeated over and over again in Shimazaki's account: 3, 4, 14, 194, 256, etc.

115. Ibid. Also, the villagers' conservative obstinacy (*korō*) and boorish country traits (*inakamono no kuse*): 53, 222, 259, 364, etc. For *fukei*, meaning disrespect but used for lèse majesté: 68, 334-35, etc. On the prefectural governor: 238, 244.

116. Ibid., 335.

117. Ibid., 28-29, 88.

118. Shimazaki's father was the model for the protagonist, Aoyama Hanzō, of Shimazaki Tōson's novel on the Restoration: *Yoakemae* (1929-1935), 4 vols. (Shinchō bunko, 1955).

119. *Shinano mainichi shinbun* (9 Aug. 1905); Aoki, *Shiryō*, 522. Also, Machida Masami, *Kiso goryōrin jiken* (Nagano: Ginga shobō, 1982), 607-14.

120. Hōjō Hiroshi, *Mura to iriai no hyakunenshi* (Ochanomizu shobō, 1978), 3-6, 100-57.

121. See below, Chapter Seven.

122. Matsuura Rei, *Nihonjin ni totte tennō to wa nan de atta ka* (Henkyōsha, 1974), 253-54.

123. On the railroad: Harada Katsumasa and Aoki Eiichi, *Nihon no tetsudō: 100-nen no ayumi kara* (Sanseidō, 1973); Suzuki Jūzō, *Meiji tetsudō nishiki-e* (Kōtsū kyōikukai, 1971); Nagata Hiroshi, *Meiji no kisha* (Kōtsū Nihonsha, 1978). Sorimachi Shōji, *Tetsudō no Nihonshi* (Bunken shuppan, 1982).

CHAPTER FIVE

1. At the behest of Occupation authorities, the Diet finally declared the Rescript invalid in June, 1948: Supreme Commander for the Allied Powers, Civil Information and Education Section, *Education in the New Japan*, vol. 2 (Washington: U.S. Government Printing Office, 1948), 172; SCAP, *Political Reorientation of Japan* 2:585. Also, Toshio Nishi, *Unconditional Democracy: Ed-*

ucation and Politics in Occupied Japan, 1945-1952 (Stanford: Hoover Institution Press, 1982), 146-57.

2. Representative secondary treatments: Takeda Kiyoko and Nakauchi Toshio, "Tennōsei kyōiku no taiseika," *Iwanami kōza: gendai kyōikugaku*, vol. 5, *Nihon kindai kyōikushi* (Iwanami shoten, 1965), 64-117; Naka Arata, *Meiji no kyōiku* (Shibundō, 1967), 172-76, 212-15, 239-45. Mori's "statism" (*kokkashugi*): Hall, *Mori Arinori*, 397-408.

Basic sources on education include: Kyōikushi hensankai, *Meiji ikō Nihon kyōiku seido hattatsushi*, 14 vols. (hereafter *Hattatsushi*), which generally reprints documents in full. For a comprehensive account: Kokuritsu kyōiku kenkyūjo, *Nihon kindai kyōiku hyakunenshi*, 10 vols. (hereafter *Hyakunenshi*). For a brief summary: Monbushō, *Gakusei hyakunenshi* (2 vols.). Also, Herbert Passin, *Japanese Education: A Bibliography of Materials in the English Language* (New York: Teachers College Press, 1970), 14-32.

3. "Shōgakkō o mōkeru koto," no. 10 of 13 points in "Fuken shisetsu junjo," sent to the new government's provincial territories, not to the domains. *Hattatsushi* 1:228-31. Nativist scholars (*kokugakusha*) influential in the early months of the regime included Tamamatsu Misao, Hirata Kanetane, and Yano Harumichi. *Hyakunenshi* 3:263-74.

4. "Daigaku kisoku oyobi chūshōgaku kisoku," *Hattatsushi* 1:139-42; Kurasawa Takashi, *Shōgakkō no rekishi*, vol. 1 (Japan raiburarii byūrō, 1963), 33-38; *Hyakunenshi* 3:279-87. These and other education laws and ordinances are reprinted in chronological order in Naikaku kirokukyoku, *Hōki bunrui taizen*, vol. 58 (Hara shobō, 1981).

5. Ōkubo Toshimichi, "Seifu no teisai ni kansuru kengensho" (Feb. 1869); Itō Hirobumi, "Kokuze kōmoku" (Feb. 1869); Kido Kōin, "Futsū kyōiku no shinkō o kyūmu to subeki kengenshoan" (Jan. 1869), *Hyakunenshi* 3:258-62.

6. "Monbushō futatsu" (Feb. 1872), *Hattatsushi* 1:250-51.

7. *Gakusei* and its preamble, *Ōseidasaresho* (Sept. 1872), ibid., 275-99; Kurasawa, *Shōgakkō no rekishi* 1:256-71. Preamble translated (with slight differences) in Herbert Passin, *Society and Education in Japan* (New York: Teachers College Press, 1965), 209-11.

8. "Kyōgaku taishi," *Meiji Tennō shōchoku kinkai*, 592-95. Translated, with slight differences, in Passin, *Society and Education*, 226-28.

9. *Motoda Sensei shinkōroku* (1910), 94; also, Kaigo Tokiomi, *Motoda Eifu* (Bunkyō shoin, 1942), 133; Shively, "Motoda Eifu," 327.

10. *Meiji Tennō shōchoku kinkai*, 592-93; *Meiji Tennōki* 4:757-59; Passin, *Society and Education*, 227-28.

11. Karasawa, *Kyōkasho no rekishi*, 60-64.

12. Kaigo, *Motoda Eifu*, 1-69; Shively, "Motoda Eifu," 302-33. Kaigo Tokiomi, *Nishimura Shigeki, Sugiura Jūgō* (Hokkai shuppansha, 1937), 8-92; also, Shively, "Nishimura Shigeki: A Confucian View of Modernization," in *Changing Japanese Attitudes Toward Modernization*, ed. Marius B. Jansen (Princeton: Princeton University Press, 1965), 193-241; Egi Kazuyuki-ō keirekidan kankōkai, *Egi Kazuyuki-ō keirekidan* (1935), vol. 1.

13. *Hyakunenshi* 3:589-91.

14. Egi Kazuyuki, "Kyōiku chokugo no kanpatsu," *Kyōiku gojūnenshi* (1923), 152-53.

15. Translation of Marcus Willson, *The First Reader*, Lesson V (1873), Karasawa, *Kyōkasho no rekishi*, 70.

16. Nishisonogi-gun kyōikukai, *Shōgakkōchō kōshūkai kōenroku* (Nagasaki: Jūseisha, 1918), 19.

17. E.g., "Kokkyōron" (1884): *Kyōiku chokugo kanpatsu kankei shiryōshū*, vol. 2 (Kokumin seishin bunka kenkyūjo, 1940), 297-98.

18. Itō Hirobumi, "Kyōiku-gi" (1879): Inada Masatsugu, *Kyōiku chokugo seiritsu katei no kenkyū* (Kōdansha, 1971), 46-47; Kaigo Tokiomi, *Kyōiku chokugo seiritsushi no kenkyū* (Kōtokusha, 1965), 95-97; translated in Passin, *Society and Education*, 229-33.

19. Motoda Eifu, "Kyōikugi fugi" (1879): Inada, *Kyōiku chokugo*, 50-51; Kaigo, *Kyōiku chokugo*, 98-101.

20. Inada, *Kyōiku chokugo*, 47; Kaigo, *Kyōiku chokugo*, 96; Passin, with slight differences, 233.

21. Kurasawa, *Shōgakkō no rekishi* 2:200-2.

22. *Hattatsushi* 2:493-97. The Ministry also established its own textbook section which published an ethics text by Nishimura Shigeki entitled *Shōgaku shūshin kun* as its first volume in 1881. *Nihon kyōkasho taikei* 2:6-37.

23. "Shōgakkō kyōin kokoroe" (1881), in which the first of sixteen articles was on loyalty and morality, the fourteenth on politics; "Shōgakkō kyōin menkyojō juyohō kokoroe" (1881), *Hyakunenshi* 3:946-50.

24. E.g., Naka Arata, *Meiji shoki no kyōiku seisaku to chihō e no teichaku* (Kōdansha, 1962), 816-49; *Nagano-ken kyōikushi*, vol. 1 (Nagano-ken kyōikushi kankōkai, 1978), 372-437; *Hyakunenshi* 3:953-77.

25. *Egi Kazuyuki-ō keirekidan* 1:124; also, Karasawa, *Kyōkasho no rekishi*, 150.

26. "Pesutarojii-shi den," *Higashichikuma-gun kyōikukai zasshi*, nos. 1-5 (Oct. 1884); "Kōshūin Ōta Tsuruo Sensei kuju kakitori" (Oct. 1884); for these and others: *Nagano-ken kyōikushi* 6:496-502.

27. E.g., "Gakusei yōryō" (c. 1885), *Mori Arinori zenshū* 1: 351-56. In the different drafts, "national education" appears as the gloss to *kokusetsu kyōiku, kokutai kyōiku,* and *kokka kyōiku.* Mori repeated these sentiments in speeches and writings of the late 80s. See also Hall, *Mori Arinori*, 390-447.

28. "Fukushima-ken gijidō ni oite kenkan gunkuchō oyobi kyōin ni taisuru enzetsu" (1887), *Mori Arinori zenshū* 1:549; Hall, *Mori Arinori*, 437.

29. See especially "Mori Bunshō ni taisuru kyōiku ikensho" (1887), Kaigo, *Motoda Eifu*, 207-9; Hall, *Mori Arinori*, 443-44.

30. Motoda Eifu, "Kyōiku taishi," Inada, *Kyōiku chokugo*, 188-92; Kaigo, *Kyōiku chokugo*, 217-29.

31. Nishimura Shigeki, "Meirin'in kengi" and "Shūshinsho chokusen mondai kiroku," *Kyōiku chokugo kanpatsu kankei shiryōshū* 2:395-400. Also, Shively, "Nishimura Shigeki," 237-38.

32. Kurasawa, *Shōgakkō no rekishi* 2:980-1028.

33. *Nagano-ken kyōikushi* 6:520-31.

34. "Shugi to iu koto ni tsukite," *Shinano kyōiku* (May 1897): 1-9.

35. "Bunmei to kinsen to no kankei," and "Eibei no idō," *Ozaki Yukio zenshū* (1926) 3: 146-59, 232-35.

36. Aizawa Kikutarō, *Aizawa nikki*, 130.

37. Legal arguments: "Hōten hensan ni kansuru hōgaku shikai no iken" (May 1889); Masujima Rokuichirō, "Hōgaku shikai no iken o ronzu" (June 1889); "Meiji nijūnen no hōritsu shakai oyobi hōri seika" (Jan. 1890); and others in Hoshino, *Minpōten ronsō shiryōshu*, 14-21, 35-37. For a representative bureaucratic comment: Ishii Shōichirō, Governor of Iwate-ken, on "wives bringing suit" (Oct. 1888), in Toshitani Nobuyoshi, "Meiji minpō ni okeru 'ie' to sōzoku," *Shakai kagaku kenkyū* 23, no. 1 (1971): 41. Hozumi's famous article, which both summed up the conservative position of 1888-90 and launched the main phase of the dispute over the civil code: "Minpō idete chūkō horobu" (Aug. 1891), in Hoshino, 82-85.

38. Sasakawa Rinpū, *Meiji sakigaeshi* (Ajiasha, 1946), 18-19.

39. *Shinano mainichi shinbun*, 8 Apr. 1890.

40. Representative rhetoric of the conservative establishment: early issues of *Meijikai sōshi*, e.g., nos. 1-6 (Dec. 1888-May 1889), journal of the Meijikai, founded by Sasaki Takayuki and others. Its principles of reverence for the gods, loyalty to the throne, and patriotism were printed in every issue from no. 6. Also, *Kōdōkai sōshi* (Nov. 1887-July 1889), journal of Nishimura's Nihon kōdōkai, which flourished in this period. For its guidelines and goals: *Nihon kōdōkai shijūnenshi* (1918), 67-94, 161-66. Also, *Nihon kokkyō daidō sōshi* 1, nos. 1-10 (July 1888-Apr. 1889); its manifesto advocating the combined ways of Shintō, Confucianism, and Buddhism was printed in the front of each issue (see above, pp. 22-23).

41. See Pyle, *The New Generation*, esp., 53-98. For this use of "national" words: Kuga's editorials in the *Tōkyō denpō* (1888-89), *Kuga Katsunan zenshū* 1:397-400, 533-34, 564-66, 638-39, etc.

42. *Nihonshugi* (Gumma-ken, Maebashi), no. 1 (11 Feb. 1890): 1-6.

43. Although the nationalists were called *hoshuteki* (conservative), they assigned the term *hoshuronka* (conservatives) to anti-Western moralists. "*Korō*" was the common term for hidebound, or reactionary. E.g., Tokutomi Sohō, *Shin Nihon no seinen* (1887), in *Meiji bungaku zenshū* 34:134-37; Kuga Katsunan, "Kinji seironkō" (1890), *Kuga Katsunan zenshū* 1:62-63; Yamaji Aizan, "Gendai Nihon kyōkai shiron" (1906), *Kirisutokyō hyōron, Nihon jinminshi* (Iwanami shoten, 1966), 99-103. Also, Pyle, *The New Generation*, 94 and passim.

44. "Gobyū chūairon no moedashi," *Nihon* (6 Aug. 1890), *Kuga Katsunan zenshū* 2:644-45.

45. "Shakai reishūron," *Nihon* (3-4 Jan. 1892), *Kuga Katsunan zenshū* 3:365-68; "Fukyū mugen," *Nihon* (23 Sept. 1892), ibid. 3:615-16.

46. On the imperial institution: e.g., "Ise no taibyō, kōshitsu to gyōseifu to no kankei" (21 Sept. 1888), *Kuga Katsunan zenshū* 1:532-34. On Confucius and Buddha: "Kinji seironkō" (1890), ibid., 64. Also, Pyle, *The New Generation*, 94-96, 124-26.

47. Tatebe Tongo, "Meiji shisō no hensen," *Nihon*, 22 Apr. 1898.

48. "Kokuminteki no kannen," *Nihon* (12 Feb. 1889), *Kuga Katsunan zenshū* 2:7-8.

49. Inō Tentarō, *Jōyaku kaiseiron no rekishiteki tenkai* (Komine shoten, 1976); Inoue Kiyoshi, *Jōyaku kaisei* (Iwanami shoten, 1955). Assessment of the peaks of protest: Yamamoto Shigeru, *Jōyaku kaiseishi* (Takayama shoin, 1943), 436.

50. Sakeda Masatoshi, *Kindai Nihon ni okeru taigai kō undō no kenkyū* (Tōkyō daigaku shuppankai, 1978), 1-11 and passim.

51. *San'in shinbun*, 29 July 1889.

52. Sakeda, *Kindai Nihon*, 13-30; *Kuga Katsunan zenshū* 2: passim.

53. "Jōyaku kaisei," Soeda, *Enka no Meiji Taishōshi*, 28-30; writers of popular fiction took advantage of the publicity value of treaty revision in their titles, which had little to do with the stories they told. E.g., Shibugakien Shujin, *Seiji shōsetsu jōyaku kaisei* (1889); Suehiro Masanori, *Seiji shōsetsu chigai hōken, Jōwahen* (1889). See Inō, *Jōyaku kaiseiron*, 604.

54. Full record of the governors' debates: "Meiji nijūsannen nigatsu chihō chōkan kaigi hikki" (1890), Chihōkan kaigi giketsusho narabi hikki (ms). Unless otherwise indicated, all quotations below are taken from this transcript. Discussions and text of the memorial: Inada, *Kyōiku chokugo*, 163-69; Kaigo, *Kyōiku chokugo*, 137-40.

55. "Tokuiku kan'yō no gi ni tsuki kengi," Inada, *Kyōiku chokugo*, 168-69; Kaigo, *Kyōiku chokugo*, 137-38.

56. For a list of prefectural governors (which in 1890 consisted largely of a few nearly professional prefectural governors who moved from one prefecture to another [e.g., Yasuba], well-connected, up-and-coming career bureaucrats in the central government [e.g., Komatsubara], loyal Satsuma or Chōshū men [e.g., Takasaki], members of the old elite [Matsudaira of the *daimyō* family], and officials at the end of their careers): Kuribayashi Teiichi, *Chihō kankai no hensen* (1930); Taikakai, *Naimushōshi* 4:552-646.

57. *Tōkyō mainichi shinbun*, 16 Feb. 1890; also, Tokutomi, *Yamagata Aritomo den* 2:1097-1103.

58. "Gaikō seiryakuron," *Yamagata Aritomo ikensho*, 199-200.

59. "Kokkai kaisetsu ni kansuru kengi," *Yamagata Aritomo ikensho*, 85. Translated, with slight differences, in Hackett, *Yamagata Aritomo*, 93.

60. Ibid.

61. "Gunjin kunkai" (1878), in Tokutomi, *Yamagata Aritomo den* 2:769. Like the Rescript to Soldiers and Sailors in 1882, this earlier document was drafted for Yamagata by Nishi Amane.

62. Tokutomi Ichirō (Sohō), *Waga kōyūroku* (Chūō kōron, 1938), 9.

63. *Tōkyō mainichi shinbun*, 28 Feb. 1890, 4-7 Mar.; also, Inada, *Kyōiku chokugo*, 170-71; *Kyōiku chokugo kanpatsu kankei shiryōshū* 2:449.

64. "Kyōiku chokugo happu ni kansuru Yamagata Aritomo danwa hikki" (1916), *Kyōiku chokugo kanpatsu kankei shiryōshū* 2:453-55.

65. Ibid., 464. For Motoda: Inada, *Kyōiku chokugo*, 172.

66. Nakamura's drafts: ibid., 177-87.

67. "Kyōiku chokugo ni tsuki Sōri Daijin Yamagata Haku e atauru iken" (June 1890), *Inoue Kowashi den* 2:231; Inada, *Kyōiku chokugo*, 196.

68. Ibid., 197, 268-74; Kaigo, *Kyōiku chokugo*, 328-30, 359-60.

69. *Inoue Kowashi den* 2:231-32; Inada, *Kyōiku chokugo*, 196.

70. Ibid., 217-20; Kaigo, *Kyōiku chokugo*, 259-62.

71. *Inoue Kowashi den* 2:232; Inada, *Kyōiku chokugo*, 196.

72. "Kyōiku taishi" (June 1890): ibid., 188-92; Kaigo, *Kyōiku chokugo*, 229-36.

73. Inada, *Kyōiku chokugo*, 243-44; Kaigo, *Kyōiku chokugo*, 281.

74. Inada, *Kyōiku chokugo*, 227-42; Kaigo, *Kyōiku chokugo*, 280-327.

75. "Ōshū mohō o hi to suru setsu" (1874 or 1875); "Jukyō o zonzu" (1881 or 1882): *Inoue Kowashi den* 1:47-54, 3:497-500.

76. Inoue's speech at the Kōten kōkyūjo (1888), quoted in Nakashima Michio, "Meiji kokka to shūkyō: Inoue Kowashi no shūkyōkan, shūkyō seisaku no bunseki," *Rekishigaku kenkyū*, no. 413 (Oct. 1974): 37.

77. "Jukyō o zonzu," *Inoue Kowashi den* 3:500. For Inoue's eclectic views on moral education: Kaigo Tokiomi, ed., *Inoue Kowashi no kyōiku seisaku* (Tōkyō daigaku shuppankai, 1968), 934-45.

78. Inada, *Kyōiku chokugo*, 227-56, 268-97; Kaigo, *Kyōiku chokugo*, 355-80. Other accounts of the drafting, which are less complete in documentary presentation but offer slightly different interpretations of the final ideological mix: Umetani Noboru, "Kyōiku chokugo seiritsu no rekishiteki haikei," in *Meiji zenpanki no nashonarizumu*, ed. Sakata Yoshio (Miraisha, 1958), 85-128; Ienaga Saburō, *Nihon kindai kenpō shisōshi kenkyū* (Iwanami shoten, 1967); Joseph Pittau, "Inoue Kowashi, 1843-1895, and the Formation of Modern Japan," *Monumenta Nipponica* 20, nos. 3-4 (1965): 270-76.

79. Foreign Minister Aoki Shūzō was said to have objected because of possible reaction in Christian countries. "Kyōiku chokugo happu ni kansuru Yamagata Aritomo danwa hikki" (1916), *Kyōiku chokugo kanpatsu kankei shiryōshū* 2:455; Inada, *Kyōiku chokugo*, 252.

80. Text of the *Shōgakkōrei: Hattatsushi* 3:56-73. Article 1 stated the purpose of elementary education in terms of *dōtoku kyōiku, kokumin kyōiku* and the knowledge and skills (*chishiki ginō*) necessary in everyday life.

For the Privy Council's role in education policy, which was strengthened by Yamagata when he was prime minister in 1900: Kubo Yoshizō, *Tennōsei kokka no kyōiku seisaku* (Keisō shobō, 1979), 2-61 and passim.

81. Ebihara Haruyoshi, *Gendai Nihon kyōiku seisakushi* (San'ichi shobō, 1965), 111-18; Inada, *Kyōiku chokugo*, 257-67.

82. Ibid., 290-92.

83. *Tōkyō asahi shinbun*, 1 Nov. 1890; also, *Tōkyō nichi nichi shinbun*, 2 Nov.; *Yūbin hōchi shinbun*, 17 Nov.; *Tōkyō asahi shinbun*, 5 Nov.; etc. Also, *Kyōiku chokugo kanpatsu kankei shiryōshū* 3:471-555.

84. *Jiji shinpō*, 5 Nov. 1890.

85. *Tōkyō nichi nichi shinbun*, 2 Nov. 1890.

86. "Kindoku chokugo," *Nihon* (1 Nov. 1890), *Kuga Katsunan zenshū* 2:748.

87. "Shidōron," *Nihon* (3 Nov. 1890), ibid., 749-50.

88. E.g., *Kyōiku hōchi*, nos. 241-42 (8-15 Nov. 1890); *Kyōiku jiron* (Dec. 1890-May 1891): passim.

89. *Yūbin hōchi shinbun*, 17 Nov. 1890.

90. *Tōkyō asahi shinbun*, 1 Nov. 1890.

91. "Kyōiku hōshin no chokugo," *Kokumin no tomo*, no. 100 (13 Nov. 1890): 42.

92. Minister of Education Yoshikawa's recollections of hostility to the Rescript on these grounds: "Kyōiku chokugo gokashi jijō," *Kyōiku chokugo kanpatsu kankei shiryōshū* 2:460-61. Institutional decline of Confucianism between 1868 and 1918: Warren W. Smith, Jr., *Confucianism in Modern Japan: A Study of Conservatism in Japanese Intellectual History* (Hokuseido Press, 1959), 41-102.

93. Cited in Shively, "Nishimura Shigeki," 238.

94. "Shigeno Yasutsugu-shi ayamareri," *Kokumin no tomo*, no. 100 (13 Nov. 1890): 42-43. Tokutomi's earlier criticism: *Shin Nihon no seinen* (1885), *Meiji bungaku zenshū* 34:125- 37.

95. *Tōkyō nichi nichi shinbun*, 13 Nov. 1890.

96. "Rinri to seirigaku to no kankei," *Nihon*, 7 Nov. 1890; cited in part in Inada, *Kyōiku chokugo*, 202-3.

97. Yokoi Tokio, "The Moral Crisis in Japan," *The Far East* 2, no. 4 (20 Apr. 1897): 154 (original in English; quote from the Rescript is here corrected to match the official translation, which appeared later). Similar analyses had been commonplace since 1890: e.g., *Tōkyō nichi nichi shinbun*, 13 Nov. 1890.

98. "Kongo no tokuiku o ronji awasete kyōikusha no rikkyaku ni oyobu," *Shinano kyōiku* (May-June 1897): 5-13.

99. Tanimoto Tomeri, *Jitsuyō kyōikugaku oyobi kyōjuhō* (Rokumeikan, 1894), 36. The book began, "Ah, Herbart! Awake or asleep, we cannot forget the name of Herbart. Ah, Herbart! Day or night we do not fail to propound the theories of Herbart." See Horimatsu Buichi, *Nihon kindai kyōikushi: Meiji no kokka to kyōiku* (Risōsha, 1972), 219-22.

100. Inoue Kowashi, "Kyōiku chokugo ni tsuki Sōri Daijin Yamagata Haku e atauru iken" (1890), *Inoue Kowashi den* 2:232.

101. Bibliography of 595 commentaries: Gotō Seiichi, *Kyōiku chokugo kankei bunken mokuroku* (Kyōiku chokugo hōsenkai, 1940).

102. E.g., Inoue Tetsujirō, *Kokumin dōtoku gairon* (1912); *Kyōiku to shūyō* (Kōdōkan, 1910); *Rinri to kyōiku* (1908); *Sonken kōwashū* (1903), etc. A brief account of his work: Yamazaki Masakazu and Miyakawa Tōru, "Inoue Tetsujirō: The Man and His Works," *Philosophical Studies of Japan* 7 (1966): 111-25.

103. Yoshikawa Akimasa, "Tokkyō ni kansuru chokugo no gi," *Kyōiku chokugo kanpatsu kankei shiryōshū* 2:452; Egi Kazuyuki, "Kyōiku chokugo no kanpatsu," ibid., 467.

104. Saigusa Hiroto and Shimizu Ikutarō, eds., *Nihon tetsugaku shisō zensho*, vol. 3, *Shisō ideorogii hen* (Heibonsha, 1956), 768.

105. Inoue Tetsujirō, "Meiji tetsugakkai no kaiko" (1932), in Shimomura Toratarō and Furuta Hikaru, eds., *Gendai Nihon shisō taikei*, vol. 24, *Tetsugaku shisō* (Chikuma shobō, 1965), 70-71. Inoue's Confucian compilations included *Nihon Yōmei gakuha no tetsugaku* (1900), *Nihon kogakuha no tetsugaku*

(1902), *Nihon Shushigakuha no tetsugaku* (1905); also, Inoue Tetsujirō and Kanie Yoshimaru, *Nihon rinri ihen* (1902). His best-known philosophical essays were *Genshō soku jitsuzairon* (1894) and *Ninshiki to jitsuzai to no kankei* (1901).

106. Inoue Tetsujirō, Preface, *Chokugo engi* (Keigyōsha, 1891), reprinted in *Kyōiku chokugo kanpatsu kankei shiryōshū* 3:232.

107. Among the more than 80 people Inoue is said to have consulted as he drafted the commentary were Katō Hiroyuki, Nakamura Masanao, Nishimura Shigeki, and Inoue Kowashi. *Kyōiku chokugo kanpatsu kankei shiryōshū* 3:2. On its many printings: 3:4; Yamazaki and Miyakawa, "Inoue Tetsujirō," 121. On the drafting: Inada, *Kyōiku chokugo*, 337-76.

108. See Ishida Takeshi, "Kazoku kokkakan no kōzō to kinō," *Meiji seiji shisōshi kenkyū*, 39-96. Inoue's commentary, unlike the Rescript itself, aroused criticism from progressive and conservative intellectuals alike: Minamoto Ryōen, "Kyōiku chokugo no kokkashugiteki kaishaku," in *Meiji zenpanki no nashonarizumu*, ed. Sakata, 191-98.

109. Inoue Tetsujirō, "Meiji tetsugakkai no kaiko," 66.

110. Inoue Tetsujirō, Preface, *Chokugo engi* (1891), in *Kyōiku chokugo kanpatsu kankei shiryōshū* 3:230-31.

111. *Tōkyō nichi nichi shinbun*, 15 Mar. 1891; also, *Nihon*, 2 May; etc.

112. *Tōkyō nichi nichi shinbun*, 14 May 1891; also, Osatake Takeshi, *Konan jiken* (1963).

113. *Nihon*, 14 May 1891; *Chōya shinbun*, 20 May.

114. *Nihon*, 16 July 1891; *Tōkyō mainichi shinbun*, 12 July.

115. *Tōhō kyōkai hōkoku*, no. 1 (May 1891). See Sakeda, *Kindai Nihon ni okeru taigai kō undō*, 65-68.

116. Ōhama Tetsuya, *Meiji no bōhyō* (Shūei shuppan, 1970), 12.

117. "Ajia no zento," in Soeda, *Enka no Meiji Taishōshi*, 48. Also, Ōhama, *Meiji no bōhyō*, 10-13.

118. See Ozawa Saburō, *Uchimura Kanzō fukei jiken* (Shinkyō shuppansha, 1961).

119. Letters to D. C. Bell, 6, 9 Mar. 1891, *Uchimura Kanzō zenshū*, vol. 20 (Iwanami shoten, 1933), 207-12.

120. Kume's essay, "Shintō wa saiten no kozoku," appeared in the scholarly *Shigakkai zasshi* (Oct.-Dec. 1891), and aroused controversy when it was reprinted by Taguchi Ukichi in his general magazine, *Shikai* (June 1892). Examples of press response: *Tōkyō nichi nichi shinbun*, 4 Mar. 1892; *Nihon*, 8 Apr. From the Shintō point of view: Shintō bunkakai, *Meiji ishin Shintō hyakunenshi*, vol. 3 (Shintō bunkakai, 1967), 83-94. From the viewpoint of academic freedom: Ōkubo Toshiaki, "Yugamerareta rekishi," in *Arashi no naka no hyakunen*, ed. Sakisaka Itsurō (Keisō shobō, 1952), 42-51.

121. *Nihon*, 18 Sept. 1892; also, Takeda Kiyoko, *Ningenkan no sōkoku: kindai Nihon no shisō to Kirisutokyō* (Kōbundō, 1959), 281-97.

122. The main articles in this controversy are collected in Seki Kōsaku, ed., *Inoue Hakase to Kirisutokyōto: "kyōiku to shūkyō no shōtotsu" no tenmatsu oyobi hyōron*, 3 vols. (Tetsugaku shoin, 1893). On the controversy, see Mi-

yakawa Tōru et al., *Kindai Nihon shisō ronsō* (Aoki shoten, 1971), 234-61; also, Takeda, *Ningenkan no sōkoku*, 136-90.

123. Fujishima Ryōon, "Yasokyō no matsuro," in Seki, *Inoue Hakase to Kirisutokyōto* 3:18.

124. Inoue Tetsujirō, "Kyōiku to shūkyō to no shōtotsu" (1892), ibid. 1:70-71.

125. Ibid., 71.

126. "Shūkyō to kyōiku no kankei ni tsuite: Inoue Tetsujirō-shi no danwa," *Kyōiku jiron* (1892), ibid. 1:2-3.

127. "Kyōiku to shūkyō to no shōtotsu," ibid., 94, 101-02.

128. Ibid., 115.

129. Yoshida Kyūichi, *Nihon kindai Bukkyōshi kenkyū* (Yoshikawa kōbunkan, 1959), 153, 222.

130. Ozawa, *Uchimura Kanzō fukei jiken*, 28; the "two J's" is translated in Tsunoda et al., *Sources of Japanese Tradition*, 856-57.

131. Letter to D. C. Bell, 25 Mar. 1893, *Uchimura Kanzō zenshū* 20: 243.

132. The exceptions included reasoned rebuttals by the Christians Kashiwagi Gien, Ōnishi Hajime, and Uemura Masahisa. See Takeda, *Ningenkan no sōkoku*, 174-87.

133. For Buddhism, which also suffered traumatic disestablishment and persecution at the beginning of the period: Sakurai Masashi, *Meiji shūkyōshi kenkyū* (Shunjūsha, 1971), 21-54. For Shintō, whose travails began with the westernization of the early 70s: Ashizu Uzuhiko, "Teikoku kenpō jidai no jinja to shūkyō," *Meiji ishin Shintō hyakunenshi*, ed. Shintō bunkakai, 2:183-214; Sakurai, 21-54; Hideo Kishimoto, *Japanese Religion in the Meiji Era* (Ōbunsha, 1956).

134. A quintessential exemplar of this attitude was Motora Yūjirō, whose personal and academic involvement with Shintō, Christianity, Confucianism, and Zen influenced many of the leading religious and intellectual figures of the day. For examples and descriptions of his "religion of science" (*kagakushū*): Ko Motora Hakase tsuitō gakujutsu kōenkai, *Motora Hakase to gendai no shinrigaku* (Kōdōkan, 1913), 149-64, 406, 444-48.

135. For his denial of both "national essence-ism" and Buddhism as reasons for his attack: Inoue Tetsujirō, *Kyōiku to shūkyō no shōtotsu* (Keigyōsha, 1893), Preface.

136. Inoue Tetsujirō, "Nihon no kyōdai naru gen'in," *Nihonjin* 3, no. 400 (5 Dec. 1904): 13.

137. Speech to Tōhō gakkai, June 1892, *Inoue Hakase kōenshū* (Keigyōsha, 1895), 37-40.

138. See Tsunemitsu, *Meiji no Bukkyōsha* 1: 174-81. Inoue was an active philosophical defender of Buddhism. At the Academy of Philosophy (*Tetsugakudō*) he built in 1903, he held the ceremony of the four sages for the benefit of disseminating philosophy (and Buddhism) to the general population. The academy is preserved in Tokyo today.

139. Yamamoto Tetsuo, "Kyōiku to shūkyō no shōtotsu ronsō o meguru Bukkyōgawa no taiō," *Kyōikugaku zasshi* (1977): 12-24; also, Yoshida Kyū-

ichi, *Nihon kindai Bukkyōshi kenkyū*, 153-66, and *Nihon kindai Bukkyō shakaishi kenkyū* (Yoshikawa kōbunkan, 1964), 195-200. Colonization was the Buddhists' most frequent theme.

140. Naitō Konan, "Meiji ni jūichinen kitareri" (1888), *Naitō Konan zenshū*, ed. Kanda Kiichirō and Naitō Kenkichi, vol. 1 (Hakkōsha, 1970), 429-31; Ōuchi Seiran, "Hahaoya wa tanin ni naru ka," *Bukkyō*, no. 71 (20 June 1893). At the time of Naitō's comment, he was writing for Ōuchi's Buddhist journal, *Meikyō shinshi*.

141. Tanimoto Tomeri, "Yasokyō kengi," *Tetsugaku zasshi* 8, no. 79 (1893): 1400.

142. Inoue Tetsujirō, "Kyōiku to shūkyō," *Taiyō* 18, no. 6 (May 1912): 146.

143. Tokonami Takejirō, "Sankyō kaidō ni kansuru shiken," in Yoshida Kumaji, *Waga kokumin dōtoku to shūkyō* (1912), 78-79; *Shimin* 6, no. 1 (Mar. 1912): 114-18. Also, Sakurai, *Meiji shūkyōshi*, 444-55.

144. Yoshida, *Nihon kindai Bukkyōshi kenkyū*, 385-88.

145. E.g., "Ryūkō no kazu kazu," *Tōkyō asahi shinbun*, 7 Oct. 1894, also, 28 Sept.-30 Oct.; *San'in shinbun*, 12 Aug., also, 3 Aug.-24 Sept.; *Miyako shinbun*, 28 Apr.-2 May 1895; *Fukuoka nichi nichi shinbun*, 29 Aug. 1894.

146. E.g., *Nisshin sensō jikki* (Hakubunkan), nos. 1-50 (25 Aug. 1894-7 Jan. 1896); Kakubari Eisaburō, *Nisshin sensōshi no hanashi* [P] (Uedaya honten, 1895); *Tsūzoku Nisshin sensō mondō* [P] (1894); *Nisshin sensō gentō eiga setsumeisho* (1895); *Nisshin sensō gentōkai* (1895); *Nisshin sensō sugoroku* (1894, 1895); etc. Also, Donald Keene, "The Sino-Japanese War of 1894-95 and Japanese Culture," *Landscapes and Portraits: Appreciations of Japanese Culture* (Kōdansha, 1971), 259-99.

147. Soeda, *Enka no Meiji Taishōshi*, 62-71; Ōhama, *Meiji no bōhyō*, 46-63.

148. Takayama Chogyū, "Meiji shisō no hensen" (1897), *Chogyū zenshū*, vol. 4 (Hakubunkan, 1905), 434-35. For "Japanism": " 'Nihonshugi' hakkan no shui," and "Nihonshugi hakkan ni tsukite," *Nihonshugi*, no. 1 (May 1897), 1-39; and subsequent issues.

149. For a comment and bibliography: Inō Tentarō, *Jōyaku kaiseiron no rekishiteki tenkai*, 507-51, 627-39.

150. Inoue Tetsujirō, *Naichi zakkyoron* (1889), in *Meiji bunka zenshū*, vol. 11, *Gaikōhen*, 473-520.

151. Ozaki Yukio, *Naichi gaikō* (Hakubunkan, 1893), 13, 57-60. A representative etiquette guide: *Shichigatsu koi!—Naichi zakkyo kokoroe* [P] (1898), 49-65.

152. Yasuda Kyūshū, *Zakkyo junbi yūkoku no namida* (Kokkōsha, 1897), 3. On the Buddhists: Inō Tentarō, "Bukkyōtogawa no naichi zakkyo taiundō: sono shiryō ni tsuite," *Chūō daigaku bungaku kiyō* 3 (1957): 35-50.

153. Katō Totsudō, *Bukkyō kokumin:zakkyogo no kokoroe* (Ōmeisha, 1898); *Shichigatsu koi!* [P], 33-39, 129-31.

154. Ōkuma: Bōkyūkai, *Naichi zakkyo ni taisuru shotaika no iken* (Kōeki tosho, 1899), 6-7; Suzuki Jun'ichirō, *Kokumin yōi: naichi zakkyo kokoroe* [P] (1894), 54.

155. Yasuda, *Zakkyo junbi*, 6-18; Ōkuma, *Naichi zakkyo*, 66-69; etc.

156. For a relevant classification of attitudes toward the foreign: "Zakkyoha to hizakkyoha no kubun," *Nihonjin* 2, no. 1 (Oct. 1893): 5-9.

157. On the previous presence of foreigners: Imai Shōji, "Meiji nijūnendai ni okeru naichi zakkyoteki keikō ni tsuite," *Kokushigaku*, no. 104 (Jan. 1978): 1-22.

158. Otis Cary, *A History of Christianity in Japan*, vol. 2 (New York: Fleming H. Revell Co., 1909), 266-67; Kishimoto, *Japanese Religion*, 277-79.

159. Kuyama Yasushi et al., *Kindai Nihon to Kirisutokyō, Meiji hen* (Sōbunsha, 1956), 226-64; Yoshida, *Nihon kindai Bukkyō shakaishi kenkyū*, 381-470.

160. Ashizu, "Teikoku kenpō jidai no jinja to shūkyō," 191-204. Murakami, *Kokka Shintō*, 77-119. Also, D. C. Holtom, *The National Faith of Japan: A Study in Modern Japan* (1938) (New York: Paragon reprint, 1965).

161. Ashizu, "Jingikan kōfuku undō ni okeru no katsudo," *Meiji ishin Shintō hyakunenshi* 5: 354-98; Nishida Hiroyoshi, "Meiji ikō jinja hōseishi no ichi danmen: 'kokka no sōshi' no seidoteki jūjitsu to jingikan fukkō undō," ibid. 4:60-143.

162. "Kyōdōshoku haishi iken an" (1884), *Inoue Kowashi den* 1:386-92; "Jingiin setsuritsu iken" (1890), ibid. 2:280-81.

163. E.g., in memorials to the Diet such as "Jingikan fukkō no gi ni tsuki kengi" (1895): Ashizu, "Jingikan kōfuku undō," 371-73. Also, Ashizu, "Teikoku kenpō jidai no jinja," 205-13.

164. Ashizu, "Jingikan kōfuku undō," 381, 369-82. Also, "Zenkoku dōshi shokun ni gekisu," *Zenkoku shinshokukai kaihō*, no. 2 (Sept. 1899): 1-6. This was the journal of the priests association.

165. "Jinjakyoku shinsetsu seraru," *Zenkoku shinshokukai kaihō*, no. 7 (Feb. 1900): 47-48.

166. "Meiji sanjūkunen o okuru," *Jinja kyōkai zasshi* 5, no. 12 (Dec. 1906): 2. The Shrine Association was associated with the Home Ministry's Shrine Bureau.

167. *Zenkoku shinshokukai kaihō*, no. 61 (Aug. 1904): 49; no. 62 (Sept. 1904): 31-32; no. 64 (Nov. 1904): 7.

168. Shrines as monuments were related to the "non-religion" issue: e.g., *Jinja kyōkai zasshi* 1, no. 4 (June 1902); also, Kōmoto Mitsugi, "Shisō konnan to jinja," in *Nihon ni okeru kokka to shūkyō*, ed. Shimode Sekiyo Sensei kanreki kinenkai (Daizō shuppan, 1978), 322-33. On shrine reorganization: e.g., Kōno Shōzō, "Jinja Shintō no konpon mondai," *Jinja kyōkai zasshi* 7, no. 10 (Oct. 1908): 1-7, and (1907-10): passim; *Zenkoku shinshokukai kaihō* (1908-10): passim. Also, Wilbur Friedell, *Japanese Shrine Mergers, 1906-12* (Tokyo: Sophia University Press, 1973), 81-93.

169. E.g., Mizuno Rentarō, "Jinja ni tsuite," *Jinja kyōkai zasshi* 7, nos. 4-5 (Apr.-May 1908): 1-6, 1-7; Mizuno Rentarō, "Jinja o kyōdōtai no chūshin to subeshi," *Shimin* 3, no. 1 (Apr. 1908): 3-10; Inoue Tomoichi, "Jinja chūshin no setsu," *Zenkoku shinshokukai kaihō*, no. 122 (Dec. 1908): 1-8. Tsukamoto Seiji, "Jinja ni kansuru chūi," *Zenkoku shinshokukai kaihō*, nos. 208-10 (1916). Friedell, *Japanese Shrine Mergers*, 45-79.

170. "Naimushō jinja tōkyoku dan," *Zenkoku shinshokukai kaihō*, no. 209 (Mar. 1916): 29-31; also cited in Kōmoto, "Shisō konnan to jinja," 325.

171. Kōmoto, ibid., 320-25.

172. Shrine bureau activities: Taikakai, *Naimushōshi* 2:1-60. Monbushō directive issued by Komatsubara in 1911: Holtom, *The National Faith of Japan*, 73.

173. "Shintō daigaku hitsuyōron," *Zenkoku shinshokukai kaihō*, no. 55 (Feb. 1904): 25.

174. Inoue Tetsujirō, *Kyōiku to shūkyō no shōtotsu* (1892), 8; or, Seki, *Inoue Hakase to Kirisutokyōto* 1:53. See Minamoto, "Kyōiku chokugo no kokka-shugiteki kaishaku," in *Meiji zenpanki no nashonarizumu*, ed. Sakata, 205.

175. "Shintō ga shūkyō to shite no seiryoku," *Zenkoku shinshokukai kaihō*, no. 106 (Aug. 1907): 35.

176. Inoue Tetsujirō, *Kokumin dōtoku gairon* (1912), cited in Kishimoto Yoshio, "Shintō to kokumin dōtoku," *Meiji ishin Shintō hyakunenshi*, ed. Shintō bunkakai, 3:319-20.

177. Festivals (*Shinnensai, Niinamesai*): *Jinja kyōkai zasshi* 7, no. 2 (Feb. 1900): 63. State Shintō as effective from the late Meiji period: Murakami, *Kokka Shintō*. Full national administration occurring only in the 30s: Nishida, "Meiji ikō jinja hōseishi," *Meiji ishin Shintō hyakunenshi* 4:63-64, 119-36.

178. For another view: Friedell, *Japanese Shrine Mergers*, 70.

179. Miyata Noboru, *Ikigami shinkō: hito o kami ni matsuru fūzoku* (Hanawa shobō, 1970), 52-75.

180. Nagano-ken jinjachō, *Nagano-ken jinja hyakunenshi* (Nagano-ken jinja sōdaikai, 1964), 492-94.

181. E.g., Tenrikyō, which was the last of the thirteen religious "sects" of Shintō to be so designated in 1908. The following year, to preserve the designation, Tenrikyō began to teach that the emperor in the Rescript was to be considered a god, but the religion continued to suffer persecution nonetheless: Oguri Junko, *Nihon no kindai shakai to Tenrikyō* (Hyōronsha, 1969), 263-67.

182. On the 30s: Fujitani Toshio, *Shintō shinkō to minshū-Tennōsei* (Hōritsu bunkasha, 1980), 209-37; Holtom, *National Faith of Japan*, 298-316. On the abolition: "The Shinto Directive Staff Study" (Dec. 1945), in William P. Woodard, *The Allied Occupation of Japan and Japanese Religions* (Leiden: E. J. Brill, 1972), 322-41.

183. For a list of modern definitions: Richard Minear, *Japanese Tradition and Western Law: Emperor, State, and Law in the Thought of Hozumi Yatsuka* (Cambridge: Harvard University Press, 1970), 64-71.

184. Fukuzawa Yukichi, "Bunmeiron no gairyaku," in *Fukuzawa Yukichi zenshū* 4:18-19; or, *An Outline of a Theory of Civilization*, 23-26.

185. Pittau, *Political Thought in Early Meiji Japan*, 93-171.

186. Kōshaku Sasaki Takayuki-kun shokan: kokutai mondō, Shoryōbu, Imperial Household Agency, Tokyo (ms).

187. Ibid. With the words "*nao yoku kangaeyo*," Itō ended the conversation.

188. *Aikoku* (Gifu), Feb. 1893; *Nihonjin* (Gumma), May 1889, etc.

189. Toyama Kakusuke, *Nihon no Nihon* (Hakubunkan, 1892), 3.

190. E.g., Katō Hiroyuki, "Nisshi ryōkoku no kokutai no idō," *Taiyō* 5, no. 16 (20 July 1899): 1-5. A typical presentation: Haga and Shimoda, *Nihon katei hyakka jii* (1906), 411-12.

191. Katō Totsudō, "Kokutai no seika," *Shakai kyōiku: tsūzoku kōwa* (Bunseidō, 1918), 215-18.

192. Katō Totsudō, "Banpō muhi no kokutai," ibid., 237-40.

193. See Tsurumi Shunsuke's famous 1946 article, F. J. Daniels, trans., "Mr. Turumi-Syunsuke on the 'Amuletic' Use of Words: A Translation with Commentary," *SOAS Bulletin*, no. 18 (1956): 514-33. "Amuletic" is "o-mamoriteki."

194. Kōshaku Sasaki Takayuki-kun shokan: kokutai mondō (ms). Also, for Itō's speech, Kaneko, *Itō Hirobumi den* 3:739-43. By Japanese count 1908 was the 20th anniversary (*nijūshūnen*) of the promulgation of the Constitution, though ceremonies were also held the following year, the same anniversary according to the Western reckoning.

195. Tokutomi, *Waga kōyūroku*, 9.

196. *Japan Chronicle*, 15 Feb. 1907.

197. Yamamoto and Konno, *Meijiki gakkō gyōji no kōsatsu*, 74-80.

198. "Shōgakkō shūshinsho hensan no kengi," *Teikoku gikai*, ed. Abe, 2:81.

199. Karasawa, *Kyōkasho no rekishi*, esp. 191-329. Also, Harold J. Wray, "Changes and Continuity in Japanese Images of the Kokutai and Roles Toward the Outside World, A Content Analysis of Japanese Textbooks, 1903-1945" (Ph.D. dissertation, University of Hawaii, 1971). Texts were revised in 1910, 1918-1923, 1933-1939, and 1941-1945.

200. *Hyakunenshi* 4:681-766; Maki Masami, *Nihon kyōin shikaku seidoshi kenkyū* (Kazama shobō, 1971), 196-225.

201. Kubo, *Tennōsei kokka no kyōiku seisaku*, 12-24.

202. "Chokugo haidoku ni kansuru sahō" (1900), *Nagano-ken kyōikushi* 6:556. Example of the progress of directives: ibid., 531-56. A typical village initiative celebrating the Rescript: Shinano-no-kuni Saku-gun Shimokaise-mura, Tsuchiya-ke monjo, no. 4182, Monbushō shiryōkan, Tokyo (ms).

203. Watari, *Kyōiku chokugo to gakkō kyōiku*, 55-78; Yamamoto and Konno, *Meijiki gakkō gyōji no kōsatsu*, 86-129.

204. *Nagano-ken kyōikushi* 6: 555-56; Karasawa Tomitarō, *Meiji hyakunen no jidōshi*, vol. 1 (Kōdansha, 1968), 219-21, 282-83.

205. "Shōgakkō kyōsoku taikō" (1891), Kyōikushi hensankai, *Hattatsushi* 3: 95-103. Also, Shindō, *Kyōiku chokugo shinnyū katei*, 11-12.

206. Kaigo, *Inoue Kowashi no kyōiku seisaku*, 944-45; Kokuritsu kyōiku kenkyūjo, *Hyakunenshi* 4:211.

207. *Shūshin* schedule: *Hyakunenshi* 4:170. Lesson plans and notes: *Nagano-ken kyōikushi* 6:546-54. A barely fictionalized recollection of ethics class in the nineties: Naka Kansuke, *The Silver Spoon* (*Gin no saji*, 1913), trans. Etsuko Terasaki (Chicago Review Press, 1976), 87-88.

208. *Kyōiku chokugo sugoroku* (1890).

209. This and other extracurricular renderings of the Rescript: Karasawa, *Meiji hyakunen no jidōshi* 1:221-25.

210. Kakurentaiku kannai minjō fūzoku shisōkai no genjō, II, Takada (ms).

211. Composition, fifth grade (May 1894), Shimofusa-no-kuni Sōma-gun Fujishiro-mura Iida-ke monjo, no. 4173, Monbushō shiryōkan, Tokyo (ms).

212. Monbushō directives: *Hattatsushi* 3: 144-45. For "*shōbu, shōbu*": *Kyōiku jiron*, no. 383 (5 Dec. 1895). Naka, *The Silver Spoon*, 124-28. See Umihara Tōru, *Meiji kyōinshi no kenkyū* (Minerubua shobō, 1973), 214-27; Chiba Toshio, *Meiji no shōgakkō* (Hirosaki: Tsugaru shobō, 1969), 221-25; Ubukata, *Meiji Taishō kenbunshi*, 33-41.

213. Kaigo Tokiomi and Yoshida Kumaji, *Kyōiku chokugo kanpatsu igo ni okeru shōgakkō shūshin kyōju no hensen* (Kokumin seishin bunka kenkyūjo, 1935), 68-70.

214. In 1895 the average monthly salary of an elementary schoolteacher was 7.36 yen; a typesetter, 8.79 yen; a roofer, 8.9 yen; a shipyard carpenter, 10.05 yen; and a civil servant of *hannin* rank, 12 yen and above. Umihara, *Meiji kyōinshi no kenkyū*, 229-39.

215. Ueda Shōzaburo, *Seinen kyōshi no sho* (Kenbunkan, 1936), 166-67; Umihara, *Meiji kyōinshi*, 173-82.

216. *Saikin chōsa shūshoku no tebiki* [P] (Seibunsha, 1911), 17.

217. Training: ibid., 157; Maki, *Nihon kyōin shikaku*, 224-40. The "unfit": Watanabe Masamori, *Seinen kyōshi jidai* (Tōyō tosho, 1937), 70.

218. "Kyōin no hinpan," *Kyōiku jiron* (25 Sept. 1897); Umihara, 239-40.

219. Ibid., 241; also, *Hyakunenshi* 1:1158-68.

220. Karasawa Tomitarō, *Kyōshi no rekishi* (Sōbunsha, 1968), 85-93, 139-50, 265-82.

221. Umihara, *Meiji kyōinshi*, 169-82, 246-52.

222. For fine fictional caricatures of such principals by writers who taught under them: Ishikawa Takuboku, *Kumo wa tensai de aru* (1906), *Takuboku zenshū*, vol. 3 (Chikuma shobō, 1967), 3-34; Tayama Katai, *Inaka kyōshi* (1904), *Tayama Katai zenshū* 2:313-595.

223. Ibid., 52. Reminiscences of this kind of teacher: Inage Sofū, *Gendai kyōikusha no shinseikatsu* (Daidōkan shoten, 1913), 353-423; Watanabe, *Seinen kyōshi jidai*, 48-80.

224. Watanabe, 225-33.

225. Ibid., 216.

226. Chiba-ken shihan gakkō, *Sōritsu rokujū shūnen kinen: Chiba-ken shihan gakkō enkakushi* (Chiba: 1934), 323.

227. Ishitoya Tetsuo, *Nihon kyōinshi kenkyū* (Kōdansha, 1967), 371-462; Karasawa, *Kyōshi no rekishi*, 164-87.

228. Mizuhara Yoshiyuki, " 'Shihankei' mondai hassei no bunseki to kōsatsu," *Nihon no kyōiku shigaku*, no. 20 (Oct. 1977): 20-35; Karasawa, *Kyōshi no rekishi*, 28-93.

229. "Kyōiku chokugo ni kansuru kengi" (1900), *Teikoku gikai*, ed. Abe, 2:90.

230. To this praise by the president of the Chicago Board of Education,

the IWW responded with its own appraisal of the Rescript as "the veriest commonplaces of capitalist morality." *Industrial Union Bulletin*, International Workers of the World, 2 Nov. 1907.

231. Ōkuma: *Tōkyō mainichi shinbun*, 8 Jan. 1907. Ukita: "Shinjidai no shimei," *Kokumin zasshi* 3, no. 7 (Sept. 1912): 19.

232. Ebina Danjō, "Shūkyōka no mitaru gendai shakai," *Taiyō* 17, no. 3 (Feb. 1911): 29.

233. "Nihonjin no dōtoku," *Tōkyō asahi shinbun*, 18 Apr. 1909; *Miyako shinbun*, 13 June 1911.

234. Sawayanagi Masatarō, "Futatabi shūshin kyōju wa jinjō yonen yori hajimubeki o ronzu," *Sawayanagi zenshū* 6:457; "Nisan no seinenron," *Rinri kōenshū*, no. 101 (Jan. 1911): 77.

235. Kajiyama Masafumi, "Meiji makki no tokuiku rongi—taigyaku jikengo no teikoku gikai," *Nihon shisōshi*, no. 7 (1978): 112-33.

236. Akimoto Kōchō, "Kazoku no mitaru gendai shakai," *Taiyō* 17, no. 3 (Feb. 1911): 23.

237. Kaigo and Yoshida, *Kyōiku chokugo kanpatsu igo*, 95-96.

238. Watari, *Kyōiku chokugo to gakkō kyōiku*, 78-95.

239. Watari, *Kyōiku chokugo shakugi zenshō*, 536-38.

CHAPTER SIX

1. Fujii Masata, *Gunshichōson hattensaku gunshichōsonze chōsa hyōjun* (Himeji: 1910), 1-11.

2. Yamagata: letter to Terauchi (27 July 1906), Terauchi Masatake kankei monjo, Kensei shiryōshitsu, National Diet Library (ms). Typical of the paeons to empire: "Meiji yonjūnen o mukau," *Tōkyō mainichi shinbun*, 1 Jan. 1907. Confucius: Kawai Kiyomaru, "Meiji yonjūnen o mukau," *Nihon kokkyō daidō sōshi*, no. 223 (25 Jan. 1907): 2-5.

3. "Meiji yonjūnenshi," *Taiyō* 14, no. 3 (Feb. 1908): 201.

4. A representative discussion: "Sengo keiei," *Taiyō* (*zōkan*) 12, no. 9 (15 June 1906), esp. Kubota Jō, "Sengo no shakai," 50-51, and Tatebe Tongo, "Shakai mondai no kontei," 132-48.

5. E.g., second restoration and "twentieth-century issues of social livelihood" (*shakai minsei*) and "agricultural problems" (*nōmin mondai*): Eto Kōsaburō, "Kongo no Nihon," *Nihonjin*, no. 454 (1 Mar. 1907): 22-25. A typical retrospective account: Tanaka Hozumi, *Seikatsu mondai to nōson mondai* (Jitsugyō no Nihonsha, 1913).

6. Inoue Tomoichi, preface to Mori, *Chōsonze chōsa shishin* (1909), 1-2. For a chronology of Inoue's activities as founder of the central Hōtokukai with its journal *Shimin* and as dedicated bureaucrat in the Naimushō's *chihōkyoku*: Inoue Tomoichi, *Inoue Meifu ikō*, ed. Ōmi Masao (Sanshūsha, 1920), 6-54. For a brief sketch: Taikakai, *Naimushōshi* 2: 101-105.

7. Yokoi Tokiyoshi, "Tokainetsu no kekka," *Kyōikukai* 6, no. 5 (Mar. 1907): 27-30. Also for *tokainetsu*: Nakasone Saburō, "Tokainetsu to kyōiku,"

ibid., no. 12 (Oct. 1907): 20-22; Yokoi Tokiyoshi, "Tokai to inaka" (1913), *Yokoi Hakase zenshū* 4:531-652; "Shakai no ranchō, gakusei no fuhai," *Taiyō* 3, no. 24 (5 Dec. 1897): 253-72; Yamazaki Enkichi, "Nōson jichi no kenkyū" (1908), *Yamazaki Enkichi zenshū* 1:406-7; Kakurentaiku kannai minjō fūzoku shisōkai no genjō, V, Fukuyama (ms).

8. Kishimoto Minoru, "Meiji Taishōki ni okeru rison chiiki no keisei to toshi jinkō no shūseki katei," *Meiji kōki no rekishi chiri, Rekishi chirigaku kiyō*, ed. Rekishi chiri gakkai, no. 8 (1966): 155.

9. Tokyo metropolitan survey, 1908: "Tōkyō jumin no kenkyū," *Kokumin zasshi* 3, no. 13 (July 1912): 63; Kobayashi Ichirō, "Tokai no bōchō," *Rinri kōenshū*, no. 58 (1907): 3. Similarly for Yokohama: Yamada, *Keihin toshi mondai*, 24-26.

10. Yamaguchi Keiichirō, "Meiji kōki no toshi keisei," *Meiji kōki no rekishi chiri*, ed. Rekishi chiri gakkai, 199.

11. "Chōson no jichi": Ishida Denkichi, *Jichi sōsho: Mohan chōson to yūryō shōgakkō* (Daigakkan, 1910), 1-6.

12. Farming population: Nojiri Shigeo, *Nōson rison no jisshōteki kenkyū* (1942) (Nōson gyōson bunka kyōkai, 1978), 11, 74. "Recklessly pressing": "Shakai no ranchō, gakusei no fuhai," *Taiyō* 3, no. 24 (5 Dec. 1897): 256.

13. Labor outmigration from the farms, both male and female: Watanabe Makoto, *Nihon nōson jinkōron* (1938), 80-100, 137-98. Eldest, second, and third sons: Nojiri, *Nōson rison no jisshōteki kenkyū*, 466-87. Although based on data from the late twenties and thirties, his general findings apply to the earlier period as well. A helpful study of labor outflow in Niigata-ken: Ushiyama Keiji, *Nōminsō bunkai no kōzō: senzenki* (Ochanomizu shobō, 1975), 21-38. Contemporary references: Yokoi Tokiyoshi, "Toshi seinen to inaka seinen," *Yokoi Hakase zenshū* 5:202-4; Yamazaki Enkichi, "Nōson kyōikuron" (1914), *Yamazaki Enkichi zenshū* 3:1-20. Daughters marrying into provincial cities: Kakurentaiku kannai minjō fūzoku shisōkai no genjō, VI, Matsuyama (ms).

14. Sawayanagi Masatarō, "Gakusei no fūki mondai," *Jindō* 1, no. 6 (15 Sept. 1905): 6. Also, Kakurentaiku kannai minjō fūzoku shisōkai no genjō, III, Tsu; IV, Tsuruga; V, Hamada; etc. (ms).

15. Kamiya Chikara, *Ie to mura no hōshi kenkyū: Nihon kindai hō no seiritsu katei* (Ochanomizu shobō, 1976), 152-54. Data vary in different parts of the country, and some Tōhoku villages lost far greater portions of their population between 1906 and 1909. This Aichi village was probably more typical of general household mobility in the period. For similar data which also locate the increase in families leaving for the city in the decade from 1897-1907: *Ibaraki-ken Kita Sōma-gun Omonma sonze* (1914). For impact on farming of economic developments between 1888 and 1908: Nakamura, *Kindai Nihon jinushi seidoshi kenkyū*, 133-40. A contemporary survey of economic reasons for migration to Tokyo in 1911: Miyachi Masato, *Nichiro sengo seijishi no kenkyū: teikokushugi keiseiki no toshi to nōson* (Tōkyō daigaku shuppankai, 1973), 204.

16. *Shiga-ken Kōga-gun Ishibe chōze* (1910).

17. Yanagita Kunio, "Tsuka to mori no hanashi," *Shimin* 6, no. 10 (1 Jan. 1912): 46-48.

18. Examples of change in status and livelihood of families in the post Russo-Japanese War period: Takeda Tsutomu, "Meiji kōki Setouchi ichi nōson ni okeru nōminsō no bunka," *Nōgyō sōgō kenkyū* 17, no. 4 (Oct. 1963): 76-89. Also a DaiNihon nōkai study of 18 villages around the country between 1899 and 1916, which showed that of the households that shifted from self-cultivation as owner-farmers, 68.8% became tenants, 8.4% became landowners, 15% left farming for commerce or wage labor, and 1.2% became "propertyless." In the latter two categories *dekasegi* and permanent migration of individuals were common: DaiNihon nōkai, *Honpō jisakunō no jōkyō* (1918), 6-8.

19. Saitō Mankichi, *Nōgyō shikin: jitchi keizai* (Aokisūzandō, 1911), 37-38.

20. Business fever: "Kigyōnetsu no bokkō, I," *Kokumin zasshi* 3, no. 8 (15 Apr. 1912): 7-8. "Get-rich-quick market fever": Kakurentaiku kannai minjō fūzoku shisōkai no genjō, V, Himeji (ms).

21. Kobayashi Ōri, *Meiji bunmei shi* (1915), 1176.

22. Criticism of "jitsugyōnetsu" from the late 90s: Tatebe Tongo, "Meiji shisō no hensen," *Nihon*, pt. 8 (23 Mar. 1898); Yokoi Tokio, "Dōshisha no shugi hōshin ni kanshite," *Sekai no Nihon*, no. 18 (Aug. 1897): 21; also, Okuda Yoshito, "The Career of Constitutional Government in Japan," *The Far East* 2, no. 4 (Apr. 1897): 146; *Taiyō* 3, no. 24 (5 Dec. 1897): 253-72. "Political fever" replaced by "enterprise fever" in youth: Tokutomi Ichirō (Sohō), "Chōson no shitei," *Nichiyō kōdan*, vol. 1 (Min'yūsha, 1900), 52-53; similarly, among newspaper readers, "Shinbun dokusha no hensen," *Chūō kōron* 15, no. 5 (May 1900): 85.

23. Success fever: Hirata Tōsuke, *Jikyō sadan* (1911), advertisement in *Shimin* 6, no. 5 (Aug. 1911). Small success fever and Roosevelt: Oshikawa Shunrō, "Keikai subeki Nihon," *Bōken sekai* (Dec. 1910). Also, *jitsugyō* and small successes: Kakurentaiku kannai minjō fūzoku shisōkai no genjō, VII, Ōita (ms).

24. *Fukushima-ken Tamura-gun Koizumi-mura sonze chōsasho*, 1902.

25. Inoue Tomoichi, lecture at Shiminkai monthly meeting (15 Mar. 1908), *Shimin* 3, no. 1 (Apr. 1908): 86.

26. *Fukushima-ken Tamura-gun Koizumi-mura sonze chōsasho*, 1902; *Fukushima-ken Iwase-gun Nishibukuro-mura sonze chōsa*, 1902; *Aichi-ken Kaitō-gun Ifuki-mura sonze*, 1904; *Kenritsu Nakanojō nōgyō gakkō kōyūkaihō* (Gummaken), no. 2 (1907): 8-9; no. 6 (1912): 4-6.

27. Early opposition to the railroad: Nagata, *Meiji no kisha*, 98-101. Local elite: Haga Noboru, "Gōnō to jiriki saisei," *Meiji kokka to minshū*, 213-235; also, *Aizawa nikki* 1:134. Ideologues: below, note 30.

28. "Tetsudō shōka" began with the famous line "Kiteki issei Shinbashi o," the melody still heard over Japan National Railway loudspeakers. Komota, *Nihon ryūkōkashi*, 29, 220; Kindaichi and Anzai, *Nihon no shōka*, 115-21. A representative railway guide that found wide circulation in the countryside: "Riku no Nihon," *Taiyō (rinji zōkan)* 9, no. 7 (June 1903).

29. The 5,000-mile (8,100 km.) mark, including public and private railroads, was celebrated in a "Tetsudō 5000-ri shukugakai" in Nagoya in 1906. Nationalization took place in 1906-7, and new lines were constructed continuously. In 1912 the National Railway recorded 86.9 million freight and passenger kilometers and 155.4 million passengers: Nihon kokuyū tetsudō, *Nihon kokuyū tetsudō hyakunen shashinshi* (Kōtsū kyōryokukai, 1972), 132; *Kokutetsu rekishi jiten* (Nihon kokuyū tetsudō, 1973), 66-67.

30. "Tōkyō kara Matsue e," *San'in shinbun*, 6 May 1912; Kakurentaiku kannai minjō fūzoku shisōkai no genjō, III, Hamamatsu, Toyama; IV, Tsuruga; V, Himeji; VI, Matsuyama, Marugame; VII, Kurume; etc. (ms).

31. Kokuritsu kyōiku kenkyūjo, *Hyakunenshi* 4:223, 1008.

32. Oct. 1906 proposal: ibid., 903-5. Also, Minister of Education Makino Nobuaki, speech to prefectural governors' conference (28 Apr. 1907), Chihō chōkan kaigi kunji yōryō, Chihōkan kaigi giketsusho narabi hikki, 1907 (ms); *Kyōiku jiron*, nos. 765-791 (July 1906-Apr. 1907): passim.

33. Chiba, *Meiji no shōgakkō*, 255-57.

34. Early opposition: Kurasawa, *Shōgakkō no rekishi* 1:1002-19; *Nagano-ken kyōikushi* 1:604-21; Horimatsu, *Nihon kindai kyōikushi*, 49-53.

35. "Gimu kyōiku no enchō" (1922), *Sawayanagi Masatarō zenshū* 3: 442-44.

36. Kokuritsu kyōiku kenkyūjo, *Hyakunenshi* 4:916.

37. "Shōgakkō kyōiku ni taisuru shiken," *Yamanashi kyōiku*, no. 118 (Sept. 1904): 26, cited in Ebihara, *Gendai Nihon kyōiku seisakushi*, 222.

38. Monbushō view on spiritual education (*seishin kyōiku*): e.g., Kunrei no. 3, "Sengo kyōikujō ni kanshi tōkyokusha o ryūihō" (Oct. 1905), Kyōiku hensankai, *Hattatsushi* 5:6-7. Representative *minkan* advocacy of moral education (*tokuiku*): Ōkuma Shigenobu, "Kyōrai ryōseiki ni okeru sekai rekkoku to Nihon to no ichi," *Taiyō* 6, no. 8 (June 1900): 2; Yokoi Tokio, "Wagakuni tokuiku no zento," and Inoue Tetsujirō, Yoshida Kenryū, Miyake Yūjirō, Koyanagi Shikita, Fukasaku Yasufumi, Ōshima Masanori, "Migi ni taisuru iken," *Rinri kōenshū*, no. 72 (Sept. 1908): 1-28ff.

39. Kakurentaiku kannai minjō fūzoku shisōkai no genjō, III, Azabu (ms).

40. *Fukushima-ken Iwase-gun Nishibukuro-mura sonze chōsa*, 1902; *Fukushima-ken Tamura-gun Koizumi-mura sonze chōsasho*, 1902; *Aichi-ken Kaitō-gun Ifuki-mura sonze*, 1904.

41. In Miyagi-ken the number of agricultural continuation schools at the village level increased from 73 in 1900 to 5,530 in 1912, the local demand for agricultural subjects overwhelming the original intent of the central government in the early 1890s to emphasize industrial skills: Yamagishi Haruo, "Meiji kōki nōson ni okeru jitsugyō hoshū gakkō: Miyagi-ken no baai," *Kyōiku shakaigaku kenkyū* (Tōhoku daigaku) 32 (Sept. 1977): 139-49.

42. Kakurentaiku kannai minjō fūzoku shisōkai no genjō, II, Hirosaki (ms).

43. Naimushō objection to the costs of extending compulsory education: Kokuritsu kyōiku kenkyūjo, *Hyakunenshi* 4: 910-15.

44. Ōshima Mitsuko, "Chihō zaisei to chihō kairyō undō," in Furushima, *Meiji Taishō kenkyūhō*, 65-66.

45. Criticism of Toyama: *Kokumin zasshi* 2, no. 1 (Jan. 1911): 102. Nagano schools: *Shinano mainichi shinbun*, 5-6 Oct. 1912, 8 Jan. 1913. Other examples: *Kyōiku jiron*, nos. 987-96 (15 Sept.-15 Dec. 1912): passim.

46. Suzuki Masayuki, "Nichiro sengo nōson saihen seisaku no tenkai ni kansuru ichikōsatsu: nōson shōgakkō mondai o chūshin ni," *Ibaraki-kenshi kenkyū*, no. 27 (Dec. 1973): 21.

47. In his chronology of village disturbances, Aoki Kōji lists 249 risings between 1906 and 1911, 97 of which concerned elementary schools. In the same period there was an annual average of 35 disturbances related to village government, compared to an average of only 20 tenant uprisings per year: *Meiji nōmin sōjō nenjiteki kenkyū* (Shinseisha, 1967), 153-214. Also cited by Ariizumi, who uses the date 1905 instead of 1906, with the same count: "Meiji kokka to minshū tōgō," 262.

48. *Tōkyō asahi shinbun*, 23 Feb. 1908.

49. *Niigata shinbun*, 30 Apr. 1907.

50. Speech to prefectural governors conference (28 Apr. 1907): Chihōkan kaigi kunji yōryō, Chihōkan kaigi giketsusho narabi hikki, 1907 (ms).

51. Sawayanagi Masatarō, "Tenka no chūgakusei ni gekisu" (1910), *Sawayanagi zenshū* 6:521-31; "Yūmin o tsukuru kyōiku," *Gifu nichi nichi shinbun*, 17 May 1912; Kakurentaiku kannai minjō fūzoku shisōkai no genjō, II, Takada; III, Sakura; V, Yamaguchi, Matsue, Fukuchiyama; VI, Marugame (ms).

52. *Ryōsai kenbo* (good wives, wise mothers): Komatsubara Eitarō, "Monbu tōkyoku no mitaru gendai shakai," *Taiyō* 17, no. 3 (Feb. 1911): 10-14; "Kumamoto-ken no joshi kyōiku," *Kyūshū nichi nichi shinbun*, 30 Nov. 1910; "Iwayuru atarashiki onna," *Shinano mainichi shinbun*, 3 Jan. 1910; also Kokuritsu kyōiku kenkyūjo, *Hyakunenshi* 4:1122-25.

53. "Kentōhazure no gakumon," *Chōshū nichi nichi shinbun*, 21 July 1912; readers' column, *Shinano mainichi shinbun*, 5 Dec. 1912.

54. "Kyōiku aru yūmin no shochi mondai," *Chūō kōron* (July 1912): 75-90.

55. Ishida, *Jichi sōsho* (1910), 85-86.

56. Fukaya Masashi, *Gakurekishugi no keifu* (Reimei shobō, 1969), 349-50; Nihon joshi daigaku joshi kyōiku kenkyūjo, *Meiji no joshi kyōiku* (Kokudosha, 1967), 200-1; Kokuritsu kyōiku kenkyūjo, *Hyakunenshi* 4: 854, 1085.

57. Kakurentaiku kannai minjō fūzoku shisōkai no genjō, V, Fukuchiyama (ms).

58. In 1908-10 it cost approximately 10 yen a month to attend middle school and board in town. At that time elementary schoolteachers earned an average of 15 yen 85 sen a month; laborers and shopkeepers, 10-15 yen; and new graduates of a first-ranked vocational high school, 30 yen. Thus, even schoolteachers and middle-rank bureaucrats could not afford these fees, much less the small farmer or tenant. *Hyakunenshi* 4:1082-84. Also, Fukaya, *Gakurekishugi*, 342-49.

59. Kusumoto Tōkichi, *Mura no kurashi: aru kosakunin no nikki* (Ocha-nomizu shobō, 1977), 304.

60. "Naramaru-ku zushi," Soeda, *Enka no Meiji Taishōshi*, 158; *Danshi kyōiku shusse sugoroku*, 1906.

61. "Gakusei no shisō fūki torishimari kunrei," Kyōikushi hensankai, *Hattatsushi* 5:7-8. For debates on this directive, which aroused more controversy among educators and in the press than the extension of compulsory education: *Kyōiku jiron*, nos. 763-65 (June-July 1906).

62. The eighth of the numbered public higher schools was established in 1908; Tōhoku and Kyūshū Imperial Universities in 1907 and 1910. *Hyaku-nenshi* 4:1198-1204, 1254.

63. E.g., "Enseikan to jisatsu," *Taiyō* 12, no. 8 (June 1906): 31-32; "Ensei to hanmon no kyūji," *Shinkōron* (July-Aug. 1906); also, Oka Yoshitake, "Nichiro sensōgo ni okeru atarashii sedai no seichō," *Shisō*, nos. 512-13 (Feb.-Mar. 1967): 1-13, 89-104; Kinmonth, *The Self-Made Man*, 206-40; Donald T. Roden, *Schooldays in Imperial Japan: A Study in the Culture of a Student Elite* (Berkeley: University of California Press, 1980), 165-73.

64. *Jiji shinpō*, quoted in *Kyōiku jiron*, no. 763 (25 June 1906): 33.

65. Rural youth and novels: Yamamoto Takinosuke, "Inaka seinen" (1896), *Yamamoto Takinosuke zenshū*, 350; *Tōkyō asahi shinbun*, 26 Feb. 1898. Novels and naturalism: *Gifu nichi nichi shinbun*, 4 May 1912. Criticism of newspapers: "Kono shakai ni shite kono seinen ari," *Kyōiku jiron*, no. 764 (5 July 1906): 1-2. The "hanging pine" analogy is here attributed to Professor Motora (Yūjirō?).

66. "Kasho igai no yomimono," *Miyako shinbun*, 5 Apr. 1912.

67. *Yomiuri shinbun*, quoted in *Kyōiku jiron*, no. 763 (25 June 1906): 33.

68. Komatsubara as *kunrei daijin*: *Tōkyō nichi nichi shinbun*, 23 Apr. 1911. Komatsubara on reading, libraries, social education: *Komatsubara Bunshō kyōikuron* (1911), 1-15, 233-46, 259-66; *Komatsubara Eitarō-kun jiryaku* (Kinoshita Ken, 1924), 114-15. Also, on social education: Kurauchi Shirō, *Meiji makki shakai kyōikukan no kenkyū: tsūzoku kyōiku chōsa iinkai seiritsuki* (Kōdansha, 1961), 11-26.

69. E.g., Naimushō, *Chihō kairyō jiseki* (Shinshinsha, 1910), passim; To-yama-ken kyōikukai, *Seinendan shidō chōsa hōkoku* (Toyama, 1918), 1-25; Chiba-ken tsūzoku kunkai bunko tosho mokuroku (Chiba: 1908) (ms); Miyamoto Muraji, *Chōhei tekireisha kokoroe* [P] (Tokyo, 1905); Monbushō futsū gakumukyoku, *Zenkoku seinendan no jissai* (Monbushō, 1921), 8-11. Kumagai Tatsujirō, ed., *Seinen yomimono ni kansuru chōsa* (DaiNihon rengō seinendan chōsa, 1928), 5-47. Also, Ono Noriaki, *Nihon toshokan shi* (Genbunsha, 1970), 255-56; Kanagawa-ken toshokan kyōkai, *Kanagawa-ken toshokan shi* (Kanagawa kenritsu toshokan, 1966), 28-36.

70. Uchikawa Yoshimi, "Shinbunshihō no seitei katei to sono tokushitsu—Meiji kōki ni okeru genron jiyū henshitsu no ichi sokumen," *Tōkyō daigaku shinbun kenkyū kiyō*, no. 5 (1956): 88; *Shinbun sōran* (Nihon denpō tsūshinsha, 1911), 537. The seven largest dailies (*Kokumin, Hōchi, Yorozu chōhō, Tōkyō asahi, Ōsaka asahi, Ōsaka mainichi*, and *Yamato*): Yamamoto

Taketoshi, *Kindai Nihon no shinbun dokushasō* (Hōsei daigaku shuppankyoku, 1981) 410-12.

71. "Shinbun sōmakuri," *Chūō kōron* 29, no. 1 (Jan. 1914): 36-37.

72. Popularity of pocketbooks: "Pocket Analects, pocket Mencius, pocket history, pocket this and pocket that. How is it that a great people *(taikokumin)* is so fond of pocket-size?" *(Nihon oyobi Nihonjin,* Mar. 1910) cited in Asakura and Inamura, *Meiji sesō hennen jiten,* 558. On the Pocket Analects: Mori Senzō, *Meiji Tōkyō itsubunshi,* vol. 2 (Heibonsha, 1969), 349. On Tachikawa bunko, which began in 1911 and published 196 titles by 1923, including *Mito Kōmon* and *Sarutobi Sasuke*: a fictionalized account by Ikeda Ranko, *Onna mon* (Kawade shobō, 1960).

73. *Shōnen sekai, Jogaku sekai, Chūgaku sekai, Nōgyō sekai,* etc. In 1911, Hakubunkan published 20 periodicals each month and 78 book titles a year. The special supplements *(rinji zōkan)* of *Taiyō,* which had thematic titles, were particularly well circulated. "Hakubunkan tokubetsu tenrankai ni tsuite," *Taiyō* 17, no. 10 (July 1911), 230-32; also, *Hakubunkan gojūnenshi* (Hakubunkan, 1936).

74. E.g., *Nanshin zasshi* (Nagano), no. 10 (Oct. 1908); "Konnichi no toshokan," *Gifu nichi nichi shinbun,* 4 May 1912; Kakurentaiku kannai minjō fūzoku shisōkai no genjō, II, Takada (ms); Aichi kyōikukai, *Sengo shakai kyōiku ni kansuru chōsa* (1906), 25, 229, and passim. *Nikudan* by Sakurai Tadayoshi: *The Human Bullet,* trans. Masujirō Honda (Boston: Houghton Mifflin, 1907).

75. Haga and Shimoda, *Nihon katei hyakka jii* (1906), 741-67. For its publishing history: *Fuzanbō* (Fuzanbō, 1932), 75-80. Another popular one-volume encyclopedia of the time: *Kokumin hyakka jiten* (Fuzanbō, 1908).

76. *Kyōiku jiron* (15 Mar. 1907): 35.

77. Yamamoto Taketoshi, "Meiji kōki no riterashii chōsa," *Hitotsubashi ronsō* 61, no. 3 (Mar. 1969): 345-55. Also, Yamamoto, *Kindai Nihon no shinbun dokushasō,* 164-81. Recruit literacy rose at the rate of elementary school enrollments of 10 to 14 years earlier, which meant that the effect of nearly universal enrollment would not be felt until after 1915.

78. Watanabe Kazuo, *Jitsuroku gōgai sensen* (Shinbun jidaisha, 1963).

79. Newspapers as *shōbai no taiteki*: *Hōchi shinbun* (28 Nov. 1897); learning to read: *Shōgyō sekai* (15 Apr. 1901); cited in Yamamoto, *Kindai Nihon no shinbun dokushasō,* 187. The rise in literacy by self-education on the job and postcards to the editor: *ibid.,* 168-69, 359-64.

80. Namekawa Michio, *Nihon sakubun tsuzurikata kyōikushi I* (Kokudosha, 1977), 171, 282-86.

81. An informal survey in the regimental district of Takada in 1913 showed that 20 newspapers were sold locally. The top four sellers were local papers, the fifth and sixth from Tokyo (*Kokumin* and *Tōkyō asahi*). The best-selling local papers were listed as having "readers in every class"; the Tokyo papers, "middle class and above." Kakurentaiku kannai minjō fūzoku shisōkai no genjō, II, Takada (ms). Also on rural and urban newspaper readers, Yamamoto, *Shinbun to minshū; Kindai Nihon no dokushasō.*

82. *Shimin byōdō* and the Ebisu beer hall: *Chūō shinbun*, 4 Sept. 1889; also, *Tōkyō asahi shinbun*, 9 Sept. 1889. Newspapers: "Shinbun dokusha no hensen," *Chūō kōron* (May 1900): 85-86. Also, "Shinbunshi no tachiba," *Daifukuchō*, no. 27 (Mar. 1906): 1-4.

83. 28 subscriptions, mostly to the low-cost *Niroku shinbun*, were recorded in a tenement with 27 households and 150 people. Yamamoto, *Kindai Nihon no dokushasō*, 193.

84. Nishichikuma-gun Ōkuwa jinjō kōtō shōgakkō (Nagano), "Gakudō shinbun," *Shinano kyōiku*, no. 255 (Nov. 1908); *Nagano-ken kyōikushi* 12:591-92.

85. Fear of socialism: e.g., *Tōkyō nichi nichi shinbun*, 4 June 1889, 20 Nov. 1890; Hozumi Yatsuka, "Minpō oyobi kokumin keizai," *Tōkyō nichi nichi shinbun*, 17-18 Nov. 1891. Labor as social problem: *Yomiuri shinbun*, 1 Aug. 1891. Strikes as *yakubyō*: *Ōsaka asahi shinbun*, 19 Apr. 1897, etc. Socialism and *bunmei no shinpo*: *Tōkyō nichi nichi shinbun*, 27 Aug. 1908, etc.

86. See Pyle, "Advantages of Followership," esp. 148-60; Hirata Tōsuke on "calamity," ibid., 156.

87. Chian keisatsuhō (1900): Nakamura Kichisaburō, *Meiji hōseishi* 1:216.

88. Letter to Yamagata (2 Sept. 1906) in Tokutomi Ichirō, *Katsura Tarō den*, vol. 2 (Katsura Kōshaku kinen jigyōkai, 1917), 296; also in Okamoto, *The Japanese Oligarchy*, 185. Hibiya riots: ibid., 197-223.

89. *Miyako shinbun*, 31 Oct. 1914; *Yorozu chōhō*, 2 Feb. 1913.

90. "Sutoraiki sawagi no ryūkōnen," *Jitsugyō no Yokohama* 3, no. 12, cited in Yamada, *Keihin toshi mondai*, 14.

91. Figures vary; here factory workers are defined more narrowly than laborers (*rōdōsha*) in general, for which the numbers are higher (see Ch. 2, p. 32). Kazuo Okochi, Bernard Karsh, and Solomon Levine, *Workers and Employers in Japan* (Tokyo: University of Tokyo Press, 1973), 40; Miyachi, *Nichiro sengo seijishi*, 168-89. In the late Meiji division of the urban poor among *saimin*, those workers and laborers who could just manage, *hinmin*, those who could not, and *kyūmin*, the unemployed and the destitute, a Tokyo municipal survey set the *hinmin* monthly income at 20 yen in 1911. In effect, the day laborers comprised much of the *hinmin* poor, and the regular factory workers hovered close to their level. Miyachi, 201-08.

92. Factory law: Oka Minoru, *Kōjōhōron* (Yūhikaku, 1913), 2-101; Ronald P. Dore, "The Modernizer as a Special Case: Japanese Factory Legislation, 1892-1911," *Comparative Studies in Society and History* 11 (1969): 433-50.

93. E.g., *San'yō shinpō*, 30 June 1908; *Tōkyō nichi nichi shinbun*, 23 June-27 Aug. 1908, *passim*.

94. Yamagata Aritomo, "Shakaihakaishugiron," *Yamagata Aritomo ikensho*, 315-16. Also, Tokutomi, *Yamagata Aritomo den* 3:764-67. For accounts of *tenchōsetsu jiken* (also known as the Open Letter Incident of Nov. 1907), *akahata jiken* (June 1908), and the *taigyaku jiken* trial (Dec. 1910-Jan. 1911): Itoya Toshio, *Zōho kaitei taigyaku jiken* (San'ichi shobō, 1970), 51-92, 125-95; more briefly, Itoya, *Nihon shakaishugi undō shisōshi* (Hōsei daigaku shuppan kyoku, 1979), 178-95; also, Notehelfer, *Kōtoku Shūsui*, 145-61, 187.

95. "Shakaihakaishugiron," *Yamagata Aritomo ikensho*, 319.

96. Social relief policy: Yoshida, *Nihon shakai jigyō no rekishi*, 171-240. "Pneumonia": *Kokumin to hikokumin* (Min'yūsha, 1911), 9.

97. Haga Yaichi, *Kokuminsei jūron* (Fuzanbō, 1908), 257.

98. Raymond Williams, *The Country and the City* (Oxford: Oxford University Press, 1973), 1-12.

99. Ogyū Sorai, *Seidan* (1727). J. R. McEwan, *The Political Writings of Ogyū Sorai* (Cambridge: Cambridge University Press, 1962), 50-51.

100. "Tohi kyōiku no rigai," *Nihonjin*, no. 53 (Aug. 1890): 24-27; "Toshi no bōchō o nan to miru beki," *Nihonjin* 3, no. 455 (15 Mar. 1907): 9-11; Kobayashi Ichirō, "Tokai no bōchō," *Rinri kōenshū*, no. 58 (1907): 1-15; Machida Kyōu, "Busshitsuteki bunmei no yokei," *Sen'yū*, no. 26 (1 Dec. 1912); Sawayanagi Masatarō, "Tokai to chihō," *Fukyōkai* (Nov. 1915), *Sawayanagi Masatarō zenshū* 5:444-52, etc.

101. Tokutomi Ichirō (Sohō), "Inaka to tokai," *Seikatsu to shosei* (Min'yūsha, 1900), 67-68.

102. Soda Osamu, *Maeda Masana* (Yoshikawa kōbunkan, 1973), 134-50; Soda, *Chihō sangyō no shisō to undō*, 132-73. Also, on oligarchic infighting in the late 80s: Mikuriya, *Meiji kokka keisei to chihō keiei*, 231-43. Agrarian thought in this period: Havens, *Farm and Nation*, 56-132.

103. Yamazaki Enkichi, *Chihō jichi kōshū nikki* [P] (Shimane: 1912), 8-9, 56-58; "Nōson kyōikuron" (1914), *Yamazaki Enkichi zenshū* 3:24-25; "Nōmin no kunren" (1916) 3:459-66, 477-84.

104. Yokoi Tokiyoshi, "Hōmon-dōtoku to keizai," *Jindō* 3, no. 9 (15 Jan. 1906): 3-4; also, "Nōgyō kyōikuron" (1901), *Yokoi Hakase zenshū* (1925) 9:88-90, paraphrased in Havens, *Farm and Nation*, 103-04; Yamazaki later wrote in a similar vein, e.g., "Nōmindō" (1930), *Yamazaki Enkichi zenshū* 5:1-90.

105. Yokoi Tokiyoshi, "Tokai to inaka," *Yokoi Hakase zenshū* (1925) 5:544.

106. "Nōhonshugi" (1897), *Yokoi Hakase zenshū* (1925) 8:225-231; also, Havens, *Farm and Nation*, 100-01.

107. Yanagita's *Jidai to nōsei* on agricultural administration (*Yanagita Kunio shū*, vol. 16 [Chikuma shobō, 1962], 1-160) and his *Tōno monogatari* (ibid. 4:5-54), the well-known collection of legends that marked the beginning of his folkloric interests, were both published in 1910. Translation of the latter by Ronald Morse, *The Legends of Tōno* (Tokyo: The Japan Foundation, 1975). Also on Yanagita: Morse, "The Search for Japan's National Character and Distinctiveness: Yanagita Kunio (1875-1962) and the Folklore Movement" (Ph.D. diss., Princeton University, 1974). Morse's study in Japanese: *Kindaika e no chōsen: Yanagita Kunio no isan* (Nihon hōsō shuppankai, 1977). For Nitobe Inazō: *Nōgyō honron* (1912), *Nitobe Inazō zenshū*, ed. Nitobe Inazō zenshū henshū iinkai, vol. 2 (Kyōbunkan, 1969), 5-540; "Jikata no kenkyū," *Shimin* 2, no. 2 (May 1908); also, "Jikata no kenkyū," *Tōkyō asahi shinbun*, 16-24 Feb. 1907.

108. E.g., Tanaka Giichi, "Chihō to guntai to no kankei," and "Chihō to guntai to no kankei ni tsuite" (speeches to Tokyo officers, Apr., May 1911,

and to local officials, Aug. 1911), *Kaikōsha kiji*, nos. 427, 432 (Apr., Sept. 1911): 1-17, 1-34; also, Kakurentaiku kannai minjō fūzoku shisōkai no genjō, II, Takada, Hirosaki; III, Azabu; V, Tottori, Fukuchiyama; VII, Kurume; etc. (ms).

109. E.g., "Seinen no tairyoku to zaigō gunjin," *Tanaka Chūjō kōenshū* (Fuji shoin, 1916), 208-15; Kakurentaiku kannai minjō fūzoku shisōkai no genjō (ms), passim.

110. Kakurentaiku kannai minjō fūzoku shisōkai no genjō, III, Azabu. "Unabashed," "calmly," "coolly," etc. are quoted from the reports.

111. Tanaka Giichi, "Guntai to chihō to no kankei," *Sen'yū*, no. 7 (1 May 1911): 9-14, and above, note 106; Tanaka, "Guntai kyōiku shikan" (1911), *Tanaka Chūjō kōenshū* (1916), 58-113.

112. E.g., Tanaka, "Zaigō gunjin no kokoroe" (1912), ibid., 114-22; "Kokumin to zaigō gunjinkai," 123-27. Reservists associations and Tanaka's role in the *seinendan*: Smethurst, *A Social Basis for Prewar Japanese Militarism*, 6-33.

113. *Zenkoku minji kanrei ruishū* (Shihōshō, 1880), 258.

114. "Hōritsu komon," *Shinano mainichi shinbun*, 1 Oct. 1912.

115. Hōten chōsakai minpō giji sokkiroku, Box 124-130 (vols. 42-43), Faculty of Law, Tokyo University (ms). On the debates: Hirano Yoshitarō, *Nihon shihonshugi shakai to hōritsu* (Hōsei daigaku shuppankai, 1971), 79-102.

116. Yanagita Kunio, *Kokyō shichijūnen* (Asahi shinbunsha, 1974), 119-20; also *Yanagita Kunio shū*, supp. 3:3-99. Samurai customs as legal model: Kawashima Takeyoshi, *Ideorogii to shite no kazoku seido* (Iwanami shoten, 1957), 1-125.

117. E.g., Oka, *Yamagata Aritomo*, 35-37; Kuga Katsunan, *Nihon*, 2-3 Jan. 1892, cited in Pyle, *The New Generation*, 124; Inoue Tetsujirō, *Kyōiku to shūyō* (1910), 36-39.

118. Tokutomi Roka's *Shizen to jinsei* (1900) was particularly popular, appearing in 200 printings by the 20s: *Higuchi Ichiyō, Tokutomi Roka, Kunikida Doppo, Meiji no bungaku* (Chūō kōronsha, 1968), 546-47.

119. Tayama's criticism of Yanagita: Morse, "The Search for Japan's National Character," 27. *Furusato* (1899) and *No no hana* (1901), *Tayama Katai zenshū* 14:3-117, 185-305; *Inaka kyōshi* (1904), ibid. 2:313-595. Tayama also wrote literary accounts of his country travels that appeared in periodicals and, like Roka's, were well received. *Meiji bungaku zenshū* 67:383-87.

120. Ishikawa Takuboku, "Hyakkai tsūshin," *Iwate nippō* (11 Oct. 1909), *Takuboku zenshū* 4: 182.

121. "Keian no furegaki" (1649), in George B. Sansom, *Japan: A Short Cultural History* (New York: Appleton-Century-Crofts, Inc., 1962), 465; Inoue Kangai, "Nōmin no shinnenryoku o ronzu," *Shinano mainichi shinbun*, 11 Nov. 1912.

122. Inoue Kamegorō, *Nōmin no shakai kyōiku* (Kinkyōdō, 1902), 1-21; Aichi kyōikukai, *Sengo shakai kyōiku ni kansuru chōsa* (1906), 16.

123. Ichiki Kitokurō, "Shimin sonsei no kaisei to shakai kyōiku," speech in Fukuoka-ken (May 1911), *Shimin* 6, no. 3 (June 1911): 4-6.

124. Watanabe Takayoshi, "Kyūhei isshin," in "Meiji jibutsu kigen jiten,"

Kaishaku to kanshō, Rinji zōkan (Jan. 1968): 33; Ono, *Meiji wadai jiten*, 2-10, 180-84.

125. A compendium of "high-collar" fashions: Uchiyama Sōjūrō, *Meiji haikara monogatari* (Jinbutsu ōraisha, 1968), esp. 10-48. Typical criticisms of extravagant customs: Kakurentaiku kannai minjō fūzoku shisōkai no genjō, V, Iwakuni, Yamaguchi, Okayama, Fukuchiyama; VI, Matsuyama (ms); Machida Kyōu, "Busshitsuteki bunmei no yokei," *Sen'yū*, no. 26 (1 Dec. 1912): 5-8. Representative later criticism of such customs in the villages: Yokoi Tokiyoshi, "Tsūzoku nōson kairyōan," *Yokoi Hakase zenshū* (1925)7:60-78.

126. E.g., Inoue Tomoichi, "Jichi no kaihatsu kunren," *Inoue Hakase to chihō jichi* (Zenkoku chōson chōkai, 1940), 419-31; Naimushō, *Chihō kairyō jiseki* (1910), 310-24; Naimushō chihōkyoku, *Kanka kyūsai jigyō kōenshū*, vol. 2 (Naimushō, 1909), 931-1015. Representative examples of custom reform in a Home Ministry "model village": *Miyagi-ken Natori-gun Oide-mura sonze chōsasho* (1902); also, *Shizuoka-ken Haibara-gun Katsumata-mura sonze chōsa* (Katsumata-mura nōkai, 1903).

127. *Hyōgo-ken Iibo-gunze narabi ni chōsonze* (Himeji: 1908), 103-5.

128. Naimushō chihōkyoku, *Chihō kairyō jitsurei* (1912), 73-83. Yokoyama Masao, *Chōsonze chōsa kōyō* (Morioka: Iwate-ken naimubu shomuka, 1909), 30-32; Noda Sentarō, *Shichōsonze* (Shichōson zasshisha, 1903), 42-44; Kakurentaiku kannai minjō fūzoku shisōkai no genjō, III, Sakura; IV, Wakayama; VI, Tokushima (ms).

129. "Iho-mura fūzoku kyōsei kitei," in Fuwa, "Nichiro sengo ni okeru nōson shinkō to nōmin kyōka, I," 162.

130. Kakurentaiku kannai minjō fūzoku shisōkai no genjō, III, Sakura (ms).

131. On Nagai Kafū: Edward G. Seidensticker, *Kafū the Scribbler* (Stanford: Stanford University Press, 1965), 32-52. Kōda Rohan, "Ikkoku no shuto," *Kōda Rohan zenshū* 27:8.

132. On the cultural meaning of modern Tokyo: Isoda Kōichi, *Shisō to shite no Tōkyō: kindai bungaku shiron nōto* (Kokubunsha, 1978).

133. Yamamoto Tsuneo, *Kindai Nihon toshi kyōkashi kenkyū* (Reimei shobō, 1972). Also, below, pp. 201-202.

134. Katō, *Shakai kyōiku: tsūzoku kōwa* (1918): "Edo to Tōkyō," 293-94; "Aishishin no ketsubō," 299-300; "Nihon no shuto to shite," 301-2. Also, Takashima Heizaburō, "Kyōfū ni tsuite," *Tōkyō-shi kyōikukai zasshi*, no. 31 (Apr. 1907): 1-4.

135. Katō, "Kokutai no seika," 215-17, part of "Bushiteki seishin," *Shakai kyōiku* (1918), 215-35; also, Katō, "Shinbushidō" (lecture in Honjo, 15 June), *Tōkyō-shi kyōikukai zasshi* (Aug. 1912): 27-30.

136. Home Ministry circular to Mie prefectural governor (Oct. 1908), cited in Friedell, *Japanese Shrine Mergers*, 57.

137. "Sosenkyō wa kōhō no minamoto nari" (1892), *Hozumi Yatsuka Hakase ronbunshū*, ed. Hozumi Shigetaka (Yūhikaku, 1943), 256-66. Similarily, in popular form: Hozumi, *Kokumin dōtoku: aikokushin* (1897). Also, Minear, *Japanese Tradition and Western Law*, 71-76; and Hirai Atsuko, "Ancestor Wor-

ship in Yatsuka Hozumi's State and Constitutional Theory," in *Japan's Modern Century*, ed. Edward Skrzypczak (Tokyo: Sophia University Press, 1968), 41-50.

138. Ukita Kazutami, "Shōrai no Nihon ni kansuru sandai gimon," *Taiyō* 14, no. 1 (Jan. 1908): 36-41; Yanagita Kunio, *Jidai to nōsei, Yanagita Kunio shū* 16:44; Fukasaku Yasufumi, *Kokumin dōtoku yōgi* (Kōdōkan, 1916), Ch. 4. On Nogi and ancestor worship: Gakushūin, *Nogi Inchō kinenroku* (Sankōdō, 1914), 544-55. In the press, e.g., on Japanese ancestor worship as inferior to the West because Westerners hang ancestral portraits and Japanese only offer food before ancestral tablets: "Shintō to sosen sūhai," *Chōshū nichi nichi shinbun*, 16-18 July 1912. A contemporary account written in English in 1899 by the legal scholar Hozumi Nobushige, whose views differed from those of his brother, Yatsuka: *Ancestor Worship and Japanese Law* (Tokyo: Maruzen, 1912). Also, Morioka Kiyomi, "The Appearance of 'Ancestor Religion' in Modern Japan: The Years of Transition from the Meiji to the Taishō Periods," *Japanese Journal of Religious Studies* 4, nos. 2-3 (June-Sept. 1977), 183-212.

139. A seminal article on family-state ideology: Ishida Takeshi, "Kazoku kokkakan no kōzō to kinō," *Meiji seiji shisōshi kenkyū*, 1-216. On changes in Meiji views of the family: Arichi Tōru, *Kindai Nihon no kazokukan—Meijihen* (Kōbundō, 1977); also, Aoyama Michio et al., *Kazokukan no keifu, Kōza kazoku*, vol. 8 (Kōbundō, 1974), 28-118; Kawashima, *Ideorogii to shite no kazoku seido*, 1-191.

140. For Kawaji: Hironaka Toshio, *Sengo Nihon no keisatsu* (Iwanami shoten, 1968), 5. For Maeda: Soda, *Chihō sangyō no shisō to undō*, 148-50. For the scholars: Ishida, *Meiji seiji shisōshi kenkyū*, 67-138; Arichi, *Kindai Nihon no kazokukan*, 108-20, 233-40.

141. Kawada Shirō, "Kazokuseido no hakai ga shakai seikatsu ni oyobosu eikyō," *Kyōto hōgakkai zasshi* 6, no. 2 (1911): 110; Arichi, *Kindai Nihon no kazokukan*, 323.

142. Address to prefectural governors, *Tōkyō asahi shinbun*, 23 Apr. 1910.

143. "Iede no hitobito," *Tōkyō asahi shinbun*, 21-31 Oct. 1910; Arichi, *Kindai Nihon no kazokukan*, 164.

144. "Backbone owner-farmers" and changes in proportion of owner-farmers: Havens, *Farm and Nation*, 67, 34.

145. "Nōson kakumeiron," *Tōkyō asahi shinbun*, 2 June 1914; Arichi, *Kindai Nihon no kazokukan*, 304-05. For similar concern for *jisakunō* on the local level: *Ehime-ken Unsen-gun Yoto sonze chōsa shiryō* (1903).

146. For *iegoroshi*: *Jidai to nōsei* (1910), *Yanagita Kunio shū* 16:38-39. Also, Irokawa, *Meiji no bunka*, 309-11.

147. Arichi, *Kindai Nihon no kazokukan*, 309-12.

148. "Katei no kokoroe" (1904), *Nagano-ken kyōikushi* 12:370. Other examples of *katei kyōiku*: Aichi kyōikukai, *Sengo shakai kyōiku ni kansuru chōsa* (1906), 13-15; "Tsūzoku kyōiku to chūtō shakai," *Tsūzoku kyōiku*, no. 23 (Jan. 1913): 13-15; Yamazaki Enkichi, "Nōson kyōikuron" (1914), *Yamazaki Enkichi zenshū* 3:84-90.

149. Ōkubo Masunobu, "Zaiei kashisotsu no katei to guntai to no renraku

ni tsuite mottomo ryōkō naru hōhō o ronzu," *Kaikōsha kiji*, no. 445 (July 1912): 1-9. Also, "Guntai to katei," *Gifu nichi nichi shinbun*, 3 May 1912; Kakurentaiku kannai minjō fūzoku shisōkai no genjō, II, Hirosaki (ms). Inoue Tomoichi made the same point about family education in regard to agricultural reform, "since it is bad form in a farm family [to undertake such change] without the agreement of the wife": "Jichi no kaibatsu kunren," *Inoue Hakase to chihō jichi*, 408.

150. Koyama Masatake, "Katei to keishin kannen to no kankei," *Nihonjin*, no. 446 (5 Nov. 1906): 14.

151. Arichi, *Kindai Nihon no kazokukan*, 120, 205-06.

152. *Sangyō kumiai* and *nōkai*: Havens, *Farm and Nation*, 72-84.

153. E.g., Tomeoka Kōsuke, "Jidai no shin'un to hōtokusha no taido," *Shimin* 6, no. 12 (Mar. 1912): 85-88. A collection of articles on Sontoku by leading ideologues of the day, Kiyoura Keigo, Okada Ryōhei, Yokoi Toki-yoshi, Inoue Tetsujirō, Ukita Kazutami, Tokutomi Sohō, Yamaji Aizan, Inoue Tomoichi, and others, including Shimada Saburō, Kōda Rohan, and Uchimura Kanzō: Tomeoka Kōsuke, ed., *Ninomiya-ō to shoka* (1906), which was a reprint of Tomeoka's Hōtoku magazine, *Jindō*, no. 8 (Dec. 1905). According to an advertisement for the book, this special issue commemorating the fiftieth anniversary of Sontoku's death had sold 20,000 copies in a month. *Jindō*, no. 13 (May 1906).

154. Emori Itsuo, "Meijiki no hōtokusha undō no shiteki hatten," *Nihon sonraku shakai no kōzō* (Kōbundō, 1976), 399-462; Sasaki Ryūji, "Hōtokusha undō no kaikyūteki seikaku," *Shizuoka daigaku hōkei kenkyū* 17, no. 3 (Dec. 1968): 31-69; 18, no. 1 (Jan. 1969): 31-60; Ogawa Nobuo, "Meiji kōki ikō ni okeru sonraku hōtokusha no tenkai," *Chihōshi kenkyū* 24, no. 2 (Apr. 1974): 22-36; Havens, *Farm and Nation*, 41-49.

155. Emori, "Meijiki no hōtokusha undō," 440-50.

156. "Shimin kōenkai" (Feb. 1908), *Shimin* 3, no. 1 (Apr. 1908): 84. Brief reports of lecture meetings: *Shimin*, "Iho" (Bulletins), vols. 2-4 (Apr. 1907-Jan. 1910).

157. Nakagawa Nozomu, "Nōson kairyōka to shite no Rōzubueruto," *Shimin* 6, no. 10 (Jan. 1912): 37-40. Egg savings: 3, no. 1 (Apr. 1908), 79.

158. Hayakawa, later managing director of Mitsui Bank and eminent supporter of Hōtokukai activities after the Russo-Japanese War, here writing as a university student: *Kyūchōkan dōsōkai zasshi*, no. 9 (1890): 15-16.

159. Karasawa, *Kyōkasho no rekishi*, 672-87.

160. The *Hōtokukai* (Hōtoku associations), like the *Shiminkai*, were often founded with official encouragement after the Russo-Japanese War; the *Hōtokusha* (Hōtoku societies) usually dated from the earlier period. Emori, "Meijiki no hōtokusha undō," 460-62.

161. Yamazaki Enkichi, *Chihō jichi kōshū hikki* [P] (Shimane-ken, Daito-chō: 1912), 1.

162. Tomeoka Kōsuke, *Chihō kairyō kōen sokki* [P] (Okayama, 1912), 1.

163. Kikegawa, *Jichi gojūnenshi seidohen*; Staubitz, "The Establishment of the System of Local Self-Government (1888-1890) in Meiji Japan."

164. "Chihō chōka ni taisuru kunji" (13 Feb. 1890), Chihōkan kaigi gi-ketsusho narabi hikki (ms); also, Staubitz, 150.

165. "Chihō jichi iken," Inoue Kowashi den 2:28.

166. Ōshima Mitsuko, "Chihō zaisei to chihō kairyō undō," in Meiji Taishō kyōdoshi kenkyūhō, ed. Furushima, 50-92.

167. Inoue Tomoichi, "Jichi no kaihatsu kunren," Inoue Hakase to chihō jichi, 21, 16-32; Jichi yōgi (Hakubunkan, 1909), 21-22.

168. Ibid., 83-280.

169. E.g., Cleveland, Lombardy, garden cities: Inoue, Jichi yōgi (1909), passim. Garden cities, Chicago, and others: Naimushō, Chihō kairyō jiseki (1910), 240-52; Ikeda Jōtarō, Mohan chōson no genkyō (Yomiuri shinbunsha, 1911), 30-37.

170. Inoue Tomoichi, Inoue Hakase to chihō jichi, 19. The rhetoric is stand-ard: e.g., Naimushō, Senji kinen jigyō to jichi keiei [P] (Seitō shobō, 1906), 1.

171. Tokonami Takejirō, Chihō jichi oyobi shinkōsaku (Jitsugyō no Nihon-sha, 1912), 12-13.

172. Ibid., 1-3.

173. Ibid., 5, 7.

174. Hirata Takeji, "Mohan chōson to furyō chōson," Shimin 3, no. 1 (Apr. 1908): 42-46; also, "Seiseki furyō naru chōson gyōsei seirei suru ki" (Fukushima: 1908), in Fuwa, "Nichiro sengo ni okeru nōson," 17.

175. "Nōson kyōikuron" (1914), Yamazaki Enkichi zenshū 3:124.

176. For Yanagita: Hashikawa Bunzō, Yanagita Kunio: sono ningen to shisō (Kōdansha, 1977), 104-05. Yokoi Tokiyoshi on shrine and village mergers: "Nōson kaizōron," Yokoi Hakase zenshū (1925)4:147-82. On model villages: "Nōson no kairyō," ibid. 4:305; also, "Mohan nōson to naru nakare," 7:90-96.

177. Yamazaki Enkichi, "Nōson kensetsu" (1927), Yamazaki Enkichi zen-shū 2.

178. Nōson jichi no kenkyū (1908), Yamazaki Enkichi zenshū 1:13.

179. Speeches at the first Chihō kairyō jigyō kōshūkai held in July 1909: Naimushō, Chihō kairyō jigyō kōenshū, 2 vols. (Hakubunkan, 1909). On the Local Improvement Movement: Miyachi Masato, "Chihō kairyō undō no ronri to tenkai: Nichiro sengo no kokka to 'kyōdōtai'," Nichiro sengo seijishi no kenkyū, 1-127; also, Kenneth B. Pyle, "The Technology of Japanese Na-tionalism: The Local Improvement Movement, 1900-1918," Journal of Asian Studies 33, no. 1 (Nov. 1973): 51-66.

180. Mohan senshō: Okayama-ken Kawakami-gun Uji-mura chiseki (Okayama: 1911). On model villages: Endō Shunroku, "Mohanson no seiritsu to kōzō," Nihonshi kenkyū, no. 185 (Jan. 1978): 33-60.

181. Toyama-ken Imizu-gun Yokota sonze chōsasho (1911). Other examples of local organizations: Naimushō chihōkyoku, Chihō kairyō jitsurei (1912), 160-252.

182. Ikeda, Mohan chōson no genkyō (1911), 1-37. Fishing boats: Naimushō chihōkyoku, Mohanteki chōsonji (Naimushō, 1903), 19-20. Shōtoku Taishi kō: Ikeda Gengo, Boshin shōsho to chihō jiseki (Sapporo: Ikeda shoten, 1911), 112.

183. For *hankan hanmin*: Ishida, *Meiji seiji shisōshi kenkyū*, 180-202.

184. *Yamamoto Takinosuke zenshū*, 1-93. Yamamoto and the *seinendan*: Kumagai Tatsujirō, *DaiNihon seinendan shi* (Nihon seinenkan, 1942).

185. Hirayama Kazuhiko, *Seinen shūdanshi kenkyū josetsu*, vol. 2 (Shinsensha, 1978), 14-15.

186. "Seinen dantai ni kansuru kunrei an," and "Seinen dantai no setchi ni kansuru hyōjun," Terauchi Masatake kankei monjo, Tanaka Giichi, no. 44, Sept. 1915 (ms). Also, Smethurst, *A Social Basis for Prewar Japanese Militarism*, 25-33.

187. E.g., Yamamoto on *ichinichi ichizen*: *Yamamoto Takinosuke zenshū*, 811-30, 1152-66, and passim; Tanaka Giichi, "Seinen to zaigō gunjinkai" (1915), and "Seinendan no igi" (1915), in *Tanaka Chūjō kōenshū*, 197-207, 250-64.

188. E.g., Hamanaka Nisaburō, ed., *Chihō jichi seinen dantai mohan jiseki* (DaiNihon gokokukai, 1910), Preface.

189. Smethurst, *A Social Basis for Prewar Japanese Militarism*, 33-41, 74-76.

190. On social education: Tsūzoku kyōiku kenkyūkai, *Tsūzoku kyōiku ni kansuru jigyō to sono shisetsu hōhō* (1911); Kurauchi, *Meiji makki shakai kyōikukan no kenkyū*; Kokuritsu kyōiku kenkyūjo, *Hyakunenshi* 7:379-744.

191. Reverence for gods: *Shimin* 6, no. 2 (May 1911) through 7, no. 3 (May 1912): passim. Trash: *Shinano mainichi shinbun*, 1 Oct. 1912. Evening study: Kozuka Saburō, *Yagaku no rekishi: Nihon kindai yakan kyōiku shiron* (Tōyōkan shuppansha, 1964).

192. Itō Keidō, *Shūshoku tebikigusa* [P] (1909), 32.

193. *Tsūzoku kōdankai* and *tsūzoku kōwakai*: Tōkyō-to kyōikukai, *Tōkyō-to kyōikukai rokujūnenshi* (1944), 413-14.

194. *Miyako shinbun*, 17, 23 May 1911.

195. Yamamoto Tsuneo, *Kindai Nihon toshi kyōkashi kenkyū*, 93.

196. Sasagawa Kiyoshi, *Ganzen shōki* (Keibunkan, 1912), 1-2.

197. Yamamoto, *Kindai Nihon toshi kyōkashi kenkyū*, 108.

198. E.g., Yamagata Aritomo, "Shisei chōsonsei gunsei fukensei ni kansuru genrō-in kaigi enzetsu" (Nov. 1888), *Yamagata Aritomo ikensho*, 193; Staubitz, "The Establishment of the System of Local Self-Government," 147-59. On the *Seiyūkai*: Tetsuo Najita, *Hara Kei and the Politics of Compromise, 1905-1915* (Cambridge: Harvard University Press, 1967); and below, pp. 234-36. Also, on local elite: Kanno Tadashi, *Kindai Nihon ni okeru nōmin shihai no shiteki kōzō* (Ochanomizu shobō, 1978), 81-104.

199. *Chōya shinbun*, 20 Feb. 1889; Ishikawa, *Kokkai giin senkyo kokoroe* (1889) [P], 9-10.

200. E.g., rice riots: *Akita sakigake shinpō*, 26 June 1890. Poor children: *San'in shinbun*, 8 May. Schools and Western hall: *Shinano mainichi shinbun*, 9, 12 Apr.

201. *Aizawa nikki* 1:130 and passim.

For a typical group of local "men of influence," see illustration following page 228. These men were responsible in 1911 for conducting the survey and preparing the plan (*ze*) for their village (Toyama-ken Imizu-gun Yokota-mura). The present village mayor, his predecessor, and the head of the credit union were all members of the Hori family, an established landowning family. The Hori house in the picture had a clapboard second story in the Western style, a local badge of wealth and fashion. The personages in the photograph were identified in the side captions according to the varieties of their dress, as follows:

Right—Village Mayor and Chairman of the Committee Hori Yutaka ("furokku kōto" = frockcoat)

Center—Former Village Mayor and Consultant to the Committee Hori Nisaku ("shiruku hatto" = silk hat)

Left—Executive Director of the Credit and Purchasing Union and Committee Member Hirooka Mankurō ("haori hakama" = traditional dress)

Extreme Left—Prefectural Agricultural Association Engineer Nakagawa Shigeharu ("sebiro" = suit)

Next Left—Chairman of the Credit and Cooperative Union and Committee Member Hori Nihei ("gunpuku" = military uniform)

202. See Denda Isao, Gōnō (Kyōikusha, 1978); also, Haga Noboru, "Gōnō to jiriki saisei," Meiji kokka to minshū, 165-256.

203. Akita sakigake shinpō, 4 Nov. 1905; Shinano mainichi shinbun, 10 Sept. 1908.

204. "Kinbara Meizen-ō no seikō ni tsuite," Shimin 1, no. 5 (Aug. 1905): 56-58. One of many biographies of Kinbara: Nakayama Noritomo, Kinbara Meizen: saisei hogo jigyō no senkakusha (Shizuoka: Shizuoka saisei hogo kyōkai, 1966). Similar examples of Meiji local worthies: Inabo chōsa: ichimei, Komeyasu daimyōjin (Hakubunkan, 1918) and Iwadani Kyūjirō seiden (Shimane-ken Anno-gun kyōikukai, 1919).

205. Inoue Tomoichi, Inoue Meifu ikō (1920), 416-18; "Chihō tokushika no utsukushiki jigyō," Shimin 6, no. 4 (July 1911): 14-19.

206. E.g., "Seinen dantai no setchi ni kansuru hyōjun," Terauchi Masatake kankei monjo (ms); Naimushō, Chihō kairyō jiseki (1910); Ishida Denkichi, Risō no mura (Shōyōdō, 1914), etc.

207. Hirata Tōsuke, speech to prefectural governors, announcing the new Home Ministry awards "to cultivate the foundations of jichi and aid in its advancement" (June 1907), Miyachi, Nichiro sengo seijishi no kenkyū, 32.

208. Tanaka Giichi, "Ōbei shutchō ni saishite, II," Tanaka Chūjō kōenshū (1916), 175-78.

209. Gratuitous advice: Shinano mainichi shinbun, Oct. 1912. Shrine mergers began in 1906, consolidation of common lands from 1909, and new village mergers occurred in 1910. See also Aoki's chronology of rural disputes, Meiji nōmin sōjō no nenjiteki kenkyū; Suzuki, "Nichiro sengo nōson saihen seisaku no tenkai," 15.

210. "Nōmin no genkyō," San'in shinbun, 2 Apr. 1910.

211. Gifu nichi nichi shinbun, 8 May 1912.

212. Yamanashi-ken gikai jimukyoku, Yamanashi-ken gikaishi 3:426-27; Ariizumi, Meiji seijishi no kiso katei, 330-31.

213. E.g., "Sonmin oshiyose," Tōkyō asahi shinbun, 28 Oct. 1903; "San-

byakunin gunga ni oshiyosu," *Gifu nichi nichi shinbun*, 30 Aug. 1908; "Fukai gunga ni oshiyosu," *Gifu nichi nichi shinbun*, 16 May 1906; "Gohyakunin no oshiyoshi," *Tōkyō asahi shinbun*, 24 Sept. 1907. Also, Ōshima Mitsuko, "Chihō zaisei to chihō kairyō undō," in *Meiji Taishō kyōdoshi kenkyūhō*, ed. Furushima, 50-92; Suzuki, "Nichiro sengo nōson saihen seisaku no tenkai," 11-28.

214. Ishida Denkichi, *Jichi sōsho: mohan chōson to yūryō shōgakkō* (1910), 1-3; Kakurentaiku kannai minjō fūzoku shisōkai no genjō, V, Tottori (ms); *Kokumin zasshi* 3, no. 17 (1 Sept. 1912): 23.

215. "Jichisei kaizen," *San'in shinbun*, 9 Jan. 1910.

216. E.g., "Tsukasawa no sonmin taikai," *Kokumin shinbun*, 5 Mar. 1909; "Ōkuma no fuon," *Jiji shinpō*, 7 Sept. 1902; "Oshiyoshi ryūkō," *Tōkyō asahi shinbun*, 30 Mar. 1908, etc.

217. Compare, e.g., speech by *gunchō* in 1894 urging village mayors to "raise attendance rates, hire good teachers, build schools, buy equipment . . . for the sake of your village, for the sake of your honor" (*Ōtsuka Kajima Gunchō chōsonchō ni taisuru enjutsu* [P] Osaka: 1894, 6-7) with 1909 Home Ministry injunctions regarding "local improvement" (Naimushō, *Chihō kairyō jigyō kōenshū* 1:1-166 and passim).

218. Kakurentaiku kannai minjō fūzoku shisōkai no genjō, I, Kushiro; III, Sakura; V, Hiroshima, Okayama (ms). "Odorokubeki mugisaku shinpo no kiin: seinenkai jigyō kōka no ichirei," *Shimin* 6, no. 1 (Apr. 1911): 71, etc.

219. Kakurentaiku kannai minjō fūzoku shisōkai no genjō, II, Takada.

220. Kinmonth, *The Self-Made Man*; also, Maeda Ai, "Meiji risshin shusseshugi no keifu," *Bungaku* 33, no. 4 (Apr. 1965): 10-21; Morishita Kimio, "Meijiki ni okeru risshin shusseshugi no keifu: masukomi no hatashita yakuwari," in Fukuchi Shigetaka Sensei keireki kinen ronbunshū kankō iinkai, *Kindai Nihon keisei katei no kenkyū* (Yūzankaku, 1978), 187-211.

221. Yoshida Noboru, "Meiji jidai no jōkyō yūgaku," in Ishiyama Shuhei, ed., *Kyōiku no shiteki hatten* (1952), 429-442.

222. Koike, "Meiji kōki ni okeru chihō seinen no shisō to kōdō II," 71-72, 88.

223. *Saikin chōsa shūshoku no tebiki* (Seibunsha, 1911), 42.

224. Abe Isoo, "Sanko no kaiketsuan," in "Kyōiku aru yūmin no shochi mondai," *Chūō kōron* (July 1912), 78-83.

225. "Aa, kane no yo," (1907), Komota et al., *Nihon ryūkōkashi*, 26, 227-28. This refrain echoed throughout the late Meiji literature of job-seeking.

226. Takayanagi Junnosuke, *Shōgaku sotsugyō risshin annai* (Ikuei shoin, 1907), 4-5.

227. Examples drawn from *Danjo hikkei: shūshoku annai* (Eirakudō, 1905); Takayanagi, *Shōgaku sotsugyō risshin annai* (1907, 1910); *Saishō shihon: Shin-shokugyō annai* (Tanizaki hanbaibu, 1909); *Shōgaku sotsugyō kugaku seikō shū-shoku tetsuzuki: risshin annai* (Seikōdō, 1910); *Shūshoku no hiketsu: kyūshokusha no fukuin* (Yokohama: 1910); *Shūshoku tebikigusa* (Tōkyō kōbunkan, 1909); *Shokugyō annai zensho* (Tōkyō jitsugyōsha, 1911); *Saikin chōsa shūshoku no tebiki* (Seibunsha, 1911); *Jokō tokuhon* (Jitsugyō kokumin kyōkai, 1911) [P].

228. Lecture: Fujii Kenjirō, "Seizon kyōsō to dōtoku," *Teiyū rinrikai rinri kōenshū* 108 (10 Aug. 1911): 1.

229. *Saikin chōsa shūshoku no tebiki,* 3.

230. *Shōgaku sotsugyō kugaku seikō shūshoku tebiki: risshin annai,* 2-4.

231. From nations to individuals: Fujii, "Seizon kyōsō to dōtoku," 4-8. Momotarō: Torigoe Shin, *Momotarō no unmei* (Nihon hōsō shuppan kyōkai: 1983), 12-48.

232. Oshikawa Shunrō, "Keikai subeki Nihon," *Bōken sekai* (Dec. 1910) in *Meiji daizasshi,* 174.

233. Morality and economics: e.g., Tatebe Tongo, *Boshin shōsho engi* (Dōbunkan, 1908), approved by both Home and Education ministries. Bushidō: e.g., Inoue Tetsujirō, "Bushidō to jitsugyōkai to no shūkyō," *Taiyō* 5, no. 12 (June 1899): 62-65; "Shifū taihai no ichi sen'in," *Shimin* 4, no. 6 (July 1909): 3-5. Self-help: *Shimin* 1, no. 7 (Oct. 1906): 82.

234. Inoue Tetsujirō, "Shifū taihai no ichi sen'in," 3-9.

235. Hayakawa Yokichi, "Hito no haha," "Uma no waraji: seinen risshi" in *Kyōiku kōdan* (Ōe shobō, 1919).

236. "Shihan gakkōchō no kōan to shakai chizu," Naimushō, *Chihō kairyō jiseki,* 43-46.

237. "Dōtoku to kisha no hiyu," ibid., 46-47.

CHAPTER SEVEN

1. Account of the ceremony drawn from numerous eyewitness accounts: "Meiji Tennō gotaisōgō," *Fūzoku gahō,* no. 438 (Oct. 1912); Sugi Kenji, *Meiji Tennō gotaisō* [P] (Shiseisha shuppanbu, 1912); "Gotaisō kinengō," *Taiyō* 18, no. 14 (Oct. 1912); *Nihon,* 13-16 Sept.; *Tōkyō asahi shinbun,* 13-18 Sept.; *Yomiuri shinbun,* 13-17 Sept.; *Yorozu chōhō,* 14 Sept. Comments of the "special worshiper," and the "Japan no one imagined": *Taiyō,* 44-50, 12. Unprecedented ceremony was *mizou no seigi, kūzen no seishiki,* etc.

2. *Aizawa nikki (Zokuzoku),* 463-65; also, *Akita sakigake shinpō, Niigata shinbun, Fukuoka nichi nichi shinbun,* 12-15 Sept. 1912.

3. Strong, *Ox against the Storm,* 196-97. Tanaka had earlier written a message of prayer for the emperor's recovery on behalf of his village, the same village whose destruction by Ashio mine pollution had been the cause of Tanaka's long struggle against the state.

4. *Akita sakigake shinpō,* 2 Aug.-13 Sept. 1912. Instructions for mourning were printed verbatim in provincial newspapers throughout August. Other details from *Shinano mainichi shinbun,* 31 July-10 Aug.

5. *Shinano mainichi shinbun,* 10, 14 Sept. 1912; *Fukui nippō,* 18 Sept.

6. Ubukata, *Meiji Taishō kenbunshi,* 191. Details of the emperor's illness: e.g., *Tōkyō asahi shinbun,* 22-29 July 1912.

7. *Yomiuri shinbun, Jiji shinpō,* 3-4 Sept. 1912.

8. Speeches: Sugi, *Meiji Tennō gotaisō,* 52. Imperial gift: 42-43.

9. *The Daily Telegraph,* 30 July 1912. Mochizuki Kotarō, *The Late Emperor of Japan as a World Monarch* (Tokyo: Liberal News Agency, 1913), 19. This

collection of foreign opinion was published in Japanese as *Sekai ni okeru Meiji Tennō* (Eibun tsūshinsha, 1913). Newspapers and magazines also reprinted or summarized quantities of foreign comment.

10. "Emperor Mutsuhito could say with pride that he had in one generation created a great power out of nothing." *Neue Freie Presse* (30 July 1912), in Mochizuki, *The Late Emperor of Japan as a World Monarch*, 183.

11. Arthur May Knapp, "Who are the Japanese?" *Atlantic Monthly* 10, no. 3 (Sept. 1912): 335; also, George Kennan, "Can We Understand the Japanese?" *The Outlook* (10 Aug. 1912): 822. Both articles were reported in the Japanese press.

12. *Tōkyō nichi nichi shinbun*, 12 Sept. 1912.

13. Translated in *Japan Times*, 1 Sept. 1912, from *Nan-yüeh pao*, a Kuomintang paper published in Canton.

14. E.g., "Meiji no hokori," *Fukui nippō*, 5 Aug. 1912; "Meiji no kaiko," *Fukui nippō*, 4 Aug.-22 Sept.; "Taikōtei goseitokuki," *Kyūshū nichi nichi shinbun*, 1-7 Aug.; "Aa sentei!" *Chūgai shōgyō shinpō*, 30 July.

15. "Meiji taitei oyobi sono jidai," *Kokumin zasshi* 3, no. 16 (15 Aug. 1912): 4-21; 3, no. 17 (1 Sept. 1912): 1-11. Also, Ōkuma Shigenobu, "Tsutsushinde Meiji taitei o tsuikai su," *ShinNihon* 2, no. 9 (Sept. 1912): 2-17. A lengthy example of the genre, parts of which were printed in newspapers around the country: Miyake Setsurei, "Meiji nenkan no hensen," *Dōjidaishi* 4:160-397.

16. E.g., Shōmu: *Shinano mainichi shinbun*, 31 July 1912. Napoleon and Victoria: "Meiji Tennō goichidai goseitokuki," *Taiyō* 18, no. 13 (Sept. 1912): 7-12. On comparison, some found him peerless: e.g., Suematsu Kenchō, "Taikō Tennō to rekkoku kōtei," *Akita sakigake shinpō*, 4 Aug. 1912.

17. *Shinano mainichi shinbun*, 25 Aug. 1912.

18. "Gotaisō to chihōjin," *Tōkyō asahi shinbun*, 6 Sept. 1912.

19. "Ōbei tokushi no kangei," *Tōkyō asahi shinbun*, 11 Sept. 1912; "Misou no taisō," *Tōkyō asahi shinbun*, 12 Sept.; "Ippan shimin no hōsō chūi," *Tōkyō asahi shinbun*, 13 Sept.; "Raigetsu jūsannichi no keisatsu," *Yomiuri shinbun*, 30 Aug.; "Reikyū hōsō no kokoroe," *Jiji shinpō*, 4 Sept.

20. E.g., Seki Naohiko, "Gotaisō ni yorite arawaretaru Nihonjin no tokushitsu," *Taiyō* 18, no. 14 (Oct. 1912): 62; "Hangetsu hyōron," *Kokumin zasshi* 3, no. 17 (1 Sept. 1912): 12.

21. Makino Nobuaki, *Kaikoroku*, vol. 2 (Chūkō bunko, 1978), 61.

22. *Ehime shinpō*, 24 Jan. 1913.

23. For accounts of press coverage, including photographs: Shashi hensan iinkai, *Mainichi shinbun shichijūnen* (Mainichi shinbunsha, 1952), 148-52; Asahi shinbunsha shashi henshūshitsu, *Asahi shinbun no kyūjūnen* (Asahi shinbunsha, 1969), 265-71.

24. The emperor's illness was announced in the press on July 21, only nine days before his death. "Tenjitsu kuraku shinjin kokusu," *Yorozu chōhō*, 30 July 1912; *Tōkyō asahi shinbun*, 27-30 July; *Fūzoku gahō*, no. 437 (Sept. 1912); "Ōinaru kanashimi," *Haimi* (Sept. 1912). Also, diaries of the period: e.g., Tashiro Kōji, ed., *Tashiro Zentarō nikki, Meijihen* (Sōgensha, 1968), 471; *Aizawa nikki (Zokuzoku)*, 457-58.

25. "Aa! Meiji no owari: kisha chū no zakkan," *Tōkyō asahi shinbun*, 31 July 1912. Popular reaction: *Niigata shinbun*, 16-17 Aug. 1912; *Akita sakigake shinpō*, 1-15 Aug.; *Kyūshū nichi nichi shinbun*, 1-9 Aug., etc.

26. Mourning bands: *Tōkyō asahi shinbun*, 13 Sept. 1912. Home Ministry: Kindai Nihon shiryō kenkyūkai, *Nihon shakai undō shiryō*, 2d ser., vol. 2-1, *Tokubetsuyō shisatsunin jōsei ippan* (Meiji bunken shiryō kankōkai, 1957), 177-84.

27. "Tōkyō no sanjūnen," *Tayama Katai zenshū* 15: 685-86.

28. Uchimura, letter to Miyabe Kingo (31 July 1912), *Uchimura Kanzō zenshū* 20; Ebina Danjō, "Meiji Tennō no seitoku," *Shinjin* 13, no. 9 (Oct. 1912): 13-18.

29. *Sōseki zenshū* (Iwanami shoten) 13:701; 15:156. Eulogy: *Natsume Sōseki zenshū* (Chikuma shobō) 10:165.

30. Natsume Sōseki, *Kokoro*, trans. Edwin McClellan (Chicago: Henry Regnery Co., 1957), 295.

31. "This autumn morning / Meiji 45 by a slip of the pen. / Rewrite it Taishō and it is still sad. / Seeing the black bands on the passersby, / Tears come to my eyes." "Chidoribushi," in Soeda, *Enka no Meiji Taishōshi*, 156. The press also reported the difficulties of schoolchildren and others in writing Taishō instead of Meiji.

32. Businesses changing name: *Niigata shinbun*, 22 Aug. 1912.

33. Tokutomi Roka, "Meiji Tennō hōgyo no zengo," *Mimizu no tawagoto* (1913), *Meiji bungaku zenshū* 42:335-38.

34. *Atarashii otoko, atarashii onna*: *Tōkyō asahi shinbun*, 31 July 1912; also, "Shichigatsu sanjūnichi no asa," *Akita sakigake shinpō*, 11 Aug.

35. Account of the suicide: Ōhama Tetsuya, *Meiji no gunshin: Nogi Maresuke* (Yūzankaku, 1972), 184-96; "following the lord" (*taikun no miato shitaite ware wa yuku nari*), 192.

36. E.g., Haga Yaichi, "Taisōgi suiju no ki," *ShinNihon* 2, no. 10 (Oct. 1912): 7-11; Ubukata, *Meiji Taishō kenbunshi*, 212-19.

37. Ukita Kazutami, "Nogi Taishō no junshi o ronzu," *Taiyō* 18, no. 15 (Nov. 1912): 2.

38. *Nihon oyobi Nihonjin* (Oct. 1912): 3; "Rōshū daharon," *Shinano mainichi shinbun*, 19 Sept. 1912.

39. *Yorozu chōhō*, 16-18 Sept. 1912; *Niigata shinbun*, 16-21 Sept.; *Fukui nippō*, 15-26 Sept.; *Chōshū nichi nichi shinbun*, 17 Sept.-23 Oct.; *Shinano mainichi shinbun*, 15-25 Sept.

40. Ubukata, *Meiji Taishō kenbunshi*, 228. One of the most vocal critics of Nogi's act was the scholar Tanimoto Tomeri, who was condemned for his views and eventually resigned from Kyoto Imperial University.

41. "Junshi no heifū," *Tōkyō asahi shinbun* (10 Aug. 1912), cited in Ōhama, *Meiji no gunshin*, 205. An elderly man's suicide in Saga on July 31 provoked this and other comments: *Saga shinbun*, 1-3 Aug. 1912.

42. *Tōkyō asahi shinbun*, 15 Sept. 1912. This separation of reason and feeling was a common approach: e.g., *Shinano mainichi shinbun*, 22 Sept.

43. *Jiji shinpō*, 16 Sept. 1912; *Tōkyō nichi nichi shinbun*, 17 Sept. *Nihon*, 18 Sept.; *Chūgai shōgyō shinpō*, 18 Sept.

44. *The Times* (London), reprinted in *Tōkyō asahi shinbun*, 30 Aug., 14 Sept. 1912. Tokutomi Sohō's *Kokumin shinbun* (17 Sept. 1912) recorded pleasure at the response of the foreign press.

45. *Shinano mainichi shinbun*, 9 Aug. 1912. An article by Tōyama Mitsuru entitled "Seishinteki ni junshi seyo," *Tōkyō asahi shinbun* (14 Aug. 1912) had resulted in newspapers being banned by the Home Ministry: *Niigata shinbun*, 17 Aug. 1912.

46. "Shōrai no Nihon ni kansuru sandai gimon," *Taiyō* 14, no. 1 (Jan. 1908): 37. Ukita's more tempered version of the same theme: "Bushidō ni kansuru sanshu no kenkai," *Taiyō* 16, no. 10 (July 1910): 1-7. Also, Yamaji Aizan, "Shinbushidō" (1899), *Aizan bunshū*, 361-62.

47. *Taiyō* 18, no. 15 (Nov. 1912): 9.

48. Uemura Masahisa, "Meiji Tennō no jisha o hōsō su," *Fukuin shinpō*, 12 Sept. 1912; Kashiwagi Gien, "Nogi Taishō to jisatsu," *Jōmō kyōkai geppō* (15 Oct. 1912), cited in Ōhama, *Meiji no gunshin*, 215-20.

49. Ōhama, *Meiji no gunshin*, 187-203, 291-94; Ōya Sōichi, *Honoo wa nagareru* (Bungei shunjū, 1972), 21-32.

50. E.g., *Miyako shinbun, Tōkyō asahi shinbun*, 15-16 Sept. 1912; also, Ōhama, *Meiji no gunshin*, 210-13.

51. Kurata, *Meiji Taishō no minshū goraku*, 116-29; Shisō no kagaku kenkyūkai, *Yume to omokage* (Chūō kōronsha, 1950), 293-301. Popular songs about Nogi: Soeda, *Enka no Meiji Taishōshi*, 156.

52. Karasawa Tomitarō, "Nihon ni okeru jidō bungaku no kindaiteki hatten to sono kyōikushiteki igi: Meiji-Shōwaki no jidō zasshi o chūshin ni," *Nihonjin no kindai ishiki keisei katei ni okeru dentōteki keiki to seiōteki keiki, "Nihon kindaika" kenkyūhō*, no. 2 (Tōkyō kyōiku daigaku, 1968), 25-28. On Kōdansha: Suzuki, *Shuppan*, 164-68.

53. Inoue Tetsujirō "Shisō no keitōjō yori mitaru Nogi Taishō," *Jinkaku to shūyō* (Kōbundō, 1915), 342.

54. The suicide inspired Ōgai to the writing of historical fiction, and immediately relevant to *junshi* are "Okitsu Yagoemon no isho," written five days after the event, and "Abe ichizoku," written in Nov. 1912: David Dilworth and J. Thomas Rimer, eds., *The Incident at Sakai and Other Stories* (Honolulu: University of Hawaii Press, 1977), 15-69. Akutagawa's story, "Shōgun" (1922) is translated as "The General" in W.H.H. Norman, *Hell Screen and Other Stories* (Tokyo: Hokuseido Press, 1948), 135-67.

55. E.g., Satō Haruo, "Nogi Taishō o itamu," in *Kaishaku to kanshō, Rinji zōkan* (Jan. 1968): 135.

56. *Kokumin zasshi*, 3, no. 19 (1 Oct. 1912): 8; 3, no. 20 (15 Oct. 1912): 9.

57. G. M. Young, *Victorian England: Portrait of an Age* (New York: Doubleday Anchor, 1954), 269.

58. Ōya, *Honoo wa nagareru*, 32-37; Ōhama, *Meiji no gunshin*, 270-90.

59. Letters to Yamagata from Katsura, temporarily in the imperial household, and from Watanabe Chiaki, former Home Ministry official who had entered the palace bureaucracy and was now Imperial Household Minister. Yamagata Aritomo monjo, Aug.-Oct. 1912 (ms); also excerpted in Yama-

moto Shirō, *Taishō seihen no kisoteki kenkyū* (Ochanomizu shobō, 1970), 114, n. 2.

60. *Hara Kei nikki*, ed. Hara Keiichirō, vol. 5 (Kangensha, 1951), (1, 20 Aug. 1912), 90, 101. Although Hara's interpretation of Yamagata's motivations was not generous, it was probably not incorrect. Oka, *Yamagata Aritomo*, 121-22. Katsura was Grand Chamberlain and Lord Keeper of the Privy Seal from 13 Aug. to 21 Dec. 1912.

61. Asada Kōson, "Naikaku hakaisha," *Taiyō* 19, no. 1 (Jan. 1913): 19-28.

62. Letter from Yamagata to Terauchi (12 Dec. 1912), Terauchi Masatake kankei monjo, no. 360-106 (ms); also cited in Yamamoto, *Taishō seihen*, 271.

63. Letter from Yamagata to Katsura (14 Jan. 1913), Katsura Tarō monjo, no. 70-151. For *ikkai no buben* in Yamagata's recounting of the events of December: Tokutomi, *Yamagata Aritomo den* 3:819. Also, Hackett, *Yamagata Aritomo*, 256. Yamagata's version of the events of 1912-13: Taishō seihenki, Kensei shiryōshitsu, National Diet Library (ms); also, Yamamoto, *Taishō seihen*, 641-52.

64. On the Taishō change: Yamamoto, *Taishō seihen*; Masumi, *Nihon seitō shiron* 3:1-124; Banno Junji, "Keien naikaku to Taishō seihen," *Iwanami kōza Nihon rekishi*, vol. 17, *Kindai* 4 (Iwanami shoten, 1976), 263-304; also, Banno, *Taishō seihen: 1900 nen taisei no hōkai* (Minerubua shobō, 1982); Najita, *Hara Kei*, 80-184.

65. E.g., "Giin o kanshi seyo," *Niroku shinpō*, 5 Jan. 1913; "Shinnaikaku to mintō no taikō," *San'yō shinpō*, 23 Dec. 1912; "Kōshitsu to seisō," *Jiji shinpō*, 14 Jan. 1913.

66. "Shinjidai no shimei," *Kokumin zasshi* 3, no. 17 (1 Sept. 1912): 18; also, *Tōkyō asahi shinbun*, 13 Jan. 1913. Second restoration: e.g., Hayashi Kiroku, "Kyōhaku saretaru Saionji naikaku," *Taiyō* 18, no. 14 (Oct. 1912): 227. Taishō restoration: "Taishō seijiteki ishin no kaishi," *Tōkyō asahi shinbun*, 5 Dec. 1912; "Taishō ishin no koe," *Tōkyō asahi shinbun*, 2 Feb. 1913; *Fukuoka nichi nichi shinbin*, 10 Feb.; *Kōchi nippō*, 14 Jan.; also, the issue entitled "Taishō ishin no fūun," *Taiyō* (*rinji zōkan*) 19, no. 4 (15 Mar. 1913); etc.

67. E.g., Sasakawa Rinpū, "Kan ka min ka," *Nihon oyobi Nihonjin*, no. 597 (Jan. 1913).

68. "Seihen monogatari: genkon no seikai wa," *Ōsaka mainichi shinbun*, 23 Jan. 1913.

69. "Thirty years": editorial, *Fukuoka nichi nichi shinbun*, 10 Feb. 1913. "Blights": "Taishō shosei no kekkaku," *Nihon oyobi Nihonjin*, no. 597 (Jan. 1913); etc.

70. Examples of the "constitutional-unconstitutional" epithets: *Tōkyō asahi shinbun*, 22 Jan. 1913, and throughout Jan.-Feb. 1913.

71. *Kensei no kiki*, a standard phrase of the time: e.g., *Ōsaka mainichi shinbun*, 16 Jan. 1913; *Tōkyō asahi shinbun*, 18 Jan., 26 Feb. "Sekigahara": editorial, *Nihon oyobi Nihonjin*, no. 598 (Feb. 1913); also, Yamamoto, *Taishō seihen*, 134-38.

72. *San'yō shinpō*, 16 Feb. 1913.

73. Najita, *Hara Kei*, 147. For a typical response to the rescript: editorial, *Ōsaka asahi shinbun*, 10 Feb. 1913.

74. Letter from Tanaka to Terauchi (21 Feb. 1912), Terauchi Masatake kankei monjo, no. 315-9 (ms); also, Banno, "Keien naikaku to Taishō seihen," 286. Letter from Yamagata to Katsura (9 Feb. 1912), Katsura Tarō monjo, no. 70-150 (ms); also, Najita, *Hara Kei*, 92.

75. Masumi, *Nihon seitō shiron* 3:109-13. Also, Banno Junji, "The Taishō Political Crisis and the Problem of Japanese Government Finance, 1906-1914," *Papers on Far Eastern History*, no. 19 (Australian National University, March 1979), 181-202.

76. Tokutomi Ichirō (Sohō), *Taishō seikyoku shiron* (Min'yūsha, 1916), 10; also, Banno, "Keien naikaku to Taishō seihen," 265.

77. *Dakyō seiji* and *jōi tōgō*, the last particularly referring to the 1911 agreement between Hara and Katsura. For the common use of "compromise": e.g., "Seijijō no dakyō," *Tōkyō nichi nichi shinbun*, 27 May 1910.

78. Mitani Taichirō, *Taishō demokurashiiron* (Chūō kōronsha, 1974), 23-24.

79. E.g., readers' column, *Shinano mainichi shinbun*, 5 Dec. 1912; "Shin-naikaku to mintō no taikō," *San'yō shinpō*, 23 Dec.

80. Peter Duus, *Party Rivalry and Political Change in Taishō Japan* (Cambridge: Harvard University Press, 1968), 12-16.

81. "Seitō kakushin no ki," and "Seitō ni taisuru gojin no giwaku," *San'yō shinpō*, 15-16 Feb. 1913; "Tenka izure no toki ka sadamaran," *Shinano mainichi shinbun*, 21 Jan. 1913.

82. For daily reports of the provincial meetings, which often attracted between 1,000 and 4,000 people: *Tōkyō nichi nichi shinbun*, *Ōsaka mainichi shinbun*, and local papers such as the *Shinano mainichi shinbun* and *Fukuoka nichi nichi shinbun*, 18 Jan.-12 Feb. 1913. For a partial list of meetings with attendance figures: Masumi, *Nihon seitō shiron* 3:114-16.

83. "Battlefield": *Jiji shinpō*, 11-14 Feb. 1913; also, "Aa! Nigatsu tōka," in "Taishō ishin no fūun," *Taiyō* 19, no. 4 (15 Mar. 1913): 233-40. Earlier crowds around the Diet: *Tōkyō asahi shinbun*, 6 Feb. 1913; also, Yamamoto, *Taishō seihen*, 594-610. "Bureaucratic papers" (*kanryōshi*) attacked by the Tokyo rioters were the *Kokumin*, *Yamato*, *Miyako*, *Niroku*, *Hōchi*, and *Yomiuri* (*Tōkyō asahi shinbun*, 11 Feb. 1913). For similar attacks in the provinces on the *Kōchi shinbun*, *Chūgoku shinbun*, etc.: *Fukuoka nichi nichi shinbun*, *Tōkyō nichi nichi shinbun*, 13-15 Feb. 1913; Yamamoto, *Taishō seihen*, 604-10.

84. Letter from Tanaka to Terauchi (15 Feb. 1913), Terauchi Masatake kankei monjo, no. 315-14 (ms).

85. Najita, *Hara Kei*, 100; letter from Hirata to Katsura (10 Dec. 1912), Katsura Tarō monjo, no. 10-19 (ms).

86. *Goyō shinbun*, government, or official, newspaper: letter from Tokutomi to Terauchi (11 Dec. 1912), Terauchi Masatake kankei monjo, no. 330-14 (ms). For the attack: *Tōkyō asahi shinbun*, 11 Feb. 1913.

87. Yamamoto, *Shinbun to minshū* (Kinokuniya shinsho, 1973), 123.

88. "Rejoicing": letter from Yamagata to Tokutomi (15 Aug. 1908), To-

kutomi Sohō monjo. Sohō kinenkan (ms). This and other private communications to Tokutomi are discussed in Itō Takashi and George Akita, "The
Yamagata-Tokutomi Correspondence: Press and Politics in Meiji-Taishō Japan," *Monumenta Nipponica* 36, no. 4 (Winter 1981): 391-423.

89. Examples of the *kisha taikai: Jiji shinpō,* 9 Jan. 1913; *Tōkyō nichi nichi
shinbun,* 14 Jan.; *Tōkyō asahi shinbun,* 18 Jan.

90. Ono Hideo, *Nihon shinbunshi* (Ryōsho fukyūkai, 1948), 123.

91. Mention of a "white rainbow piercing the sun," an ancient Chinese
portent of civil disturbance, resulted in a Home Ministry ban and also the
resignation in protest of the newspaper's leading liberal writers: Ariyama
Teruo, "Asahi shinbun 'Hakkō jiken,' " *Ryūdō* (Oct.-Nov. 1972).

92. Mainichi shinbunsha, *Mainichi shinbun hyakunenshi, 1872-1972* (Mainichi shinbunsha, 1972), 419; Yamamoto, *Shinbun to minshū,* 130-34, 198. Another, but in some cases unreliable, source of circulation figures for the major
papers at the end of 1912: Ono Hideo, "Wagakuni shinbun zasshi hattatsu
no gaikan," in "Meiji Taishō no bunka," *Taiyō (Sōgō shijūnen kinen zōkan)*
33, no. 8 (15 June 1927): 377-95.

93. Asahi shinbunsha shashi henshūshitsu, *Asahi shinbun no kyūjūnen,* 318-
23. The phrase remains in the motto of the present-day *Asahi* and is echoed
in similar words by the other two of Japan's three major dailies, the *Mainichi*
and *Yomiuri*: Yamamoto, *Shinbun to minshū,* 185.

94. Masumi, *Nihon seitō shiron* 3:118-23.

95. Examples of local *rikken seinenkai, kensei yōgo seinendan: Fukuoka nichi
nichi shinbun,* 13-17 Feb. 1913; *San'yō shinpō,* 13 Feb.; etc. Political fever: e.g.,
Tōkyō nichi nichi shinbun, 27 Feb.; *Ōsaka nichi nichi shinbun,* 1 Mar.; *Ōsaka
mainichi shinbun,* 19 Mar.

96. Kakurentaiku kannai minjō fūzoku shisōkai no genjō, II, Takada (ms).

97. See Matsuo Takayoshi, *Taishō demokurashii no kenkyū* (Aoki shoten,
1966), 106-22; Ariizumi Sadao, *Meiji seijishi no kiso katei,* 371-87.

98. Yamagata Aritomo, "Chihōkan ni taisuru kunji" (25 Dec. 1889), translated in McLaren, *Japanese Government Documents,* 419-22; "Chihōchōkan ni
taisuru kunji" (Feb. 1890), cited in Kanno, *Kindai Nihon ni okeru nōmin shihai
no shiteki kōzō,* 87; also, Yamagata, speech to the Diet (1899), in Kikegawa,
Jichi gojūnenshi seidohen, 426-28.

99. Kakurentaiku kannai minjō fūzoku shisōkai no genjō, II, Takada (ms).
Emphasis added. Similar comments are found throughout the country: II,
Hirosaki; IV, Wakayama; V, Tottori; VII, Saga; etc. For similar remarks:
Yamaji Aizan, *Kokumin zasshi* 1, no. 1 (Dec. 1912): 5-6.

100. Yamagata to Katsura (14 Jan. 1913), Katsura Tarō monjo, no. 70-
151 (ms).

101. Mitani Taichirō, *Nihon seitō seiji no keisei* (Tōkyō daigaku shuppankai,
1967), 70-132; Najita, *Hara Kei,* 35-55. For abolition, which went into effect
in 1923, followed by the abolition of the *gun* offices in 1926: Kikegawa, *Jichi
gojūnenshi seidohen,* 500-16, 552-58.

102. Like all generalizations involving localities, these characterizations

miss the regional distinctions that made the socioeconomic behavior of local elite vary considerably from region to region. For a study of this Meiji-Taishō transition in Yamanashi: Ariizumi, *Meiji seijishi no kiso katei*, 328-70.

103. Ariizumi, "Meiji kokka to minshū tōgō," 247-54; *Meiji seijishi no kiso katei*, 244-327.

104. E.g., Naimushō, *Chihō kairyō jigyō kōenshū* (1909) 1:25-26.

105. Among many examples, Ueda school construction, Toyooka kumin taikai on village river funds, Nobuta jikyōkai meeting on Meiji commemoration: *Shinano mainichi shinbun*, 5 Oct., 6 May, 5 May 1912.

106. *Shinano mainichi shinbun*, 5-10 Oct. 1912.

107. Mitani, *Taishō demokurashiiron*, 17-22.

108. This is the France of Eugen Weber's description: "Comment la Politique Vint aux Paysans: A Second Look at Peasant Politicization," *The American Historical Review* 87, no. 2 (Apr. 1982): 380-89.

109. Tetsuo Najita, *Japan* (Englewood Cliffs, N.J.: Prentice-Hall, 1974), 121.

110. "The denial of politics" in Taishō socialism: Mitani, *Taishō demokurashiiron*, 80-92.

111. Hashikawa, *Yanagita Kunio*, 64. On the late Meiji-Taishō withdrawal from politics: Harry D. Harootunian, "Between Politics and Culture: Authority and the Ambiguities of Intellectual Choice in Imperial Japan," in *Japan in Crisis*, ed. Silberman and Harootunian, 110-55.

112. For an argument that Tanaka's view of parties was consistent from as early as 1912: Banno Junji, "Taishō shoki ni okeru rikugun no seitōkan: Tanaka Giichi o chūshin to shite," *Gunji shigaku* 11, no. 4 (Mar. 1976): 54-62.

113. Tanaka Giichi, "Kokumin to guntai" (1911) and "Rokushūkan gen'ekihei no kakugo" (1913), in *Tanaka Chūjō kōenshū* (1916), 55, 303. Also, Smethurst, *A Social Basis for Prewar Japanese Militarism*, Chs. 1, 2, and passim.

114. See Richard H. Mitchell, *Thought Control in Prewar Japan* (Ithaca: Cornell University Press, 1976), 39-96.

115. A typical complaint: *Tōkyō-fu kyōikukai zasshi*, no. 82 (27 May 1911): 5.

116. "Shōrai no Nihon ni kansuru sandai gimon," *Taiyō* 14, no. 1 (Jan. 1908): 40.

117. Proposed in the 28th Diet, Mar. 1912; passed in the 30th Diet, Mar. 1913 (but without the provision that the Rescript also be read at election time); government questioned about its implementation, 31st Diet, Mar. 1914. (Hara replied that directives had been sent to elementary and middle schools, but that the village offices presented more of a problem and had not yet been so instructed.) "Seijiteki chitoku kan'yō no kengi," etc. in *Teikoku gikai*, ed. Abe, 3:128-31, 168-70, 182.

118. Minobe Tatsukichi, preface to *Kenpō kōwa*, lectures to the Monbushō's summer conference of middle school teachers in 1911, the publication of which in 1912 sparked Uesugi's attack ("Kokutai ni kansuru isetsu," *Taiyō*

18, no. 8 [June 1912]: 69-80) and the debate. Collection of articles in the controversy: Hoshijima Jirō, ed., *Uesugi Hakase tai Minobe Hakase saikin kenpōron* (Jitsugyō no Nihonsha, 1913). On the debate: Matsumoto Sannosuke, "Nihon kenpōgaku ni okeru kokkaron no tenkai: sono keiseiki ni okeru hō to kenryoku no mondai o chūshin ni," *Tennōsei kokka to seiji shisō*, 254-308; Nakamura Yūjirō, "Minpōten ronsō to Minobe-Uesugi kenpō ronsō," in *Kindai Nihon shisō ronsō*, ed. Miyagawa, 85-95; also, Frank O. Miller, *Minobe Tatsukichi: Interpreter of Constitutionalism in Japan* (Berkeley: University of California Press, 1965), 27-38. For Uesugi's position and the views of his teacher Hozumi: Minear, *Japanese Tradition and Western Law*, 105-47.

119. Uesugi taught at Tōdai from 1910 to his death in 1929; a second chair in constitutional law created in 1920 was filled by Minobe until his retirement in 1934, a year before the "Minobe incident." For the incident: Miller, *Minobe Tatsukichi*, 196-253. Minobe had been appointed to the Peers in 1932.

120. Katō, *Shakai kyōiku: tsūzoku kōwa* (1918), 253-54.

121. Kakurentaiku kannai minjō fūzoku shisōkai no genjō, e.g., II, Himeji, Okayama; and I-V, passim.

122. Vernacular uses of "unconstitutional": *Tōkyō nichi nichi shinbun*, 27 Feb. 1913; *Ōsaka mainichi shinbun*, 12 Feb.; etc.

123. E.g., *Tōkyō asahi shinbun*, 2-12 May 1912; "Kokumin no seiji shisō," *Gifu nichi nichi shinbun*, 3 May; *San'in shinbun*, 4, 9, and 16 May. Also, in cautionary material on local education: e.g., Nishisonogi-gun kyōikukai, *Shōgakkōchō kōshūkai kōenroku* (1918), 52-53.

124. Abe Isoo, "Senkyo ni reitan naru kokumin," here quoted from *San'in shinbun*, 5 May 1912.

125. E.g., *fuhai giin*: Ukita Kazutami, "Shinjidai no shimei," *Kokumin zasshi* 3, no. 7 (Sept. 1912): 18-20. *Furyō giin*: *San'in shinbun*, 12 May 1912. *Erai daraku*: Kiyama Kumajirō, "Nisan no seinenron," *Rinri kōenshū*, no. 101 (Jan. 1911): 82-83. Other examples: "Daigishi kishitsu," *Tōkyō asahi shinbun*, 26, 29-31 Jan., 1, 23 Feb. 1912; "Gikai fūunroku," *Nihon oyobi Nihonjin*, nos. 598-602 (1 Jan.-15 Mar. 1913).

126. For "fools become Dietmen": "Aa wakaranai," Soeda, *Enka no Meiji Taishōshi*, 126. To Taishō youth: Nitobe Inazō, "Taishō seinen no shinro," *ShinNihon* (Nov. 1915), *Taishō daizasshi* (Ryūdō shuppan, 1978), 36-39.

127. See Kinmonth, *The Self-Made Man*, 277-87.

128. E.g., *Saikin chōsa shūshoku no tebiki* [P], 19-21.

129. Itō Keidō, *Shūshoku tebikigusa* [P], 10.

130. Yamaji Aizan, "Yo to tatakaubeki wareware no gunki," *Kokumin zasshi* 1, no. 1 (Dec. 1910): 4.

131. "Kanryō seiji," *Ōsaka mainichi shinbun*, 21 Jan. 1913 (continued, 23-29 Jan.).

132. For a cogent argument on this structural adaptation of the parties to the bureaucracy: Bernard S. Silberman, "The Bureaucratic Role in Japan, 1900-1945: The Bureaucrat as Politician," in *Japan in Crisis*, ed. Silberman and Harootunian, 183-216.

133. "Dokusha to kisha: kurashi no raku ga daiichi," *Miyako shinbun*, 13 Feb. 1914.

134. E.g., editorials, *Tōkyō mainichi shinbun*, 17 May 1907; *Shinano mainichi shinbun*, 25 May 1912; *San'in shinbun*, 6 May; *Gifu nichi nichi shinbun*, 11 May. Also, from an approving point of view: Kakurentaiku kannai minjō fūzoku shisōkai no genjō, III, Tsu, and passim (ms).

135. "Kokuminteki daihankō: Ōkuma Hakushaku no dan," *Tōkyō mainichi shinbun*, 8 Jan. 1907.

136. "Rikken kokumin no kyōiku," *Tōkyō mainichi shinbun*, 17 May 1907.

137. Abe Isoo, "Senkyo ni reitan naru kokumin," *San'in shinbun*, 5 May 1912.

138. Aizawa Tetsudō, "Chihō seinen ni gekisu," *Shinano mainichi shinbun*, 5 Dec. 1912.

139. E.g., Naikaku kanpō naikaku chōsashitsu, *Nihon no seijiteki mukanshin* (1961); Nihon hōsō kyōkai hōsō yoron chōsajo, *Daini Nihonjin no ishiki: NHK yoron chōsa* (Shiseidō, 1980), 55-69; English résumé, 639-44. Also, Bradley M. Richardson, *The Political Culture of Japan* (Berkeley: University of California Press, 1974), 29-82.

CHAPTER EIGHT

1. Suzuki, *Meiji tetsudō nishiki-e*, iii-viii; Nagata, *Meiji no kisha*, 29-31. On the baleful influence of the railroad in the provinces: e.g., Kakurentaiku kannai minjō fūzoku shisōkai no genjō, III, Tsu, Sakura; IV, Tsuruga, Nara; V, Himeji, Kobe, Okayama, Matsue (ms); *San'in shinbun*, 6 May 1912; *Shimo Ina-gun seinenkaihō*, no. 1 (Mar. 1913): 18. For the American counterpart of the intrusion of technology into the agrarian "garden": Henry Nash Smith, *Virgin Land: The American West as Symbol and Myth* (Cambridge: Harvard University Press, 1950).

2. Coolness (*reiketsu*) and sparrows: Kakurentaiku kannai minjō fūzoku shisōkai no genjō, II, Hirosaki. Military's use of emperor and village: *Sen'yū*, nos. 1-40 (Nov. 1910-Feb. 1914), passim; also, Smethurst, *A Social Basis for Prewar Japanese Militarism*.

3. E.g., "One family, one village" autonomy (*ikka itchōson no dokuritsu*): Maeda Masana, *Sangyō*, no. 38 (Feb. 1897): 9. Spirit of savings (*chochikushin*): *Aichi-ken Kaitō-gun Ifuki-mura sonze* (1904), 134; Naimushō chihōkyoku, *Chihō kairyō jitsurei* (1912), 26. Unit of the state: Yokoyama, *Chōsonze chōsa kōyō* (1909), 1.

4. Mori, *Chōsonze chōsa shishin* (1909), 18-19.

5. Samurai: Katō, "Bushiteki seishin," *Shakai kyōiku: tsūzoku kōwa* (1918), 215-34. Obedience: Katō, *Shūyō shohin* (1915), 101. Rothschild: Tagawa Daikichirō, "Shōjikimono no hanashi," (talk at *tsūzoku kōdankai* in Shiba, Mar. 1911), *Tōkyō-fu kyōikukai zasshi*, no. 78 (Apr. 1911): 60.

6. Middle-school compositions on entrepreneurship in the name of loyalty and filial piety: Chiba, *Meiji no shōgakkō*, 290. Asahi beer advertisement: *Ōsaka mainichi shinbun*, 15 July 1913.

7. Kakurentaiku kannai minjō fūzoku shisōkai no genjō, II, Takada (ms).

8. Kindaichi and Anzai, *Nihon no shōka*, 284. A typical example of *ittōkoku*: Takekoshi Yosaburō, *Jinmin tokuhon* (1913), 1-5. Textbooks, second edition (1910): Kaigo, *Nihon kyōkasho taikei* 3:63-109; 2:115-18.

9. For the term "national villagers": Smethurst, *A Social Basis for Prewar Japanese Militarism*, xvi and passim.

10. Kondō Seigetsuya, "Ikō ka kaerō ka: kokumin no yūshūsei," *Shimo Ina-gun seinenkaihō*, no. 1 (Mar. 1913): 16-27. A frequent lecturer to local youth organizations, Kondō put his thoughts to paper in this essay when illness prevented him from delivering them in person.

11. Watanabe, *Seinen kyōshi jidai* (1937), 15-20.

12. A relevant discussion of the several kinds of meanings often lumped together as "consensus": Charles Taylor, "Interpretation and the Sciences of Man," *The Review of Metaphysics* 25, no. 1 (Sept. 1971): 3-51.

13. For 1890: Mason, *Japan's First General Election*, 148. *Kenmin taikai* proceedings: e.g., *Shinano mainichi shinbun*, 2-13 Feb. 1913.

14. Kita Ikki, *Kokutairon oyobi junsei shakaishugi* (1906), reprinted as *Kokutairon* (Kita Ikki icho kankōkai, 1950), 68-69; also, *Kita Ikki chōsaku shū*, vol. 1 (Misuzu shobō, 1959), 213. Familial emperor: e.g., Ōkuma Shigenobu, *Kokumin tokuhon* (Hōbunkan, 1910), 2.

15. See Murray Edelman, *Politics as Symbolic Action* (New York: Academic Press, 1971), 10; and *The Symbolic Uses of Politics* (Urbana: University of Illinois Press, 1964), 1-21.

16. Mountains and rivers: Sakatani Shiroshi, "The Irregular Route to a Popularly Elected Assembly," *Meiroku zasshi*, no. 27 (Feb. 1875), in Braisted, *Meiroku Zasshi*, 334. Mt. Fuji: Ozaki Yukio, "Ōbeimanyūki" (1888-90), *Ozaki Yukio zenshū* 3:48.

17. Civilization and socialism: *Tōkyō nichi nichi shinbun*, 27 Aug. 1908. Evils of the city: Kakurentaiku kannai minjō fūzoku shisōkai no genjō, V, Hamada (ms). Changes in ways of living (*seikatsu hōhō*): *Chōshū nichi nichi shinbun*, 7 July 1912. Suicide: "Jisatsu zehi," *Taiyō* 9, no. 9 (Aug. 1903): 56. Lefthandedness: *Gifu nichi nichi shinbun*, 3 May 1912.

18. Clifford Geertz, "Common Sense as a Cultural System," *The Antioch Review*, no. 33 (1975): 8.

19. "Civilization" as a new word: Nishimura Shigeki, "An Explanation of Twelve Western Words, Part I," *Meiroku zasshi*, no. 36 (May 1875), in Braisted, *Meiroku Zasshi*, 446-49. An argument that "new" should be dropped from its association both with "civilization" and "Japan": "Kyū-Nihon shinNihon no sabetsu o haisu," *Nihonjin*, no. 400 (5 Dec. 1904): 3-6. For earlier uses of *bunmei*: Suzuki Shūji, *Bunmei no kotoba* (Bunka hyōron shuppansha, 1981), 33-68.

20. The *Meiroku zasshi* offers as convenient a compendium as any of this usage: e.g., Braisted, 93, 117, 132, 159, 196, 272, 458, etc.

21. A typical account of "the appurtenances of civilization," beginning with the railroad and ending with empire: *Ōsaka mainichi shinbun*, 1 Jan. 1907.

22. Evil consequences of civilization: Tanaka Giichi, "Bunmei no yokei," *Tanaka Chūjō kōenshū* (1916), 128-36. Underside (*rimen*): Yamazaki Enkichi,

Chihō jichi kōshū hikki [P], 82. Ornaments (*sōshoku*): Koyama Masatake, "Katei to keishin shinnen to no kankei," *Nihonjin*, no. 446 (5 Nov. 1906): 15-17. Empty trappings (*kyoshoku*): letter to the editor, *San'in shinbun*, 26 May 1890.

23. Factory law: Dore, "The Modernizer as a Special Case: Japanese Factory Legislation, 1892-1911," 444. Nogi: *Niigata shinbun*, 16 Sept. 1912. *Bunmeiteki sengoku jidai*: Oshikawa Shunrō, "Keikai subeki Nihon," *Bōken sekai* (Dec. 1910), *Meiji daizasshi*, 174. Throwing stones: *Niigata shinbun*, 21 Aug. 1912. Local debts: "Chihōsai to kokusai," *Chōshū nichi nichi shinbun*, 7 July 1912.

24. References to airplanes as the latest product of civilization became increasingly common from 1910: e.g., "Those who do not know of airplanes do not know modern civilization (*kindai bunmei*)," advertisement, *Shinano mainichi shinbun*, 3 Oct. 1912; also, *Fūzoku gahō*, Oct.-Nov. 1911, and often thereafter.

25. *Fukushima-ken Iwase-gun Nishibukuro-mura sonze chōsa* (1902).

26. *Ibaraki-ken Kita Sōma-gun Omonma sonze* (1914).

27. "Uncivilized": Nishisonogi-gun kyōikukai, *Shōgakkōchō kōshūkai kōenroku* (1918), 20. Kōtoku: "Bunmei no fūzoku wa gizen nomi ōshi," *Shinkōron* 21, no. 5 (May 1906): 25-26.

28. Kaneko Chikusui, "Kokuun no shinpo to taiho," *Taiyō* 18, no. 15 (Nov. 1912): 14.

29. E.g., Kakurentaiku kannai minjō fūzoku shisōkai no genjō, V, Hamada, Fukuyama; VI, Marugame (ms).

30. For a different view: Irokawa, *Meiji no bunka*, 315.

31. The many variations included *ureubeki mono ari, ikan nari, taerarezaru koto nari*, and even *tsūtan no nen ni taerashimuru wa jitsu ni ikan shigoku de ari*, etc.

32. Pre-selection meetings: above, p. 66. Village riots: "Shakai kasō no haran," *Taiyō* 3, no. 30 (Oct. 1897): 263-64. Wartime women: e.g., Tokushima-kenfu, *Meiji sanjūshichihachinen: Tokushima-ken senjishi* (Tokushima, 1907), 644-56; Ibaraki-ken, *Ibaraki-ken senji jōkyō ippan* (Mito, 1906). *Chihō kairyō undō* funds: Yamanashi-ken gikai jimukyoku, *Yamanashi-ken gikaishi* 3:426.

33. Katō, *Shakai kyōiku: tsūzoku kōwa* (1918), 229-30.

34. E.g., Kakurentaiku kannai minjō fūzoku shisōkai no genjō, III, Tsuruga; VII, Ōita; etc. (ms).

35. E.g., Maruyama Masao, *Nihon no shisō* (Iwanami shinsho, 1961), 44-50; Smethurst, *A Social Basis for Prewar Japanese Militarism*. Collectivist ethic: Ronald P. Dore and Tsutomu Ōuchi, "Rural Origins of Japanese Fascism," in *Dilemmas of Growth in Prewar Japan*, ed. James W. Morley (Princeton University Press, 1971), 181-209.

36. *Fukui nippō*, 22 Sept. 1912.

37. "Gods of draft exemption": Kakurentaiku kannai minjō fūzoku shisōkai no genjō, III, Sakura; IV, Nara; VII, Fukuoka; etc. (ms).

38. Mori, *Chōsonze shōsa shishin* (1909), 6-12.

39. "As the world moves on to civilization and all confront the struggle for survival. . . . Improve Your Memory," cover advertisement for *Kioku-ryoku zōshinjutsu* (1909). *Shinkei suijaku*: e.g., *Shinano mainichi shinbun*, 7 Aug., 10 Oct. 1912; *Niigata shinbun*, 19 Aug., 4 Sept.; etc.

40. Yokoi Tokiyoshi, "Nōson kaizōron," *Yokoi Hakase zenshū*, 4: 277.

41. Representative examples: Naimushō, *Chihō kairyō jiseki* (1910), passim.

42. Bushidō: Katō, *Shakai kyōiku: tsūzoku kōwa* (1918), passim. Reverence for the gods: e.g., "Keishin no shisō to zenkō shōrei," *Shimin* 6, no. 1 (Apr. 1911): 32-35; Hirata Tōsuke, "Keishin no seishin yōsei" (speech to prefectural governors, Apr. 1911), Chihōkan kaigi giketsusho narabi hikki (ms).

43. *Seikatsunan* and *dekasegi*: e.g., Kakurentaiku kannai minjō fūzoku shisōkai no genjō, III, Tsu; V, Himeji, Fukuchiyama, Iwakuni, Yamaguchi, Matsue; VII, Kurume (ms). *Amerika goke*: IV, Wakayama. Labor out-migration: Watanabe Makoto, *Nihon nōson jinkōron*, 78-173; also Kuwabara Makoto, "Meiji-Taishō no Hokkaidō ijū," *Atarashii dōshi* 7, no. 5 (1969): 1-15.

44. Tenants and *tatami*: editorial, *Yomiuri shinbun*, 3 Jan. 1913.

45. Agricultural sector employment: Ohkawa and Shinohara, *Patterns of Japanese Economic Development*, 392. Rural population: Ōsato, *Meiji ikō honpō shuyō keizai tōkei*, 14.

46. Nōshōmushō nōmukyoku, *Tochi shoyūken idō no jōkyō* [P] (Nōshōmushō, 1910).

47. Old men of Tenpō, young men of Meiji: Tokutomi Sohō, *ShinNihon no seinen* (1887), discussed in Pyle, *The New Generation*, 32-36, 42-47; Pierson, *Tokutomi Sohō*, 118-24.

48. This second Meiji generation: Uchida Yoshihiko, "Chishiki seinen no shoruikei," *Nihon shihonshugi no shisōka* (Iwanami shoten, 1967), 157-202; Irokawa, *Meiji no bunka*, 209-32.

49. Pierson, *Tokutomi Sohō*, 381-97.

50. Ōkuma Shigenobu, "Teikoku gikai o tsūjite mitaru gendai shakai," *Taiyō* 17, no. 3 (Feb. 1911): 8.

51. Mason, *Japan's First General Election*, 196; Duus, *Party Rivalry and Political Change*, 15.

52. Takane, *Nihon no seiji eriito*, 34; also, Mannari Hiroshi, *Bijinesu eriito* (Chūkō shinsho, 1975). Another example of unusual Meiji presence is provided by the peerage. 85% of all the "new peers" in the prewar period were awarded to Meiji political and military figures, and their political influence, which was considerable in the Meiji era, apparently ended with their generation (Takane, 35-36, 51).

53. A brief chronology is included in *Aizawa nikki* 1:285.

54. The exception perhaps is the other unusual generation born between 1925 and 1935, some of whose members became prominent when still very young after the defeat in 1945 and have remained influential throughout the postwar period.

55. Samurai consciousness: Fukuchi Shigetaka, *Shizoku to shizoku ishiki: kindai Nihon o okoseru mono horobosu mono* (Shunjūsha, 1967).

56. Kaneko Chikusui, "Kindaishugi no engen," *Taiyō* 17, no. 14 (Nov. 1911): 11.

57. Miyake Setsurei, *Meiji shisō shōshi* (1913); *Nihon no meichō*, ed. Kano Masanao, vol. 37 (Chūō kōronsha, 1971), 416-27.

58. Ebina Danjō, "Shūkyōka no mitaru gendai shakai," *Taiyō* 17, no. 3 (Feb. 1911): 29.

59. *Kyōiku chokugo Boshin shōsho haidoku shiki oyobi dainikai chihō jigyō kōrōsha hyōshō shiki kiji* [P], 67.

60. Yamaji Aizan, "Gendai Nihon kyōkai shiron" (1906), *Kirisutokyō hyōron, Nihonjinminshi*, 8.

61. Curriculum: Ariizumi, "Meiji kokka to minshū tōgō," 229. The Ishin shiryō hensankai was accused in educational circles of historiographical bias that favored the government's prejudice toward Chōshū's view of the Restoration: *Kyōiku jiron* (15 Jan. 1911): 60, 68. Similar concerns for history at the local level: e.g., "Shinanoshi dankai setsuritsu shushisho," *Shinano kyōiku*, no. 270 (Apr. 1909).

62. "Shiseki shōchi kinenbutsu nado no hozon ni kansuru ken" (presented to the prefectural governors' conference, Apr. 1911), Chihōkan kaigi giketsusho narabi hikki (ms). Discussion of the issue: *Shimin* 6, nos. 1-4 (Apr.-July 1911).

63. "Shokakokoro o itsu no shi," *Meiji Tennō shōchoku kinkai*, 1377-78. The Charter Oath was also quoted approvingly and in full in the Imperial Rescript denying the emperor's divinity (*Tennō ningen sengen*) of 1 Jan. 1946: Supreme Commander for the Allied Powers, *Political Reorientation of Japan*, 470.

64. "Seiyō no mane wa mappira gomen," *Kokumin zasshi* 2, no. 1 (Jan. 1911): 8.

65. E.g., Hayakawa Tetsuji, "Jinshin isshinron," *Kokumin zasshi* 3, no. 14 (15 July 1912): 28.

66. E.g., letters to Terauchi Masatake (16 Aug. 1911); Hirata Tōsuke (19 Mar. 1907); Terauchi (19 Sept. 1906); Katsura Tarō (9 Dec. 1902, 2 June 1903): Yamagata Aritomo monjo (ms). Letter to Tokutomi (3 Oct. 1903), Tokutomi Sohō monjo (ms).

67. E.g., Tokutomi Ichirō (Sohō), *Taishō no seinen to teikoku no zento* (Min'yūsha, 1916); *Jimu ikkagen* (Min'yūsha, 1913). Sunday chats: *Nichiyō kōdan*, 11 vols. (Min'yūsha, 1900-11), and widely reprinted. Historical works: especially the revision of his well known *Yoshida Shōin* (Min'yūsha, 1908).

68. Pierson, *Tokutomi Sohō*, 307.

69. "Kako oyobi shōrai," *Ōsaka mainichi shinbun*, 1 Jan. 1907.

70. World War I: *Yamagata Aritomo ikensho*, 342. Revolution and rice riots: Itō and Akita, "The Yamagata-Tokutomi Correspondence," 421.

71. Pierson, *Tokutomi Sohō*, 307.

72. Yamagata's pencil markings in Kakurentaiku kannai minjō fūzoku shisōkai no genjō (ms), passim.

73. 15 May 1907, *Aizawa nikki (Zokuzoku)*, 192-93.

74. Pierson, *Tokutomi Sohō*, 307.

75. Kiyama Kumajirō, "Nisan no seinenron," *Rinri kōenshū*, no. 101 (Jan. 1911): 74.

76. Shiga Shigetaka, "Nihonjin no jōtō o sensu," *Nihonjin* (Apr. 1888): 3-4. For Mannheim: "Conservative Thought," *Essays on Sociology and Social Psychology* (New York: Oxford University Press, 1953), 74-164.

77. Tsubotani Suisai, "Meiji hyakunen Tōkyō hanshōki," *Bōken sekai*, 20 Apr. 1910; *Miyagi-ken Natori-gun Oide-mura sonze chōsasho*, 1902.

78. *Kado jidai*: "Gendai shisō no tōitsu," *Kokumin zasshi* 3, no. 13 (1 July 1912): 86; Akimoto Kōchō, "Kazoku no mitaru gendai shakai," *Taiyō* 17, no. 2 (Feb. 1911): 23; etc.

79. Basil Hall Chamberlain, *Things Japanese* (London: John Murray, 1905), v.

80. Fukasaku, *Kokumin dōtoku yōgi* (1916), 456.

81. Roland Barthes, *Mythologies* (New York: Hill and Wang, 1972), 155.

82. George Orwell, original "Preface" to *Animal Farm* (1945), first printed as "The Freedom of the Press," *The Times Literary Supplement* (15 Sept. 1972): 1037-39.

83. Taishō schools: Nakano Akira, *Taishō jiyū kyōiku no kenkyū* (Reimei shobō, 1968). *Seinendan*: Hirayama, *Seinen shūdanshi kenkyū josetsu*, 108-257. Landlord associations: Ann Waswo, "In Search of Equity: Japanese Tenant Unions in the 1920s," in *Conflict in Modern Japanese History: The Neglected Tradition*, ed. Tetsuo Najita and J. Victor Koschmann (Princeton: Princeton University Press, 1982), 366-411.

84. *Yamanashi sansō jihō* (1906), quoted in Takizawa Hideki, *Mayu to kiito no kindaishi* (Kyōikusha, 1979), 167-76.

85. Natsume Sōseki, "My Individualism," trans. Jay Rubin, *Monumenta Nipponica* 34, no. 1 (Spring 1979): 45.

CHAPTER NINE

1. E.g., a series of essays on the subject: "Rikkokuron," *Chūō kōron* 26, no. 4 (Apr. 1911): 15-132.

2. E.g., lectures to local *kyōikukai* meetings printed in *Shinano kyōiku*: Ukita Kazutami, "Dōtoku no kiso," (Dec. 1913), Kakehi Katsuhiko, "Kyōiku chokugo to jidai shichō," (Aug. 1915). For "progressivism" and other typical rhetoric: Yoshida Kumaji, "Dōtoku kyōiku no kakushin," *Rinri kōenshū*, no. 125 (Mar. 1913).

3. Tsuda Gentoku, "Risō no shōgakkōchō," *Shōgakkōchō kōshūkai kōenroku* (Nishisonogi-gun kyōikukai, 1918), 14-15.

4. "Abnormalities"; "Kyōiku no kōka o mattakarashimubeki ippan shisetsu ni kansuru kengi," presented to the Rinji kyōikukai, 17 Jan. 1919, in Kyōikushi hensankai, *Hattatsushi* 5:1196-1204. For the Kyōiku chōsakai (1913-17) established by the Ministry of Education: *Kyōiku jiron* (Mar.-Aug. 1913). For the Rinji kyōikukai (1912-19) established by the Terauchi cabinet with such Yamagata men as Komatsubara, Hirata, and Ichiki among its

members: Kaigo Tokiomi, *Rinji kyōikukai no kenkyū* (Tōkyō daigaku shuppankai, 1960); Ikeda Susumu, "Rinji kyōiku kaigi o megutte," in *Taishō no kyōiku*, ed. Ikeda Susumu and Motoyama Yukihiko (Daiichi hōki shuppan, 1978), 163-76.

5. E.g., Shintoists: Kōmoto, "Shisō konnan to jinja," 315-35. Monbushō: Kokuritsu kyōiku kenkyūjo, *Hyakunenshi* 1:273-323. Naimushō: Taikakai, *Naimushōshi* 1:338-44.

6. *Miyako shinbun*, 29 Mar. 1919.

7. Educators: e.g., "Kongo no kokumin shisō shidōjō kyōikusha no chūi subeki ten ikan," *Teikoku kyōiku*, no. 446 (Sept. 1919). Assemblymen: Haga Noboru, "Chihō bunka to fūzoku shūkan," in *Meiji Taishō kyōdoshi kenkyūhō*, ed. Furushima, 199-200.

8. Taikakai, *Naimushōshi* 1:338; 3:361-98; Pyle, "Advantages of followership," 127-64; Morita Yoshio, *Nihon keieisha dantai hattatsushi* (Nikkan rōdō tsūshin, 1958), 57-59; Sydney Crawcour, "The Japanese Employment System," *Journal of Japanese Studies* 4, no. 2 (Summer 1978): 225-46.

9. From Home Minister Tokonami Takejirō's directive no. 94 to the prefectural governors (Mar. 1919). *Naimushōshi* 1:340-44.

10. E.g., the "Keizai saisei undō" of the Home and Agricultural and Forestry Ministries was begun in 1932; the term *"jiriki saisei,"* which was used by bureaucratic and agrarianist ideologues alike, dates from the same time. For this movement seen through local materials: Nakamura Masanori, *Kindai Nihon jinushi seidoshi kenkyū*, 321-83.

11. Suzuki Masayuki, *Katsuta-shi shiryō*, vol. 3 (Katsuta-shishi hensan iinkai, 1973), 15.

12. Awaya Kentarō, *Shiryō Nihon gendaishi*, vol. 2, *Haisen chokugo no seiji to shakai* (Ōtsuki shoten, 1980), 389-90, 495-96.

13. Examples of this usage include Kita Ikki's *Nihon kaizōan genri taikō* (1919), a text of the "radical right"; *Kaizō no risō* (1920), by Nagai Ryūtarō, a Taishō "new liberal"; the preeminent journal of Taishō democracy, *Kaizō*, founded in 1919; and the statements calling for *shakai kaizō* (social reform) on the part of the new student and labor movements, especially the Yūaikai, in 1919-21. See Stephen S. Large, *The Rise of Labor in Japan: The Yūaikai, 1912-19* (Tokyo: Sophia University Press, 1972), and Henry DeWitt Smith, II, *Japan's First Student Radicals* (Cambridge: Harvard University Press, 1972).

14. On Taishō textbooks: Karasawa, *Kyōkasho no rekishi*, 330-430.

15. Ukita Kazutami, "Shinjidai no shimei," *Kokumin zasshi* 3, no. 17 (1 Sept. 1912): 19-20.

16. Employment figures: Ohkawa and Shinohara, *Patterns of Japanese Economic Development*, 392. Urban population: Ōsato, *Meiji ikō honpō shuyō keizai tōkei*, 14.

17. Landlord paternalism: Waswo, *Japanese Landlords*, 66-93. Industrial paternalism: Crawcour, "The Japanese Employment System," 225-46.

18. As an example of cooperative spirit, the fourth prewar edition of the elementary school textbooks (1933-39) offered five village headmen whose collective efforts at dam-building helped the locality prosper—a phenomenon

familiar in late Meiji but less and less possible in the mid-thirties. Kaigo, *Nihon kyōkasho taikei* 3: 340.

19. "Miso mo kuso mo issho ni torishimattari suru koto, " literally, "control the beanpaste with the dung": "Nisan no seinenron," *Rinri kōenshū*, no. 101 (Jan. 1911): 80. *Konchū shakai*, a biological text on social insects questioned by the censors because of the word "society": Jō Ichirō, *Zoku hakkinbon* (Tōgensha, 1965), 170. For volumes censored from 1888 to 1934: Naimushō keihōkyoku, *Kinshi tankōbon mokuroku*, vol. 1 (Kohokusha, 1976). On thought control: Richard H. Mitchell, *Thought Control in Prewar Japan* (Ithaca: Cornell University Press, 1976). For the major rebellion against the state: Ben-Ami Shillony, *Revolt in Japan: The Young Officers and the February 26, 1936 Incident* (Princeton: Princeton University Press, 1973).

20. Mitchell, *Thought Control in Prewar Japan*, 62-68; Minear suggested the comparison between accusations of "inimical to *kokutai*" with "un-American": *Japanese Tradition and Western Law*, 65-67.

21. *Kokutai no hongi*, trans. Hall and Gauntlett, 59. The manual was produced under the direction of the Ministry of Education whose Compilation Committee included such noted scholars as Watsuji Tetsurō and Hisamatsu Sen'ichi.

22. Uete Michiari, "Kokutai ron o megutte" ("Geppō," no. 31), *Nihon shisō taikei*, vol. 36, *Ogyū Sorai* (Iwanami shoten, 1971), 8. Uete also recollects looking in vain for a book about the *Kojiki* in a department store in 1940 with his "loyal and patriotic" (*chūkun aikoku*) father, who showed no interest in the subject. The clerk misunderstood his request and thought he had said "beggar" (also *kojiki*). Yet the *Kojiki* was one of the basic scriptural sources both for State Shintō and *kokutai*, of which 1940 was celebrated as the 2600th anniversary year.

23. E.g., "Kakuha seisaku tōronkai: kenpō mondai to tennōsei," in *Sengo shisō no shuppatsu*, ed. Hidaka, 105-06.

24. *Kokutai goji*: Awaya, *Shiryō Nihon gendaishi* 2: 459-61, 483-84, 256-77. Constitution: Ishida Takeshi, "Sengo minshu kaikaku to kokumin no taiō, *Iwanami kōza Nihon rekishi*, vol. 22, *Gendai* 1 (Iwanami shoten, 1977), 135-41.

25. For this definition, see the Cabinet's Exposition on the New Constitution (Nov. 1946), excerpted in Hall and Gauntlett, *Kokutai no hongi*, 198-202.

26. Irokawa, *Meiji no bunka*, 266.

27. *Kokutai no hongi*, 181.

28. E.g., Kaigo, *Nihon kyōkasho taikei* 3:312, 405, 412.

29. Leon Festinger's conception of "cognitive dissonance" is relevant here: Festinger, Henry W. Riecken, and Stanley Schachter, *When Prophecy Fails* (New York: Harper and Row, 1964).

Index

Abe Isoo (1865-1949), 207, 245
academic ideologues: and institutionalization of Shintō, 143; in patriotic controversies, 132; and Rescript on Education, 129. See also *goyō gakusha* ("government scholars"); *minkan* ideologues
Aesop: *Fables*, 106
Agatsuma Kyōaikai (youth group; later Agatsuma Alumni Association), 52
agrarian myth, 41, 265, 276, 282; and *jichi*, 178-204
agrarianism (*nōhonshugi*), 180
agrarianist ideologues, 34, 179-80, 185, 186, 189-91, 195, 248, 265, 282
agricultural associations (*nōkai*), 179, 190, 197, 198, 200, 204, 281
agricultural side-employments (*fukugyō*), 96, 162, 194, 265
agriculture, 158, 266, 273; enterprise fever in, 161-62; as foundation of nation, 34, 179, 195, 248; ideology about, 13, 34, 159, 265 (*see also* agrarian myth); improvement of, 189-91, 194; percent of population in, 31-32, 267, 282; problems in, 33, 158, 180, 266, 282. *See also* countryside
Aizawa Kikutarō (1866-1933), 47, 86, 110, 203, 214, 269, 273
Aizawa Seishisai, 122
Akutagawa Ryūnosuke, 225
Althusser, Louis, 7
ancestor worship, 141, 142, 156, 186
ancestors, imperial, 42, 44, 77, 78, 93, 127, 139, 226; presentation of Constitution to, 43, 44
ancestral customs, 159, 162, 177-78, 181
ancestral property, occupation, etc. (*sosen denrai no zaisan hongyō*, etc.), 9, 117, 160, 162, 180, 182, 195, 248, 261, 266
anti-Westernism (anti-foreignism), 20-21, 38-39, 115, 284. *See also* foreigners

Arisugawa, Prince (1835-1895), 63, 74
army. *See* military (the)
Army Ministry, 9
Asahi (newspaper), 154, 232; *Osaka asahi*, 68, 232-33; *Tokyo asahi*, 46, 68, 82, 125
Asia: expansion in, 114, 131

Barraclough, Geoffrey, 37, 39
Barthes, Roland, 29, 275
benevolence (beneficence), 127, 135; imperial, 81, 91, 92, 93, 99-100, 214, 215, 216; local, 202-204
Berger, Peter L., 7
Boshin Imperial Rescript (*Boshin shōsho*), 87, 91-92, 177, 198, 206, 258, 271
Buddhism, Buddhists, 22-23, 128, 134, 135, 138, 141, 204; as antidote to foreignism, 137; in conflict with Christianity, 133-35; in mixed residence issue, 137, 138; schools of, 137-38
bunmei kaika. See "civilization and enlightenment" (*bunmei kaika*)
bureaucracy, bureaucrats: 5, 43; aging of, 268-69; ambition of educated youth, 62-63, 162, 243-44; relation to popular parties, 60-61, 68-69, 230-31, 234-35, 238; national and local, 63, 69; palace, 76, 80-81; political participation forbidden to, 53, 55-57. *See also* officials, local officials
bureaucratic ideologues, 9, 186, 197-98, 283; attitude toward farmers, 183, 184, 248; in Shrine Bureau, 141-42; and social problems, 28, 157-58. *See also* local officials; and under individual government ministries
bureaucratic politics (*kanryō seiji*), 58, 244-46
Burke, Edmund, 144
bushidō, 136, 155, 180, 185, 210, 248, 259-60; and Nogi's suicide, 222, 223-24, 226; spirit of, 265, 273

use of metaphor in, 38, 135, 137, 187, 222-23, 226-27, 265
ideological process, 6, 7, 9-16, 17, 26; anachronism in, 39-40, 267-68, 278, 282; characteristics of (naturalization of meaning, expansion of usage, elusive completion), 35-36, 154-55, 157, 228, 230, 249-61; congruence in, 262-68, 275, 281-82, 284; consent/coercion in, 7, 29, 263, 277, 278, 281-82; contradiction and inconsistency in, 4, 7, 13-15, 16, 35, 39, 209-11, 226-27, 258-59, 264, 284 (*see also* ideology, plural renderings of); dominant ideology (hegemony) produced by, 7, 8, 15, 29, 39, 41, 246, 262, 275, 281-82; factors affecting efficacy of (timing, inventory of values, historical corroboration, immediacy), 262-67; interactions/intersections in, 103, 120, 142-43, 186-87, 197, 249-62, 275; institutions of ideological dissemination in, 7, 10-12, 276-77; in Japan, compared to other national contexts, 37-40; "non-ideological" sources in, 14-15, 171-74, 204, 206-209; not controllable, 12, 14-15, 147, 153-54, 205-206, 209, 248-49; in prewar years, 279-85; in postwar, 285-86; reinforcement and repetition in, 39, 128, 182, 197, 249-53, 254, 257; unreliability of agents of, 11-12, 87, 147, 152-54, 204-205, 234-37, 277
ideologues (ideologists), 5, 8, 13, 14, 40, 250, 253, 259; belief in exhortation, 3, 34, 59, 60, 102, 118-19, 177, 280-81; competing and diverse, 8-9, 11, 15-16, 204, 275-78; as diverse contributors to agrarian myth, 178-86; as diverse sources of Rescript on Education, 103, 111, 115, 120, 127-28; as diverse agents of denaturing of politics, 50, 60, 71-72, 245-46; and the emperor, 74, 78, 80-83, 95, 97-99; fear of politics/need for unity as spur to ideological production, 8-9, 21-26, 117-18, 120, 262, 276; fear of social disorder as spur, 26-35, 90-92, 157, 175-78, 274, 276, 279-80; impelled by sense of crisis, 8, 26; intensification of effort by, 282-83; and local elite, 12, 197, 203-205; local elite as, 20-21, 95, 97-99; provoked by change, 18-20, 32-34, 186-89, 211, 265-66, 273-75; and Shintō, 138-43; social class of, 270; of

two Meiji generations, 268-75; types of, 9-10. *See also* academic ideologues; agrarianist ideologues; bureaucratic ideologues; *minkan* ideologues; interest groups
ideology: "apparent invisibility" of, 262, 282; audiences of, 12, 13, 15, 25, 48, 147, 248-49; conservative nature of, 268, 272-75, 276; credibility of, 262-63, 266, 268, 277-78, 284; definition of, 6-9; effectiveness of, 259-60, 276, 278, 285; formed in and limited by late Meiji context, 36-37, 39-40, 262, 267, 278, 279; imperial and parliamentary, 237-42, 245-46, 264; not monolithic, 6, 41, 285; of nation and society, compared, 34-35, 263-67; and orthodoxy, 275-76, 283-84; orthodoxy and diversity in, 16, 276-78, 281-83, 285; plural rendering of, 9, 15, 39, 277, 285-86; politics and, 51, 58-60, 71-72, 228, 230, 237-38, 244-45; of success, 13, 206-11, 257, 259, 276, 278; versions of, 13, 248-49, 284. See also *tennōsei* ideology
impartiality, 55-56, 58-59, 71, 228-29
imperial family: visits to localities, 96-97
Imperial Forest Bureau, 203
Imperial Household Law of 1889, 78, 139
Imperial Household Ministry (Kunaishō), 80-81, 83, 91, 94, 109, 155, 216; grants, 85, 91; and Kiso forestlands, 97-100. (*See also* benevolence [beneficence])
imperial institution (house): constitutional conception of, 43, 76-78, 241-42; as ideological axis, 76, 146; and *lèse majesté*, 98, 132; as source of morality, 82, 112-13. *See also* emperor
imperial "line unbroken for ages eternal" (*bansei ikkei*), 77, 82, 93, 121, 123, 139, 142, 143-46, 156, 187
Imperial Poetry Bureau, 89
Imperial University (Tokyo), 55, 84, 85, 129, 132, 242
imperialism, 36, 137, 143, 250
India, 145
individual rights, 110-11
individualism, 153; in grammar of ideology, 251, 259; as negative value, 13, 38, 113, 134, 177, 188, 277, 284
industrialization, 17, 31-33, 34, 37, 158, 175, 179, 265, 266; emperor and, 93-94

Library of Congress Cataloging in Publication Data

Gluck, Carol, 1941-
Japan's modern myths.

Bibliography: p.
Includes index.
1. Japan—History—1868-1945.   2. Ideology.   I. Title.

DS881.95.G58 1985   952.03   85-600
ISBN 0-691-05449-5
ISBN 0-691-00812-4 (pbk.)